Developmental Issues in Contemporary India

The Editor

Dr. M.R. Biju (*b. 1965*) currently works as Director of Asian Institute of Development Research and Reader in the Post Graduate and Research Department of Political Science, Sree Narayana College, Kollam, Kerala. Also, he is Editor of *South Asian Journal of Socio-Political Studies* (SAJOSPS). Presently he is heading two research projects on decentralized governance funded by Ministry of Panchayati Raj and University Grants Commission, New Delhi.

Dr. Biju has written extensively on socio-political and developmental issues. He has to his credit nineteen books and ninety research papers published in various national and international journals of repute.

Developmental Issues in Contemporary India

Edited by

M.R. Biju

CONCEPT PUBLISHING COMPANY PVT. LTD.
NEW DELHI-110059

ISBN-13-978-81-8069-714-2

First Published 2010

Published and Printed by

Concept
Since 1974

Concept Publishing Company Pvt. Ltd.
Regd. Office :
A/15-16, Commercial Block, Mohan Garden
New Delhi-110059 (India)
Phones : 25351460, 25351794, *Fax* : 091-11-25357109
Email : publishing@conceptpub.com
Website: www.conceptpub.com

Editorial Office :
H-13, Bali Nagar, New Delhi-110 015, India

Cataloging in Publication Data--*Courtesy:* D.K. Agencies (P) Ltd. <docinfo@dkagencies.com>

Developmental issues in contemporary India / [edited by] M.R. Biju.
p. cm.
Contributed articles.
Includes bibliographical references and index.
ISBN 9788180697142

1. Economic development projects--India. 2. Human rights--India. 3. Education and state--India. 4. Rural development--Government policy--India. 5. India.--Politics and government--1947- I. Biju, M. R., 1965-

DDC 338.954 22

Preface

The founding fathers of the Constitution of India choose democracy as a form of governance, because it is the best and most suited form of government that has ever evolved over centuries. The other reasons include, democracy responds to the needs and aspirations of the people; sustained by the consent of the governed; address their concerns; accountable and responsible to the people. Moreover, India is the largest democracy on earth in terms of its size and population. The very magnitude of its function is daunting, baffling and astonishing. It is a gigantic organization that commands respect and admiration from its friends and foes alike. It is a fledging democracy which has just completed six decades of existence, which is infinitesimal period in the life of a nation. Certainly it is in the process of evolving, developing and maturing. It has survived four wars thrust upon it by its hostile neighbours and it is constantly threatened by its enemies both externally and internally. It is compacting ruthless, unrelenting, dreadful terrorism since its inception as a sovereign state.

Against this backdrop, this collection of 29 articles contributed by renowned academics, embodies critical analysis of the various aspects of the topic. The volume has been broadly categorized under five categories. Part-I examines developmental projects, action plans and good governance. Part- II highlights issues on human rights. Topic of discussion in Part-III is on education and development. Part-IV highlights the issues and concerns of the marginalized and the concluding part presents the various aspects of regionalism.

Before concluding, I would like to express my gratitude to those who have been kind enough to help me in the preparation of this volume. I wish to express a deep sense of gratitude to the esteemed contributors to this anthology of articles. The views and opinions expressed by the contributors are of immense value for researchers, policy makers, planners for rejuvenating policies and strategies on Indian Politics. Finally I am extremely thankful to Shri Ashok Kumar Mittal of Concept Publishing Company Pvt. Ltd., New Delhi who brought out the volume in an elegant form. I am also grateful to my wife Jaya, daughter Aishwarya and son Anantha Padmanabha for kindly sparing me the time for completing the volume.

29th January, 2009 M.R. Biju

Contents

SECTION - II

HUMAN RIGHTS IN DEMOCRACY

SECTION - III

EDUCATION AND DEVELOPMENT

Introduction

The founding fathers of the Indian Constitution chose democracy as a form of governance, because it is the best and most suited form of government that has ever evolved over centuries. The other reasons include, democracy responds to the needs and aspirations of the people; sustained by the consent of the governed; address their concerns; accountable and responsible to the people. Moreover, India is the largest democracy on earth in terms of its size and population. The very magnitude of its function is daunting, baffling and astonishing. It is a gigantic organization that commands respect and admiration from its friends and foes alike. It is a fledging democracy which has just completed six decades of existence, which is infinitesimal period in the life of a nation. Certainly it is in the process of evolving, developing and maturing. It has survived four wars thrust upon it by its hostile neighbours and it is constantly threatened by its enemies both externally and internally. It is compacting ruthless, unrelenting, dreadful terrorism since its inception as a sovereign state.

Against this backdrop, this collection of 29 articles contributed by renowned academics, embodies critical analysis of the various aspects of the topic. The volume has been broadly categorized under five categories. Part–I examines developmental projects, action plans and good governance. Part–II highlights human rights and Democracy. Topic of discussion in Part–III is on education and development. Part–IV highlights the issues and concerns of the marginalized and the concluding part presents the various aspects of regionalism.

In the very first chapter *Prasenjit Maiti*, highlights the key

Concepts of Social Impact Assessment and Resettlement Action Plan for Infrastructure Development Projects. In his paper Maiti observes that, resettlement of affected persons and rehabilitation of their lost assets (land and/or structures) and livelihood are critical yet imperative social development exercises of linear road projects that require displacement of individuals and groups in order to either upgrade/widen existing road networks or else to construct new road systems for better transport facilities and streamlined movement of vehicular traffic essential for economies undergoing reforms. Involuntary resettlement caused by road projects should be informed by comprehensive mitigation measures in order to reduce adverse impacts on the existing social fabric of Project Affected Persons. After his detailed observations and analysis he came to the conclusion that—

(a) Implementation of the Resettlement Action Plan on the part of Non Government Organization(s) appointed by the Project Authority would require sensitive handling of the critical issue of involuntary displacement that is a necessary result of infrastructural development projects involving roads and highways, flyovers and interchanges etc.
(b) Legal owners of land and structures would suffer in terms of loss of immovable assets while their tenants would suffer losses either in terms of residence or livelihood or both.
(c) Resettlement of affected persons and rehabilitation of their lost assets (land and/or structures) and livelihood are critical yet imperative social development exercises of infrastructure development projects that require displacement of individuals and groups.

In chapter two *Jayanta Sinha* and *Amrita Pal* focusses on the Economics of the Sustainable Environment. To them, in our society the environment has become a scarce resource.

Since economics is about how to tackle scarce resources, it can often be useful when dealing with environmental problems. This gives birth to a branch designated as environmental economics as a subfield of economics concerned with environmental issues. Environmental economics is about the proficient utilization of resources, generally expressed in monetary terms. One way of them is using economics to ensure that the costs and the benefits of environmental measures are well balanced. In this sense, there are various theories regarding sustainable use of resources that can be made applied to economic sustainability. Apart from that, in monetary terms, one resource can generally stand in for another. The economic sustainability concept is subject, on all levels, and pertains to different inputs and outputs. The economic sustainability of a farm or a company is conditional on the viability of, and markets for, an enterprise or product. In furtherance, the economic sustainability of a nation is dependent on the whole economy at local, national and international level. In describing economics pertaining to sustainability there is the advent of new economic theory in contradiction to the old one. The new economic theory seems to be much holistic and organismic in nature and follows the principles of quantum theory. A sustainable human society has to conserve, recycle, and salvage materials and energy, if it is to slow, rather than hasten, the process of entropy. Above all, human population and per capita consumption must consider the restricted carrying capacity of the earth. This earth's carrying capacity depends on much of our efficiency in nurturing and using living systems to capture and store solar energy and go for renewable and non-consumptive resources.

Both the authors further states that performance of various countries in terms of sustainability and environmental quality is assessed in terms of ESI and EPI. India ranked quite below in both the index. Such a low rank is due to India's low per capita consumption level which is far below world standards furthered by the inefficient management of this consumption that drags down India's environmental record. Thus to better such a rank India should establish quality health measures, control population, reduce stress on ecosystem, develop arid regions having low natural resources and promulgate systematic natural resource management.

In chapter three *Manuka Khanna* and *Poornima Tripathi* made a study on the Administrative and Organisational Aspects of Environmental Policy making. Both the authors observes that the ever-increasing zeal for ecological modernization has constantly come in the way of environmental preservation and development. The introduction of technology and electronics in all aspects of man's life has created environmental hazards .These are increasing rapidly with the constantly accelerating pace of globalization. Though the people of the world share a global culture in certain aspects, there is a lack of consensus in others due to the confusion between globally local and locally global phenomena. Further both the authors also hails that at the international and national level implementation of international laws and standards is required. It cannot be assumed that international standards, which by tacit consent may have become binding *vis-a vis* states, are thereby automatically effective on the national level. Even without formal ratification, some governmental action is necessary. Depending on the requirements of national constitutional law, this usually takes the form of implementing legislation or statutory regulation. While this ultimate state of law-making and law enforcement is normally considered beyond the range of international machinery, certain ways need to be adopted to ascertain and supervise the proper national implementation of standards. This would also lead to a partial harmonization or approximation of existing national environmental laws, consequently eliminating a substantial number of transnational legal disputes.

Swami Prakash Srivastava in his Chapter on Special Economic Zones (SEZ) and its Future Role in Export Promotion states that SEZ is a geographical region that has economic laws that are more liberal than a country's typical economic laws. To Srivastava, SEZ is a trade capacity development tool, with the goal to promote rapid economic growth by using tax and business incentives to attract foreign investment and technology.

The author further observes that SEZs are meant for creating industrial, commercial and social infrastructure. Industrial infrastructure such as factories, warehouses and access roads has to be estimated a minimum 50 per cent of the SEZ area, even in the non-processing area social and commercial infrastructure needs to be developed for supporting the people working at the SEZ. As social and commercial infrastructure included educational institutions, entertainment areas, hospitals, housing power stations, and effluent treatment plants as SEZ was nothing but an infrastructure project and had to be treated accordingly. RBI needs to revise its guidelines and classify SEZs as infrastructure projects. Several developers also voiced concern on the issues of service tax and benefit of scheme and duty drawback on supplies to their facilities and interpretation of Section 10AA of the Income Tax (IT) Act. Though the clause under Section 10B of the IT Act was proposed to be revoked and it had been extended by a year threatening it impede the growth of the EoU sector.

He also believes that SEZs ensure better investment climate by offering three major advantages over the rest of the economy : provision of fiscal incentives, infrastructure facilities and hassle free governance. These advantages reduce production and transaction costs for exporting and hence provide an edge to EPZ units over the others. For exploring the factors responsible for the poor performance of the zones in India, we need to evaluate various micro aspects of the investment climate offered by the SEZs, especially the incentive package, quality of governance and the state of physical and financial infrastructure. Recent literature however indicates that the importance of corporate tax incentives has been increasing in attracting FDI. The renewed debate on the effectiveness of tax incentives on FDI suggests that changes in the way multinational firms structure their operations abroad have made low tax rates increasingly important to a country's ability to attract foreign capital.

In chapter five *Pranab K. Dan, Kousik Guhathakurta* and *Shatadru Gupta* discusses the modelling for land acquisition for SEZ. According to the authors, Special Economic Zones (SEZs) are specific geographical regions that have economic laws different from and more liberal than a country's typical economic laws. The goal is usually an increase in Foreign Direct Investment (FDI) in the country. According to them this process of planning and development is under question, as the States in which the SEZs have been approved are facing intense protests, from the farming community, accusing the government of forcibly snatching fertile land from them, at heavily discounted prices as against the prevailing prices in the commercial real estate industry.

In chapter six *Ritu Narang* has made an innovative study on Health Care System in Rural India : Need for Public- Private Partnership. According to Ritu Public-Private Partnership (PPP) is an approach under which services are delivered by the private sector, both non-profit and for-profit organizations, while the responsibility for providing the resources rests with the government. This kind of a partnership refers to the sharing of resources needed to work together towards a common goal while respecting one another's identity. Ritu concludes her study by stating that to foster the health care system in India impetus needs to be given to PPPs. The resources at the disposal of private sector make it an attractive partner for undertaking any kind of major developmental initiative. Though the private sector may be viewed with suspicion due to its profit motive but its performance in various sectors namely banking, insurance, telecom and communications etc. has undisputedly established its credentials to penetrate both the rural as well as the lower income groups. It makes good sense to encourage the private sector in the rural health sector which is in poor state and raises question over the prevalent disparity in terms of health facilities between the rural and urban areas. On its own the private sector may have scepticism in making big inroads into the villages where the people are used to almost free treatment from the existing public health centres and infrastructure deficiencies in the form of roads, electricity, water may strengthen entry barriers. Involving private player with its resources, expertise and efficiency in the public health delivery system can prove to be a boon.

R. Sunita in her Chapter on Stress Management of Women in IT Sector states that Stress is a body reaction to any demand or any changes in its internal and external environment. Whenever there is a change in external environment such as temperature, pollution, humidity and working conditions, it leads to stress. In these days of competition when one wishes to surpass what has been achieved by others leading to an imbalance between demands and resources, it causes psycho-social stress. It is part and parcel of everyday life. She further reveals that stress reduces productivity and increases pressure to the management. Today companies prefer women to men because of the hope that they bring additional qualities like innovation, patience and dedication in the work place. But due to increased pressure for women both at work place and home they face stress. Sunita concludes her study by saying that any employee will give the maximum effort and contribution when kept happy and without any stress. Hence it is the responsibility of the employer to keep the employees without any stress to increase productivity.

Moreover women should also take necessary steps to reduce their stress and increase their productivity. Stress only leads to depression and constant depression may prove to be fatal. Hence, it is necessary that stress be managed properly and effectively. Thus, this issue acquires importance in the context of the employee's behaviour, on which the effectiveness of the organization depends to a large extent. In this connection, the personality traits of the employee and the characteristics of the organization may induce stress, ultimately affecting their performance and efficiency. Hence it is essential to take steps to minimize the effects of determinants of stress and help individual and organizations evolve newer and effective coping strategies.

In chapter eight, *Arjun Sharma* has made a study on Good Governance and E-Governance : Prospects for Rural Bihar. Sharma highlights the feasibility of adopting ICT – Computer, Internet, RTI access, IT tools, Communication Skills, PCOs, PIOs and other Facilitation Centres – have been kept in mind. Strategies, scopes, steps etc. are the key factors for the psyche of the rural poor in ICT friendly environment. Knowledge management, feasibility and desirability of new techniques, nature and modes of self-government and other related issues. Good governance has become an integrated part of democratic system of Bihar. According to Sharma e-governance has been accepted as a tool to accomplish good governance. It focusses in bringing improvements in the service delivery, dissemination of information, transparency, public and private partnership, efficiency and accountability. Government and its numerous agencies being the largest service providers in rural Bihar feel the need to make extensive use of ICTs for its major services. There are many stumbling blocks and constraints in the growth of e-governance that must be removed. E-governance should demonstrate its potentiality in ensuring good governance. It should also cover the issues which are not covered by IT Act, 2000 like IPRs, privacy, e-taxation, data protection,

protection of e-consumers. Successful implementation of e-governance in rural Bihar requires more then skills in ICTs, good programme management techniques, good programme managers, involvement of stakeholders and teamwork. Thus, for the development and prosperity of rural Bihar in the area of e-governance, a proper planning and adjustment is inevitable. E-governance projects should be guided by a clearly focused objective, clearly spellout funding, strong ICT infrastructure, awareness and commitment, continuous training, sustainability, appropriate mechanism, secure environment, participatory structure, rural development, strengthening of PRIs, social settings, educational extension, unempowered section, enrichment of democratic outlook, knowledge management, proper utilization of resources and so on. Our resources—human, natural and man-made—should be properly utilized by the better knowledge management of Good Governance through the ICTs or e-governance.

Security Challenges in e-commerce is the topic of discussion in chapter nine. This Chapter is presented by Seyed Reza Mousavizadeh and H. Rajshekar. In their chapter the authors analyses the role of e-commerce security issues, identify the major risks, and describe the variety of solutions currently available. According to them, e-commerce is a tool for businesses to make great success possible. This chapter aimed to expose the warning signs for these e-commerce entities from being a few nodes away from the professional and amateur intruders. There are both legitimate opportunists as well as those who are in the criminal element. The latter ones hope to seek small fortune or destroy someone else's dream. The scary part is that an e-commerce star can lose all it gained throughout its success path at the speed of light. The hope is that a greater awareness of this problem and also the security of this problem and also the security culture necessary in innovative ideas being brought to the market.

In chapter ten *M.R. Biju* unfolds Human Rights and

Social Justice under Decentralization. According to him, the notion of social justice has emerged out of a process of evolution of societal norms, order, law and morality. The core element of social justice is the social equity for preservation of rights, privileges and established practices to sustain social peace and harmony. The basic of social justice as the equal well-being or individual helps to bring out a just society.

In his study he further states that in order to achieve the goal of perfect democracy, the ideology of social justice calls for to obey rule of law and evolve a democratic government at the grass roots. Rural potentials for growth and development can be sustained only in the preservation of social democracy and strengthening the local political institutions. Therefore, an institutionalized action to a desired goal could be achieved only through democratic decentralization. Democratic decentralization is conceived as a vehicle of social transformation of enlightened humanity to screen out democracy in action. Democratic decentralization is a process whereby some duties, responsibilities, authorities and power are devolved to the institutions of the people by higher authority to discharge and manage their own affairs. In fact, democratic decentralization may be regarded as an efficient method of formulation and execution of local plans consistent with the democratic trends towards local self-government.

In chapter elevan *Amita Agarwal* critically examines the link between Human Rights and Mass Media. According to Amita, in the age of globalization today when information technology is advancing and spreading at a very rapid pace, the role of media in generating awareness and its responsibilities have also increased manifold. Due to advancement of technology news travels very fast and both print media and electronic media have entered virtually every household on this planet. If one has access to electronic media (which is a normal feature in the forms of T.V. and internet) one can witness the events occurring hundreds and thousands miles apart simultaneously or if there be still a person who due to one reason or other has access only to print media will have access to all the details of the event on the morrow. Due to such an easy accessibility media has become a dual edged sword, which if used responsibly can help transform the entire society in a constructive manner and can help create a positive public opinion and if fallen in irresponsible hands can destroy the very fabric of a society and culture by putting the facts in a negative manner. Dangers of yellow journalism have today increased manifold.

Amita further believes that media influences people at the social and cultural levels and its impact is more popular, lasting and far-reaching than all the government agencies put together. Media can also establish an effective and impressive dialogue among people and between government and people, hence its role and responsibility increases manifold. It provides a free platform for popular dialogue and is dreaded by wrong doers and violators of human rights.

The problem of refugees or just of asylum seekers but of migrants owing to push and pull factors in economic terms that factor into ethnic divides everywhere. These raise concerns of resettlement with dignity around which human rights theorization has taken place, since the England Bill of Rights to American and France and to United Nation Convention. Against this background in chapter twelve, Chunnu Prasad has made a study on Refugees and Human Rights. It is a comparative enquiry between Chakmas in India and Biharis in Bangladesh. According to Prasad, the problem of Chakmas in India and Biharis in Bangladesh is one of the oldest human problems and this problem has to be taken in deep concern by both the government either a democratic in case of India and Islamic religious fundamentalist or totalitarianism in case of Bangladesh. Both the countries should try to solve the refugee problem so that these people who are being discriminated their basic fundamental rights and dignity to survive should also reclaim their human rights which they lost just because of partition. Also both the country should follow the directions of the United Nations Human Rights Commission for Refugees (UNHRCR) to solve the refugee problem within a time bound and provide all sort of help and legality which is related to the Chakmas and Biharis of both the country and also open the positive and middle path so that the possibility of building of nation-state would be possible in future.

The working of Right to Information Act in a Democratic Political System is the topic of discussion in chapter thirteen. This chapter is presented by *S.P. Guru, Johani Xaxa* and *Bibhuti Kalyan Mahakul.* According to the authors, the citizen's right to information is increasingly being recognised as an important instrument for a fair and free Public administration. The demand for Right to Information is the outcome of long standing collective action against arbitrariness and corruption of agencies of the state. The greater the access of the citizen to information the greater the responsiveness of government to community needs. Alternatively, the greater the restrictions that are placed on access, the greater the feelings of powerlessness and alienation. Without information, people cannot adequately exercise their rights as citizens. It has been observed that a government, which operates in greater secrecy, is more prone to corruption as compared to a government, which operates in greater openness. That is why, the right to information is considered as a significant step in empowering people to combat corruption. The authors conclude their study by stating that a democratic culture is synonymous with participation, openness, transparency and good governance. The Right to Information Act is to promote transparency and accountability in governance by enabling the citizen to have effective access to information and thus to have the ability to question and correct the process of governance. To them, the Act recognizes that democracy requires an informed citizenry which in turn thrives on transparency of information. It also seeks to check corruption and to hold governments and their instrumentalities accountable to the governed. It seeks to curb the anti-democratic attitude and activities of the public authorities.

Sujan Singh in chapter fourteen dwell upon the linkage between Education on Human Rights. According to Dr. Sujan education is undoubtedly the single most potent remedy for making human rights a reality because 'knowledge is power' and it is 'power' that brings about change in the situations. Therefore, education of human rights has been made a right itself and has been underlined amongst the list thereof.

Singh clearly mentions that the human rights are the inalienable rights emanating from a superior source having universal character but needed to be adopted in the national legal regimes as the enforceable laws. Social actions are in the background of such rights aimed at all-round development of human beings and therewith of their societies. Therefore, the Human Rights Commissions and the NGOs are required to adopt a proactive approach for the protection and promotion or human rights. Education of human rights with the methodology of case studies of social action groups and practice of such efforts can keep the *mashal* burning and the movement of human rights marching.

N.R. Madhava Menon presents a study captioned 'Equal Opportunities for Deprived Groups: Need for Fresh Thinking'. According to Menon in the Indian context it is not necessary to canvass affirmative action for deprived groups because it is a Constitutional mandate for the implementation of which there are positive obligations put on the State. This includes not only prohibition of discrimination [Art.15(1)], but also creation of equality promoting conditions including reservation of seats in educational institutions [Art.15(4) and (5)]. Besides, several provisions in Part IV of the Constitution directs the State to remove inequalities in status, facilities and opportunities not only amongst individuals but also amongst groups of people residing in different areas or engaged in different occupations [Art. 38(2) read with Articles 39, 41, 45, 46]. This is the affirmative action agenda set by the Constitution itself towards fulfilment of the equal opportunity guarantee in respect of deprived groups of citizens.

Menon laments that, it is unfortunate that even after 60 years of Independence, only 9 per cent of the eligible age group of youth find their way into higher education in India. The National Knowledge Commission recommended to increase the gross enrolment ratio to 20 per cent in the medium term by doubling the scale of higher education institutions in the next decade with constant improvement in standards to meet the needs of a knowledge society. This has tremendous implications to access, quality, ownership, control and accountability in higher education. Reservation of seats in higher education is a useful tool to provide access to certain disadvantaged groups; but it can happen only with some trade-offs which, some people argue is not sustainable with merit and equality for all. This is also the rationale for the Supreme Court in capping reservations at 50 per cent.

Judicial Activism and Protection of Human Rights in India is the topic of discussion of *Ashutosh Pandey* in chapter sixteen. According to Pandey Judicial Activism is a state of mind. It has its genesis in the inactivity and apathy of the legislature and the executive. It is nothing but the performance of the judicial activities. It is creativity to fill the gulf between the positive and the normative aspects of the law.

He further wants to say that the Judicial Activism manifested in the strategy of PIL paves the way for the participation of public spirited and enlightened people in India's development process and displays the potentiality of the legal system to offer justice to the poor and the oppressed. The strategy has brought to light many a medieval practice still prevalent in India such as relief to prisoners, plight of women in protective homes, untouchables, tribal etc. An attempt has been made to show how in taking up such cases, the Supreme Court is emerging as the guardians of the rights and liberties of the victims of repression, cruelty and torture. No wonder, the people of the country are now looking towards judiciary for protection of life, liberty and pursuit of happiness. By enlarging the scope of Article 32 and by accelerating the process of socio-economic revolution it has brought justice to the doorstep of the weak, the unprivileged and exploitative section of society. But the inadequacy of what has been accomplished stands out the moment the issue of human rights is brought up. One reason why the advance in this area of operations has been striking slow is that, without some drastic restructuring of the legal system, human rights cannot be protected as they ought to be protected. This is precisely where the bottleneck lies.

Amal Mandal presents the progress and pitfalls of *Sarva Shiksha Abhiyan* as a tool for achieving basic education for all in India. This chapter is a critical reflection on a few crucial operational aspects of the SSA: the status of micro planning and availability and utilisation of fund. Mandal in this chapter comments that the national resolve and proclaiming a new deal for universal elementary education in India the *Sarva Shiksha Abhiyan* (SSA), a comprehensive and integrated flagship public programme, sets out with emphatic objectives and encompassing strategy, like decentralised framework and community ownership. Regarding the questions how the SSA is performing, how far its objectives are realistic or have the potential to come to fruition, contradictory contentions ranging from optimistic expectation to apprehension may leave one wondering but one thing is unequivocal: the progress and success of the

SSA will, for the moment at least, determine when and whether India will attain the cherished goal of satisfactory level of basic education for all.

Deepa Awasthi and *U.C. Vashishtha* in their chapter analyse the rationale for Depriviation and its Role in Universalization of Elementary Education in chapter eighteen. According to the authors, education enables the individual to develop harmony in a social culture. Education develops desirable habits, skills and attitudes which make an individual a good citizen. Education plays an important role in enabling a person to face a real life situation with adequate knowledge. It plays a pivotal role in shaping up a person. A balanced education should give total opportunity to the learner to discover and use his fullest potential. It is not just inborn talent or educational achievements that guarantee the success of children. Without sound values, good habits and self discipline, even the most gifted child cannot blossom into a good achiever.

Ira Das in her chapter explains the crucial significance of the rural-urban divide in accessing the educational facilities in the State of Assam with the help of available secondary data. The study reflects rural-urban disparity in educational attainment still prevailing both for the State and the national average. Although the disparity is falling down more significantly in the State than the national level regarding the indicators of literacy rate, GER, ATN and DRP, percentage of persons acquired higher education and diploma/certificate course is less in the State than all India average. Moreover, private sector investment in education sector is occurring mostly in urban area and thereby contributing in favour of urban sector which have been excluded in this study. This point needs further study. Government should direct private investment equally to rural area also for balanced development and not to further already existing rural-urban disparity.

In chapter twenty *Reena Agarwal* has made a study on the Phychological Basis of Value Education. According to

Reena, today we are passing through a critical stage of battle between the best possibilities and the worst possibilities, which give experience of value crisis in our lives. Rapid social changes, globalization, materialistic society, population explosion, goal oriented society, environmental pollution, difference between thinking and action, self centeredness are some of the causes leading to distortion of personality. Disregard shown to basic values like honesty, tolerance in personal and public life have become a matter of grave national concern. Crime, violence, cruelty, greed, meanness, selfishness and indifference and apathy to human sufferings have spread to all aspects of our living—political, social and economic. The values of idealism, altruism, selflessness, and service to fellowmen are becoming increasingly rare in the younger generation who are not able to find any meaning in life and adopt escapist means as drug addiction and alcoholism. Campus violence and indiscipline have become integral part of each and every working day. Reena cautions that pursuit of material wealth and selfish ends at any cost has become the lifestyle of modern man. Sensitivity to beauty, arts, literature, craft, nature and life has declined and the object of life is now considered to make oneself as comfortable materially as one can.

She further feels that mere knowledge providing in the school and home does not guarantee good or right behaviour because behaviour is motivated by factors other than knowledge. Social pressure, how children feel about themselves how they are treated by family members and peers, desires at the moment and many other factors influence how child will behave in a situation. The behaviour of 'true morality' not only confirms to social standards but also is carried out voluntarily. It comes from the transition from external to internal authority and consists of conduct regulated from within. It is accompanied by a feeling of personal responsibility one's act. Learning to behave in a socially approved manner is a long and slow process. There are mainly three approaches to learning – Behaviouristic, Socio-cognitive and Constructivistic. All these approaches can guide teachers and parents about the learning process of their children, especially the learning of various values.

A. N. Panda in his research paper examines political participation of rural leaders of Kuchinda Scheduled Area by making a case study of the positional leaders of different Panchayati Raj institutions. After a detailed enquiry on the area, the author concludes that positional leaders of the grass roots level in Kuchinda Scheduled Area are active in the political process of the country. They are performing their responsibilities as the common citizens of the country besides doing their duties as the representatives of people, though there may have been deviations in some cases. They are not only active in doing their jobs at the grass roots institutions but also try to solve the problems of the people by taking recourse to meeting officers, higher political leaders and utilising their contacts. Some of them also engage themselves in propagating for some causes and politically socialising others. Thus, the tribal leaders of the Kuchinda Scheduled Area are politically active not only at election time but also play dynamic roles at the time when there is no election. They are politically active in all respects though in some cases they are more active.

In chapter twenty two *T.N. Pati* critically examines the interrelationship between political communication and mass-media. The author has made a conceptual analysis of these two concepts. According to him, in the socio-political process, mass-media may play roles as political socializer, political communicators, and performance of these roles by the mass-media may entail significance for the salability, viability and overall dynamics of the political society. The detailed study undoubtedly reveals that political communication may play a vital role in the survival, stability, growth and development of the political system. In the process of political communication, mass-media such as the newspaper, the radio and the television and cinema tend to play significant roles. While playing roles as political communicators, they may contribute significantly towards the formation of patterns of political culture in the individual as well as the collectivity by way of transmission of explicitly political information, news and views and also politically relevant non-political information and values. Such transmissions and communications may help shape the individual's political self of political culture which, in turn, may influence the performance of his political roles and behaviour. Simultaneously, the political behaviour and roles of the people tend to determine political dynamics and working of the political system. If the pattern of political culture of the people is congruent and allegiant to the structure or form of the political system, the latter is likely to remain stable and viable. On the contrary, if the pattern of political culture is incongruent and alienated to the structure of the political system, the latter is likely to experience instability and to undergo change.

Niranjan Mandal and *Asit Kumar Banerjee* in their paper examines how Gram Panchayats play a positive role in reducing rural poverty by adopting and implementing different developmental schemes. In this study, the authors examines the trends in the incidence of rural poverty by studying some sample villages by taking family-wise data and by studying the perceptions of the beneficiaries of different developmental schemes. The detailed study came to the conclusion that in implementing centrally sponsored Poverty Alleviation Programmes (PAPs), the Panchayats have played a formidable role for alleviating rural poverty in our study area. Experience shows that Gram Panchayats could play an effective role in PAPs through the process of planning, execution, monitoring and evaluation. At the same time the Panchayati Raj (PR) leaders could provide help to the PRIs in identifying the beneficiaries, in selection of priority areas and also in monitoring the works of the

Panchayats. Sometimes it is reported that PRIs and Government officials behave negatively with the general masses. Their attitude towards the rural people is not favourable for smooth functioning of the Panchayat. Inadequacy of fund is reported to be another constraint in the implementation of plans and programmes. To combat the situation there is a need to enhance the quantum of aid under various programmes, thereby enabling the beneficiaries to generate enough income to raise Above the Poverty Line (APL). In our analysis it is also observed that in some of the cases, proper care has not been taken at the time of preparing BPL list. It appears that some non-poor are included wrongly in the BPL list instead of including real poor and, therefore, non-poor are relatively getting higher benefits than the poor. In West Bengal, PRIs have become synonymous with rural development. They have become perfect agencies of welfare state system. From the study it is noticed that only thing PRI's need is to reduce political interference, which sometimes becomes unhealthy for democracy.

In chapter twenty four *Ranjit Karmakar* and *Bhola Nath Ghosh* highlights the problems of milk-cooperatives in West Bengal. Their major concern is that, there are many aspects of milk-cooperatives, which need to be probed critically, and how it is affecting or benefiting the rural producers who always have been the victims of market mechanism—are they be farm producers or milk-producers. As in the age of market economy, market plays a very important role and whoever has more control over the market will gain in the long run. But the farmers in many times do not get fair prices due to lack of control and infrastructure for their produces. The milk co-operative is free from these handicaps as the Milk Marketing Federation at the State level wholly controls the marketing affairs. But it is a matter of serious concern that co-operative milk business is being dependent on the donation of the EEC and technology imported from the foreign countries.

According to the authors in spite of some success of cooperatives, it is mostly blamed for inefficiency and corruption but it is co-operatives, which have social objectives and best quality control capacity. Process of co-operation also exists alongside the competition in the society. But unhealthy competition not only ruins oneself alone but it accelerates another process, which is known as isolation. So let give co-operation a chance to succeed.

Vishnu Bhagwan in his paper entitled "National Rural Employment Guarantee Act : A SWOT Analysis" states that in the history of post-Independence India, Panchayati Raj Institutions are expected to be directly involved in this scheme in such a way that they would implement the scheme as an integral part of rural development plan. Gram Panchayats and Gram Sabhas would decide types of work to be undertaken in the villages and use of funds earmarked under the scheme. Gram Sabhas would discuss and approve this plan. Gram Sabhas would also supervise and monitor the implementation of the NREGA.

Anup Sekhar Chakraborty in his chapter on Mizo Politics states that the church and the State are the two instruments through which the majority dectates their terms to the minorities including women. According to him the State-building process in Mizoram requires the systematic mapping of the discourses and narratives of inclusion and exclusion at all levels.

He further adds that the State has grown from a hills district to a Union Territory to full Statehood, from a three-district State to an eight-district State. The Peace Accord apparently seems to have ended in success but the fact remains that ethnic identities are further mushrooming and minorities including women in Mizoram *today,* are raising their voices against the domination of *the majority* i.e. the Zos/Mizos and the Church and the State. These dissenting voices reflect themselves through the *various strategies* ranging from that of *Whisperings* at the private spaces; to camouflagings and that of violent anti-Mizo/Zo movements spearheaded at the public spaces as a response to the State-led *Politics of Silencing* operating against the *marginals*.

The multi-ethnic and culturally plural character of our society and multi-party system of our polity seems to rule out the possibility of a single party government, strong enough to govern the country effectively. Rather, it requires the coalition politics for adjusting various social formations in the power-structure. Against this backdrop.

Bhupinder Singh in chapter twenty seven examines the dynamics of coalition politics with special focus on Punjab.

According to Singh coalition is likely to continue till a serious challenge is posed to them with the emergence of such new combinations in Punjab politics or any one of the partner take a strong ideological shift in its electoral game plan. But at present both of these kinds of scenarios are unlikely to develop. Hence possibility of continuation of this coalition is not ruled out at present. The SAD(B)-BJP coalition government has been working in Punjab during the 2007 Assembly Elections. On the whole, the SAD(B)-BJP coalition made a healthy impact on society of Punjab. The divide that had been created between the Sikhs and the Hindus during the militancy and had continued for more than a decade was bridged by this coalition. The coalition also strengthened the roots of the democracy in the State. Besides, it has opened a new chapter in Centre-State relations, ushering in the age of co-operated federalism in the country. The era of confrontations has been effectively ended and replaced with a forward looking thrust on working together for the overall good of the State and the nation.

Jogendra Kumar Das and *Haren Ch. Kalita* in their chapter captioned Role of the Asom Gana Parishad in Assam Politics and the future of Regionalism seeks to review the genesis the role of the party in State politics, its present status and the future of regionalism in Assam as such. The authors have taken up a historical documentary approach in dealing with the issues relating to the role of the AGP.

According to them the present status of regionalism in Assam is quite unhealthy and the future is also not bright as is expected and as it was during 1980s. The failure of the leaders of the AGP to fulfil the regional hopes and popular expectations along with its failure to work as a stable political party with a determinate programme of action are reflection of the futile effort of a regional movement. The decline of the AGP clearly shows that regionalism in isolation of a larger nation-wide democratic movement in the federal democracy like India is barren. It is also evident from the fact of the past, that regionalism parallel to national politics is sick, cripple and in fact, a fruitless attempt. Moreover, regionalism, as is evident from the specific historical exigencies of Assam society, is a difficult task where sub-national and innumerable ethnic movements are endemic.

The latest UN statistics shows that by the year 2025 as many as 500 crore of people will be facing water shortage, as many as 270 crore will face severe water shortage, if the world continues consuming water at the present rate. With the misuse and overuse of water is becoming scarce all over the world. Several prognostications made from knowledgeable quarters indicate that there could be a war over it in not too distant a future. "Fierce national competition over water resources has prompted fears that water issues contain the seeds of violent conflict". Against this background *Midatala Rani* examines the historical background of Krishna Water dispute in an analytical way. According to Rani the dispute in the Krishna basin between Karnataka, Maharashtra and Andhra Pradesh has brought into sharp focus the issue of scarcity and struggles with regard to water resources and other important issues like water politics, displacement of people by raising the dams, large scale farmer suicides in the States. The riparian States in the river basin are making attempts to establish their water rights. The existing situation demands a clear cut National Water Policy with a Constitutional stand on waters and scientific Water Management Control. It also calls for a review of Inter-State Water Disputes Act, 1956 consistent with the changing trends of disputes. Further the Inter-State Council needs to be given more impetus in resolving inter-State river water disputes. The proposed inter-linking of rivers is still in a speculative realm and its feasibility depends upon on adventurous course of an unimaginable magnitude which may face more interruptions and insurmountable barriers when it comes to the stage of implementation involving a budget estimate in astronomical figures.

M.R. Biju

SECTION-I

DEVELOPMENT PROJECTS, ACTION PLANS AND GOOD GOVERNANCE

1 Key Concepts of Social Impact Assessment and Resettlement Action Plan for Infrastructure Development Projects

Prasenjit Maiti

Resettlement of affected persons and rehabilitation of their lost assets (land and/or structures) and livelihood are critical yet imperative social development exercises of linear road projects that require displacement of individuals and groups in order to either upgrade/widen existing road networks or else to construct new road systems for better transport facilities and streamlined movement of vehicular traffic essential for economies undergoing reforms. Involuntary resettlement caused by road projects should be informed by comprehensive mitigation measures in order to reduce adverse impacts on the existing social fabric of Project Affected Persons.

Resettlement Action Plan

One of the most crucial aspects of implementing infrastructure development projects (such as roads and highways projects) is acquisition of land and/or properties and resettlement thereof of Project Affected Persons and their families/households.

Land Acquisition Act 1984

The Land Acquisition Act I of 1984 (along with its

modifications) usually forms the basis of the land acquisition process in India. [The National Highways (Amendment) Act 1997 may be applied if the project road is declared as a National Highway.] The value of land depends upon its area and location along with its type that is classified as residential, agricultural, ponds, barren etc. besides Government Land being used for railways, roads, canals, public utilities etc.

National Policy on Resettlement and Rehabilitation 2003

In case of projects relating to Railway Lines, Highways, Transmission Lines and laying pipelines wherein only a narrow stretch of land extending over several kilometres is being acquired, the Project Affected Families will be offered an *ex gratia* amount of Rs. 10,000 per family, and no other Resettlement and Rehabilitation benefits shall be available to them.[1]

The system of extending cash compensation does not by itself, in most cases, enable the affected families to obtain cultivable agricultural land, homestead and other resources, which they have to surrender to the State. The difficulties are more acute for persons who are critically dependent on the acquired assets for their subsistence/livelihoods, such as landless agricultural workers, forest dwellers, tenants and artisans, as their distress and destitution is more severe, and yet they are not eligible for cash compensation.[2]

Project Affected Family means a family/person whose place of residence or other properties or source of livelihood are substantially affected by the process of acquisition of land for the project and who has been residing continuously for a period of not less then three years preceding the date of declaration of the affected zone or practicing any trade, occupation or vocation continuously for a period of not less than three years in the affected zone, preceding the date of declaration of the affected zone.[3]

Affected zone, in relation to a project, means declaration by the appropriate Government area of villages or locality under a project for which the land is being acquired under Land Acquisition Act 1894 or any other Act in force.[4]

The National Resettlement and Rehabilitation Policy displays concern for the more vulnerable sections of society that may be unevenly impacted by project interventions. It is to be realized that Resettlement and Rehabilitation is centrally about securing justice in nearly all its forms to Project Affected Persons. The unique feature that sets Resettlement and Rehabilitation apart is its attempt to explore new institutional mechanisms outside the scope of the conventional legal framework.

National Policy Guidelines

The Government of India has prepared a Resettlement and Rehabilitation Policy that strives to standardize the good practices related to involuntary displacement of persons and their assets in the national context. State governments as well as Central Government Agencies more or less adhere to this policy in the case of development projects. This is evident from the review of different Entitlement Matrices of road projects spread across the country.

It is imperative that best practices and lessons learnt continuously evolve during the preparatory and operational phases of development projects so that change management in difficult situations may be efficaciously handled by the concerned project authorities. So information dissemination and knowledge-sharing exercises have to be constantly upgraded with regard to the problems as well as the solutions in the context of projects involving Resettlement and Rehabilitation.

The National Policy on Resettlement and Rehabilitation for Project Affected Families (2003) prepared by the Ministry of Rural Development (Department of Land Resources) of the Government of India states that "Compulsory acquisition of land for public purpose including infrastructure projects displaces people, forcing them to give up their homes, assets and means of livelihood. Apart from depriving them of their lands, livelihoods and resource-base, displacement has other traumatic psychological and socio-cultural consequences. The Government of India recognizes the need to minimize large scale displacement to the extent possible and, where displacement is inevitable, the need to handle with utmost care and forethought issues relating to Resettlement and Rehabilitation of Project Affected Families. Such an approach is especially necessary in respect of tribals, small and marginal farmers and women."

"The system of extending cash compensation does not, by itself, in most cases enable the affected families to obtain cultivable agricultural land, homestead and other resources which they have to surrender to the State. The difficulties are more acute for persons who are critically dependent on the acquired assets for their subsistence/livelihoods such as landless agricultural workers, forest dwellers, tenants and artisans, as their distress and destitution is more severe, and yet they are not eligible for cash compensation."

This is a limitation of the National Resettlement and Rehabilitation Policy. The primary stakeholders who are not entitled to any cash compensation from the project can subsequently become a social problem in terms of their relative deprivation.

". . . The Policy essentially addresses the need to provide succour to the assetless rural poor, support the rehabilitation efforts of the resource poor sections, namely, small and marginal farmers, SCs/STs and women who have been displaced. Besides, it seeks to provide a broad canvas for an effective dialogue between the Project Affected Families and the Administration for Resettlement and Rehabilitation. Such a dialogue is expected to enable timely completion of projects with a sense of definiteness as regards costs and adequate attention to the needs of the displaced persons, especially the resource poor sections. The intention is to impart greater flexibility for interaction and negotiation so that the resultant (Compensation/Support/Assistance) Package gains all-round acceptability in the shape of a workable instrument providing satisfaction to all stakeholders/Requiring Bodies."

Dialogues in the context of involuntary resettlement of Project Affected Persons is essential in order to provide the necessary interactive space within the framework of entitlements and benefits designed for PAPs. This dialogue must continue throughout and even beyond the project cycle in order to ensure that PAPs have secured adequate representation during the policy formulation stage and comprehensive participation during the project implementation stage.

This policy further states that "In case of projects relating to Railway Lines, Highways, Transmission Lines and laying pipelines wherein only a narrow stretch of land extending over several kilomteres is being acquired, the Project Affected Families will be offered an *ex gratia* amount of Rs 10,000 per family, and *no other Resettlement and Rehabilitation benefits shall be available to them*" (emphasis added). This contradicts the long-term income/livelihood restoration objective of development projects that induce displacement as per the World Bank's policy guidelines.

"The National Policy on the Resettlement and Rehabilitation of Project Affected Families will be in the form of broad guidelines and executive instructions for guidance of all concerned and will be applicable to Projects *displacing 500 families or more* en masse in plain areas and 250 families *en masse* in hilly areas, Desert Development Programme (DDP) Blocks, areas mentioned in Schedule V and Schedule VI of the Constitution of India" (emphasis added).

This is another limitation of the National Resettlement and Rehabilitation Policy due to its mentioning of the specific number of Project Affected Families. It implies that development projects displacing less number of families would not be covered by this policy. This shortcoming may be corrected in the future to ensure social safeguards. It is essential to impart social and economic justice to Project Affected Persons. It is also imperative to ensure that their community fabric and kinship ties and cultural identities are not destroyed by way of project interventions.

World Bank Policy Guidelines

The World Bank has extended different categories of bilateral support to facilitate implementation of development projects since its inception. It also simultaneously ensures that Structural Adjustment Programme are duly implemented by the countries receiving monetary support (loans/credit grant) as a condition attached to such financial assistance. So adherence to the World Bank's Resettlement and Rehabilitation Policy Guidelines on the part of national and/or State governments is imperative in order to be eligible for any project support.

"The World Bank's involuntary resettlement policy states that project planning must avoid and minimize involuntary resettlement, and that if people lose their homes or livelihoods as a result of Bank-financed projects, they should have their standard of living improved, or at least restored."[5]

Project implementing authorities who seek World Bank funding must ensure proper adherence to the Bank's policy guidelines in order to qualify for long-term financial support and assistance. Comprehensive Resettlement and Rehabilitation policy frameworks must be prepared in this connection as one of the preliminary tasks during the project preparatory phase.

"Involuntary resettlement may cause severe long-term hardship, impoverishment and environmental damage unless appropriate measures are carefully planned and carried out. For these reasons, the overall objectives of the (World) Bank's policy on involuntary resettlement are the following :

- Involuntary resettlement should be avoided where feasible, or minimized, exploring all viable alternative project designs.
- Where it is not feasible to avoid resettlement, resettlement activities should be conceived and executed as sustainable development programme, providing sufficient investment resources to enable the persons displaced by the project to share in

project benefits. Displaced persons should be meaningfully consulted and should have opportunities to participate in planning and implementing resettlement programme.

- Displaced persons should be assisted in their efforts to improve their livelihoods and standards of living or at least to restore them, in real terms, to pre-displacement levels or to levels prevailing prior to the beginning of project implementation, whichever is higher."[6]

It is evident that the World Bank intends to maintain all possible social safeguards in order to mitigate/reduce negative impacts caused by development project interventions. So policy planners of the concerned implementing agencies who accept World Bank funding should prepare their Resettlement and Rehabilitation guidelines in accordance with the Bank's social and environmental prescriptions. Such guidelines must also be in tune with the national context and ground realities of specific projects.

World Bank Funded Road Projects

Several State governments in India such as Andhra Pradesh, Gujarat, Karnataka, Kerala, Uttar Pradesh, Mizoram and Tamil Nadu and government agencies like the National Highways Authority of India have in recent times undertaken road improvement projects funded by the World Bank.

Resettlement and Rehabilitation Policy Guidelines were prepared by the concerned implementing agencies in accordance with the World Bank's Operational Directive 4.30/Operational Policy 4.12 related to involuntary resettlement. A few road projects can be cited in this regard such as :

1. Third National Highway Project (TNHP) ,
2. Grand Trunk Road Improvement Project (GTRIP),

3. Allahabad Bypass Project (NHAI Project),
4. Lucknow-Muzaffarpur National Highway Project (NHAI Project),
5. Andhra Pradesh State Highways Project (APSHP),
6. Karnataka State Highways Improvement Project (KSHIP),
7. Tamil Nadu Road Sector Project; and
8. Uttar Pradesh State Roads Project.

Certain changes have taken place over time in the policy formulation stage of different road projects funded by the World Bank. Such moderate policy shifts indicate that road or any other development projects require streamlining in accordance with the local-level situation and ground realities although the general policy framework with regard to involuntary resettlement of Project Affected Persons remains almost the same.

This is a lesson learnt i.e. specific projects require specific planning attuned to the ground realities in order to ensure that Resettlement and Rehabilitation Policy guidelines are properly followed as mandated by the World Bank. Lacunae identified in earlier road projects can be addressed in subsequent projects (especially with regard to the entitlements of PAPs) in this process that strategizes continuous knowledge upgradation underpinned by change management mechanisms.

Case Studies

For instance: the Entitlement Matrix of the Allahabad Bypass Project mentions that "PAPs will be explained the process (of acquisition of land and assets and compensation against such acquisition at replacement cost or actual market value) and their views will be taken into consideration while determining the market value."

This concern was not reflected in similar terms in the Entitlement Matrix of the Lucknow-Muzaffarpur National Highway Project. But it was duly reflected in the case of the

Kerala State Highways Project. The National Highways Authority of India's Detailed Entitlement Matrix for the National Highway Corridor (Public-Private Partnership Project) also includes this people's participation factor in its design (2002).

The provision of verification of mortgage clearance by the Project Authority is included in the Allahabad Bypass Project while it is not included in the Lucknow-Muzaffarpur Project. Categories of land loss were included in the Entitlement Matrix of the Andhra Pradesh State Highways Project (1996). This was a novel approach to identify the types of land loss in terms of magnitude (>25% and <25%).

The provision of "Unforeseen impacts shall be documented and mitigated based on the principles agreed upon in this policy framework" was absent in the Andhra Pradesh State Highways Project. This provision is essential to address new factors that may emerge at different points of the project cycle.

The Kerala State Highways Project (2000) provided "For those who choose self-relocation, the Project Displaced Persons will be entitled to plots . . . even if they do not opt for resettlement sites." This was a unique effort to incorporate an adequate social space required for Project Affected Persons in their pursuit of alternative places of residence and/or work.

This project also mentioned that "Easily replaced resources such as cultural properties will be conserved (by means of special protection, relocation, replacement etc.) in consultation with the community." This provision respects the cultural identities of Project Affected Persons and ensures that participatory development is safeguarded under the project so that the primary stakeholders are properly benefited from the positive impacts of the civil works undertaken in connection with the project. It is also reflected in the Entitlement Matrix of the Uttar Pradesh State Roads Project Phase I (2002).

The Tamil Nadu Road Sector Project (2003) remarked in its Detailed Entitlement Matrix that "The land (agricultural or otherwise) purchase grant will be available if alternative land is purchased and registered within one year of receiving the compensation amount. The grant will be released on the submission of copy of registered sale deed".

This provision (available to those Project Affected Persons who lost more than 25 per cent of their land holding and were left with less than the minimum economic land holding) is a good practice as it considerably streamlined the land compensation mechanism and ensured social safeguard for PAPs. This project also included the option of built houses depending on the size of houses lost. This may be replicated elsewhere if practicable.

The Karnataka State Highways Improvement Project (Raichur and Bijapur Bypasses) pinpointed the budgetary provisions for implementation of the Resettlement Action Plan by mentioning that "All the costs calculated will be pegged to the inflation costs after 2 years from the Cut-Off Date". It also proposed in its Entitlement Matrix that "The maintenance of common property resources and infrastructure will be handed to the Local Authority."

This provision ensures that the benefits of the project percolate to the grass roots as a result of decentralization of power and devolution of resources. The project also included a "Scope for making amendments in the Resettlement and Rehabilitation Policy." This is critical in order to accommodate any factor(s) not conceived during the project preparatory stage.

The Detailed Entitlement Matrix of the Gujarat State Highways Project (Phase IIB) included the institutional arrangement of an Independent Committee entrusted to decide the replacement cost or actual market price of agricultural land and assets of private property owners. This was a good practice and can be emulated elsewhere. This provision made the assessment procedure of land and assets transparent and also made this committee accountable to the Project Affected Persons.

The organizational structure of the Resettlement and Rehabilitation Cell has been mentioned in the Assam State Roads Resettlement and Rehabilitation Policy (2004). This is important because such organizational structures and institutional arrangements ultimately help implement the Resettlement Action Plan and facilitate entrenchment of good practices as per World Bank guidelines.

Review of different project policies reveal that a uniform set of guidelines apply to the Detailed Entitlement Matrices with minor inclusion and exclusion of certain provisions. The key beneficiaries have already been identified and the principal entitlements have been decided upon. Such policy continuity is essential for the long-term sustainability of benefits accruing from road projects funded by the World Bank.

Legal Framework

The Land Acquisition Act I of 1984 allows Government Agencies to expropriate any private land for a public purpose (by exercising Eminent Domain), provided the owners in possession of legal titles to occupy the land and structures are duly compensated. Current land acquisition compensation packages include the following :

1. Market value of the land.
2. A solatium of 30 per cent on the market value of land.
3. An interest of 12 per cent on the market value of land from the Date of Notification to the Date of Declaration of Award.
4. Additional compensation is also allowed for loss of trees, crops, houses and other immovable assets.
5. The compensation for loss of earning to the sharecropper would be not more than six times of net average annual income derived during the three years immediately preceding the Date of Acquisition.
6. Damage due to severing of the land holding from adjoining land.

7. Damage due to land acquisition leading to change of residence or place of business.

Whenever it appears to the appropriate Government that the land in any locality (is needed or) is likely to be needed for any public purpose (or for a company), a Notification to that effect shall be published in the Official Gazette (and in two daily newspapers circulating in that locality of which at least one shall be in the regional language), and the District Collector shall cause public notice of the substance of such Notification to be given at convenient places in the said locality.[7]

Where land acquisition is required the practice is to refer to the Date of Notification under law as the Cut-Off Date. Compensation is paid on the basis of value of the land at the time of Notification. The District Collector would issue a Notification announcing the public purpose for which the land or property is to be acquired. This would be followed by a period of one month during which objections may be filed by concerned persons with an interest in the land/property to be acquired. Hearing of objections and the award of compensation by the District Collector would follow subsequently. All legal procedures would be meticulously followed while awarding compensation packages to Project Affected Persons in possession of legal titles to the land and (residential/commercial) structures to be acquired for the project.[8]

Resettlement and Rehabilitation Guidelines

Every conceivable effort should be made during the project design and preparation stages to minimize acquisition of land and other assets in order to reduce adverse socio-economic impacts. The structures/assets falling outside the Right of Way/Corridor of Impact should be left undisturbed as far as practicable. Road and/or flyover projects may have to deal with Project Affected Persons who fall under the following categories :

1. Legal owners and/or tenants getting adversely affected due to the acquisition of their land and assets or due to the fact that such land or assets so acquired are their sources of livelihood; and
2. Encroachers and/or squatters who are the illegal occupants/users of public property/land/structures falling within the Right of Way and accordingly live and/or earn their livelihood by operating within the Right of Way.[9]

The Project Authority would take final decision with regard to compensation and/or Resettlement and Rehabilitation assistance. No compensation for land may be provided to the encroachers and squatters keeping in mind their illegal status. Resettlement and Rehabilitation assistance may be provided to encroachers and squatters who belong to the disadvantaged and vulnerable groups. Compensation for structures and other lost assets (required for the project) may be paid at the replacement value[10] to encroachers/squatters who belong to the vulnerable groups.[11] The Project Authority would take final decision in this regard.

Resettlement and Rehabilitation Compensation

Legal owners of land and property shall be entitled to compensation. Squatters and encroachers who are not ordinarily entitled for compensation may receive certain benefits as per their respective entitlements if they belong to vulnerable groups. The compensation for land and buildings shall be provided within the ambit of the Land Acquisition Act 1894 and assistance would be provided to meet the replacement value. All losses, including loss of income, should be compensated within the overall Resettlement and Rehabilitation package as per the (proposed) Entitlement Framework. The Project Authority shall take the final decision in this regard.

Compensation and assistance would be extended to

Project Affected Persons who were identified on or prior to the Cut-Off Date. Where land acquisition is required the practice is to refer to the Date of Notification under law as the Cut-Off Date. Compensation is paid on the basis of value of the land during Notification. The Project Authority would ensure that a Notification is issued by announcing the public purpose for which private land and/or property are to be acquired. This would be followed by a period of one month during which concerned persons may file objections with an interest in the land/property to be acquired. The Grievance Redress Committee would deal with claims regarding assistance.

Payment of compensation against land acquired by the Project Authority may be made on the basis of updated official records and ground-level information. Land records of title/classification/current land use may be updated to ensure adequate cost compensation and allotment of land to the Entitled Persons/Project Displaced Persons. Official records as they are on the Cut-Off Date may be consulted in order to determine the classification and current use of land. If 75 per cent or more land holding of a Project Affected Person/Project Displaced Person is acquired or when the part of a plot of land remaining after acquisition becomes economically unviable after acquisition, the owner of such land/property shall have the right to seek acquisition of his/her entire contiguous land holding/property provided the residual land is less than the Minimum Economic Holding.[12]

The compensation amount for the land and properties to be acquired by the Project Authority shall be paid according to the provisions of the Land Acquisition Act. The Project Authority shall pay the difference as assistance if the provisions are less than the replacement value. The Project Authority may decide on the magnitude of loss to structures (in terms of percentage of the existing area or otherwise) in order to consider the owners of such affected structures to be Project Displaced Persons.

The Project Authority shall determine the possible replacement cost of land and assets to be acquired. Land rate surveys may be carried out by the Project Authority for this purpose in association with representatives of Project Affected Persons and external assessment agencies. The Project Authority may utilize the following systems of assessment while determining the replacement cost of land:

1. Taking into account such prescribed rates or the average of the actual transaction rates of similar lands for contemporary years for which sale deeds are registered.
2. Taking into consideration twenty times of the annual value of gross production of the concerned land averaged over the preceding five years.
3. Fixing up market value of land equal to the minimum land value if so prescribed by the State Government under the Indian Stamp Act for the purpose of registration of sale deeds under the Indian Registration Act of 1908.

The replacement cost of land to be fixed by the Project Authority would be the amount that shall be the highest among the three amounts arrived at by the aforesaid three alternative methods. The difference shall be paid in the form of assistance in case the replacement cost is higher than the market value determined by the Project Authority.

The value of the houses, buildings and other immovable properties of the Project Affected Persons (including the Project Displaced Persons) shall be determined for the purpose of payment of compensation without depreciation.

Compensation for properties belonging to the Project Affected Community or for common places of religious worship that would be acquired for the project shall be provided to enable construction of the same at the relocation site(s) (if any) through the offices of the concerned local self-governing bodies in accordance with the modalities determined by such bodies to ensure proper utilization of the compensation amount.[13]

Persons (belonging to the vulnerable groups) who derive their livelihood from the common places of religious worship may be supported by the project's special assistance scheme (if any).

Compensation for trees would be based on their market value in case of timber bearing trees and replacement cost in case of fruit bearing trees as per the rates decided by the Project Authority in consultation with the concerned Government Departments. Loss of income may also be considered when assessing the compensation amount.

Compensation shall be paid and efforts would be made to complete the Resettlement and Rehabilitation of Project Affected Persons/Project Displaced Persons before taking possession of their land and/or properties. The Project Affected Persons/Project Displaced Persons shall hand over their land and properties to the Project Authority free from all encumbrances such as mortgage, debt etc. for the purpose of acquisition.

In the case of any loan on such acquired land and properties extended to the Project Affected Persons by any Government Agency remaining unadjusted as per the information furnished by the Project Affected Persons or by the loaner agency such amounts shall be deducted from their total compensation.

All transaction costs (including transportation costs/ wages lost due to the project) shall be assessed and compensated for. The payment of this amount shall be made in accordance with the relevant clauses of the Land Acquisition Act.

All payments shall be made into the joint bank accounts of the husband and the wife while all new titles issued shall be in the joint names of the husband and the wife. All payments shall be made in public to ensure transparency.

Disposal of acquired properties shall be carried out as follows :

- The acquired land and properties shall vest in the Government Department(s) paying compensation for such land and properties.
- Project Displaced Persons shall be allowed to collect the materials salvaged from their houses and shops etc. acquired by the project even after payment of compensation. The Government would levy no charges upon them for the same. A notice to that effect would be issued to take away the materials so salvaged within 48 hours of demolition of structures. If not collected then the Project Authority without giving any further notice shall dispose the same.
- The Project Displaced Persons receiving compensation for trees shall be allowed to take away timber from their trees (acquired by the project) for domestic use. Trees standing on Government Land shall be sold by public auction to be organized by the concerned Government Department(s).

The Project Authority can take appropriate action to demolish structures within the project's Corridor of Impact after the expiry of the notified deadline. The Project Authority can also dismantle structures and evict individuals within the Corridor of Impact of the project if it is established that such structures and individuals occupied the public Right of Way after the duly notified Cut-Off Date. Any grievances and objections in this connection would be referred to the Grievance Redress Committee.

Information Dissemination Campaign

Information dissemination exercises for Project Affected

Persons may be carried out prior to implementation of the Resettlement Action Plan. This campaign may be facilitated by the Project Authority and executed by the Partner Non Government Organization(s) that would be appointed to implement the Resettlement Action Plan.

Impact Categories

Project-induced displacement may lead to loss of income or reduced income for Project Affected Persons. The main categories of impact expected as a result of the project include the following types of loss :

1. Loss of commercial establishments,
2. Loss of commercial space,
3. Loss of residential (dwelling) units,
4. Loss of livelihood, and
5. Loss of common property resources.[14]

Loss of temporary commercial structures is a complex problem since the issue of retaining the present customer base must be considered in this regard. Another problem pertains to the tenants and owners. Mitigation measures delivered under this Resettlement Action Plan may include reconstructing demolished commercial structures in an adjacent area so that the present customer base is retained. The Project Authority should duly consider the means of accomplishing this and addressing ownership of the new structures. The Project Authority would make final decision with regard to all aspects of this matter. There is also the need to respond to more generalized impacts of disturbance in the lives and livelihood of Project Affected Persons. Such adverse impacts may be mitigated by payment of Maintenance Allowance.

Institutional Arrangements

Implementation of this Resettlement Action Plan requires staff, resources and close coordination with different agencies and organizations working in the project area. This Resettlement Action Plan seeks to provide a strategy for developing the required implementation capacity on the part of the Project Authority.

Capacity building and training may be coordinated with the project implementation schedule in order to ensure that skilled staff members are available to implement this Resettlement Action Plan without any delay in civil works.

Orientation workshops may be organised by the Project Authority (Project Implementation Unit) and Partner Non Government Organizations. A Resettlement and Rehabilitation Cell may be established within the Project Implementation Unit. Partner NGOs would be engaged to support the Project Authority and counterparted with PIU personnel to foster transfer of social development expertise. An independent external agency may provide professional services for monitoring and evaluating the Resettlement and Rehabilitation process.

The Project Authority may initiate high priority actions to establish institutional linkages necessary for time-bound delivery of the Project Affected Persons' entitlements and assure coordination across agencies as well as between the various social and economic mitigation measures outlined in this Resettlement Action Plan.

Institutional Context

Effective implementation of this Resettlement Action Plan would require institutional relationships and responsibilities, rapid organizational development and collaborative efforts on the part of the Project Authority, State Government, Partner NGO(s) and Project Affected Persons.

Resettlement and Rehabilitation Coordination

The Project Implementation Unit would be responsible for

coordinating with different government agencies. The Resettlement and Rehabilitation Cell would establish operational links to facilitate the critical process of project induced resettlement. It may establish an effective process of dialogue between the Project Authority and the Project Affected Persons/Communities.

The Resettlement and Rehabilitation Cell would have to provide the means and mechanisms for coordinating the efficacious delivery of compensation and assistance entitlements to those adversely affected due to implementation of the project.

The Resettlement and Rehabilitation Cell would have to contribute social development perspectives and field-level inputs to ongoing project design and implementation by working closely with project planners, contractors and construction supervision consultants.

It would link the project with the concerned Government Agencies, provide liaison with Affected Communities, establish decentralized (grass roots) committees to coordinate social development and resettlement operations in the field, mobilize Partner NGO(s) and motivate local-level Community Based Organizations to represent and safeguard the interests of Project Affected Persons.

It would also engage training services, oversee a grievance redress process, actively monitor Resettlement Action Plan implementation and cooperate with project evaluation exercises. The Resettlement and Rehabilitation Cell would be responsible for disseminating project related information to the public and providing additional opportunities for civil societal feedback.

Inter-Departmental Coordination

Resettlement Action Plan entitlements for Income Restoration Programmes and Project Affected Groups are exclusively the responsibility of the Project Authority (apart from the land acquisition and compensation components in which the Revenue Department and the Project Authority would jointly provide entitlements). Several entitlements comprise services and benefits ordinarily provided by other government sponsored social development programmes such as the vulnerable groups' housing schemes.

The Resettlement and Rehabilitation Cell may establish liaison with these ongoing programmes to facilitate access of the Project Affected Persons and take advantage of services and programmes already in place. It may negotiate cost sharing arrangements wherever feasible. Restoration of community assets would require coordination with the Public Health Engineering Department.

The Resettlement and Rehabilitation Cell's coordination with the Education Department would be required in the event schools are adversely impacted. A variety of State and Central Government programmes addressing women's needs may be associated with other group entitlements, including those responding to potential transmission of sexually transmitted diseases as well as reproductive and child health.

Grievance Redress Mechanism

The Resettlement Action Plan's participatory processes as well as its compensation and support mechanisms are expected to enhance acceptance of the resettlement programme and reduce complaints. There may nevertheless be individuals or groups who perceive that they have not received adequate support or that their needs have not been properly addressed.

The Project Authority would, therefore, establish a Grievance Redress Committee. This Committee would have representation from Project Affected Persons, NGO(s)/ CBO(s) involved in the Resettlement Action Plan implementation, local level Government Officials and the Project Authority.

This Committee would hear complaints and facilitate solutions. This process is expected to promote settlement of disputes through mediation in order to reduce the volume of time-consuming litigation. The Project Authority would take final decision on different aspects related to grievance redress of Project Affected Persons.

Monitoring and Evaluation

Monitoring and Evaluation are critical activities in the process of involuntary resettlement. Monitoring involves periodic checking to ascertain whether Resettlement and Rehabilitation activities are going according to the Resettlement Action Plan. It provides required feedback to the Project Authority to ensure that the Resettlement Action Plan implementation programme runs on schedule. Evaluation is basically the post-project assessment of whether the implementation programme was finally able to achieve its stated objectives. An independent external agency may be engaged by the Project Authority to carry out the (impact) Monitoring and Evaluation of the project with regard to implementation of the Resettlement Action Plan. Monitoring and Evaluation would measure project performance against project objectives.

Long-term impact indicators may be examined during the project evaluation stage. The Project Authority may contract an external agency (such as an academic institution) that would undertake independent evaluation studies at least twice during the life-time of the project. These evaluations would provide inputs to the mid-term review and the post-project report. Independent evaluation exercises may focus on assessing whether the overall objectives of the project are being met and would utilize the impact indicators as a basis for evaluation. The Project Authority would take final decisions on all Monitoring and Evaluation (and related) aspects of the project.

Monitoring of involuntary resettlement operations require an application of general project monitoring procedures to the processes occurring in resettlement with particular attention to the specific high risks intrinsic in such operations. This means that monitoring of Resettlement and Rehabilitation requires certain specialized skills. To meet this requirement a sub-unit within the Resettlement and Rehabilitation Cell may be established.

An external agency may be appointed to monitor and evaluate the Resettlement and Rehabilitation programme on a periodic basis. This additional perspective in Resettlement Action Plan implementation is critical because conventional Monitoring and Evaluation exercises carried out by government agencies may not adequately focus on certain aspects of importance to the implementing agencies. This external agency would be required to streamline the Resettlement and Rehabilitation process. External Monitoring and Evaluation studies may synchronize with the implementation of the Resettlement Action Plan. The external agency may submit periodic reports on the progress of Resettlement Action Plan implementation to the Project Authority. It may also identify the issues and concerns that require attention and subsequent action on the part of the Project Authority.

Conclusions

- Implementation of the Resettlement Action Plan on the part of Non-Government Organization(s) appointed by the Project Authority would require sensitive handling of the critical issue of involuntary displacement that is a necessary result of infra-structural development projects involving roads and highways, flyovers and interchanges etc.
- Legal owners of land and structures would suffer in terms of loss of immovable assets while their tenants would suffer losses either in terms of residence or livelihood or both.
- Resettlement of affected persons and rehabilitation of their lost assets (land and/or structures) and liveli-hood are critical yet imperative social development exercises of infrastructure development projects that require displacement of individuals and groups.

Recommendations

- The Project Authority may set up a dedicated

office in order to provide information with regard to the Resettlement and Rehabilitation guidelines and the Resettlement Action Plan.

- Fixation of compensation to the legal owners of affected land and structures should be based on the present market rate.
- The Grievance Redress Committee may expedite the process of redress of grievances. Project Affected Persons may be counselled by Partner Non-Government Organization(s) as and when required.
- Unauthorized encroachers and squatters as such do not have any legal rights to their occupied land and structures but the vulnerable groups among such illegal occupants may be considered by the Project Authority for Resettlement and Rehabilitation support/assistance.
- Illegal encroachers and squatters may be allowed to salvage the dismantled materials. The Project Authority may consider appointing such persons (belonging to vulnerable groups) as casual workers during the construction stage of the project in order to provide livelihood at least on a short-term basis in order to mitigate the adverse impacts of involuntary displacement.
- Representatives from the local bodies such as municipalities/panchayats, officials from the local administration and police, local Community-Based Organizations/Non Government Organizations may be consulted on a periodic basis to ensure efficacious implementation of the Resettlement Action Plan.
- Involuntary resettlement caused by infrastructure development projects should be informed by comprehensive mitigation measures in order to reduce adverse impacts on the existing social fabric of Project Affected Persons.

NOTES

1. *Source*: National Policy on Resettlement and Rehabilitation for Project Affected Families 2003 (published in The Gazette of India Extraordinary Part I, Section I, No. 46, Dated 17th February 2004), Chapter VI (Resettlement and Rehabilitation Benefits for Project Affected Families).
2. *Ibid.* Chapter I (Policy: Preamble).
3. *Ibid.* Chapter III (Definitions).
4. *Ibid.*
5. http://www.ciel.org/Ifi/wbinvolresettle.html
6. http://wbln0018.worldbank.org/Institutional/Manuals/OpManual.nsf/toc2/CA2D01A4D1BDF58085256 B19008197F6?OpenDocument#foot
7. http://www.indiahousing.com/general/acquisition.asp
8. Public sector organizations have in certain cases directly purchased land/property through negotiations due to project exigencies.
9. Identification of encroachers and squatters may be sought from the voters' lists or from any other legal documents or information from the community (in the absence of ration cards/photo identity cards).
10. Replacement cost shall be equivalent to an amount required to acquire substitute land of equal productive value as well as to replace any structures or other assets. The difference is to be paid by the project in the form of assistance in case the replacement cost is more than the compensation at market price as determined by the Project Authority.
11. Vulnerable categories include Women Headed Households, Landless Agricultural Workers, Scheduled Castes, Scheduled Tribes, Persons from households with income less than 20 per cent above the Poverty Line, Elderly Persons (above 65 years of age) who are the single earning members of their respective households, Persons with Disability and Orphan Children.
12. The Minimum Economic Holding is equivalent to two hectares of non-irrigated or one hectare of irrigated land.
13. This provision would be applicable in those cases where relocation site(s) may be developed for Project Affected Persons/Project Displaced Persons.
14. Common Property Resources may include playgrounds,

community meeting platforms, bus bays, public stand posts, hand pumps, wells, vats, cattle grazing areas, solid waste disposal sites, sewerage and drainage systems, water supply and sanitation systems, electrical infrastructure, educational institutions, primary health centres, local markets etc. that are utilized by the affected community members for their everyday civic requirements.

ANNEXURE I : KEY DEFINITIONS

Corridor of Impact

The Corridor of Impact is defined as the construction width or the operational width plus a safety zone on either side of the road. Within the Corridor of Impact there should not be any structure or other hindrances. The Corridor of Impact would vary depending on site requirement.

Compensation and Assistance

Compensation refers to restitution made to legal property owners in possession of title deeds under the Land Acquisition Act. Compensation is payment made by the Government to legal owners when Eminent Domain is exercised to transfer ownership of private property/land to the State. Assistance refers to all other support mechanisms such as grants, assets, services etc. provided to Entitled Persons (or their groups).

Project Affected Persons

Project Affected Persons are individuals who would be adversely impacted by implementation of the civil works of the project. They would lose land/property/livelihood in this process. So a Project Affected Person is an individual who (as a direct consequence of the project) sustains damages :

1. due to severance of his/her land, or
2. due to negative impacts on his/her immovable properties in any manner, or
3. due to adverse effects on his/her livelihood calculated on the basis of an objective assessment.

Project Affected Persons include Project Displaced Persons. These are individuals who are compelled to change their place of residence/work/business due to implementation of the project. Project Affected Persons are categorized as follows :

1. Private Property Owners,
2. Tenants,
3. Sharecroppers,
4. Squatters, and
5. Encroachers.

Depending upon their category, Project Affected Persons would be entitled to either compensation or assistance or both. Each category is described as follows :

Private Property Owners have legal titles to land, structures and/or other assets. They are entitled to compensation under the Land Acquisition Act. They are also entitled to shifting (relocation) assistance. They may also be facilitated for voluntary relocation to alternative site(s) (if any).

Tenants have *bona fide* tenancy agreements with private property owners to occupy a structure or land for residence, business or cultivation purposes. They are eligible for certain compensation/assistance as per existing norms.

Share-Croppers are those individuals who have formally or informally entered into an agreement with private property owners to cultivate their land.

Squatters have illegally occupied Government Land for residential, commercial and/or other purposes. They are not eligible for compensation but would qualify for certain assistance and targeted support if they belong to vulnerable groups (defined subsequently). They would be entitled to shifting assistance. They would also be assisted for voluntary relocation to alternative sites.

Encroachers have extended their buildings, land holdings, business premises or work places illegally into Government Land. They are not eligible for either compensation or assistance. Vulnerable groups would be entitled for project support.

Persons Losing their Livelihood

Persons losing their livelihood are Project Affected Persons who are at least 18 years of age at the time of displacement and who stand to lose their primary occupation or primary source of income as a result of project interventions. Such persons are eligible for support extended by the Project Authority on the basis of their contributions to household income.

Vulnerable Groups

Vulnerable groups may receive special targeted support and assistance under the project because they would be unevenly impacted by developmental interventions. It is desirable that such groups receive special support from the project in order to ensure social safeguards. The human face of the project would be duly maintained if adequate attention is paid to these vulnerable groups. The following categories may be considered vulnerable :

- Women Headed Households,
- Landless Agricultural Workers,
- Scheduled Castes,

- Scheduled Tribes,
- Persons from households with income less than 20 per cent above the Poverty Line,
- Elderly Persons (above 65 years of age) who are the single earning members of their respective households,
- Persons with Disability, and
- Orphan Children.

Project Affected Households

Project Affected Households are those that would be adversely affected by implementation of the civil works. Project Affected Households are entitled to certain benefits as a household unit.

Project Affected Groups

Project Affected Groups are communities (with a focus on the more vulnerable and weaker sections) that may be adversely/disproportionately affected by the project.

Entitled Persons

Entitled Persons are Project Affected Persons who qualify for (or are entitled to) assistance/compensation since they would be resettled or otherwise be negatively impacted by the project. Entitled Persons include Project Affected Households and Project Affected Groups.

Cut-Off Date

The Cut-Off Date would be announced in consultation with the concerned District Magistrates in order to ensure that squatter settlements do not proliferate in the affected area due to lack of proper information. A Project Affected Person not identified at the Cut-Off Date may be considered for support if he/she can produce the necessary documentary evidence of his/her residential proof (of not less than three years) before declaration of the Cut-Off Date. The Cut-Off Date identifies Project Affected Persons (within the existing/ proposed Right of Way) who are entitled to compensation and/or assistance. Persons occupying the Right of Way after the Cut-Off Date would not be considered as Project Affected Persons under this project. Such persons would not be entitled to any assistance. The list of Project Affected Persons may be made public to ensure that Entitled Persons are duly covered under the project. Project Affected Persons may be allowed to lodge complaints (if any). Appropriate measures may be taken by the Project Authority to avoid any further encroachment(s) or squatter settlement(s) in the project area after announcement of the Cut-Off Date. Information dissemination exercises are critical to make the Cut-Off Date credible *vis-à-vis* the general public. The Project Authority may ensure that the Cut-Off Date is suitably publicized in the project area. Public Notifications in this regard should be prominently displayed in Government Offices, Post Offices, market places, telephone booths, shop windows, public notice boards in the local language. Word of mouth may also be spread by deploying public address systems.

Household Unit

The Household Unit is defined as all persons living and eating together as a single unit. The household as a collective entity shall be entitled to compensation and assistance in certain cases.

Family

A family shall mean the husband, wife and their minor children. Every son or unmarried daughter who has attained 18 years of age on or before the Cut-Off Date would be treated as a separate family. Every divorced or widowed daughter living separately or with the family on or prior to the Cut-Off Date would be treated as a separate family. Orphans in one single household would be clubbed together as one single family. Mentally handicapped persons irrespective of age and sex would be treated as one single family.

Landless Agricultural Worker

A landless agricultural worker is a person who does not hold any agricultural land and who has been deriving his/her principal income by working on the lands of others as a sub-tenant or as an agricultural labourer prior to the Cut-Off Date.

Small Farmer

A farmer holding two hectares of non-irrigated or one hectare of irrigated land shall be treated as a small farmer.

Marginal Farmer

A farmer holding one hectare of non-irrigated or ½ hectare of irrigated land shall be treated as a marginal farmer.

Minimum Economic Holding

The Minimum Economic Holding is equivalent to two hectares of non-irrigated or one hectare of irrigated land.

Income

The Income of a Project Affected Person shall mean the amount of income as shown in his/her Income Tax Return prior to the Cut-Off Date. His/her income shall be calculated (in the absence of any Income Tax Return) by an objective assessment applying the same method as adopted by the Government Agencies to identify Below Poverty Line families.

2 Economics of the Sustainable Environment

A Review

Jayanta Sinha and **Amrita Pal**

Over the past three decades, there is increasing consciousness about environmental problems facing communities, nations, and the world. During this period, natural resource and environmental issues have grown in scope and urgency. In 1970, the Environmental Protection Agency was created in the United States to address to a new problem of air and water pollution. In 1972, the first international conference on the environment, the United Nations Conference on the Human Environment, was held in Stockholm. In 1992, the United Nations Conference on Environment and Development (UNCED) was the result of growing world-wide attention to environmental issues. This conference focussed on major global issues including depletion of the earth's protective ozone layer, depletion of tropical and old-growth forests and wetlands, species extinction, and the steady build-up of carbon dioxide and other "greenhouse" gases causing global warming and climate change. Eight years later, the United Nations Environmental Programme (UNEP) report *Global Environmental Outlook 2000* found that "environmental gains from new technology and policies are being overtaken by the pace and scale of population growth and economic development." In 2002, the follow-up report *Global Environmental Outlook 3* stated that, in spite of great strides the state of the global environment continues to deteriorate. Moreover, UNEP points to nitrogen pollution in freshwater and oceans, exposure to toxic chemicals and hazardous wastes, forest and freshwater ecosystem damage, water contamination and declining groundwater supplies, urban air pollution and wastes, and overexploitation of major ocean fisheries. Underlying all these problems is global population growth, adding more than 70 million people a year and would pass 8 billion by the year 2030. As a result, scientists, policy-makers, and the general public have begun to ponder over questions like :

- What will the future look like?
- Can we respond to these multiple threats adequately and in time to prevent irreversible damage to the planetary systems that support life?

Here come the questions of economic analysis of environmental issues. The policies for environmental protection are often measured – and sometimes rejected – in terms of their economic costs although environmental issues surpass economics sometimes. For instance, it is extremely difficult to preserve open land that has high commercial development value. Either large sums must be raised to purchase the land, or strong political opposition to "locking up" land must be overcome. Environmental protection organizations often face a continued battle with ever-increasing economic development pressures.

Often public policy issues aim at the conflict between development and the environment. This leads to even more critical questions :

- Does economic development necessarily require a high environmental price?
- Although all economic development must affect the environment to some degree, is "environment-friendly" development possible?
- If we have to make a trade-off between development and environment, how shall we decide the proper balance?

Questions such as these highlight the importance of environmental economics. Most economics text starts with the three vital economic questions :

1.What should be produced?
2. How should it be produced?
3. For whom should it be produced?

This is achieved by having a better understanding of human activities in a market system.

Considering environmental aspects the questions become :

1. What should be produced and what should be maintained?
2. How should production and maintenance be accomplished?
3. For whom should economic activity be undertaken?

'Environmental Economics' is a different branch of Economics that acknowledges the value of both the economic activity and environment and makes choices based on those values. The goal is to achieve balance between the economic activity and the environmental impacts considering all the relevant costs and benefits. The theories are designed to take into account pollution and natural resource depletion, which the traditional model of Economics fails to do. This failure can be addressed by correcting prices so that they can take into account external costs[1] . Central to environmental economics is the concept of externality. This means that some effects of an activity are not taken into account in its price. For instance, pollution in excess of the socially optimal level may occur if the prices a producer pays do not include the impacts (costs) experienced by those adversely affected. Externality occurs in connection to public goods (goods that are non-excludable and rival, that is, they are open to all, but potentially exhaustible). Visitors to an open-access recrea-tional area often use the resource more than they should pay for visit to that place. This leads to environmental degrada-tion in the absence of any policy instrument (for example, permits, regulation) used to control access. In economic terminology, these are examples of market failures. Market failure is defined as the inability of markets to reflect the full social costs or benefits of a good, service, or state of the world. So, when markets fail, the result will be inefficient or unfavourable allocation of resources[2]. Although the aim of economic theory is to achieve efficiency, Environmental Economics is used as a tool to find a balance in the world's system of resource use[3]. Another key term in environmental economics is scarcity. Historically, goods and services provided by the environment were not considered scarce. Scarcity is a misallocation of these services (which are not limitless) due to pricing problem. If resources were properly priced to include all costs, then the resource could not be over-exploited because the actual cost would be too high. So proper pricing is a major problem in environmental economics.

Approaches to Natural Resource and Environmental Economics

There are two approaches to address the problem of natural resource and environmental economics. The first, or traditional or conventional approach uses a set of models and techniques embedded in the standard *neo-classical mainstream* of economic thoughts to employ economic concepts to the environment. The second approach, recognized as ecological economics[4], takes a different viewpoint. Rather than applying economic view to the environment, ecological economics seeks to place economic activity in the perspective of the biological and physical systems that sustain life, together with all human activities. Environmental economics is distinguished from ecological economics, which takes as its premise that economics is a strict sub-field of ecology. Ecological economics adopts a more pluralistic approach to environmental problems and focusses more explicitly on long-term environmental sustainability and issues of scale.

The Traditional Economics Approach

Several models in economic theory specifically address

environmental issues. One important application of neo-classical economic theory deals with the allocation of non-renewable resources (oil and mineral resources), renewable resources (agricultural soils), common property resources (atmosphere and oceans) and public goods (national parks and wild life preserves). Since these resources are not privately owned, the pricing of these resources differ from those goods traded in the market. Another central concept in neo-classical economic analysis of the environment is that of externalities (sometimes referred as third-party effects) or external costs and benefits. The theory of externalities analyzes the costs of environmental damage caused by economic activities or the social benefits created by economic activity that improves the environment. Modern environ-mental economic theory, built on this foundation, addresses many issues varying from overfishing to fossil fuel depletion to parkland conservation.

The Ecological Economics Approach

Ecological Economics capture a broader perspective in framing environmental questions by incorporating laws derived from the natural sciences. Ecological economics theorists emphasize the importance of energy resources, especially fossil fuels, in existing economic systems. Although ecological systems depend on energy inputs natural systems rely almost entirely on solar energy. The rapid growth of economic production requires enormous energy inputs, and global economic systems will make even greater energy demands growing with time. Energy availability and environmental implications of energy use are fundamental ecological problem. Basic principle of ecological economics is that human economic activity must be constrained by the environment's carrying capacity. Carrying capacity is defined as the population level and consumption activities of humans or animals that the available natural resource base can carry on without depletion. Although the standard economic theory gives these factors insufficient weight major structural changes in the nature of economic activity are required to adapt to environmental constraints. Sometimes the theories show significant agreement, and sometimes they produce widely varying results. Now consider the relationship between the economic system, natural resources, and the environment.

A Framework for Understanding the Ecological Perspective

The relationship between environment and economic activities can be explained by the traditional 'circular flow diagram' (Figure 2.1). Circular flow model is able to explain a simplified model of relationships relating households and business firms in two markets *i.e.*, the market for goods and services and the market for factors of production. The

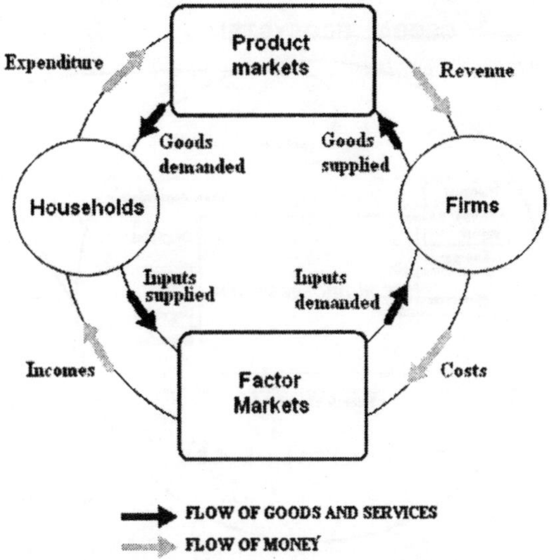

Figure 2.1: The circular flow of income is a simple model of the economy depicting flows of goods and services and factors of production concerning firms and households. In the absence of government and international trade this simple model shows that households provide the factors of production for firms who produce goods and services. In return the factors of production obtain factor payments, for instance wages, which conse-cutively are spent on the output of firms.

services of production factors (land, labour, and capital) are 'inputs' to the production of goods and services for households consumption needs. In both markets the interaction of supply and demand determines a market-clearing price and an equilibrium level of output. Natural resources (minerals, water, fossil fuels, forests, fisheries, and farmland) fall under the inclusive category of "land." The two other major production factors, labour and capital, continually regenerate through the economic circular flow process. But the regeneration of natural resources for future economic use is completely different. To understand this process it is necessary to construct a larger 'circular flow' which takes into account ecosystem processes as well as economic activity (Figure 2.2). Moreover, the standard circular flow

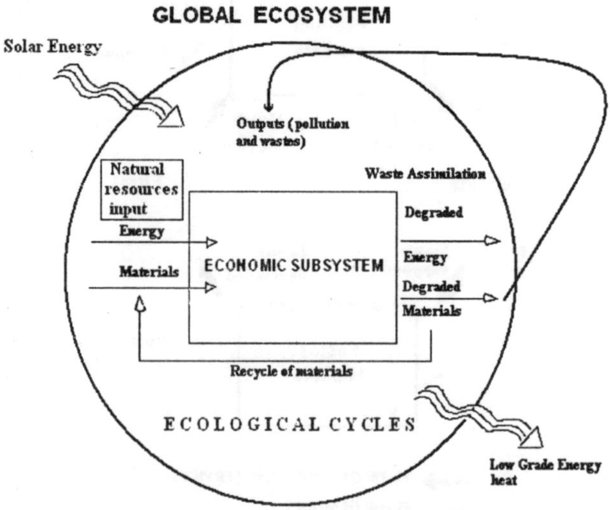

Figure 2.2: Broader circular flow model. The economy is an open subsystem contained by the environment. The economic process is sustained by irreversible and unidirectional flow of low entropy energy and recyclable material flow from economic subsystem to environment. This generates pollution and wastes which affect the environment. The economic subsystem is the flow of goods, services and money (Figure 2.2). (Modified from Hall *et al.*, 1986 [5])

diagram also omits effects of wastes and pollution generated in the production process. These wastes from both firms and households must somewhere flow back into the ecosystem, either through land disposal or as air and water pollution. In addition to the simple processes of extracting resources from the ecosystem and returning wastes to it, economic activities also affect broader natural systems in different ways. For example, modern intensive agriculture transforms the composition and ecology of soil and water systems, thereby affecting nitrogen and carbon cycles in the environment. The ecological system has its own circular flow, determined by physical and biological rather than economic laws. In Figure 2.2, the 'broader flow' has only one net 'input' i.e. solar energy (extra planetary); and only one net 'output' i.e. waste heat. To detail, natural resources supply inputs in the form of energy and materials to economic subsystem. In the economic subsystem these inputs are utilized and converted into other form of materials or energy and may be termed as degraded materials or energy (may be heat energy). Some part of it is again recycled inside the ecosystem that includes the economic subsystem. Such an artificial ecosystem where apart from the solar energy input other energies are artificially generated and utilized and gets incorporated in the ecological cycles as a subsidy. This cooperates in the conversion of artificial material input into wastes of which many are polluting and adds upto the global ecosystem.

Points of Contact between Economic and Ecological Flows

Understanding the relationships between economic systems, natural resources, and the environment requires defining the different functions the natural systems serve.

- The environment's *source function* is its ability to make services and raw materials available for human use. Degradation of the source function can occur by two factors :

  (1) Resource depletion : The resource declines in

quantity because humans have drawn on it more rapidly than it could be regenerated; and

(2) Pollution : Contamination of the resource reduces its quality and usefulness.

- The environment's *sink function* is its ability to absorb and make harmless the waste by-products generated by human activity. The sink function is overburdened when waste volume is too great in a given time period or when wastes are too toxic. If it happens, aspects of the environment on which we depend (most often soil, water, and atmosphere) become damaged, polluted, or poisoned.

These relationships between human activity and the environment are explained by the points of contact between the inner circle of economic flows and the outer circle of ecological flows.

Environmental Micro-economics and Macro-economics

The difference between standard and ecological approaches can be explained in terms of micro-economic and macro-economic perspectives of the environment. A micro-economic perspective focusses on individual resource and environmental issues. Standard environmental economic analysis relies largely on micro-economic theory. The macro-economic view is concerned with the inter-relationship of economic growth and ecosystems. Environmental macro-economics places the economic system in its broader ecological context.

Valuation of Natural Resources

Valuation is an attempt to put a monetary value on a certain asset, which can be tangible or intangible. When a commodity has a market, its value is reflected in the price for which the commodity is being exchanged. However, not all assets have markets for trading. Therefore, an asset that has economic value may not have a price. For example, in this country, surface water is indeed valuable but it has no market and is, therefore, not priced. Drinking water, on the other hand, has a market and, therefore, has a price.

The Economic Valuation Approach

The traditional economic approach to the valuation of natural resource and waste flows uses the same method of economic valuation applied to factors of production, goods, and services. The theory of economic valuation is based on individual preferences and choices. Economic Valuation measures human preferences for or against changes in the state of environments but the value of environment is not considered on its own. There must be human attachment to it. Although other types of value are often important, economic values are useful in making economic choices choices that involve trade-offs in allocating resources.[2] People express their preferences through the choices and they make trade-offs, subject to certain constraints, such as income or available time. 'Willingness to Pay' for something is defined as how much of all other goods and services they are willing to give up to get that item. This analysis requires pricing of each natural resource and environmental input to the economy, including an estimated price for inputs not usually included in market transactions, like clean air and water. Economic techniques help to assess the money value of damages done by pollution and waste disposal. Imputing a money value on natural resources and environmental functions helps us to include them in the inner or economic circular flow[6].

The main method used for valuation is 'Cost-Benefit Analysis (CBA)'[7]. This analysis is basically comparing the costs of a project as well as the benefits, by translating them into monetary terms and discounting them over time. (Discounting is the process of determining the present value of future benefits and costs.) As a result, the projects with benefits greater than costs should be accepted. Micro-economics play a very important role in this regard.

The Ecological Economics Approach

Traditional economic valuation expressed in prices is incapable to capture the complexity of ecological processes, and indeed sometimes results in serious conflict with ecosystem requirements. For example, in dealing with the problem of global climate change, an ecological economics approach looks first at the physical requirements for a stable climate, in particular the limitation of carbon dioxide and other heat trapping gases in the atmosphere. When the physical requirements for a stable climate are determined, the economic measures necessary to achieve this are analyzed. But application of a standard economic approach directly to the problem of global climate change often results in a recommendation for more limited policy action, to avoid excessive economic costs. In contrast, the ecological approach usually suggests more drastic action to preserve atmospheric balance. Cost minimization is also a concern for ecological economists, but only when the basic bio-physical requirements for ecosystem stability have been achieved[8].

Environmental Micro-Economics

Standard micro-economic theory helps to explain the process of achieving equilibrium in markets for natural resources and for environmental services. Analytical techniques which play an important role in environmental micro-economics include :

- Measuring external costs and benefits. for example, we can internalize externalities by imposing a tax on the polluting activity.
- Valuing resources and the environment as assets, (private or public). This involves inter-temporal resource allocation. This is done by using discount rate.
- Imposing appropriate property rights rules for

environmental resources and establishing rules for use of common property resources and for provision of public goods.

- Balancing economic costs and benefits through some form of cost-benefit analysis.

Environmental Macro-Economics

Standard micro-economic valuation techniques are less effective in handling important unquantifiable values such as aesthetics, ethical issues, and biodiversity (the maintenance of many different inter-related species in an ecological community). They are also unable to capture the scope of global environmental problems, the importance of which has grown in recent years. Issues such as global climate change, ozone depletion, loss of species, widespread degradation of agricultural lands, regional water shortages, forest and ocean ecosystem damage, and other large-scale environmental issues require a broader platform. According to the ecological economist, Herman Daly, here comes the requirement of environmental macro-economics. Developing such a macro-economic perspective on environmental issues requires placing the economic system in its broader ecological context. With economic growth, the dependence of the economic system on the ecological cycles grows. Thus the environmental macro-economic issue deals with the technique how to balance the size of the economic system, or macro-economic scale, with the supporting ecosystem[9].

Implications of Ecologically Oriented Economics

An ecologically oriented macro-economics introduces new concepts of national income measurement that explicitly consider environmental pollution and natural resource depletion. Moreover, ecological economists have introduced new forms of analysis at both micro-economic and macro-economic levels. These new analytical techniques are derived from the physical laws that govern energy and materials flow in ecosystems. Applying these laws to the economic process offers a contrasting perspective to the standard micro-economic analysis of environmental issues. Maintaining a balance between economic growth and ecosystem health has given rise to the concept of *sustainable development*. Renewable energy use, organic and low-input agriculture, and resource-conserving technologies preserve rather than degrade the environment. On a global scale, the promotion of sustainable development responds to the many resource and environmental issues in terms of ecosystem impacts rather than as individual problems.

Sustainable Development

Sustainable development is a socio-ecological process characterized by the fulfilment of human needs keeping the quality of the natural environment indefinitely. The word 'sustain' comes from the Latin *sustenare* meaning "to hold up" *i.e.* to support. These days, the closest synonym of sustainability is 'maintain'. Sustain and its derivatives (e.g. sustainability, sustainable, sustaining) were first used in a micro or personal context. During the 1960s and 70s, sustainability was used in the macro context of environmental issues where there was a need to sustain the whole environment and human society. This usage was established by the time of the 1972 UN Conference on the Human Environment held in Stockholm. From then sustainability was most often talked about in terms of 'sustainable development'. In 1980, the International Union for the Conservation of Nature (IUCN) published in the *World Conservation Strategy* and used the term "Sustainable Development"[10]. In 1987, came the Brundtland Report . The most often-quoted definition of sustainable development is coined by the Brundtland Commission. It is the development that "meets the needs of the present generation without compromising the ability of future generations to meet their own needs".[11-12] Then the 1992 UN Conference on Environment and Development (UNCED) in Rio stated that sustainability equals the integration or balancing of environmental, social and economic issues often in the context of strong programmes of consultation and participation. So, over time 'sustainability' and 'sustainable development' were treated by many people as synonyms. As the scale of the task of achieving a sustainable environment and society has become lumpy many people have tried to cut off themselves from the enormity of the challenge by retreating into small incremental changes. So it came up that sustainability is a process of change, that is the journey that counts towards the destination. As the terms sustainability and sustainable development have been used more and more in government and corporate circles, the business world has started using the terms more and more for its own purposes. As a result, the word 'sustainable' has quickly reverted to its earlier simple meaning of 'able to be maintained'.

Sustainability is about *continuity* and *development* is about *change*. In our life we want to sustain (maintain) as well as want to change many thing's. So the notion of '*sustainable development*' that combines desired change and desired continuity is quite implicative. Treated in this way *sustainable development* doesn't have to be an oxymoron (a combination of conflicting term). But sometimes quite a bit of negotiation arises before a society, what should be maintained and what should be changed.

Since humans depend in countless ways on the physical environment (both natural and human constructed) environmental sustainability is very much required for social sustainability. Moreover, the feasibility of the economy depends on environmental resources and service flows. So, economic sustainability depends on environmental sustainability. More generally, it can be seen that environmental, social and economic policies are greatly inter-related giving rise to an intersection of sustainable policies[13] (Figure 2.3). The Figure 2.3 exhibits the interactive outcome of various environments *viz.*, social and economic domains relates to equitable outcome; social and environmental domains relates to produce a bearable outcome; environment

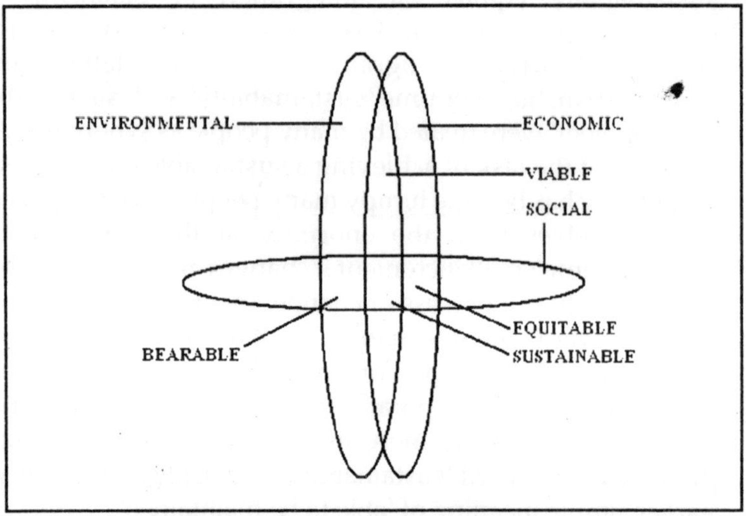

Figure 2.3: Interaction and confluence of the social, economic, environmental domains to produce a sustainable outcome

and economic domains relate to produce a viable outcome but above all the arenas relate to produce a sustainable outcome.

Old *versus* New Economics

Maximization of profits and consumer satisfaction in an open-market economy is consistent with maximization of human well-being, and market failures can be corrected through public policies. Conventionally economics of sustainability is based on a belief that short-run maximization of profits and individual consumer satisfaction ultimately will exhaust both the natural and social resources upon which human well-being and survival of the species depend. So, problems arising from old economic thinking cannot be solved using old economic thinking. A new economics of sustainability cannot be based on the economics of the old belief system which is at the root of most sustainability issues. It must be started with a new belief system.

Inadequacies of the 'Old' Economics

The old economics is a unidimensional, consumptive science. The discipline of economics addresses the allocation of scarce resources to produce consumer goods and services which reflect the tastes and preferences of the consumers even under the assumptions of perfect competition. But old economics is not capable to ensure the regeneration or sustainability of the stocks of resources, either natural or human, which are required to support production of consumer goods and services for current and future generations.

Moreover, it considers the society, the environment, and even preferences for non-consumption goods as external to the economic decision-making process. Along with this, consumer tastes and preferences, societal restrictions or regulations, and environmental constraints are all taken as given. Generation of human satisfaction through social interactions and through resource stewardship is beyond the explanation of the old economics. The old economics is regarded as a reductionist science. It assumes a world of separability. Economic theory is meaningless without the assumption of the term *ceteris paribus* that is other things held constant. The most fundamental law of economics, diminishing marginal returns, also assumes *ceteris paribus*. Economics is fundamentally incompetent of addressing issues of interconnectedness in a holistic world. In a world made up of wholes rather than pieces, there can be no *ceteris paribus*. It is quite unrealistic to think that one may manage those things called economic without simultaneously and unavoidably impacting those things called social and spiritual as well[14].

Industrial development, neo-classical economics, and reductionist science are paradigms of 'dead systems'. They have led to the destruction of ecological, cultural, and economic boundaries and the extraction of stored energy from land, water, air, plants, animals, and people. They provide no means of restoring boundaries, no means of recreating matter, and thus, no means of renewing sources of energy for the future. The mechanistic world view of modern science is fundamentally incapable of addressing the most critical issues of life — of healthy interdependent relationships among diverse elements within holistic, living systems.

Economics of Sustainability

Considering all the drawbacks of old economic theory, a new theory of economics is developed to explain the problem of "sustainability." A theory for management or human decision-making for sustainability is an economic theory of sustainability. The basic purpose of an economy is to facilitate interactions among people and between people and their natural environment. Under the old economics, non-transactional interactions among people and between people and their natural environment were considered non-economic. When economics is expanded to mean "*oikonomia*" (management of the household, community, society, humanity, and biosphere so as to increase its value to all members over the long-run), it must include all interactions within society and between society and the environment.

Theory of Economics of Sustainability : Advent of 'New' Economics :

- To sustain a desirable quality of life is the basic purpose of all human activities.
- A dynamic balance among inseparable ecological, social, and economic dimensions of quality of life is required for its sustainability.
- Energy is finite in quantity and availability.
- The capacity of the natural environment to absorb and detoxicate waste is limited.
- Solar energy and human life are associated through non-human, biological processes.
- Nature and humanity are linked through spiritual, and physical bonds.

- Humans are a social species, and thus, are inherently interdependent.
- The basic purpose of an economy is to facilitate mutually beneficial relationships among people and between people and their natural environment.
- People of any future generation have also basic right to have opportunities for a quality of life equal to or better than those of any current generation.

Paradigm of 'New' Theory of Economics

The new economics of sustainability is absolutely different from the old theory. The new theory has different boundaries, different goals, and different rules[15,16]. According to this theory, social and environmental strategies are equally important as economic strategies in ensuring long-run sustainability contrary to the old. Thus, society and the environment must be considered inside, rather than outside. The goal of sustainability is to ensure opportunity for a desirable 'quality of life' for the current generation as well as all generations to follow. Quality of life has inseparable ecological, social, and economic dimensions. These three are different dimensions of a single holistic goal[17]. All are necessary and none, alone or in pairs, is sufficient to guarantee sustainability. All three are essential dimensions of the goal of sustainability.

Model for New Economics

New models of economic sustainability must be built upon a set of principles quite different from those of old models. This axiom precludes the mechanical separation of sustainability into different components. As societies and ecosystems are living organisms, a strong case can be made for using Quantum rather than Newtonian models for living systems[18].

To develop new economic theory (Figure 2.4) an organismic model of the economic sustainability paradigms

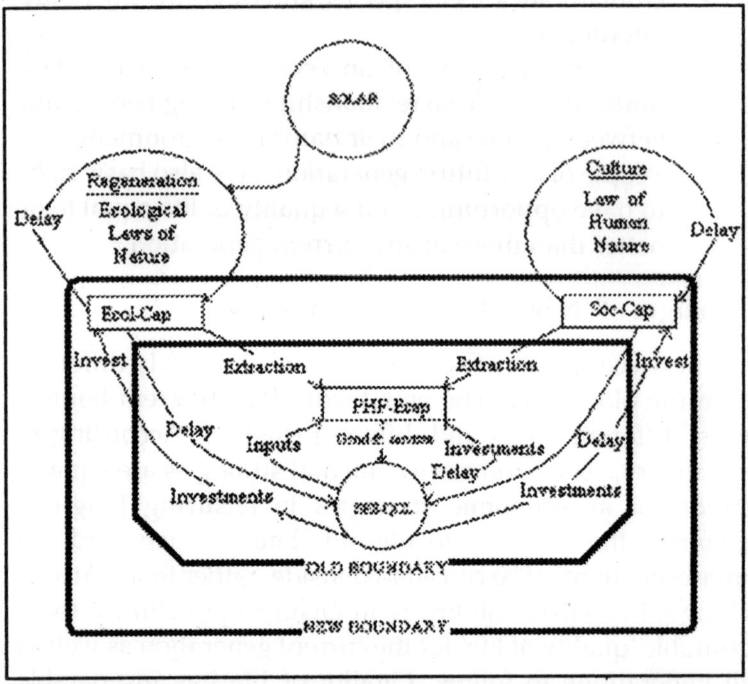

Figure 2.4: Economics of Sustainability Paradigm in terms of Old and New Economics (adapted and modified from 'Economics of Sustainability by John E. Ikerd', www.web.missouri.edu/~ikerdj/papers). Where, SEE-QOL: Social, Economic, Ecological: Quality of Life; PHF-ECap: Physical, Human, Financial: Economic Capital; Soc-Cap: Social Capital; Ecol-Cap: Ecological Capital

is developed which is based on the axioms and principles of Quantum Theory [19]. The basic purpose is to point out what a biological model of economic sustainability might appear and how it might differ from the "old" mechanical model of economics. First, consumers are represented by the SEE-QOL circle whereas the PFH-ECap box represents producers in traditional economic terms within the "old boundaries" of economics. Goods and services flow from producers to consumers and the inputs (labour, management) and investments (land, capital) flow in the opposite direction. The "delay" or break between "investment" and the resulting flow of goods and services implies a multi-period time lag[20]. It is very well known that consumers are directly or indirectly affected by economy (society and environment) but only the indirect effect through ECap are taken care in old economies. In turn Soc-Cap and Ecol-Cap are all externalities to the old economics. In old economy ECap is the composition of Physical capital (P), Human capital (H) in combination with the Financial capital (F).In old economy SEE-QOL represents the consumers but in contrary it is 'people' in new economics. Here new economy exemplifies the significance of Quality of Life in terms of economic, ecological and social dimensions. So social and ecological capital stocks are included within the new economic boundaries Thus, the extraction of economic capital from ecological and social capital also takes place within the new boundaries. There are no flows directly from the economy to either ecological or social capital. Direct economic investments in human capital and environmental protection are internal investments made only to enhance the extractive process. Sustainability requires that the stocks of ecological and social capital be maintained. Thus, the total of direct and indirect extraction cannot be sustained at levels in excess of levels of regeneration. The balance of intentional extraction minus intentional regeneration – those flows within the "new" economic boundaries – cannot be sustained at levels that exceed the rate of natural regeneration.

Figure 2.5, exhibits the simplified model of sustainable economic system. This model shows the interaction between cycles of human need, production and maintenance of resource stocks which is important to sustain production and meet needs of the people. Production capacity is interrelated with stocks of economic, social, and ecological resources and available technologies for resource use and regeneration. Investments in technology can only enhance the ability of resources to support production and meet the needs of

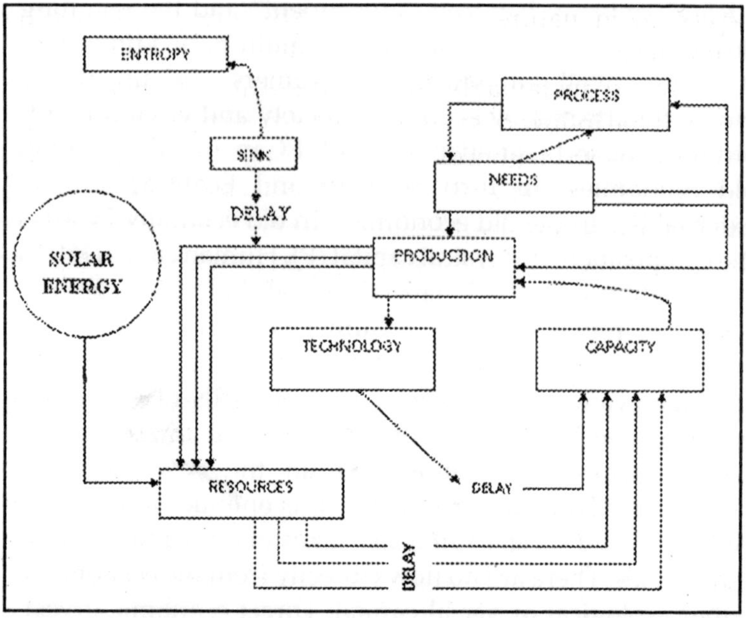

Figure 2.5: Sustainable Economic System; integration of new economics (adapted and modified from 'Economics of Sustainability by John E. Ikerd', www. web.missouri.edu/~ikerdj/papers)

people. In this model, production includes all those things that contribute to quality of life – economic, social, and ecological. The production process includes recycling and regeneration of resources as well as conversion of resources to direct human use. Wastes are directed to "sinks" for absorption, detoxification, regeneration and ultimate re-entry into the productive resource base. But sink capacity, and thus, rate of regeneration, is limited. Delays in various cycles imply the existence of "chaotic" interconnections – the basic organization is stable but precise cause and effect relationships are chaotic. A sustainable dynamic balance requires that the inflow of solar energy must match the outflow of "entropy" – the rate at which energy loses its availability. Needs are identified as individual, shared (which are realized collectively with larger community), and spiritual in nature, *i.e.* to fulfil one's responsibility for humanity.

To be sustainable in the long-run, entropy cannot exceed the inflow of solar energy. No one can imagine a life on the earth without the inflow of solar energy and receptive mineral and biological systems to capture and transform it into human useful form. The economics of sustainability should provide guidance for the holistic management of the ecological, social, and economic resources upon which long-run human sustainability depends. Allocation of resources through the private markets can satisfy self-interest and also meet individual needs. Social resources are allocated as public goods and services for community need. Ecological resources are allocated by ethics and values. Economic resources are allocated through private markets to satisfy self-interest and meet individual needs. Social and ecological resources cannot be allocated through private markets.

Environmental Performance and Sustainability Index and India

The 'Environmental Performance Index (EPI)' is a procedure of quantifying and numerically benchmarking the environmental performance of a particular country's policies. This index emerged from the Pilot Environmental Performance Index, that was first published in 2002, and designed to adjunct the environmental targets proposed in the U.N. Millennium Development Goals[21]. The EPI was led by the Environmental Sustainability Index (ESI), published between 1999 and 2005. The 'Environmental Sustainability Index (ESI)' is a composite index tracking 21 elements of environmental sustainability covering natural resource endowments, past and present pollution levels, environmental management efforts, contributions to protection of the global commons, and a society's capacity to improve its environmental performance over time. Up till January 2008, two EPI reports have been prepared and released – the Pilot 2006 and Environmental Performance Index and the 2008 Environmental Performance Index [22],the basic indicators on which the EPI score is made is Environmental Burden of Disease, adequate sanitation, drinking water, indoor air pollution, urban particulates, local ozone, regional ozone, sulphur dioxide emissions, water quality, water stress, conservation risk index, effective conservation, critical habitat protection, marine protected areas, growing stock, marine trophic index, trawling intensity, irrigation stress, agricultural subsidies, intensive cropland burnt land area, pesticide regulation, emission/capita, emission/electricity generated and industrial carbon intensity.

The country with the highest EPI score is Switzerland with a score of 95.5. Niger has the lowest EPI score of 39.1 with a rank of 149. India has a score of 60.1 and rank of 120 in EPI[23].

India ranked 101 with an ESI score of 45.2 whereas Finland has the highest ESI score of 75.1 (rank 1) and the lowest scored country is North Korea with ESI score of 29.2 and a rank of 146. India falls in the cluster 7 which is characterized by high population density, middle-tier developing countries with strained ecological systems but middle-range scores across the rest of the components.[24] While assessing the Indian sustainability it was observed that there is a varied degree of environmental sustainability and unsustainability in India. Highest sustainability is noted in case of Madhya Pradesh whereas lowest sustainability (extremely unsustainable) is observed in case of Punjab, Haryana, Orissa, Andhra Pradesh, Kerala and Assam are moderately sustainable[25].

Conclusion

In our society the environment has become a scarce resource. Since economics is about how to tackle scarce resources, it can often be useful when dealing with environmental problems. This gives birth to a branch designated as Environmental Economics as a subfield of Economics concerned with environmental issues. Environmental Economics is about the proficient utilization of resources, generally expressed in monetary terms. One way of them is using economics to ensure that the costs and the benefits of environmental measures are well balanced. In this sense, there are various theories regarding sustainable use of resources that can be made applied to economic sustainability. Apart from that, in monetary terms, one resource can generally stand-in for another. The economic sustainability concept is subject, on all levels, and pertains to different inputs and outputs. The economic sustainability of a farm[26] or a company is conditional on the viability of, and markets for, an enterprise or product. In furtherance, the economic sustainability of a nation is dependent on the whole economy at local, national and international level. In describing economics pertaining to sustainability there is the advent of new economic theory in contradiction to the old one. The new economic theory seems to be much holistic and organismic in nature and follows the principles of quantum theory. A sustainable human society has to conserve, recycle, and salvage materials and energy, if it is to slow, rather than hasten, the process of entropy[27]. Above all, human population and per capita consumption must consider the restricted carrying capacity of the earth. This earth's carrying capacity depends on much of our efficiency in nurturing and using living systems to capture and store solar energy and go for renewable[28] and non-consumptive resources.

Performance of various countries in terms of sustainability and environmental quality is assessed in terms of ESI and EPI. India ranked quite below in both the index. Such a low rank is due to India's low per capita consumption level which is far below world's standards furthered by the inefficient management of this consumption that drags down India's environmental record[29]. Thus to better such a rank India should establish quality health measures, control population, reduce stress on ecosystem, develop arid regions having low natural resources and promulgate systematic natural resource management.

NOTES

1. The Chartered Institution of Water and Environmental Management (CIWEM). *Environmental Economics*. http://www.ciwem.org.uk/policy/policies/economics/index.asp, 2003.
2. King, D. and Marisa, M. 2000. *Ecosystem Valuation*. www.ecosystemvaluation.org.
3. Turner, R.K.; David, P. and Bateman, I. 1993. *Environmental Economics: An Elementary Introduction*, John Hopkins University Press, p. 8.
4. Costanza, R.; Cumberland, J.; Daly H.; Goodland, R. and Norgaard, R. 1998. *An Introduction to Ecological Economics*. St. Lucie/CRC Press, Boca Raton, Florida.
5. Hall, C. A. S.; Cleveland, C. J. and Kaufmann, R. K. 1986. *Energy and Resource Quality : The Ecology of the Economic Process*, Wiley Interscience, New York.
6. Cleveland, C. J. 1999. Biophysical Economics: From Physiocracy to Ecological Economics and Industrial Ecology. In *Bioeconomics and Sustainability*: Essays in Honour of Nicholas Georgescu-Roegen, J. Gowdy and K. Mayumi, Eds. (Edward Elgar Publishing, Cheltenham, England), p 125.
7. Per Olov, J. 1993. *Cost-Benefit Analysis of Environmental Change*, Cambridge University Press.
8. Costanza, R. (ed.) 1991, *Ecological Economics: The Science and Management of Sustainability*. New York: Columbia University Press.
9. Daly, H. 1991. Elements of Environmental Macro-economics; ed. by Costanza R. *Ecological Economics: The Science and Management of Sustainability*. New York: Columbia University Press, p. 32.
10. *National Strategies for Sustainable Development, 2004*. "World Conservation Strategy: Living Resource Conservation for Sustainable Development", www.nssd.net.
11. United Nations, 1987."*Report of the World Commission on*

Environment and Development," General Assembly Resolution 42/187, 11 December 1987.

12. Brundtland, G.H. (ed.) 1987. (Our Common Future): The World Commission on Environment and Development, published as Annex to General Assembly Document A/42/427, Develop-ment and International Co-operation: Environment.
13. *World Summit Outcome Document, 2005.* World Health Organization, www.ony.unu.edu/seminars/2007/R2P/2005/World Summit Outcome, pdf.
14. Brewster, J. M. 1970. *Philosopher among Economists,* ed. by J. Patrick Madden and David E, Brewster, J.T. Murphy Co, Philadelphia, PA.
15. Barker, J. 1993. Paradigms: The Business of Discovering the Future, Harper Business, a Division of Harper Collins Publishing, New York, NY.
16. Savory, A.; Butterfield, J.; and Butterfield, J. 1988. Holistic Resource Management, Island Press, Covelo, CA.
17. Capra, F.1982. *The Turning Point: Science, Society, and the Rising Culture,* Simon and Shuster, New York.
18. Anatoly, V. K.2005. *Physical Modelling of Economic Systems. Classical and Quantum Economies.* MPRA Paper, No. 6123. University Library of Munich. http://mpra.ub.uni-muenchen.de.
19. Landau, L.D. and Lifshitz, E.M. 2002. Theoretical Physics, Vol. 3, Quantum Mechanics. Non-Relativistic Theory. Fizmatlit, Moscow.
20. Senge, P.M. 1990. The Fifth Discipline. Doubleday Publishing Co., New York, NY.
21. Yale Center for Environmental Law and Policy, and Center for International Earth Science Information Network at Columbia University. *Environmental Performance Index.*www. research. yale.edu/envirocenter.
22. Yale Center for Environmental Law and Policy, 2005 *Environmental Sustainability Index,* Yale University.www. yale.edu/esi/ESI2005_Main_Report.pdf.
23. *Environmental Performance Index (EPI).*2008, Yale Center for Environmental Law and Policy. Center for International Earth Science Information Network (CIESIN), Columbia University.www.epi.yale.edu.

24. Environmental Sustainability Index (ESI), 2005. Environmental Sustainability Index, New Haven, Conn: Yale Center for Environmental Law and Policy.
25. "*Food Insecurity Atlas of Rural India*", M. S. Swaminathan Research Foundation (MSSRF) and World Food Programme (WFP) (2001), Table 2.4, Appendix 5.3.
26. Tellarini, V. and Caporali F. 2000. An input/output methodology to evaluate farms as sustainable agroecosystems: An application of indicators to farms in central Italy. Agriculture, Ecosystems and Environment. 77(1-2), p.177.
27. Georgescu-Roegen, N.1993. Thermodynamics and We, the Humans, in: Dragan, J. C., E. K. Seifert, M. C. Demetrescu (eds), *Entropy and Bioeconomics*, Proceedings of the First International Conference of the E.A.B.S, Nagard, Milanno, p. 184.
28. Valente, S. 2005. Sustainable Development, Renewable Resources and Technological Progress. Environmental and Resource Economics, European Association of Environmental and Resource Economists, 30(1), p. 115.
29. Ewing, T. 2005.India ranks 101 on Environmental Sustainability Index, *The Hindu*, February 4.

3 Administrative and Organisational Aspects of Environmental Policy Making

Manuka Khanna and Poornima Tripathi

The ever-increasing zeal for ecological modernization has constantly come in the way of environmental preservation and development. The introduction of technology and electronics in all aspects of man's life has created environmental hazards. These are increasing rapidly with the constantly accelerating pace of globalization. Though the people of the world share a global culture in certain aspects, there is a lack of consensus in others due to the confusion between globally local and locally global phenomena.[1]

In the nineties the international scene came to be governed by new assumptions and parameters. The environmental factors transcended the boundaries of nations and lead the governments towards international forums to find amicable solutions. The revolution in the field of information and communication as well as the flow of financial capital brought the world closer. It came to be accepted that the global biosphere is a single system and the environmental impact of each nation ultimately affects the whole. The human impact on environment has had a very long history. However, the speed and scale of current global socio-economic change in the nineties has overwhelmed the political leaders, planners, policy-makers and academics.[2] The concept of national security had been expanded in the seventies to include international economics. It was upheld that the economy of a country could not operate independently, and was necessarily linked with the economies of several other nations. The concept extended its limits further to include resource, environment and demographic issues in the nineties.[3]

Environmental factors emerged as the most potent threat to international security in the twenty first century. The major components of the biosphere including the atmosphere, the oceans, soil cover, the climate system and the range of animals and plant species have been altered by the intensity of human exploitation of the earth's resources in the twentieth century. The constantly growing population imposed an unprecedented stress on the physical and biological system of the Earth. Man has succeeded in conquering several dreaded diseases as well as a number of social and economic problems but the current crisis of disappearing forests, endangered wildlife, crowded cities and conflicts between mankind still need to be dealt with. It is a time when all the countries need to take up the cause of environmental conservation to shape the future of our planet and determine the quality of our life. The issues of sustainable development and protection of environment have received priority within the framework of the United Nations and other international bodies. However, listing of priorities in discussions is not sufficient. Today there is a political need for laws and institutions that could operate beyond the zones of sovereignty. Policy-making is essential for dealing with the environmental concerns, but there are several difficulties in framing and implementing an environmental policy. Environmental policy-making is conditioned by the situations and motivations that influence the behaviours respectively of politicians, administrators and environmental protectionists.[4] The incentives that motivate politicians, administrators and projectionists differ from each other substantially. On scrutinizing their behaviours and motiva-tions it is observed that certain organizational and admini-strative factors play a significant role in this context. The administrative and organizational barriers to environmental policy-making prevent the adoption of a well-defined policy. Some of the significant aspects of the issue are discussed herewith.

Nature of the Environmental Problem

The nature of the problem to be solved conditions the entire policy-making process and the specific tasks of organization and administration. In this context, the nature of environmental problems make organization and administration especially critical to the solution of these problems. The environmental problems are characteristically complex and dynamic, do not conform to the boundaries of political jurisdiction and pervade all levels and sectors of human organization. Problems of development and the environment, even when localized at a given organizational level – local, national or international – cannot be dealt with without co-operation from other levels.[5] Since these problems have multiple causes and implications, any successful imple-mentation of environmental policies hinges upon a variety of factors that span the political, economic and security arenas. They can, therefore, not be addressed in isolation. There is a need of a holistic world-view which will look at man as an integral part of the ecology.[6] An integrated approach that connects environmental concerns to the complicated concerns like development and security is vital to the effective implementation of environmental initiatives. A collective responsibility and effort as well as laws and institutions that operate beyond the zones of sovereignty are needed for effective governance. Effective policies require the strengthening of the global and local ends of the political spectrum. Markets, credits, labour supply, information, political ideologies and energy cycles are in constant flux and it is not possible for any nation to unilaterally isolate itself from the worldwide environmental and economic trends.[7]

The development of an effective global environmental governance is required. Lamont Hempel has defined global governance as the "people, political institutions, regimes and NGOs at all levels of public and private policy-making that are collectively responsible for managing world affairs." Global governance is not yet feasible due to the absence of a global government or a central institution with sufficient authority to craft strong environmental protections at the international level and insist on compliance. The current situation witnesses a fractious community of nations which lacks effective co-operation. For instance, it has been observed that the pollution control laws, currently envisaged by several international and regional organizations, require an integrated approach to comparative research, in order to balance the economic effects of national legal constraints.[8] The lack of co-operation prevents the implementation of any measures.

The environmental policy is fragmented at the international level and the situation is not any different within the nation. The domestic environment policy has not been able to develop a well-defined form. In most countries the governmental structure for policy and administration perpetuates a 'fractional approach' to environmental problems. Generally the governments are divided into departments to serve the interests of particular groups in society and fulfil certain functions. Each section is governed by its own laws, structures and goals.[9] The environment has an inter-related cross-media character, which requires a comprehensive and coherent policy. Though there is a general awareness of the need for holistic strategies, creating organizational and legal structures and appropriate processes to achieve this end has still not been successful.[10] The various departments are at cross-purposes with one another with regard to environmental policies.

It raises the call for 'cooperative environmentalism' or what has been referred to as 'civic environmentalism' by

Stan Johnson and De Witt John. They suggest the adoption of a new style of environmental politics that would replace the traditional command-and-control top-down style of environmental regulations. It visualizes a more decentralized system to address the environmental problems.[11] In this new paradigm the primary responsibility for pollution prevention and ecological management is placed on the state and the local officials and citizens, rather than the federal government.[12] There is a growing awareness to mobilize indigenous knowledge and promote community participation so as to improve people's lives in the developing world. The local groups and communities are not regarded as mere victims of the ecological breakdown. They are assumed to know some solutions also.[13]

It is also observed that the environmental problems and the approach to its solution have been changing. The targets involved are not only changing with time but are altered with cross customary boundaries, as science and societal circumstances change the way in which environmental problems are perceived.[14] The administrative organization and procedure are adversely affected by the constantly accelerating rate of change in the present times. Every society is developing, but the rates and degrees of change differ greatly within and among the nations. New problems and technologies strain the adaptive capabilities of governmental organization and administration designed for a slower moving and less innovative age. There is a requirement of a world governance which would have an operational flexibility with the capacity to reassign priorities, regroup personnel and reallocate funds.[15]

Low Priority to Environmental Issue

Secondly, for a coherent policy to be adopted national governments need to recognize the significance of natural environment and take the necessary measures to implement economically sound and sustainable development. However, a low priority is assigned to environmental issues. This trend is often reflected in the low budgets, limited staff and limited authority provided to most of the national environmental agencies.[16] In the past, governments generally treated the environment as just one more factor in decision-making, rather than as the basis of all the actions. Consequently, the responsibility for environmental protection was left to the environmental agencies and departments with their limited resources and 'traditionally junior portfolios with relatively little clout at the cabinet table'.[17] The governments need to change their priorities in order to make an effective policy regarding the environment.[18]

Financial Factor

Another aspect that plays a significant role is the financial factor. The developing countries are the worst affected by the financial aspect of the policy-implementation. Some of the measures needed to control environmental degradation would require only a reallocation of money but others would require sizable capital investment. Though the amounts involved may not be globally unaffordable, yet they raise apprehensions in the developing world. The developing countries are chiefly concerned about the high cost of adapting to climate change. In order to adjust to the inevitable effects of climate change there will be a requirement of investing in sustaining food production. For instance, it has been estimated by the UNCED Secretariat that $100 million would be needed in international assistance annually to support the development of new crop varieties and farming practices that will be more resilient to heat and drought. Certain other areas of concern include sea wall construction, disaster relief and resettlement as well as species protection. Though the financial needs of these programmes have not been accurately ascertained, they are likely to be many times greater than those needed for climate-control measures.[19]

International actors, particularly transnational financial

institutions and multilateral donors can play a critical role in the environmental field by channelling resources to environmentally friendly investments. While these institutions have unprecedented leverage to provide environmentally responsible projects, their practices often fall short . For example, the International Monetary Fund and the World Bank increasingly advocate environmental considerations, their efficacy is limited by their suspicion of public regulatory authorities, and by lending priorities and portfolios still consisting of traditional investments in major infrastructure projects. There are few incentives for private investment banks to use environmental criteria in financing or selecting investments, while trade treaties such as GATT (WTO now) have no formalized criteria for environmental accountability.[20]

Ineffective Laws

Environment is currently an important issue. It has been widely discussed and several environmental policy studies have been conducted since 1970. However, international environmental diplomacy is still in its 'infancy' and will require some time to develop.[21] The national as well as global environmental policy-making in the last decades has focussed on principles and declarations rather than concrete devices and mechanisms to alter incentives. The global environ-mental management system is not adequately equipped to meet the world community's needs and its expectations.[22] The national laws at times are not able to co-ordinate with the international system. If the national environmental laws could be partially harmonized or approximated several transnational legal disputes could be eliminated.[23] Conse-quently, the environment protection agencies are not effective and show weak administrative and organizational behaviour. The national as well as global environmental policy-making in the last decade has focussed on principles and declarations rather than concrete devices and mechanisms to alter incentives. Nations should be bound by certain laws but International Law, broadly speaking, has declined in influence in recent years.[24] At the same time, the inter-national environmental law is plagued by vague agreements, imprecise requirements, tax enforcement and underfunded support. Effective implementation of treaties requires tremendous effort of the governments.[25] The arrangements like the Law of the Sea Treaty, the Nuclear Non-proliferation Treaty, Convention to Protect the Ozone Layer are not adequate. Generally these arrangements take about fifteen years to negotiate and enter into force and perhaps another ten years before substantial changes in behaviour are observed. (The NPT was an exception requiring only 7 years to complete these processes). International agreements which can respond quickly to the growing scientific understanding, which have new economic methods for assessing risks, a more active political role for biologists and chemists than they have been accustomed to and far greater technical competence in the natural and planetary sciences among policy-makers will be required.[26]

Feasible Solutions

The environmental crisis is threatening the future of our planet, making environmental protection and relevant policy-making one of the most pertinent issues. An attempt to improve the environmental quality of life has been and will continue to be conditioned by the rapid population growth. A majority of the developing countries have sound family planning policies. Nevertheless, what they achieve is far from what they need. It is necessary that the governments should deal with population growth, that is the perpetrator of poverty, inequality and the environmental problems. As far back as 1969, the Report on the Problems of the Human Environment (May 26, 1969) had identified three basic causes for the deterioration of the environment accelerated population growth, increased urbanization and expanded an efficient new technology, with their associated increase in demands for space, food and natural resources. By controlling population growth, the nation would succeed in reducing administrative cost since there would be lesser number of persons to deal with.[27]

Organizational challenges can be minimized by increasing the involvement of all major stakeholders in the decision-making process *i.e.*, sovereign governments, their negotiating teams, NGOs, including citizen's forum.[28] Reorganizing the agencies to provide for a comprehensive approach to environmental problems may facilitate co-ordination. To bring the environment shaping agencies together within a common organizational structure is only a logical first step towards coherent administration of environmental policies. The Minister or cabinet-level official responsible for the co-ordination of environmental policy and action cannot be effective unless equipped with adequate resources of information and tools for the analysis of programmes subject to his administration.[29] Thus, the governments have the prime role to play in tackling the inequality that encourages the rich to be wasteful and the poor to overexploit the environment.[30] However, a greater involvement and constructive role for the private sector could speed up the process. It was witnessed in the case of the ozone agreement that it was made possible in a short period due to the co-operation of the chlorofluorocarbon producers. In order to be effective the policies should include provisions for monitoring, enforcement and compensation, even when damage cannot be assigned a precise monetary value.[31]

At the international and national level implementation of international laws and standards is required. It cannot be assumed that international standards, which by tacit consent may have become binding *vis-a-vis* states, are thereby automatically effective on the national level. Even without formal ratification, some governmental action is necessary.[32] Depending on the requirements of national constitutional law, this usually takes the form of implementing legislation or statutory regulation. While this ultimate state of law-making and law enforcement is normally considered beyond the range of international machinery, certain ways need to be adopted to ascertain and supervise the proper national implementation of standards.[33] This would also lead to a partial harmonization or approximation of existing national environmental laws, consequently eliminating a substantial number of transnational legal disputes.[34]

NOTES

1. Samir Dasgupta:*The Changing Face of Globalization,* Sage Publications,New Delhi, California, London, 2004, pp. 23-24.
2. *Ibid.,* p. 15.
3. Jessica Tuchman Mathews: The *Environment and International Security,* in Michael T. Klare and Daniel C. Thomas (ed): *World Security-Trends and Challenges at Century's End,* St. Martin's Press, New York, 1991, p. 362.
4. Lynton K. Caldwell: *Environment as a Problem for Policy,* in Lynton K. Caldwell and Robert V. Bartlett (ed.): *Environmental Policy – Transnational Issues and National Trends,* Quorum Books, Westport, Connecticut, London, 1997, p. 12.
5. Lynton K. Caldwell: *Environment as a Focus for Public Policy,* Texas A & M University Press, College Station, 1995, p. 187.
6. Samar Bagchi: *Environment and Development,* in N.P. Chaubey and D. Panda (ed.): *Crisis of the Modern Civilization, Vol. 1,* Indian Academy of Social Sciences, Allahabad, 2005, p. 142.
7. Lynton K. Caldwell: *Environment as a Focus for Public Policy, op. cit.,* p. 187.
8. Sheila Jasanoff and M.L. Martelts (ed.): *Earthly Politics: Local and Global in Environmental Governance,* MIT Press, Cambridge, Massachusetts, London 2004, p. 84.
9. Lynton K. Caldwell: *Environment as a Problem for Policy, op. cit.,* p. 13.
10. Odelia Funke: *Prospects for Integrated Environmental Policy,* in Lynton K.Caldwell and Robert V. Bartett: *op. cit.,* pp. 173-174.
11. De Witt John:*Civic Environmentalism: Alternatives to Regulations in States and Communities,* Congressional Quarterly Press, Washington D.C., 1994, p. (xiv).
12. Jacqueline V. Switzer and Gary Bryner: *Environmental Politics: Domestic and Global Dimension,* St. Martin's Press, New York, 1998, pp. 305.

13. Sheila Jasanoff and M. L. Martelts: *op. cit.*, p. 8.
14. Lynton K. Caldwell and Robert V. Bartlett: *op. cit.*, preface, p. (x).
15. Lynton K. Caldwell: *Environment as a Focus for Public Policy, op. cit.*, pp. 196-7.
16. Jacqueline V. Switzer and Gary Bryner: *op. cit.*, pp. 16-8.
17. Michael Keating: *Toward a Common Future: A Report on Sustainable Development and its Implications for Canada*, in Resource Book of the Invitational Seminar: Ethics and Environment-Perspectives on Sustainable Development November 1991, Vancouver Island, B.C.
18. Jessica Tuchman Mathews: *op. cit.*, p. 374.
19. Patti L. Petesch: *North-South Environmental Strategies*, Costs and Bargains, Overseas Development Council, Washington DC, 1992, pp. 6.
20. Jacqueline V. Switzer and Gary Bryner: *op. cit.*, pp. 16-7.
21. White *et al.*, 1990, in Lawrence E. Susskind, Rau K. Jain and Andrew O. Martyniuk: *Better Environmental Policy Studies: How To Design and Conduct More Effective Analyses*, Island Press, Washington, 2001, p. 139.
22. J.G. Speth (ed.): *Worlds Apart: Globalization and the Environment*, Island Press, Washington, Covelo, London, 2003, p. 80.
23. Sheila Jasanoff and M. L. Martelts: *op. cit.*, p. 123.
24. W.P.Bundy:*The1950s versus the 1990s*, in E.K. Hamilton(ed.): America's Global Interests : A New Agenda, W.W. Norton and Co., NewYork, 1989, pp. 33—81.
25. J. G. Speth (ed.): *op. cit.*, p. 9.
26. Jessica Tuchman Mathews : *op. cit.*, p. 378.
27. J.G.Starke: *International Law*, p. 362.
28. Patti L. Petesch: *op. cit.*, p. 35.
29. Lynton K. Caldwell: *Environment as a Focus for Public Policy, op. cit*, p. 195.
30. Peter Calvert and Susan Calvert: *The South, The North and the Environment*, Pinter Publishers London and New York, 1999, p. 216.
31. Jessica Tuchman Mathews: *op. cit.*, p. 378.
32. Seidl-Hohenveldern: *Transformation or Adoption of International Law into Municipal Law*, International and Comparative Law Quarterly, No. 12, 1963, p. 88.
33 Sheila Jasanoff and M.L. Martelts (ed.): *op. cit.*, p. 27.
34. *Ibid.*, p. 125.

4 Special Economic Zones and its Future Role in Export Promotion

Swami Prakash Srivastava

SEZ is a geographical region that has economic laws that are more liberal than a country's typical economic laws. A SEZ is a trade capacity development tool, with the goal to promote rapid economic growth by using tax and business incentives to attract foreign investment and technology. There were 176 zones across 47 countries in 1986. Today, there are approximately 3,000 SEZs operating in 120 countries, which account for over US$ 600 billion in exports and about 50 million jobs. By offering privileged terms, SEZs attract investment and foreign exchange, spur employment and boost the development of improved technologies and infrastructure. In a large scale effort transforming India's competitiveness in the global market, enacted the SEZ Act in 2005. India was one of the first countries in Asia to recognize the effectiveness of the Export Processing Zone (EPZ) model in promoting exports. Asia's first EPZ was set up in Kandla in 1965. With a view to attract larger foreign investment in India, the Special Economic Zones (SEZs) Policy was announced in April 2000. This policy was intended to make SEZs an engine for economic growth supported by quality infrastructure and by an attractive fiscal package, both at the Centre and the State level, with the minimum possible regulations. Union Commerce Ministry figures indicate that in India , after the notification of the SEZ Act 2005, 439 SEZs have been given formal approval, 138 SEZs have in principle approvals, while 195 are notified SEZs. The current investment in SEZs is Rs. 67,347 crore and the employment generated is 61,015.

In India, the first zone was set up in Kandla as early as 1965. It was followed by the Santacruz export processing zone which came into operation in 1973. The Government set up five more zones during the late 1980s. These were at Noida (Uttar Pradesh), Falta (West Bengal) Cochin (Kerala), Chennai (Tamil Nadu) and Visakhapatnam (Andhra Pradesh). Surat EPZ became operational in 1998. The EXIM Policy, 2000 launched a new scheme of Special Economic Zones (SEZs). Under this scheme, EPZs at Kandla, Santacruz, Cochin and Surat were converted into SEZs. In 2003, other existing EPZs namely, Noida, Falta, Chennai, Vizag were also converted into SEZs. In addition, approval has been given for the setting up of 26 SEZs in various parts of the country. Apparently, India is now promoting the EPZ programme much more vigorously than in the initial phases of their evolution. Huge amounts of public resources are being invested in the zones. This warrants an in-depth analysis of the performance of EPZs and their contribution to the country's export performance. Out of the 462 formal approvals given till date, 159 approvals are for sector specific and multi-product SEZs for manufacture of Textiles and Apparels, Leather Footwear, Automobile Components, Engineering etc. which would involve labour intensive manufacturing. SEZs are going to lead to creation of employment for large number of unemployed rural youth.

Brief History of the EPZ Policy in India

The first zone was set up in Kandla as early as 1965. It was followed by the Santacruz export processing zone which came into operation in 1973. There was, however, no clarity of objectives that the Government wanted to achieve. Kandla and Santacruz EPZs were set up with multiple objectives

(Tondon Committee, 1980). Operationally, an overall inward looking trade policy with umpteen controls and regulations influenced the EPZ policy also (Kundra, 2000). The policies were rigid and the package of incentives and facilities was not attractive. Zone authorities had limited powers. There was no single window facility within the zone. Entrepreneurs had to acquire individual clearances from various State Government and Central Government departments. Day-to-day operations were subjected to rigorous controls. Custom procedures for bonding, bank guarantees and movement of goods were rigid. FDI policy was also highly restrictive. According to the business environment rating index which rated investment climate in 43 countries on the basis of 18 independent factors, Indian zones were placed at the bottom for FDI (TCS, 1976).

Attempts to promote the EPZ as an export platform on the basis of economic incentives, such as the free provision of infrastructural services and tax holidays, has been a feature of Indian development thinking since the 1960s. The EPZ policy in India underwent gradual relaxation of procedural and operational rigidities. The changes effected in this policy since 1991 have been far reaching and significant. It is believed that the overall and EPZ investment climate has an overwhelming bearing on the EPZ performance. In India, however, a conducive policy framework has had only a limited impact on the zone performance. Though the gross exports, foreign exchange earning and employment increased phenomenally in absolute terms, their growth rates declined substantially. Growth in exports per unit of employment also slowed down indicating deterioration in the export performance. Net value addition performance compares favourably with other Asian countries but it has not been consistent and the trend growth rate in value addition had not been statistically different from zero. Furthermore, zones also failed to promote non-traditional exports. Traditional sectors namely electronics and gems and jewellery dominate the zones. This could be due to the piecemeal nature of the policy changes. Various committees were set up to examine the performance of the zones. These committee made far-reaching recommendations regarding incentive package, development of infrastructure and improvement in governance. However, policy changes remained slow and extremely cautious. Even the introduction of the SEZ policy did not impact on the SEZ performance. Their performance continued to slide. SEZs are often developed under a public-private partnership arrangement, in which the Public Sector provides some level of support (provision of off-site infrastructure, equity investment, soft loans, bond issues, etc.) to enable a private sector developer to obtain a reasonable rate of return on the project (typically 10-20 per cent depending on risk levels).

The category 'SEZ' covers a broad range of more specific Zone types, including Free Trade Zones (FTZ), Export Processing Zones (EPZ), Free Zones (FZ), Industrial Estates (IE), Free Ports, Urban Enterprise Zones and others. Usually the goal of a Special Economic Zone structure is to increase foreign investment. One of the earliest and most famous Special Economic Zone was founded by the Government of the People's Republic of China under Deng Xiaoping in the early 1980s. The most successful Special Economic Zone in China Shenzhen, has developed from a small village into a city with a population over 10 million within 20 years. Following the Chinese examples, Special Economic Zones have been established in several countries, including Brazil, India, Iran, Jordan, Kazakhstan, Pakistan, the Philippines, Poland, Russia, and Ukraine. North Korea has also attempted this to a degree, but failed. Currently, Puno, Peru has been slated to become a "Zona Economica" by its President Alan Garcia. A single SEZ can contain multiple specific Zones within its boundaries. The two most prominent examples of this layered approach are Subic Bay in the Philippines and the Aqaba Special Economic Zone in

Jordan. According to World Bank estimates, as of 2007 there are more than 3000 projects taking place in SEZs in 120 countries world-wide. SEZs have been implemented using a variety of institutional structures across the world ranging from fully public to 'fully' private. In many cases, public sector operators and developers act as quasi-government agencies in that they have a pseudo-corporate institutional structure and have budgetary autonomy. The following Table 4.1 indicate the number of countries having EPZs , number of EPZs and employment in EPZs.

Table 4.1 : Estmates of EPZs

Years	*1975*	*1986*	*1995*	*1997*	*2003*
No. of countries having EPZs	25	47	73	93	116
No. of EPZs	79	176	500	845	>3000
Employment in EPZs (million)	—	—	—	22.5	42

Source : WEPZA.

The policy provides for setting up of SEZs in the public, private, joint sector or by State governments. It was also envisaged that some of the existing Export Processing Zones would be converted into Special Economic Zones. Accordingly, the Government has converted Export Processing Zones located at :

- Visakhapatnam (Andhra Pradesh),
- Ahmedabad, Baroda, Kandla and Surat (Gujarat),
- Cochin (Kerala),
- Pithampur (Madhya Pradesh),
- Nagpur also refer MIHAN, Pune and Santacruz-Mumbai (Maharashtra),
- Noida, Greater Noida (Uttar Pradesh),
- Falta (West Bengal).

Currently, India has 1,022 units in operational SEZs, each an average size of 200 acres. 8 Export Processing Zones (EPZs) have been converted into SEZs are in various parts of the country in the private/joint sectors or by the State

Government. But this process of planning and development is under question, as the States in which the SEZs have been approved are facing intense protests, from the farming community, accusing the Government of forcibly snatching fertile land from them, at heavily discounted prices as against the prevailing prices in the commercial real estate industry also some reputed companies like Bajaj and others have commented against this policy and have suggested using barren and wasteland for setting up of SEZs the special economic zones. Attempts to set up a special Economic Zone in Nandigram have led to protects by villagers in the area. A Parliamentary Committee to study and give recommendations on SEZs has said that no further SEZs be notified unless the existing law is amended to incorporate the zone. Thus it is a useful act for the growth of economic zone of the country.

Main Objectives of the SEZ Act

The basic objective of setting up EPZs in India is to promote exports and foreign exchange earnings. Though the objectives of EPZs were not clearly spelt out in India until the late 1980s , in actual practice the predominant condition in selecting EPZ units had been the expected value addition component of exports (Kumar, 1989). In 1989, a report of the 'Comptroller and Auditor General of India' clarified that EPZs were meant for earning foreign exchange, develop export oriented industries, stimulate investment and generate employment opportunities besides creating an internationally competitive environment for export production at low cost. Subsequent policy documents have however, reiterated that EPZs are meant to provide an internationally competitive environment for export production at low cost. Some prominent objectives of SEZs in India are :

- Generation of additional economic activity;
- Promotion of export of goods and services;

- Promotion of investment from domestic and foreign sources;
- Creation of employment opportunities; and
- Development of infrastructure facilities.

SEZ Act, 2006

Considering the need to enhance foreign investment and promote exports from the country and realizing the need that a level playing field must be made available to the domestic enterprises and manufacturers to be competitive globally. The Government of India had in April 2000 announced the introduction of Special Economic Zones policy in the country, deemed to be foreign territory for the purposes of trade operations, duties and tariffs. As of 2007, more than 500 SEZs have been proposed, 220 of which have been created. This has raised the concern of the World Bank, which questions the sustainability of such a large number of SEZs. The Special Economic Zones in India closely follow the PRC model. To provide a stable economic environment for the promotion of export-import of goods in a quick, efficient and hassle free manner, Government of India enacted the SEZ Act, which received the assent of the President of India on June 23, 2005. The SEZ Act and the SEZ Rules, 2006 ("SEZ Rules") were notified on February 10, 2006. The SEZ Act is expected to give a big thrust to exports and consequently to the foreign direct investment ("FDI.") inflows into India, and is considered to be one of the finest pieces of legislation that may well represent the future of the industrial development strategy in India. The new law is aimed at encouraging public-private partnership to develop world class infrastructure and attract private investment (domestic and foreign), boosting economic growth, exports and employment.

Present Role of SEZs in Indian Economy

SEZs is a policy response to the changing global scenario and a committed effort to make its implementation is a necessary condition to succeed in promoting export-led industrialization in the country. In a development that strengthens hands of pro-SEZ policy quarter at the Centre, particularly the Commerce Ministry, a Government sponsored study has rejected alarmist positions of the Finance Ministry on the issue. The study, which was commissioned by the Finance Ministry, found its claims of revenue loss exaggerated and maintained that tax incentives will have a positive impact on investment, productivity and growth. The study was commissioned following policy wrangling between Finance and Commerce Ministries. The findings of the study have emphatically countered reservations raised by the Finance Ministry. On its stand that SEZs would cause a huge loss in revenue, the report said that policy-makers have to be concerned with overall benefits to the economy. In other words, if the overall gains to the economy far outweigh potential revenue loss, SEZs should be an acceptable policy choice.

According to the study, new SEZs are expected to yield a net benefit to the economy of Rs. 1,13,000 crore to over Rs. 1, 54,000 crore in the next three years. The report, which contested the Finance Ministry's estimates of over Rs one lakh crore revenue loss, said the loss would be between Rs 19,000 crore to Rs. 23,000 crore. Therefore, the net direct benefits to the economy far outweigh possible revenue losses, the report said, and maintained that even these losses would disappear when the indirect and induced benefits/incomes generated by the SEZs are taken into account. "Induced effects arise when wage incomes are generated. Because of its linkage effects , this is expected to create additional economic activity in the domestic mainland that generate additional tax revenue. While evaluating the overall dynamic benefits from SEZs, we find that Government will net revenue generation instead of loss," said the report. The study said since all new SEZs will be developed by private players, investment in infrastructure should be seen as additional net savings for the Government. "Even in the two alternative scenarios when 60 per cent IT sector production represents diversion from the domestic area or when 75 per cent total investment is expected to be diverted from domestic areas to SEZs , the average net benefits remain positive over the period of three years," the report argued. The study has argued that there would be direct employment generation for almost 8 to 12 lakh people. It said induced and indirect employment could be more than 14 lakh. In addition, building new infra-structure could generate upto 7.5 lakh employment. The report has made three major suggestions :

1. One, capacity-building by Government to ensure effective implementation of SEZ policy. This, the report said, will prevent transfers, maximize additionally and minimize transfer pricing,
2. Second, approval of IT-SEZs should be discouraged but fiscal incentives to EOUs and STPIs should be restored, and
3. Third, dissemination of information about the performance of new SEZs those are in operation.

On human development issues the study further reveals that the working conditions in these firms were better in terms of social security benefits, transport facilities, health facilities, food facilities, working environment and working space which have a direct link to the standard of living of the workers.

After the enactment of SEZ Act, there have been quantum jumps in the SEZs full potential. This is due to the fact that while only eight zones could be set up during 1965-2000. After the act was passed, there have been a rush for setting up SEZs in the country. As of June 6, 2007, there were 19 operational corporate governance panels to watch over SEZ units. The Union Commerce Ministry has expedited the process of creating a corporate governance structure for upcoming SEZs in the country. It plans to set up a Governing Committee for SEZs in each State comprising SEZ developers, representatives at an SEZ. The committee will also have representatives from among the employees. The process has been stepped up after the Commerce Ministry received complaints from some States regarding the functioning of SEZ developers. A number of stakeholders are involved in this process. Commerce Ministry is taking views from existing SEZ developers in Gujarat and Maharashtra before framing the corporate governance structure. Commerce Ministry has to create a prototype on the governance structure before advising State governments. Incidentally, the Parliamentary Standing Committee on SEZs had also expressed apprehension that in the absence of a representative governing committee, infrastructure and other needs of SEZs may not be adequately addressed. The Urban Development Ministry, too, has voiced the need to come up with guidelines on governance structure for SEZ Township. At present, the number of valid SEZ approvals is 232 and notified SEZs are 172. Once all these SEZs become functional, 4 million additional jobs will be created. The Commerce Ministry is expecting an investment of Rs. 3,00,000 crore in these SEZs. This figure will rise further when the 165 in-principle approvals get a formal status.

Impact of SEZs on Farmers

Estimates of number of people to be displaced by the approved SEZs are as yet unavailable. People's struggles against displacement to be caused by SEZs, however, are already intense and in some cases, violent. The violence witnessed in Nandigram in the State of West Bengal is a case in point. In March 2007, 14 people died in police firing when protesting notification of land acquisition of 25,000 acres of land under the LAA 1894 for a SEZ towards a chemical hub slated for the Salim Group of Indonesia. None of the local residents whose lands were to be acquired had been consulted or informed prior to this notification by the concerned authorities and the people of the area organized themselves by blocking access to their area only to encounter violent State retaliation. The Government backed out of its claim of approval for the SEZ in the aftermath of State and nation-wide protest and inquiry by concerned citizens 'groups and the media,' and even as the violence subsided in the following months, people organised under the banner of the Bhumi Uchhed Pratirodh Committee (BUPC) to resist any further land acquisition moves by the State. Government will initiate a study to assess the impact of Special Economic Zones on farmers whose land has been acquired for the tax free enclave. The study to be commissioned by the Commerce Ministry.

The State governments have been advised by the Centre that in case of land acquisition for special Economic Zones, first priority should be for acquisition of waste and barren land and if necessary single crop agricultural land could be acquired for the SEZs. If perforce a portion of double cropped agricultural land has to be acquired to meet the minimum area requirement, especially for multi product SEZs , the same should not exceed 10 per cent of the total land required for the SEZ. Various issues related to setting up of SEZs in the country including issues raised by various political parties , have been addressed by the Empowered Group of Ministers (EGoM). Pursuant to the decision taken by the EGoM, all State governments have been informed that the Board of Approval will not approve any SEZs where the State governments have carried out or propose to carry out compulsory acquisition of land for such SEZs after April 5, 2007.

Incentives and Facilities offered to the SEZs

Special Economic Zones are primarily meant to provide an operating environment free from legal hassles relating to import and export, boost manufacturing and augment exports, earn foreign exchange and generate employment opportunities. SEZ units are allowed to import construction material, capital goods and raw materials without paying duty or import license. Benefit derived from SEZs is evident from the investment, employment, exports and infrastructural developments additionally generated. The benefits derived from multiplier effect of the investments and additional economic activity in the SEZs and the employment generated thus will far outweigh the tax exemptions and the losses on account of land acquisition. Stability in fiscal concession is absolutely essential to ensure credibility of Government intentions. The policy framework of special economic zones are getting weakened to meet the aspirations of all stakeholders. One of the latest regulations on the anvil pertains to land acquisitions. Following the recommendation by an Empowered Group of Ministers (EGoM), private developers should buy 70 per cent of the land at prevailing market prices and the Government acquiring the rest. The incentives and facilities offered to the units in SEZs for attracting investments into the SEZs, including foreign investment include :

- Duty free import/domestic procurement of goods for development, operation and maintenance of SEZ units.
- 100 per cent Income Tax exemption on export income for SEZ units under Section 10AA of the Income Tax Act for first 5 years, 50 per cent for next 5 years and thereafter 50 per cent of the ploughed back export profit for next 5 years.
- Exemption from minimum alternate tax under section 115JB of the Income Tax Act.
- External commercial borrowing by SEZ units upto US $ 500 million in a year without any maturity restriction through recognized banking channels.
- Exemption from Central Sales Tax.
- Exemption from Service Tax.

- Single window clearance for Central and State level approvals.
- Exemption from State Sales Tax and other levies as extended by the respective State governments.

India's Experiment with SEZ

India's experiment with SEZ is not good. Some months ago (in January 2008), Goa Chief Minister Digamber Kamath cancelled the notification to all approved SEZs in the State. The decision was taken after a panel set up to study the viability of the SEZs, observed that these tax free havens were not "right" for Goa's development. It added that the proposed SEZs would not match the talent skills in Goa, but would further burden the existing infrastructure and will not create any employment. Goa has three notified SEZs -- a pharma hub and two other Information Technology (IT) and IT enabled Services (ITeS) ones. The State had also sought permission to set up seven more SEZs, and allotted over 1,500 acres of land through the Goa Development Corporation. The proposal came under fire after villagers alleged misappropriations in land sale to real estate majors. The opposition is on three main issue: displacement from prime agricultural lands, access to water resources and large scale migration from other States. Migration, the protestors believe, will upset the State's harmony and create law and order problems—not to mention, put pressure on available resources. The other main reasons, and this is common to anti SEZ protests across the country, is the perceived role of the State in acquiring lands on behalf of industry. The State is seen as colluding with industry in 'grabbing' arable land and, thus, the livelihood of people. Considering that there is no data of the employment generation by SEZs with their thrust on IT, ITeS sectors, which are not labour intensive, such fears are understandable. While the people are losing land, the industry is perceived to be in a win-win situation with the tax breaks provided. Prime Minister Dr. Manmohan Singh had expressed his reservations, saying that "Prime agricultural land should not be normally diverted to non-agricultural uses" and called for satisfactory compensation to be paid when agricultural land is taken over. The SEZ will only become attractive if the approach is inclusive. They will be attractive if the compensation is commensurate. Gujarat has shown how the process can be carried out effectively, the State needs to be seen as a protector, not as an aggressor. The scramble among Chief Ministers for rosy figures will not take us anywhere, because figures seldom tell the true story. For the sake of the reputation of SEZs – not to mention the well-being of people—the State must understand this.

According to the SEZ Act, SEZs are also interpreted as "public facility or infrastructure" wherein fact they are enclaves for transnational capital to flourish in the "free market" competition inherently skewed to capitalist advantage. While in the decades following Independence, land was acquired mostly by State for development projects and deemed the property of the State, hence public, the shift that the SEZ act in 2005 marks is the acquisition of land by the State for "public purpose" and the transfer of the ownership of this land to private developers. The trajectory of neo-liberal corporate growth through accumulation by dispossession thus becomes clearer in this land acquisition process.

Beneficial Impact of the Special Economic Zones

The overwhelming response to the SEZ scheme is evident from the flow of investment and creation of additional employment in the country. The SEZ scheme has generated tremendous response amongst the investors, both in India and abroad, which is evident from the list of Developers who have set up SEZs :

- Nokia SEZ in Tamil Nadu,
- Quark City SEZ in Chandigarh,
- Flextronics SEZ in Tamil Nadu,
- Mahindra World City in Tamil Nadu,
- Motorola, DELL and Foxconn,
- Apache SEZ (Adidas Group) in Andhra Pradesh,
- Divvy's Laboratories, Andhra Pradesh,
- Rajiv Gandhi Technology Park, Chandigarh,
- ETL Infrastructure IT SEZ, Chennai.

SEZ Approval Status (Sector-wise SEZ Approvals)

Consequent upon the SEZ Rules coming into effect w.e.f. 10th February, 2006, twenty-five meetings of the Board of Approvals have since been held. During these meetings, formal approval has been granted to 462 SEZ proposals. There are 135 valid in-principle approvals. Out of the 462 formal approvals, 222 SEZs have been notified. The Sector-wise SEZ approvals are shown in the following graphs :

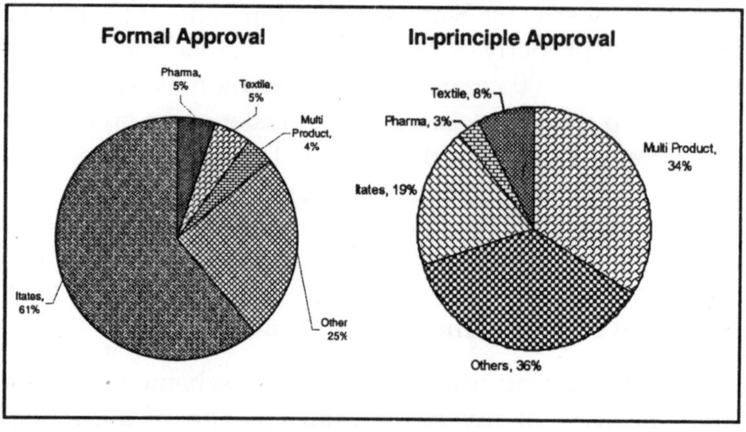

Export Performance of Functioning SEZs

The Export Oriented Units (EOUs) Scheme is complementary to the SEZ scheme which was introduced in early 1981. It adopts the same production regime but offers a wide option in locations with reference to factors like source of raw materials, ports of export, hinterland facilities, availability of technological skills, existence of an industrial base and the need for a larger area of land for the project. 2037 units were in operation under the EOU scheme as on 31st March, 2006. Physical exports in the year 2007-08 accounted for 84 per cent of the total turnover of SEZs. 381 per cent increase in exports over four years (2003-04 to 2007-08). Exports from the functioning SEZs during the last five years are as under :

Table 4.2 : Export Performance of Functioning SEZs

Year	*Value (Rs. Crore)*	*Growth Rate (over previous year)*
2003-2004	13,854	39 %
2004-2005	18,314	32 %
2005-2006	22 840	25 %
2006-2007	34,615	52 %
2007-2008	66,638	92%

As indicated from the above Table 4.2, export from SEZs have been showing steady increase . As compared to exports of Rs. 22,840 crore made by SEZs in 2005-06, exports to the tune of Rs. 34,615 crore have been effected in the year 2006-07, registering a growth of 52 per cent. Projected exports for 2007-08 from special Economic Zones is Rs. 66,638 crore. Following Tables 4.3 and 4.4 indicate the export from EOUs/SEZs and share of EOUs/SEZs in India's overall exports.

Table 4.3 : Export from EOUs/SEZs (Rs) Crore

Year	*SEZs*	*EOUs*
2002-03	10,057	23,591
2003-04	13,814	28,828
2004-05	18,655	39,228
2005-06	22,840	49,462
2006-07	34,787	69,965
2007-08*	66,838	1,25,000

* Provisional.

Table 4. 4 : Share of EOUs/SEZs in India's Overall Exports (Rs) Crore

Years	*EOUs/SEZs*	*Exports*
2002-03	33,647	2,55,137
2003-04	47,641	2,93,367
2004-05	57,883	3,75,340
2005-06	72,302	4,56,418
2006-07	1,04,752	5,71,779
2007-08*	1,91,638	6,26,200

* Provisional.

Highlights of Export Policy in SEZ (2003-07) (as amended upto 31.3.2007)

Service Exports

Duty free import facility for service sector having a minimum foreign exchange earning of Rs. 10 lakh. The duty free entitlement shall be 10 per cent of the average foreign exchange earned in the preceding three licensing years. However, for hotels, the same shall be 5 per cent of the average foreign exchange earned in the preceding three licensing years. This entitlement can be used for import of office equipments, professional equipments, spares and consumables. However, imports of agricultural and dairy products shall not be allowed for imports against the entitlement. The entitlement and the goods imported against such entitlement shall be non-transferable.

Agro Exports

Corporate sector with proven credential will be encouraged to sponsor Agri Export Zone for boosting agro exports. The corporates to provide services such as provision of pre/post-harvest treatment and operations, plant protection, processing, packaging, storage and related R&D. DEPB rate for selected agro products to factor in the cost of pre-production inputs such as fertiliser, pesticides and seeds.

Special Economic Zones Scheme

Sales from Domestic Tariff Area (DTA) to SEZs to be treated as export. This would now entitle domestic suppliers to Drawback/DEPB benefits, CST exemption and Service Tax exemption. Agriculture/Horticulture processing SEZ units will now be allowed to provide inputs and equipments to contract farmers in DTA to promote production of goods as per the requirement of importing countries. This is expected to integrate the production and processing and help in promoting SEZs specialising in agro exports. Foreign bound passengers will now be allowed to take goods from SEZs to promote trade, tourism and exports. Domestic sales by SEZ units will now be exempt from SAD. Restriction of one year period for remittance of export proceeds removed for SEZ units.

Exports, Investment and Employment in the SEZs set up prior to the SEZ Act, 2005

The benefits derived from SEZs is evident from the investment, employment, exports and infrastructural developments additionally generated. The SEZ Act 2005 , supported by SEZ Rules, came into effect on February 10, 2006 . The main objectives of the SEZ Act are generation of additional economic activity, promotion of exports of goods and services, promotion of investment from domestic and foreign sources, creation of employment opportunities and development of infrastructure facilities. Various incentives and facilities are offered to both units in SEZs for attracting investments into SEZs (including foreign investment) as well as for SEZ developers. These incentives and facilities are expected to trigger a large flow of foreign and domestic investment in SEZs, particularly in infrastructure and productive capacity, leading to generation of additional economic activity and creation of employment opportunities. The SEZ Rules provide for different minimum land requirement for different classes of SEZs. Every SEZ is divided into a processing area where alone the SEZ units are set up and a non-processing area where the supporting infrastructure is to be created. The SEZ Rules also provide for simplified procedure for development, operation and maintenance of the SEZ and setting up units in SEZs, single window clearance both relating to Central as well as State governments for setting up of an SEZ and units in a SEZ and simplified compliance procedures/documentation with emphasis EOUs and SEZs were playing a *stellar* role in India's overall exports, their contribution having risen from 13 per cent in 2002-03 to 31 per cent in 2007-08.Exports from these areas had surged 5.7 times over the last five years, from Rs. 33.65 crore to Rs. 191.64 crore. Last year alone, exports from SEZ went up from Rs. 34.79 crore to Rs. 66.64 crore, registering a 93 per cent growth , while exports from EOUs swelled 82 per cent, from Rs. 69.97 crore to Rs. 125 crore.

EPZ exports increased in India from less than Rs. one million in 1966 to over Rs. 97727 million in 2002. Over the same period, total employment increased from 70 to around 89,000, net foreign exchange earnings increased from Rs. 0.16 million to Rs. 43,195 million and value addition increased from 21 per cent to 44 per cent. Table 4.5 presents a comprehensive picture of the growth in exports, employment, imports and value addition. Three things may be observed. One, gross EPZ exports registered an impressive growth rate over the period 1966 to 2002. Two, gross exports rose much faster than employment in these zones. As a result, exports per employee increased at the annual growth rate of 24 per cent and a trend growth rate of 14.6 per cent (Table 4.5).

The growth of value addition had not been promising over this period. Average annual growth rate of value addition was as low as 2.9 per cent. The trend of growth rate in value addition was 1.5 per cent, which was not significantly different from zero. Apparently, imports also

Table 4.5 : Growth Rates in Exports, Imports and Employment (1966-2002)

	Average annual growth rate	*Trend growth rates*
Export	42.4	39.2*
Import	39.9	38.8*
Value addition	2.9	1.5
Employment	21.2	21.6*
Exports/employment	24.3	14.6*

* Significant at 1%.

Source : Ministry of Commerce.

grew approximately at the same rate as exports. The above analysis suggests that exports and foreign exchange earnings of Export Processing Zones (EPZs), in absolute terms, increased substantially but the value addition remained stagnated. There were thus no significant trends towards strengthening backward linkages with the domestic markets.

Investment

SEZ were the key to increasing India's share of global trade, which currently stood at $ 200 billion. SEZs could help to boost the foreign trade share to 5 per cent by 2015 from the current share of 1.5 per cent, while a stable policy regime would continue for SEZs. They must be allowed to run for five years before any alterations are made. SEZs have generated 2.5 lakh direct employment opportunities and the new investments of Rs. 74,000 crore constituted 95 per cent of the total investments in the SEZs. At present, 1,819 units are in operation in the SEZs. In the SEZs established prior to the Act coming into force, there are 11,22 units providing direct employment to over 1.93 lakh persons; about 37 per cent of whom are women. Private investment by entrepreneurs in these SEZs established prior to the SEZ Act is of the order of over Rs. 7,860 crore.

Private Investments

Private investments in the 19 SEZs which were set up prior

to coming into force of the SEZ Act , 2005, is of the order of about Rs. 7,104 crore. Investment of the order of Rs. 67,347 crore has already been made in the newly notified SEZs which came up after February. 10, 2006.

Total investment in Special Economic Zones as on 31.3. 2008: Rs. 77,210 crore
Incremental investment since February, 2006: Rs. 73,174 crore

Investment in notified SEZs (as on 31.3.08.)	Rs. 69350 crore (all Incremental employment generated after February, 2006)
Investment in Private/State Govt. SEZs which came into force prior to SEZ Act, 2005 (as on 31.3.08.)	Rs. 3960.44 crore (incremental investment generated since Feb. 2006 is Rs. 2204.13 crore)
Investment in 7 SEZs established by the Central Government (as on 31.3.08)	Rs. 3899.49 crore (incremental investment generated since Feb. 2006 is Rs. 1620.29 crore)

Employment

In the SEZs which have been set up/notified prior to the coming into force of the SEZ Act , 2005, at present there are 1,277 units in operation, providing direct employment to over 2 lakh persons (about 40 per cent of whom are women). Out of this, 36,463 persons are in the private. State government SEZs, most in which had come up after February 2006. The newly notified SEZs, which have come up after February 10, 2006, have provided direct employment to 61,015 persons

Apprehensions have been expressed on misuse of the scheme and relocation of existing industries into SEZs. However, experience has shown that these apprehensions are ill founded and fresh investments and employment have been flowing into the SEZs.

For example, Nokia electronics hardware SEZ in Sriperumbudur is already providing employment to 6,637 persons, majority of whom are women. Hyderabad Gems SEZ has already employed 2,000 persons after providing training to them, out of which 1,200 are girls. They have projected direct employment of about 30,000 persons. Apache SEZ, being set up in Andhra Pradesh, is expected to employ 20,000 persons to manufacture 10,00,000 pairs of shoes every month. Current employment in Apache SEZ is 4,500 persons. Brandix Apparels, a Sri Lankan FDI project, is expected to provide employment to 60,000 workers over a period of three years. Even in the services sector, 12.5 million sq metres space is expected to be created in the IT/ITEs SEZs which is estimated to translate into 12.5 lakh jobs. The benefits derived from multiplier effect of the investments and additional economic activity in the SEZs along with the employment generated is estimated to far outweigh the revenue losses on account of tax exemptions given to the SEZs. These SEZs are freshly developed industrial clusters and are not relocated from elsewhere.

Direct Employment in Special Economic Zones (as on 31. 3. 2008)

Total employment in SEZs: 3,36,235 lakh persons. Total incremental employment generated in SEZs since Feb., 2006: 2,01,531 persons

Break up

DIRECT Employment created in notified SEZs (as on 31.3.08.)	97, 993 persons (all Incremental employment generated after February 2006)
DIRECT Employment in Private/State Govt. SEZs which came into force prior to SEZ Act, 2005 (as on 31.3.08.)	44,768 persons (Incremental employment generated since Feb. 2006: 32,300 persons)
DIRECT Employment in 7 SEZs established by the Central Government (as on 31.3.08.)	1,93,474 persons (Incremental employment generated since Feb. 2006: 71,238 persons)

[In addition to this, current Indirect employment (construction workers/labourers etc.) in the newly notified SEZs is of the order of 2,20,506 persons.]

SEZs Leading to the Growth of Labour Intensive Manufacturing Industry

Out of the 462 formal approvals given till date, 159 approvals are for sector specific and multi-product SEZs for manufacture of Textiles and Apparels, Leather Footwear, Automobile components, Engineering etc., which would involve labour intensive manufacturing. SEZs are going to lead to the creation of employment for large number of unemployed rural youth. Nokia and Flextronics electronics hardware SEZs in Sriperumbudur are already providing employment to 13,623 and 1,272 persons, majority of which are women. Hyderabad Gems SEZ for jewellery manufacturing in Hyderabad has already employed 2,000 persons, out of which 1175 are women, majority of whom are from landless families, after providing training to them. They have a projected direct employment for about 2,000 persons. Apache SEZ being set up in Andhra Pradesh will employ 20,000 persons to manufacture 10,00,000 pairs of shoes every month. Current employment in Apache SEZ is 4,750 persons.

Conclusion

The EPZ policy in India underwent gradual relaxation of procedural and operational rigidities. The changes effected in this policy since 1991 have been far reaching and significant. It is believed that the overall and EPZ investment climate has an overwhelming bearing on the EPZ performance. In India, however, a conducive policy framework has had only a limited impact on the zone performance. Though the gross exports, foreign exchange earning and employment increased phenomenally in absolute terms, their growth rates declined substantially. Growth in exports per unit of employment also slowed down indicating deterioration in the export performance. Net value addition performance compares favourably with other Asian countries but it has not been consistent and the trend of growth rate in value addition had not been statistically different from zero. Furthermore, zones also failed to promote non-traditional exports. Traditional sectors namely electronics and gems and jewellery dominate the SEZs. This could be due to the piecemeal nature of the policy changes. Various committees were set up to examine the performance of the zones. These committees made far reaching recommendations regarding incentive package, development of infrastructure and improvement in governance. However, policy changes remained slow and extremely cautious. Even the introduction of the SEZ policy did not impact on the SEZ performance. Their performance continued to slide. SEZs are expected to induce dynamism in the export performance of a country by eliminating distortions resulting from tariffs and other trade barriers, the corporate tax system, excessive bureaucracy, and missing infrastructure. Fall in the protective walls and reforms in the tax system reduced the gap between EPZ and other units in the wider economy in respect of tax incentives. There should have been significant improvement in the quality of infrastructure and governance to compensate them for the lost benefits. But this did not happen. Dysfunctional policies, regulations, lack of single window clearance facilities, poor attitude of the officials, centralized governance, stringent labour laws and poor physical and financial infrastructure, all accounted for an undesirable investment climate.

SEZs are meant for creating industrial, commercial and social infrastructure. Industrial infrastructure such as factories, warehouses and access roads has to be estimated a minimum 50 per cent of the SEZ area, even in the non-processing area social and commercial infrastructure needs to be developed for supporting the people working at the SEZ. As social and commercial infrastructure included educational institutions, entertainment areas, hospitals, housing, power stations, and effluent treatment plants the SEZ was nothing but an infrastructure project and had to be treated accordingly. RBI needs to revise its guidelines and classify SEZs as infrastructure projects. Several developers also voiced concern on the issues of service tax and benefit of scheme and duty drawback on supplies to their facilities and interpretation of Section 10AA of the Income Tax (IT) Act. Though the sunset clause under Section 10B of the IT Act was proposed to be revoked it had been extended by a year threatening it impede growth of the EoU sector.

SEZs ensure better investment climate by offering three

major advantages over the rest of the economy : provision of fiscal incentives, infrastructure facilities and hassle free governance. These advantages reduce production and transaction costs for exporting and hence provide an edge to EPZ units over the others. For exploring the factors responsible for the poor performance of the zones in India, we need to evaluate various micro aspects of the investment climate offered by the SEZs, especially the incentive package, quality of governance and the state of physical and financial infrastructure. Recent literature however indicates that the importance of corporate tax incentives has been increasing in attracting FDI. The renewed debate on the effectiveness of tax incentives on FDI suggests that changes in the way multinational firms structure their operations abroad have made low tax rates increasingly important to a country's ability to attract foreign capital.

NOTES

1. *The Times of India*, March 7, 2008, p. 15.
2. The *FRONTLINE*, April 11, 2008, pp. 11-12.
3. *The Hindustan Times*, January 2, 2008, p. 8.
4. *EPW*, July 12, 2008, pp. 27-28.
5. *The Economic Times*, January 12, 2008, p. 3.
6. *Times of India*, June 12, 2008, p. 6.
7. Dhawan, Jitin, *the Changing face of Indian Economy*, 2007, p. 111.
8. *The Economic Times*, August 8, 2008, p. 3.
9. *Economic Survey*, 2007-08 p. 146.
10. *Business India*, August 10, 2008, p. 123.
11. *Business Line*, August 2, 2008, p. 15.

5 Modelling for Land Acquisition for Special Economic Zones (SEZs)

Pranab K. Dan, Kousik Guhathakurta and Shatadru Gupta

Special Economic Zones (SEZs) are specific geographical regions that have economic laws different from and more liberal than a country's typical economic laws. The goal is usually an increase in Foreign Direct Investment (FDI) in the country. There is a clear understanding that a well-implemented and designed SEZ can bring about many desired benefits for a host-country: increases in employment, FDI, attraction, general economic growth, foreign exchange earnings, international exposure, and the transfer of new technologies and skills. Hence, many developing countries are also developing the SEZs with the expectation that they will provide the engines of growth for their economies to achieve industrialization (World Bank, 1994).

The Government of India had in April 2000 announced the introduction of Special Economic Zones policy in the country, deemed to be foreign territory for the purposes of trade operations, duties and tariffs. After the SEZ Rules of 2006, the board of approval has granted formal approval to 439 SEZ proposals. There are 138 valid in-principle approvals. Out of the 439 formal approvals, 195 SEZs have been notified. The total area under these SEZs is 220,000 hectares (550,000 acres) (Sezindia, 2008).

But this process of planning and development is under question, as the States in which the SEZs have been approved are facing intense protests, from the farming community, accusing the Government of forcibly snatching fertile land from them, at heavily discounted prices as against the prevailing prices in the commercial real estate industry (Fernandes *et al*, 2006).

Nevertheless, Government intervention is required to ensure that the farmer gets a better deal than through direct negotiations with businessmen. A big company always has the upper hand in negotiations with the small farmer or with members of a community of farmers. It can offer a price that appears attractive to the farmer but does not reflect the present or potential value of the land. But at present, the Government is giving the farmer a worse deal.

In many cases, farmers are being offered a price that is attractive considering their meagre earnings from their small holdings (Ramesh *et al.*, 1997, Murickan, 2003). Besides, owners of land in the surrounding areas benefit from a sharp escalation in land prices down the road. For example in Sriperambadur near Chennai where 750 acres of land were acquired from 1,500 farmers at Rs. 500,000 per acre. The price has now shot up to Rs. 8 million per acre and 15,000 farmers in the vicinity stand to benefit.

Therefore the compensation must have two elements: a down payment in cash and an upside in the form of a call option on the value of the land a few years down the road. Thus ensuring that the farmer selling his land for a project becomes a partner in the prosperity that the project generates. Rehabilitation needs to be pareto-optimal. Those currently displaced should be compensated to cover the value of land, and their current incomes rising at the planned growth rates of the economy need to be protected, through compensation.

The model discussed in this chapter, suggests a novel land acquisition plan which envisages acquiring land in surplus to reallocate the land among those displaced from the core area. This would ensure that the appreciation of land prices or upward revision of land prices due to land development and change in land type would accrue to the ones displaced and hence it would minimize the possibilities of protests. Further, the relocation in the same habitat would the sociological change that a person undergoes as a result of rehabilitation is minimal.

Model Development

The displaced should be compensated to cover the value of land and their current incomes. Their current incomes rising at the planned or expected growth rates of the economy need to be protected (Ray, 2006). So the onus would be on the project to ensure that incomes of all affected are protected at their expected dynamic levels.

In addition proper compensation has to be given to the sharecroppers and those depended on the Common Property Resources (CPRs) (Pattanaik *et al.*, 1987, NCHSE, 1986). If the sharecroppers are registered, they are to get 25 per cent of the compensation paid to the zamindar when their land is acquired. Around 250 of the sharecroppers cultivating some of the 997 acres being acquired at Singur have not been registered so they will not be compensated or resettled. Also, the 1,000 landless agricultural labourers and others like barbers who sustain themselves by rendering services to the village as a community will lose their livelihood when that land is acquired.

Land Price Appreciation

Land has always been a scarce resource and property prices follow basic economics of demand and supply. Looking at the price trend in the last few years in the areas with close proximity to Special Economic Zone the expected infrastructural development causes a sharp appreciation in land prices. As for example in Singur, 40 km. from Kolkata, before work began on the Tata Motors' small car project, the price per acre in this fertile potato-growing belt was for Rs. 4,50,000 which has jumped to Rs. 22.5 lakh (Rs. 20.5

million) per acre now. Similarly in Delhi's neighbourhood, land prices have moved from Rs. 22 lakh an acre to Rs. one crore in Greater Noida.

The model using the above land appreciation envisages a unique land acquisition policy which is discussed below: Let

- k be extension factor indicative of the additional and to be procured
- p be the distribution factor for reallocating to the sharecropper and CPR
- r be the ultimate land reallocation ratio that represents the inverse of the times of price escalation
- x be the exact area of land required to set up the industry as per layout

Then, $$\frac{k.x - p.x}{(1+k)x} = r$$

$$k = \frac{r+p}{1-r}$$

So if we assume the land price appreciation to be 4.5 times and 10 per cent of the land to be acquired has to be allocated to sharecroppers.

$$k = \frac{0.222 + 0.100}{1 - 0.222}$$

$$k = 0.413$$

Therefore, 41.3 per cent land has to be acquired in excess to relocate those displaced from the layout. The loss in area of landholding is compensated by proper monetary compensation at the present value of land or at the negotiated rate. The area allocated for the benefit of sharecroppers and this model inherently also addresses the problems faced by people dependent on the CPR and sharecroppers.

The compensation package can be further modified according to the expectations of land price appreciation. We discuss two models in addition to the above, with the same underlying objective but with difference in the compensation amount.

So, for a higher expected land price appreciation of 6 times the extension factor can be calculated as :

$$k = \frac{0.166 + 0.100}{1 - 0.166}$$

$$k = 0.319$$

Therefore, 31.9 per cent of excess land has to be acquired to rehabilitate those displaced from the planned industry layout.

In a scenario of even higher expectation of land price escalation where an appreciation of 8 times, k can be calculated as :

$$k = \frac{0.125 + 0.100}{1 - 0.125}$$

$$k = 0.257$$

The total compensation amount borne by SEZ promoter for x acres can be calculated as,

$$= \frac{c}{u} \times (1 + k)x$$

where, c is the current land price

u is the negotiation factor subject to $u \leq (1 + k)$

Table 5.1 shows the comparative figures of different alternatives of compensation for an expected land price appreciation of 4.5 times.

Table 5.1: Comparison of Compensation Schemes

	Negotiation factor, u	*Totally compensation amount borne by SEZ promoter per 100 acres (in Rs. lakh)*	*Land price per 100 acre received by Landowner (in Rs. lakh)*	*Compensation Land for Land owners (in acres)*	*Compensation Land for Share-croppers and CPR dependents (in acres)*
1.	NA	100	100	0	0
2.	1.413	100	58.7	31.3	10
3.	1.3	108.7	67.4	31.3	10
4.	1.2	117.75	76.45	31.3	10
5.	1.1	128.45	87.15	31.3	10
6.	1	141.3	100	31.3	10

The above information can be used to construct a graph, where each point on the line represents a unique compensation point (Figure 5.1).

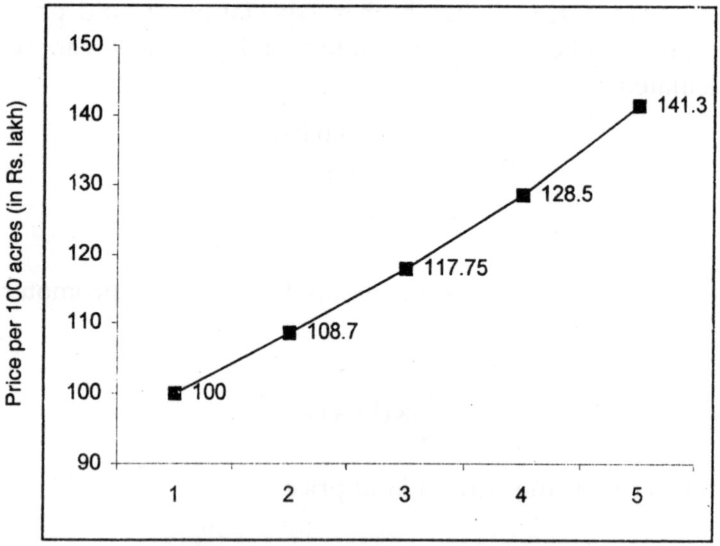

Figure 5.1 : Compensation Possibility Curve

Similarly the compensation curves for different expected price appreciation rates can be constructed. Further, the allocation for share croppers and CPR dependants can be varied as per requirement. These curves are indicative of the various compensation possibilities and will form the basis of negotiation. The rehabilitation package thus designed provides adequate compensation to share croppers and CPR dependents and the relocation in the vicinity ensure that the benefits of land price appreciation accrues to the land owners and they are made partners in the prosperity that such projects generate.

Conclusion

Rehabilitation issues have been compounded by the inherent unfairness of the acquisition process (Modi, 2006). Correction of the same would go a long way towards better and risk reducing rehabilitation.

The objective of this chapter is to design a model for land acquisition and relocation so as to offer a package whose basic thrust will be helping land owners get sustained income life long. So that it provides a level of compensation that would allow the affected person to retain his current living standard in the foreseeable future. The required specification, shortcomings of the model and environment of development has been keenly observed. The scope of the project is very wide and may pave the way for further studies and experiments to develop better models which will aim at providing equitable compensation and catapult India into achieving still higher rates of growth.

REFERENCES

Fernandes, Walter (2004): 'Rehabilitation Policy for the Displaced', *Economic and Political Weekly,* 39, No. 12, March 20-26, pp. 1191-93.

Fernandes, Walter and Gita Bharali (2006): *Development-Induced Displacement in Assam 1947-2000: A Quantitative and Qualitative Study of its Extent and Nature,* North Eastern Social Research, Centre, Guwahati.

http://sezindia.nic.in/HTMLS/about.htm..Special Economic Zones in India, Ministry of Commerce and Industry, Government of India, Feb. 2008.

Jhunjhunwala, Bharat 'Of Land Reclamation Exchange', *The Sentinel,* December 7, 2006.

Modi, Hari. 'Managing Resettlement in India: Approaches, Issues and Experiences', *Journal of Refugee Studies,* 2006; 19: 264-267.

Murickan, Jose, M.K. George, K.A. Emmanuel, Jose Boban and Prakash Pillai R. (2003): *Development-Induced Displacement : Case of Kerala,* Rawat Publications, New Delhi.

NCHSE (1986): Rehabilitation of Displaced Persons due to Construction of Major Dams, Vol. I, National Centre for Human Settlements and Environment, New Delhi.

Pattanaik, S. K.; B. Das and A. B. Mishra (1987): 'Hirakud Dam: Expectations and Realities' in PRIA(ed), *People and Dams,* Society for Participatory Research in Asia, New Delhi, pp. 47-59.

Ramesh, M. K.; and Francis Guntipilly (1997): 'A Critique of the Karnataka Project-Displaced Persons Resettlement Act, 1987' in Walter Fernandes and Vijay Paranjpye (eds), *op. cit.,* pp. 201-14.

Ray, Bibekananda (2006): 'Das Capital' I and II, *The Statesman,* December 17 and 18.

Sequeita, D., 1994 'Gender and Resettlement : An Overview of Impact and Planning Issues in Bank assisted Projects', Bank Resettlement Review, World Bank.

Singh, Chatrapati (1989): 'Rehabilitation and the Right to Property' in Walter Fernandes and Enakshi Ganguly Thukral (eds.), *Development, Displacement and Rehabilitation: Issues for a National Debate,* Indian Social Institute, New Delhi, pp. 91-103.

Stanley, William (1996): 'Machkund, Upper Kolab and NALCO Projects in Koraput District, Orissa', *Economic and Political Weekly,* 31, No. 24, June 15, pp. 1533-38.

Vaswani, Kalpana (1992): 'Rehabilitation Laws and Policies: A Critical Look' in Enakshi Ganguly Thukral (ed.), *Big Dams, Displaced People: Rivers of Sorrow, Rivers of Change,* Sage Publication, New Delhi, pp. 155-69.

World Bank (1994): *Resettlement and Development: The Bankwide Review of Projects Involving Involuntary Resettlement, 1986-93,* Environment Department, World Bank, Washington DC.

6 Health Care System in Rural India

Need for Public-Private Partnership

Ritu Narang

Public-Private Partnership (PPP) is an approach under which services are delivered by the private sector, both non-profit and for-profit organizations, while the responsibility for providing the resources rests with the government.[1] This kind of a partnership refers to the sharing of resources needed to work together towards a common goal while respecting one another's identity.[2] (Patel, *et al.*, 2007).

There are many ways of defining the term "public" and "private"[3] (Wang, 2000). In general, however, the 'public sector' includes organizations or institutions that are financed by state revenue and that function under government budgets or control. Private sector comprises those organizations and individuals working outside the direct control of the state[4] (Bennet, 1991). Broadly the private sector includes all non-state actors, some explicitly seeking profits (for-profit) and others operating on a non-profit (not-for-profit) basis. The former are conventionally called 'private enterprise'; the latter as 'non-governmental organizations' (NGOs). In health sector, for-profit providers may include individual physicians, diagnostic centres, ambulance operators, blood banks, commercial contractors, polyclinics, nursing.

Some of the definitions of public-private partnership used are :

"Means to bring together a set of actors for the common goal of improving the health of a population based on the mutually agreed roles and principles"[5] (WHO, 1999)

"a variety of co-operative arrangements between the government and private sector... in delivering public goods or services... provides a vehicle for coordinating with non-governmental actor to undertake integrated, comprehensive efforts to meet community needs.... to take advantage of the expertise of each partner, so that resources, risks and rewards can be allocated in a way that best meets clearly defined public needs"[6] (Axelsson *et al.*, 2003)

"A partnership means that both parties have agreed to work together in implementing a programme and that each party has a clear role and say in how that implementation happens"[7] (Blagescu and Young, 2005).

"A form of agreement [that] entails reciprocal obligations and mutual accountability, voluntary or contractual relationships, the sharing of investment and reputational risks, and joint responsibility for design and execution,"[8] (World Economic Forum, 2005).

Three themes emerge among these definitions. First, a relative sense of equality between the partners; second, there is mutual commitment to agreed objectives; and third, there is mutual benefit for the stakeholders involved in the partnership.

Partnership is, therefore, a collaborative effort and reciprocal relationship between two parties with clear terms and conditions, clearly defined partnership structures, and specified performance indicators for delivery of a set of health services in a stipulated time period. The core elements, therefore, of a viable partnership are beneficence (joint gains), autonomy (of each partner), jointness (shared decision-making and accountability) and equity (fair returns in proportion to investment and effort)[9] (Raman and Bjorkman, 2004). PPP may take the form of contracting in, contracting out, social franchising and social marketing.

Health Scenario in India

Health is the foundation of a better quality of life. The constitution of World Health Organization, which was drafted and signed in 1946, stated "Health is a state of complete physical, mental and social well-being and not merely the absence of disease and infirmity". The preamble of WHO further states that "the enjoyment of highest attainable standard of health is one of the fundamental rights of every human being." Health has been accepted as one of the Fundamental Human Right in the Indian Constitution. The Indian healthcare sector comprises the following :

- Service providers: doctors, hospitals, nursing homes, specialist clinics,
- Pathology labs and diagnostic centres,
- Manufacturers of medical equipments and Pharmaceutical products,
- Support service providers : laundry, catering, building maintenance.

India accounts for 16 per cent of the world's population and 21 per cent of the world's global burden of disease[10]. Over the past 57 years, substantial gains in health included increased life expectancy, reduced infant mortality, reduced fertility rates, eradication of smallpox and guinea worm, reduction of poliomyelitis, and reduction of leprosy. The Crude Death Rate (CDR) and Crude Birth Rate (CBR), declined from 27.4 per thousand in 1951 to 9.0 in 1998, and from 40.8 per thousand in 1951 to 26.4 in 1998, respectively. Life expectancy at birth increased from 32.1 in 1951 to 63 in 2005, and the Infant Mortality Rate (IMR) declined from 146 per thousand in 1951 to 56 in 2005[11]. The Maternal Mortality Ratio (MMR) and Under Five Mortality Rate were estimated to be 540 per 100,000 live births in 2000 and 74 per 1,000 live births in 2005 respectively[12]. It is estimated that 30 per cent of newborns are low birth weight (less than 2,500 grams at birth), over 50 per cent of children less than five years of age are malnourished, and over 80 per cent of pregnant women are anaemic[13]. However, in a country as vast as India, health indicator averages mark the wide disparities that exist between urban and rural populations, between States, between districts within States, and between communities within districts. For example, in 1996, IMR ranged from 77 per thousand in rural areas to 46 per thousand in urban areas, and from over 90 per thousand in Orissa and Madhya Pradesh to less than 20 per thousand in Kerala[14].

Post-liberalisation the entry of private service providers has opened up tremendous opportunities in the health care sector. The health care industry has emerged as one of the largest service sector industries in the country with estimated revenue of $34 billion in 2007[15]. This sector has experienced a growth rate of over 12 per cent in the past few years and is estimated to grow at a much faster pace than before. Despite much public and private expenditure there are major deficiencies in this sector. It has failed to address the issue of accessibility, affordability, quality and efficiency. The hitherto availability of the health facilities is largely urban centric and the rural areas have failed to lure the private investment which is driven by profits. This dramatic disparity between the rural and urban areas needs immediate and serious attention as the majority (70 per cent) of the Indian population still resides in the villages and the Human Development Index ranking of the country can improve only when the rural sector is taken care of.

Health Sector Development

The health sector in India is characterized by: (i) a

government sector that provides publicly financed and managed curative and preventive health services from primary to tertiary level, throughout the country and is almost free of cost to the consumer [these account for about 17.3 per cent (2004) of the overall health spending and 0.9 per cent (increased to 2-3 per cent with the adoption of NRHM) of the GDP as against the world average of 5 per cent], and (ii) a fee-levying private sector that plays a dominant role in the provision of individual curative care through ambulatory services and accounts for about 82.7 per cent (2004) of the overall health expenditure and 4.2 per cent of the GDP[16].

Our health policy envisages a three-tier structure comprising the primary, secondary and tertiary health care facilities to bring health care services within the reach of the people. The primary health care system has been developed as a three-tier structure in rural India, namely, a Sub-Centre (SC) for a population of 3,000-5,000, a Primary Health Centre (PHC) for a population of 20,000 to 30,000 and a Community Health Centre (CHC) as a referral centre for every four PHCs covering a population of 80,000 to 1.2 lakh. The objective is two fold; to make modern health care services accessible to the rural people and to ease the overcrowding at the district hospitals. The basic unit of health care, the sub-centre, is manned by one multi-purpose male worker and one multi-purpose female worker or Auxiliary Nurse Midwife (ANM). There is a Local Health Worker (LHW) supervising six sub-centres. Maintained under the Minimum Needs Programme (MNP) of the State governments, each PHC is staffed by a Medical Officer, 14 paramedical and other staff and acts as a referral unit for 6 sub-centres. Above the PHCs come the Community Health Centres staffed by 4 medical specialists and established under the State governments MNP/BMS programme. A CHC has a surgeon, medicine, Gynaecologist and a Paediatrician along with 21 paramedical and other staff. Each CHC serves as a referral centre for 4 PHCs and has facilities such as operation theatre, X-ray machine, labour rooms and a laboratory. Since the launch of the Community

Development Programme in 1951, India has gradually developed a vast public health infrastructure, which currently includes 1,46,026 sub-centres, 23,109 Primary Health Centres (PHCs) and 3,346 Community Health Centres (CHCs), providing services to 742.49 million rural people (72.2 per cent of the country's population). Besides, over 5,479 sub-divisional and district hospitals and other specialized hospitals are also in the public sector. The District hospitals are supposed to function as the secondary tier for the rural health care, and as the primary tier for the urban population. The tertiary health care is provided by health care institutions in urban areas, which are well equipped with sophisticated diagnostic and investigative facilities.

During 1950s and the early 1960s the Government focussed on basic healthcare including Maternal and Child Health Care (MCH). The latter programme got neglected when achieving targets under family planning programme became the focus of the health care centres. This trend of neglecting maternal and child health care persisted with the introduction of universal immunization programme in the mid 1980s and the polio eradication programme in the mid 1990s. Subsequent to the ICPD conference the Government reorganised its Family Planning and MCH programmes under the new one called Reproductive and Child Health (RCH). The National Rural Health Mission (NRHM) was launched in April 2005 clearly indicating the Government's commitment to increase public spending on health from 0.9 per cent of India's Gross Domestic Product (GDP) to 2-3 per cent of GDP and also undertake architectural correction of the health system. The National Rural Health Mission aims at providing effective, efficient and accountable health care programmes to the rural population in the country with special attention being focussed on the 18 States of India: Arunachal Pradesh, Assam, Bihar, Chattisgarh, Himachal Pradesh, Jharkhand, Jammu & Kashmir, Manipur, Mizoram, Meghalaya, Madhya Pradesh, Nagaland, Orissa, Rajasthan, Sikkim, Tripura, Uttaranchal and Uttar Pradesh, which have either weak public health indicators or weak infrastructure or both. The mission also seeks revitalization of local health traditions, bringing AYUSH (*Ayurveda, Yoga, Naturopathy, Unani, Siddha, Homoeopathy* which are the Indian systems of medicine) into mainstream public health system, strengthening the delivery mechanism for primary health services and integrating health determinants such as sanitation, nutrition, drinking water. These will, it is hoped, positively impact the health care access of the rural population. Other than this, NRHM seeks to address the issue of inter-State disparities in the area of health services and public health infrastructure. Under the NRHM programme, Accredited Social Health Activists or ASHA workers chosen by and accountable to the *Panchayat* (council of elected members at the village level) shall act as the interface between the public health care system and the community; she shall serve as a bridge between the village and the ANM. These workers shall be trained and mentored on a curriculum developed by National Experts Group, modelled on the best health care practices and implemented with an active participation of the community members. The cost of training, incentives and medical kits to be provided to the ASHA shall be borne by the Government. The models to be adopted by the States would be State specific. ASHA shall be an active participant in chalking out the Village Health Plan along with the ANM, community workers and the *Anganwadi* worker working under the guidance of the *Panchayat Health Samiti*. Her major responsibilities would involve promotion of universal immunisation, referral and escort services for RCH, promotion of construction of household toilets and other health care programmes; these responsibilities would be linked with incentives reflecting her performance.

Evaluation of Health Delivery System in Rural Areas

According to S.K. Satpathy and S. Venkatesh[17], "Despite the well-developed administrative system, good technical skills in many fields and an extensive network of public health institutions for training, research, diagnostics and other services, the health outcome is still behind the set goals". They further point out that, " Despite the vast institutional network and diverse human resource, that includes physicians, AYUSH practitioners, dentists, nurses, midwives, pharmacists, technicians, and community health workers, the public health system in India suffers from shortages, imbalances, misdistribution, poor work environments, low productivity of personnel, vacant posts, high staff turnover, loss of personnel to private sector, and migration of health personnel to urban areas or overseas. Information on health workforce is sparse, available data are fragmentary and their search is limited".

The health system in India is a mix of public and private sector with the Non Governmental Organizations (NGOs) playing a small yet important role. However, in spite of a vast network of health care institutions in India, there exists a wide gap between the rural and urban areas in terms of availability and accessibility of health care infrastructure, as the urban areas are found better equipped with these facilities[18]. Moreover, health being a state subject, there are imbalances and variations in availability and accessibility of these services in the rural areas across the States. The lopsided emphasis on health policy in favour of urban areas has led to disparity in the health status of the rural people, as reflected in the high birth, death and infant mortality rates. As most of the curative health care centres are located in the urban areas the villagers have to travel long distances to seek relief from ailments that perhaps could have been handled at the CHC level thus contributing to congestions, duplication of efforts and wastage of resources as revealed by a study[19]. The Fifth Five-Year Plan document also admits the shortfalls in the health delivery system in the rural areas and the rising disparities in the availability of facilities in the rural and urban areas. "CHCs have not made any significant contributions towards realization of the intended objectives even after two decades of their establishment"[20] has been the evaluation.

Though there were 1,46,026 sub-centres operating in 2005 according to Union Ministry of Health and Family Welfare but this figure fell 12 per cent short of the prescribed number. Similarly, despite an increase in number of PHCs from 23,109 to 23,236 during 2004-05 there was still a shortfall of 6 per cent PHCs as per required norms and the presence of 3,346 community health centres indicates a shortage of 50 per cent. Moreover, various reports point out the lack of medical facilities, equipments, medicines, basic facilities such as electricity backup and 24 hours supply of water. The major problem confronting the public health system in rural areas refers to its inability to attract, motivate and retain trained manpower. There is paucity of manpower across all cadres in the posts of ANM, LHV, trained doctors, lab technicians etc. According to the report of Ministry of Health and Family Welfare, about 50 per cent of the sanctioned posts of specialists (6,110 in number) were vacant in September 2005[21]. Shortage of manpower is indicated in Table 6.1. Another study conducted by IIPS for Ministry of Health and Family Welfare on round two of RCHS reveals that only 37.5 per cent of villages have trained birth attendants while only 25 per cent of villages have visiting doctors. Though 95.3 per cent of villages have 'any health provider' which is mainly *Anganwadi* workers and under liberal definition of health provider may qualify for inclusion under this category. It is not only the paucity of service providers that has caught the attention but the glaring absence of those who are currently employed on (Table 6.2) the payrolls of Government for this purpose. A study[22] (Chaudhury *et al.*, 2006) conducted on absenteeism among the primary health providers across various countries reveals that it is highest (40 per cent) in India and Indonesia (40 per cent) followed by Uganda (37 per cent) and Bangladesh (35 per cent). The primary reason for their absence was the lack of amenities and basic facilities

Table 6.1a: Shortfall in Manpower

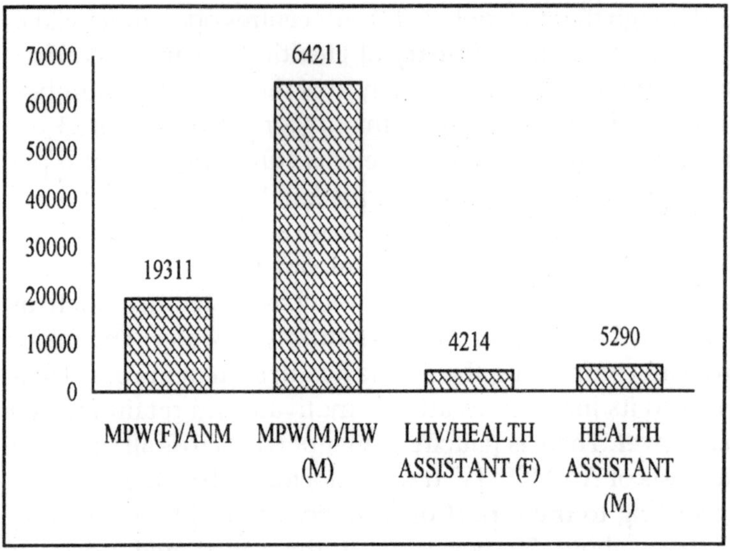

Table 6.1b : Percentage Shortfall of Manpower in PHCs

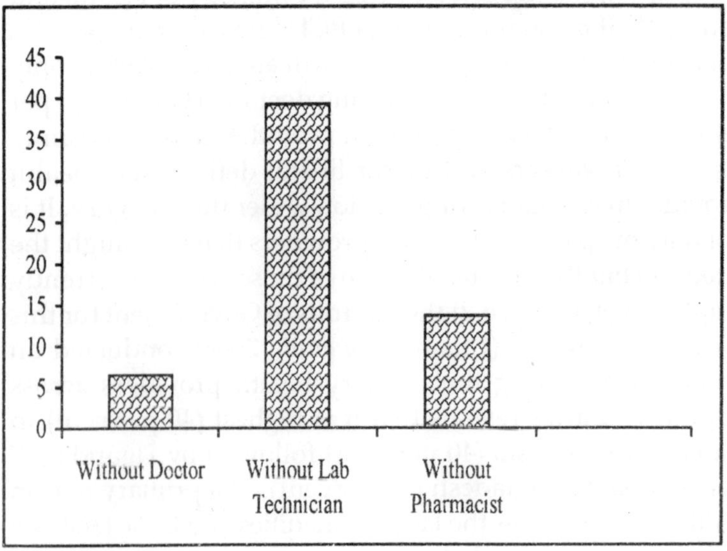

Table 6.1c : Vacancy-Percentage of Sanctioned Posts Vacant

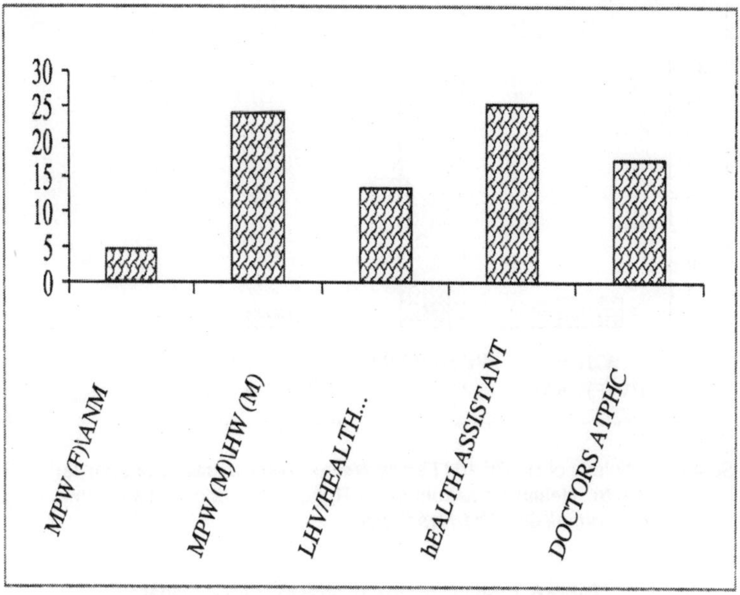

Table 6.1d : Percentage of Sanctioned Posts of Specialists Vacant

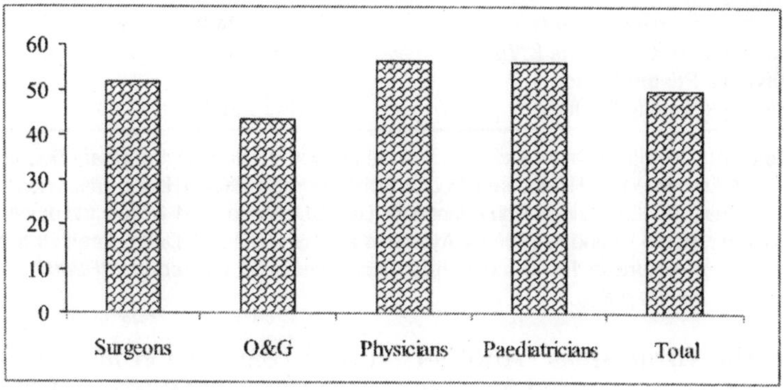

Table 6.1e : Percentage of Sub-centres functioning without ANMs and/ or HW

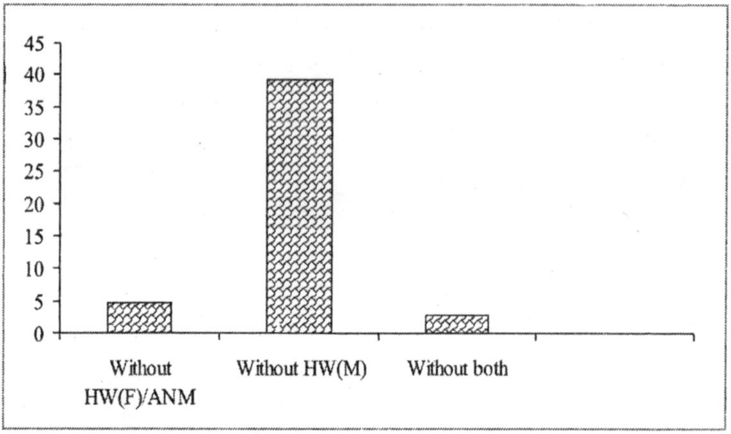

Source: Ministry of Health and Family Welfare 2005, available at Bhandari L., S. Dutta, Health Infrastructure in Rural India, *http://www.3inetwork.org/Reports/IIR2007/11-Health.pdf*

Table 6.2: Status of Health Infrastructure in Villages

Infrastructure/Services	*%Villages*
Connected with Roads	73.9
Having any Health Provider	95.3
Having Trained Birth Attendant	37.5
Having Anganwadi Worker	74.2
Having a Doctor (Private & Visiting)	43.5
Having a Private Doctor	30.5
Having a Visiting Doctor	25.0

Note : Any Health Provider includes: Private Doctor, Visiting Doctor, Unani Doctor, Ayurveda Doctor, Homoeopath Doctor, Sidha Doctor, Tarditional Healer, Village Health Guard (VHG), Tarined Birth Attendants, Dai, ICDS/Anganwadi worker and others.

Source : RCHS Round II, 2002-04 Available at Bhandari L., S. Dutta, Health Infrastructure in Rural India, *http://www.3inetwork.org/reports/IIR2007/11-Health.pdf*

in the rural areas. Another study[23] (Banerjee *et al.,* 2004) conducted in rural Rajasthan further corroborates these findings. It also throws light on the unpredictability of opening of these centres as well as the trend of absenteeism.

A report on health care system prepared by Price-waterhouse Coopers in 2007 throws light on the inadequate infrastructure available in the country. India has approximately 860 beds per million population that is only one-fifth of the world average which is 3,960 according to World Health Organization[24]. It is estimated that 70 per cent of all hospitals and 40 per cent of hospital beds are being provided by private sector (Table 6.3). 450,000 additional hospital beds

Table 6.3a : Health Infrastructure in India

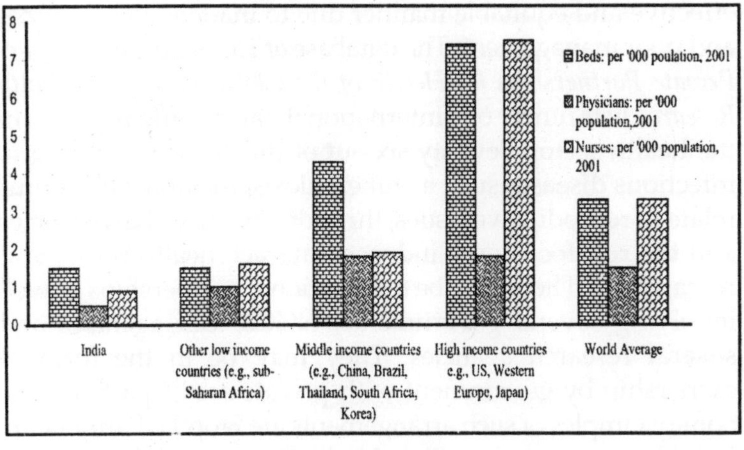

Table 6. 3b : Health Infrastructure in India

Per lakh (100K) population	*Beds*	*Hospitals*	*Dispensaries*
Urban	178.78	3.6	3.6
Rural	9.85	0.36	1.49

Source: Review of Health Care India, 2005 Available at: http://www.pwc.com/extweb/pwcpublications.nsf/docid/3100DC81746FA2308525734F 007458DF/$File/emerging-market-report-hc-in-india.pdf

will be required by 2010 requiring an investment of $ 25.7 billion and the private sector will be expected to play a major role[25].

The message emerging from the various studies and the review of the literature available on the subject is loud and clear. The present health care system has not been effective as well as efficient in its delivery system. It lacks adequate infrastructure and support system, presence of staff, and appropriate locations. The need of the hour is to suggest alternative model in order to achieve the health goals.

Public–Private Partnership (PPP)

Public private partnerships are being encouraged world-wide in view of the former's inability to meet the requirements in an effective and equitable manner due to inadequate resources and poor management. The database *of The Initiative on Public-Private Partnerships for Health of the Global Forum for Health Research* lists ninety one international partnership relations in the health sector. Seventy six out of this list is pertaining to infectious diseases such as tuberculosis, malaria, AIDS; four relate to reproductive issues, three on nutritional deficiencies and the rest focus on blindness, cataract, health policy and research etc. There may be transnational partnerships as well involving several governments, NGOs, UN agencies and several research agencies. They may be in the form of ownership by government with private sector participants. Some examples of such arrangements are Stop TB Partnership, HIV Vaccine Initiative, Global Polio Eradication Programme, Global Alliance for Vaccines and Immunization, Malaria Vaccine Initiative, Roll Back Malaria. The GATES Foundation and Global Fund for AIDS, TB and Malaria aids the government institutions at East Africa to strengthen the health delivery system.

The restructuring of the British National Health Service under Prime Minister Margaret Thatcher and the restructuring of Mexican health care system as a part of the inter-national response to its economic crises were examples of the movement towards privatization[26]. In November 2002, the WHO Centre for Health Development in Kobe, Japan convened the Global Symposium on Health and Welfare

Systems development, in which the participants stressed PPP as a strategy to improve the health and welfare services in developing countries[27]. The Mectizan Donation Programme is another example of successful partnership between Merck and Task Force for Child Survival and Development, an NGO.

Though the term PPP has become popular recently in India but the private sector has been involved in the various sectors hitherto considered to be the domain of public sector for the past several years in the form of contracts. At the local level there have been super speciality hospitals (Apollo Hospital), and primary care centres (Karuna Trust in Karnataka). Examples of partnerships at the State level can be of Malaria Control Society in Gujarat and private agencies for information dissemination, and the Government of Orissa allowing an NGO to run some of its primary health care centres. At the national level, the Government of India has hired private providers to run the tuberculosis control programmes at different sites across the country. The National AIDS Control Organisation (NACO) has also successfully collaborated with corporations such as ACC, BILT, and Godrej on National AIDS Control Programme for making available the anti-retroviral drugs, diagnostic and other care and support facilities[28].

The scope of PPP initiatives in India has spanned disease surveillance, purchase and distribution of dugs in bulk, contracting specialists for high risk pregnancies; national disease programmes, social marketing, adoption and management of primary health centres; collocation of private facilities (blood banks, pharmacy); subsidies and duty exemptions; joint ventures; contracting out medical education and training ; engaging private sector consultants; pay clinics; discount vouchers; self regulation; R&D investments; telemedicine; health cooperatives; and accreditation[29].

According to World Bank PPI database though India has fifth highest value of PPPs of any developing or transition country (only considering infrastructure), it is still one of the lowest as a share of GDP. Investment in Argentina averages 51 per cent of GDP followed by Malaysia (41 per cent), Philippines (37 per cent), Brazil (32 per cent) and so on. However, in India PPP accounts for only 8 per cent of GDP (Table 6.4). By sector, the largest share of PPPs in India has been in telecommunications followed by energy[30]. It is clear that there is tremendous scope for developing Public-Private Partnerships.

Table 6.4 : PPPs by Value

Countries	*$ billion*	*Per cent GDP*
Brazil	174	32
Argentina	73	51
China	72	4
Mexico	70	10
India	51	8
Malaysia	48	41
Philippines	36	37
Indonesia	32	13
Russia	32	7
Turkey	30	11
Thailand	29	18
Poland	28	12
Czech Republic	22	27
Hungary	21	23
Colombia	20	22

Source : World Bank PPI Database.

Partnerships in their true sense are quite different from the interventions observed in India. A true partnership requires shared objectives, shared risks, shared investments, and shared rewards[31]. For instance, giving contracts of cleanliness to private sector cannot be considered partnership in true sense whereas contracting out the management of a primary health centre like the *Karuna* Trust is a true partnership[32].

To develop true partnerships, much work needs to be done on[33]:

- Facilitating improved attitudes and trust between the public and private sectors,

- Designing transparent and accountable management and financial systems,
- Establishing an accreditation and oversight structure that ensures quality,
- Developing management capacity for both the government and implementing partners, instilling an atmosphere of shared responsibility, investment, and accountability.

To engage PPP more judiciously in health sector certain factors/challenges need to be kept in mind apart from working on the various issues outlined above.

- Pursuance of shared goals with each party with a commitment to quality and efficiency.
- Control over corruption that is likely to emerge in the absence of proper monitoring be made.
- Timely payment is essential to the private party to ensure their interest and continued motivation in further partnerships.
- Need analysis of each State of the country should be done so that need specific PPP model is adopted rather than aping a model for the entire country to yield significant results for the heterogeneous population of India.
- Sharing of experiences of different models of PPP currently operating in India and abroad across the different State governments and other stakeholders of the health sector to facilitate learning from sharing.
- Monitoring and controlling the PPP programmes with emphasis on quality control, in the absence of which the entire effort is likely to get diluted even with the involvement of private sector.
- Involving the Insurance Sector in the rural areas and developing a new model whereby insurance agencies are involved in improving the effectiveness and reach of the health delivery system.

- Role of each partner should be made very explicit at the onset of the partnership and efforts be made to develop trust.
- Accountability for the outcomes of such partnerships should be clear and there should be co-ordination across various departments within the government and various implementing agencies.[34]
- Apart from ensuring transparency and accountability emphasis should be laid on sustainability of such relations for which the selection criteria and governance pattern should be spelt out at the beginning.
- A framework on rules and regulation pertaining to such partnerships should be framed at the broad level *i.e.* national level and formulation of PPPs should be done within those guidelines.

Conclusion

It is clear from the above discussion that to foster the health care system in India impetus needs to be given to PPPs. The resources at the disposal of private sector make it an attractive partner for undertaking any kind of major developmental initiative. Though the private sector may be viewed with suspicion due to its profit motive but its performance in various sectors namely banking, insurance, telecom and communications etc. has undisputedly established its credentials to penetrate both the rural as well as the lower income groups. It makes good sense to encourage the private sector in the rural health sector which is in poor state and raises question over the prevalent disparity in terms of health facilities between the rural and urban areas. On its own the private sector may have scepticism in making big inroads into the villages where the people are used to almost free treatment from the existing public health centres and infrastructure deficiencies in the form of roads, electricity, water may strengthen entry barriers. Involving private player with its resources, expertise and efficiency in the public health delivery system can prove to be a boon.

NOTES

1. World Bank, 2001. India: Raising the Sights: Better Health Systems for India's Poor, Washington, DC: HNP Unit-India, Report #22304.
2. Patel A.; Ramani K.V.; Mavalankar D.V.; Agarwal A.; Maiya S.; Nayak B, *Implementing a Public-Private Partnership Model for Managing Urban Health in Ahmedabad,* W.P. No.2007-09-03 September 2007, available at *http://www.iimahd.ernet.in/publications/data/2007-09-03AmitPatel.pdf.*
3. Wang Y., 2000 *'Public-Private Partnerships in Social Sector: Issues and Country Experiences in Asia and the Pacific'*, ADBI policy paper No. 1, ADBI Tokyo, Japan.
4. Bennet S., 1991. *'The Mystique of Markets: Public and Private Health Care in Developing Countries'*, PHP Departmental Publication No. 4, London School of Hygiene and Tropical Medicine, London.
5. World Health Organization 1999, *WHO Guidelines on Collaborations and Partnership with Commercial Enterprise, Geneva: WHO.*
6. Axelsson H.; F. Bustreo and A. Harding 2003. *'Private Sector Participation in Child Health: A Review of World Bank Projects, 1993-2002'*, The World Bank, Washington, DC.
7. Blagescu and Young, 2005. *Partnerships and Accountability: Current Thinking and Approaches among Agencies Supporting Civil Society Organizations.* Working Paper 255, London: Overseas Development Institute.
8. World Economic Forum, 2005. *'Building on the Monetary Consensus: The Growing Role of Public- Private Partnerships in Mobilising Resources for Development.'* Geneva: United Nations high-level plenary meeting on financing for development (September).
9. Venkat Raman and James Warner Bjorkman, 2004. *'Public/Private Partnership in Health Care Services in India'*, available at *http://www.idpad.org/pdf/DR.%20A.%20VENKAT%20RAMAN%20AND%20Bjorkman-%2004.pdf.*
10. http://cms.johnshopkinsinternational.com:8001/CCG/country/india/.
11. WHO available at http://www.who.int/whosis/database/core/core_select_process.cfm.

12. *Ibid*
13. *http://www.who.int/countries/en/cooperation_strategy_ind_en.pdf*
14. *Ibid.*
15. Healthcare in India: Emerging Market Report 2007, Pricewaterhouse Coopers available at http://www.pwc.com/extweb/pwcpublications.nsf/docid/3100DC81746FA2308525734F007458DF/$File/emerging-market-report-hc-in-india.pdf.
16. See note 11.
17. S. K. Satpathy and S. Venkatesh, *"Human Resources for Health in India's National Rural Health Mission: Dimension and Challenges", Regional Health Forum – Volume 10, Number 1, 2006.*
18. National Advisory Committee on Rural Health and Human Services, 2003.
19. A study conducted on *'Functioning of Community Health Centres'* under the Advisor (Evaluation), Mr.S.P. Paul (September 1999).
20. *Ibid.*
21. MHFW (2005).*Rural Health Care System in India,* Ministry of Health and Family Welfare, Government of India, New Delhi.
22. Chaudhury N.; J. Hammer; M. Knemer; K. Muralidharan, and F.H. Rogers (2006) 'Missing in Action: Teacher and Health Worker Absence in Developing Countries', Volume 20, November 1, *Journal of Economic Perspectives*, Pittsburg.
23. Banerjee A.; Esther C. Duflo; and Angus Deaton (2004). 'Health Care Delivery in Rural Rajasthan', *Economic and Political Weekly*, 39(9), pp. 944-949, Mumbai.
24. See note 14.
25. *Ibid.*
26. Goel Naveen Krishan; Abhiruchi Galhotra; Hari Mohan Swami: Public-Private Partnerships in the Health Sector, *The Internet Journal of Health,* 2007, Volume 6, Number 2 available at *http://www.ispub.com/ostia/index.php?xmlFilePath=journals/ijh/vol6n2/ppp.xml#r3.*
27. *Ibid.*
28. Legislative and Institutional Framework for Public-Private Partnerships in India *http://www.thegbcweb.org/leadersforum/en/documents/PPP_India_Framework_eng.pdf.*
29. Legislative and Institutional Framework for Public-Private

Partnerships in India *http://www.thegbcweb.org/leadersforum/en/documents/PPP_India_Framework_eng.pdf* quoted from Bjorkman J. W. and A.V. Raman (2006), *'Public/Private Partnership in Health Care Services in India'*, Paper presented at the Conference on 'India's Development: Even or Uneven? Reflections on Development Theory and Practice' organized by Centre for Economics and Social Studies, Hyderabad, India; and Institute of Social Studies, The Hague, The Netherlands; Hyderabad, India 1-3 November, 2006.

30. Legislative and Institutional Framework for Public-Private Partnerships in India *http://www.thegbcweb.org/leadersforum/en/documents/PPP_India_Framework_eng.pdf* quoted from Thomsen, S.(2007), *'Infrastructure and Indian Development: Reform First, Invest Later'*, Chatham House Briefing Paper, January 2007.
31. An Assessment of Public-Private Partnership Opportunities in India, Annigeri B. Vinod, Prosser L., Reynolds J., Roy R. *http://pdf.dec.org/pdf_docs/PNADC694.pdf.*
32. *Ibid.*
33. *Ibid.*
34. Gupta A. Public-Private Partnerships in Health, *Health for the Millions,* 2006; 32 (6, 7): 7-13.

ANNEXURE

Annexure Table 6.1 : Some Health Parameters–India and its Neighbours

Country	*Life Expectancy at birth (yrs)*	*Under-five mortality rate (per 1,000 live births)*		*Infant-mortality rate (per 1,000 live births)*		*Maternal mortality ratio (per 100,000 live births)*
	2000-05	*1990*	*2004*	*1990*	*2004*	*2004*
China	71	49	31	38	26	51
India	**63**	**123**	**85**	**80**	**62***	**540***
Nepal	61	145	76	100	59	740
Pakistan	63	128	101	96	80	530
Sri Lanka74		23	14	19	12	92
Bangladesh	63	144	77	96	56	380
South Asia	63	126	84	84	62	NA

NA: Not Available.

* Figures shown for India are at variance with the official figure of the Office of Registrar General of India for MMR and IMR. Data shown in the table are as per the methodology and adjustment made by UNDP.

Source : UNDP, Human Development Report, 2006.
Available at http://indiabudget.nic.in/es2006-07/esmain.htm

Annexure Table 6.2 : Births attended by Skilled Health Personnel in India

Indicator	*Value (year)*
Births attended by skilled health personnel (%) rural	33.5 (1999)
Births attended by skilled health personnel (%) urban	73.3 (1999)
Births attended by skilled health personnel ratio urban-rural	2.2 (1999)
Births attended by skilled health personnel (%) lowest wealth quintile	16.4 (1999)
Births attended by skilled health personnel (%) highest wealth quintile	84.4 (1999)
Births attended by skilled health personnel (%) lowest educational level of mother	23.6 (1999)
Births attended by skilled health personnel (%) highest educational level of mother	74.0 (1999)

Source: *http://www.who.int/whosis/database/core/core_select_process.cfm?countries=all&indicators=sba.*

7 Stress Management of Women in I.T. Sector

R.Sunitha

Stress is a body reaction to any demand or any changes in its internal and external environment. Whenever there is a change in external environment such as temperature, pollution, humidity and working conditions, it leads to stress. In these days of competition when one wishes to surpass what has been achieved by others leading to an imbalance between demands and resources, it causes psycho social stress. It is part and parcel of everyday life.

Stress refers to the pressure or tension faced by people in certain situations. Stress has become a major concern now-a-days because of its serious implications which affect both the physical and mental conditions. As human beings are put up in hectic conditions at times stress is an unavoidable consequence. Stress can be due to various reasons *viz.*, hectic work schedules, pressure at work place and other physical and mental health problems.

When stress is left untreated for a long time, it can develop into anxiety and depression. According to business week, stress and depression share a common chemistry in the brain. A hormone called Corticotrophin Releasing Hormone (CRH) puts a defense against stress. Even after the stress subsides, the body keeps realising the hormone sometimes for years. When stress gets out of mind, it results in service depression, and depression, if untreated can be fatal. Depressed individuals make up some 60 per cent of all suicides.

Definition

According to Hans Selye, "stress is an adaptive response, mediated by an individual characteristics and/or psychological processes, that is a consequences of any external action, situation, or event that places special physical and/or psychological demands upon a person"

S = P > R

Stress occurs when the Pressure is greater than the Resource

Symptoms of Stress

The following are the symptoms seen in an individual when there is stress.

- Breathing becomes faster,
- Lack of sound sleep,
- Frustration,
- Consumption of alcohol in excessive quantities,
- Memory lapses,
- Difficulty in making decisions,
- Attempt to suicide,
- Lack of social behaviour,
- Prefer to be alone.

Women in IT Sector

India being a developing economy has seen a major change over the last few decades in social and economical status of women. Gone are the days where women played the role of wife and mother, doing household chores and be a dependent. Today women are independent, voicing their concerns and exhibiting their talents apart from the usual role played by them.

As a result of this, women have ventured beyond the traditional role of wife and mother, and have sought employment and careers outside the home, and have participated in economic and social development of nation (Liddle and Joshi, 1986). Indian women have taken up challenging careers in IT sector.

One can notice that more and more women in India are getting into IT-related jobs at all levels. According to the recent Nasscom study, the men-women ratio in Indian software industry stands at 76 : 24. This ratio is expected to have been increased to 65 : 35(men : women) in 2007.

IT giant Wipro Technologies is proud to announce that the ratio of women workers in Wipro rose to 21.22 per cent in April 2005 compared to 18.75 per cent in April 2004. Infosys quotes a steady increase in the number of its women employees from 19 per cent in 2003 to 22 per cent in 2004 and 24 per cent in 2005 and the number still in the increasing trend.

Significance of the Study

Stress reduces productivity and increases pressure to the management. Today companies prefer women to men because of the hope that they bring additional qualities like innovation, patience and dedication in the workplace. But due to increased pressure for women both at workplace and home they face stress. In this context **"Stress management of women in IT sector"** aims to analyse the factors influencing stress and the ways to overcome them.

Objectives of the Study

The research is carried on with the following objectives :

- To examine the level of stress of women.
- To study the factors influencing stress.
- To study the level of satisfaction in the working environment.
- To provide suitable suggestions to reduce stress.

Research Methodology Area of Study and Sampling Technique

The study is confined to Coimbatore City. The data has been collected using Random Sampling Method, wherein the researcher collected the questionnaire from women of various IT companies in and around Coimbatore.

Sample Size

Hundred and fifty respondents were selected in and around Coimbatore City.

Sources and Collection of Data

For the purpose of the study, primary data were collected through questionnaire from the respondents directly. The questionnaire was designed in such a way that it analyses the various factors influencing stress. The first part of questionnaire sought the general information about the respondents. The remaining part was directed towards finding out the views of the respondents on different area of the objectives in the study.

Tools and Techniques for Analysis

The researcher applied the following statistical tool to analyse and interpret the data collected from the respondents.

- Percentage analysis,
- Weighted average analysis using ANOVA,
- Weighted average rank analysis,
- Test of independence attributes based on Chi-Square.

Analysis and Interpretation

Percentage Analysis

Personal details of the respondents are analyzed using percentage analysis, which reveals that majority of the respondents are graduates, in the age group of 20-25 years and had one dependent in their family.

Weighted Average Analysis

To estimate and compare the mean satisfaction scores on factors among the respondents, weighted average analysis is performed using five rating score by assigning 1 for highly dissatisfied, 2 for dissatisfied, 3 for neither satisfied nor dissatisfied, 4 for satisfied and 5 for highly satisfied and the results are presented in the following tables.

Null Hypothesis

There is no significant difference in the mean satisfaction scores on different items of working conditions among the respondents.

Anova Table 7 : I

SOURCE	*DF*	*S S*	*M S*	*F*
Between groups	4	56.846	14.211	19.53*
Within groups	745	542.013	.728	

* Significant at 1 % level.

Since the *F* is significant the null hypothesis of no difference in the mean satisfaction scores among group of respondents is rejected and there is significant difference in the mean satisfaction scores among respondents. The mean satisfaction scores among the respondents are furnished below:

Table 7.1 : Level of Satisfaction about Working Conditions

Working Conditions	*Weighted Average Satisfaction Score*	*Rank*
Place of work	4.047	3
Work group	3.720	4
Hours of working	3.467	5
Work load	4.447	1
Relationship with colleague	4.093	2

Source : Primary data.

Table 7.1 shows that mean satisfaction score on working conditions namely work load is higher and stood at first, followed by relationship with colleague is higher and stood at second, place of work stood at third, work group belong stood at fourth and hours of working has secured least mean score and stood at last among the respondents.

Null Hypothesis

There is no significant difference in the mean satisfaction score on items of career development among respondents.

Anova Table 7. II

SOURCE	*DF*	*S S*	*M S*	*F*
Between groups	2	7.337	3.669	4.05*
Within groups	447	404.894	.905	

* Significant at 1% level.

Since the *F* is significant the null hypothesis of no difference in the mean score among group of respondents is rejected and there is significant difference in the mean score among group of respondents. The mean score among group of respondents is furnished below:

Table 7.2 : Level of Satisfaction about Career Development

Career Development	*Weighted Average Satisfaction Score*	*Rank*
Pursue higher education	3.340	3
Opportunity for promotion	3.440	2
Possibilities to shift when an offer comes	3.640	1

Source : Primary data.

Table 7.2 revealed that mean satisfaction score on career development, namely possibilities to shift when an offer comes is higher and stood at first, followed by opportunity for promotion is higher and stood at second, and pursue higher studies has secured least mean score and stood at last among the respondents.

Null Hypothesis

There is no significant difference in the mean satisfaction scores on items of monetary benefits among respondents.

Anova Table 7. III

SOURCE	*DF*	*S S*	*M S*	*F*
Between groups	7	152.583	21.789	25.81*
Within groups	1192	1006.587	.844	

* Significant at 1 % level.

Since the *F* is significant the null hypothesis of no difference in the mean score among group of respondents is rejected and there is significant difference in the mean score among group of respondents. The mean score among group of respondents is furnished below :

Table 7. 3 : Level of Satisfaction on Monetary Benefits

Monetary Benefits	*Weighted Average Satisfaction Score*	*Rank*
Salary	3.860	1
Perquisites and other benefits	3.267	6
Allowances	3.447	4
Group insurance scheme	3.020	7
Overtime salary	3.480	3
Leave encashment	3.413	5
Advance paid	3.647	2
Loans	2.627	8

Source : Primary data.

Table 7.3 shows that mean satisfaction score on monetary benefits namely for salary is higher and stood at first, followed by advance paid is higher and stood at second, overtime salary stood at third, allowances stood at fourth and leave encashment has secured next higher and stood at fifth, perquisites stood at six, group insurance stood at seventh and loans stood at eighth rank among the respondents.

Null Hypothesis

There is no significant difference in the mean satisfaction score on items of timing of work among respondents.

Anova Table 7.IV

SOURCE	*DF*	*S S*	*M S*	*F*
Between groups	4	84.836	21.209	31.21*
Within groups	745	506.312	.679	

* Significant at 1 % level.

Since the *F* is significant the null hypothesis of no difference in the mean score on items of timing of work among respondents is rejected and there is significant difference in the mean score among respondents. The mean score among group of respondents is furnished below :

Table 7.4 : Level of Satisfaction about Timing of Work

Timing of Work	*Weighted Average Satisfaction Score*	*Rank*
Working hours suitable and adjustable	3.393	4
Adequate leave facilities	3.807	1
Time allowed for overtime	3.553	3
Time spend with family	2.827	5
Working on holidays is rewarded	3.640	2

Source : Primary data.

Table 7.4 shows that mean satisfaction score on timings of work namely for adequate leave facilities is higher and stood at first, followed by reward for working on holidays is higher and stood at second, time allowed for overtime stood at third, working hours suitable and adjustable stood at fourth and time spend with family has secured next higher and stood at fifth rank among the respondents.

Null Hypothesis

There is no significant difference in the mean satisfaction score on items of decision-making among respondents.

Anova Table 7. V

SOURCE	*DF*	*S S*	*M S*	*F*
Between groups	3	6.793	2.264	2.25 ns
Within groups	596	598.48	1.004	

ns= Significant at 5 % level.

Since the *F* is significant the null hypothesis of no difference in mean score among different size groups is accepted and there is no significant difference in the mean score among different size groups. The mean satisfaction score is furnished below:

Table 7.5 : Level of Satisfaction about Decision-Making

Decision-Making	*Weighted Average Satisfaction Score*	*Rank*
Authority given is sufficient	3.300	1
Responsibility given commensurate with authority	3.193	3
Freedom and authority given to the job	3.207	2
Opportunity to take part in decision-making	3.007	4

Source: Primary data.

Table 7.5 revealed that mean satisfaction score on the various items of decision-making is on par among the respondents.

Null Hypothesis

There is no significant difference in the mean satisfaction score on security and safety items among the respondents.

Anova Table 7. VI

SOURCE	DF	S S	M S	F
Between groups	4	38.075	9.519	12.04*
Within groups	745	588.72	.790	

* Significant at 1 % level.

Since the *F* is significant the null hypothesis of no difference in mean score on safety and security items among respondents is rejected and there is significant difference in the mean score on security and safety items among different respondents. The mean satisfaction score is furnished below:

Table 7.6 : Level of Satisfaction about Safety and Security

Safety and Security	*Weighted Average Satisfaction Score*	*Rank*
Safe and sound working condition	4.167	1
Safeguard the interest of the respondents	3.493	4
Job security	3.660	3
Transportation facilities	3.873	2
Safety measure	2.820	5

Source : Primary data.

Table 7.6 revealed that mean satisfaction score on safety and security items namely safe and sound working condition secured higher score and stood at first, followed by the mean score for transportation facility is higher and stood at second, job security stood at third, safeguard the interest of the respondents stood at fourth, and the item namely safety measure stood at fifth among the respondents.

Null Hypothesis

There is no significant difference in the mean satisfaction score on items of welfare aspects among the respondents.

Anova Table 7. VII

SOURCE	DF	S S	M S	F
Between groups	2	30.521	15.26	30.08*
Within groups	447	226.759	.507	

* Significant at 5 % level.

Since the *F* is significant the null hypothesis of no difference in mean score on welfare aspects among respondents is rejected and there is significant difference in the mean score on welfare items among the respondents. The mean satisfaction score is furnished below:

Table 7.7 : Level of Satisfaction about Welfare Aspects

Welfare Aspects	*Weighted Average Satisfaction Score*	*Rank*
Recreational facility	3.927	3
Cleanliness	4.447	2
Drinking water facilities	4.507	1

Source : Primary data.

Table 7.7 revealed that mean satisfaction score on welfare aspects namely drinking water facility has secured higher score and stood at first, followed by cleanliness the mean satisfaction score is higher and stood at second, recreational facility has secured next higher score and stood at third among the respondents.

Weighted Average Rank Analysis

To estimate and compare the mean satisfaction scores on factors among the respondents, weighted average analysis is performed using seven ranks, assigning the score 7 for rank 1, the score 6 for rank 2, the score 5 for rank 3, the score 4 for rank 4, the score 3 for rank 3, the score 2 for rank 6 and the score 1 for rank 7 and the results are presented in the following tables.

Null Hypothesis

There is no significant difference in the mean satisfaction score on factors that cause stress in the job among the respondents.

Anova Table 7. VIII

SOURCE	*DF*	*S S*	*M S*	*F*
Between groups	6	622.053	103.675	34.02*
Within groups	1043	3178.205	3.047	

* Significant at 1 % level.

Since the F is significant the null hypothesis of no difference in mean score on welfare items among respondents is rejected and there is significant difference in the mean score on welfare measures among the respondents. The mean satisfaction score is furnished below :

Table 7.8 : Level of Satisfaction about Welfare Aspects

Welfare Aspects	*Weighted Average Satisfaction Score*	*Rank*
Working condition	4.670	3
Monetary benefits	5.180	1
Career development	3.520	5
Timing of work	3.253	6
Safety and security	4.447	4
Decision-making	3.227	7
Welfare aspects	4.973	2

Source : Primary data.

The above Table 7.8 revealed that mean score on factors that cause stress in the job and the factor namely monetary benefits is higher and stood at first, followed by welfare aspects is higher and stood at second, working condition the score is next higher and stood at third, the factor safety and security stood at fourth and the factor career development has secured next higher and stood at fifth rank, the factor time of work stood at sixth place and decision-making has secured least score and stood at last among the respondents.

Chi Square Analysis

In order to study whether there is any association between

two attributes namely socio-economic characteristics such as working condition, career development, welfare aspect and decision-making, Chi square analysis is performed and the results are presented in the following tables.

Null Hypothesis

There is no association between level of satisfaction and working conditions.

Table 7.9 : Working Conditions *Vs.* Level of Satisfaction

Working Conditions	*Level of satisfaction*					*Total*
	HS	*S*	*N*	*DS*	*NS*	
Place of work	46	69	32	2	1	150
Work group	18	86	33	12	1	150
Hours of working	15	61	55	17	2	150
Work load	21	52	55	17	5	150
Relationship with colleague	48	74	23	4	1	150
Total	148	342	198	52	10	750

Source : Primary data.

Working conditions and level of satisfaction— χ^2 test

Factor	*Calculated χ^2*	*Table Value*	*DF*	*Remarks*
Working conditions	88.506	26.22	12	Significant

Since the calculated χ^2 value is significant, the null hypothesis of no association between the two attributes is rejected and there is association between the two attributes among the respondents. Thus the study reveals that there is association between working conditions and level of satisfaction.

Null Hypothesis

There is no association between level of satisfaction and working conditions.

Table 7.10 : Career Development *Vs* Level of Satisfaction

Career Development	*Level of satisfaction*					*Total*
	HS	*S*	*N*	*DS*	*NS*	
Pursue higher education	11	57	58	20	4	150
Opportunities for promotion	22	51	54	17	6	150
Possibilities to shift when there is an offer	31	52	52	13	2	150
Total	64	160	164	50	12	450

Source : Primary data.

Working conditions and level of satisfaction- χ^2 test

Factor	*Calculated* χ^2	*Table Value*	*DF*	*Remarks*
Career development	12.490	12.59	6	Not Significant

Since the calculated χ^2 value is significant, the null hypothesis of no association between the two attributes is accepted and there is no association between the two attributes among the respondents. Thus the study reveals that there is association between career development and level of satisfaction.

Null Hypothesis

There is no association between level of satisfaction and working conditions.

Table 7.11 : Decision-Making *Vs* Level of Satisfaction

Decision-Making	*Level of satisfaction*					*Total*
	HS	*S*	*N*	*DS*	*NS*	
Authority given is not sufficient	9	56	60	21	4	150
Responsibility commensurate with authority	11	42	68	23	6	150
Freedom & autonomy given to do the job	14	51	48	26	11	150
Opportunity to take part in decision making process	13	39	49	34	15	150
Total	47	188	225	104	36	600

Source: Primary data.

Working conditions and level of satisfaction— χ^2 test

Factor	*Calculated χ^2*	*Table Value*	*DF*	*Remarks*
Decision-making	73.917	13.28	4	Significant

Since the calculated χ^2 value is significant, the null hypothesis of no association between the two attributes is rejected and there is association between the two attributes among the respondents. Thus the study reveals that there is association between working conditions and level of satisfaction.

Null Hypothesis

There is no association between level of satisfaction and welfare aspects.

Table 7.12 : Welfare Aspects *Vs.* Level of Satisfaction

Welfare Aspects	*Level of satisfaction*					*Total*
	HS	*S*	*N*	*DS*	*NS*	
Recreational facility offered by the company	45	57	40	8	-	150
Cleanliness of work place	75	68	6	1	-	150
Drinking water facilities available	82	64	3	-	1	150
Total	202	189	49	9	1	450

Source : Primary data.

Working conditions and level of satisfaction— χ^2 test

Factor	*Calculated χ^2*	*Table Value*	*DF*	*Remarks*
Welfare aspects	73.917	13.28	4	Significant

Since the calculated χ^2 value is significant, the null hypothesis of no association between the two attributes is rejected and there is association between the two attributes among the respondents. Thus the study reveals that there is association between welfare aspects and level of satisfaction.

Findings

1. It is observed that, the majority of the respondents had high level of satisfaction towards different aspects of working condition.
2. The study noted that the salary under monetary benefits secured the first rank among the respondents.
3. It is observed that, majority of the respondents are satisfied with the adequate leave facilities provided by the company.
4. The respondents were found to be satisfied with the authority given to them under the decision-making aspect.
5. It is noted that the safety and security offered by the IT companies was attracted by the women em-ployees.
6. It is clear from the study, all the respondents are satisfied with the welfare aspects opted by the company.
7. It is found that the possibilities to shift when an offer comes is higher and stood at first among the respondents

Suggestions

The researcher suggests the following remedial measures to improve the existing practices of the stress management, namely,

1. Majority of the respondent's opinion about the working hours were not satisfactory. Therefore, it is suggested that, the company must take appropriate steps to manage the hours of working effectively.
2. On the basis of opinion given by the respondents, it is suggested that the company should let them pursue higher education.

3. It is suggested that majority of the respondents opinion about the safety measures provided by the company is not satisfactory. Hence, it is suggested that the IT sectors should provide these facilities to women employees which in turn will reduce their stress.
4. On the basis of opinion given by the respondents, the company should provide the opportunity to take part in decision-making.
5. It is also suggested that considerable percentage of respondents have experienced poor recreational facilities. Therefore, the IT Company must take appropriate steps to offer those facilities to women to reduce their stress.
6. Women can also manage their stress through various measures like listening to soft music, creating favourite hobbies, meditation, proper time management and other effective methods.

Conclusion

Any employee will give the maximum effort and contribution when kept happy and without any stress. Hence it is the responsibility of the employer to keep the employees without any stress to increase productivity. Moreover women should also take necessary steps to reduce their stress and increase their productivity. Stress only leads to depression and constant depression may prove to be fatal. Hence it is necessary that stress be managed properly and effectively. Thus, this issue acquires importance in the context of the employee's behaviour on which the effectiveness of the organization depends to a large extent. In this connection, the personality traits of the employee and the characteristics of the organization may induce stress, ultimately affecting their performance and efficiency. Hence, it is essential to take steps to minimize the effects of determinants of stress and help individual and organizations evolve newer and effective coping strategies.

REFERENCES

HRD Times - Managing Stress among IT Professional, P. Nambi Raja Sudalai, the survey published in November 2007.

HRD Times – a multifaceted monthly Magazine, Vol. 9, published in September 2007.

HRM Review - Dr. SC. Poornima, The Icfai University Press, *Organizational Behavior*, January 2008.

Arun Bhatia and Rashmi Bhatia, *Stress Management*, Icfai University Press, 2007.

Aziz, M (2004). Role stress among women in the Indian Information Technology Sector. *Women in Management Review*. 19(7): 356 – 363.

Chandraiah, K.; Agrawal, S.C.; Marimuthu, P.; and Manoharan, N. (2003). Occupational Stress and Job Satisfaction Among Managers. *Indian Journal of Occupational and Environmental Medicine*. 7(2).

Chang, E.M.; Hancock, K.M.; Johnson, A.; Daly, J.; and Jackson, D. (2005). Role stress in nurses: Review of related factors and strategies for moving forward. *Nursing and Health Sciences*. 7: 57 – 65.

Green, P.E.; Tull, D.S.; and Albaum,G. (1999). (5th Ed.), *Research for Marketing Decisions*. India: Prentice Hall of India Private Limited.

Lu, L. (1999). Work motivation, Job stress and employees' well-being. *Journal of Applied Management Studies*. 8(1): 61-72.

Matthews, G.; Sparkes, T.J.; and Bygrave, H.M. (1996). Attentional overload, stress, and simulated driving performance. *Human Performance*. 9(1): 77-101

Stordeur, S., D'Hoore, W., Vandenberghe, C. (2001). Leadership, Organisational Stress, and Emotional Exhaustion among Hospital Nursing Staff. *Journal of Advanced Nursing*. 35(4): 533–542.

Olofsson, B.; Bengtsson, C.; and Brink, E. (2003). Absence of response: a study of nurses' experience of stress in the workplace. *Journal of Nursing Management*. 11: (351-358).

WEB SITES

- www.Stress.com.
- www.depthom.brooklyn.cuny.com
- www.Stress*Counseling.com*
- www.edindoro.com
- www.iowapsych.com

8 Good Governance and E-Governance

Prospects for Rural Bihar

Arjun Sharma

In his recent visit of Bihar our Hon'ble Vice President Bhairon Singh Sekhawat has expressed his concern over the poor socio-economic conditions of Bihar. In his speech he says that the rural development of Bihar is directly connected with the improvement of the poor conditions of '*Kisan*' and '*khet- khalihan*' (farmers and the farm). Earlier, in his tours to Bihar His Excellency President of India A. P. J. Abdul Kalam used to keep telling the people, the Governments – Centre and the State, industrialists, investors and NRIs to exploit their rich resources—human and natural—for the betterment of Bihar. The Prime Minister of the UPA Government, Manmohan Singh in 'Zonal Meet' appealed the NRIs and industrialists to invest in Bihar only if they wish to see India a developed ones. If Bihar remains backward India will never be a challenge to the Super Powers.

After the end of '*Jungle-Raj*' (the term coined not only by the people all over India but also by the Superior Courts), the '*Sushasan*' came last year in Bihar under the leadership of a rural man but a technocrat Chief Minister, Nitish Kumar. He always (during and after the elections) proclaims a '*Sushasan*' will solve all the problems that our State has been facing in the areas of law and order, infrastructure, education, health, energy, irrigation, agriculture, resource distribution, industries, sciences, technologies and so on all through the information and communication technology.

In view of the expressed desired of the Government of Bihar to catch the faster pace of development, Global Meet, Mirror Conference, NRIs and BDIC (Bihar Development and Investment Council) have invest more and more in the State. UGC and higher academic institutions like A.N. College have been organizing seminars, conferences, workshops where scholars and social scientists think over the strategies for all round development of agrarian society like ours.

Currently the 'Good Governance' becomes the central quest in the development discourse. It implies effective political institution and the responsible use of political power and management of public resources by the State. Essentially, it is about the interaction between democracy, social welfare and the rule of law. Good governance thus extends beyond the Public Sector to include all other actors from the private sector and society. Further, it is guided by human rights and by the principles of the rule of law and democracy such as equal political participation for all. Particular attention is devoted to the needs of the weaker members of society.[1] It is against the authoritarian rules and bureaucracy with the ruling attitude. This is evident from the nature of governance in the countries like Chile and Indonesia.[2] All these aspects place the greatest premium on the people and their participation in the decision-making process and public affairs. Good governance has another aspect related to fast growing information and communication technology. The ICT can facilitate the poor to voice their grivances as well as influence the decision-making process, not only as information receiver but also as information provider.[3] It has been argued that 'Good Governance' is 'E-Governance'.[4]

The gradual penetration of information technology in all facets of human existence is leading to multi-dimensional and often unpredictable changes. It is changing the way individuals interact with each other and with society and the way in which societies involve individuals in its evolution process. The way of governing a country is no exception to this changing scenario which is sweeping across the world.

Government around the world is carefully weighing electronic developments and their consequences.[5] The ICT has enmeshed the globe in a web that cuts across all barriers of nationality, culture, language, tradition, religion, caste and class.

India is one of the countries where this trend sees to be catching on. Information Technology enables governments to explore new ways of creating knowledge and getting citizens involved in the decision-making process.[6] It is expected that IT would be the great enabler for responsive and good governance in times to come when 'E' for E-Governance would stand for 'Excellence' particularly for Bihar.[7] E-Governance is one such crucial IT driven initiatives that will allow the NDA Government in Bihar to make information easily available, transparent and in interactive manner.[8] In fact, E-Governance is a step of Bihar Government towards creating smoother interface between Government business, citizen and tillers for SMART (Simple, Moral, Accountable, Responsive and Transparent) governance.[9]

ICTs have also provided a relevant ground for the development to knowledge sector.[10] India has yet to adequately cultivate that potential into full fruition. One of the reasons for this may be that there is not yet enough appreciation of the need for the proper management of knowledge for development.[11] To provide knowledge to the rural people of Bihar is more important than to give bread and butter as the following saying goes on, "Don't catch fish for your children; but give them knowledge on how to catch fish instead. If you catch the fish and give them to your children, you feed them for only one meal. But if you give them the knowledge on how to catch fish for themselves, they can be fed for their life time". Thus, the rural people of Bihar have a great need to understand the importance of knowledge management today.[12] Look at the huge waste of knowledge being created in our day-to-day lives, without being used, reused, collected and processed. It is like a waste dumped over without any treatment on the street, which can be otherwise transformed into resources through proper waste management technologies. It is true to say that one man's garbage is another man's vital information.[13]

Out of 94, 163 sq. km. area of Bihar, 92,258 sq. km. belongs to rural Bihar containing 8,471 village Panchayats, 534 Panchayat Samitis and 38 Zila Parishads. This area covers nearly 80 per cent of our population depending on agricul-ture and traditional occupations. The participation of the rural people in grass root democracy like PRIs will make them efficient in rural environment but their educational backwardness, social settings, lack of infrastructure, power-shortage, financial crunch, less e-readiness etc. will make them handicapped. Until or unless they are not equipped properly for the meeting of challenges of the global economy, they will not succeed in achieving the aims of good governance. They not only have to change the traditional modes of living but also have to adopt the new information communication technologies. They have to be empowered in the area of problems and prospects of use of ICT and proper management of knowledge.[14]

It is in this context this chapter deals with the conceptual clarities of the terms involved – Good Governance and E-Governance. The feasibility of adopting ICT–Computer, Internet, RTI access, IT tools, Communication Skills, PCOs, PIOs and other Facilitation Centres have been kept in mind. Strategies, scopes, steps etc. are the key factors for the Psyche of the rural poor in ICT friendly environment. Knowledge Management, feasibility and desirability of new techniques, nature and modes of self-government and other related issues are also involved in the topic I touch.

Good Governance

Good Governance : Conceptual Framework

Before going through some facets of 'Good Governance,' it is quite essential to clarify the conceptual framework. 'Governance' has been meant as the process of decision-making and the process by which decisions are implemented or not implemented. It has been defined by the UNDP in 1997 as "the exercise of political, economic and administrative authority in the management of a country's affairs".[15] It has been used in several ways such as corporate governance, local governance, national governance, international governance and so on. Although governance is the mechanism to implement a nation's development plan, yet it implies to provide feedback into planning and to ensure judicious management of the nation's resources.[16] But with the emergence of concept of public management in the early 1990s, the scholars of America have advocated the need of structural changes in the process of governance by the statecraft in order to involve the beneficiaries themselves and seek the better results at the lowest cost.[17] This has the genesis of 'Good Governance'.

Good governance accomplishes governance in a manner essentially free of abuse and competition and with due regard for the rule of law. The true test of good governance is the degree to which it delivers on the promise of human rights – civil, cultural, social, economic and political rights. It is also responsive to the present and future needs of the society. It implies effective political institutions and the responsible use of political power and management of public resources by the State. The 'E-Governance' is the outcome of 'Good Governance'.[18]

Good Governance in short can be well understood by trifurcating its dimensions-components, instrument and goals.[19] All these are placed below in a tabular form (Table 8.1) so we can have better understanding of the term.

E-Governance

E-Governance : Conceptual Clarities

The beginning of the twenty-first century has been so much dominated by Information Technology that it has become a joke that in the dictionary all words will now begin with the

Table 8.1 : Dimensions of Good Governance

Components	*Instruments*	*Goals*
• Participation and Consensus	• Participatory Structures • Representation of Weaker sections • Public-private Partnership	• Maintaining Social Order • Recognizing the voice of the poor
• Accountability	• Effective and responsible political institutions	• Judicious management of natural and other resources
• Equitability and Rule of Law	• Judicious allocation of development resources	• Equity in distribution of benefits • Maintaining law and order
• Transparency	• E-Governance • Making people aware	• Minimizing Corruption
• Responsiveness and Efficiency	• Bureaucracy made responsible • Providing ICT network accessible to people	• Commitment to people
• Result Orientation	• Structural changes committed to people's cause • Decentralized decision-making	• Efficiency in delivery
• Low Costing	• Optimum use of Human and other local resources	• Results within the available resources
• SMART*	• All	• Sustainable Development

* **S**—Simple, **M**—Moral, **A**—Accountable, **R**—Responsive and **T**—transparent.

Source: Reference 19.

letter 'e'. Perhaps existence itself would now become 'e-existence'. It is, therefore, not surprising that everybody is talking about 'E-Governance.' If we try to define it, we can say, "E-Governance or Electronic Governance or Digital Governance is the effective use of IT to improve the system of governance that is in place and thus provide better services to the citizens."[20] IT (Information Technology) is a multi-disciplinary field emerging from computer technology, software technology, database technology and

Internet Technology. IT and Communication Technology now popularly referred to as ICT, embody Satellite Broadcasting Network, Television, Video, Digital Radio, Internet, Extranets, Wireless Communations Divices (Mobile Phone), Digital Video Disk (DVD), CD-Roms, Video or Voice Mail E-mail, E-Commerce and E-Conferencing. Thus, we have moved from IT to ICT and now are advancing towards IS (Information Society).[21]

Generally, governance refers to the system of directing and controlling the action, affairs, policies and function of a political unit, organization or nation.[22]

'E-Governance' is an attempt of government to harness IT to improve the efficiency of the executive function of the government including the delivery of public services. It can be defined as "The application of electronic means in the interaction between government and citizen (G2C), and business (G2B), as well as in internal government operations (G2G) to simplify and improve democratic government and business aspects of governance" So, 'E-Governance' is lot more than online voting or electronic town hall or just delivering services online. It is all about how Government business and citizens interact on an ongoing basis.[23]

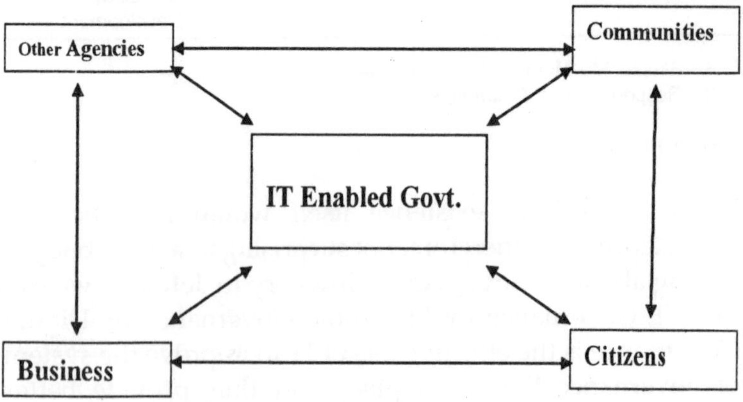

Figure 8.1 : E-Governance Interaction

Source : Reference 14.

The system of 'E-Governance' is supported by five pillars :

(i) *Computer :* It refers to all the hardware and software requirements of government.
(ii) *Connectivity :* It refers to all the information carriers system, bandwidth, etc.
(iii) *Content :* It refers to the information that is exchange between 'consumer' of the system.
(iv) *Consumer :* It refers to the entire human and human substitutes system that access and uses the 'Content' in the E-Governance system.
(v) *Confidence Building :* It refers to such of these measures that helps the citizens develop a confidence in the E-Governance and encourage them to take to E-Transformation.

Prospects for Rural Bihar

A brief scenario of rural Bihar has already been mentioned in general introduction. Bihar has been the agriculture and labour surplus economy. The huge human and natural resources have not been tapped properly for the prosperity of the State. The significance of the human capital or resource has been largely ignored and the Governance has paid least attention towards improvement of its working hands for better results. The corporate world in these days is pondering upon improvement of human resources to achieve the success and effectiveness in the market. Scholars like Christopher Hood has stressed upon.

To make structural changes in the public administration with an objective to introduce managerial attitude for setting better results on low expenses. In his sevenfold Paradigm of new Public Management, he has suggested the down sizing of the bureaucracy and devolving decision-making power on the grass roots level in order to match the local requirements.[24] N. Vittal talks for the better governance through accountability means responsibility for performance.[25]

Vast rural populace in Bihar depends, in one way or another, on agriculture. Therefore, any attempt at bringing overall development must lay greater emphasis on rural development of Bihar. It is a multi-dimensional concept encompassing social, educational, cultural, economic, political, agricultural, technological and so on.

Good governance must pass attention to the strategies of stimulation and inducement of rural development. Government should encourage changes in individual aspects regarding their perceptions and of motivation attitudes, world outlook and skills and management. People must know the nature of knowledge and the importance of its management for which traditional culture of Bihar must undergo radical changes.[26] If we mean development, we must deal with the issue of knowledge.[27] Government should also induce organizational change in rural communities in terms of leadership, structure made of people's participation and institutional linkages.[28] A sufficient level of environment support in terms of political leadership commitment, supportive policy measures, political and administrative framework and other social and economic supporting linkages should be provided by the policy-makers.[29] The rural leadership forms an important fabric of rural socio-economic and political system. Their perception of the local institution goes a long way in improving and delivering the appropriate service to the village community.[30]

Our social settings, economic conditions, political culture, educational standard, environmental pollution, ecological balances, participatory structure, infrastructural locking, ICTs initiatives etc. are so poor that we cannot progress. We must do away all those obstacles lying on the way of all-round development and it is possible through 'E- Governance' for and by the 'Good Governance'.

E- Governance : Constraints

The world has shrunk within the world-wide websites-www-Information Technology. No. society can afford to go within it. ICT revolution has changed the character of not only the economic world order rather it has effected the social change in its own way. The issue requires the examination of such societies that are poor and facing hindrances. Bihar society is such a society that it is hostile to ICT and its proliferation down at the village level. Social, administrative and political constraints should be removed to bring the projected changes in governance. Disparities in e-governance initiatives, rigidity of bureaucracy, lack of adequate infrastructure, political instability, digital divide, rural and underprivileged, gender divide, illiteracy, poverty, lack of awareness among women, lack of political will and so on are some of the constraints which have to be removed to meet the challenges of 'Good Governance' through 'E-Governance'.[31]

The ICT should also be accessible to suppressed, *dalit*, women and educational instituitions.[32] Schemes and projects should be launched to make it accessible to villagers to ensure their shares in good governance. The lack of infrastructure like road and electricity is one of the major factors responsible for the failures in sustaining the e-governance benefits. Likewise, lack of adequate funding for e-governance has restrained its reach to the masses. Administrative reforms are also very essential prerequisite for the success of e-governance. For e-governance to succeed, a strong political will commitment are necessary. Capability of use of local language in the ICT Sector is also required. Scope and areas of implementation of e-governance by the government must not be only the citizen and business men but also the farmers. Government funded projects, associations, Private companies and joint venture all should attempt to uplift the poor through the e-governance initiatives and strategies in rural Bihar.

Good Governance : Initiatives

Jaankari, the ICT based facilitation centre under RTI Act, is likely to go on stream before the end of the current month. It is a monitoring mechanism for RTI and public grievances. It would be another first for the State which happens to be the only one where RTI applications can be filed on the phone by the entire population of 85 million scattered over 1162 BSNL exchanges in 19 telecom districts covering 38,475 villages. Authorization was given to review all arrangements including monitoring as well as qualitative analysis on regular basis with all the stakeholders– Facilitation Centre, Telecom Department, the PIOs, BELTRON (Bihar State Electronics Development Corporation Ltd.), the administrative department, NGOs and most importantly feedback from common man. The State Government has also set up an independent office of the State Information Commissioner having the powers and the final responsibility to monitor compliance of public authorities to the RTI Act. Chief Minister Secretariat, Chief Secretary and Department Bosses have to keep tabs on *babus* responses to public requests and complaining. A cell has been created in the CM Secretariat to monitor movement of complaints.[33] Recently, 20 Ministers out of 26 were provided Laptops of I-Dm Lenova Company each costing the State exchequer Rs. 60,000. Rest six including the Chief Minister will soon be handed over their Laptops and all will be trained by the BELTRON. State Science and Technology Minister Anil Kumar said once all the Ministers and top-ranking administrators were equipped with computers, the State would furnish computers and necessary software to each district and Block officers in order to bring the ICT revolution in the State Government. The Science and Technology Department has also approved the purchase of over 250 servers, 100 of desktop computers and 40 projectors to give a massive boost to the State non-existent infrastructure. The State Government also gave away brand-new luxury SUVs to all its Ministers and MLAs at a whopping cost of Rs. 3.8 crore.[34]

Bihar Government has taken bold steps to implement e-governance to provide benefits for rural development. The following may be mentioned :

(i) Deliver essential services to the rural poor.
(ii) Improving agricultural productivity.
(iii) Improving resource management.
(iv) Producing same output lower at total cost.
(v) Opportunities to earn a living by learning a new skill in the knowledge based economy.
(vi) Reduction in time and paper work.
(vii) Easily performing functions like collection of various taxes and charges.
(viii) Opportunities to trade and banking online.
(ix) Enhancing access to information and communication across large distance.
(x) Increasing the accessibility of individual citizens to information and services that allows them to influence Government operations.
(xi) Ensuring transparency and Right to Information in governmental activities.
(xii) Encouraging people's participation in governance.
(xiii) Improving the overall quality of life of the common man.
(xiv) Covering rural educational institutions for high-tech.

Services offered particularly to the farmers are as follows:

(a) Land records.
(b) Crop loans.
(c) Weather forecasting at district level.
(d) Crop disease management.
(e) Natural calamities and emergencies.
(f) Information regarding prices of commodities in different markets.
(g) Crop protection guidance.
(h) Information regarding new methods and technology of cultivation.
(i) Other services of general nature like income and caste certificates, birth and death records, registration, licence, education, examination

collection, health, medicines, technical and women education and so on.[35]

Conclusion

Good governance has become an integra part of demo-cratic system of Bihar. E-Governance has been accepted as a tool to accomplish good governance. It focusses in bringing improvements in the service delivery, dissemination of information, transparency, public and private partnership, efficiency and accountability. Government and its numerous agencies being the largest services providers in rural Bihar feel the need to make extensive use of ICTs for its major services. There are many stumbling blocks and constraints in the growth of e-governance that must be removed. e-governance should demonstrate its potentiality in ensuring good governance. It should also cover the issues which are not covered by IT Act, 2000 like IPRs, privacy, e-taxation, data protection, protection of e-consumers. Successful implementation of e-governance in rural Bihar requires more than skills in ICTs, good programme management techniques, good programme managers, involvement of stakeholders and teamwork. Thus, for the development and prosperity of rural Bihar in the area of e-governance, a proper planning and adjustment is inevitable. E-governance projects should be guided by a clearly focussed objective, clearly spell out funding, strong ICT infrastructure, awareness and commitment, continuous training, sustainability, appropriate mechanism, secure environment, participatory structure, rural development, strengthening of PRIs, social settings, educational extension, unempowered section, enrichment of democratic outlook, knowledge management, proper utilization of resources and so on. Our resources—human, natural and man-made—should be properly utilized by the better knowledge management of Good Governance through the ICTs or e-governance. More we apply *Sushasan* our skill power, better will be the drainage of output as revealed by the following Diagram.

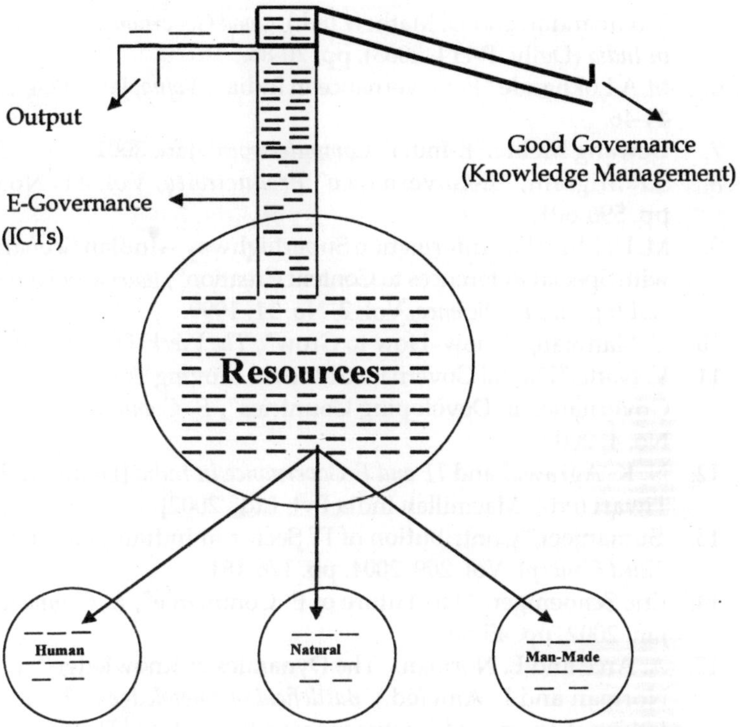

NOTES

1. G.T.Z. Themes, Downloaded from <http://www.gtz.de/en/themen/politische-reformen/882.htm>for further information please contact : Email : political-reforms@gtz.dec.
2. Atta El-Battahni, *Crisis, Politics and Governance in Sudan* as downloaded from< httm://www.ossrea.net/rw/goodgover-03.htm>
3. Richard Heeks,"Information and Communication Technology: Poverty and Development", *Development Informatics,* <www.man.ac.uk> Institute of Development Policy and Management, Manchester.
4. B. K. Dey, "E- Governance in India : Problems, Challenges and Opportunities – A Further Vision," *Indian Journal of Public Administration* Special No. on E- Governance.
5. S. Jaju, "Information Technology and Governance" in E.

Vayunandan and D. Mathew (ed.), *Good Governance Initiatives in India* (Delhi, P-H I, 2003), pp. 70-85.

6. M.A Lokhande "E- Governance in India", *Yojna,* Jan. 2004, pp. 44-46.
7. Dewang Mehta,"E-India" *Computerworld,* Jan. 2001.
8. S.P Miglani, "E-Governance" *Productivity,* Vol. 41, No.4, pp. 596-601.
9. M. U. Munshi, "Information Superhighway – Indian Scenario with Special References to Content Creation", *Journal of Library and Information Science,* Vol. 2, No. 11, 1999.
10. G. Natrajan, "Know-How to Grow", *The Week,* Dec. 28, 2003.
11. V. Nath, "Digital Governance Models: Moving Towards Good Governance in Developing Countries", *E- Commerce,* Vol. 2, No. 4, 2002.
12. N. K. Agrawal and *IT and E-Governance in India* [Delhi, M. D. Tiwari (ed.), Macmillan India Pvt. Ltd., 2002].
13. Sumanjeet,"Contribution of IT Sector in Indian Economy", *Third Concept,* Vol. 209, 2004, pp. 176-181.
14. Eric Schoeniger, "The Future of E- Commerce", *E- Commerce,* Jan. 2002, pp. 45-50.
15. A. Arce and L. Norman, "The Dynamics of Knowledge" in L. Norman and L. Ann (ed.), *Battlefield of Knowledge : The Interlocking of Theory and Practice in Social Research and Development* (N. Y. Routledge, 1992).
16. M. Moni and N. Vijayditya, *Convergence and E-Governance : National Informatics Centre – An Active Catalyst and Facilitator in India,* 2002 : http: // waterinfo. nic.in /news/ egover-convergence. htm/.
17. Nasscom, Jan. 17, 2003, E-Governance in India accelerating http: www. ispai. com/expresscomputer 07 feb 2003. html.
18. President of India, A. P. J. Abdul Kalam, Inaugural address at the International Conference on E- Governance, IIT, Delhi, 18 Dec. 2003: http : // www. iitd. ac. in / iceg. R. K. Verma and N. Sinha, "Good Governance and Rural Development : A Study in Context of People's Participation", *Bihar Journal of Public Administration,* Vol.1, No. 2 and Vol. 2, No. 1, New Series Combined, 2005, pp. 51-64.
19. Anupma Saxena, " E- Governance and Good Governance : The Indian Context" *The Indian Journal of Political Science,* Vol. LXVI, No. 2, April- June, 2005, pp. 313-327.

20. A. P. Yadav, "Information Technology and Our Society : An Overview in Context of Poor", *Bihar Journal of Public Administration,* No.19, pp. 91-95.
21. S. Majumdar, "Government Information in the Digital Era", *Libraries, Information and Knowledge,* Vol. 21, No. 1, pp. 27-42.
22. Sumanjeet, "E- Governance : An Overview in the Indian Context", *The Indian Journal of Political Science,* Vol. LXVII, No. 4, Oct.-Dec., 2006, pp. 857-866.
24. Christopher Hood, "A Public Management of All Seasons", *Public Administration,* Vol. 69, Spring 1991, pp. 3-19.
25. N. Vittal, "Towards Batter Governance Through Acccountability", *Fifty Years of Indian Parliament,* pp. 216-234.
26. C. D. Duffy, "Cultural Revolution", *CIO Magazine,* 15 Jan. 1999: http: / / www.cio.com/ archive/ enterprise/ 011599_rah.html.
27. Y. G. Lee and R. Singh, "Knowledge Management—Some Theoretical Considerations" *Bihar Journal of Public Administration* No. 19, pp. 26-37.
28. The World Bank, *Reading the Rural Poor: Strategy for Rural Development,* 2001.
29. UNDP, *Governance for Sustainable Human Development : A UNDP Policy Document, Jan. 1997.* http: / / magnet.undp.org/ policy / default.htm.
30. Y. Misra, *Empowering People : Grassroot Organisations and Rural Development* (No. Delhi, Kanishka, 2002).
31. B. R. Bajaj, http: / / in.news.yahoo.com / 041107 / 43 / 2hqsl.html.
32. B.S.Padmanabhan, *Frontline,* Sept. 24, 2004, p.120.
33. Amitabh Jha. "e-monitoring of public grievamces on anvil," *Hindustan Times,* Patna, May 13, 2007.
34. Vijay Swaroop "Rapid Stride towards E-governance," *Hindustan Times,* Patna, May 06, 2007.
35. *Dainik Jagaran,* Patna, May 16, 2007.

9 Security Challenges in E-commerce

Seyed Reza Mousavizadeh and **H. Rajshekar**

Doing business on the web is more risky than doing business with local customers. Stolen credit cards, disputed charges, off-shore shipping destinations, the power of credit card companies to force merchants to pay for fraud, and the lack of international laws governing global e-commerce problems are just some of the security problems with which e-commerce merchants must grapple. For consumers, on the other hand, the risk in e-commerce is really no greater than in ordinary commerce. Although there have been some spectacular losses of credit card information involving a tiny percentage of companies, because of the variety of laws, consumers are largely isolated from the impact of stolen credit cards and credit card information. Nevertheless, as the transactions volumes and monetary value of e-commerce continue to expand, so do the risks for both merchants and consumers. This article aim is to examine e-commerce security issues, identify the major risks, and describe the variety of solutions currently available.

What is a Good Security for e-commerce?

The Internet has evolved far beyond a collection of research and government technology labs and communication centres for which it was founded. The opening of access points on this global collection of local networks to commercial enterprises in the early 1990's spurned numerous innovations to produce immense increases in speed of transfer and quantity of storage of data capital. The means of competing in a free market economy adapted, and productivity increased at a much faster pace in the last decade than the century and a half since the dawn of the Industrial Revolution. The manipulation of digital capital shaping the progress of the Information Age must be secured in order for massive change in market space and transaction processes to become accepted and cost effective for producers, sellers, and buyers. What has transpired in commerce in the last ten years may send armed guards at physical bank buildings toward extinction. Some of these armed guards might just find new employment at massive secured data centres. However, their importance will diminish as more and more data is stored behind the gates of these data centres where the most lethal of firearms and high voltage chain link fences will not stop the growing class of electronic thieves, terrorists, and vandals.

What is a safe and secure commerce transaction? Anytime, somebody go into a market place, they take several risks, such as the loss of privacy, not getting what they paid for, or worse, paying and getting nothing, and stealing their money while they are in the market. As a merchant, the risk is not getting paid for what being sold. Thieves may take goods, and then either walk away without paying anything, or pay with a fraudulent instrument, stolen credit or debit card, or faked currency.

Merchants and consumers in E-commerce market space face many of the same risks as participants in traditional commerce. Theft is theft, regardless of whether it is traditional theft or digital theft. But, to reduce risks in e-commerce, we need a complex process that involves new technologies, organizational policies and procedures, and new laws and industry standards that empower law enforcement officials to investigate and prosecute offenders.

Using new technologies to achieve the highest degree of security possible is one thing, but to ensure the technologies are not subverted, we need another layer of action called organizational policies and procedures. At the same time, to enforce payment mechanisms, as well as investigate and prosecute violators of laws designed to protect the transfer of property in commercial transactions, there is another security layer called industry standards and government laws.

History tells us that any security can be cracked by enough resources used against it. Security is not absolute. Moreover, perfect security forever is not required especially in information age. There is time value to information—just there is to money. Also, security is costly. We always have to weigh the cost against the need. We have also learnt that security is a chain, a chain that breaks most often at the market link.

Dimensions of the e-commerce Security

E-commerce can be simply defined as conducting business over a data network that in some logical way has access to the all-encompassing Internet. The major market researchers have weighed in with revenue projections to push the fervour higher to new extremes. Gartner Group predicted in August 2000 that the year would end with an Internet retail revenue tally in North America up to 75 per cent of 1999's figure of \$16.8 billion and 15.7 per cent from 1998. E-commerce security has six key dimensions :

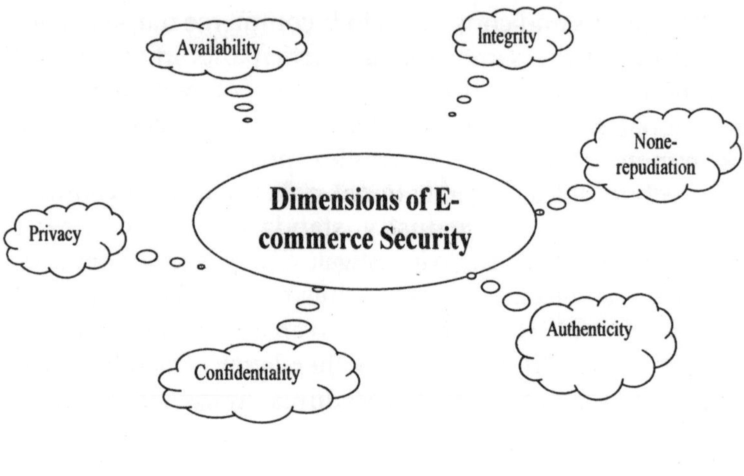

1. *Integrity*

It refers to the capability of ensuring the data and information being displayed on a website, or transferred (transmitted or received) over the Internet has not been changed by an unauthorized party.

2. *Non-repudiation*

This dimension of the e-commerce security refers to the ability to create a situation in which none of the e-commerce participants repudiate or deny their on line actions.

3. *Authenticity*

It is the e-commerce participants' ability to identify a person or entity with whom they are dealing on the Internet. Someone who claims to be someone they are not is "spoofing" or misrepresenting themselves.

4. *Confidentiality*

Here, the aim is to create the ability to ensure that messages and data are available for authorized parties to view them.

5. *Privacy*

Privacy dimension of e-commerce refers to the ability to control the use of information a customer provides about himself or herself to an e-commerce merchant.

There are two concerns related to privacy for e-commerce merchants:

- Establishing an internal policy governing their own use of customer information.
- Protecting that information from illegitimate or unauthorized use.

6. *Availability*

Ensuring that an e-commerce site continues to function as intended is referred to as availability.

E-commerce security is designed to protect these six dimensions. When anyone of them is compromised, it is a security issue.

Security Threats in the e-commerce Environment

From technology perspective, three key points of vulnerability emerges when dealing with e-commerce; the client, the server, and the communication pipeline. Each of the aforesaid vulnerable points can be a place where the security threats can cause great damages.

Seven most common and most damaging forms of security threats are :

1. Malicious Code

The term "computer virus" was formally defined by Fred Cohen in 1983, while he performed academic experiments on a Digital Equipment Corporation VAX system. Viruses are classified as being one of the two types: research or "in the wild." A research virus is one that has been written for research or study purposes and has received almost no distribution to the public. On the other hand, viruses which have been seen with any regularity are termed "in the wild." The first computer viruses were developed in the early 1980s. The first viruses found in the wild were Apple II viruses, such as Elk Cloner, which was reported in 1981.

Viruses and *worms* are related classes of malicious code; as a result they are often confused. Both share the primary objective of *replication*. However, they are distinctly different with respect to the techniques they use and their host system requirements. This distinction is due to the disjoint sets of host systems they attack. Viruses have been almost exclusively restricted to personal computers, while worms have attacked only multi-user systems.

Viruses

The following are necessary characteristics of a virus:

- Replication.
- Requires a host programme as a carrier.
- Activated by external action.
- Replication limited to (virtual) system.

In essence, a computer programme which has been infected by a virus has been converted into a Trojan horse. The programme is expected to perform a useful function, but has the unintended side effect of viral code execution. In addition to performing the unintended task, the virus also performs the function of replication. Upon execution, the virus attempts to replicate and "attach" itself to another programme. It is the unexpected and generally uncontrollable replication that makes viruses so dangerous. Viruses are currently designed to attack single platforms. A platform is defined as the combination of hardware and the most prevalent operating system for that hardware. As an example, a virus can be referred to as an IBM-PC virus, referring to the hardware, or a DOS virus, referring to the operating system. "Clones" of systems are also included with the original platform.

Personal computer viruses exploit the lack of effective access controls in these systems. The viruses modify files and even the operating system itself. These are "legal" actions within the context of the operating system. While more stringent controls are in place on multi-tasking, multi-user operating systems, configuration errors, and security holes (security bugs) make viruses on these systems more than theoretically possible.

This leads to the following conclusions :

- Viruses exploit weaknesses in operating system controls and human patterns of system use/misuse.
- Destructive viruses are more likely to be eradicated.
- An innovative virus may have a larger initial window to propagate before it is discovered and the "average" anti-viral product is modified to detect or eradicate it.

Worms

Worms were first used as a legitimate mechanism for performing tasks in a distributed environment. Network worms were considered promising for the performance of network management tasks in a series of experiments at the Xerox Palo Alto Research Center in 1982. The key problem noted was "worm management;" controlling the number of copies executing at a single time. This would be experienced later by authors of malicious worms.

Worms were first noticed as a potential computer security threat when the *Christmas Tree Exec* attacked IBM mainframes in December 1987. It brought down both the world-wide IBM network and BITNET. The *Christmas Tree Exec* wasn't a true worm. It was a *Trojan Horse* with a replicating mechanism. A user would receive an e-mail Christmas card that included executable (REXX) code, if executed the program claimed to draw a Xmas tree on the display. That much was true, but it also sent a copy to everyone on the user's address lists.

The *Internet Worm* was a true worm. It was released on November 2, 1988. It attacked Sun and DEC UNIX systems attached to the Internet (it included two sets of binaries, one for each system). It utilized the TCP/IP protocols, common application layer protocols, operating system bugs, and a variety of system administration flaws to propagate. Various problems with worm management resulted in extremely poor system performance and a denial of network service.

The *Father Christmas* worm was also a true worm. It was first released onto the worldwide DECnet Internet in December of 1988. This worm attacked VAX/VMS systems on SPAN and HEPNET. It utilized the DECnet protocols and a variety of system administration flaws to propagate. The worm exploited TASK0, which allows outsiders to perform tasks on the system. This worm added an additional feature; it reported successful system penetration to a specific site.

This worm made no attempt at secrecy; it was not encrypted and sent mail to every user on the system. About a month later another worm, apparently a variant of *Father Christmas*, was released on a private network. This variant searched for accounts with "industry standard" or "easily guessed" passwords.

The history of worms displays the same increasing complexity found in the development of PC viruses. The *Christmas Tree Exec* was not a true worm. It was a *Trojan Horse* with a replicating mechanism. The *Internet Worm* was a true worm; it exploited both operating system flaws and common system management problems. The DECnet worms attacked system management problems, and reported information about successful system penetration to a central site.

The following are necessary characteristics of a worm :

- Replication.
- Self-contained; does not require a host.
- Activated by creating process (needs a multi-tasking system).

- For network worms, replication occurs across communication links.

A worm is not a *Trojan Horse;* it is a programme designed to replicate. The programme may perform any variety of additional tasks as well. The first network worms were intended to perform useful network management functions. They took advantage of system properties to perform useful action. However, a malicious worm takes advantage of the same system properties. The facilities that allow such programmes to replicate do not always discriminate between malicious and good code. This leads to the following conclusions :

- Worms exploit flaws (*i.e.,* bugs) in the operating system or inadequate system management to replicate.
- Release of a worm usually results in brief but spectacular outbreaks, shutting down entire networks.

Trojan Horse

A *Trojan Horse* is an e-mail virus usually released by an e-mail attachment. If opened, it will scour your hard drive for any personal and financial information such as your social security, account, and PIN numbers. Once it has collected your info, it is sent to a thief's database.

Just what is a *Trojan* then? A *Trojan* is a programme that appears to be legitimate, but in fact does something malicious. Quite often, that something malicious involves gaining remote, surreptitious access to a user's system. Unlike viruses, a *Trojan* does not replicate (*i.e.* infect other files), nor does it make copies of itself as worms do.

There are several different types of Trojans. Some of these include: Remote access Trojans (RATs), backdoor Trojans (backdoors), IRC Trojans (IRCbots), and keylogging

Trojans. Many Trojan encompass multiple types. For example, a Trojan may install both a keylogger and a backdoor. IRC Trojans are often combined with backdoors and RATs to create collections of infected computers known as botnets.

But why is it important to know the difference between a virus, a worm, and a Trojan? Because a virus infects legitimate files, thus if antivirus software detects a *virus*, that file should be *cleaned*. Conversely, if antivirus software detects a worm or a Trojan, there is no legitimate file involved and action should be to *delete* the file.

2. Hacking and Cybervantalism

Technically, a hacker is someone who is enthusiastic about computer programing and all things relating to the technical working of a computer. There is in fact more to it than that – hackerdom is an entire culture in its own right. Within the hacking community, the term *cracker* is typically used to denote a hacker with criminal intent, although in the public press, the terms *hacker* and *cracker* are used interchangeably (Sinrod and Reilly, 2000).

Crackers are people who try to gain unauthorized access to computers. This is normally done through the use of a 'backdoor' programme installed on your machine. A lot of crackers also try to gain access to resources through the use of password cracking software, which tries billions of passwords to find the correct one for accessing a computer. Obviously, a good protection from this is to change passwords regularly. Another good move is the use of software that supports intruder lockout, where no further passwords are accepted after a certain number of bad passwords have tried. Even the correct password wouldn't allow access. Such blocks are normally released after a period of time has elapsed (*e.g.* 15 minutes). Of course, an even better idea is never to put security-sensitive resources on the Internet in the first place. If you don't want something to be accessed from the Internet, then make it so that it is only accessible from your local network, or even just from one computer. However, backdoor programmes are programmes that can expose files to the Internet that were never meant to be shared with other people.

Hackers and crackers are computer aficionados excited by the challenge of breaking into corporate and government websites. Sometimes they are satisfied merely by breaking into the files of e-commerce sites. Others have more malicious intentions and commit *Cybervantalism.* The damages the Hacker can do depends upon what backdoor programme(s) are hiding on your PC. Different programmes can do different amounts of damage. However, most allow a hacker to smuggle another programme onto your PC. This means that if a hacker can't do something using the backdoor programme, he can easily put something else onto your computer. Hackers can see everything you are doing, and can access any file on your disk. Hackers can write new files, delete files, edit files, and do practically anything to a file that could be done to a file. A hacker could install several programs on to your system without your knowledge. Such programs could also be used to steal personal information such as passwords and credit card information. Some backdoor programs even allow a hacker to listen in on your conversations using your computer's microphone if one is attached! Hackers can do great damage to your computer. They could delete vital files from your hard disk, without which your computer could not work.

3. Credit Card Fraud or Theft

Credit card theft is one of the most feared occurrences on the Internet. This fear prevents users from making on-line purchases, it appears to be largely unfounded. For instance, only 2 per cent credit card theft was reported, according to a study by Activemedia Research, but 58 per cent of the consumers reported a fear of credit card theft.

The greatest threat to the e-commerce websites' consumers is that the merchant's server with which the consumer is transacting will lose the credit information or permits it to be diverted for criminal purposes.

4. Spoofing

Spoofing is that kind of attack in which hackers try to conceal their true identity—misrepresent themselves. They do this by using fake e-mail address or masquerading as someone else. Sometimes hackers redirect a web link to an address different from the intended one, with the site masquerading as the intended address. Hackers can benefit from this by resetting the links to send users to a totally unrelated site, which the hackers want.

The treads associated with spoofing is about the *integrity* of a site. Spoofing does not damage files or network servers. The hacker's site which look almost exactly like the true site can collect and process orders, and effectively steal business from the true site. Sometimes the interrupting is the intent rather than stealing, by which hackers can change the orders, for example, inflating them or changing products ordered. These altered orders are then sent to the true site for processing and delivery. Therefore, it can turn satisfied customer into an unsatisfied person by improper order shipment. Also the companies may have huge inventory fluctuations that impact their operations.

Authenticity is also threatened by making it difficult to distinguish between the true senders of the message. Smart hackers are able to make it nearly impossible to discern a true and fake identity or web address.

5. Denial of Service Attacks

Sometimes, hackers flood a website with useless traffic to inundate and overwhelm the network. This is called Denial of Service (DoS) attacks. A special type of DoS attack is Distributed Denial of Service attack in which numerous computers are used to attack the target network for numerous launch points.

DoS attacks make it impossible for users to access the site by shutting down a network. While the site is shut down, customers cannot use the site. This can be very costly for busy sites such as eBay or Amazon.com, since customers can not make purchases while the site is shut down. Damage on site's reputation increases in case the site is shut down longer.

In February 2000, a series of hacker attacks caused many websites to shut down for several hours. eBay was shut down for 5 long hours, Amazon for just under 4 hours, CNN for 3.5 hours, and e-trade for under 3. Yahoo, Buy.com, ZDNet were also affected for 3 to 4 hours (McConnell).

6. Sniffing

Sniffing can be used both positively as well as negatively. Sniffer is a type of eavesdropping program. It monitors information travelling over a network. Sniffers can be damaging and very difficult to detect in case they are used for criminal purposes. On the contrary, when used legitimately, sniffers can help identify potential network trouble spots.

Sniffers enable hackers to steal proprietary information from anywhere in a network, including e-mail messages, company files, and confidential reports.

Confidential or personal information being made public is the threat of sniffing for both companies and individuals.

7. Insider Jobs

The largest financial threat to businesses does not come from robberies, but from insiders' embezzlement. We normally think that security threat to a business is what coming from outside of the organization, which is not true. E-commerce sites are no longer exception to this rule. Some of the largest disruption to service, destructions to sites, and diversion of the customer credit data and personal information originate from the insiders, that is, once trusted employees. Employees, having access to privileged information, due to sloppy internal security procedures, are able to roam throughout an organization's systems without leaving a trace.

One of such insiders' misuses is what happened to collegeboardwalk.com. Jose Oquendo worked as a company security specialist who shared office space and a computer network with Five Partners Asset Management, one of its investors. Oquendo altered the start-up commands on the Five Partners Network to automatically send the password file from the system to an e-mail account he controlled and each time the Five Partners system was rebooted. After College-boardwalk.com failed, Oquendo secretly installed a sniffer program that intercepted and recorded electronic traffic on the Five Partners network, including unencrypted pass-words. Oquendo was later caught when he used the sniffer to snare a password into the network of another company, and then erased that company's database (NIPC press release, 2001).

Technology Solution

To secure e-commerce sites against outsiders' threats, there are a set of tools that can make it difficult for outsiders invade and destroy a site. The following figure illustrates the major tools available to achieve site security.

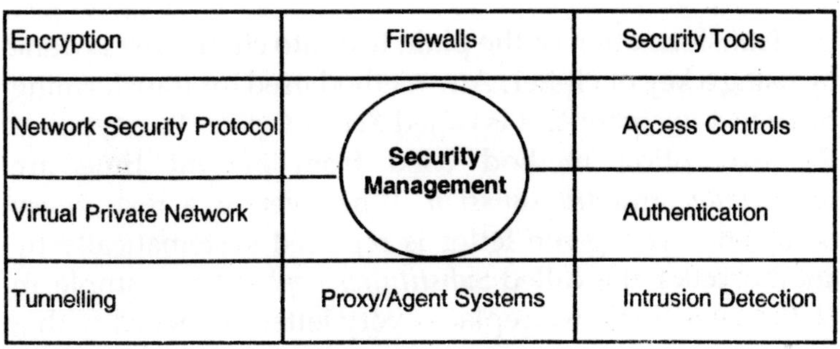

E-commerce transactions must flow over the public Internet. internet connection involves thousands of routers and servers through which the transaction packets flow. Therefore, security experts believe the greatest security threats occur at the level of internet communications. This is against another type of internet connection, namely, *private network,* in which a dedicated communication line is established between two parties. To protect the security of the internet communications, several tools are available among which *message encryption* is the most basic one.

Encryption

The process in which the plain text or data is transformed into cipher text in order not to be read by anyone other than the sender and receiver is called *encryption*. The purposes of encryption are :

- To secure the stored information.
- To secure information while transmitting.

Four of the six key dimensions of e-commerce security is targeted by encryption :

1. Message integrity.
2. Non-repudiation.
3. Authentication.
4. Confidentiality.

Transformation of the plain text into cipher text is done by using a key or cipher. Any method used for transforming plain text to cipher text is called *Key* or *Cipher*. Two types of the encryption method used from ancient time are *substitution* and *transmission*. Whenever in a text, every occurrence of a given letter is replaced systematically by another letter, it is called *Substitution Cipher*. For example, in "letter plus two", we replace every letter in a word with a new letter two places forward. "HELLO" in plain text would be transformed into the "JJNNQ" cipher text. When the ordering of the letters in each word is changed in some systematic way, the *Transposition Cipher* has taken placed. For example, what Leonardo Da Vinci turned his shop notes reversed, making it readable only by mirror (HELLO becomes OLLEH).

In a more sophisticated cipher, we would (a) break all words into two words; and (b) spell the first word with every other letter beginning with the first letter, and then spell the second word with all the remaining letters. Therefore, HELLO would be written as HLOEL.

After encrypting and sending messages, the secret cipher that was used to encrypt the plain text would have to be known by receiver. In *Symmetric Key Encryption* or *Secret Key Encryption*, both the sender and the receiver use the same key to encrypt and decrypt the message. Therefore, the sender and the receiver have to send the *Key* over some communication media or exchange it in person.

There are endless possibilities in using simple substitution and transposition ciphers, but they all suffer from common flaws :

1. First, in the era of digital explosion, computers are so fast and powerful that these ancient means of encryption can be broken quickly.
2. Second, in symmetric key encryption, sender and receiver need to share the same key over a presumably insecure medium where it could be stolen or used to decipher messages. The entire encryption system fails in case the secret key is lost or stolen.
3. Third, being in commercial activity, we are not all part of the same team or army. Therefore, for each of the parties with whom we transact, we need a secret key. In a population of millions of Internet users,

thousands of millions of keys would be required to accommodate e-commerce customers that would be a situation which is too unwieldy to work in practice.

Encryption systems which now are in use are digital. This means that the ciphers or keys used for encrypting a text are what we call digital string. Computers use binary strings composed of 0s and 1s to store text or other data.

In 1950s, the US National Security Agency (NSA) and IBM developed a systematic key encryption on the Internet called Data Encryption Standard (DES) which is most widely used now. In DES a 56-bit encryption key is used and in order to handle faster computers, it has been improved by triple DES. Triple DES means that it encrypt the message three times each with a separate key. Here also, DES requires the sender and the receiver to exchange and share the same key, and requires a different set of keys for each set of transactions.

Whitfield Diffle and Martin Hellman invented Public Key Cryptography in 1976. Public Key Cryptography solved the problem of exchanging the keys. This method uses two mathematically related digital keys; *A Public Key* and *A Private Key*. *Public Key* is widely disseminated while the *Private Key* is kept secret by the owner. The message can be encrypted and decrypted by both keys. However, once the keys are used to encrypt a message, that same key cannot be used to unencrypt the message. *One way function* is the mathematical algorithm used to produce the keys. Public Key Cryptography is based on the idea of irreversible mathematical functions.

In Public Key Encryption, a *Hash Function* is used first to create the digest of the message. It is used to check the confidentiality of a message and ensure it has not been altered in transit. *Hash Function* is an algorithm that produces a fixed length number called a *"Hash"* or *"Message Digest"*. A *Hash Function* can be simple (count the number of digital 1s in a message) or complex (produce a 128-bit number that reflects the number of 0s and 1s, the number of 00s, 11s, and so on.

After the *Hash function* has been applied, the results are sent by the sender the recipient. After receiving, the recipient applies the *Hash Function* to the received message and checks to verify the same results is produced. If so, the message has not been altered. The sender then encrypts both the hash result and the original message using the recipient public key, producing a single block of cipher text. In order to ensure the authenticity and non-repudiation, the sender encrypts the entire block of cipher text once more using the sender's *Private Key*. By doing this, a *Digital Signature* is produced. This signed cipher text can be sent over the Internet.

When this signed cipher text reached to the recipient, she first uses the sender's *Public Key* to *authenticate* the message. Then, she uses her *Private Key* to obtain the hash result and original message. Finally, the recipient should apply the same hash function to the original text and compare the result with the result sent by the sender. If the results are the same, the message has not been changed during transmission and the message has integrity.

However, the problem with the *Public Key* encryption is its slowness in computation. If, for example, a large document is to be encoded using 128 or 256-bit keys, the transmission speed will decline significantly and the processing time would increase. Though symmetric key is computationally faster, it has the flaw of sending symmetric key over insecure transmission lines. One solution to this is to integrate these two, which is called *Digital Envelope.* In digital envelope, a more efficient symmetric encryption and decryption for large documents is used, but a public key encryption is used to encrypt and send the symmetric key.

By using the recipient's *Public Key,* the symmetric key used by recipient to decrypt the document is encrypted. So, there is "a key within a key"—*Digital Envelope.* The encrypted report and the *Digital Envelope* are sent across the web. By using her *Private Key*, the recipient first decrypt the symmetric key. Then, symmetric key is used to decrypt the report.

But there are still some flaws in the message security described above. For instance, how is it possible for you to be sure that people and institutions are who they claim to be? Anyone can create a combination of public and private key and claim to be the defense department. You might plan to place an online order in Amazon.com. but before that, you must be ensured that it really is Amazon.com you have on the screen and not a spoofer masquerading as Amazon.

For solving this problem, *Digital Certificates* and the supporting *Private Key Infrastructure* are offered. A *Digital Certificate*, issued by a trusted *Certification Authority* (CA), is a digital document. It includes the name of the subject or the company, the subject's *Private Key*, a *Digital Certificate* serial number, an expiration date, an issuance date, the digital signature of the *Certification Authority*, and other identifying information. A CA is an institution or a *Trusted Third Party. Private Key* infrastructure refers to the certification authorities and *Digital Certificate* procedures accepted by all parties.

The process of creating a *Digital Certificate* starts when the user generate a public/private key pair and sends a request for a certification to a CA along with the users public key. The CA, upon receiving the information, starts verifying that information. Each CA has its own way to accomplish this task. Then, the CA issues a certificate, which contains the user's *Private Key* and other related information. Finally, a message digest—like a hash digest—is created by CA from the certificate itself, signed with the CA's private keys, which is called a *Signed Certificate*. This is totally unique cipher text document. It means that there can be only one *Signed Certificate* like this in the world.

The usages of the certificates are numerous in e-commerce. For instance, the customer, before initiating any transaction, can request the merchant's signed digital certificate and decrypt it by using the merchant's public key to obtain both the message digest and the certificate as issued. The merchant and the public key are authenticated in case the message digest matches the certificate. In turn, the merchant also may request certification of the user. In this case, the user would send the merchant her individual certificate. There are several types of certificate; personal, institutional, web server, software publisher, and CAs themselves.

Limitations to Encryption Solutions

Though public key infrastructure is a powerful technological solution to security issues, it suffers from many limitations :

1. First, PKI is used mainly to protect messages in transit on the Internet. It is not an effective tool against employees inside an organization, who have legitimate access to corporate systems including customer information.
2. Second issue refers to the protecting of the private key. *Private Key* are stored on insecure desktops or laptops machines. How is it possible to guarantee the person using a computer—and a *Private Key*—is really the person who claims to be? Under many digital signature laws, you are responsible for whatever your private key does, even if you were not the person using the key :
3. Third issue relates to the security of the verifying computer of merchant. There is no guarantee the verifying computer of the merchant is secure.
4. Fourth issue relates to the CAs. CAs are self-selected organizations seeking to gain access to the business of the authorization. They may not be authorities in the corporations or individuals they certify. Also, the question arises around the method used by the CAs

to identify the certificate holder. Was this an e-mail transaction verified only by claims of applicants who filled out an online form?

5. Last issue refers to the matter of revoking or renewing certificate. It is the function of the frequency of use and vulnerability of the systems which use the certificate that determine the expected life of a *Digital Certificate* or *Private Key*. But, most CAs have no policy or just an annual policy for reissuing certificate (Ellison and Schneier, 2000).

Securing Channels of Communication

Web server certificates are the practical means of implementing PKI and digital certificates. ***SSL (Secure Socket Layers) Certificates,*** by allowing websites to offer safe, secure information exchange to their customers, form the basis of an internal trust infrastructure. The most common form of securing channels is through SSL of TCP/IP.

When a message is reached to a person from a server on the web communicating through a secure channel, this means SSL is used to establish a secure *Negotiated Session*. A secure *Negotiated Session* is a client-server session in which the URL of the requested document, along with the contents, contents of forms, and cookies exchanged, are encrypted. The browser and server, through a series of handshakes and communications, establish each other's identity *via* exchanging digital certificates, agree upon the most powerful shared form of encryption, and finally, by using an agreed upon session keys, proceed to communicate. A *Session Key* is unique, one-time used symmetric key chosen just for this high secure session.

SSL structure is designed in a way to address the threat of authenticity by allowing users to identify another user's identity, or identity of the server. Integrity of the message exchanged is also protected by SSL. Yet, the encrypted credit and order information received by merchant is typically stored in unencrypted format on the merchant's server.

However, provision of the secure transactions between merchants and consumers by SSL protocols only guarantees server side authentication. Client authentication is optional. Moreover, SSL cannot provide no-repudiation assurance. This means that consumers can order goods or download information products, and then claim transaction never occurred.

Another method in security channel data transfer is called *Secure Hypertext Transfer Protocol* (S-HTTP). S-HTTP, which is used in conjunction with HTTP, is a secure message-oriented communication protocol. S-HTTP coexists with HTTP and is easily integrated with HTTP applications. Unlike SSL, which is designed to establish a secure connection between two computers, S-HTTP is designed to send individual messages securely. It is not supported by all browsers and websites. When the URL starts with S-HTTP, we realize, we are dealing with supporting site. When it is used as an anchor tag, the target server is S-HTTP capable. The aim is to make HTTP more secure.

Virtual Private Network (VPN), using the *Point-To-Point Tunnelling Protocol* (PPTP), permit remote users to access internal networks *via* the Internet securely. PPTP, which is an encoding mechanism, allow one local network to connect to another using the Internet as the conduit. A remote user can dial into a local ISP and PPTP make the connection from the ISP to the corporate network as if the user had dialled into the corporate network directly. When one protocol (PPTP) is connected to another protocol (IP), *tunnelling* occurs. PPTP creates a private connection by adding an invisible wrapper around the message to hide its content. As the message travels through the Internet between ISP and corporate network, it is shielded from prying eyes by PPTP's encrypted wrapper.

We call VPN a *virtual* network because it appears to users as a dedicated secure line when in fact it is a temporary secure line. The primary use of VPN is to establish secure communication among business partners such as larger suppliers and customers. It is very costly to use a dedicated connection to a business partners. Internet and PPTP connection method significantly reduces the cost of secure communications.

Protecting Networks

The next set of tools, after protecting communications as well as possible, to consider are those that can protect the networks, and the servers and clients on those networks. Two tools intended to build a wall around the networks and the attached servers and clients are *Firewalls* and *Proxy Servers.* These two tools share some similar functions, but they are quite different.

As software applications, *Firewalls* act like filters between the Internet and a company private network. They create a kind of wall between remote client machines and the companies' internal network. All incoming and outgoing communications are monitored and validated by Firewalls. *Firewall* software process every message sent or received from the network. They determine if the message meets security guidelines established by the business. If such security criteria are met, it is permitted to be distributed; otherwise, the message is blocked.

Pocket Filters and *Application Gateways* are two major methods used by *Firewalls* to validate traffic. *Pocket Filters* scrutinize data packets to make sure if they are destined for a prohibited port, or originated from a prohibited IP addresses. *Filter* do this by looking at the source and destination information, and the port and packet type. But this method is susceptible to spoofing because authentication is not one of its roles.

The next method is *Application Gateways* filtering communications based on the application being requested, rather than the source and destination of the message. They also process requests at the application level, rather away from the client computer than packet filters. Though compromising system performance, they provide greater security than packet filters, by providing *Central Filtering Point.*

Proxy Servers, usually located on a dedicated machine, are software servers handling all communications originating from or sent to the Internet. Though some *Proxy Servers* act like *Firewalls,* they primarily act as a limitation force for internal clients to access external internet servers. Because of having two networks, proxy servers are sometimes called *Dual Home Systems.* To internal machines, a proxy server is known as *Gateway,* while to external machines, it is known as a *Mail Server* or *Numeric Address.*

The proxy server is the first place where a user requests on an internal network is routed. *The User* and *the Nature of Request* is validated by the proxy servers, and then proxy server sends the request onto the Internet. Proxy server also validates the pages sent by the external Internet. The pages pass onto the internal network web server and then to the client desktop, in case they are acceptable.

Companies can limit access to certain types of sites such as pornographic, auction etc. by prohibiting users from communicating directly with the Internet. Also, by storing frequently requested web pages locally, reducing upload times, and hiding the internal network's address, proxy servers improve web performance.

Protecting Servers and Clients

There are two tools which can help further protect servers and clients from certain types of attacks. The first one is the *Operating System Controls,* typically having a built-in username and password requirement by which a level of authentication is provided. An *Access Control Function* automating user access or denying access by clients to various areas of network is a function which is found in some operating systems control. For example, to create a network path to which only authorized personnel can obtain access to payroll information; operating system security can be used.

Anti-virus software is the easiest and least expensive way to prevent threats to system integrity. For example, companies like McAfee and Symantic, to identify and eradicate the most common types of viruses as they enter a computer, provide inexpensive tools. These tools also destroy those viruses already lurking on a hard drive. ANTI-VIRUSES should be updated regularly since new viruses are being developed daily.

Intrusion Detection System, being more complex and expensive, is a similar type of software. Such programmes look for recognized hacker tools and signature actions. In order to work properly, these systems, which are designed to trigger an alarm when such an action is noted, must be monitored by staff members or intrusion-detection services. Hundreds of alarms will be triggered by sensors, set up on a computer network. Only a few small percentages are a potential security threat. By monitoring and analyzing regularly, we can weed out the insignificant alarms from the potentially harmful ones.

Conclusion

When it comes to the bottom line results coming to the winners and losers, there will continue to be those who operate so powerfully blocking all the sophisticated and random attacks, and those who lose from their lack of planning and implementation of defenses. Competing to gain more wealth electronically is and will be expanding at a frantic pace in transactions over wires and through the air and those applications storing and processing digital codification of information. Therefore, practicing the best techniques to reach to a point where the threats are controlled is a must for e-commerce companies and practitioners.

E-commerce is a tool for businesses to make great success

possible. This chapter aimed to expose the warning signs for these e-commerce entities from being a few nodes away from the professional and amateur intruders. There are both legitimate opportunists as well as those who are in the criminal element. The latter ones hope to seek small fortune or destroy someone else's dream. The scary part is that an e-commerce star can lose all it gained throughout its success path at the speed of light. The hope is that a greater awareness of this problem will further the security of this problem will further the security culture necessary in innovative ideas being brought to the market.

REFERENCES

"E-Commerce Growth Predicted for North America" *CyberAtlas,* August 8, 2000, URL: "http://cyberatlas. int ernet.com/ markets/ ret ailing/articl e/0,6061_408451, 00.html"

Gary P. Schneider. *Electronic Commerce.* Thompson Asia Pvt. Ltd. Singapore, 2004.

Royce, Walker. *Software Project Management.* Pearson Education Asia, Pearson Education, Inc.: Copyright © 1998.

Goyal, P.K., *Adaptation and Implementation of e-commerce.* Delhi: Vista International Publishing House, 2005.

McManus and Wood-Harper. *Information Systems Project Management, Methods, Tools, and Techniques.* Delhi: Pearson Education, 2003.

Pankaj, S., *"E-commerce"*, APA Publishing Corporation, New Delhi, 2005.

Strause, El-Ansari, and Frost, *E-marketing.* Pearson Education: Pearson Education Inc. Copyright © 2003.

Lauder and Traver, *E-commerce, Business, Technology, Society.* Pearson Education, Lauder and Traver, Published by Dorling Kinersly (India) Pvt. Ltd. Copyright © 2002.

Rayprot and Jaworski, *Introduction to E-commerce.* McGraw Hill, Market Space LLC: Copyright © 2004, 2002.

James A. O'brien. *Introduction to Information Systems, Essential for the E-business Enterprise.* McGraw Hill/Irwin, the McGraw Hill Inc. Copyright © 2003.

SECTION-II

HUMAN RIGHTS IN DEMOCRACY

10 Human Rights and Social Justice under Decentralization

M.R. Biju

The concept of human rights has assumed great significance globally during the recent past and it has become a matter of serious concern all over the globe in the present day-to-day life. In all the societies irrespective of social, political, economic ethnic, ideological disparities and differences, it has been observed that people treat each other depending upon their motivations may be of love, gratitude, hatred, greed etc. Human beings display certain needs, which must be satisfied if they have to survive, grow and develop their pretensions as well as for the development of the society. These basic needs have been incorporated in almost all the national constitutions, which contain catalogues of human rights and basic fundamental freedoms.

Human rights are no doubt the inherent rights of a man, without which one cannot live with dignity. During the ancient and medieval period the concept of human rights was unknown. The ruler of a country was considered to be the fountain of all honours and all powers. The rulers just safeguarded the country from foreign invasions and the subjects in turn obeyed the dictation of the ruler. Rights do exist in a state of anarchy. It is essential to enquire into the relation between the concept of law of nature and natural rights of man. The concept of human rights has been evolved from the concept of natural rights. These natural rights are derived from natural law, which helped for the development of human rights.

According to Aristotle man is a social animal. He cannot live alone. The gregarious instinct in man compels him to live in the company of others. He has got rights only in the society of which he is a member. Man seeks social approval and wants to abide by the rules and regulations of society. Thus the rights of man become meaningful only when the rights are properly enforced. Our rights as human beings remind us of the rights of other human beings. To protect our rights we are under an obligation not to encroach upon the rights of others.

Though the concept of human rights is very old it assumed great importance only after the Second World War. The aftermath of the Second World War witnessed tremendous concern for humanity. As a result great progress was made in the field of human rights. The Universal Declaration of Human Rights, which was adopted by the UN General Assembly on 10th December 1948, has been proclaimed "as a common standard of achievement for all peoples and all nations". It incorporates not only the traditional Civil Liberties but also Social, Economic and Cultural Rights. Together with it, the two international human instruments, namely, the International Covenant on Civil and Political Rights, 1966, and The International Covenant on Economic, Social and Cultural Rights, 1966 have given wide connotation to the concept of human rights.

Originally the rights of man as a legal or moral concept appeared in the form of natural rights, "moral rights which every human beings, everywhere, at all times, ought to have simply because of the fact that, in contradiction with other beings, he is rational and moral". The theories of natural rights advocated that the natural rights were derived from the nature of man. These are inherent in man and form part of his intrinsic nature. It was argued that since man is endowed with reason, he is also endowed with certain rights without which he ceased to be a human being. For John Locke, these rights consist of the "right to life, liberty and property".

The natural right theory was closely associated with the natural law theories. The latter played a vital role in universalizing the concept of natural rights. The natural law theory was developed systematically by the Stoic philosophers. The central notion of the Stoic Philosophy was that the principles of natural law were universal in nature. Their application was not limited to any class of persons of a certain state. It applied to everybody; everywhere in the world it was the embodiment of the higher principle of justice, which could be discovered by human reason. Stoic thinkers preached the idea of universal brotherhood of mankind and laid stress upon the equality and freedom of all.

The conception of natural law was used by the Romans in the formulation of legal rules for the administration of justice. They developed a body or rules on the basis of custom and reason. They modernized the old law and incorporated high ethical standards in legal procedure.

Scholastic thinkers of the medieval period like Abelard and Thomas Aquinas laid great stress on the concept of natural law as divine law. An obstruction to the development of the concept of natural rights was the teachings of Machiavelli in the sixteenth century. To him human nature was bad and selfish. This necessitated the establishment of the state to crush the anti-social elements. The concept of natural rights was revitalized by the rise of Reformation, which challenged the authority of the Church. It provoked wide-spread demand for the natural rights of freedom of conscience and religious belief. The social contract doctrine also played a key-role in making the natural rights re-emerge.

In the seventeenth century the protagonists of the social contract theory, particularly Rousseau, tried to explain the state as an artificial creation of individuals surrendered some of their rights to the state. The state is the result of a social contract by which the individuals surrendered some of their rights to the state. The state in return granted some rights. Rousseau began with the state of nature in which man was free and independent in all respects. From this state of nature there emerged a political society by the separate acts of individuals. They agreed to set up a government, which would be responsible to promote their common interests.

The American War of Independence, the French Revolution, the two World Wars, all contributed to the development and universalisation of the concept of human rights.

Classification of Human Rights

Louis. B. Sohn has classified human rights into the following three categories :

(a) *The Human Rights of First Generation:* The International Covenant on Civil and Political Rights. These are not new rights. These are the rights that had developed in the course of a long period of time, since the time of the Greek city-states. It concretized in the form of Magna Carta, the American Declaration of Independence and the French Declaration of the Rights of Man and of the Citizen.

(b) *The Human Rights of Second Generation:* The International Covenant on Economic, Social and Cultural Rights. These rights are considered to have originated in the Russian Revolution of 1917 and the Paris Peace Conference of 1919. The significance of Paris Conference was the establishment of the International Labour Organization. It emphasized the concept of social justice and proclaimed that "peace can be established by only if it is based upon social justice". The credit goes to the efforts of the American President Roosevelt. He expressed his hope for an instrument dealing with economic and social rights. In his message to the congress on

January 6, 1941, Roosevelt referred to the four essential freedoms – freedom of speech and expression, freedom of every person to worship God in his own way, freedom from want and freedom from fear.

(c) *The Human Rights of Third Generation:* Collective Rights Individuals are also members of such units of groups or communities as family, religious community, social club, trade union, professional association, social group, nation and state. It includes the right to the self-determination, the right to development and the right to peace.

All human rights are interdependent. Human rights and fundamental freedoms are indivisible. The full realization of civil and political rights without the enjoyment of economic, social and cultural rights is impossible.

The concept of human rights is not purely western. The *Vedas, Upanishads, Bhagavad Gita,* the *Manusmriti, Kautilya's Arthasastra* all reveal that Indians had a high moral and ethical code. The rulers were always aware of the rights of the ruled. The Indus Valley Civilization throws light on the fact that there were *Darbar Halls* where discussions were held. The reign of Ashoka, the Great, reveals that even at that time, the Indian rulers had high sense of justice. Equality of religions was practiced by Akbar the Great Mughal Emperor. There was equality, freedom and peace in those days.

Meaning

Various definitions of human rights have been offered by different scholars. According to Bosanquet, "A right as a claim recognized by society and enforced by the state". Earnest Barker says, "Any particular right which we have, is a capacity of enjoying some particular status or employing some particular power of action, which has been secured and guaranteed to me by law". A perusal of the above definitions of rights shows that there are certain inherent characteristics of rights. The rights are guaranteed by the State. The demand of an individual becomes a right only after it is accepted by other members of the society and recognized by the State. It may be further observed that the rights are available not to a few persons only, but to all. The rights conferred on some and denied to the others are privileges and not rights. Moreover, the rights are conditions of good life and without them the human personality cannot develop. Again, the rights are intimately related to duties. They are not static and have a tendency to grow according to the circumstances. This explains why some of the rights, which could never be imagined about a century back, are recognized as absolutely essential at present *viz.* right to social security. Rights are also not absolute and are subject to reasonable restrictions in the larger interest of the society. A State does not create rights; it merely recognizes them. A state is known by the rights it enjoys.

Human Rights in Developing Countries

Observance of human rights poses problems everywhere, and no country's record, be it highly industrialized or economically underdeveloped, is faultless. In most of the countries which have acceded to independence only recently the problems are aggravated. Many of these countries have implacable enemies: poverty, ignorance, disease, and inertia. Western commentators have tended to underestimate the importance of illiteracy and ignorance, particularly in unsophisticated rural societies (De Smith 1964, p. 237). At the Kabul Conference it was agreed that there could be no meaningful exercise of many human rights in a country where economic resources were scarce and the bulk of the population lives on the margins of subsistence. It was argued that in such matters as the development of the whole economy and the improvement of health, education and housing, the state needed the necessary powers to implement its plans meanwhile, the rights of individuals or groups might be temporarily curtailed. Some speakers wondered, however, whether the governments of some developing countries did not show an excessive concern for the internal and external security of the state and apply unnecessary restrictions on human rights.

Developing countries experience difficulties not only in regard to economic and social rights, the enjoyment of which clearly presupposes a certain economic standard, but also in regard to the "classical" civil and political rights. A basic prerequisite of the right to a fair trial is the existence of an adequate number of well-trained lawyers, and "crash programmes" or their training were recommended at the Kabul Conference. The scarcity of competent and efficient public officials is also an obstacle to progress in the human rights field. Another specific problem of the underdeveloped world arises in the very sensitive area of "labour mobilization". In some countries, it was alleged at the conference, it is not yet possible to rely exclusively upon systems of voluntary labour to satisfy the basic needs of the nation. Recourse has sometimes to be had to certain forms of labour mobilization involving the compulsory removal of people to arear other than those of their residences. It was claimed, however, that such national labour service should be distinguished from the practices of forced labour which were forbidden by international conventions.

Neither the human rights provisions of the United Nations Charter and the Universal Declaration of Human Rights nor the other treaties and declaration mentioned above have brought about the millennium. It is, therefore, not the purpose of this article to convey the idea that the rights set forth in these instruments are, in act, respected and observed throughout the world. In 1952, 1957, and again, in 1962 the General Assembly of the United Nations reiterated that notwithstanding the obligations arising from the charter and notwithstanding the Universal Declaration of Human Rights, violations of human rights continue to occur in various parts of the world, and that notwithstanding some progress the situation in many parts of the world was unsatisfactory.

Human Rights under the Indian Constitution

India became independent in 1947 and gave to ourselves a Constitution which guaranteed to all its citizens liberty, equality and justice – social and political irrespective of caste, colour, creed or sex. The chapter of Fundamental Rights unambiguously recognized the basic rights of all individuals. It suggested a mechanism for realizing the cherished goals of the nation and outlined a clear direction for removing all kinds of inequities from the lives of its people in the chapter on the directive principles of State Policy. Many significant directions were given, one of the most important being that the State will endeavour to give free and compulsory education to every child in the age of 6 to 14.

After the promulgation of the Constitution many amendments were made, many laws were enacted to realize the aims and purposes enshrined in the Constitution.

Today, if we review the position of human rights available to the people of India in the right of the direction envisaged by the Constitution in 1950, we find the picture as a mix of many successes with occasional failure due to strange condition available in our country.

India has played the most significant role in the promotion of the cause of Human Rights. With the attainment of Independence, a declaration of rights, the most elaborate in the world, was incorporated in the new Constitution. India has made the most sincere efforts for the protection and promotion of human rights the world over and is the greatest champion of the human rights in the Third World. India has not only incorporated an elaborate Bill of

Rights in her Constitution but efforts have been made to translate these into reality. Thus we find that India has incorporated the most elaborate Declaration of Human Rights, 1948 in its Constitution.

The Constitution of India further provides enough inputs for working an effective machinery for the enforcement of fundamental rights. If a fundamental right is interfered with by an Act of the executive, any person entitled to the right can move the Apex Court to get the Act or Law declared unconstitutional.

Initially the attitude of judiciary in India towards the Directive Principles was not favourable and it had nullified many important legislations embodying Socio-Economic Reforms. However, with the passage of time there has been a shift in the attitude of the Indian judiciary towards Socio-Economic rights contained in Part IV of the Constitution of India.

Directive Principles of State Policy and Human Rights

Directive Principles of the State Policy covered under Part IV of the Constitution of India could be safely said to be fundamental in respect of regulation and governance of the country. Basically these Directive Principles could be intended to promote social welfare in consonance with basic object of the human rights, which acclaim global recognition, and needs to be enforced at national level.

Directive Principles of the State Policy play a significant role by imposing obligation upon the State to implement them so as to protect the interest of common masses including the working class. The Directive Principles of State Policy are mainly intended to promote welfare of the people and strive for securing social and economic justice to the workers. In furtherance of these objectives various directives for providing living wages to the workers ensuring just human conditions of work, motivating the workers to participate in the management of a company, providing equal opportunity to all workers irrespective of their sex in terms of employment and promotion opportunities, prohibiting employment of children in hazardous occupation and regulating their working conditions in non-hazardous occupational employment, etc. have been explicitly included in Part IV, from Article 36 to Article 51 of the Constitution of India. For accomplishing these objectives relevant legislations have been enacted and enforced which mainly include the Factories Act, 1948; The Minimum Wages Act, 1948; Employees State Insurance Act, 1948. The Mines Act, 1952; Employees Provident Funds and Miscellaneous Provisions Act, 1952; Payment of Bonus Act, 1965; The Payment of Gratuity Act, 1972; etc. and undoubtedly these legislative measures have come in rescue of the workers, particularly, the industrial workers and those engaged in organized sector of employment. It would not be out of place to bring forth at this juncture significant observations of Dr. Nagendra Singh that the Universal Adult Franchise and democratic form of Government envisaged by the Constitution provides guarantee against violation of human rights. Ultimately democracy, public opinion and awareness of one's own rights would be the best guarantee for protection of human values and basic freedoms. There could not be an iota of doubt that these basic human rights which have been duly recognized in the form of constitutional guarantees have been duly taken care of particularly, in a democratic set-up of society and have provided to be of much relevance for protecting the interest of a common man and more specifically that of the worker. With regard to the working class engaged in the organized sector of employment, these constitutional mandates have certainly played a significant role so as to ensure them social and economic stability. But at the same time the outcome is very much disappointing so far as the workers engaged in unorganized sectors are concerned, who are subjected to exploitation and victimization by their employers mainly due to absence of strong trade unions over there as well as on account of ineffective implementation process due to corruption and political interference. Due to these reasons unorganized workers are presently compelled to lead a miserable life in contravention of basic human rights.

Role of the Judiciary for Protecting Human Rights

It would not at all be unjustified to state that the judiciary has played a vital role for the protection of human rights and unlimited number of cases decided by the Supreme Court during the last two decades for achieving this goal would establish in undisputed terms such a tall claim. In this context it was quite appropriately observed by the Justice Chandrachud long back in historic case of Keshavananda Bharti *Vs.* State of Kerala under :

> "...it is really the poor, starved and mindless millions who need the Court's protection for securing to themselves the enjoyment of human rights. In the absence of explicit mandate the Court should abstain from striking down a Constitutional amendment which makes an endeavour to wipe out every tear from every eye".

It is well known fact that the judiciary has been in a position to achieve success in terms of protection of human rights, more particularly, through Social Action Litigation also popularly known as Public Interest Litigation by providing relief to poor, downtrodden, exploited and victimized categories of people including bonded labour, women and the children.

Protection of Human Rights and the Bonded Labour

Abolition of bonded labour would undoubtedly be said to be the urgent need of time otherwise all the achievements made so far would prove to be meaningless in terms of protection of human rights. Under Article 32 (1) of the Constitution of India various forms of forced labour has been prohibited and its contravention has been declared to be an offence punishable under the law. The power to enact legislation has been conferred on the Parliament and under Article 35 of the Constitution of India this power has been explicitly taken away from the State Legislature. The Supreme Court in case of People's Union for Democratic Rights *Vs.* Union of India while considering the scope of Article 23 in the context of bonded labour observed that not only *begar* rather all forms of forced labour would be prohibited under this Article as it declares illegal any form of forced labour being violative of human dignity and contrary to basic human values. Therefore, every form of forced labour has been prohibited under Article 23 as the practice of forced labour has been condemned in almost every international instrument dealing with human rights. If labour supplied was not willingly but as a result of force or compulsion, it would be a forced labour even if remuneration might be paid to a person but the labour supplied by such person would be hit by the mandate of Article 23. Even if a person might have come with another to perform service and there could be even consideration in the hope of liquidation of debt but he could not be forced by compulsion to continue to perform such service otherwise it would be considered to be forced labour within the meaning of Article 23 (1) of the Constitution of India due to the reason that no one could be compelled to provide labour or render service against his will. Supreme Court in case of Bandhua Mukti Morcha *Vs.* Union of India observed that under 'Bonded Labour System' the labour was required to work on some economic consideration and the process relating to discovery of bonded labour and their rehabilitation posed a serious problem, since the social and economic conditions in which it might be accomplished would be confronted with financial constraints involved therein. But this problem would have to be solved if we want to emancipate those who might be living in bondage in order to make them equal participants in the fruits of freedom and liberty. This problem undoubtedly needed urgent attention of Government of India and the concerted State Government and when the Directive Principles of State Policy obligated the Central and the State governments to adopt appropriate measures for the purpose of ensuring social justice to the have nots and the oppressed class of people because it would not be justified on the part of the concerned governments to overlook the inhuman exploitation to which the bonded labour would be exposed in gross violation on human rights. Undoubtedly, judiciary has played a vital role for the abolition of the Bonded Labour by providing a liberal meaning to the term 'Bonded Labour' and in Bandhua Mukti Morcha case it as observed by the Supreme Court would raise a presumption that he was required to do so in consideration of an advance or other economic consideration received by him and accordingly he would be declared to be a bonded labourer unless this presumption might be rebutted by the employer as well as the appropriate Government. The Supreme Court reiterated its stand by providing more extended scope of the term 'Bonded Labour' in case of Neeraja Chaudhary *Vs.* State of Madhya Pradesh by observing that whenever it was found that any workman was forced to provide labour for remuneration or nominal remuneration, the presumption might be drawn that he was bonded labour unless the employer was in position to prove otherwise by rebutting such presumption.

Violation of human rights is a global phenomenon. The difference is only of degree. Where the people, like India, in majority, are illiterate, ignorant, poor and exploited ones, the violation of human rights are bound to be more but where the people are educated, advance they are likely to be less prone to inhuman treatment and exploitations, India being a vast country, with greater part of masses being poor, ignorant and illiterate, they are bound to suffer more atrocities and inhuman treatment at the hands of the richer ones or the governmental agencies.

India adopted the International covenants on human rights but did not incorporate the human rights embodied in such covenants in its municipal laws. The judiciary particularly the apex Court of India has played a vital role in enforcing the human rights spelled out in the International Covenants, which were adopted by India. The Supreme Court of India, adopting the creative role has done a wonderful job by incorporating virtually all the human rights in the express provisions of our Constitution. The judicial activism occurred the historic case of Maneka Gandhi. It is, in fact needed, as the judiciary is only the hope under the present political chaos. Merely delivering the lectures is not enough. The practical approach has to be adopted to make the human rights really meaningful to those who need them most.

The role of the NHRC is appreciable. It is doing a wonderful job by entertaining complaints regarding violation of human rights in different parts of India. Since, India is a vast country, single Commission would not be enough. As submitted above, the Commissions, under the control of NHRC be established even at the district level to monitor the human rights violation from a close range. The NHRC though has recommendatory character, but is a step in right direction.

The proper implementation of the human rights also needs the full co-operation of the government and governmental agencies. The government is required to be more responsive to the public opinion regarding inhuman or repressive laws in force in India. Such laws should be repealed or confined to States, which need them most.

To make the human rights really meaningful to the society and to check the human rights violations, the social organizations have a vital role to play. The judiciary has made their task easy by evolving the concept of Social Action Litigation. It is submitted that the social law about human rights and to help them when their human rights are violated by individual or the state. In fact, to make the human rights more meaningful a realistic approach is needed to be adopted by all those who are really interested to serve the humanity. Mere talks, discussions, making laws will not be enough.

The horizons of human rights are expanding. It is gratifying to note that both the government and non-governmental organizations are taking the necessary lead in protecting human rights. It is recognized on all hands that access to justice is one of the most basic human rights and without it, the realization of many other human rights may become difficult. Gradually a revolution is taking place in the legal and judicial process as a result of legal aid and social action litigation. For this credit goes to former Chief Justice P.N. Bhagawati of Supreme Court of India. This type of social action litigation initiated by means of writ petitions or even letters addressed by social activists, lawyers, journalists, law academics and social action groups and using their constitutional power of intervention with a view to ameliorating the miseries of the people, arising from repression, government lawlessness and administrative deviance.

In our society around 50 per cent people are living below poverty line and around 70 per cent of the people are illiterate, and large masses of people are suffering untold hardship and misery on account of exploitation. These people cannot live as ordinary human beings with basic human dignity. The activists are generally talking of protection of all persons from being subjected to torture and other cruel, inhuman or degrading treatment or punishment. But the vast majority of men, women, and children are today living a sub-human existence in conditions of abject poverty. The only solution for making fundamental rights meaningful to them would be to remake the material conditions and restructure the social and economic order so that they may be able to realize the economic, social and cultural rights.

It is also now realized that the right to development is a

basic human right without the realization of which it is not possible enjoy any other human rights. People are also demanding safe environment as fundamental human right. It is a healthy sign that there is concern about saving the world environmental degradation. The World Watch Institute (WWI), a human rights policy research organization of the USA, has demanded safe environment as a matter of human right. This also called for sustainable development.

As women's rights are aimed too at the elimination of one of the most widespread forms of discrimination, sex discrimination they are perfectly in tune with human rights ideology. Human rights perspective of women's rights tries to enhance the scope of women's issues in the best interests of both women and society. The child's rights are an interval part of the human rights which has its umbrella stretched in the Universal Declaration of Human Rights adopted in 1948. Public conscience is taking time to wake up gradually to the realization that it must take steps to restore to every child, the birth rights to develop in freedom and creativity. A large number of provisions under the Constitution provide protection to the religious and linguistic minorities, scheduled tribes, scheduled castes and other backward castes. But introduction of adult franchise and competitive politics have not been fully utilized. The concrete solution lies with the strengthening of human rights movement at the grass roots level.

PRIs and Human Rights

Panchayati Raj Institutions, as part and parcel of direct democracy, have inestimable potential to promote and uphold human rights in their areas of jurisdiction. Through decentralization of power by inculcating democratic culture at the local level and by changing the existing unequal social, political and economic order into a more equitable and generally acceptable social order. The historic 73rd Constitution Amendment Act, 1992 has given the power of decision-making to the PRIs both in the preparation and execution of plans for social, political and economic advancement, and thereby ensuring the very novel concept of Social Justice. Article 243 G of the Indian Constitution says that, the legislatures of a State may, by law, endow Panchayats with such power and authority as may be necessary to enable them to function as institutions of self-government and such law may contain provisions for the devolution of powers and responsibilities upon Panchayats at the appropriate level, including preparation of plans for economic development and social justice as may be entrusted to them, including those listed in the 11th Schedule. This Schedule contains the following 29 subjects.

1. Agriculture, including agricultural extension.
2. Land improvement, implementation of land reforms, land consolidation and soil conservation.
3. Minor irrigation, water management and watershed development.
4. Animal husbandry, dairying and poultry.
5. Fisheries.
6. Social forestry and farm forestry.
7. Minor forest produce.
8. Small-scale industries, including food processing industries.
9. Khadi, village and cottage industries.
10. Rural housing.
11. Drinking water.
12. Fuel and fodder
13. Roads, culverts, bridges, ferries, waterways and other means of communication.
14. Rural electrification, including distribution of electricity.
15. Non-conventional energy sources.
16. Poverty alleviation programme.
17. Education, including primary and secondary schools.

18. Technical training and vocational education.
19. Adult and non-formal education.
20. Libraries.
21. Cultural activities.
22. Markets and fairs.
23. Health and sanitation, including hospitals, primary health centres and dispensaries.
24. Family welfare.
25. Women and child development.
26. Social welfare, including welfare of the handicapped and mentally retarded.
27. Welfare of the weaker sections, and in particular, of the Scheduled Castes and Scheduled Tribes.
28. Public distribution system.
29. Maintenance of community assets.

In conformity with this Amendment, States have enacted their separate Panchayat Acts and devolved certain powers to these institutions, for execution of various plans and programmes both for ensuring rural development and for implementing the concept of social justice.

Besides constituting Gram Panchayats at village level, Panchayat Samitis at Block level and Zila Panchayats at district level, all the State Panchayat Acts have also made provisions for forming of Gram Sabha (Village Assembly) at the lowest tier of the Panchayati Raj System as it gives opportunity to each and every adult of the Gram Panchayat to involve and participate in decentralized governance, planning and development. At least two meetings of the Gram Sabha will be held in a year. However, in some states like Madhya Pradesh, frequency of holding meetings of Gram Sabha is four times in a year. In some States like Bihar and Rajasthan provision for forming of Vigilance Committees by the Gram Sabhas have been made to oversee and monitor work of the Gram Panchayat. These provisions will again strengthen people's supervision, monitoring and evaluation on the functioning of the Gram Panchayats.

In addition to the above, in the Fifth Scheduled Areas of Andhra Pradesh, Bihar, Maharashtra, Madhya Pradesh, Orissa, Gujarat, Rajasthan and Himachal Pradesh, Gram Sabhas have further been empowered :

(i) to safeguard and preserve the traditions and customs of the people, their cultural identity, management of community resources and customary mode of dispute resolution;

(ii) to approve the plans, programmes and projects, selection of beneficiaries under poverty alleviation programmes and issue certificate of utilization of funds by the Panchayats;

(iii) prior consultation before making the acquisition of land for projects and before resettling or rehabilitating persons affected by such projects;

(iv) prior recommendation for granting license for mining lease for minor minerals;

(v) to enforce prohibition, ownership or minor produce, alienation of land, management of village market and money lending to SCs and STs, control over institutions and functionaries in all social sectors, preparation of local plan and mobilization of resources for such plan including tribal sub-plan. In this way, the entire scheme of decentralized governance in the Fifth Scheduled Areas has been put in the hands of Gram Sabha.

Human Rights Values through Elected Representatives

Article 243-K of the Indian Constitution says that "the superintendence, direction and control of the preparation of electoral rolls, for and the conduct of all elections to the Panchayats shall be vested in a State Election Commission to be appointed by the Governor. On the basis this constitutional provisions, elections to the PRIs were held in almost all States. As a result there are about 34 lakh elected representatives as members, chairpersons, at all levels of Panchayats in the country. Further, Article 243-D of the Constitution says that "in every Panchayat and the member of seats so reserved shall bear, as nearly as may be, the same proportion to the total number of seats to be filled by direct election in that Panchayat as the population of the Scheduled Castes in that Panchayat area or of the Scheduled Tribes in that Panchayat area bears to the total population of that area and such seats may be allotted by rotation to different constituencies in a Panchayat". Article 243-D (2) also states that "not less than one-third of the total number of seats reserved under Clause(1) shall be reserved for women belonging to Scheduled Castes or as the case may be the Scheduled Tribes". Article 243-D(3) further illustrates that "not less than one-third (including the number of seats reserved for women belonging to the scheduled castes and scheduled tribes) of the total number of seats to be filled by direct election in every Panchayat shall be reserved for women and such seats may be allotted by rotation to different constituencies in a Panchayat". Article 243-D (4) depicts that "the office of the chairpersons in the Panchayats at the village or any other level shall be reserved for scheduled castes, the scheduled tribes and women in such manner as the legislature of a State may, by law, provide". Provided that the number of offices of chairpersons reserved for the scheduled castes and scheduled tribes in the Panchayats at each level in any State shall bear, as nearly as may be, the same proportion to the total number of such officer in the Panchayats at each level as the population of the scheduled castes in the State bears to the total population of the State. Provided further that not less than one-third of the total number of office of chairpersons in the Panchayats at each level shall be reserved for women. Provided also that the number of offices reserved under this clause shall be allotted by rotation to different Panchayats at each level". Article 243-D(5) underlines that, "the reservation of seats under clauses (1) and (2) and the reservation of office of chairpersons (other than the reservation for women) under clause (4) shall cease to have effect on the expiration of the period specified in Article 334." Article 243-D (6) observes that, "nothing in this part shall prevent the legislature of a State from making any provision for reservation of seats in any Panchayat or office of chairpersons in the Panchayats at any level in favour of backward class of citizens".

As a result of reservation provided to SCs, STs and women under Article 243 D, about seven lakh members and chairpersons are from SC and ST categories. Of them, about two lakh are women belonging to these categories. Besides, of the total elected representatives at all levels, more than 11 lakh are women belonging to different castes and communities of rural society of India, which is perhaps the broadest representative base in the whole world.

Certainly, this will strengthen and promote human rights values and awareness in the rural areas and PRIs can be very well utilized as platform for the promotion of the ideals of human rights. For promoting and guaranteeing human rights in the countryside, transformation of unequal social order into more egalitarian social order is a *sine qua non*. This is no a simple task. It could happen only after a long struggle and sacrifice by people. Panchayats have the potential to achieve such a social order in villages. Experience of marginalized sections such as SCs, STs and women as members and chairpersons of Panchayats during the last three/four years reveal that they have been struggling and sacrificing a lot for weakening the established forces in the form of higher castes and landlords. Of course, the weaker sections, including women in most cases, have not been participating effectively as they ought to be. But, they are definitely learning the art of governance through these institutions. To conclude Dr. Mahi Pal has suggested the following measures for using PRIs as instruments for spreading human right values :

1. More functional, financial and administrative autonomy should be accorded to Panchayats, keeping in view the letter and spirit of Article 243G, which designated Panchayats as institutions of self-government. In other words, clear-cut demarcation of functions, adequate financial resources to perform devolved functions and sufficient personnel to handle the assigned responsibilities should be operationalised. Because the problems the elected representatives have been facing are mostly related to the fact that the district and sub-district bureaucracy is not in Panchayat's control. Why did elected representatives not get the desired cooperation from local bureaucracy? Why did they not get earmarked money for development of their village? The reason is that the bureaucracy considers itself superior to Panchayats. This makes a strong case of putting all district and sub-district government personnel under the control of the Panchayats for their smooth functioning.
2. Orientation about powers and functions of Panchayats and capacity-building in performing devolved functions among elected representatives is very important for creating confidence among them for shouldering the responsibilities of decentralized governance, planning and development. Example of Atima Bi, Sarpanch of the Kalva Gram Panchayat in Koomul district of Andhra Pradesh is a telling reference here, who after getting orientation about powers and functions of the Panchayat went from

strength to strength. Hence, imparting training to elected representatives about their functions and powers is a must for promoting human rights.

3. For the first time, SCs, STs and women got elected as member and chairperson of Panchayats. Most of them are inexperienced in governing the Panchayats. Hence, the support of non-governmental and voluntary organizations besides Central and State governments is important to them to prepare and map out economic and social justice plan for promoting human rights.
4. Central, State and district level associations of elected representatives have to be formed and promoted so that they can interact themselves, share their experience and unitedly assert for more power and authority for Panchayats.
5. The Constitution (Seventy-third Amendment) Act has given constitutional status to the Panchayats endowing them with the powers of preparation and execution of plans for economic development and social justice, including the subjects listed in the 11th Schedule of the Constitution. But, no legal framework has been made at local level to settle disputes while implementing schemes and programmes relating to 29 subjects listed in the 11th Schedule of the Constitution. Although, some States have provision for constituting *Nyaya* Panchayat, in most of the cases, they are dormant and defunct. The existing courts at district and sub-district level already have been burdened thus enlarging the number of pending cases. In this connection, Prof. Menon (1995) commented that: "Despite such an elaborate hierarchy of civil and criminal courts which number nearly (10,000 with country) the judicial system is unable to provide access to justice to common man. Over two crore cases are pending in

these courts for more than a decade". There are possibilities that the disputes at local level might be increased in future as reservation given to SCs, STs and women have created animosity among the established social forces which resulted in conflict and disputes on various issues relating to decentralized governance, planning and development. In view of the above, it becomes necessary to create an institution of justice at local level, having representation of weaker sections, including women for dispensing speedy and inexpensive justice to the masses. For this purpose, a constitutional amendment may be carried out for providing a viable and sustainable decentralized judicial system for administering justice, expeditiously and economically at village level itself.

The above discussion reveals that Panchayats have potential to promote human rights in the country. But, to accelerate this process, Panchayats have to be strengthened further by awarding functional, financial and administrative autonomy at different levels enabling elected representatives to have full freedom to play their role effectively. Besides developmental functions, policing should also be brought under the control of Panchayats. And, as developmental works have been assigned to Panchayats, the judicial system should also be decentralized at local level for settling the disputes arising in the implementation of the different schemes and programmes connected with 29 subjects listed in the 11th Schedule of the Constitution at grass roots level enabling weaker sections of rural society to get speedy and inexpensive justice at their doorsteps. It has been noticed that gradual awakening about their rights, power, authority and responsibility has been taking place among elected representatives of the Panchayats at local levels. This has been creating an urge among them for local governance. This development, over a period of time, shall create such an environment at decentralized level where human rights would be guaranteed and respected.

Panchayati Raj and Social Justice

The champions of democratic decentralization preach for promoting development and change from grass root level. India has followed a policy of active support of decentralized rural development as a strategy designed to improve the economic and social life of the rural poor. It is presumed that the existing politico-administrative apparatus in the country would strengthen the public policy so as to help in fulfilling the aspiration of the common man. Since the ultimate objective of decentralization is 'development'. It is considered necessary to find out the ways and means to ensure direct participation of weaker sections in planning and implementation of decentralized programme. In the planned process of development, every effort was made and innovative practices were directed from time to time for the achievement of this goal. In the initial stage, the aim of the planned process of development was sought to be achieved for a change and transforming the socio-economic life of Indian villages. At the same time, decentralization of rural development is assumed as a necessary precondition of social transformation and development with the resolve to reconstruct the country economically and socially strong.

With the enactment of the New Act of Panchayati Raj (1992) the dynamic interplay of dispersal of power and authority entrusted to local leaders (people's representatives) of Panchayati Raj Organization has affected the internal and external changes in the social system. The structural and contextual factors call for the process of institutionalized actions to a desired goal aiming at development and change. This could be achieved through democratic decentralization process in a welfare society. But, over a period of time, decentralized administration as a vehicle of social transformation has witnessed many twists and turns due to ever-changing politico-administrative culture, which has virtually eclipsed direction of development. The demand of social democracy for enlightened humanity in searching out democracy in action, has accentuated the local leaders and forced the power structure to rebuild, 'From Below" a progressive broad-based social structure for accelerating the welfarism in the country.

Concept of Social Justice

The concept of social justice has been conceptualized by Plato in his *'Republic'*, Aristotle in his *'Nicomachean'* characterized social justice as the sum of virtues and set of not only positive laws but a system of rights. In the sociological analysis, justice is treated as a social phenomenon. David Hume's *Treatise of Human Nature* (1739) and *Enquiry Concerning the Principles of Morals* explore the concept of justice intensively. Since long, Sociologists have ever remained engaged in identifying and describing the problem of social justice as 'identical of social equilibrium' and a precondition of social progress (Spencer), social solidarity (Durkheim) sociologists have outlined in detail the 'Sociology of Law' and have shown their interest in issues of procedural justice, while the sociologists of social stratification have concerned themselves with studying distributive justice. Social inequality has always been one of the central problems in the field of sociology. As an instrument of value judgment, social welfare administration addresses itself for universalization of a kind of means end relationship in the moral fabric of government and the governed. It proceeds from social pathology to social legislation and social policy. "In the Theory of Distributive Justice", it is presumed that it would strengthen in public policy so as to help in fulfilling the aspirations of common men.

Justice, equality and freedom are the fundamental rights

of individual. Social justice is a function of social process in a given society at a given time. Sociological analysis of justice to each according to his right, to each according to his desert and to each according to his need." (Miller) shows that these three criteria of social justice are conceptually distinct and logically presents conflicting prescriptions for action. Thus, the existing political theories of Spencer, Hume, Mill, Rawls find no place rationally about its interpretation in the democratic society. Moreover,, Democratic Welfare State due to inherited nature of conflict between right of freedom and 'right of equality', there are likely the chances of gross inequality of income distribution or even equal opportunities as accorded in the Constitution of India. The principle of equality - equality of treatment among unequal alone cannot be treated as criteria of social justice. As such, equalitarian justice entails the notion of just distribution and not equal distribution of benefits. To this extent Vlastos asserts, "equalitarian justice has a direct stake in equalizing the distribution of those goods whose enjoyment constitutes well-being". Therefore, social justice is to be viewed in relation to a particular society.

Social Justice in the Constitution of India

Fundamental Rights and the Directive Principles of State Policy have been incorporated in the Constitution of India. The founding fathers provided general content to the concept of social justice in Article 38 which reads as under:

1. The State shall strive to promote the welfare of the people by securing and protecting, as effectively as it may, a social order in which justice — social, economic, and political, shall inform all the institutions of the national life.
2. The State shall, in particular, strive to minimize the inequalities in income and endeavour to eliminate inequalities in status, facilities and opportunities, not

only amongst individuals but also amongst groups of people residing in different areas or levels.

Areas or engaged in different vocations, (a) To ensure equality, Article 15 of the Constitution prohibits any discrimination on the grounds of religion, race, caste, sex, etc. Not only this, clause 3 of Article 15 also clarifies that this provision will not prevent the State from making any special provision for women. This special favour may be given because of the fact that the women are considered as one of the weaker sections in the Indian Society. Hence, till women reach the same footing as men, they have to be taken care of as a special group needing special attention. Hence, reservation of seats for women in election is protected by Article 15 (3).

Article 15 (4) was also added in 1951, which provides that nothing shall prevent the State from making any special provision for the advancement of any socially and educationally backward classes of citizens or for the Scheduled Castes and the Scheduled Tribes. Thus, the Article permits the State to make any special provision for the following :

(a) Women,
(b) Socially and educationally backward classes of citizens,
(c) Scheduled Castes,
(d) Scheduled Tribes.

Special provisions for women have been widely resorted to and the courts have upheld the validity of special measures in legislation or executive orders favouring women. In particular, provisions in the criminal law, in favour of women or in the procedural law discriminating in favour of women, have been upheld. There are relevant judgments as under :

(i) Girdhar *vs.* the State (Section 154 IPC),

(ii) Yusuf *vs.* the State of Bombay (Section 497 IPC) regarding adultery,
(iii) Choki *vs.* the State (Bail),
(iv) Shahbad *vs.* Abdulla (service of summons on men only in civil cases).

Similarly, provisions providing for reservation of seats for women in local bodies or in educational institutions or services are valid. Following decisions exist on this issue also :

(i) Dattatraya *vs.* the State of Bombay,
(ii) Sagar *vs.* the State.

Blanket provision in Article 15 (4), protecting any kind of beneficial discrimination for the benefit of other backward classes, may look unreasonable on the basis of general Article 14, which guarantees general right of equality to all citizens. Hence, reservation of any excessively high percentage of seats for each class would be void. Ordinarily, reservation in excess of 50 per cent of available seats may not be upheld. The under mentioned decisions have been reported on this issue also :

(i) The State of AP *vs.* Balram,
(ii) Rajindran *vs.* the Union of India,
(iii) Balaji *vs.* the State of Mysore,
(iv) Jayashree *vs.* the State of Kerala,
(v) Perria Karanppan *vs.* the State of Tamil Nadu,
(vi) Abdul Latif *vs.* the State of Bihar,
(vii) Anil *vs.* the Dean, Government Medical College, Nagpur.

Article 46 of the Directive Principles provides that the State shall promote with special care the educational and economic interests of "the weaker sections of the people" and in particular, "of the Scheduled Castes and Scheduled Tribes".

Part XVI of the Constitution also contains special provisions relating to certain classes. Article 330 provides for reservation of people and Article 332 in the legislative assemblies of the States.

Article 334 mentions that reservation of seats and special representation will cease after 50 years from the commencement of the Constitution.

Ensure Social Justice through the Constitution (73rd Amendment)

Panchayati Raj was launched in 1959 to ensure people's participation in the development process, associate rural people in grass root democracy and devolve powers to the people below at the village level. Even in 1959, the Panchayati Raj Acts contained a provision that :

1. A woman member shall be co-opted if no woman member is elected;
2. A Scheduled Caste member shall also be co-opted if no such member has been elected; and
3. Similarly, a Scheduled Tribe member shall be co-opted in Panchayat bodies where the population of such tribes is 5 per cent or more of the population of the area.

Though provisions existed in the Article 15 of the Constitution and women, SC/ST members were co-opted in the Panchayati Raj Institutions (PRIs) during the period 1959-1993 also, but the Girdharilal Vyas Committee, Rajasthan (1973), observed that "co-option in fact is nothing but a corrosion and infringement of the true democratic process and the representatives of the Scheduled Castes, Scheduled Tribes and women getting a place through co-option in the

Panchayats, Panchayat Samitis or Zila Parishads are nothing but a creation of the generosity of the members of these bodies and consequently their participation in the deliberations of such bodies is far from action or objective".

The Constitution (73rd Amendment) Act, 1993 provides in Article 243 (D) for reservation of seats of members as well as of chairpersons for Scheduled Castes and Scheduled Tribes as well as women in the Panchayats at the village, block and district levels. Article 243 (D) (1) mentions that seats shall be reserved for the Scheduled Castes and the Scheduled Tribes in every Panchayat and the number of seats so reserved shall bear, as nearly as may be, the same proportion to the total number of seats to be filled by direct election in that Panchayat as the population of the Scheduled Castes in that Panchayat area bears to the population of that area and such seat may be allotted by rotation to different constituencies in a Panchayat.

Article 243 (D) (2) also provides that not less than one-third of the total number of seats reserved under clause (1) shall be reserved for women belonging to the Scheduled Castes, or as the case may be, the Scheduled Tribes.

Article 243 (D) (4) further mentions that offices of the chairpersons in the Panchayats at the village or any other level shall be reserved for the Scheduled Castes, the Scheduled Tribes and as nearly as may be, in same proportion in the total number of such offices in the Panchayats at each level, as the population of the Scheduled Castes in the State or of the Scheduled Tribes in the State bears to the total population of the State. Provided further that not less than one-third of the total number of offices of chairpersons in the Panchayats at each level shall be reserved for women and provided also that the number of offices reserved under this clause shall be allotted by rotation to different Panchayats at each level.

Article 243 (D) (6) also authorizes the State governments

to make any provision for reservation of seats in any Panchayat or the offices of the chairpersons in the Panchayats at any level in favour of backward class of citizens.

The notion of social justice has emerged out of a process of evolution of societal norms, order, law and morality. The core element of social justice is the social equity for preservation of rights, privileges and established practices to sustain social peace and harmony. The basic of social justice is the equal well-being or individual helps to bring out a just society. Thus, social justice is related to the way the law in many ways: First it is related to the way the law is modified, second the nature of social justice effectuated by the law is applied by administrative agencies, which in turn, influence the public attitudes through government agencies. It is an irony that despite several jurisprudential explorations and universal theory of social justice has not evolved. At the academic level it is easy to argue that social justice must be prevailed. But the fact is that it is extremely difficult to operationalise the social justice in concrete term. Justice Krishna Iyer in his book "Social Justice in Crisis" considered social justice as "legally untouchable, factually inappropriate and intellectually vague". In fact, the basic ideology of social justice inherited in the notion of legitimacy, welfare and entitlement, is still hanging in the minds of men as how to remove the imbalances in political, social and economic life of individual. Therefore, in order to achieve the goal of social justice within a given social, political and administrative culture, the heterogeneous nature of society demands a fair play in distribution of material goods for the survival of individual. For the growth of social justice and maintenance of social order in the country, it is presumed to strengthen the social welfare policy in fulfilling the aspiration a common man. To follow up the genuine spirit of democratic decentralization, it is therefore, essential to create a strong and sound sub-structure of local government and entrust to local leaders the task of policy formulation and implementation of rural development programmes.

The existence of caste pyramid institution, " 'where there is a political equality but not social equality' (Ambedkar), has forced the constitution makers, political thinkers and policy makers 'to rebuild from below' and restructure the polity by the enactment of the Constitution Seventy Third Amendment (Act), 1992 which has come into force with effect from 20th April 1993 in the democratic society. In search of alternative paradigm of development and governance, rural local government a morbid system of Panchayati Raj has been revitalized with the power of devolution and power equation in favour of oppressed, weaker and backward classes of society. This paradigm shift from nucleus/core to periphery protoplasm of the system is due to preservation of human rights and retention of administrative culture in the country. In the newly created Panchayati Raj institutions, the dynamic interplay of power dispersal and authority to local leaders has affected both by the internal and external changes in the social system. The established pattern of social relationship in the democratic society based on the complexities of 'core' and periphery of the system has brought forth a change in he social outlook of super-ordinate (dominant castes) and sub-ordinate (weaker sections). In this context, it is imperative to spell out the basic ideology of social justice as enunciated in the Preamble of the Constitution of India, 'to' secure to all citizen-justice, social, economic and political equality of status and opportunities". To screen the Public Policy Agenda for Distributive Justice the problem of upliftment of weaker sections and backward classes, has been studied from sociological perspective.

To achieve the goal of perfect democracy, the ideology of social justice calls for to obey rule of law and evolve a democratic government at the grass roots. Rural potentials for growth and development can be sustained only in the preservation of social democracy and strengthening the local political institutions. Therefore, an institutionalized action to a desired goal could be achieved only through democratic decentralization. Democratic decentralization is conceived as a vehicle of social transformation of enlightened humanity to screen out democracy in action. Democratic decentralization is a process whereby some duties, responsibilities, authorities and power are devolved to the institutions of the people by higher authority to discharge and manage their own affairs. In fact, democratic decentralization may be regarded as an efficient method of formulation and execution of local plans consistent with the democratic trends towards local self-government.

REFERENCES

Biju, M.R., *Human Rights in a Developing Society*, Mittal, New Delhi; 2005.

Agarwal, R.K., *National Security Act*, The Law Book Company, Bombay, 1986.

B.R.P. Bhaskar (Ed), *Human Rights 2001*, Vigil India Movement, 2001.

Bhagawati, P.N., Human Rights and Democratization of Remedies, *Indian Bar Review*, Vol. 10, No. 4, 1983.

Constituent Assembly Debates, Official Report, Vol., 1949.

Cowen Denis, V., *Human Rights in Contemporary Africa*, Natural Law Forum, 9: 1-24, 1964.

De Smith Stanley, A., *The New Commonwealth and its Constitutions*, Stevans London, 1964.

Dholakia, R.P., 'Human Rights and Expressions of Global Conscience', *Banaras Law Journal*, Vol. 26, 1990.

Diwan, P. and Peeyushi, D., *Human Rights and the Law*, Deep & Deep, 1998.

Egon Schwelb, *International Encyclopaedia of the Social Sciences*, Vol. V. The MacMillan Co., New York, 1972.

Friedrich Carl, J., Rights, 'Liberties, Freedom— A Reappraisal', *American Political Science Review*. 57:841-854.

Ganji Manonchehr, *International Protection of Human Rights*, Droz, Geneva, 1964.

Gokulesh Sharma, *Human Rights and Social Justice*, Deep & Deep, 1998.

Gupta, R.K., *Implementation of Human Rights* in B.P. Singh (Ed). *Op. cit.*

Gursharan Varandani, *Human Rights: Constitutional Mandate and the Worker*, in B.P. Singh (Ed.) *op. cit.*

Jacob Punnose, *Human Rights Commission*, ASC, University of Kerala, 2002.

Jagannath Mohanty, *Human Rights Education*, Deep & Deep, New Delhi, 2000.

Jariwala, C.M. Preventive Detention in India: Indian Constitution Trends and Issues. *Journal of Indian Law Institute*, 1978.

Macpherson, C.B., *The Political Theory of Possessive Individualism*, Oxford, 1962.

Man of Mitta, 'Human Rights Commission', *India Today*, 15 January 1994.

Nagendra Singh, *Enforcement of Human Rights*, Eastern Law House, 1986.

Nicholas, J.H., *Democracy and the Churches*, Westminster Press, Philadelphia.

Pandey, J.N., *Constitutional Law of India*, Central Law Agency, Allahabad, 1988.

Paramasivam, S., *Human Rights – A Study*, Sriram, 2000.

Rajni Kothari, Party System, *Economic Weekly*, Bombay, 3 June 1961.

Raphael, D.D., *Poliical Theory and Rights of Man*, MacMillan London, 1967.

Rekha Choudhary, *Ideology and Politics of Ruling Party in India*, Deep & Deep, New Delhi, 1991.

Singh, B.P., *Human Rights in India*, Deep & Deep, New Delhi, 1999.

Singhvi, L.M., *Horizons of Freedom*, NPH, New Delhi, 1969.

Tarkunde, V.M., 'Abrogation of Civil Liberties and Democratic Rights', *Civil and Military Law Journal*, Vol. 24, No. 2, 1998.

The Code of Criminal Procedure, 1898 (Act of 1898).

Tripathi, T.D., 'Human Rights and TADA', *Kanpur Law Journal*, Issue 8, 1992.

Winlelband, W., *A History of Philosophy*, MacMillan, New York, 1956.

World Bank, *World Development Report*, 1980.

Abdul Aziz, *Poverty alleviation in India : Policies and Programmes*, New Delhi: Ashish Publishing House, 1994.

Adiseshiah, Malcolm S. *et. al.*, *Decentralized Planning and Panchayati*

Raj, proceedings of the D.T. Lakdawala Memorial Symposium, New Delhi: Institute of Social. Sciences, 1994,

Ambedkar, B.R., *Ambedkar and Social Justice*, New Delhi: Publications Division, Ministry of Information and Broadcasting, 1992, 2 Vols.

Bajpai, Ashok and Verma, M.S., *Panchayati Raj in India: A New Thurst*, Delhi, Sahitya Prakashan, 1995,

Bhatt, Anil, *Development and Social Justice Micro Action by Weaker Sections*, Delhi, Sage, 1989.

Bhattacharjee, Ajit (ed.), *Social Justice and the Constitution*, Shimla: IIAS, 1997.

Borgohain, Bani, *Human Rights: Social Justice and Political Challenge*, New Delhi, Kanishka, 1999.

Chaubey, P.K., *Poverty Measurement: Issues, Approaches and Indices*, New Delhi: New Age International, 1995.

Dahal, Madan K., *Structural Adjustment and Strategies for Poverty Alleviation: The Nepalese case*, New Delhi: Haranand, 1994.

Datta, Prabhat, *Major Issues in the Development Debate: Lessons in Empowerment from India*, New Delhi, Kanishka, 1998.

Social Justice, from Hume to Walzer, edited by David Boucher and Paul Kelly, London : Routledge, 1998.

Gandhi, P.K. *Social Action Through Law: Partnership for Social Justice*: Delhi: Concept Publishing Company, 1985.

Hanumantha Rao and Linnemann, *Economic Reform and Poverty Alleviation in India*, New Delhi, Sage, 1996.

Hobhouse, L.T. *The Elements of Social Justice*, London: Allen and Unwin, 1949.

Hoshiar Singh, *Administration of Rural Development in India*, New Delhi: Sterling, 1995.

India, Ministry of Social Justice and Empowerment, *Annual Report*, New Delhi, Library, 1998-99.

Jha, Himanshu Shekhar, *Culture of Poverty: A Sociological Study*, Varanasi: Ganga Kaveri Pub., 1994.

Jha, S.N. and Mathur, P.C. (Ed). *Decentralization and Local Policies*, New Delhi, Sage Publication, 1999.

Joshi, R.P. (Ed). *Constitutionalization of Panchayati Raj: A Reassessment*, Jaipur, Rawat Pub., 1998.

Kamta Prasad, *New Economic Policy: Eighth Plan and Prospects* for *Poverty Alleviation*, New Delhi, Deep & Deep, 1994.

Kaushik, Susheela, *Panchayati Raj in Action: Challenges to Women's Role*, New Delhi, 1995.

Khanna, B.S., *Panchayati Raj in India: Rural Local Self Government*, Delhi: Deep & Deep, 1994.

Krishna Iyer, V.R., *Ambedkar Centenary Social Justice and the Undone Vast*, Delhi, B.R. Pub., 1991.

Maheshwari, Shriram, *Rural Development in India: A Public Policy Approach*, 2nd , New Delhi: Sage, 1995.

Menon, Madhava N.R (Ed), *Social Justice and Social Process in India*, Indian Academy of Social Sciences, 1988.

Mier, Robert, *Social Justice and Local Development Policy*, Newbury Park: Sage, 1993.

Mishra. S.N., *Poverty Alleviation Programmes and Gram Panchayats*, New Delhi, IIPA, 1997.

Oommen, M.A.; Dutta, Abhijit, *Panchayats and their Finance*, New Delhi: Institute of Social Sciences, 1995.

Prakash, S.S., *Bonded Labour and Social Justice*, New Delhi, Deep & Deep, 1990.

Raj Sabastin and Mathias, Edward, *People's Power and Panchayati Raj: Theory and Practice*, New Delhi: Indian Social Institute, 1998.

Shanmugasundaram, Yasodha, (ed.) *A Study of Social Justice Movement: Life and Times of T.R. Kothandarama Mudaliar*, Madras: Emerald, 1991.

Thimmaiah, G. *Power Politics and Social Justice: Backward Castes in Karnataka*, New Delhi: Sage, 1993.

UNDP Poverty Report, New York: United Nations Development Programme, 1998.

United Nations, *Rural Poverty Alleviation and Sustainable Development in Asia and the Pacific*, New York: United Nations, ESCAP, 1996.

De Souza, Victor S., *Development Planning and Structural Inequalities: The Response of the Under Developed*, New Delhi, Sage Publication, 1990.

Verma, B.M., *Social Justice and Panchayati Raj*, Mittal, 2002.

11 Human Rights and Mass Media

Amita Agarwal

Concept of human rights is a result of human beings struggle to remain human beings. This struggle has always been present in all the societies against political, economic, social and cultural oppression as well as against injustices and inequalities. During the course of this struggle concept of certain basic rights gradually emerged. These basic rights are paramount, sacrosanct and eternal and every human being is entitled to enjoy these rights without any type of differentia-tion or discrimination e.g. caste, class, region, sex, place, birth, status etc. etc. These rights are so basic and fundamen-tal in nature that they are to be treated as inalienable and inviolable for preserving the dignity of human life. These rights cannot be snatched away by any other individual, organisation or State on any grounds whatsoever and even a human being himself or herself cannot renounce these rights even of ones own will, in any circumstances, as these are vital for the development of human personality.

(A) Development of Human Rights—The Global Framework

Though the concept of human rights is not new in both the Eastern and the Western cultures, a formal global framework of human rights was laid down for the first time by the United Nations General Assembly on December 10, 1948 in the form of Universal Declaration of Human Rights (UNDHR). Both, the United Nations charter and the declaration reaffirm faith in fundamental human rights in the dignity and worth of the human person and in the equal rights of men and women.

The Declaration (UNDHR) covers the entire canvass of human rights *i.e.,* civil, political, economic, social and cultural and thus provides, "a common standard of achievement for all peoples and all nations." The rights are termed universal as they are interdependent, inalienable and inviolable.

(B) Three Generations of Human Rights

Three generations of human rights have evolved based on three competing schools of thought.

1. First Generation Rights

This term is applicable to all those rights that comprise all civil and political rights *i.e.,* voting, expression, religion, movement, assembly, equality, fair trial and life. These rights are individual and immediate rights.

Here the term generation does not imply a chronological order or hierarchy of human rights. It is more of a political, ideological or conceptual categorization. The use of the concept of generations in discussing human rights is now increasingly, being avoided and discouraged.[1]

2. Second Generation Rights

This term is used to describe that class of human rights that comprises all economic, social and cultural rights.

These rights are said some to be more "collective type of rights". By their very nature they are thought to be "progressive or pragmatic rights", meaning that their implementation requires progressive measures or programmes by a State within the States economic resources *e.g.,* the right to health care, work, food, shelter and education.[2]

3. *Third Generation Rights*

These are historically newer rights, though the term generation does not necessarily connote any chronological difference or hierarchy of human rights. It is simply a political, legal, conceptual categorization and a way of classifying "these rights".

These rights are also known as "solidarity rights" or "rights of solidarity". These later terms should not be confused with the "right to solidarity" which itself is one of the third generation rights. These rights are complex, ill defined conceptually, collective and the subject of much dispute as to whether they are even rights. In theory they are rights that can only be realized through the concerted and good faith efforts of all the actions in the international scene; States, NGO's, individuals and other public and private bodies *i.e.* the international community as a whole.[3]

Most scholars consider these claimed rights to contribute *lex ferenda* at best and not yet *lex later* though some may argue in favour of such later status for the right to development.

Third generation rights are said to include the following separate rights—

(a) right to development,
(b) right to peace,
(c) right to a clean environment,
(d) right to humanitarian assistance,
(e) right to a common heritage,
(f) right to a communication, and
(g) right to solidarity.

(C) Human Rights Tiers

All human rights can be for the convenience of study, put in a hierarchial order *i.e.*

1. UN Charter,

2. UN Declaration (no state had voted against the declaration and there were only 08 absentations by Soviet Union and five of its allies, Saudi Arabia and South Africa.[4]
3. The two Covenants of 1966—
   (a) The Covenant on Civil and Political Rights, and
   (b) The Covenant on Economic, Social and Cultural Rights.

Both the covenants came into force in 1976 and by 1998 the first covenant was ratified by 140 states/countries and the second covenant was ratified by 138 states/countries. Here it is important to note that Communist China has also ratified the second covenant in 1999 after having reservations about it for a long time.

4. Treaties on Human Rights

At the lowest rung, in the hierarchy of human rights come various treaties on human rights e.g.,—

(a) The Convention on the Prevention and Punishment of the Crime of Genocide, 1948.
(b) The International Convention on the Elimination of All Forms of Racial Discrimination, 1965.
(c) The Convention on Elimination of All Forms of Discrimination Against Women, 1979.
(d) The Convention Against Torture and other Cruel, Inhuman or Degrading Treatment or Punishment, 1984, and
(e) The Convention on the Rights of the Child, 1989 (176 parties).[5]

United Nations through its various organs and agencies has been trying to spread awareness about human rights. The Economic and Social Council (ECOSOC), UNICEF, ILO and Commission on Human Rights (established in 1946) have been active to fulfil and achieve this objective. To spread human rights awareness December 10 is celebrated as "Human Rights Day" annually the world over. Years 1995 to 2004 have been declared as the decade for human rights education and 1998 was declared as the year of human rights.

(D) Right to Communicate, Freedom of Expression and Media

A basic and significant entitlement to human survival and development is right to communicate. Some governments, notably the United States and India have included communication right as a basic right for their citizens. The Universal Declaration of Human Rights under Article 19 states: Everyone has the right to freedom of opinion and expression. This right includes freedom to hold opinions without interference and to seek, receive and impart information and ideas through any media and regardless of frontiers. As a result the right to information and communication is receiving greater attention in the contemporary affairs.

The media can mobilize public opinion by spreading awareness of human rights policies and highlighting their violations. In many countries the media already is a major force for reporting such violations and demand accountability. A related tool for influencing norms is the Internet. Cyber networks have brought attention to rights, diss e-minate information on good practices and on rights violations. A coalition of African NGOs working for the right to food and food security uses the Internet to exchange experiences and lessons.

All those working in the mass media should contribute to the fulfilment of human rights, both individual and collective, in the spirit of the UNESCO Declaration on the Mass Media and the International Bill of Human Rights. The contribution of the media in this regard is not only to foster these principles, but also to expose all infringements, wherever they occur, and to support those whose rights have been neglected or violated. Extension of these communication freedoms to a broader individual and collective right to communicate is an evolving principle in the democratization process. Among the human rights to be emphasized are those of equality for women and between races. Defence of all human rights is one of the media's most vital tasks.

(E) Human Rights and Mass Media

At the time when the UN declaration was adopted neither the print media nor the electronic media were as influential and spread over as they are today. Also due to lack of widespread literacy and easy reach to electronic media a large section of world population remained unaware of their rights.

In the age of globalization today when information technology is advancing and spreading at a very rapid pace, the role of media in generating awareness and its responsibilities have also increased manifold. Due to advancement of technology news travels very fast and both print media and electronic media have entered virtually every household on this planet. If one has access to electronic media (which is a normal feature in the forms of T.V. and internet) one can witness the events occurring hundreds and thousands miles apart simultaneously or if there be still a person who due to one reason or other has access only to print media will have access to all the details of the event on the morrow. Due to such an easy accessibility media has become a dual edged sword, which if used responsibly can help transform the entire society in a constructive manner and can help create a positive public opinion and if fallen in irresponsible hands can destroy the very fabric of a society and culture by putting the facts in a negative manner. Dangers of yellow journalism have today increased manifold.

(F) Role of Mass Media

Though nowadays we emphasize more upon rights than duties and it cannot be denied that no right can exist without a corresponding duty. In fact one's duty is other's right and *vice versa*. Same is true about human rights and human duties. If we have a right to enjoy our rights we have a duty to protect other's rights or at least to enjoy our rights in a manner which doesn't hinder others in enjoying their rights.

Mass media "The Fourth Estate" after the legislature, the executive and the judiciary, has become the prime educative, informative and catalytic agent in safeguarding human rights. It is the most systematic and effective means of reaching quickly and communicating convincingly with a large number of people in a very short span of time.

Media is rightly called the "watch dog" of peoples rights and the "mirror of contemporary society". Vigilant and enlightened mass media can go a long way in spreading human rights awareness to achieve this objective; and it is essential that agencies of mass media should remain free, independent and impartial and media personnel are responsible, responsive, trained in human rights and committed to social welfare. Then and then only they will be able to do their duty with a clear conscience and commitment. It is easy to talk and fight for one's rights but it is equally difficult to perform one's duty in earnest and this is as true for media personnel as for every other person in other walks of life.

The issue of human rights is as important as it is complex and is equally, if not more, confusing. There are different types of cultures the world over and still more varied are expressions used by people of different cultures in such a situation in sensitive circumstances care should be taken to avoid eruption of misunderstandings among peoples of different cultures. Electronic and print media, both have long lasting impact on the masses so whatever is being said, shown or printed in the media should have a positive perspective and aura and must be able to provide proper leadership and form effective and correct public opinion. Media personnel should cultivate a deep understanding of the concept of human rights then and then only they will be able to bring forward issues of human rights, protection and violation, before the public at large in a correct perspective.

Media influences people at the social and cultural levels and its impact is more popular, lasting and far-reaching than all the government agencies put together. Media can also establish an effective and impressive dialogue among people and between government and people, hence its role and responsibility increases manifold. It provides a free platform for popular dialogue and is dreaded by wrong doers and violators of human rights.

(G) Human Rights and Human Wrongs and Mass Media

In an era of globalisation when the entire world has turned into "a global village" and entire humanity in "a big human family", the noble cause of human rights is also being used as a means of interference in other sovereign people's "domestic jurisdiction" by the vested interests of a few people and governments which has given birth to "politics of human rights". At times mass media becomes a tool in the hands of such reactionary forces and their vested interests, disguised in the holy garb of 'human rights' find place and publicity through this noble instrument which should, in all events and eventualities, be at the service of human kind.

A glaring example of this is "human rights of terrorists".

In the name of protection of human rights "terrorists" are being shielded and thus encouraged at the cost of innocent masses and police and army personnel who are only performing their sacred duty of defending people and nation, as has been happening in Kashmir for a long time. In such cases instead of playing in the hands of enemies of the people the mass media has to play a proactive, positive and constructive role and has a duty to highlight whose rights are being actually violated and by whom? Are foreign invaders, who have been waging proxy wars with foreign arms and assistance, worthy of human rights is a million dollar question. Do we need to ask the question, in the same way whether the persons and properties of the innocent people need protection in the disturbed areas? or does this question needs to be answered that should a country have or have not the right to intervene in other sovereign country's affairs on the pretext of violation of human rights?

In a liberal democratic country the classical dilemma of security of the nation and human rights of insurgents, billigerents and terrorists is always present before the nation-state and its government, that poses a serious challenge to the very existence of the State as well its honour and prestige.

In a positive manner media can also bring out violation of human rights of children, woman, child and bonded labourers, *dalits* and other backward classes, prisoners, refugees and victims of communal riots by the government and its various agencies leading to public awareness and a big hue and cry that can force the government and community to take corrective measures without any delay.

All said and done one shouldn't forget in this debate of mass media's role, rights and duties that mass media personnel too are human beings and they too face the risk and difficulties in reporting cases of human rights violations during terrorist activities, insurgencies, other war like situations and even during national emergencies in all the countries. Every dictatorial ruler tries to control, first of all the media and to use it to fulfil vested interests. In such circumstances role and responsibility of media personnel as well as their desire to leave it all, let it be and feel safe, also increases manifold.

The task of promotion and protection of human rights is a complex one and requires the cooperation of all sections and strata of society *i.e.* political parties, NGO's, lawyers, judges, public servants, doctors, teachers, police, army and media personnel. This noble task cannot be completed if any one section of the society lags behind and is unwilling to contribute its share of work and responsibilities.

NOTES

1. *A Handbook of International Human Rights Terminology*, The University of Nebraska Press, USA, 1999, p. 46.
2. *Ibid.*, pp. 133-34.
3. *Ibid.*, pp. 148-49.
4. Baylis, John and Smith Steve, "The Globalization of World Politics", Oxford University Press, New York, 1997, p. 476.
5. Alfredsson Gudmunder and Eide Asbjorn (ed.), "The *Universal Declaration of Human Rights – A Common Standard of Achievement*, Kluwer Law International, The Netherlands, 1999.

12 Refugees and Human Rights

Comparative Studies between Chakmas in India and Biharis in Bangladesh

Chunnu Prasad

World refugee problem has escalated from one million refugees in 1951 to 17.5 million with 15 million internally displaced persons. 25 million cared by United Nations in Palestine.

The problem of refugees or just of asylum seekers but of migrants owing to push and pull factors in economic terms that factor into ethnic divides everywhere. These raise concerns of resettlement with dignity around which human rights theorization has taken place since the England Bill of Rights to American and France and to United Nations Convention. Practically all governments suffer on some count or the other and so the pressure on them is to incorporate these into domestic laws with regard to refugees, notwithstanding the fact that the term refuge is loaded with confusion *viz.,* as their classification around political, economic, ecological axes.

Most of it involves citizenship rights as well as rights to basic amenities, *e.g.* in refugee camps in terms of shelter, water protection from diseases, caloric intake. States adopt various strategies on inclusion and exclusion for nation building purposes depending on the nature of their polity. Cambodians exclude Vietnamese on the basis of lineage or ethnic Russian face citizenship problems in Lithuania.

Since this is happening one has to look at the political variable of the nature of polity to look at the problem that may have come on origin and different trajectories of evolution as far instance in South Asia. Hence, the problem of Chakmas and Biharis get related to Redcliff Commission and yet follow their different courses owing to the democratic polity in India and authoritarianism and Islamic military and civilian governments of the theocratic state. Secondly the political culture of integration in assimilation contributes to recognition and denial of citizenship and human rights.

It is in the nature of the polity that lays the possibilities of comparisons and contrasts in our two case studies of how nation-building is taking place. In case of India the dangers of *ad hoc* measures accompanying the happy situation of homogenization of Chakmas in the North East region while in Bangladesh it is the segmentation of Biharis around language and community that is compared with inter-state Bangla-Pakistan conflict that leads to the denial of human rights.

In an age when international standards are continually refined to ensure protection and empowerment for all, millions of people are still prevented from exercising their legitimate rights. They are the 'non-citizens' people who are denied the right of citizenship[1]. Citizenship is denied for reasons of political power and is most prevalent in situations of conflict. Non-citizens are denied access to suffrage, justice, services, and rights in their countries and often become political scapegoats.

Most people become citizens at birth. All but three States have ratified the 1990 Convention on the Rights of Child which *inter alia* provides that a child should be granted citizenship at birth. It is, therefore, a globally recognized right. Nevertheless, it is as yet far from universal in its application[2]. There are a number of people and groups who are denied citizenship, either at birth or later. There are people who lose their citizenship and cannot obtain basic human rights and their dignity.

A case of refugee groups in the States of India like Chakma refugees and Biharis in case of Bangladesh are to be focussed in detail. The genesis of each of these refugee groups and the area of human rights in their treatment has to be looked out. Also, review the shifting *adhoc* and confusing stands of the state machineries and treatment of various refugees' streams. The inadequacies of the international regime for the protection of the refugees in India and Bangladesh have also been examined. My research largely focussed on the case of two major refugee groups, Chakmas in India and Biharis in Bangladesh respectively. It looks on the various aspects of problems on their settlement, institutional setups, various policies and human rights violation. The fate of Chakma refugees in India and Biharis in Bangladesh is dissimilar though both issues originate initially in partition with added dimension of the Chakmas in secession of East Pakistan and formation of Bangladesh. The Chakma and Bihari refugee problems relate to the state policies of India, Pakistan and Bangladesh as well as internal policies in East Pakistan then Bangladesh and Pakistan. The nature of the three politics get reflected in the attitudes and policies they develop in issue of resettlement of refugees, who have legitimate human rights as they have allowed since Bill of Rights in England and through French and American position to the United Nations Convention. The latter has been flouted across the world and South Asia. A comparative perspective on this with regard to Chakmas in India and Biharis in Bangladesh is possible to develop around the nature of polity in the two countries *viz.* democracy and secularism in India and communal and ethnic segmentation in army regime of Bangladesh as also Islamising experiences in civilian regimes.

The problem of the world's refugees and internally displaced is among the most complicated issues before the world community today. Much discussion is taking place at the United Nations as it continues to search for more effective ways to protect and assist these particularly vulnerable groups, while some call for increased levels of cooperation and coordination among relief agencies, others point to gaps in international legislation and appeal for further standard setting in this area. Everyone, however, agrees that the problem is both multidimensional and global. Any approach or solution would, therefore, have to be comprehensive and to address all aspects of the issue, from the causes of mass exodus to the elaboration of responses necessary to cover the range of refugee situations from emergencies to repatriation. In this debate, some facts remain beyond dispute. The first is that while some mass displacements may be preventable, none is voluntary. No one likes or chooses to be a refugee. Being a refugee means more than being an alien. It means living in exile and depending on others for such basic needs as food, clothing and shelter. Information on the number of the world's refugees, their geographical distribution, and the causes of their exodus is generally available. The refugee problem has undergone drastic quantitative and qualitative changes in the past five decades. Since its creation, the United Nations has worked to protect refugees around the world.

In 1951, the year in which the office of the United Nations High Commissioner for Refugees (UNHCR) was established, there were estimated one million refugees within UNHCR's mandate. Today that number has grown to an estimated 17.5 million refugees, an additional 2.5 million refugees cared for by the United Nations Relief and Works Agency for Palestine refugees in the Near East (UNRWA) and more than 25 million internally displaced persons. In 1951, most of the refugees were European. The majority of today's refugees are from Africa and Asia.

Current refugee movements, unlike those of the past, increasingly take the form of mass exoduses rather than individual flights. Eighty per cent of today's refugees are women and children. The causes of exodus have also multiplied and now include natural or ecological disasters and extreme poverty. As a result, many of today's refugees do not fit the definition contained in the Convention relating to the Status of Refugees. This refers to victims of persecution for reasons of race, religion, nationality, membership of a particular social group or political opinion. The United Nations system has also been very concerned by the rise in the number of mass internal displacements in recent years. The "internally displaced" are persons who are forced to flee their homes but remain within the territory of their own country. Since they remain inside their own countries, these persons are excluded from the present system of refugee protection. Most of the internally displaced populations are in developing countries are largely women and children. In some countries, the internally displaced make up more than ten per cent of the population. The refugee situation has become a classic example of the interdependence of the international community. It fully demonstrates how the problems of one country can have immediate consequences for other countries. It is also an example of interdependence between issues.

There is a clear relationship between the refugee problem and the issue of human rights. Violations of rights of minorities and ethnic conflicts are increasingly at the source of both mass exoduses and internal displacements. Disregard for the minimum rights of refugees and internally displaced persons are another dimension of the relationship between the two issues. During the process of seeking asylum, a growing number of people are faced with restrictive measures, which deny them access to safe territories. In some instances, asylum-seekers and refugees are detained or forcibly returned to areas where their lives, liberty and security are threatened, some are attacked by armed groups, or recruited into armed forces and forced to fight for one side or the other in civil conflicts. Asylum-seekers and refugees are also victims of racist aggression. Refugees have rights which should be respected prior to, during, and after the process of seeking asylum. Respect for human rights is a necessary condition for both preventing and resolving today's refugee flows. In the words of the United Nations High Commissioner for Refugees, Sadako Ogata, "the refugee issue must be put to all governments and peoples as a test of their commitment to human rights".

In the post-World War-II period refugee problem emerged to be the biggest problem before the international community. India has also experienced it at a large scale. Factors such as rise of religious nationalism, ethnisization of politics, state terrorism, and anarchic-majoritarianism and above all state's refusal to confirm to norms set by the international refugee regime rendered the refugees stateless and subjects for inhuman treatment. The incident of human rights violation has been taking place at an alarming rate despite a worldwide awareness about human rights. Among various occurrences of human rights violation, refugees constitute an important category. In fact, the phenomenon of refugees by itself is a phenomenon of violation of human rights and is the greatest blot on human civilization[3].

The historical forces like religious, linguistic or ethnic nationalism, religion and economic disparity continue to generate refugees in various parts of India and Bangladesh face with unfriendly state, both in the country of origin and the country of adoption, the refugees struggle to find the ways and means for a healthy living and whenever possible they make efforts to put up an organized movement for their 'human rights'.

A case of refugee groups in the States of India like

Chakmas refugees and Biharis in case of Bangladesh are to be focussed in detail. The genesis of each of these refugee groups and the area of human rights violation in their treatment has to be looked out. Also, review the shifting *ad hoc* and confusing stands of the state machineries and treatment of various refugees' streams. The inadequacies of the international regime for the protection of the refugees in India and Bangladesh have also been examined.

Man is born free and is everywhere in chains. Human rights are inherent to man as being human person, variously known as 'fundamental rights' or natural rights everybody everywhere is entitled to enjoy the privilege of human rights. Universal Declaration of Human Rights and subsequent all covenants on human rights to which most of the nation-states are signatory and ensuring the cause of human rights. Despite all the statutory provisions, we come across the cases of human rights violations.

Being a human being one is entitled to have basic rights. All human rights derive from the dignity and worth inherent in the human person and that the human person is the central subject of human rights and fundamental freedoms. In simple terms, whatever adds to the dignified and free existence of a human being should be regarded as human rights.

For the first time human rights was coined independence in 1776 and the United States Constitution embodied a bill of rights. French revolution gave birth to the declaration of rights of man and citizen in 1789. In 1929, Institute of International Law, New York (USA) prepared a declaration of human rights and duties. Finally, on 10 December 1948 the United Nations proclaimed the Universal Declaration of Human Rights[4]. Coming to the case of India, the Constitution of India, which came into effect in 1950, incorporate a part on 'fundamental rights' of the citizens. The United States defined human rights in a policy document in 1978 as;

> *"Freedom from arbitrary arrest and imprisonment, torture, unfair trial, cruel and unusual punishment and invasion of privacy, Right to food, shelter, health care and education and freedom of thought, speech, assembly, religion, press, movement and participation in government"*[5].

Human rights are the natural born rights for every human being universally. People cannot live in dignity without these basic standards. To violate someone's human rights is to treat that person as though she or he is not a human being. To advocate human rights is to demand that the human dignity of all people be respected.

The refugee problem has assumed an unprecedented dimension in the international sphere. Some scholars have viewed present century as the century of uprooted people. The total number of refugees is believed to be twenty million. Refugees is quite complex involving many countries and so many issues. According to United Nations, a refugee is,

> *"Any person who owing to well founded fear of being persecuted for reasons of race, nationality membership of a particular social group or political opinions is outside fear, is unwilling to avail of the protection of that country"*[6].

The term 'refugee' is an evolutionary as well as a contested concept. There is considerable confusion and a lack of clarity in its meaning, nature, scope and usage (Dordrecht: Martinus Nijhoff, 1997). The terminologies that are used relating to the term political refugees, economic refugees, environmental refugees, resource refugees, developmental refugees, eco-migrants, internal refugees or internally displace people, external refugees etc. indicate its multi-context usages and a certain degree of confusion over its definition[7].

The Bihari Refugees in Bangladesh

The history of the Bihari refugees goes back to the partition of India in 1947[8]. Their displacement occurred in the wake of communal violence during and in the aftermath of the partition (for example, 30,000 Muslims were killed in the 'Great Bihar Killing' in October-November 1947). About a million of them migrated to the eastern wing of Pakistan[9] (East Pakistan), mostly from the eastern Indian States of Bihar, West Bengal, Assam, Orissa, Nagaland, Manipur, Tripura and Sikkim[10]. During the period of united Pakistan (1947-1971), the Urdu-speaking Biharis were not assimilated within the society of East Pakistan and remained as a distinct cultural-linguistic group. They generally associated and identified themselves with the West Pakistani society primarily based on a shared linguistic heritage and supported the West Pakistani governing elite, in the process of capturing the economic and political power in East Pakistan[11].

Initially the arrival of Biharis and the positive discrimination of the Pakistan Government in terms of refugee rehabilitation were not resented by the Bengalis. However, the euphoria of the formation of Pakistan and the positive attitude of the Bengalis towards the Biharis was short-lived. It was over as early as March 1948 when Mohammad Ali Jinnah announced in Dhaka that "Urdu and Urdu alone shall be the State language of Pakistan." During the Language Movement, the Biharis instead of supporting the Bengalis sided with the West Pakistani ruling elite[12]. Further, in the 1954 provincial elections and in the 1970 general elections, they extended their support to the Muslim League, which symbolized and championed the domination of the West Pakistanis over the Bengalis. They also supported the West Pakistani ruling elite and many of them actively participated in the military actions against the Bengalis in the 1971 Bangladesh Independence War. The exclusive attitude of the Biharis and their pro-West Pakistani political activities culminated with the growth of an anti Bihari sentiment among the Bengalis[13].

Against the above backdrop and, more importantly, because of their active anti-independence role (for example, their participation in the East Pakistan Civil Armed Forces, *i.e.* Razakars and Al-Shams, raised by the Pakistani authorities to carry out atrocities over the East Pakistanis), the Biharis became subject to widespread political persecution preceding and during the Independence War, as well as in the aftermath of liberation. Following independence, the Bihari political persecution continued and their properties and houses were taken over by the Bengalis. Several government promulgations for example, the Acting President Order I of 1972, the Bangladesh Abandoned Property (Control, Management and Disposal) Order, 1972, President's Order 16 etc. did facilitate the dispossession of Bihari properties. As a result, by the middle of 1972, a total of 1,008,680 Biharis were domiciled in various shanty camps spreading all over Bangladesh[14].

The Bangladesh Government announced the Presidential Order 149 in 1972 as a step towards offering the Bangladeshi citizenship to the Biharis. According to Bangladesh Government sources, 600,000 Biharis accepted the offer, by the Ministry of Relief and Rehabilitation, Government of the People's Republic of Bangladesh, Stranded Pakistanis in Bangladesh[15] while 539,669 registered with the International Committee of Red Cross (ICRC) opting to return to their 'country of nationality', Pakistan. Islamabad, however, was less interested and showed a lax attitude about the repatriation of the Biharis except those who joined the East Pakistan Civil Armed Forces (CAF) and surrendered with the Pakistan Army[16].

Bangladesh in its formative phase insisted that it would establish formal diplomatic relations with Pakistan only if that country agreed to expeditious repatriation of the non-Bengalis including Biharis from Bangladesh. This insistence forced the Pakistan Government to move back from its original stance and agreed to receive a sizeable number of Biharis in the 1973, New Delhi Agreement as well as in the Tripartite Agreement of 1974 in exchange for the return of the Bengalis from Pakistan. As the first step towards implementing these agreements, the International Committee of Red Cross (ICRC) registered 539,639 Biharis who intended to return to Pakistan. The United Nations High Commissioner for Refugees (UNHCR) facilitated the return of 108,750 Bihari refugees by June 1974. After that date, the UNHCR had to suspend the repatriation process due to exhaustion of funds. The Bangladesh Government complained to Islamabad about the slow repatriation of the Biharis and raised the issue during the 1974 Mujib-Bhutto summit. The Pakistani side, as it was earlier, showed little interest in the matter[17].

The post-Mujib Government undertook new diplomatic initiatives to persuade Islamabad to resume the repatriation of the Biharis. It approached the Islamic countries to exert pressure on Pakistan as well as to provide assistance to resolve the matter. Despite initial reluctance, President Zia-ul Haq subsequently, however, desired a solution to the Bihari issue on humanitarian ground. He asserted during a visit to Dhaka in December 1985 that Pakistan was ready to accept the Bihari refugees if sufficient financial resources could be raised for their transfer and rehabilitation. In 1988, a trust agreement was signed between Pakistan and Rabita Al-Alam Al-Islami (an Islamic charity organization, hereafter Rabita) to expedite the process of Bihari resettlement in Pakistan. A repatriation and resettlement plan was drawn up which included the construction of 36,000 houses spread over 80 sites costing about $278 million and with approximately $30 million for community services and $10 million for the transportation of the refugees. Despite elaborate preparations, the repatriation process could not get off the ground.

Benazir Bhutto was traditionally opposed to the idea of transferring the Biharis to Pakistan and followed the party politics [Pakistan Peoples Party (PPP)] and the state policy of her father (Zulfikar Ali Bhutto) after she came to power in 1988. Zulfikar Ali Bhutto, it is noteworthy, introduced the restrictive entry regulations for the Bihari refugees in the early 1970s. During her tenure as Prime Minister, Benazir did not grant the citizenship rights either to the refugees in Bangladesh or to the 100,000 Biharis who moved to Pakistan illegally since 1977. During a visit to Bangladesh in October 1989, Benazir asserted that the Biharis should be permanently settled in Bangladesh and Pakistan would help to raise funds from the Muslim world for their settlement. Prime Minister Newaz Sharif, was generally supportive to the repatriation of the Bihari refugees from Bangladesh. He undertook meaningful initiatives for the return of the Biharis. He was ready to rehabilitate them in his home province (Punjab) and officially domiciled issuing identity cards. Although definite steps were taken for repatriation and a symbolic return of 235 Biharis did occur on 10 January 1993, it was subsequently shelved for 'logistical and practical' problems. All subsequent Pakistani governments showed disinterest in ending the Bihari issue that it is indeed a political question rather than an economic problem[18].

There are an estimated 300,000 Bihari non-citizens currently in Bangladesh. They have been wilfully denied citizenship by the state since the early 1970s[19]. The vast majority still resides in refugee camps and the prospects for a change in their status or condition seemed until recently very dim[20]. The case of the Biharis in Bangladesh is different from other cases of denial of citizenship because the government considers them as a foreign group of individuals that ought to return to Pakistan. In fact Biharis never resided in Pakistan, but originally entered East Pakistan as refugees fleeing from India at the time of its accession to Independence. The Biharis assimilated quickly and with support from the ethnic Punjabis, who dominated the politics of the newly indepen-dent State of Pakistan, established themselves in key positions over the Bengali majority. This situation prevailed until the secession of East Pakistan and the creation of the independent state of Bangladesh. At the time, the new Government of Bangladesh granted citizenship to the Bihari, but soon revised its position. Biharis came to be seen as Pakistanis who had supported the armed intervention of West Pakistan during the Bengali struggle for independence. They were subsequently stripped of their citizenship and related rights and placed in camps to await "repatriation" to Pakistan. Some 170,000 Biharis were indeed resettled in Pakistan after a tripartite agreement was concluded between India, Pakistan and Bangladesh[21]. Thereafter, the Govern-ment of Pakistan has refused to accept further resettlement, fearing possible ethnic conflict and instability. In 1999, the Government of Pakistan reiterated that the Biharis were Bangladeshis and not Pakistanis. Indeed, by that time almost all the Biharis living in Bangladesh had been born in that country[22]. In June 2003, a decision of the Bangladeshi High Court granted citizenship to ten Biharis. It was hoped that the High Court's decision would eventually pave the way for Bangladeshi citizenship to all Biharis and finally allow them to leave the camps and enjoy the full rights of nationals[23]. However, the government appealed the case. Moreover, the ten persons who obtained Bangladeshi citizenship met with rejection and opposition from the part of their own community[24] and were threatened with being evicted from the camps. The generational split within the Bihari community is likely to further complicate the issue. Many, older generation Biharis still hope to return to Pakistan while the younger generation is increasingly seeking citizenship rights in Bangladesh[25].

The Chakma Refugees in India

The Chakmas of India were expatriated from their abode in the Hill Tracts of Bangladesh in year 1964. They migrated to India through the Mizoram and Tripura border. They have been rehabilitated and allotted land in the Balijan Circle of the Lower Subansiri district, Miao Sub-Division of the Changlang district and Chowkham Circle of the Lohit district of the Indian State of Arunachal Pradesh[26]. They are the Mongloid tribes probably of Arakanese origin. Popular myth belief that the Chakmas migrated from Champanagar in the Champaran area of Bihar to the Arakan Hills, and finally settled down in the Chittagong district area as mentioned in British India, is not at all a historical fact. However, detail studies conducted earlier suggest that they might have migrated from a place somewhere in South-East Asia (Lewin, 1869 and Choudhury, 1975). Whatever the case may be but the Chakmas are the inhabitants of the Chittagong Hill Tract (CHT) are perhaps the least known people of Asia being the residents of a remote and backward area which is of little political or economic consequence. This place has been the home land of the Chakmas particularly for centuries. Though the origin of the Chakmas is too murky, their history connects them with the mountainous kingdom of Kapilnagar (an ancient place of the Lord Buddha, presently in Nepal) in the Himalayan ranges[27]. It is learnt that from 1052 A.D the Chakmas started moving from Arakan into the bordering area of Bengal right down the plain areas of Chittagong (Bangladesh) and made it their home.[28]

The Chittagong was ruled by the British as a part of India from 1787 to 1947 by providing the status of an autonomous area exclusively for the tribal people[29]. To equip the hill subjects of Chittagong with some kind of administration the British Government formulated an act in 1860 making way for the appointment of a superintendent of hill tribes in charges of the hill Tracts which was hence, known as the 'Hill Tract of Chittagong'.

The awfully inauspicious British Raj came to an end with the tragic partition of the Indian sub-continent. But this was even more catastrophic for the ill-fated Chakmas[30]. In 1947 when the country was to be partitioned it was expected that the CHT with over ninety eight per cent non-Muslim population would be included in India, contemplating this, an Indian flag was hoisted by the optimist Chakmas in Rangamati district for three days from August 15, 1947.[31] But brushing aside all the expectations Sir Cyril Radcliffe chairman of the Punjab and Bengal Boundary Commission, awarded the CHT to Pakistan on 17 August 1947 in contravention of the Indian Independence Act 1947 for political ends. Even Alastair Lamb was very critical about this arrangement when he stated, "Sir Cyril Radcliff's major qualification for this, it appeared was his almost total ignorance of Indian affairs"[32].

As archival materials amply show, Mountbatten, Nehru and Patel also wanted the CHT to remain as a part of India. Yet, 600,000 Buddhist, like other '*Kafirs*' were thrown to the wolves and offered on a platter to East Pakistan[33] through no specific reasons were given by the Boundary Commission for taking such an unethical division. Thus, the fate of the Buddhist Chakmas was decided by a treacherous appeasement plan put forward by the shrewd representatives of the dominating communities[34]. To their great dismay no referendum was held to elicit the opinion of the Chakmas regarding the future of their destiny. To register proclamation, a delegation of the Chakmas set out for Delhi to vindicate the apprehension of the Buddhist Tribes to Nehru despite all the assurance that their viewpoint would be due respect by the Radcliff Commission, unceremoniously the CHT was gifted away to the Islamic Nation of Pakistan. Thus, the authority committed one of the earliest mistakes in handling the minorities issue ineptly objection from some disgruntled student leaders of the CHT only amplified their agony inviting the wrath of the Pakistani Army. The storm measures taken by the army thus, made the students flee, leading to the first Chakma exodus to India since Independence[35].

The Chakma problem in India goes back to post-1971 and

post-Bangladesh issue[36]. The Chakma influx into India can be traced to the partition of the sub-continent from the beginning, 'inconsistency and political expediency' governed India's CHT policy[37]. Until the 1970's, its policy *vis-à-vis* Chakmas was lackadaisical and short-sighted. The first influx of the refugees took place shortly after partition when 40,000 Chakma families fled into India. Having housed and absorbed a large number of non-Muslims Chakmas from East-Pakistan, India did not treat the Chakma differently and rehabilitated them in North Indian States and later to the North eastern States of India. The manageable number of the Chakmas, their widespread dispersal in the sparsely populated North East and their ethnic proximity largely mitigated any potential for opposition from the indigenous population. Furthermore, absorption was feasible party because ethnic consciousness in the North East was still in its infancy[38].

In 1964 a second wave of Chakma exodus was precipitated by the events surrounding the Kaptai Dam Project across river Karnaful, in Chittagong Hill Tract. Arable land used by the inhabitants for plough cultivation, it displaced an estimated 100,000 people mostly Chakmas. A faulty and inefficient resettlement policy resulted in about 40,000 seeking refugee in India[39]. Geographical, as well as, tribal proximity provided an additional incentive to the Chakmas fleeing to India, as they felt alienated by the Bengali Muslims[40].

Unlike the past, however, India viewed this wave of influx with some apprehension. Though not demanding their repatriation into East Pakistan, it sought to minimize the friction between the immigrants and the local population of Tripura and Mizoram. If the Indo-Pakistan war of 1965 prevented the repatriation of Chakmas into CHT[41].

In an age when international standards are continually refined to ensure protection and empowerment for all, millions of people are still prevented from exercising their legitimate rights. They are the 'non-citizens' people who are denied the right of citizenship. Citizenship is denied for reasons of political power and is most prevalent in situations of conflict. Non-citizens are denied access to suffrage, justice, services, and rights in their countries and often become political scapegoats.

Denial of citizenship is closely linked to conflict and State building. Emerging States often deny citizenship to population groups they believe constitute a menace to their fragile integrity and the power base of influential groups. Post-conflict State-building in the Balkans, for example, has seen a number of cases where citizenship was denied to populations whose ethnic origins associated them with former enemies. Beyond perceived direct threats to their territorial integrity, new States are also generally concerned with controlling citizen participation in the governance of their territory and resources. The outcome of the referendum held in Slovenia in April 2004 has shown that such concerns do not abate easily. More than a decade into the State-building process, an overwhelming majority of voters still confirmed their desire to exclude from citizenship sizeable communities of former Yugoslavs. In countries where State-building is led by a culturally or ethnically distinct group, non-members are liable to exclusion and denial of citizenship[42]. In such cases, the right to citizenship is often denied in the context of voting rights. For instance, in Cambodia, extensive criteria pertaining to lineage were introduced to exclude ethnic Vietnamese from receiving Cambodian citizenship prior to elections. Cambodia is by no means unique and this practice has been repeated frequently around the world. Over time, as States mature, some exclusionary situations may be resolved through the assimilation and cooption of fringe groups[43].

Other situations, however, linger because States may find it more convenient or safer not to acknowledge their root causes. Fear of change and fear of eventual shocks to established structures are other reasons for States to continue denying population groups citizenship. Short-term goals of entrenched governments may lead to reversals as well. In some such cases, discrimination and the denial of citizenship have contributed to social unrest and armed conflict.

The question of citizenship polarized the country's population and exacerbated internal tensions; it caused the civil war and brought the issues to the brink of international conflict. While denial of citizenship is, for States who practice it, a radical instrument of exclusion, there exist other forms of discrimination which may erode people's citizenship right and other norms of the human right violations.

Conclusion

What are the consequences of statelessness for an individual? The short-term consequences of statelessness are similar to being an illegal alien. Except that illegal aliens can return to the country of their citizenship but the statelessness can't. The consequences often start with a lack of recognition of the education, training, skills or professional achievements. From there it degenerates into unemployment or massive underemployment, lack of economic opportunities and exploitation (by State, employers and private citizens), absence of any political rights, inability and unwillingness of the statelessness to seek justice, general poverty follows with unavailability of medical care and education for the statelessness and their off-spring, lack of security of person and protection of property from other citizens and the State. Inabilities to travel or the ability to improve one's condition in life are just some of the consequences of statelessness. These have been proven in numerous academic studies. Statelessness is depriving these individuals from uplifting themselves and their countries[44] .

The problem of Chakmas in India and Biharis in Bangladesh is one of the oldest human problems and this problem has to be taken in deep concern by both the government either a democratic in case of India and Islamic religious fundamentalist or totalitarianism in case of Bangladesh. Both the countries should try to solve the refugee problem so that these people who are being discriminated their basic fundamental rights and dignity to survive should also reclaim their human rights which they lost just because of partition. Also both the country should follow the directions of the United Nations Human Rights Commission for Refugees (UNHRCR) to solve the refugee problem within a time bound and provide all short of help and legality which is related to the Chakmas and Biharis of both the country and also open the positive and middle path so that the possibility of building of nation-state would be possible in future.

NOTES

1. Prasad, Chunnu (2006), Migration and the Question of Citizenship: People of Chittagong Hill Tract in Arunachal Pradesh, *Indian Journal of Political Science*, Vol. LXVII, No. 3, July-September, 2006, pp. 471-490.
2. Naorem, Sanajeoba (1994), *Human Rights: Practices and Abuses*, Cosmos Publication, New Delhi, p.1.
3. S.C. Joshi (2006), *Human Rights Concepts: Issue and Law*, Akansha Publishing House, New Delhi, p.1-3.
4. *Ibid.*, p.3.
5. The 1951 UN Convention relating to the Status of Refugees, UN Treaty, Vol. 189, No. 2545, p. 137.
6. Pirkko Kourula, Broadening the Edges: Refugee Definition and International Protection Revisited.
7. Ravinder Kaur (2006), The Last Journey; Exploring Social Class in the 1947 Partition Migration, *Economic and Political Weekly* June, No. 3, pp.2221-2228.
8. Minority Rights Group, *The Biharis in Bangladesh*, Report 11, 4th edition, January 1982, p. 7.
9. Minority Rights Group, *The Biharis in Bangladesh*, Report 11, 4th edition, January 1982, p. 7.
10. See the website article title, Condition of Statelessness in Bangladesh and Pakistan, www.statelesspeopleinbangladesh.

net/www.strandedpakistani.org/Stateless People in Bangladesh and Pakistan – Stranded Pakistanis in Bangladesh – Urdu Speaking Minority in Bangladesh – Biharis in Bangladesh, 2004, 2005, 2006. Stateless People in Bangladesh Inc., USA

11. The Bihari Refugees, by South Asia Forum for Refugee Rights, taken from "*Bangladesh State and Refugee Phenomenon*" Date/ Time Page Created: 12/15/2004, Date/Time Last Modified: 12/15/2004 10:27:52 AM.
12. See the Information and Article on *Biharis in Bangladesh and their Human Rights* published by the South Asian Forum for Human Rights, http://www.safhr.org.
13. *Ibid.*
14. Reported by the Ministry of Relief and Rehabilitation Dhaka: Government of Bangladesh, 1982, p. 3.
15. According to a Pakistani Foreign Ministry official: "What are we supposed to do with them (the Biharis)? We have enough problems already. Besides, you must remember that they are really Indian refugees." Zulfikar Ali Bhutto, the first post-1971 civilian President of Pakistan, was even unwilling to admit any sizeable number of 'Bihari refugees' to be repatriated to Pakistan, (Constantin Sokoloff, Denial of Citizenship: a Challenge to Human Security, Report was made on the support of Ford Foundation on February 2005).
16. *Ibid.*
17. Information Displayed by the South Asian Forum for Human Rights.
18. Constantin Sokoloff, *Denial of Citizenship: A Challenge to Human Security*, Report was made on the support of Ford Foundation on February 2005.
19. Bangladesh, Country Report, *Country Information and Policy Unit*, Immigration and Nationality Directorate, Home Office, United Kingdom, April 2004.
20. *Citizenship and Statelessness in South Asia*, Gerrard Khan, The Fletcher School of Law and Diplomacy, October 2001.
21. Case#3 of "Being Recognized as Citizens: A Human Security Dilemma in South and South East Asia", A paper prepared for the Commission on Human Security by John W. Hefferman, November 2002.

22. U.S. Committee for Refugees, Press Release, 16 June 2003; BBC News - Mixed Feelings over Bihari Ruling, 28 May 2003.
23. Bangladeshi identity brings miseries to 10 youths in Geneva Camp - New Age, Dhaka, Bangladesh 19 Oct 2004, http://www.newagebd.com/2004/oct/19/met.html#2.
24. Biharis demands Bangladeshi citizenship, *The Bangladesh Observer*, 15 July 2004, http://www.bangladeshobserveronline.com/new/2004/07/15/front.htm.
25. Singh, Deepak K. Refugee question in Arunachal Pradesh: Some conflicting currents' *Journal of Anthropological Survey of India*, 50(4), 2001, December, pp. 95-102.
26. Prasad, Chunnu (2007), Student Movement in Arunachal Pradesh: A Case of Chakma-Hajong Refugee Problem, *Economic and Political Weekly*, Vol. XLII, No. 15, April 14-20, pp.1373-1379.
27. *The Observer*, 23, September 1994.
28. Prasad, Chunnu (2007), Arunachal Pradesh and the Inner-Outer Line Regulation of 1873-1874 of North East Frontier Agency, *Third World Impact*, Vol. XVIII, No.173, January-March, pp. 15-19.
29. Prasad, Chunnu (2006), Victims of Partition: A Case of Chakma and Hajong Refugees of Arunachal Pradesh, *Think India*, Vol. 9, No. 4, October-December, 2006, pp. 59-71.
30. *The Hindustan Times*, 25th September, 1994.
31. *Patriot*, 19th May, 1993.
32. *The Pioneer*, 21st October, 1994.
33. Singh, Deepak K. Refugee question in Arunachal Pradesh: Some conflicting currents' *Journal of Anthropological Survey of India*, 50(4), 2001, December, pp. 95-102.
34. Singh, Deepak K. (2003), The Elsewhere People: Cross Border Migration, Refugee Protection and State Response, in a edited book by Om Prakash Mishra and A.J.Majumdar, Lancer Publication, New Delhi, pp. 94-105.
35. Talukdar, S.P, Chakmas: *An Embattled Tribes*, Uppal Publishing House, New Delhi, pp. 64-65.
36. Saeed, Amera (1987), The Chakma Unrest in Bangladesh, Regional Studies, Vol. 6, No.1, Winter, p. 63.
37. Singh, Deepak K. Refugee question in Arunachal Pradesh: Some conflicting currents' *Journal of Anthropological Survey of India*, 50(4), 2001, December, pp. 95-102.

38. Verghese, B.G (1997), *India's northeast resurgent: Ethnicity Insurgency, governance development*, Konark Publication, New Delhi, p. 225.
39. Singh, Deepak K. Refugee Question in Arunachal Pradesh: Some Conflicting Currents', *Journal of Anthropological Survey of India*, 50(4), 2001, December, pp. 95-102.
40. *Ibid.*
41. Constantin Sokoloff, *Denial of Citizenship: A Challenge tó Human Security*, Report was made on the support of Ford Foundation on February 2005.
42. *Ibid.*
43. *Ibid.*
44. See the website article title, Condition of statelessness in Bangladesh and Pakistan, www.statelesspeopleinbangladesh.net/www.strandedpakistani.org/ Stateless People in Bangladesh and Pakistan – Stranded Pakistanis in Bangladesh– Urdu Speaking Minority in Bangladesh – Biharis in Bangladesh, 2004, 2005, 2006. Stateless People in Bangladesh Inc., USA

REFERENCES

Aziz, Qutubuddin (1974), *Blood and Tears*, United Press of Pakistan, Karachi.

B.S. Chimni (2000), *International Refugee Law: A Reader*, Sage Publications, New Delhi.

Baehr, Peter R. (1999), *Human Rights: Universality in Practice*, Macmillan Press Ltd.

Bauer, Jaanner R. and Beel, Daniell. A (ed.) (1999), *The East Asian Challenge for Human Rights*, Cambridge University Press.

Beetham, David (ed.) (1995), *Politics and Human Rights*, Blackwell Publishing.

Borgohain, Bani (1999), *Human Rights, Social Justice and Political Change*, Kanishka Publisher, New Delhi.

Bose, Shikha (1993), Victims of Security Dilemma: Chakmas and Refugees from Bangladesh, In Muni and Baral (ed.), *Refugees and Regional Security in South Asia*, Konark Publication, New Delhi.

Bose, Tapan K. and Manchanda, Rita (ed.) (1997), *States, Citizens and*

Outsiders: The Uprooted People of South Asia, South Asian Rights for Human Rights, Kathmandu.

C.R. Abrar and Shahdeen Malik (2000), *Towards National Refugee Laws in South Asia* (Refugee and Migratory Movement's Research Unit; University of Dhaka, Bangladesh).

Chakarvarty, Manik (1998), *Human Rights and Refugees Problems, Law and Practices,* Deep and Deep Pvt. Ltd. New Delhi.

Chiranjivi J. Nirmal (ed.) (2000), *Human Rights in India: Historical, Social and Political Perspectives,* New York: Oxford University Press.

Diwan, Paras and Diwan, Peeyushi (1996), Human Rights and the Law, Deep and Deep Publication Pvt. Ltd., New Delhi.

Dunne, Tim and Wheeler, Nicholas J. (ed.) (1999), Human Rights in Global Politics, Cambridge University Press.

Ganguly, Rajat and Macduff Ian (ed.) (2003), *Ethnic Conflict and Secessionism in South and Southeast Asia: Causes, dynamics, solution,* Sage Publication, New Delhi.

Ganguialy, Rajat and Phadnis, Urmila (2001), Ethnicity and *Nation-Building in South Asia,* Sage Publication, New Delhi.

Gupta, D.N and Singh, Chandrachud (2003), *Human Rights: Acts, Statutes and constitutional provisions,* Vol.I, Kalpaz Publication, Delhi.

Hutchinson, R.H.S. (1978), *Chittagong Hill Tracts,* Vivek Publishing House, New Delhi.

Jala, Avesha (1995), *Democracy and Authoritarianism in South Asia,* Sang-e-Meel Publication,

Khana, D.P. (2001), *Reforming Human Rights,* Manas Publication, New Delhi.

Mahendra P. Lama (2000), *Managing Refugees in South Asia: Protection Aid, State Behaviour and Regional Approach,* Occasional Paper, No.4, Refugee and Migratory Movement, Research Unit, University of Dhaka, Bangladesh.

Mamta, Rajwat (ed.) (2001), *Burning Issue of Human Rights,* Kalpaz Publications, Delhi.

Manoj Kumar Sinha (2000), *Basic Documents on International Human Rights and Refugee Laws,* Manak Publications, New Delhi.

Mirza, Loraine (1998), *Internment camps of Bangladesh,* Crescent International, Markham, Canada.

Mishra, Omprakash and Majumdar, Anindyo J. (ed.) (2003), *The Elsewhere People,* Lancer Book Publisher, New Delhi.

Muni, S.D. and Baral, Lok Raj (ed.) (1996), *Refugees and Regional Security in South Asia,* Konark Publishers Pvt. Ltd., Delhi.

Narasimham, R.K. (1999), *Human Rights and Social Justice,* Commonwealth Publishers, Delhi.

Nautiyal, Annpurna (ed.) (2002), *Fifty Years of Human Rights: Expectations and Challenges,* Sarita Book House, Delhi.

Patil, V.T and Trivedi, P.R. (2000), *Migration, Refugees and Security in the 21st Century,* Authors Press, Delhi.

Perry, Michael J. (1998), *The Idea of Human Rights,* Oxford University Press, New York.

Pradip Kumar Bose (ed.) (2000), *Refugees in West Bengal: Institutional Practices and Contested Identities,* Calcutta Research Group, Calcutta.

Rahman, Dr. Mizanur (2003), *Biharis in Bangladesh: A Community in Transition,* Dhaka, Bangladesh.

Roy, Sanjay K. (ed.) (2001), *Refugees and Human Rights,* Rawat Publication, New Delhi.

Rushbrook, L. Williams (1972), *The East Pakistan Tragedy,* Drake.

Sachar, Rajinder (2004), *Human Rights: Perspectives and Challenges,* Gyan Publishing House, New Delhi.

Saksena, K.P. (ed.) (2003), *Human Rights and the Constitution: Vision and Reality,* Gyan Publishing House, New Delhi.

Sanajaoba, Naorem (ed.) (1994), *Human Rights Principles: Practice and Abuses,* Omson Publication, New Delhi.

Savic, Obrad (ed.) (1999), *The Politics of Human Rights,* Verso, London.

Sen, Sankar (1998), *Human Rights in a Developing Society,* APH Publishing Corporation, New Delhi.

Sharma, N.R. (1999), Human rights in the world, Pointer Publisher, Jaipur.

Singh, K.P. (ed.) (1994), *Human Rights Perspective and Challenges,* Institute for World Congress on Human Rights (IWCHR), New Delhi.

Singh, K.P. (ed.) (1999), *Human Rights: Fifty Years of India's Independence,* Gyan Publishing House, New Delhi.

Sinha, Manoj Kumar (1999), *Implementation of Basic Human Rights,* Manak Publications Pvt. Ltd., Delhi.

Sinha, Manoj Kumar (2000), *Basic Documents on International Human Rights and Refugee Laws,* Manak Publication Pvt. Ltd.

Sinha, P.C. (2003), *India's Human Rights Regime: A Comprehensive Presentation,* Kaniska Publishers and Distributors, New Delhi.

Talukdar, S.P. (1988), *The Chakmas: Life and Struggle,* Gian Publishing House, New Delhi.

Talukdar, S.P. (1994), *Chakmas: An Embattled Tribes,* Uppal Publishing House, New Delhi.

UNHCR (2000), *The State of the World's Refugees: Fifty Years of Humanitarian Action,* Oxford University Press, Oxford.

Vijapur, Abdulrahim P. and Kumar, Suresh (ed.) (1999), *Perspectives on Human Rights,* Manak Publication, Pvt. Ltd, New Delhi.

13 Right to Information and the Democratic Political System
The Indian Experience

S.P. Guru, Johani Xaxa and
Bibhuti Kalyan Mahakul

Democracy revolves round the basic idea of citizens being at the centre of governance as the sovereignty lies with them. A democracy 's well-being cannot be ensured without effective participation of its citizenry. Transparency and information are the most important prerequisites of participatory, responsive, accountable democratic governance. It is widely believed that access to government information is one of the conditions for democratic participation through which the common people can exercise democratic control over the government authorities. The citizen's right to information is increasingly being recognised as an important instrument for a fair and free Public Administration. The demand for Right to Information is the outcome of long standing collective action against arbitrariness and corruption of agencies of the State. The greater the access of the citizens to information the greater the responsiveness of government to community needs. Alternatively, the greater the restrictions that are placed on access, the greater the feelings of powerlessness and alienation. Without information, people cannot adequately exercise their rights as citizens. It has been observed that a government, which operates in greater secrecy, is more prone to corruption as compared to a government, which operates, in greater openness. That is why, the right to information is considered as a significant step in empowering people to combat corruption.

The right to information helps to strengthen the foundation of democracy. Unlike a totalitarian government, a democratic government needs to be based on the trust of the governed. It should, therefore, function in public view as much as possible so that the citizens know its aims, policies and programmes and help the government to accomplish them. To quote the Franks Committee of the United Kingdom, "A government which pursues effective conduct of its proper functions require, or which turns information services into propagandas agencies, will lose the trust of the people. It will be countered by ill informed and destructive criticism" (Frank Committee Report: 1972). Openness in governmental functioning is, therefore, regarded as an essential ingredient of democracy, and the right to information as a fundamental democratic right.

Democracy, to be effective and meaningful, should also have responsive administration, which is a bilateral process. On the one side, administration is required to be responsive the citizen's legitimate needs and grievances. The citizens, on the other side, are required to be co-operative and yet vigilant, for it is the eternal vigilance of enlightened citizens, which facilitates accountability and prevents arbitrariness in Public Administration, and brings it closer to the citizens. An eternal and enlightened vigilance is, thus, the best guarantee of democratic government. There is no denying in fact that the right to know is an effective means for the citizen's enlightenment, for it is the right, which gives them access to government departments and documents and thereby enables them to acquire knowledge of what is happening in the government.

The right to information tends to remove unnecessary secrecy surrounding the decision-making process in the government, and thereby helps to improve the quality of decision-making in Public Policy and Administration. It enables the citizens to know about the government decisions, and the basis on which they are made, so that they can exercise sound judgment on the merits of public policies and respond appropriately to influence the process of policy formulation and decision-making in public governance. To quote James, Madison, one of the founding fathers of the American Constitution, "A Popular Government without Popular Information or means of acquiring it, is but a prologue to a farce or a tragedy or perhaps both" (Guha Roy, 1-3; 2006).

Historical Antecedents

The history of Right to Information could be traced back to Sweden when it introduced a freedom of information law in 1766. During the second half of the twentieth century, the Right to Information became a powerful human rights movement. The United Nations recognized the Freedom of Information as a fundamental right. In 1946, at its first session, the UN General Assembly adopted Resolution 59(1), which stated "freedom of information is a fundamental human right and the touch stone of all the freedoms to which the UN is consecrated". The international Institutions through different resolutions—the Universal Declaration of Human Rights, the International Covenant on Civil and Political Rights, the European Convention on Human Rights, the African Charter on Human and People's Rights also contained an inherent component of Right to Information that has been legally guaranteed. The UDHR states: " Every one has the right to freedom of opinions and expression; this right includes freedom to hold opinions without interference, and to seek, receive and impart information and ideas through any media and regardless of frontiers" (Article 19). The protection and exercise of these rights are essential components of a democratic society.

The International Covenant on Civil and Political Rights provides: Everyone shall have the right to freedom of expression: this right shall include freedom to seek, receive and impart information and ideas of all kinds, regardless of frontiers, either orally, in writing or in print, in the form of art, or through any other media of his choice. [(Article 19 (2)]. The exercise of freedom of opinion and expression 'carries with it special duties and responsibilities and may thus be ' subject to certain restrictions but these shall be such as provided by law and are necessary for the respect of the rights and reputation of others, for the protection of national security or public order or public health or morals.

Thereafter the right to information has gained wide recognition at global level. In many commonwealth countries like Canada, Australia and New Zealand the concept of secrecy has lost relevance and invisible government has become obsolete in this age of liberalization and globalization. Finland enacted the Freedom of Information Legislation in 1951. The United States of America enacted its Freedom of Information Act in 1966, followed by Denmark and Norway in 1970.

In 1980, the Commonwealth Law Ministers meeting in Barbados stated that, 'is Public participation in the democratic and governmental process was at its most meaningful when citizens had adequate access to official information'. The commonwealth has taken a number of significant steps to elaborate on the content of this right. Canada enacted its Right to Information Act in 1982 and South Africa in 1966. Ireland enacted Freedom of Information Act in 1997, which came into force in 1998. In March 1999, the Commonwealth Expert Group meeting in London adopted a document setting out a number of guidelines on the right to know and freedom of information as a human right, including the following: Freedom of Information should be guaranteed as a legal and enforceable right permitting every individual to obtain records and information held by the executive, the legislative and the judicial arms of the state, as well as any government owned corporation or any other body carrying out public functions. These principles and guidelines were endorsed later at the Commonwealth Heads of Government Meeting in November 1999 (Reddy, 79: 2006). In Bulgaria the Access Information Act was enacted in June 2000, so also in Britain and Scotland in 2002.

The Freedom of Information Legislation in developed democracies have three fundamental features :

(i) a legal right of access to government records without a demonstrated need to know.
(ii) specific exemptions to protect national security, personal privacy, law enforcement and the like, and
(iii) where access is refused, a right of appeal lies independent of government officials (Bell and Watchirs, 297: 1998).

The collapse of authoritarian states and emergence of new democracies provided a new sense on the right to be informed among the people. The right to information has long proven to be a key component of a healthy democracy because it empowers citizens with the right to demand what activities and decisions are being made in their name. The demand for the people's right to information stems from long standing collective action against arbitrariness and corruption by the agencies of state that have an immediate and grave impact on issues related to survival and dignity particularly of those belonging to the most underprivileged and marginalized sections of the population. In the course of mobilization and coming together, the building of solidarities depends critically on process of democratic governance within movements and equal participation of all people affected by the denial of right (Kalpana, 17: 2006). Right to Information is redefining relationship between the government and citizens. There are no effective systems within governance, which could hold government officials accountable. With the Right to Information to be a International concern in contemporary times, different countries are increasingly incorporating it in their national policies.

Freedom of information should be guaranteed as a legal and enforceable right permitting every individual to obtain records and information held by the executive, the legislative and the judicial arms of the state, as well as any government owned corporation and any other body carrying out public functions. These principles and guidelines were endorsed later at the Commonwealth Heads of Government Meeting in November 1999 (Reddy, 79: 2006).

Right to Information : Evolution and Growth in India

Some of the major ills of the contemporary system of administration are corruption, secrecy, bureaucratic red tapism, centralized decision-making etc., where the citizen hardly acquires any freedom to express his voice or access the official domain. As a result, citizen remains as a mere receiver in the hands of the ruler. As against this development administration puts emphasis on positive 'action and activities' of the officials. It basically raises voice against the over-bureaucratic and non-cooperative attitudes of the office bearers, particularly their 'Culture of Secrecy'. In fact, as a form of new social revolution, the Right to Information Movement has emerged to address the specific issues confined to participatory democracy more particularly, peoples' right over information, transparency, accountability and social justice (Mishra and Mishra, 388: 2006).

The Constitution of India, though in Part III does not explicitly guarantee the right to information to the citizens, in Article 19(1) provides for the right to freedom and expression. The right to know, 'receive and impart information' has been recognized within the freedom of speech and expression by the judiciary activism. Right to know is as fundamental as the right to freedom of speech and expression. Right to Information flows from giving a meaningful and constructive interpretation of Article 19. The

Supreme Court of India in its various rulings made it clear that the fundamental rights guarantee the individual's right to information.

In the case of State of UP *Vs.* Raj Narain Mathew, J. the Supreme Court stated "In a government of responsibility like ours, where all the agents of the public must be responsible for their conduct, there can be but few secrets. The people of this country have a right to know every public act, everything that is done in a public way, by their public functionaries. They are entitled to know the particulars of every public transaction in all its bearing. The right to know, which is derived from the concept of freedom of speech, though not absolute, it is a factor which should make one way, when secrecy is claimed for transactions, which can, at any rate, have no repercussion on public security. To cover with veil of secrecy, the common routine business is not in the interest of the public. Such secrecy can seldom be legitimately desired. It is generally desired for the purpose of parties and politics or personal self-interest or bureaucratic routine. The responsibility of officials to explain and to justify their acts in the chief safeguard against oppression and corruption (1979, 4 Sec. 428, 453, Para 74).

The Supreme Court of India in S.P.Gupta *Vs.* Union of India, decided by Seven Judge Bench, added a fresh, liberal dimension to the need for disclosure in matters relating to public affairs. In the instant case it was held that in regard to the functioning of Government, disclosure of information must be ordinary rule while secrecy must be an exception, justifiable only when it is demanded by the requirement of public interest. It was further held that the disclosure of documents relating to the affairs of the State involves two competing dimensions of public interest, namely the right of the citizen to obtain disclosure of information, which connects with the right of the state of protecting the information relating to its crucial affairs. In addition it was also held that in deciding whether or not a disclosure of the contents of a particular document, a judge must balance the competing interests and make his final decision depending upon the particular facts involved in each individual case. It is important to note that it was conceded that there are certain classes of documents which are necessarily required to be protected such as cabinet minutes, documents concerning the national safety, documents which affect diplomatic relations or relate to state secrets of the highest importance and the like in respect of which Court would ordinarily uphold government's claim of privilege. However, even these documents have to be tested against the basic guiding principle, which is that wherever it is clearly contrary to the public interest for documents to be disclosed, then it is in law immune from disclosure (1981 Spp. Scc. 87, Para 73 and 74 of pp.284-286).

In Dinesh Trivedi *Vs.* Union of India the Supreme Court while making a reference to State of UP *Vs.* Raj Narain and S.P. Gupta *Vs.* Union of India held that in modern constitutional democracies, it is axiomatic that citizens have a right to know about the affairs of the government which having been elected by them, seeks to formulate social policies of governance aimed at their welfare. Further Article 21 of the Constitution guarantees to every citizen the right to life and personal liberty. The citizens cannot exercise this right to protect their lives unless they are informed about threats to their lives, the measures being taken by the concerned authorities and the measures available to them. Without this, information right becomes totally meaningless. Bhopal gas tragedy is a living example wherein many lives could have been saved provided people living near the plan site were provided complete information about the hazards of the plant and how they can protect themselves from the MIC Gas (Chadah, 7: 2006).

In India, the first political commitment to the citizen's right to information began on the eve of the Lok Sabha elections in 1977 as a corollary to public resentment against suppression of information, press censorship and abuse of authority during the National Emergency of 1975-77. In its election manifesto of the 1977, the Janata Party, founded by Lok Nayak Jaya Prakash Narain promised "an open government", and declared that it would not "misuse the intelligence services and governmental authority for personal and partisan ends". Pursuant to this commitment, the Janata Government headed by Morarji Desai constituted a working group in 1977 to examine as to whether the Official Secrets Act, 1923 could be modified so as to facilitate greater flow of information to the public. The working group consisting of officials from the Cabinet Secretariat and the Ministries of Home Affairs, Finance and Defence recommended that the Act of 1923 should be retained without change. This 'no change' recommendation was far from popular expectations. The very composition of the group, however, was indicative to the kinds of recommendation made by it. Bureaucracy by its nature thrives in secrecy, and hence, any other kind of recommendation would have been an exception. The matter ultimately went back to 1923 as it was intended to regulate its recommendation system with "We, the people of India" along the network of the Colonial Official Secrets Act (Maheswari, 126-27: 1980).

Again in 1989, the National Front Government renewed commitment to this right. It offered to amend the Constitution to "ensure the citizen's right to information" in addition to amend suitably the Official Secret Act, 1923. In this context, the then Prime Minister, V.P. Singh, in his first broadcast to the nation in December 1989 said, "We will have to increase access to information. If the government function in full public view, wrong doings will be minimised. To this end, Official Secrets Act will be amended and we will make the functioning more transparent. Right to Information will be enshrined in our Constitution". But the government lived short to realize its dream.

Further initiatives for strengthening the right to information in India were also taken in early 1990s. For instance, on 2nd December 1994, a grass root organization namely Mazdoor Kisan Shakti Sangathan (MKSS) working in Rajsathan held the first *Jan Sunwai* (Public Hearing) at Kot Kirana in Pali District. This public hearing focussed on the false entries in muster rolls and corruption in development works. The bills, vouchers and muster rolls were read out in public and the people were outraged when they heard the amount of money that had been fully spent on them as per records. The daily wagers were never given the amounts claimed in the muster rolls (Menon, 10: 2004). The MKSS's campaign demanded transparency of official records, a social audit of government spending, and a redressal machinery for people who had not been given their due.

Also the National Campaign for People's Right to Information formed in the late 1990s became a broad based platform for action. As the campaign gathered momentum, it became clear that the right to information had to be legally enforceable. In 1996, the Press Council of India drew up the first major draft legislation on the right to information. The draft affirmed the right of every citizen to information from any public body and also provided for penalty clauses for defaulting authorities. Public body included not only the state, but also all privately owned undertaking, non-statutory authorities, companies and other bodies whose activities affect the public interest. It asserted that information that cannot be denied to Parliament or State Legislatures cannot be denied to a citizen either.

In 1997 the Government of India decided to introduce the Freedom of Information Bill. In the same year, a conference of Chief Ministers resolved that the Central and State governments would work together on transparency and the Right to Information. Consequently, the Central Government agreed to take immediate steps for introducing the same, along with amendment to the Official Secrets Act and the Indian Evidence Act. The National Democratic Alliance

Government formed in 1998 declared, "Our first commitment to the people is to give a stable, honest, transparent, and efficient government capable of accomplishing all-round development. For this the government shall introduce time-bound programme of needed administrative reforms". Finally, the NDA Government introduced the Freedom of Information Bill 2000 in the Parliament in view of the growing recognition and demands from various sectors for Right to Information. Due to various controversies the Freedom of Information Bill 2002 could not be introduced.

Right to Information Act 2005

The Right to Information Act 2005 is a comprehensive legislation that confers statutory rights on citizen for seeking information from public authorities. The Act seeks to ensure the following-

- Maximum disclosure and minimum exemptions,
- Consistent with constitutional provisions,
- An effective mechanism for access to information and disclosure by authorities, and
- Penalties for failure to provide information as per the law.

With these objectives the Right to Information Bill was tabled in Parliament on December 23 2004, which was passed on 12th May 2005 and received President's assent on 15th June 2005.

Key Provisions of the Right to Information Act, 2005

The Preamble of the Right to Information Act speaks of a practical regime of right to information for citizens to secure access to information under the control of public authorities, in order to promote transparency and accountability in the working of every public authority. The Act extends to whole of India except the State of Jammu and Kashmir. [Section 1(2)].

Meaning

"Information" means any material in any form, including records, documents, memos, e-mails, opinions, advices, press releases, circulars, orders, log books, contracts, reports, papers, samples, models, data material held in any electronic form and information relating to any private body which can be accessed by a public authority under any other law for the time being in force [Section 2(f)]. "Public authority" means any authority or body or institution of self-government established or constituted –

(a) By or under the Constitution.
(b) By any other law made by Parliament.
(c) By any other law made by State Legislature.
(d) By notification issued or order made by the appropriate Government and includes :
  (i) any body owned, controlled or substantially financed,
  (ii) Non-Government Organization substantially financed, directly or indirectly by funds provided by the appropriate Government [Section 2 (h)].

Right to Information means the right accessible under this Act, which is held by or under the control of any authority and includes the right to,

(e) inspection of work, documents, records;
  (i) Taking notes, extracts or certified copies of documents or records;
  (ii) Taking certified samples of material;
  (iii) Obtaining information in the form of diskettes, floppies, tapes, video cassette or in any other electronic mode or through prints where such information is stored in a computer or in any other device [Section 2 (J)].

Every public authority is required to maintain all records duly catalogued and indexed in a manner and the form which facilitate the Right to Information under this Act and ensure that all records that are appropriate to be computerized are, within a reasonable time and subject to availability of resources, computerized and connected through a network all over the country on different systems so that access to such records is facilitated [Section 4 (a)]. The public authority has to publish the particulars of its organization, like its functions, duties and powers of different officers and employees [Section 4 (1)(b)]. It shall be a constant endeavour of every public authority to take steps to provide as much information *suo motu* to the public at regular intervals through various means of communications including internet, so that the public have minimum effect to the use of this Act to obtain information [Section 4 (2)].

Every Public Authority shall designate as many officers as the Central Public Information Officers or State Public Information Officers as the case may be in all administrative units or offices under it as may be necessary to provide information to persons requesting or the information under this Act. In addition, every public authority shall designate an officer, at each such divisional level or other sub-district level as a Central Assistant Public Information Officer or a State Assistant Public Information Officer.

The Information Commission: Its Structure

The Act under Sections 12 and 15 provides for creation of the Central Information Commission at the central level and State Information Commission at the State level. The Central Government shall by notification in the Official Gazette, constitute a body to be known as the Central Information Commission to exercise the powers conferred on, and to perform the functions assigned to it under this Act. The Central Information Commission shall consist of the Chief Information Commission and such number of Central

Information Commissioners, not exceeding ten as may be deemed necessary. The Chief Information Commissioner and the other Information Commissioners shall be appointed by the President on the recommendation of a Committee consisting of :

- The Prime Minister, who shall be the Chairperson of the Committee;
- The leader of opposition in the Lok Sabha; and
- A Union Cabinet Minister to be nominated by the Prime Minister.

The Chief Information Commissioner and other Information Commissioners shall be persons of eminence in public life with wide knowledge and experience in Law, Science, and Technology, Social Service, Management, Journalism, Mass Media or administration and governance, and hold office for a term of five years or till he attains the age of 65 years whichever is earlier. Salaries and allowances and terms and conditions of the Chief Information Officer shall be the same as that of the Chief Election Commissioner, and of the Information Officer as that of an Election Commissioner. Both of them can be removed from office by the order of the President on ground of proved misbehaviour or incapacity. They can be removed after an enquiry made by the Supreme Court on a reference made by the President.

Every State Government shall by notification in the Official Gazette, constitute State Information Commission consisting of the State Chief Information Commissioner and such number of State Information Commissioners, not exceeding ten, as may be deemed necessary. The State Chief Information Commissioner and the State Information Commissioners shall be appointed by the Governor on the recommendation of a Committee consisting of :

- The Chief Minister, who shall be the Chairperson of the Committee;

- The leader of opposition in the Legislative Assembly; and
- Cabinet Minister to be nominated by the Chief Minister.

The Information Officer, as the case may be, shall receive the applications for information or appeals under this Act for forwarding the same forthwith to the Central Public Information Officer or the State Public Information Officer. Every Central Public Information Officer or State Public Information Officer as the case may be, shall deal with requests from persons seeking information and render reasonable assistance to the persons seeking such infor-mation (Section 5).

Procedure for Obtaining Information

A person, who desires to obtain any information under this Act, shall make a request in writing or through electronic means in English or Hindi or in the official language of the area in which the application is being made, accompanying such fee as may be prescribed, to the Central Public Information Officer or State Public Information Officer of the concerned public authority or Central Assistant Public Information Officer or State Assistant Public Information Officer as the case may be [Section 6(1), a, b]. An applicant making request for information shall not be required to give any reason for requesting the information or any other personal details except those that may be necessary for contacting him [Section 6 (2)]. The particulars of the information required must be specified to be given by seeking information. The request for information must either be provided within a period of 30 days or the request be rejected for the reasons as specified in sections 8 and 9 [Section 7(1)]. The procedure for seeking information is free from the constraints of language and illiteracy.

Exemption from Disclosure of Information

The following information can be denied to the citizen :

(a) Information, disclosure of which would prejudicially affect the sovereignty and integrity of India, the security, strategic, scientific or economic interests of the state, relation with foreign state or lead to incitement of an offence;

(b) Information which has been expressly forbidden to be published by any court of law or tribunal of the disclosure of which may constitute contempt of court;

(c) Information , the disclosure of which would cause a breach of Privilege of Parliament or the State Legislature;

(d) Information including commercial confidence, trade secrets or intellectual property, the disclosure of which would harm the competitive position of a third party, unless the competent authority is satisfied that larger public interest warrants the disclosure of such information;

(e) Information available to a person in his fiduciary relationship, unless the competent authority is satisfied that the larger public interest warrants the disclosure of such information;

(f) Information received in confidence from foreign government;

(g) Information , the disclosure of which would endanger the life or physical safety of any person or identify the source of information or assistance given in confidence for law enforcement or security purposes;

(h) Information which would impede the process of investigation or apprehension or prosecution of offenders;

(i) Cabinet papers including records of deliberations of the Council of Ministers, Secretaries and other officers: provided that the decisions of Council of Ministers the reasons thereof, and the material on the basis of which the decisions were taken shall be made public after the decision has been taken and the matter is complete, or over; provided further that those matters which came under the exemptions specified in this section shall not be disclosed;

(j) Information which relates to personal information the disclosure of which has no relationship to any public activity or interest, which would cause unwarranted invasion of the privacy of the individual unless the Central Information Officer or the State Public Information Officer or the appellate authority, as the case may be, is satisfied that the larger public interest justifies the disclosure of such information; provided that the information which cannot be denied to the Parliament or a State Legislature shall not be denied to any person. (Section 8).

Without prejudice to the provision of Section 8, a Central Public Information Officer or a State Public Information Officer, as the case may be may reject a request for information where such a request for providing access would involve an infringement of copyright subsisting in a person other than the state (Section 9).

Power and Function of the Information Commission

The power and function of the Commission are specified in Section 18.

- Subject to the provision of this Act, it shall be the duty of the Central Information Commission or State Information Commission, as the case may be, to receive and inquire into a complaint from any person; who has been unable to submit a request to a Central Public Information Officer or State Public Information Officer, as the case may be, either by reason that no such officer has been appointed under this Act, or because the Central Assistant Public Information Officer, or State Assistant Public Information Officer, as the case may be has refused to accept his or her application for information or appeal under this Act for forwarding the same to the Central Public Information Officer or State Public Information Officer or Senior Officer.

- Where the Central Information Commission or State Information Commission, as the case may be, is satisfied that there are reasonable grounds to inquire into the matter, it may initiate an inquiry in respect thereof.
- The Central Information Commission or State Information Commission, as the case may be, shall while inquiry into any matter under this section have the same powers as are vested in a Civil Court.
- Notwithstanding anything contained in any other Act of Parliament or State Legislature, as the case may be, the Central Information Commission or the State Information Commission, as the case may be, may, during the inquiry of any complaint under this Act, examine any record to which this Act applies which is under the control of the public authority, and no such record may be withheld from it on any ground.

Appeal

The Act provides for two stages of appeals under Section 19. At first stage the appeal lies against the decision of the Central Public Information Officer or the State Public Information Officer. If the person does not receive a decision within thirty days from the expiry of such period or from the receipt of such a decision prefer an appeal to officer who is senior in rank to the Central Public Information Officer or State Public Information Officer [Section 19(1)].

When an appeal is referred against an order made by a Central Public Information Officer or a State Public Information Officer, as the case may be, to disclose third party information, the appeal by the concerned third party shall be made within thirty days from the date of the order.

A second appeal against the decision of the appellate authority in the first appeal to the Central Information Commission or the State Information Commission shall lie within ninety days from the date on which the decision should have been made or was actually received. Provided that the Central Information Commission or the State Information Commission, as the case may be, may admit the appeal after the expiry of the period of ninety days if it is satisfied that the appellant was prevented by sufficient cause from filing the appeal in time [Section 19(3)].

Penalties

The Commission can impose penalties on the Central Public Information Office or the State Public Information Officer as the case may be if they have, without any reasonable cause, refused to receive an application for information or has not furnished information within the time specified under Sub-section (1) of Section 7 or malafidely denied the request for information or knowingly given incorrect, incomplete or misleading information or destroyed information which was the subject of the request or obstructed in any manner in furnishing the information, it shall impose a penalty of two hundred and fifty rupees each day from the date the application is received to the date of information is furnished. However, the total amount of such penalty shall not exceed twenty-five thousand rupees [Section 20(1)]. In certain cases the Commission is empowered to recommend disciplinary action against the erring information officers [Section 20(2)].

Conclusion

A democratic culture is synonymous with participation, openness, transparency and good governance. The Right to Information Act is to promote transparency and accountability in governance by enabling the citizen to have effective access to information and thus to have the ability to question and correct the process of governance. The Act recognizes that democracy requires an informed citizenry which in turn thrives on transparency of information . It also seeks to check corruption and to hold governments and their instrumentalities accountable to the governed. It seeks to curb the antidemocratic attitude and activities of the public authorities. If the government expects its citizens to take their own initiatives to make themselves informed, then it is obligatory and imperative on the part of the government to create conducive and convenient conditions whereby its citizens feel encouraged to seek information. This is essentially a citizen fundamental right. The Constitution of India and important international human rights instruments have recognized its importance. Citizens Right to Information is a necessary prerequisite for a successful democracy because transparency, accountability and good governance cannot be ensured without the effective implementation of the Right to Information Act.

REFERENCES

Bell, Robin and Watchirs, Helen (1988): "Freedom of Information: The Commonwealth Experience". *Australian Journal of Public Administration*, Vol. XL.VII (4), December.

Kalpana, Kannabiran (2006): "Access, Diversity and Representation", *Yojana*, January.

Mishra, B.K. and Mishra, A.K. (2006): "Right to Information: Needs for decentralization and procedural simplification", *Social Action*, Vol. 56, No. 4, Dec.

Guha Roy, Jaytilak (2006): "Right to Information Initiatives and Impact", *Indian Journal of Public Administration,* New Delhi.

Chadah, Sapna (2006): "Right to Information Regime in India: A Critical Appraisal", *The Indian Journal of Public Administration,* Vol. LII, No.1., January-March.

Reddy, G. Gopal (2006):"The Right to Information : An Analysis", *Punjab Journal of Politics,* Vol. XXX., No.1

Maheshwari, Shriram 1980): Secrecy in Government of India in T.N. Chaturvedi (ed), *Secrecy in Government,* Indian Institute of Public Administration.

Menon, Girish, (2004): Civil Society: Potential and Opportunities, *Empower. Org.* Vol. I Issue January.

Feinberg, Latte E. (1986): "Managing the Freedom of Information Act and Federal Information Policy", *Public Administrative Review,* Nov.-Dec.

Jenkins, Rob and Goetz, A.M. (1999): "Accounts and Accountability; Theoretical Implications of the Right to Information Movement in India: *Third World Quarterly,* 20 (3).

Right to Information Act, 2005.

14 Education on Human Rights
An Analysis

Sujan Singh*

1. Introduction

Human Rights is an important topic today in academics and public debate. Many seminars, symposia and publications on the topic are available in the form of books, periodicals, special issues of journals. The topic is one of the most fashioned ones. The media is also focussing on this important area of social problems. The judiciary has also not remained behind. Rather it has proved to be the front runner and champion in this social cause. The efforts and emphasis on human rights is also not confined to any region or a nation but is equally spread over all nations on the globe – developed, developing and even the underdeveloped. The voice of human rights, if it is loud in USA it is not so feeble in Pakistan, indicating thereby that the system of state power cannot even check the voice or sway of human rights movement. India has been acclaimed to be having a good track record of adopting human rights in its legal system.

Does too much emphasis on human rights mean all satisfactory results? Does it lead to a rosy picture of human rights protections? Certainly not. The reality of the day is "Too much emphasis — Too many violations". The newspapers point out human right violations of the individuals – may they be women, children, workers, prisoners, or even

* Reader and Head, Law Department, Guru Nanak Dev University Regional Campus, Gurdaspur, (Punjab).

the groups named migrants, minorities and other vulnerable sections of all societies.

Education is undoubtedly the single most potent remedy for making human rights a reality because 'knowledge is power' and it is 'power' that brings about change in the situations. Therefore, education of human rights has been made a right itself and has been underlined amongst the list thereof. The universities, colleges of their own and under the instructions of the University Grants Commission and the Ministry of Human Resource Development are paying particular attention to the topic of human rights as a part of curriculum in various classes and courses.

To which extent this emphasis and concern in India has been able to bring about clarity in the concept of human rights, what is the content and methodology of human rights education, what are our achievements and shortcomings and what more can be done to achieve better results are the different segments of this article by a student of law.

2. Concept of Human Rights

The concept of human rights is as old as civilization itself. It has its seeds in 'natural rights' going back to the ancient periods. But the term human rights, having surfaced in the modern period, was first used in the Charter of the United Nations.[1] The Preamble of this Charter, which was drawn up to prevent a recurrence of the destruction and suffering caused by the Second World War, by setting up the international organization called the United Nations, declared that United Nations shall also have as its object: "to reaffirm faith in fundamental human rights." Furthermore, Article 1 of the Charter stated that the purposes of United Nations shall *inter alia* be : "To achieve international co-operation ... in promoting and encouraging respect for human rights, and for fundamental freedoms for all without distinction as to race, sex, language, or religion ...."

Human rights are those minimal rights which every

individual must have against the state or other public authorities by virtue of his being a 'member of the human family,' irrespective of any other consideration.[2] These equal and inalienable rights of all members of the human family is the foundation of freedom, justice and peace in the world; and disregard and contempt for human rights have resulted in barbarous acts which have outraged the conscience of mankind.[3] Through the Declaration, the UN General Assembly proclaimed :

> "This Universal Declaration of Human Rights as a common standard of achievement for all peoples and all nations, to the end that every individual and every organ of society, keeping this declaration constantly in mind, shall strive by teaching and education to promote respect for these rights and freedoms and by progressive measures, their universal and effective recognition and observance, both among the peoples of Member States themselves and among the peoples of territories under their jurisdiction."[4]

Accordingly, the International Covenant on Civil and Political Rights and International Covenant on Economic, Social and Cultural Rights were adopted in the year 1966 and national as well as regional initiatives on the same lines were taken in the form of American Convention on Human Rights (1969), African Charter on Human Rights and Peoples' Rights (1981) and European Convention for the Protection of Human Rights and Fundamental Freedoms (1950) were put into gear. India adopted the principles of Universal Declaration in its Constitution for the reason of contemporariness, ratified the Covenants in 1979, enacted category specific laws like The Protection of Civil Rights Act (1955), The Scheduled Castes and the Scheduled Tribes (Prevention of Atrocities) Act (1989), The Commission of Sati (Prevention) Act (1987), The National Commission for

Backward Classes Act (1993), The National Commission for Safai Karamcharis Act (1993), The National Commission for Women Act (1990), The Persons with Disabilities (Equal Opportunities, Protection of Rights and Full Participation) Act (1995), The Pre-Natal Diagnostic Techniques (Regulation and Prevention of Misuse) Act (1996), National Rural Employment Guarantee Act (2005), Equal Remuneration Act (1971), Prevention of Domestic Violence Act (2006), and The National Commission for Minorities Act (1992) etc. To provide machinery and mechanism for the enforcement of human rights India enacted The Protection of Human Rights Act (1993).

The 1993 Indian Act defines human rights as: "the rights relating to life, liberty, equality and dignity of the individual guaranteed by the Constitution or embodied in the International Covenants and enforceable by Courts in India."[5]

From the above reference of human rights, in terms of its nature, it can be made out that these rights are sourced in the International Conventions and Covenants but the same should have been made a part of the national legal regime because in Austinian terms 'law is the command of the Sovereign' and sovereignty has the national character. The universal character of human rights, like its source the natural law, need to be translated to national situations and realities. Julius Stone, quoting Thomas Acquinas, outlines the nature of human rights: "Natural Law" as well as "Human Law" are spheres of "practical intellect" in which as principles have to be brought down to precepts for concrete situations."[6]

As against this usual way of looking at human rights, Professor Baxi finds social action as the golden thread in human rights. For him human rights are "Protean forms of social action assembled by convention, under a portal named human rights."[7] For the reason of a critical look, the legal genius finds haunting ambiguities in the concept of human rights, which he explains as under :

> "The very term 'human rights' remains indeed problematic. In the rights – talk, the expression often masks the attempts to reduce the plenitude of its meanings to produce a false totality. One such endeavour locates the unity of all human rights to some designated totality of sentiment such as human 'dignity', 'well-being', and 'flourishing'. Another mode invites us to speak of human rights as 'basic', suggesting that some others may be negotiable, if not dispensable at least in the short run, experienced as a horrendously long run by the violated humanity. The deprived, disadvantaged, and dispossessed may indeed find it hard to accept any justifications for the very notion of human rights that may end up in their lifetime, and even inter-generationally, as a denial of their right to be, and to remain, human. Yet another mode of totalization makes us succumb to an anthropomorphic illusion that the range of human rights is limited to human beings; the new rights to environment (or what is, somewhat inappropriately, even cruelly, called 'sustainable development') take us far beyond such a narrow notion. As descriptive ventures, such attempts at totalization of human rights reduce to a 'coherent' category the forbiddingly diverse world of actually existing human rights."[8]

The ambiguities created by the selfish interests of the nations and the twists given to meet the economic interests have changed the universal and humane character of the human rights. Professor Upendra Baxi underscores the paradigm shift in the era of liberalization and the practical extinction of humanitarian law in the post-9/11 wars when he sums up :

> "The paradigm shift from the Universal Declaration

of Human Rights to that of trade-related, market-friendly human rights, now aggravated by the concurrent forms of the 'war of terror' and the 'war on terror'."

Human Rights Education

Leaving aside the changing contours of human right models, education has been given an important place in the human rights list. Article 26 of the Universal Declaration outlines the right to education of every person while emphasizing the focus of such education as 'full development of the human personality and strong terming respect for human rights and fundamental freedoms. The Declaration provides :

"Art. 26 –

(1) Everyone has the right to education. Education shall be free at least in the elementary and fundamental stages. Technical and professional education shall be made generally available and to all on the basis of merit.
(2) Education shall be directed to the full development of the human personality and to the strengthening of respect for human rights and fundamental freedoms. It shall promote understanding, tolerance and friendship among all nations, racial or religious groups, and shall further the activities of the United Nations for the maintenance of peace.
(3) Parents have a prior right to choose the kind of education that shall be given to their children."

The Declaration recognizes the right to education of all persons and it also particularly mentions that such education curriculum must strengthen the respect for human rights and fundamental freedoms. The spirit of the Declaration regarding right to education was reiterated and adopted in the binding *International Covenant on Economic, Social and Cultural Rights*, 1966.[9]

Meeting the needs of the Covenant, Indian Constitution recognizes the right to compulsory education upto 14 years of age as a fundamental right of Indian citizens.[10] It also declares all important human rights as the Fundamental Rights or the Directive Principles of State Policy. The Constitution also recognises other human rights in the International Covenant and other instruments, even if not formally included as the constitutional or legal rights of Indians. Clause (c) of Article 51 provides for promotion of international peace and security. It reads: "The state shall endeavour to ... (c) foster respect for international law and treaty obligations in the dealings of organized peoples with one another..."[11]

Fulfilling the demands of the human right instruments, human rights have been given legal protection, they have been made enforceable rights and they have been included in the curriculum of school, college and university education in India. Education on human rights has been emphasized to the extent that of the 9 functions of the National Human Rights Commission and *mutatis mutandis* applied to State Commissions 3 relate to education of human rights by the Commission directly or through non-governmental organizations. These functions are :

"(i) Undertake and promote research in the field of human rights;
(ii) Spread human rights literacy among various sections of society and promote awareness of the safeguards available for the protection of these rights through publications, the media, seminars and other available means;
(iii) Encourage the efforts of non-governmental organizations and institutions working in the field of human rights."[12]

3. Content and Methodology

Human Rights education is being imparted in India by

schools, colleges, universities, human right commissions, and the non-governmental organizations. Newspapers are playing some role in this societal task.

Regarding the contents of human rights education, there is not much difference. The difference, if any, is regarding the possible area of coverage and the areas of emphasis depending upon the nature of the course where such instruction is being imparted. At the school level human rights find a place in civics or social studies at the surface level, in humanities undergraduate students study human rights as a part of political theory and as rights under the Constitution of India. The commerce students get the knowledge of human rights as are available to workers, women and children at the workplace as a part of labour laws. The science students have relatively little information about the human rights except as professionals *e.g.* doctors have to know human right of health and medical aid[13] available to people of the land. The students of law and P.G. students in Political Science study human rights as universal rights contained in natural law ideology of inalienable rights, the constitutional rights and those contained in International Covenants and Conventions.

The major portion of human rights curriculum revolves around Universal Declaration, International Covenant on Civil and Political Rights and the International Covenant on Economic, Social and Cultural Rights. Only little emphasis is laid on the human rights as a part of the national legal regime, its enforcement and social actions and movements creating such rights and helpful in their successful implementation.

Methodology for instruction of human rights is traditional class room teaching adopting lecture method, seminar paper presentations and published articles in newspapers and periodicals. Though Human Rights Commissions owe a duty to encourage the non-governmental organizations yet they find little recognition and attract little attention of the

Commissions and Institutions engaged in human rights education and research. Case studies and Social Actions as the means of education are little known at the time when even class discussions are a rare phenomenon in our education.

4. Achievements and Shortcomings

In an effort to prepare a balance sheet of human rights in general and their education in particular, we note the important achievements that human rights have become a popular term, known to all peoples and pupils. Schools, colleges and universities in India are laying emphasis on adopting human rights as the compulsory portion in the curriculums. The media has also played some role in highlighting human right violations. The result is production of a good amount of literature on human rights, adoption of provisions under the Declaration, Covenants and Conventions in the Constitution of India[14] and the laws of the land pertaining to women, children, workers, prisoners, disabled and minorities. The creation of National and State Human Rights Commissions as the statutory bodies and assigned with well-defined functions has contributed to provide force and momentum to the cause of protecting human right violations at the hands of the state authorities. The judiciary in India deserves an applause for having played a pro-active role on the front of human rights. The invention of a remedy in Public Interest Litigation (PIL), relaxing the *locus standi* principle has served the cause of human rights protection of the deprived, weak and vulnerable sections of the Indian society. It has encouraged the social actions at the hands of non-governmental organizations. NGOs though not in sufficient numbers and strength, have appeared on the scene and some of them like People's Union for Civil Liberties, People's Union for Democratic Rights, SAHELI, *Bandhua Mukti Morcha,* Consumer Education and Research Centre, CRY and public-spirited persons like M.C. Mehta have championed the cause of human rights protection with the support of higher judiciary in India. The Supreme Court of India has also contributed to extend the cantours of the enforceable human rights by way of declaring some provisions in the Directive Principles as the Fundamental Rights of the Indian citizens[15] and also accepting that all the human rights contained in the international instruments, to which India is a party, are enforceable rights in the spirit of Article 51 (c).[16]

Achievements though many on the human rights front, these are not sufficient and satisfactory on many counts.

First and foremost, the concept of human rights needs to be saved from mutilation. Understandably human rights need to be adapted and adopted in its changing form with the change in the society. It is also accepted without doubt that human rights are available to all people and all sections of societies without any distinctions and discriminations. But in this exercise of adaptation, the basic spirit of human rights cannot be lost sight of. And the basic characteristic of these rights, like their source natural rights, is that they are the product of a higher source – the unbiased human reason. These rights are the guiding principles for the national laws and not *vice versa*. The aim of these superior rights is to serve the purpose of humanity as a step towards promoting world peace and progress. The human rights, though unbiased, recognize the focus and a leaning towards the deprived, vulnerable, low and the lost in societies. Therefore, the narrow interests of the nations and ruling groups cannot be allowed to kill the spirit of human rights in the name of development and progress. A satisfactory balance of human rights of various sections in the society, as their interests and freedoms, is being disturbed by some powerful nations, guiding the economies and also the ideologies of many nations and their groups.

The second shortfall in the study material of human rights is the absence of movements and social actions that led to the achievement of human rights. In the same area, it is also ignored that human rights are legal rights, which need a national support and substance. Therefore, to be conversant with human rights, the students and their teachers are required to understand not only the international documents and their provisions but also the national laws adopting those rights and providing for their enforcement because "human rights without effective implementation are shadows without substance."[17]

The education of human rights is based on ideology and not action. Human rights need to be realised and these are bound to be deprived. Therefore, action part of these rights, to make them realities of social life, needs to be inculcated and imparted to the students. For this purpose, social actions, jointly by the teachers and students are needed.[18] Such initiatives will also create more NGOs, which are needed to protect and promote human rights as Justice P.N. Bhagwati observed : "We can escape from this paradox and break the vicious circle by organising the poor."[19]

Conclusion

The human rights are the inalienable rights emanating from a superior source having universal character but needed to be adopted in the national legal regimes as the enforceable laws. Social actions are in the background of such rights aimed at all round development of human beings and therewith of their societies. Therefore, the human rights commissions and the NGOs are required to adopt a proactive approach for the protection and promotion of human rights. Education of human rights with the methodology of case studies of social action groups and practice of such efforts can keep the *mashal* burning and the movement of human rights marching.

NOTES

1. Adopted after the Second World War at San Franisco on June 25, 1945 and ratified by a majority of its signatories in October that year.

2. Basu, Durga Dass, (2003), *Human Rights in Constitutional Law*, Wadhwa & Company, Nagpur, p. 8.
3. *Universal Declaration of Human Rights* (1948), The Preamble.
4. *Ibid.*
5. *The Protection of Human Rights Act*, 1993, Section 2(1) (d).
6. Stone, Julius (2004), *Human Law and Human Justice*, Universal Law Publishing Co. Pvt.Ltd., Delhi, p. 221.
7. Baxi, Upendra (2006), *The Future of Human Rights*, Oxford University Press, p. xiii.
8. *Ibid.*, pp. 10-11.
9. Ratified by India in the year 1979. Article 13 of the Covenant gives a detailed description of right to education.
10. Article 21-A introduced by Amendment Act of 2002. Before this, the Supreme Court of India declared right to elementary education as a fundamental right being included in the right to life enshrined under Article 21. The cases were: *Mohini Jain* v. *State of Karnataka*, AIR 1992 SC 1858 and *Uni Krishanan* v. *State of AP*, AIR 1993, SC 2178.
11. This article has been relied upon to introduce and implement various international instruments, particularly the Declaration and two Covenants. The Apex Court has consistently held that by virtue of this Article international instruments, particularly those to which India is a party, become part of Indian law so long as they are not inconsistent with it. Therefore, they can be very well relied upon and enforced. For reference the cases are: *Prem Shankar Shukla* v. *Delhi Administration*, AIR 1980 SC 1535. *Sheela Barse* v. *Secretary Children's Aid Society*, (1987), 3 SCC 50; *Viskakha* v. *State of Rajasthan*, (1997) 6 SCC 24; *People's Union for Civil Liberties* v. *Union of India*, (1997) 3 SCC 433; DK Basu *v.* State of WB, (1997) 1 SCC 416.
12. Clauses (g), (h) and (i) of Section 12.
13. *Paschim Banga Khet Mazdoor Samiti* v. *State of West Bengal*, (1996) 4 SCC 37.
14. Articles 14, 15, 16 (1), 19 (1) (a), 19 (1) (b), 19 (1) (d) and (e), 20 (1), 20 (2), 20(3), 21, 22, 23, and 25 of the Constitution as Fundamental Rights find a place in the Covenant on Civil and Political Rights with Articles 14(1), 26, 25(c), 19(1) and 19 (2), 21, 22(1), 12(1), 15(1), 14(7), 14(3) (g), 6(1) and 9 (1), 9(2), 9 (3) & 9 (4), 8 (3) and 18 (1). Similarly Articles 21-A, 39(d), 39 (f), 41, 42, 43, 45 and 47 are in the International Covenant on Economic, Social and Cultural Rights.

15. *Supra* note 10.
16. *Supra* note 11.
17. Professor Humphrey quoted by Richard B. Lillich, "Civil Liberties' in Thedor Meron (ed.), *Human Rights in International Law: Legal and Policy Issues*, Vol. I, Clarenden Press, p. 134.
18. Professor Upendra Baxi undertook such actions while in Delhi University.
19. Quoted by Dr. Ramesh K. Tilak, (1998), "NGO's and Their Role in Promotion and Protection of Human Rights," *Journal of the Institute of Human Rights*, Vol. I, No. 1.

15 Equal Opportunities for Deprived Groups

Need for Fresh Thinking

N.R. Madhava Menon

In the Indian context it is not necessary to canvass affirmative action for deprived groups because it is a Constitutional mandate for the implementation of which there are positive obligations put on the State. This includes not only prohibition of discrimination [Art.15(1)], but also creation of equality promoting conditions including reservation of seats in educational institutions [Art.15(4) and (5)]. Besides, several provisions in Part IV of the Constitution directs the State to remove inequalities in status, facilities and opportunities not only amongst individuals but also amongst groups of people residing in different areas or engaged in different occupations [Art. 38(2) read with Articles 39, 41, 45, 46]. This is the affirmative action agenda set by the Constitution itself towards fulfilment of the equal opportunity guarantee in respect of deprived groups of citizens.

Need for a Neutral Mechanism

The question which requires discussion, therefore, is not so much about the desirability or legitimacy of affirmative action measures in favour of certain disadvantaged groups; rather, it is about the criteria for determining the beneficiary groups, the process of their selection and the extent of benefits to be given to overcome the disadvantages and consequent denial of equal opportunities. It is here vested interests have developed, reverse discrimination tended to appear, and politics got to play a dubious role distorting the Constitutional balance of equality and freedom. If affirmative action measures were to succeed in rendering social justice to the deprived groups, Parliament should constitute an independent statutory watchdog body to advise the government on implementing equal opportunity schemes fairly and efficiently without creating new inequalities. Justice should not only be done but seen to have been done by all the affected groups. Experience shows that there is no alternative to recognizing the reality of the historical burden of direct and indirect discrimination as well as extreme forms of deprivation. Wisdom lies in developing a credible mechanism independent of government for gathering and publishing hard evidence about persisting inequalities and advocating remedial action to restore equality of opportunity to such groups without compromising the right to equality of other sections of society.

Groups cannot be predetermined any more on the basis of caste identities alone as changes occur constantly and intra-group inequalities develop simultaneously. The evidence gathered on one occasion may soon become irrelevant to demonstrate inequality or discrimination in a different situation. Therefore, equalization of opportunities is a process which require professional analysis of a wide range of factors which do not allow preconceived ideas to take the place of quantitative and qualitative data on status and facilities. It is to make good this data deficit in the determination of beneficiaries of affirmative action and to design proactive creation of conditions within the Constitutional Scheme that a professional mechanism capable of assembling and evaluating evidence is needed in the present context. A duly empowered Equal Opportunity Commission is an obvious answer to the challenges ahead.

Given the vast number who are in the disadvantaged

category and the complex nature of disabilities they have been suffering from, it is not easy to bring about equality of opportunity through rule of law alone. Entrenched attitudes and conventional mindsets constitute a major constraint in directed social change. Authoritarian and coercive methods are counter-productive in democratic societies. Social engineering through democratic processes has to necessarily acknowledge the bonds of groups, identities and seek incremental and consensual changes. The proposed Equal Opportunity Commission is, therefore, to be structured as a research body capable of evidence-based advocacy on benefits and beneficiaries for purposes of affirmative action.

Reservation alone does not Guarantee Equality in Access

It is unfortunate that even after 60 years of independence, only 9 per cent of the eligible age group of youth find their way into higher education in India. The National Knowledge Commission recommended to increase the gross enrolment ratio to 20 per cent in the medium term by doubling the scale of higher education institutions in the next decade with constant improvement in standards to meet the needs of a knowledge society. This has tremendous implications to access, quality, ownership, control and accountability in higher education. Reservation of seats in higher education is a useful tool to provide access to certain disadvantaged groups; but it can happen only with some trade-offs which, some people argue is not sustainable with merit and equality for all. This is also the rationale for the Supreme Court in capping reservations at 50 per cent.

Access is important for equality and inclusive, sustainable growth in plural societies. By increasing investment and expanding institutional infrastructure there can be substantial increase in access. This is reportedly the strategy of the Eleventh Five Year Plan. Today 40 per cent of all higher education institutions and a third of all enrolment in them are in the private sector. According to one estimate, 84 per cent of management institutes, 64 per cent of engineering colleges and 75 per cent of medical schools in the country are under private managements. Many of them are minority institutions where the scope of governmental intervention on behalf of deprived groups is limited in scope. Laws have recently been amended to compel private sector educational institutions, aided or unaided by governments, to follow official policies on reservation of seats, quantum of fees and quality standards. The issue has led to acrimonious debates on the freedom of private enterprise and the scope of government controls. While public-private partnership in higher education is universally accepted, the relative role and responsibilities of the two are not yet settled. In this context, one view is to increase user charges to allow recovery of costs and profit with the government undertaking to pay the costs of education of disadvantaged sections.

Access, however, is not the only issue posing challenges in higher education. Quality and equality have to go together if higher education is to serve its purpose to individuals and to society. Compromising quality to accommodate equality is not a policy which can be sustained in a highly competitive knowledge society of the future. Educated unemployment in large scale co-existing with acute shortage of skilled manpower in different sectors of the economy is a phenomenon now facing the country. Perhaps this is part of the reason why every year over a lakh and fifty thousand students seek admissions in higher education institutions abroad spending over a billion dollars. How to get that money invested in India to build world class institutes is an issue seeking an answer from educational planners and affirmative action advocates today.

By increasing access through reservation or otherwise, the object of affirmative action to deprived groups will not get resolved unless the quality of education imparted is raised in content and methods. This is a function government bureaucracies cannot perform to the advantage of better education. Rigid regulatory frameworks kill initiatives, investment and innovation. Industry-academic linkages are essential for improving employability of graduates and development of markets while contributing to knowledge creation. If the existing system of evaluation and accreditation is to be believed, the country has very few globally comparable institutions of higher learning; there are some which are potentially capable of reaching world standards and a vast majority which are nothing more than degree-manufacturing centres with little or no contribution to the objectives of higher education. Affirmative action can help the disadvantaged groups only if the quality of education they get is comparable to that available to others. Therefore, strategies on affirmative action should go along with quality-enhancing measures across all sectors of higher education.

Designing and Implementing Affirmative Action Schemes

Equality and affirmative action are subjects largely left to the legislature and the executive under the Constitutional Scheme as they envisage a range of positive actions supported by budgetary resources. Only in respect of the limited sphere of 'anti-discrimination[1], that the implementation of the equality guarantee got transferred to the Courts from the legislature. But when Courts assumed a primary role in implementing the right to equality through public interest litigation, it tried to stretch the anti-discrimination principle (persons similarly situated must be treated the same way) to comprehend equality of results or outcomes, rather unsuccessfully. The judicial process lacks the necessary tools to measure inequality in terms of opportunities or outcomes. The empirical dimensions of social disadvantage of groups deserving affirmative action need to be established by neutral decision-making mechanisms on the basis of their superior fact finding capacities. The judicial discourses in many of the Indira Sawhney (Mandal Case) opinions are centered around the principles and procedures by which systemic disadvantage formula is applied to determine groups for special treatment. This problem does not arise in respect of Scheduled Castes and Scheduled Tribes categories as their disadvantage was highly visible and widely acknowledged even while the constitutional provisions on equality were constructed. That is why in Indra Sawhney Case, one Judge even declared that in order to qualify for special treatment, the social disadvantage claimed by a group should be of the same nature as that suffered by the Scheduled Castes. In any case, systemic social disadvantage continues to be the guiding principle to determine the beneficiaries of affirmative action.

In the beginning, selection of groups to receive preferential treatment was left largely to State governments. Courts have repeatedly struck down schemes that seemed primarily to benefit politically powerful groups or that were based on prejudice, without any empirical data to support such assumptions. It was only in 1990s the emphasis shifted to facts rather than assumptions. This is partly a contribution of the Mandal Commission and the debates that followed its implementation. To conclude, one may submit the following propositions for consideration in the matter of affirmative action in higher education :

(1) In the context of continued prevalence of inequality, discrimination and denial of equal opportunities, there is need for more and varied affirmative action measures to implement the constitutional mandate,
(2) Equality guarantee is not to be confined to the anti-discrimination principle of "equals to be treated equally". Substantive and not merely formal equality is what is guaranteed. This envisages equality that promotes equal opportunities and, in the long run, equal outcomes. Legislature and Executive have obligations in this regard stipulated in the Directive Principles of State Policy. The basic philosophy of

affirmative action is nothing but the rationale of a just and fair social order. Affirmative action is not an exception to equality of treatment, but a method of providing it, by enabling all individuals to perform to their full potentials.

(3) The equality jurisprudence developed over the years does not follow the colour blind approach in the matter of pursuing the object to secure a society free of all distinctions based on caste, religion, sex etc. However, it permits as a necessary means to that end, caste-based remedial programmes on conditions that they are scientifically designed, limited in scope and self-liquidating over time.

(4) The most difficult problem in the sphere of affirmative action has been the identification of beneficiaries. The initial effort was structured in terms of caste. In the case of Scheduled Castes, the Constitution itself provided the methodology of identification. In the case of "Other Backward Classes", the quick and ready method of identification adopted by political parties in different States were shot down by Courts on the ground of unfair discrimination. Evidence-based identification using criteria of systemic disadvantage is what is needed for which a neutral body is now recommended. This is what the proposed Equal Opportunity Commission is expected to undertake if and when established.

(5) There is evidence to suggest that the relatively better-offs in the preferred groups appropriate most of the benefits. Again, based on facts, there is need to re-define the preferred groups in order to distribute the benefits to the most deserving among the selected groups.

(6) There is also evidence to suggest that the beneficiaries could not reach higher levels of education and

employment despite reservation because of systemic factors. This is where affirmative action has to go beyond reservation and innovate new strategies for facilitating equal opportunity facilities to deprived groups.

(7) All affirmative action measures to be acceptable have to be seen to be self-liquidating to save itself from the compulsions of electoral politics inevitable in democratic societies. Towards that end, all existing strategies should be reassessed in the light of better knowledge of social reality now available from social and behavioural sciences. Again this is a function that the EOC can profitably undertake.

(8) Equality jurisprudence is slowly shifting its emphasis from non-discrimination to equal opportunity. Simultaneously there is shift from concepts to facts to guide policies and programmes. Both these trends are welcome developments for the affirmative action agenda to develop a focus on equalizing conditions of existence for improving equal prospects of success. In the process, there is greater attention given to social conditions of group existence than equality conceived as individual rights. The affirmative action debate uses the rationale of systemic group disadvantage principle rather than individualised non-discrimination principle. The problem being addressed is of structural inequalities against which individuals are relatively helpless. It is more a question of fairness and social justice in governance rather than just a claim for non-discrimination.

16 Judicial Activism and Protection of Human Rights in India

Ashutosh Pandey

The concept of Human Rights emerged out of mankind's reasoning capacity and sensitive conscience. From their nature, human rights which are often characterized as ' basic' or 'fundamental' can hardly be considered as having been 'created' at any given moment. Thus, human rights consti-tute the vital concern of the mankind. The history of mankind has been closely associated with the struggle of individual against injustice, exploitation and humiliation. The recognition, first at national and later at international level, of human rights is one of the most remarkable mani-festations of this struggle. Recognition, protection and implementation of human rights are a very important and complicated issue because there is no agreed definition and understanding of the term 'human rights'. It is a dynamic concept and it endeavours to adopt itself to the changing historical needs. For this reason, the definition and under-standing of human rights depends upon the prevalent conditions in any given society at any time, and attaining ever new dimensions with the march of history.

The concept of human rights has evolved originally in the field of domestic legislation as in the Magna Carta in England, the Bill of Rights in the U.S. Constitution and the Declaration of Rights of Man in France[1]. Although ancient Indian wisdom has emphasized human rights consciousness through the notion of *dharma* (duty) and *danda* (punishment) which regulated the government of state and its citizens.

However, one of the first examples of international recognition of human rights and protection occurred in the 'minorities treaties' concluded after the First World War (Treaty of Versailles – Articles 86 and 93) which guaranteed life, liberty and freedom of religion to all inhabitants of the territories concerned.

Though, the first universal and comprehensive recognition of 'human rights and fundamental freedom' occurred in the Charter of the United Nations, 26th June, 1945, whose preamble speaks of the determination of the 'people' of the United Nations to reaffirm faith in human rights. "The General Assembly of the United Nations adopted the universal declaration of human rights on 10th December, 1948, which recognized a set of thirty rights. These rights are indeed broad-based and cover a very wide range[2] in its thirty Articles, the Declaration proclaims the basic human rights and fundamental freedoms to which all men and women everywhere are entitled without any distinction as to race, colour, sex, language, religion, political or other opinion, national or social origin, property, birth or other status. The text of the Declaration did not pretend to be law. It proclaimed itself a common standard of achievement for all people.[3] The Charter of UNO confers, "Primary responsibility" for maintaining international peace and security to the Security Council. However, the current thinking is that gross and persistent violations of human rights constitute threat to international peace and are, therefore, a matter of international concern.[4] At the fag end of twentieth century when we talk of being more democrat and enlightened we are awfully and paradoxically barbaric reflecting our apathy to a large scale violation of human rights.[5]

The conception and principles of human rights are now found both in international law and domestic law of many modern states. "There is a common agreement that every individual has both political and civil as well as economic and social claims upon his/her society. But in a world of nation states, the strength of commitment to human rights and the extent to which it is realized depends on the particular state and its institutions, the condition of human rights thus differ markedly in different societies. Some states and some groupings of states are identified by differing ideologies can connoting different conception and commitments to human rights."[6]

"The Indian Constitution, which was being formulated at the time the universal declaration of human rights was adopted by the General Assembly, has accepted most of these as Fundamental Rights and the rest have been drafted into Part IV as Directive Principles of State Policy. More than thirty constitutions which have come into being their contemporaneously or later have been substantially influenced by the Declaration."[7]

"The conception and principles of human rights are the hallmark of modern civilized and democratic societies. What is obvious and important in these sense that human rights being the rights of everyone, has assumed great significance at the individual group, national and international levels, state denials, infringements or blatant violations of human rights occurring in any part of the globe invariably reverberate and alert the rest of the world community. Infringed enjoyment of human rights would only remain the protective umbrella of the organized state and effective instruments are created for redressal of grievances relating to human rights."[8]

India's status of human rights is fairly high under its constitution which makes provision for fundamental rights and empowers the Supreme Court of India and High Court to enforce these rights. Equally important is the fact that India has been a signatory to international conventions on economic, social, cultural, civil and political rights, with certain conditions. Enforcement of rights and actualization of relief through remedial jurisprudence makes law the defender of the right of life. Towards this end the Constitution of India invests the Supreme Court and the High Courts with authority to grant remedies under Articles 32 and 226 of the Constitution of India. Part IV of the Constitution directs the State to apply policies and principles in the governance of the country so as to enhance the prospects of social/economic justice. Article 43 directs the state to secure for workers a living wage, decent standard of life and social and cultural opportunities. In short, the universe of human rights in India is still on an expanding horizon.[9]

The Lok Sabha has adopted in December 1993, the protection of Human Rights Bill, making possible the establishment of the National Human Rights Commission of India (NHRC). However, some misgivings were expressed for not including the Chief Justice of India as one of the members of the NHRC, for some procedural drawbacks and inadequate powers of the body as such.[10] "The appointment of such Commission can make a platform for institutionalizing the concept of the human rights in addition to the provisions of fundamental rights as enshrined in the Indian Constitution"[11]

"The judicially enforceable fundamental right, which encompasses all seminal civil and political rights and some of the rights of the minorities, are enshrined in Part III of the Constitution (Articles 12 to 35). These include the right to equality, the right to freedom, the right against exploitation, the right to freedom of religion, cultural and educational rights and the right to constitutional remedies."[12]

"The right to constitutional remedies is essentially the right to move Supreme Court of India for enforcement of the above rights (Article 32). The Supreme Court is vested with wide constitutional powers in this regard. They include the power to issue directions, orders or writing by enforcement of the Fundamental Rights [Article 32 (2)]. State High Courts too have identical powers (Article 226). As laws inconsistent with or in derogation of the right conferred by Part III of the Constitution are void (Article 13) the Courts have power to adjudge the constitutional validity of all laws. Further more, by virtue of Article 141, the law declared by the Supreme Court shall be binding on all Courts in India."[13]

The power of the High Courts under Article 226 is constitutional and it cannot be taken away by any stretch of imagination by a "Measure of Finality" given by the legislature to any administrative action or decision.[14] Article 227 is yet another important devise or measure or mechanism of Judicial Review of administrative actions in as much as it invest High Courts with the power of superintendent over administrative agencies/bodies/authorities/tribunals quasi judicial bodies exercising adjudicatory powers. Article 32, itself is fundamental right, invests the Supreme Court with the power of Judicial Review for the enforcement of fundamental rights. Since the right to move the Supreme Court for the enforcement of fundamental rights is itself a fundamental right, as such it is not only the right and power correlation, but the duty of the Supreme Court to protect and safeguard the fundamental rights of the people.[15] And in recent years people have preferred to approach before these courts for protection of their rights. And trend-setting judicial orders in recent years, to translate these constitutional goals into reality has been generally described as "Judicial Activism". This Judicial Activism is twofold, viz., first Judicial Policy, and second legal services access to justice or Social Action Litigation (SAL) or Public Interest Litigation (PIL), or third party litigation or Private Attorney of Law (PAL) which clearly shows that any public minded citizen can approach the Court with grievances of the poor and the illiterate.[16]

A strong, independent, impartial and well-organized judiciary plays an important role in the democratic system of governance. It not only prevents the arbitrary use of government authority but also safeguards the rights and liberties of citizens. Moreover under the Federal form of government, the judiciary has the additional role of the guardian of the Constitution.[17]

A comparatively recent development in the judicial field is the emergence of Judicial Activism which is essentially action by the judiciary to realize social justice. According to Justice P.N. Bhagwati, it is nothing but another form of constitutionalism which is concerned with substantivisation of Social Justice. A good example of Judicial Activism is seen in the Supreme Court ruling that legal aid to the poor, accused in a criminal trial, is an essential requirement of reasonable , fair and just procedure and is implicit in Article 21.

Judicial Activism is not a new phenomenon, way back in 1893, Justice Mahmood of the Allahabad High Court delivered a dissenting judgment which served the seed for judicial activism in India. It was a case of an under trial who could not afford to engage a lawyer. So the question was whether the Court could decide his case by merely looking his papers. Justice Mahmood held that the precondition of the case being heard would be fulfilled only when some body becomes speakers.[18]

Judicial Activism is a state of mind. It has its genesis in the inactivity and apathy of the legislature and the executive. It is nothing but the performance of the judicial activities. It is creativity to fill the gulf between the positive and the normative aspects of the law.

Indian Constitution does not contain the term "Judicial Activism" but it has become an integral part of the present day functioning of judiciary.[19] The judicial exercise in constitutional adjudication is bound to be influenced consciously and sub-consciously by the social philosophy and scales of values of those who sit in judgment.[20] Therefore, PIL/ SAL/ PAL may appear to be the invention of another legislative body, called the Supreme Court, of twenty six men who seem to be more powerful than all other legislators of both the Houses of Parliament put together; but their function in relation to the state in this perspective is limited to seeing that popular action does not trespass or intrude or freed upon right and justice as it exists in the written Constitution.[21]

In Kesavananda Bharti case,[22] the Supreme Court of India held that basic features of the Constitution of India such as democracy, rule of law, federal system, secularism and independence of judiciary cannot be amended but in Minerva Mill case also the Court held that the basic features of the Constitution cannot be amended.[23] Justice Bhagwati the father of public interests litigation in India,[24] observes that Judicial Activism is a central feature of every political system that vests adjudicatory power in a free and independent judiciary.

In this context it has rightly been pointed out that highest form of judicial activism is written into the Constitution itself. It is necessary ingredient of a written federal Constitution which demarcates the respective sphere of the Centre and the States and which embodies of Bill of Rights.[25] However, Judicial Activism refers to the phenomenon of the courts dealing with issues which they have traditionally not touched. Even at the height of its present activism, the Court has not exceeded its powers or usurped those of others. Where legal and constitutional rights of the people are involved, the Court always has jurisdiction.[26]

The working of the judicial decision-making during last four decades has been marked by two conflicting attitudes of judicial self restraint and judicial activism at different times. The period of 17 years (1950-67) reflected a trend of judicial self restraint. There was no confrontation between the judiciary and the executive though tensions, between the judiciary and the legislature and the executive were visible......................[27].

This tension, however, turned into confrontation in 1967 when the constitutionality of the Constitution (17th

Amendment) Act was challenged in I.C. Goloknath *V.* State of Punjab.[28]

PIL and judicial activism go hand in hand. PIL itself is the result of Judicial Activism under Article 32, violation of a fundamental right must first be shown before the Supreme Court can directly entertain a PIL matter, Besides other rights, life and personal liberty in Article 21 have been given a very wide interpretation, *e.g.*, in Fancis Coralie Mullin *V.* Administrator, Union Territory of Delhi.[29] Wherein the Court has observed through Bagwati J., "We think that the right to life includes the right to live with human dignity and all that goes along with it".

The exemplary role played by PIL cannot be forgotten. It was due to PIL that compensation was given to the young men whose eyes were gouged out by the police in Bhagalpur (Bihar) over two decades ago. And the widow of a lawyer killed by the police would not have been given Rs. 7.5 lakh compensation, the dependents of those killed in encounters in Punjab, U.P. and elsewhere would not have been compensated.[30]

Under the new jurisprudence of PIL followed by what is often also called Judicial Activism, it has moved far beyond judicial review to a near takeover of the administration marching through direction, supervision and participation.

Purposive Public Interest Jurisdiction and Judicial Activism are eminently necessary and have a great meaning for preventing the executive and legislature getting arbitrary and wayward.[31] And the Supreme Court of India, as constituted at present, has by its recent several judgments and directions to governmental and civic agencies depend on the foundations of the rule of law in a way that was never done before in India, or elsewhere. The purpose of public law is to ensure the citizen that they live under a legal system which aims at protecting their interests. The state is constitutionally, legally and morally bound to compensate and indemnity wronged persons. As such proponents of

Judicial Activism think that a powerful judiciary is essentially necessary to protect the rights, interest and entitlements of weaker sections of the society as well as public interest at the hands of those who may be motivated by folly or injustice.[32] Justice A.M. Ahmadi has rightly pointed out that "Changing times make it appropriate for laws and courts to adapt themselves to new situations... courts are not the only guardians of the Constitution but are last resort".[33]

The Judicial Activism manifested in the strategy of PIL paves the way for the participation of public spirited and enlightened people in India's development process and displays the potentiality of the legal system to offer justice to the poor and the oppressed. The strategy has brought to light many a medieval practice still prevalent in India such as relief to prisoners, plight of women in protective homes, etc. The attempt has been made to show how in taking up such cases, the Supreme Court is emerging as the guardians of the rights and liberties of the victims of repression, cruelty and torture. No wonder, the people of the country are now looking towards judiciary for protection of life, liberty and pursuit of happiness. By enlarging the scope of Article 32 and by accelerating the process of socio-economic revolution it has brought justice to the doorstep of the weak, the unprivi-leged and exploitative section of society. But the inad-equacy of what has been accomplished stands out the moment the issue of human rights is brought up. One reason why the advance in this area of operations has been striking slow is that, without some drastic restructuring of the legal system, human rights cannot be protected as they ought to be protected. This is precisely where the bottleneck lies.[34]

REFERENCES

1. See Dholakia, H.C., "Human Rights" in R.C. Hingorani (ed.),

International Law through United Nations, Tripathi, Bombay, 1972, p. 75.

2. K.P. Saxena (Ed), *Human Rights: Perspective and challenges, 1990 and Beyond*, Lancer Books, New Delhi, 1996, p. 540.
3. See Green, N.A. Maryan, *International Law: Law of Peace*, Macdonald, London, 1973, pp. 111- 113. Also see H.C. Dholakia, *op. cit.*, pp. 75-84.
4. See Sorabji, Soli, J., "Humanitarian Assistance", *World Focus*, 189, New Delhi, Sept. 1995, p. 23.
5. See Bharadwaj, A.N., *Failures, of the U.N.O.*, Anmol Publications, New Delhi, 1996, p.p. 358.
6. Louis Henkin, *The Rights of Man Today*, Westview Press, Coloroda, USA, 1978, p. 31.
7. K.P. Saxena (ed.), *op. cit.*, p. 542-43.
8. Justice V.R. Krishna Iyer, *The Hindu*, 23rd June, 1998.
9. Geholt, N.S., "India and Human Rights; Emerging Realities", *The Indian Journal of Political Science*, Oct. – Dec., 1994, Vol. 55, p. 381.
10. *Ibid.*
11. Arun Kumar Palai, *National Human Rights Commission of India; Formation, Functioning and Future Prospects*, Khama Publishers, New Delhi, 1998, p. 79.
12. V.S. Mani, *Human Rights in India : An Overview Occasional Paper*, Institute for World Congress on Human Rights, Paper No.4, January 1997, p. 47-48.
13. V.S. Mani, *op. cit.*, pp. 10-11
14. Bhatia , K.L., *Judicial Review and Judicial Activism*, Deep & Deep Publications, New Delhi, 1997, pp. 23-24.
15. *Ibid.*, p. 21.
16. *Ibid.*, p. 7, also see. Vijay Kumar, "Constitutional Democracy and Judicial Activism", in Vevinder Grover *et al.* (eds), India : 50 *Years of Independence*, 2, Deep & Deep Publications, New Delhi, 1997, p. 205.
17. V.L. Dudeja, Judicial Review in India, *Radiant*, New Delhi, 1988, p.1.
18. See Justice J.S. Verma's Interview with Manoj Mitra in *India Today*, March, 15, 1996, p. 122.
19. Judicial Activism: Its Impact on Public Administration, *The Administrator*, Vol. XLII (2), April-June, 1997, p. 179.

20. See Bhatia , K.L. , *op. cit.*, pp. 121-122, also see Bachan Singh *Vs.* State of Punjab (1982) 3, Supreme Court Case 24.
21. See Bhatia , K.L., *op cit.*, p. 122.
22. AIR 1973, SC 1461.
23. AIR 1980, SC 1789.
24. K.N. Bhat, Judges *Vs* Judges, *The Tribune*, December 15, 2007.
25. See Ramchandran, Raju, "Judicial Activism-11: The Sentinel Turns Saviour", *The Times of India*, New Delhi, Feb. 28, 1996, p. 10.
26. *Ibid.*
27. Supra note, 15, p. 70.
28. AIR 1967, SC 1943.
29. AIR 1981, SC 746.
30. See Bhatnagar, Rakesh, "Move to Curb PIL may be Unconstitutional", *The Times of India*, New Delhi, Feb. 18, 1997, p. 13.
31. See Dua, P.N., "A Matter of Balance," *The Hindustan Times*, Jan. 15, 1997, p. 7.
32. Bhatia, K.L., *op. cit.*, p. 115.
33. Bhatnagar, Rakesh, *op. cit.*
34. See Singh, Amrik "Judicial Activism", *The Hindustan Times*, Patna, Oct. 19, 1996, p. 7.

SECTION - III

EDUCATION AND DEVELOPMENT

17 Achieving Basic Education for All in India

Progress and Pitfall of Sarva Shiksha Abhiyan

Amal Mandal

Reaffirming the national resolve and proclaiming a new deal for universal elementary education in India the *Sarva Shiksha Abhiyan* (SSA), a comprehensive and integrated flagship public programme, sets out with emphatic objectives and encompassing strategy, like decentralised framework and community ownership. Regarding the questions how the SSA is performing, how far its objectives are realistic or have the potential to come to fruition, contradictory contentions ranging from optimistic expectation to apprehension may leave one wondering but one thing is unequivocal : the progress and success of the SSA will, for the moment at least, determine when and whether India will attain the cherished goal of satisfactory level of basic education for all.

The SSA, on the one hand, is regarded as conceptually inclusive and feted as hugely successful. Its national coverage, constituent schemes, massive investment and the phenomenal progress in the sphere of access and infrastructure are purportedly more imposing than the erstwhile schemes. 98 per cent of total habitations have already been served with primary and 86 per cent with upper primary schools (up to 2006). During 2006-07 the enrolment at elementary stage has increased to 18.15 crore. Dropout rates have declined— at primary level from 15 per cent in 2002-03 to 10.5 per cent in 2004-05. As per DISE data, the transition rate from primary to upper primary was 87 per cent in 2005-06. The gender gap has come down— 3.9 per cent at primary and 8.2 per cent at upper primary during 2005-06. Up to September 2007, 1.86 lakh new schools, 8.1 lakh teachers, 1.7 lakh school buildings, 7.1 lakh additional classrooms, 1.57 lakh drinking water facilities, 2.03 lakh toilets have been provided. Cumulative target achievement rates are commendable. As on September 2007, the achievement percentage was 78 for new school, 71 for teacher recruitment, 79 for school building construction, 88 for additional classrooms, 99.9 for Block Resource Centre, 95 for Circle Resource Centre and 82 for enrolment in informal system. Consequently, the public primary schools have, for the first time ever, seen a turnaround when children are withdrawing from private mode, getting enrolled in public schools and many private school are shutting down (as in Andhra Pradesh, *5th Joint Review Mission*, 2007, p. 18).

In contrast, the scheme is "readily" dismissed as a failure, particularly in those states where it really matters. The progress is scarcely satisfactory or the trumpet blowing largely premature[1] when the number of unserved habitation, minimum facilities in school, Pupil-Teacher Ratio (PTR), number of Out-of-School Children (OoSC), dropout rates and focus on vulnerable section are considered. In some States the enrolment across formal and informal modes is consistently declining, many States are struggling in extending universal access and equity, some are taking *ad hoc* measures and fumbling at mainstreaming the SSA (*7th Joint Review Mission*, 2008). One allegation is that the desperation of making everyone literate is substituting *Shiksha* by *Sakharata*, entrenching poor quality education through temporary structure with under-qualified, contractual teachers[2] and relegating formal public system.[3] The envisaged target dates are highly ambitious and one fallout is the proliferation of *Sarkari* success stories, saga of lies and unfounded sense of celebration. The national figures for substantiating the success are insufficient index and deceptive exercise, as these mask fatalities at disaggregated levels. The target dates for universal enrolment and quality schooling have already been missed, many others are likely to follow suit and the SSA is likely to be yet another failed promise on basic education.

This article is a critical reflection on a few crucial operational aspects of the SSA: the status of micro planning and availability and utilisation of fund. Decentralised planning and management is expected to cater to the situation specific problems and judicious use of resource will accelerate UEE much faster and effectively than otherwise possible. The analysis is based basically on the SSA monitoring, assessment reports undertaken by public agencies and research institutions. Few gaps are emphasised not to belittle but to buttress the momentum of the SSA. The underlying credence is that in order to expedite the actualisation of the hitherto elusive Universal Elementary Education (UEE) it is fundamental to identify the barriers making the initiative and resourceless effective rather than feeling complacent over strategy or breakthrough. Few areas have also been identified where renewed focus and reinventing the strategy are imperative.

II

PLANNING PROCESS

The SSA envisages bottom up approach with participatory planning process reflecting and aggregating local specificities. As an epitome of micro planning, the SSA has ordained constitution of core planning team at habitation, Block and district levels and formulation of plans through involvement and consultation with the stakeholders and grass roots organisations. Together with the ground level comprehension of the problems and selection of the solution, the local community in general and few committees in particular—Parent-Teacher Association (PTA), Mother-Teacher Association, Village Education Committee (VEC)—have been assigned key roles in the preparation of the educational plan, school improvement plan, monitoring educational issues and utilising grants.

Habitation plan is first formulated with close involvement of grass roots functionaries. This is then complied at cluster, Block and district level. Every district has to prepare both perspective plan (up to 2009-10) and annual plan, better known as Annual Work Plan and Budget (AWP&B). The district annual plan is primarily based on Block level plans and it is the prioritisation of various proposal emanated from habitation/Block levels. District plan has two parts: plans for the current financial year and spill over activities. The State plan outlines the vision of the State, the policy framework, overall strategy, State support to district etc. The district and State plans are to be approved by the Executive Committee of the State Mission, then to be forwarded to Ministry of Human Resource Development, where one appraisal team will make its recommendation, then the national Project Approval Board (PAB) will accord final approval and thereafter the Ministry will sanction the central share.

Notwithstanding the policy stipulation, the involvement of people and grass roots organisations in preparing habitation plan is markedly missing and the overall experience attests that micro planning is still a far cry. In Kerala village planning committee was non-existent. In Tamil Nadu and Bihar core planning team at habitation was missing. In Madhya Pradesh (MP) preparation of plan was minus village community. There are many instances where evidence did not corroborate that annual plan was prepared at the lowest level and then transmitted upward. VEC was, in general, neither involved nor plan proposal sought from it. Needs and aspiration of the community and target groups were neither asked for nor was it formally known to the planning team (Karnataka). The District Office unilaterally prepared district plan (Assam). Plans were prepared on the basis of certain basic data collected from schools in prescribed format, which were then consolidated Block-wise (Haryana). Somewhere the village plans were merely a wish list of Head Master/President of VEC/PTA.

Annual district plan was not always inclusive, factual or followed the SSA norms. In Bihar one district plan excluded estimates for basic components like civil works, textbooks, teachers' salary, which were subsequently incorporated by the State agency. District plans contained no details of works to be undertaken institution-wise (West Bengal, Kerala), identification of works and selection of institution did not precede target fixation, which later caused procedural problems. The projected deficiencies of school, classroom and teacher were either awry or perfunctory. Regarding requirement of additional classroom West Bengal casually adhered to four classrooms for each sanctioned primary school, disregarding enrolment and priority in requirements. Gujarat AWP&B, 2003-04, estimated only 384 additional teachers for primary stage and for a district none at all. Test checking indicated 303 vacancies in that district alone. Majority plans were concerned with supply side intervention: building classrooms, teachers etc. States in general failed to focus on strategy and vision for improving classroom transaction, learning achievement and quality related issues (5th Joint Review Mission, 2007). Such oversight is likely to have abnegating impacts and may strangulate the progress of UEE.

Apparently, the annual plans are not prepared at grass roots, or they emanate from habitation level and the plan proposals seldom include felt needs of the community or contain details of the proposed works. Basic data and information essential for meaningful AWP&B are neither readily available nor there is concerted effort to collect, compile and use those. It is imperative that authentic database is collated and used for planning purpose, without which the intervention will only be redundant.

Another issue relating to planning is preparatory activity. The SSA makes a clear departure from past programmes by envisaging Pre-Project Activities (PPA) and accepting those as essential prerequisites for comprehending the problems, developing capacity to improve the delivery and monitoring system. Filling up teachers' position, constitution of planning team, diagnostic study, household, baseline survey are few district specific activities supposed to be pivotal for the success of the SSA. Accordingly, a portion of the fund is earmarked for this purpose. However, such activities are rarely enamoured or taken up in right earnest and the follow up action is either weak or absent. Few instances are indicative. In Tamil Nadu Rs 1.55 crore (out of 1.59 crore PPA fund) was invested in fixed deposit scheme, the fund was released to districts only after 2 years. In Assam the fund was refunded, as districts could not utilise it. In Kerala 87 per cent of available fund was incurred for house-to-house survey, yet the survey report was found untraceable. In Gujarat money languished in bank account. Not much survey, capacity building effort, huge unspent amount and above all, implementation of the scheme without pre-project activities substantiate a lackadaisical approach being followed or favoured.

III

RESOURCE ALLOCATION AND UTILISATION

Regarding resource availability, it transpires that the central share is often less than the approved amount, the fund is not provided on time, release of State share is commonly disproportionate to the central share, considerable portion of the fund is withheld by the State agency and the release from the district and sub-district levels to the school is both uncertain and untimely. The situation has not improved much even after 7 years of operation, one report rued (7th Joint Review Mission, 2008). The release of State share continues to be delayed or problematic and the fund utilisation relative to the approved amount has been quite low. As to the resource allocation and transfer, the SSA guidelines are flayed and the rationale for initiating the SSA so as to ease the fund flow by pulling resource and reducing transit time is yet to materialise.

Few aberrations in fund approval and allocation are glaring and some started from the very inception. Disregarding the stipulation that districts so far uncovered by programmes like DPEP would be taken up first, many districts, particularly in Uttar Pradesh (UP), were readily offered fund from 2001-02. The prerequisites for release of second instalment of Central share are at least 50 per cent expenditure, utilisation certificate and quality of implementation justifying the demand. Yet, States having floundered such financial propriety have received fund (Assam, Tamil Nadu). The general impression is that States that submit plan and estimates usually get approval. The SSA, it seems, is flushed with fund and whatever asked for is nearly granted. Such easy money from this expenditure scheme may sound wrong signal or at worst may be a recipe for disaster.

The States in general fumble to release fund within 30 days of receipt of Central share and it is invariably in instalments. The average time between Central release and cash in hand by the school is about one year. Moreover, disbursement in several trances makes it difficult for the districts to allocate fund to Cluster, for the Cluster to school/VEC. Untimely release and that too in spells adversely affects proper planning, programming, budgeting and efficient implementation all of which aggravate the implementation process of the scheme. Though uncertainty over fund availability is one accounting factor, huge spill-over and unspent amount[4] vindicate lack of preparedness and ability of the implementing agencies.

Nevertheless, available funds are not always used optimally or for the purpose intended. They are 'regularly' diverted to activities beyond the permitted scope. CAG Report 2006, revealed that 11 States spent Rs. 99.8 crore on unauthorised items. And financial irregularities to the tune of 472.5 crore were detected in 14 States/UTs— school grant for non-existent schools, salary of non-SSA teacher, funding of training programme for implementing grading system (Kerala) are few typical examples. Excess charging of the SSA fund is not rare either—Rs.17.11 crore for paying honorarium to para teacher, 74.6 crore for repair and maintenance (Rajasthan). The SSA offers fund for free textbooks costing up to Rs 150 per child. However, the actual cost of textbooks is found to be much lower. Consequently, Haryana obtained excess claim of 6.8 crore for textbook supply, which could have been used for other productive purpose.

The monitoring reports reveal that the proportion of the fund expended is below per, unspent amount is massive, pace of civil works sluggish and expenditure on priority components scarce. Comparison of outlay and expenditure indicates that actual expenditure is 'much less' than the outlay, which undermines the programme efficacy. Even the lesser amount could not be spent by majority of States.[5] For instance, expenditure in Andhra Pradesh ranged between 17-36 per cent during 2002-06, in Assam 55 per cent during 2002-05. Nevertheless, the shortfall in expenditure will generally be higher as the test checking unfolded that the lapsable funds (*i.e.* school grant) are often shown as utilised. The SSA expenditure pattern largely corroborates DPEP experience, where most districts failed to utilise available fund.[6] This tends to confirm that shortage of fund is less critical than its optimal and effective utilisation.

In Gujarat the percentage of completed works ranged between 0-60 in 2002-04. Not even one-half of approved AWP&B fund could be expended in Assam. MP completed only 20 per cent of civil works proposed in 2004-05. No new teacher was recruited in UP and Assam during 2006-07. Upgradation of schools with additional classroom and teacher bogged down because of problems relating to selection of site and teachers (MP). In West Bengal original vacancies of regular primary teachers was 28,333 and 10,344 post sanctioned later on. Yet, only 25 per cent of those vacancies were filled up. In many pockets and States, PTR is still unacceptably high – 63 in Bihar, 49 each in MP and UP. Such huge vacancies constrict the capacity to improve the quality of education.

Regarding expenditure and intervention on focus group disconcerting dimensions are evident. In Assam only 23 per cent of approved fund was incurred on OOSC. Similar was the Gujarat case. In Karnataka physical achievement of Education Guarantee Scheme (EGS) and remedial teaching was 16 per cent in 2002-03, 2 per cent next year and Rs 42.8 lakh on remedial teaching lapsed. West Bengal reported activities relating to girls, SCs, STs on innovative category, ignoring the fact that they are integral part of the SSA. Field officials had parochial notion about innovative activity. Neither the allocation, nor utilisation on innovative activities was ample or worth mentioning. For EGS, integrated education for disabled, community training, research and evaluation, the intervention in general has proved to be "dismal" which shunts the prospect for the focus groups

Regarding dropout rates and extent of OOSC, test checking unearthed far worse scenario than that conveyed by official version, indicative is the Kerala case. In 2002 it submitted to PAB that as per the house-to-house survey the State has 3.75 lakh OOSC. In Annual Plan for 2005-06 it was, however, shown that out of total 48.18 lakh child population, 43.52 lakh were enrolled in I-VIII, effectively leaving 4.6 lakh children as out of school, which probably authenticates that the implementation of the SSA "did not help in bringing down the number of out of school children."[7]

House-to-house survey or child tracking survey results need to be treated cautiously. While house-to-house survey in Karnataka disclosed inconsiderable dropout rates, the interaction of the monitoring team with villagers confirmed far greater proportion. In two districts of MP the actual dropout rate was 22 and 17 per cent, in sharp contrast to the official rate of 0.11 and 0.05. In Rajasthan child tracking survey, 2004 divulged 5.7 per cent dropout. But cross checking in 18 primary schools pushed the rate in between 55 to 70 per cent, as majority of class I students could not be retained up to class V. In Gujarat considerable portion of primary and upper primary students left school without completing the course. The Kerala instance vindicated no visible effort to bring dropout child back to school or keeping trace of their whereabouts. In Gujarat about 65 per cent of identified children, mostly residing in two backward districts, were deprived of educational access due to lack of school and teacher.

IV
BATTLE YET TO BE WON

Some achievements as in the sphere of access, enrolment, phenomenon of out-of-school are certainly an evidence. Do they conclusively corroborate that the battle has almost been won and the final onslaught should focus only on retention and upper primary level? Like other public programme, the success of the SSA is being measured in terms of quantifiable indicators such as new school opened, classroom constructed, new teacher recruited and fund expended. Macro level figures furnish impressive advancement in many spheres and emboldened by such stride there is the tendency to emphasis on a policy shift from universal access to universal retention and from primary to upper primary stage (4th Joint Review Mission, 2006). Consequently, the Union Finance Minister in his Budget (2008-09) has declared that the focus of the SSA will now shift to enhancing retention, improving quality of learning and ensuring access to upper primary school.

Seen in overall perspective, the battle is far from being

over and the challenge looming large is no less daunting. About 50 per cent of total SSA fund is expended only on infrastructural development, which is surely significant for addressing access problems. Yet, the deficiencies in this particular sector are still substantial. NIEPA survey on infrastructure, 2006 found that 10 per cent (of total 1.04 million) public schools have only one classroom and 42,000 schools lack any sort of classroom building. 1.37 lakh are single teacher schools and 8 per cent could not boast of blackboard even. Lopsided student-teacher ratio, more so in rural schools, is still one worrisome feature. 75 per cent schools are to resort to multi-grade teaching, where teachers seldom have training over intricacies of such teaching process. The CAG Report, 2006 revealed that 31,648 habitations lacked any form of schooling within one km distance and 1.36 crore or 40 per cent of total children in the 6-14 age group remained out of school.[8] Accordingly, basic access and meaningful instruction are yet to be provided universally. Attempt to hush up the hurdles or win the war by changing goal posts will do injustice to thousands of target group population and it may undermine the functional efficacy of the public system.

Universal education is a huge challenge and it is unlikely to be achieved within twinkling of eyes, literally. The network is vast, schools do not operate in socio-political vacuum, the target groups are sharply heterogeneous in every conceivable term and the backlog to be covered in every front is substantial. In such a context when everything is sought within ten years at best (2010 being the outer limit for the SSA), failing is arguably inescapable. One does not know what convinced the SSA framers to proclaim the target dates but in the face of previous experience, persisting challenges and mode of selection, these are far too ambitious. Few target dates are already missed, and other are about to nosedive.

Bringing children to school is not enough. Enrolment,

attendance and learning do not essentially go hand in hand. Registering a child does not imply that he is attending classes, taking examination or getting equipped. Those who are attending school regularly are uniformly fewer than those enrolled. Enrolment and attendance rates are often inflated mainly to conceal the darker sides and such tendencies essentially distract attention from the needs of a considerable portion of excluded children and propagate gobbledegook. When the whooping 14 million are still playing truant and when they are the most difficult to reach segment, one can assume the magnitude of the challenge lying ahead.

Though the SSA vouches quality education, its efforts end up in extending physical infrastructure, higher PTR, TLM, teachers' training, cooked meal etc. These are obviously essential but more fundamental is the incidence of class teaching and learning achievement, without which the available facilities turn trivial. Every school must work, deliver and achieve the objectives for which it has been established. If and when any school does not perform or remains dysfunctional, it is outright wastage. The perennial problem of public system is that the teaching activity is either fairly low or lacking, the teaching process is impervious and teachers' truancy is getting ominous. Skipping of classes and closer of school rule the roost, one consequence of which is abysmally low achievement level of the learners. Indeed, the functionality of school continues to be one neglected aspect. And the SSA, unfortunately, has no definite strategy to stem such rot. Scepticism is that the rush for make shift arrangement will compromise the quality of education and will perpetuate inequity among masses more ominously than ever.

V

STRENGTHENING THE STRATEGY

The quality of planning and implementation of the SSA

requires improvement and reinventing the strategy would be exigent. Instead of the prevailing trend of garnering fund through preparation of AWP&B, the intervention must have clear linkage with the strategic objectives of the SSA. The district plan must reflect on local situation and address local problems. Situational survey with the involvement of community people should be undertaken and the down-to-earth solution should be incorporated in education plan. Customized strategies with micro level planning are needed for the hardest to reach segments, such as the urban poor, migrant children, tribals, minorities and older girls. AWP&B is not all about budgeted estimate for infrastructure development, it must contain differentiated plans, have clear thrust on gender/vulnerable groups, strategy for improving the quality of education and capacity of the delivery system. One way of enforcing strategic objective and need based planning is to abandon the lenient attitude and carefully examine the feasibility of the suggested strategy, sanction the component plans, establish linkage with past performance and utilisation of the fund. In case of casual approach or miserable performance, withholding or pruning the fund is likely to sound a tough signal. Wisdom teaches that easy money leads to misuse or no use at all !

One reason why the achievement of the target dates envisaged by public programmes is consistently falling flat is the lack of disaggregated target setting consequent upon situational assessment and micro level intervention. Given the available organisation and expertise, each Circle/Cluster should better be asked to fix its target date in terms of access and other problems. And each Circle should squarely be made responsible for achieving it. Considering the longest timeframe of the Circles, the target for each district and accordingly the State may be envisioned. Such a target setting would obviously upset the present obsession with 'miracle' but it would minimise the miss and cater to the heterogeneity of the educational needs of socio-economic groups.

Universal enrolment drive cannot succeed unless it is fairly known who are staying out and for what context specific reason and reparatory measures consequent upon such information are taken. Compilation of data-base regarding the never enrolled, out of school and dropout children has been attempted. The Village Education Register, Child Tracking system are few efforts that try to capture child's whereabouts. Unfortunately, such effort is rarely enamoured, updated and at worst, authentic. Objectively verifiable information/data-base of the target group population as well as other important aspects of education—and putting those in public domain for scrutiny/correction and enforcing accountability of the concerned agencies—is likely to capture the real situation, which will surely help in meaningful planning and devising appropriate strategy.

Within the SSA framework integral should be clear thrust on improving the schooling process, retaining children and imparting meaningful education. For ensuring basic learning conditions, the minimum number of teachers, space and facility have to be defined and streamlined. For monitoring the functionality of school few common minimum indicators—teaching days, time spent for teaching, teachers' attendance—need to be ascertained. Moreover, stipulation concerning least engagement of teacher in non-educational activities may help in petrifying the teaching process. Reinventing the role of the school inspectors and community empowerment over teachers' attendance and performance would regenerate the teaching activity. Though the department of school education of the State is in charge of fructifying the functional aspects of public schools, categorical directives in the SSA will have reinforcing impacts.

The much 'touted' decentralised planning and community control have not worked wonder for the SSA. When the community involvement is only for conforming to the scheme guideline, when community people and organisations do not have adequate decision-making power or command over resource, when the effort is lacking in converting their suggestions into action, when financial and management decisions are taken elsewhere, peoples' involvement and enthusiasm can only evaporate. The participatory planks should be broad-based, unencumbered, non-political and endowed with delineated power and responsibility.

From the perspective of the programme management, the motivation and capacity building of the implementing agencies are to improve "dramatically," if the SSA is to deliver its promise. The SSA "is an ambitious programme of a large scale and the implementation structures at all levels need to be strengthened considerably. There needs to be large scale and continuous capacity building at all levels" (5th Review Mission, 16-31 January, 2007, p. 22). Multiplicity of organisations and `lack of horizontal and vertical integration of the State, district and sub-district agencies with the institutional set-up of the State has resulted "in them not being in charge of any aspect relating to the elementary education in the State and district." The SSA is being viewed as a collection of activities having not much sense of ownership and concern for the output. The weak positioning of the State and district project officials adversely affects the planning and performance. The SSA officials tend to perceive their role as a conduit for channelling fund to others without being responsible for the strategy and outcome. At the same time, *ad hoc* officials, inadequate technical personnel and large number of vacancies aggravate the situation. Institutionalisation of parallel/additional structure tends to upset the expectation of overcoming bureaucratic barriers impinging on the efficacy and often creates complicacy, chaos or chasm.

Experience evinces that the DPEP operated as separate programme from the State department of education. Similar eventuality is getting manifested for the SSA as well.

Somewhere the SSA is working as parallel intervention without seeking or achieving any convergence in between, thus the SSA gains are likely to die down whenever it is folded up. Ideally, there should have effective integration of the SSA with school education programme at all level. Disbanding the structure(s) operating independently or at cross-purpose is one option towards achieving such synergy.

In order to take stock of the operational process, the SSA harps on regular monitoring and engages many agencies for this purpose. Over the years, the monitoring and other assessment reports have peeked into the fruition of the scheme and they are rich commentary on its progress and pitfalls. They in general authenticate that the achievements thus far are uneven across the board. They have also suggested few reparatory measures. However, it is unfortunate that such recommendations are given short shrift, there is no visible effort to improve the capacity of the delivery mechanism and strengthen need based planning and intervention. It would auger ill for UEE if the prescription continues to be prevaricated and operational strategy is not streamlined in terms of lessons learnt. After all, the stakes are extremely high and in dithering or delay "we waste our lights in vain like lamps by day."

NOTES

1. The euphoria of 'mission accomplished' tends to resemble with the proud pronouncement of the USA President Bush on Iraq War.
2. In West Bengal *Shishu Shiksha Kendras* (SSK) are severely under-resourced, extremely poor in infrastructure. If the plight of SSKs continues, two contrasting systems will probably entrench socio-economic inequity. It is apprehended that the state policy of not opening new upper primary school and meeting additional demands though alternative schools may be retrograding. SSA *Third Joint Review Mission: State Report, West Bengal*, 2006, p. 4-5.
3. Compared to formal, alternative schools are increasing by

more than 20 percentage points. Their nature of exclusively catering to the marginal sections may have ghettoising impact and the prominence of this mode would probably weaken or even dismantle the structure of primary education. Kumar, Priyam and Saxena. (2002), 'Looking Beyond Smoke screen DPEP and Primary Education in India,' *Economic and Political Weekly*, Vol. 36, No 17, pp. 560-68.

4. 76 per cent of school building and 43 per cent of additional classrooms in MP happened to be carried over, and the target achievement rate in these two aspects was 1.4 and 0.9 per cent respectively (up to June 2006). *Monitoring Report of the Institute of Social Science Research on SSA for Madhya Pradesh*, 1st April 2006 to 30th September 2006, pp. 60, 63.
5. One study pointed out the gaps between approved outlay and actual release, unsatisfactory utilisation and failure of States to adhere to the sharing ratio. Rani, Geeta, P. (2006), 'Challenges of Achieving and Financing Universal Elementary Education in India', *Journal of Educational Planning and Administration*, Vol. 20, No 4, pp 429-464. See also Jha, Das, Mohanty and Jha (2008), Public Provisioning for Elementary Education in India, New Delhi, Sage Pub.
6. Low utilisation of fund has always been one perennial problem. Karan, A.K. and Pushpendra. (2005), 'Bihar Including the Excluded and Addressing the Failure of Public Provision in Elementary Education,' in Mehrotra, S. (ed.), *The Economics of Elementary Education in India: The Challenge of Public Finance, Private Provision and Household Cost*, New Delhi, Sage Pub.
7. *Study on Monitoring the Financial Aspects relating to Sarva Shiksha Abhiyan in Kerala*. Institute of Public Auditors of India. July 2005, p. 49.
8. Though the estimate of Ministry of Human Resource Development (MHRD) and UNESCO is lower, CAG, Pratham and Social and Rural Research Institute put the figure in the range of 14 million. MHRD sponsored All India Sample Survey (2006) informed that out of total 19.4 crore estimated children in 6-13 age group, 7 per cent (1.34 crore) are OOSC, of which 11.3 crore hail from rural and 21 lakh from urban areas and 68 per cent never went to school and 32 per cent dropped out at later stages.

18 Deprivation and its Role in Universalization of Elementary Education

Deepa Awasthi and **U.C. Vashishtha**

Education enables the individual to develop harmony in a social culture. Education develops desirable habits, skills and attitudes which make an individual a good citizen. Education plays an important role in enabling a person to face a real life situation with adequate knowledge. It plays a pivotal role in shaping up a person. A balanced education should give total opportunity to the learner to discover and use his fullest potential. It is not just inborn talent or educational achievements that guarantee the success of children. Without sound values, good habits and self discipline, even the most gifted child cannot blossom into a good achiever.

Primary education is one of the cornerstones of development. This is the right time to introduce/inculcate values as well as good habits in children. It is a powerful tool for solving population problem, a catalyst for women empowerment. Education has been assigned high priority among nation's objectives. Article 45 of the directive principles of state policy in the constitution urge to provide free and compulsory education to all children below 14 years. Now this provision is shifted to Article 21(A) after 86th amendment. Through this amendment of Constitution education has been put under the category of "Fundamental Rights". Now it has been ensured that state will provide free and compulsory education to all children belonging to 6-14 years age group. Education is considered as a matter of concurrent list ; thus Central and State government both can make legislations. Now in Article 45 of Directive Principles of State Policy, provision has been made for preprimary education of children below 6 years. Through this amendment one fundamental duty has been added i.e. parents should provide opportunity for education between age group of 6-14 years.

Universalization of elementary education means making available education to all children in the age group of 6-14 years. It means opportunities of education for all and not for selected few. This concept accepts that education is the birth right of every child. All children belonging to the rich and the poor, living in towns as well as rural areas and in places which are accessible with difficulty have to be provided with facilities for elementary education.

Universalization of primary education involves the following three stages or steps –

- Universalization of provision,
- Universalization of enrolment,
- Universalization of retention.

Universalization of provision means that school facilities should be provided to all the children between the age group of 6 to 14 years in the country. The school should be easily accessible within the walking distance of a child.

Universalisation of enrolment means all of the age group of 6 to 14 years must be enrolled. For this compulsory legislations must be passed. Under legislation, parents can be fined for not sending their children to schools.

Universalisation of retention means that once a child joins a primary school he should remain there till he completes his primary education. Mere enlistment of children is not enough, they have to be retained.

Primary education plays an important role in laying the proper foundation of child's physical, intellectual, emotional, social, moral, cultural and spiritual development. Primary education contributes to national development also. Since the time of Independence the Indian Government has done its level best to implement the vision of education embodied in Article 45 of the Constitution. To cover all the children in the age-group of 6-14 years under the provision of primary education government decided to provide incentives such as mid day meal, free text books, stationary, scholarships etc. to pupils.

Even after 60 years of Independence, the goal of universal primary education has not been achieved so far. The main causes of the non-implementation of this basic objective of our national policy are –

- Problem of priority,
- Problem of finance,
- Problem of population explosion,
- Problem of restricting educations
- Problem of poverty,
- Problem of illiterate parents,
- Problem of unattractive schools,
- Problem of wastage and stagnation,
- Problem of girls education,
- Problem of States with low enrolment,
- Problem of education of backward classes,
- Problem of small habitations,
- Problem of education of the handicapped ,
- Problem of enforcing compulsory primary education,
- Lack of voluntarism.

Bhengra, Silvestor (1997) conducted a study of causal factors of unavailability of education to slum children.

The findings showed that parents are neither able to provide proper food nor education to their children. In sample of 229 parents, 70 do not want to send their children to schools because they think that if their children stay at home, they can earn money. Ninety four parents do not know about the facilities provided by the government. Fifteen parents are not aware about the economic aid such as scholarship provided by government. Thirty eight parents do not want to educate their daughters. Sixty one parents think that their children will be neglected in schools due to ordinary clothing. Forty four parents are in favour of religious education. So they do not want to send their children in schools.

Sunil Kumar Singh (2002) emphasized on need of voluntarism in context of elementary education in his article entitled, 'Voluntarism in contemporary Indian society and universalization of elementary education'.

Lack of voluntarism is a serious problem in universalization of elementary education. Voluntarism is the spirit of human being to help other fellow beings with free will. The goal of universalization of elementary education can be achieved only when voluntary community participation is ensured along with governmental efforts. Local community should step forward to provide voluntary support for proper implementation of intervention strategies initiated by government for universalization of elementary education.

Diane S. Kaplen, B. Mitchell Peck and Howard B. Kaplen (1997) established relationship between academic performance and dropout in their research note entitled, 'Decomposing the academic failure-dropout relationship: A longitudinal analysis'.

According to them poor academic performance is one of the most often reason given for dropping out of school. In this view low grades tend to make a student feel incapable and inadequate. For those students low grades may reflect the teacher's personal feelings towards them. Thus school atmosphere also plays an important role.

Primary education should be developed on priority basis

and percentage of budget under this sector should be suitably raised. Universalization of primary education should not be allowed to suffer form want of funds. Cost on primary education may be rationalized by introducing double shift system where possible, by harnessing community resources in human, material and monetary terms and by evolving a system of voluntary service in the form of teaching by young persons.

A vast majority of children in the age group of 6-14 years do not attend schools because the poverty compels the children to work at home. Illiterate parents do not recognize the importance of education for their children. The prevalence of illiteracy is one of the factors that have stood in the way of Universalization of primary education. Unattractive schools also create problems. These schools do not have sufficient attractive modes as they use traditional teaching methods and the courses of study are unrelated with daily lives of the students. There is wide gap between education of boys and girls.

Although the compulsory primary education act has been passed yet this has not been properly enforced. Wastage is the main obstacle in Universalization of elementary education. This problem of illiteracy and dropouts is quite critical in the deprived section of society *i.e.* slum. Children belonging to slum areas hardly get admission in school. Slum may be characterized by overcrowding, poor or informal housing, inadequate access to safe water and sanitation. This indicates the deprived living pattern of children living in slums.

Deprivation is very wide and relative term because facilities which are expected from each field are different. Lack of facilities in one or more than one sectors of life is known as 'Deprivation'.

According to 'The Penguin Dictionary of Sociology', deprivation may be defined broadly as inequality of access to social goods. Deprivation may occur in several areas of social life *i.e.* low income or unemployment may go together with poor housing, poor health and access to inferior education.

According to Kellmer Pringle (1965), the term deprivation is commonly used to denote three conditions:

- The child who is living in residential care (deprived of normal family life).
- The child who is unloved and rejected by his parents (emotional deprivation).
- The child who is growing up in a home which is culturally and educationally extremely unstimulating will be handicapped by environmental deprivation.

According to K. C. Panda (1997) deprived children are the children who come from socio-economically backward section of the community, who cannot profit from school because of deprivation of one sort or another and children who are seen in interior tribal and rural areas of country where educational facilities have not reached.

According to Wolman (1973), "Deprivation means low category life conditions or separation which stops some people from participating in their society's cultural achievements".

S.A. Stouffer *et al.* (1994) formulated the concept of 'Relative Deprivation'. According to this concept, people mainly experience feelings of deprivations when they compare their own situations unfavourably with those of other individuals or groups. Comparison can be made with both; with whom people interact and with outsiders.

Thus deprivation may be defined as lack of proper physical, intellectual, social, educational, moral, cultural and economic conditions which are necessary for overall development of an individual.

Causes of Deprivation

There are many causes of deprivation. Cyril Burt (1951)

described following causes which lead to deprivation; they are—

- Poverty,
- Material conditions at home,
- Intellectual conditions of home,
- Emotional and moral conditions of home,
- The conditions of neighbourhood.

Poverty

Poverty is supposed to be the main cause of deprivation. Poverty reflects those conditions in which the individual is not able to fulfil his basic needs. It implies lack of necessary facilities is one's life.

Cyril Burt (1951) defined poverty as "in sufficient earning for the full maintenance of bodily health in all the members of family."

Townsend (1979) in his study described poverty. According to him, "individuals, families and groups in the population can be said to be in poverty when they lack the resources to obtain the types of diet, participate in the activities and have the living condition and amenities which are customary or are at least widely encouraged or approved in the societies, to which they belong".

Poverty has to be understood not only as the inevitable feature of severe social inequality but also as a particular consequence of actions by the rich to preserve and enhance their wealth and so deny it to others.

Poverty may be defined in absolute as well as in relative terms. When we describe poverty in relation with the subsistence level than it is termed as absolute poverty and when we describe poverty as comparison between conditions of worse off and better off people than it is known as relative poverty.

Material conditions at home are also responsible for deprivation. The efficiency of mind varies from day to day with the state of the body and the body cannot be sustained in full working order if poverty deprives it of proper food, proper clothing, proper housing and proper sleep.

Poverty operates in two main directions, it impairs health and it limits general knowledge. By impoverishing the child's physical activity it diminishes child's capacity to learn and by restricting his mental growth it deprives him of that preparatory background which is needed for education.

According to Burt, poverty tends to stunt the young child's mental and physical growth during infancy.

Material Conditions

Improper food leads to nutritional derivation. The hungry child is in no fit conditions to wrestle with intellectual tasks. The child from the needy home seems more often to be suffering from improper food than from insufficient food. They may be dosed or overdosed with bread, potatoes and tea. The choice of food is largely determined by cheapness not by nutritional value. Thus improper and inadequate food leads to deprivation.

Inadequate sleep is another factor which is related with material condition of home and leads to deprivation. These all conditions lead to various deprivations and ultimately to educational deprivation.

Intellectual Conditions

Intellectual conditions of home are very poor in slum localities. Mostly parents are illiterate and do not understand the importance of education for their children. In well educated family the child has proper background to start his school education while with the poor *i.e.* deprived child these conditions are adverse.

Parents of deprived children not have any knowledge beyond their daily life. They do not have knowledge of many things and have neither the time nor the leisure, neither the ability nor the disposition to tell the children what little they know.Thus the vocabulary that the child absorbs is limited up to few hundred words, most of them inaccurate and mispronounced and the rest unfit for generation of new knowledge. In home there is no kind of literature.

The child's whole universe is closed and circumscribed by walls of his house. Because intellectual background of deprived children is very poor, thus they are not able to understand and grasp the instructions very well in the schools.

Emotional and Moral Conditions

Along with intellectual and cultural status, emotional and moral atmosphere of the family also equally react on the child's education and development.

Lower class families tend to be large with appearance of children in rapid succession. The parents are generally busy in their routine work of family. Thus engaged parents have very little time available for children. Thus children learn more from their siblings and peers than the adults.

If in home there is general attitude of irregularity, slackness, dishonesty and other immoral activities than the child himself is likely to become unpunctual and dishonest. The anxieties and quarrels at home are liable to upset the balance of child's self control.

Neighbourhood

School and home environment are not the only determinants of child's social life. Child is also affected by conditions of neighbourhood. The child is very much affected by his peer group and older children of his neighbourhood.

In slum living condition are very poor. These areas are overcrowded with poor or informal housing, inadequate access to safe water and sanitation, insecurity of tenure. People live in very suffocative atmosphere.

Thus various diseases and epidemics spread there. Social evils such as alcoholism, gambling, delinquency and prostitution etc. also prevail there. These all adverse conditions in neighbourhood take away the child from right direction. He also starts doing such anti social activities either due to need or due to greed of money.

So, it is clear that child may be deprived due to any cause but these all lead to educational deprivation of child. Deprivations are not limited up to a particular field of life. It may be socio-cultural deprivation, economic deprivation, parental deprivation, educational deprivation or deprivation due to individual characteristics. A deprived child may belong to any field.

Socio-culturally deprived children feel themselves isolated socially. Social status of their family is not very good. Social atmosphere is adverse for them *i.e.* lack of educational facilities, lack of means of entertainment and sports etc. They do not have proper view point regarding values such as morality, co-operation, tolerance, sacrifice and patience etc. This difference is only inter-group difference. According to Clarizio and McCoy they all are well adjusted in their own group.

Economically deprived children are not able to show their inherent talent due to lack of money. They work in hotels etc. Society discards them and then feelings of jealousy, inferiority and frustration develop in them. They get engaged in anti-social activities with bad people. They become thieves, beggars etc. to fulfil their needs.

Parental deprived children are those who used to live in residential care or who are unloved and rejected by their parents or whose parents died. They become timid, cheerless and dreamer. They feel themselves as orphan and helpless and become more sensitive. These children are not able to do free exchange of emotions.

The children who are deprived due to their individual characteristics are maladjusted either physically or mentally. They are afflicted by inferiority complex and lack of social adjustment, decision-making and logical capacities. They are not able to spend successful life.

All the above types of deprivations lead to educational deprivation. Educationally deprived children are those who are not able to attain proper education due to some reason. They appear impulsive, interruptive and inattentive. They have a low curiosity. Their range of experiences is also narrow, so they are not able to understand and generalize.

Deprivation in children is not hereditary rather it is due to lack of social, economic, cultural, intellectual and environmental facilities. Characteristics of deprived children may be described as under :

> Environment is more or less responsible for deprivation. Children attain various experiences through their environ-ment. Negative environment lays negative impact on development of child. Environmentally deprived children neither develop properly nor can they express their inherent qualities. Environment affects child's language, behaviour and thinking. Improper environmental conditions hinder the natural development of child.
>
> Deprived children feel under protection. They feel rejection either by parents or guardians. Their moral standard may be high or low. Their attitude towards education and present system is negative. They show narrow mindedness and faulty discipline.
>
> The deprived children become worried and frustrated due to lack of family, social, economic and cultural facilities. There is lack of social adjustment in deprived children. These are conservative, introvert, shy, worried, and hopeless towards future. They are afflicted by inferiority complex, prejudices and feeling of insecurity. They are emotionally less stable. They show negligible participation in social activities.

Family and social culture lays great emphasis on cognitive development of children. Adverse parental, social and cultural conditions lay negative impact on cognitive development of child. Language and vocabulary of these children is limited and below standard. They are not able to achieve their goal and their educational achievement (if any) is also not good. Their logical attitude and discrimination power is of low standard. Their memory is not very sharp. They are not able to express their feelings.

Role of socio-cultural atmosphere is very important in achievement of directed goals. A child may become social worker, orator or philosopher in future while in adverse conditions child's positive development is obstructed. Human values are disintegrating in polluted society and culture and children belonging to this society and culture have disintegrated personality. Socio-economic standard of deprived children is of low standard. Their participation in community work is negligible. They lack social adjustment, social and cultural values. They do not understand the value of cultural unity, communal unity, linguistic and religious unity.

Conclusion

Thus, it is clear that deprivation in slum localities is the main barrier in education of children living there. These children are not only economically poor, but often deprived of family support and educational environment. The problems of educating the deprived urban child in slums are complex and varied. These include poverty, inadequate schooling infrastructure; absence of specific incentives for these children, the location of schools etc. Different types of deprivations are very common in slum localities. In slum a child faces social, economic, cultural and parental deprivation. These all lead to educational deprivation. Due to many reasons the deprived children are not able to fulfil their basic needs as well as education. Some of them are illiterate and some are dropouts. In present scenario we talk about universalization of elementary education but it renders no meaning to deprived children living in slums.

Any country's development is dependent upon its educational status. Many incentives have taken place to raise the educational level but most of them are in wrong direction. Provision of literacy programme is not the solution of problem of illiteracy. This problem can be tackled only through implementation of provision of universal, free and compulsory education.

If we do not educate the children, after some time they will join one or the other literacy programme and it will become cyclic process. This will be same as if one tries to dry the floor and on the other hand the tap is opened; means useless efforts. Thus teachers, administrations and policy-makers must focus on elementary education because only through this the problem of illiteracy can be uprooted. Policy-makers should consider socio-economic factors of society which create favourable or unfavourable conditions for implementation of certain policy. If we want to implement universalization of elementary education successfully then we must consider the needs, problems, expectations and life-styles of deprived section. Adverse conditions in children's life-styles are major obstacles in universalisation of elementary education. A poor person cannot think about education of his children until he fulfils their basic needs. Universalization of elementary education can be possible only when education will be related with real life's situations of people. Thus when any policy is evolved policy-makers must consider the living patterns of the people and their local needs. Education should be related with daily life and needs of deprived sections. More practical knowledge should be provided along with theoretical knowledge. There are many reasons of non-completion of elementary education which are embodied in life-styles of children. So administrators must consider these reasons while framing any policy. Slum children are deprived of many facilities. They do not have stimulating conditions for education at home. So teachers should encourage them. Time-table of school should be flexible and according to convenience of these children. Teachers should try to make their teaching more effective and interesting to create interest of children in education. Voluntarism can play an important role in this mission of universalization of elementary education. Thus every responsible citizen of country must understand importance of education as well as his/her duty towards it, and then only we can achieve our target of universalization of elementary education.

REFERENCES

Adams, Robert (ed.) (2002); *'Social Policy for Social Work'*, Hampshire, Palgrave Hound Mills.

Bajpai, L.B. and Bajpai, Amita (2000); *'Vishishta Balak'*, Lucknow, Bharat Book Centre.

Basu, D.D. (2002); *Bharat ka Samvidhan: Ek Parichay*, New Delhi, Wadhwa Company Law Publishers.

Bhengra, Silvestor (1997), *Jhopadpatti mein rahane wale bachchon ko shiksha na mil pane ke karno ka addhayan*, Unpublished M.Ed. dissertation, University of Lucknow.

Burt, Cyril (1951): *The Backward Child*, London, University of London Press Limited.

Clarizio, Harvey F. and McCoy, George F. (1970); *'Behaviour Disorders in School-aged Children*, Scrantion Chandler Publishing Company.

Crombic, Nicholas and Hill, Stephans (ed.) (2000); The *Penguin Dictionary of Sociology*, New Delhi, Penguin Books.

Kaplen, Diane S., Peck B. Mitchell, Kaplen, Howard B.; 'Decomposing the Academic Failure-Dropout Relationship: A Longitudinal Analysis', *The Journal of Educational Research*, Vol. 90, No. 6, July/August, 1997.

Kumar, Girish (ed.) (1996); *Samajkarya ke Chhetra*, Lucknow, Uttar Pradesh Hindi Sansthan.

Panda, K.C. (1997); *Education of Exceptional Children*, New Delhi, Vikas Publishing House Private Limited.

Pringle, M.L. Kellmer (1965); *Deprivation and Education*, London, Longman Green & Co. Limited.

Sadgopal, Anil (2000); *Shiksha mein Badlav ka Sawal*, Delhi, Granth Shilpi (India) Private Limited.

Sharma, Brij Kishore (2007); *Bharat ka Samvidhan: Ek Parichay*, New Delhi, Prentice Hall of India Private Limited.

Singh, Sunil Kumar, 'Voluntarism in Contemporary Indian Society and Universalisation of Elementary Education', *The Primary Teacher*, Vol. XXVII, No. 2, April 2002.

19 Rural-Urban Divide in Education Sector in Assam

An Underdeveloped State in India

Ira Das

Education is considered as the most important instrument of beneficent social change and development in any country. Although , equity in education by gender, caste and socio-economic groups has been the major objectives of educational planning in India (Tilak, 2006), in a developing country like India there is critical gap in educational attainments across regions and population segments (Copal Partners, 2007). The largest disparity in educational attainment in India is perhaps by rural-urban location (Bajpai and Goyal, 2004). While there has been overall improvement in literacy rates both for males and females, the differences continue to be unacceptably large between rural and urban areas, especially for females. According to Census data, only 46 per cent of females in rural areas were literate against nearly 73 per cent in urban areas in 2001, a gap of around 27 percentage points. For males, the gap was lower at around 15 percentage points with 71.1 per cent of males in the rural areas and 86.4 per cent in the urban areas being literate in 2001.

The underinvestment in education and inter - and intra-sectoral pattern of allocation of resources is found to be in imbalance in the development of education in the country (Tilak, 2006). As noticed by Mazumdar (2007), "the most revealing aspect of the various school-related statistics presented in a survey is the stark reality of inequality in public spending. The rural-urban divide in the distribution of educational resources stares in the face of the reader with unfailing regularity. For example, ...a clear difference in the provision of teachers in rural and urban areas." The average expenditure per student of 5-24 years old pursuing general education by broad level of education is Rs. 570 in rural areas and Rs. 1,686 in urban areas in India in 1995-96 (NSSO, 1998). Percentage share of household expenditure on education in total household expenditure is 2.87 per cent for rural people and 5.04 per cent for urban people according to Micro Impacts of Macro-economics and Adjustment Policies (MIMAP) Survey, 1994-95. Moreover, it is said that disparities in the quality of education provided by different schools are very large and increasing and the disparities which begin with primary school are carried forward to the level of secondary and higher education (Beteille, 2008). Aicha Bah-Diallo, Deputy Assistant Director General of UNESCO's Education Sector, also said "In many cases, legislators don't assess rightfully the importance of education for rural people in the development of their countries. This indifference towards rural people is the result of a strong urban bias on the part of politicians and policy-makers" (UNESCO, 2003). It is also said that not only because of the lack of financial resources, but a strong political will that is lacking (Dreze and Sen, 1995) in this regard.

The available educational facilities in Assam, an under-developed State in India is even less than the all India average as 'Elementary Education in India, 2005-06—An Analytical Report' included a unique Education Development Index (EDI) according to elementary provision (the variables asserted to compute EDI are: access, infrastructure, teachers and learning outcomes) which ranks Assam in 17th position among the 21 major States). In Assam, 87.1 per cent people are living in rural areas as stated by the Census of 2001. As reported in the Assam Human Development

Report, 2003, there exists vast rural-urban divide in accessing the educational facilities in the State. The average expenditure per student of 5-24 years old pursuing general education by broad level of education is Rs. 506 in rural areas and Rs. 1,380 in urban areas in Assam which are found below the all India average in 1995-96 (NSSO, 1998). Therefore, although rural-urban disparity in education sector is well known, the issue relating to the disparity has not been very well analyzed in Assam. Nature and magnitude of rural-urban disparity in accessing the educational facilities in Assam compared to the national average obviously becomes the concern of the time. Since not many studies have been carried out on this issue, a systematic and empirical study in this regard is felt required. To investigate the reasons behind this divide, this chapter examines whether there exists urban bias in policy making of the government regarding educational services for rural and urban people in the State.

Objectives of the Study

The specific objectives are :

1. To assess the nature and magnitude of rural-urban disparity in education sector in Assam *vis-à-vis* India.
2. To examine whether there exists urban bias in the policy making of the government in education sector in Assam.

Data Source and Methodology

The study is based entirely on secondary data and exclusive of private sector. The secondary data are collected from various sources like National Sample Survey (NSS) Reports, National Sample Survey Organisation (NSSO); National Institute of Educational Policy Research (NIEPR), Analytical Tables; National University of Educational Policy Research (NUEPR) Analytical Tables; Census Reports; Directorate of Secondary Education, Directorate of Elementary Education,

Kahilipara, Assam; *Sarba Siksha Abhiyan,* Assam; District Office for Elementary Education, Chatribari, Guwahati-01, and from internet sources. Detailed sources are furnished in respective tables and references. There are different layers of education system in India: primary, secondary, higher, adult education etc. The nature and magnitude of rural-urban disparity from the available data in different layers in education sector is tried to capture with the help of disparity in educational outputs and educational inputs representing different students related, school related, teacher's quality related indicators. Literacy Rate (LTR), Gross Enrolment Rate (GER), Attendance Rate (ATN), Dropout Rate (DRP), General Education Level (ADL) are taken as the education outputs. Following are taken as inputs for educational attainment:

(i) Percentage distribution of schools by type of building (PKM);
(ii) Average number of classrooms (CLR);
(iii) Pupil-Teacher Ratio (PTR);
(iv) Percentage distribution of trained teachers provided in service training (STR)
(v) Percentage of schools having boundary wall (BWL);
(vi) Percentage of schools not having building (NBL);
(vii) Percentage of schools having Drinking Water Facility (DWF);
(viii) Percentage of schools having separate Girls' Toilet Facility (GTF);
(ix) Percentage of schools having Electricity Connection (ELC);
(x) Percentage of schools having Playground (PLG);
(xi) Percentage of schools conducting Medical check-up last year (MED);
(xii) Percentage of schools having Book-Bank facility (BOK);

During study period, educational outputs have been taken for years 1991, 1993-94, 1995-96, 1999-2000, 2001 and 2004-05 and educational inputs have been taken for 2002, 2004-05 and 2005-06 due to limited availability of rural-urban breakup data with the government departments. To assess the divide between the rural and urban areas, Rural-Urban Disparity Index (RUDI) is constructed from the proposal for Afghanistan Rural Development Report by AIRD (2006) as

$$RUDI = (1 - I_R/I_U)*100$$

RUDI is calculated for both educational output indicators and educational inputs indicators separately. Here, I_R is the composite index of the educational output/input indicators for rural areas with equal weights. Similarly, I_U is the composite index of the educational output/input indicators for urban areas with equal weights. Indices are calculated for available data by taking the formula as follows:

$$I = (\text{Actual value} - \text{Minimum value})/(\text{Maximum value} - \text{Minimum value})$$

Since Dropout Rate and not literate above 15 years of age are the negative indicators, the inverse of these indices are taken for calculation of the composite index for rural and urban areas calculation in line with India's Social Development Report, 2006 [Council for Social Development (2006, pp. 219)]. Similarly, *kutcha* type of building, pupil-teacher ratio, and percentage of schools not having building are also negative educational input indicators and inverse of the indices are taken for calculating the composite index.

Here, the maximum and minimum values for different indicators are taken as follows[1]:

Educational Output Indicators

LTR: Maximum value: 100, Minimum value: 0
GER: Maximum value: 100; Minimum value: 0

ATN: Maximum value: 100, Minimum value: 0
ADL: Maximum value: 100, Minimum value: 0

Educational Input Indicators :

PKM: Maximum value: 100, Minimum value: 0
CLR: Maximum value: 23.8, Minimum value: 1
PTR: Maximum value: 30, Minimum value: 1
For STR, BWL, NBL, DWF, GTF, ELC, PLG, MED, BOK: Maximum value: 100, Minimum value: 0

To examine the urban bias in the policy making of the government the different types of available financial grants are compared for rural and urban areas.

Results and Discussions

I. *Rural-Urban Disparity in Educational Attainment or Outputs in Assam compared to All India Average*

Table19.1 reveals that the rural-urban disparity in literacy level was more in Assam compared to all India average in 1991. Although the rural-urban gap for literacy rate has narrowed down by 49.17 per cent in Assam against 8.45 per cent in the national average during the period from1991 to 2004-05 showing the optimistic picture of increasing literacy rate in rural areas in the State, however, the rural-urban gap still remains significant both for the State and the country as a whole. There was a significant gap of 24.9 percentage points between rural and urban areas in the State in case of GER compared to 14.9 percentage points in the country average in 1995-96 and the gap has narrowed down by 94.42 per cent in the State against 88.46 per cent in the country as a whole during the period from 1995-96 to 2004-05. The rural-urban gap was prominent in 1991 with a gap of 19.92 percentage points in the State in case of students currently attending the educational institution. The gap has narrowed down significantly by 87.94 per cent compared to 71.11 per

Table 19.1 : Rural-Urban Disparity in Educational Attainments or Outputs in Assam compared to the All India Average

Education Outputs(%)			1991$		1993-94$		1995-96*		1999-00$		2001$	
			Rural	Urban	Rural	Urban	Rural	Urban	Rural	Urban	Rural	Urban
1. Literacy Rate (LTR)		Assam	49.32	79.39	69	88	67.3	86.4	69	86	60.92	85.76
		India	44.69	73.08	50	77	46.4	77	56	80	59.21	80.06
2. Gross Enrolment Rate (GER)		Assam	N.A	N.A	N.A	N.A	55.6#	70.5#	75.1?	79.5?	17.08a	19.07a
		India	N.A	N.A	N.A	N.A	46.4#	61.3#	71.6?	78.2?	8.99	24.5
3. Students currently attending the educational institution (ATN)		Assam	31.96+	51.88+	74.4^	81.4^	55.1#	46.1#	71.2**	83.8**	81.3v	88.8v
		India	45.8v	68.3v	63.3^	82.4^	70.2#	61.1#	69**	81.5**	79.9v	90.2v
4. Dropouts (DRP)		Assam	N.A	N.A	22^	14.6^	62.3#	56.4#	N.A	N.A	N.A	N.A
		India	N.A	N.A	33.1^	15^	58.1#	51.3#	33.6>	15.15>	N.A	N.A
5.Persons of age15+ by general education level, (ADL)	Not literate	Assam	37.94	13.79	39.8	20.2	32.7	13.6	31	13.9	29	9.82
		India	63.69	38.28	56.4	30.9	53.6	23	44	20.2	28.46	12.59
	Literate upto Primary	Assam	12.31	11.47	38.2	29.2	17.4	13.7	17.7	17.3	14.11	11.08
		India	11.48	14.72	28.5	32.2	13.3	13.8	13.5	14.7	17.83	14.25
	Middle	Assam	29.37	38.68	13.9	21.5	18.6	24.7	17.3	19.7	20.39	21.45
		India	7.61	12.84	8.3	13.2	12.6	19	12.3	16.5	18.74	18.95
	Secondary	Assam	13.77	24.15	8b	28.9b	8.5	16.1	7	13.7	18.71	28.64
		India	5.41	15.38	7.6c	19.1c	6.5	15.4	6.4	13.5	15.51	23.85
	Higher Secondary	Assam	2.1	7.51	N.A	N.A	3.7	11.1	3	9.2	5.43	14.21
		India	N.A	N.A	1.9	10.9	2.6	8.9	2.8	8.5	6.71	15.4
	Diploma/ Certificate	Assam	0.05	0.1	N.A	N.A	0.1	0.6	0.1d	0.7d	0.04	0.27
		India	0.14	0.59	N.A	N.A	0.2	0.9	0.4d	1.2d	0.43	1.08
	Graduate and above	Assam	0.22	0.68	N.A	N.A	1.8	10.4	1.5	12.1	1.39	6.56
		India	1	6.68	1.5c	12.1c	1.4	9.2	1.7	10.5	1.89	7.32

Table 19.1 *(Contd...)*

Education Outputs(%)			2004-05*		Rural-Urban Gap					
			Rural	*Urban*	*1991*	*1993-94*	*1995-96*	*1999-00*	*2001*	*2004-05*
1. Literacy Rate (LTR)		Assam	73	88.3	30.1	19	19.1	17	24.9	15.3
		India	54.5	80.5	28.4	27	30.6	24	20.9	26
2. Gross Enrolment Rate (GER)		Assam	90.81~	92.2~	-	-	24.9	4.4	1.99	1.39
		India	93.94~	95.66~	-	-	14.9	6.6	15.5	1.72
3. Students currently attending the educational institution (ATN)		Assam	54.2@	56.6@	19.9	-	-9	12.6	7.5	2.4
		India	48.5@	53@	22.5	19.1	-9.1	12.5	10.3	6.5
4. Dropouts(DRP)		Assam	22¤	24¤	-	-7.4	-5.9	-	-	2
		India	16.33¤	14.36¤	-	-18.1	-6.8	-18.5	-	-2
5.Persons of age15+ by general education level (ADL)	Not literate	Assam	26.8	11.6	-24	-19.6	-19.1	-17.1	-19	-15
		India	45.2	19.6	-25	-25.5	-30.6	-23.8	-16	-26
	Literate upto Primary	Assam	38.3	18.1	-0.8	-9	-3.7	-0.4	-3	-20
		India	23.8	20	3.24	3.7	0.5	1.2	-3.6	-3.8
	Middle	Assam	20.5	24.8	9.31	7.6	6.1	2.4	1.06	4.3
		India	15.2	18.2	5.23	4.9	6.4	4.2	0.21	3
	Secondary	Assam	8.6	13.1	10.4	20.9	7.6	6.7	9.93	4.5
		India	8.2	15.3	9.97	11.5	8.9	7.1	8.34	7.1
	Higher Secondary	Assam	3.9	15.5	5.41	-	7.4	6.2	8.78	11.6
		India	4.1	10.4	-	9	6.3	5.7	8.69	6.3
	Diploma/ Certificate	Assam	0.1	1.1	0.05	-	0.5	0.6	0.23	1
		India	0.7	2.6	0.45	-	0.7	0.8	0.65	1.9
	Graduate and above	Assam	1.6	15.7	0.46	-	8.6	10.6	5.17	14.1
		India	2.5	14	5.68	10.6	7.8	8.8	5.43	11.5

(Contd...)

Notes:

- * for persons aged 15 years and above.
- ^ for students of age 5-14 years.
- # for enrolment rate (%) and for students of age 5-24 years.
- @ for students of age 5-29 years.
- v for students of age 6-10 years and 1991 figure is the average figure taken from male and female figures as given by Premji (2004) and census india.net/cendat/datatable 15 html;figure for 2001 is from MICS-2000.
- ** for the year 1998-99 and for the students of age 6-17 years.
- < for students of age 6-17 years and data is from NFHS II,Table 2.9 as presented in India Rural Infrastructure Report, 2007.
- i implies the data is for the age of 6-14 years as presented in *Labour and Development*, Vol.11-12, No. 2 and 1, June 2006 from Srivastava, Ravi (2002).
- $ for students of age 7 years and above and the data for general education level is for the students of age 15-19 for 1991, of age 15+ for 1993-94 and of age 15-24 for 2001. The data for 1993-94 are from NSS 50th Round, Report No. 409.
- ~ for the students of age 6-13 years and data is from http://ssa.nic.in accessed on 13-10-07.
- ? implies the figure is for Net Enrolment Ratio.
- ¤ is for students of class I only.
- \+ is for the students of age 5-9.
- a is for the students of class I-XII.
- b is for secondary and above.
- c implies the data is for July 1994-June 95 from NSS 51st Round, Report No. 436.
- d implies the data is for age 7 and above and for July 2000-June 01 from NSS 56th Round, Report No. 476.

Sources:

1. WWW.censusindia.net accessed on 22-09-07
2. htp://education.nic.in/cd50years/r/6H/HI/6HHI0701.htm accessed on 16-09-07.
3. GoA(2003)
4. Tilak (2006)
5. NSSO (1997)
6. NSSO (1998)
7. NSSO (2001)
8. NSSO (2006)
9. www.childinfo.org/MICS2/newreports/india/india.pdf accessed on 30-09-07.
10. www.mospi.nic.in accessed on 19-09-07

cent in the country as a whole during the study period from 1991 to 2004-05. The rural-urban gap in percentage of dropout has narrowed down both for the State and the country as a whole. However, the rural-urban disparity persists for not literate persons of age above 15 *i.e.* adult literacy with a significant 15.2 percentage points in 2004-05 (the rural-urban gap was 24.2 percentage points in 1991) in Assam compared to the same with 25.6 percentage points in 2004-05 for the country. In case of the percentage of persons of age 15 and above attained levels of education, only a marginal fall in the gap between rural and urban areas both for the State and the country average is found. However, in case of diploma and certificate holders, the gap between rural and urban areas has increased both for the State and the country except a marginal fall in 2001. Similarly, the gap has widened significantly regarding higher education *i.e.* in the level of graduate and above both for the State and the country as a whole except a significant fall in 2001.

II. Rural-Urban Disparity in Educational Inputs in Assam Compared to All India Average

Table 19.2 reveals the disparity between rural and urban areas in case of important educational inputs. Significantly the gap between rural and urban schools in case of type of *pucca* building is much more in Assam compared to all India average and the gap has widened by 33.10 per cent from 2002 to 2005-06 in the State. It shows that infrastructure regarding school building of the rural schools in Assam is bad compared to national average. The disparity in case of average number of classrooms (CLR) is less in the State compared to the national average. However, the disparity has increased more (by 58.82 per cent) from 2002 to 2005-06 in Assam than the national average (by 39.13 per cent) for the same period. The rural-urban gap in Pupil-Teacher Ratio (PTR) is marginally existing both for the State and the national average and the gap narrows down marginally

Table 19.2 : Disparity in Educational Inputs in Assam compared to All India Average

Educational Inputs			*2002**		*2004-05***		*2005-06***		*Rural Urban Gap*		
			Rural	*Urban*	*Rural*	*Urban*	*Rural*	*Urban*	*2002*	*2004-05*	*2005-06*
1. % distribution of	a.*Pucca*	Assam	36.61	49.49	38.13	53.41	43.55	60.72	12.9	15.31	17.17
schools by type of	b.*Kuchha*	India	80.61	83.62	70.07	74.3	70.36	74.57	3	4.2	4.21
building (PKM)		Assam	16.57	6.57	11.45	3.91	9.42	3.06	-10.03	-7.59	-6.36
	c.*Multiple*	India	N.A	2.57	1.99	0.92	1.91	0.88	-1.95	-1.07	-1.03
	Type	Assam	45.06	45.09	7.47	14.05	8.13	12.84	0.03	6.58	4.71
		India	12.24	11.65	10.65	7.95	8.61	7.92	-0.59	-2.75	-0.69
2. Average number of		Assam	1.6	3.3	2	4.6	2	4.7	1.7	2.6	2.7
Classrooms (CLR)		India	2.5	4.8	3.3	6.6	3.5	6.7	2.3	3.3	3.2
3. Pupil-Teacher		Assam	30#	23#	26.41	22.74	25.17	20.82	-7	-3.66	-4.35
Ratio (PTR)		India	44#	36#	38.73	32.92	36.76	32.08	-8	-5.78	-4.68
4. % distribution of		Assam	N.A	N.A	51.14	43.82	59.32	52.79	-	-7.32	-6.53
teachers provided in service training (STR)		India	N.A	N.A	42.07	21.12	45.1	25.87	-	-20.98	-19.23
5. % of schools having		Assam	N.A	N.A	32.7	51.98	29.1	51.97	-	19.28	22.87
Boundary Wall (BWL)		India	N.A	N.A	47.5	75.87	46.89	75.79	-	28.37	28.9
6. % of schools not		Assam	1.75#	0.85#	0.78	0.45	0.54	0.28	-0.9	-0.33	-0.26
having building (NBL)		India	2.63#	2.16#	4.19	2.55	4.37	2.54	-0.47	-1.64	-1.83
7. % of schools having		Assam	53.87	60.64	63.13	71.29	70.36	74.48	6.77	8.19	4.12
Drinking Water Facility (DWF)		India	75.72	83.66	80.56	87.05	82.59	89.26	7.94	6.45	6.67
8. % of schools having		Assam	6.36	15.6	7.44	21.13	8.85	22.65	9.24	13.69	13.8
separate Girls' Toilet Facility (GTF)		India	24.58	58.23	29.41	58.85	34.17	61.9	33.65	29.45	27.73

Table 19.2 : *(Contd...)*

9. % of schools having Electricity Connection in school (ELC)	Assam	0.98	27.66	5.04	43.12	5.38	45.16	26.68	38.08	39.78
	India	10.93	53.07	23.2	67.76	25.08	69.2	42.14	44.56	44.12
10. % of schools having Playground in the school (PLG)	Assam	25.53	21.91	50.45	41.84	50.56	42.53	-3.62	-8.66	-8.03
	India	34.79	39.34	49.69	61.7	50.92	62.87	4.55	12	11.95
11. % of schools conducting medical check-up last year (MED)	Assam	3.43	8.94	3.24	7.18	4.24	7.8	5.51	3.94	3.56
	India	51.78	58.16	53.74	58.64	52.8	58.07	6.38	4.94	5.27
12. % of schools having Book-Bank facility (BOK)	Assam	N.A	N.A	23.58	30.44	26.2	30.26	-	6.84	4.06
	India	N.A	N.A	43.12	49.76	46.89	55.52	-	6.66	8.63

Notes
- * implies that the data is for primary level only.
- ** implies that the data is for all schools which include categories of primary only, primary with upper primary and secondary/higher secondary, upper primary only, upper primary with secondary/higher secondary.
- @ implies that the data is for middle (VI to VIII) level only.
- # implies that the data is for all levels of students i.e. primary, middle, secodary, higher secondary and above higher secondary students.
- < for constant prices. N.A means not available.

Sources:
1. NSSO (1998).
2. Mehta, C. (2005).
3. Bhandari Laveesh (2006) for 6th and 7th All India Educational Survey,1993 and 2002 respectively.
4. Jalaluddin, (2007) for 5th All India Educational Survey,1986.
5. Kochar, Anjini (2001).
6. http://manipur.nic.in/planning/DraftMSDR/Draft_SDR_pdf/Chapter%2014_edu.pdf accessed on 07-10-07.
7. http://censusindia.net *accessed on 08-10-07.*
8. Mehta, C (2007)
9. NUEPA (2007), Flash Statistics of Indian states, 2005-06 from http://www.dise.in/Downloads/EDI.pdf accessesd on 05-08-08

during the study period. It is significant that the percentage distribution of teachers having in-service training (STR) is more in rural areas than in urban areas in Assam as well as India. Although the rural-urban disparity in case of percentage of schools having Boundary Wall (BWL) is less in the State compared to the national average, however, the disparity persists both for the State and the national average. The disparity is significant with 19.28 percentage points in 2004-05 which has further increased to 22.87 percentage points in 2005-06 for the State. The disparity in percentage of schools not having building (NBL) has decreased in Assam while the disparity has increased in the national average during the study period. The rural-urban disparity in percentage of schools having Drinking Water Facility (DWF) is significant though it is decreasing both for the State and the national average except an increase of 20.97 percentage points in 2004-05 for the State. However, the rural-urban gap has widened by 49.35 per cent from 2002 to 2005-06 in Assam regarding percentage of schools having separate Girls' Toilet Facility (GTF) against a narrowing down of gap by 17.59 per cent in the same period in the country average. There is also significant rural-urban disparity regarding the percentage of schools having Electricity Connection (ELC) in Assam and the disparity has further widened by 49.10 per cent during the period from 2002 to 2005-06. The gap is more in the country average. Interestingly, the condition of rural schools in the State is better regarding the percentages of schools having Playground in the school (PLG) whereas better condition of the urban schools in the country average is found in this regard. Regarding percentages of schools conducting medical check-up (MED), the performance of Assam is far behind the national average both in rural and urban areas and a marginal fall has been observed in the gap between rural and urban areas in the State and the country as well. The rural-urban gap in percentages of schools having book-bank facility (BOK) has narrowed down by 40.64 per cent during the period from 2004-05 to 2005-06 in Assam against a widening gap in the same period in the country average.

To have a better idea about the disparity between rural and urban areas, Rural-Urban Disparity Index (RUDI) has been constructed. From the Table 19.3 it is evident that the RUDIs for educational output for Assam show a falling trend by 21.33 per cent during the period from 1991 to 2001 with a sharp fall by 82.31 per cent during the period from 2001 to 2004-05. RUDI for all India average fluctuates from 37.5 in 1991 to highest of 49.37 in 1993-94 followed by 45.65 in 1999-00 and finally 15.97 in 2004-05. This implies a better trend for the State compared to the national average in educational attainment over a period of about 15 years from the available data. The values of RUDI for educational inputs in the State are more than the country average except in 2004-05 showing more disparity in Assam. Although disparity in educational input is falling by 18.38 per cent in the State from 2002 to 2005-06, RUDI remains high in the State (47.64) compared to the national average (44.00) in 2005-06. The disparity in educational inputs is increasing by 38.32 per cent in national average during the period from 2002 to 2005-06.

Table 19.3 : The Value of Rural-Urban Disparity Indices (RUDI) for Educational Outputs and Inputs in Assam compared to All India Average

	Value of RUDI								
	Educational Outputs						*Educational Inputs*		
	1991	*1993-94*	*1995-96*	*1999-00*	*2001*	*2004-05*	*2002*	*2004-05*	*2005-06*
Assam	48.43	32.28	21.55	26.2	38.1	6.74	58.37	41.46	47.64
India	37.5	49.37	21.45	45.65	35.3	15.97	31.81	43.46	44.00

Examination of Urban Bias

To examine whether there exists any urban bias in the policy making of the government, different types of grants allotted to schools located in rural and urban areas are compared for available data. Higher educational institutions are located mostly in urban areas, therefore, urban areas are obviously in an advantageous position. Hence, urban bias is examined for elementary and secondary education. 11th Finance Commission granted more money for urban students in 2002-03. However, new school building grant for the same year shows a different picture of per capita expenditure of Rs. 34.38 for rural students whereas it was nil for the urban students. New school building grant in the year 2003-04 and 2006-07 show more per capita expenditure for urban students whereas the same grant in the year 2004-05, 2005-06 shows more per capita expenditure on rural students. More per capita expenditure on urban students have been observed in the year 2002-03, 2004-05 and 2005-06 regarding the additional class room and repairing and renovation grant. However, per capita expenditure on rural students is more for the same grant for the year 2003-04 and 2006-07. The 12th Finance Commission grant for supply of blackboard and cooking equipment grant in 2006-07 also shows more expenditure on rural students than on urban students. Moreover, kitchen shed and store room grant for rural student is found more than that of urban students. Therefore, it becomes difficult to make any comment regarding urban bias from this handful of data. Due to non-availability of the data for other grants, it is not easy to generalize that there exists any urban bias in the policy making of the government. Moreover, the data are mainly for elementary education for recent years and government has given more importance in universal elementary education thereby giving importance to rural areas.

Conclusion

People must have a level playing field and have equal opportunity to grow themselves. Education provide level playing field for reducing disparity among the people in the country. However, vast rural-urban disparity in the

Table 19.4 : Per Capita Expenditure for Rural and Urban Students in Assam in School Grants

Grants	*Year*	*Per Capita Expenditure on Student (Rs.)*	
		Rural	*Urban*
1. 11th Finance Commission Grant	2002-03	38.31	321.6
2. New School Building Grant*	2002-03	34.38	Nil
	2003-04	20.1	27.32
	2004-05	19.31	2.39
	2005-06	179.78	Nil
	2006-07	29.14	29.65
3. Additional Classroom and Repairing and Renovation Grant*	2002-03	186.98	1832.77
	2003-04	35.02	10.36
	2004-05	47.42	65.37
	2005-06	44.79	69.5
	2006-07	800.47	649.42
4. 12th Finance Commission grant for supply of Blackboard (Rs.489.98 per school)	2006-07	2.95	2.81
5. Kitchen shed and store room grant (Rs.60,000 per school)*	2006-07	170.2	120.28
6. For provisioning/replacement of cooking equipment grant (Rs.5000 per school)*	2006-07	23.72	10.52
7. 12th Finance Commission award for construction of Girls' Common Room (Rs.1 lakh per school)**	2006-07	46.39	36.13
8. Supply of science Kit Box to ME school (Rs. 42,000 per school)	2006-07	9.29	8.64

Notes : Per capita expenditure on rural and urban students are calculated as dividing total expenditure by total rural and urban enrolment of students for respective years. Moreover, due to non-availability of the enrolment figure for the year 2006-07, the enrolment figure for the year 2005-06 is used to calculate the per capita expenditure for the year 2006-07.

* The grants are only for elementary education in Kamrup district from *Sarva Siksha Abhijan* (SSA) except 11th Finance Commission grant.

** The grants are for secondary schools in Kamrup district, Assam and due to non-availability of data for student enrolment in Kamrup district for 2006-07 in rural-urban break up, the per capita rural and urban expenditures are calculated by dividing total grants by the student enrolment in secondary school as given in 7th All India Educational Survey.

Source : 1. Directorate of Elementary Education, Kahilipara, Guwahati-19.
2. Directorate of Secondary Education, Kahilipara, Guwahati-19.
2. District Office, Kamrup District, Chatribari, Guwahati-01.
3. Census Report, 2001 from Assam at a Glance, Directorate of Census Operations, Assam, Guwahati-07.
4. www.dpepmis.org accessed on 29-10-07.

education sector in the State was reported in Assam Human Development Report, 2003. This paper assesses the rural-urban divide in accessing the educational facilities in the State with the help of available secondary data. The study reflects rural-urban disparity in educational attainment still prevailing both for the State and the national average. Although the disparity is falling down more significantly in the State than the national level regarding the indicators of literacy rate, GER, ATN and DRP, percentage of persons acquired higher education and diploma/certificate course is less in the State than all India average. Regarding rural-urban disparity, significant disparity has been observed in almost all the education input indicators except for schools having playground facility in the State. Disparity between two areas increases over the period from 2002 to 2005-06 in *pucca* building facility, average number of classrooms, schools having boundary walls, girls' toilet facility and schools with electricity connection in the State. Regarding disparity in the educational inputs, the position of Assam is comparatively better than the all India average in CLR, BWL, DWF, GTF, ELC, PLG, MED and BOK. The values of RUDI show a somewhat better trend for the State compared to the national average in educational attainment over a period of about 15 years from the available data. However, the values of RUDI of educational inputs in the State are more than the country average showing more disparity in Assam. Although, the values of RUDI for educational inputs show a falling trend in Assam, RUDI remains high in the State (47.65) compared to the national average (44.04) in 2005-06. Due to non-availability of the sufficient information and data for grants, it is not easy to generalize that there exists any urban bias in the policy making of the Government. Government has given more importance in universal elementary education in recent years thereby giving importance to rural areas. Therefore, no clear urban bias has been observed in education sector in the State. Of course, higher educational institutions are located mostly in urban areas and, therefore, urban areas are obviously in an advantageous position in the State. Moreover, private sector investment in education sector is occurring mostly in urban areas and thereby contributing in favour of urban sector which have been excluded in this study. This point needs further study. .Government should direct private investment equally to rural area also for balanced development and not to further already existing rural-urban disparity.

NOTES

1. In case of LTR, GER, ATN, ADL, PKM, STR, BWL, NBL, DWF, GTF, ELC, PLG, MED, and BOK, the figures are in percentages and, therefore, the maximum value is taken as 100 and minimum as 0. In case of Average Number of Classrooms (CLR), the maximum value is taken as 23.8 because this is the figure for best performed State (Chandigarh) in average number of classrooms for all schools (which includes classes primary only, primary with upper primary, primary with upper primary and secondary/higher secondary, upper primary only, upper primary with secondary/higher secondary) in 2005-06. On the other hand, minimum value is taken as 1 by assuming at least one classroom for all the classes.

   In case of Pupil-Teacher Ratio (PTR), the maximum value is taken as 30 as it is stated in *India Together*, Friday, 09 November, 2007 (accessed from *www.indiatogether.org* on 09-11-07) that 3:1 has been accepted as the appropriate ratio in world-wide .Moreover, Economic Review, 2006 of Kerala Government (accessed from *http://www.keralaplanningboard.org/* on 31-07-08) worked out the pupil-teacher ratio as 30.67 : 1 by taking average of the lower primary, upper primary and high school level. On the other hand, 1 is taken as minimum value as there must be at least one teacher in schools.

REFERENCES

AIRD-Afghanistan Institute for Rural Development (2006), *A Proposal for Afghanistan Rural Development Report,* accessed from *http://www.mrrd.gov.af/aird/RDR%20Proposal%20of%20Afganistan%20%Rural%20 Development* on 26-07-07.

Bajpai, N. and S. Goyal (2004), "Primary Education: Low Coverage, Poor Quality", *Business*.

Line, Financial Daily from The Hindu Group of Publications, Wednesday, June, 09.

Beteille, Andre (2008), "Access to Education", *Economic and Political Weekly*, Vol. XLIII, No. 20, May 17-23, pp. 40-48.

Bhandari, Laveesh (2006), *Social Infrastructure: Urban Health and Education, Indian Infrastructure Report*, 2006, Chapter 11 for 6th All India Educational Survey, Copal Partners (2007), *Indian Education Sector*, Sector Research, India, Internal Reference Document, Accessed from *www.copalpartners.com/Library/PDF/Sector_Reports/Sector_Report_Education.pdf* on 22-09-07.

Council for Social Development (2006), *Indian Social Development Report*, Oxford University Press, p. 219.

Dreze, Jean and Amartya K. Sen (1995), "Basic Education as a Political Issue", *Journal of Educational Planning and Administration*, Vol. 9, No. 1, Jan, pp.1-26. GoA (2003), *Assam Human Development Report*.

GoA, Directorate of Elementary Education, Kahilipara, Guwahati-19.

GoA, Directorate of Secondary Education, Kahilipara, Guwahati-19.

GoA, District Office, Kamrup District, Chatribari-01.

GoI (2004), *Selected Socio-Economic Statistics, India, 2002*, CSO, Ministry of Statistics and Programme Implementation.

Jalaluddin, A.K *et al.* (2007), *Basic Education and National Development*, UNICEF, Compiled and cited from All India Educational Survey (NCERT).

Kochar, Anjini (2001), Emerging Challenges for Indian Education Policy, Working Paper No.97, Centre for Research on Economic Development and Policy Reform, March, Stanford from *http://scid.stanford.edu/pdf/credpv 97.pdf* accessed on 07-10-07.

Mazumdar, Manabi (2007), 'Elementary Education: Road Ahead', *The Hindu*, Tuesday, May, 8 accessed from *www.hindu.com/br/2007/05/08/stories/2007050800881500.htm* on 30-09-07.

Mehta, Arun C (2005), *Elementary Education in Rural India – Where do we stand?* Analytical Table 2005, National Institute of Educational Planning and Administration (NIEPA), New Delhi.

Mehta, Arun C. (2005), *Elementary Education in Urban India -- Where Do We Stand?* Analytical Table 2005, National Institute of Educational Planning and Administration (NIEPA), New Delhi.

Mehta, Arun C. (2007), *Elementary Education in Rural India – Where Do We Stand?* Analytical Table 2005-06, National University of Educational Planning and Administration (NUEPA), New Delhi, April.

Mehta, Arun C. (2007), *Elementary Education in Urban India – Where Do We Stand?* Analytical Table 2005-06, National University of Educational Planning and Administration (NUEPA), New Delhi, April.

National University of Educational Planning and Administration (NUEPA) (2007), *Elementary Education in India–Progress towards Universal Elementary Education*, Flash Statistics, DISE 2005-06, New Delhi from *http://www.dise.in/Downloads/EDI.pdf.* on 03-08-08.

NCERT (1993) and 7th All India Educational Survey and NCERT (2002) from *www.3inetwork.org/reports/IR2006/social_infra.pdf* accessed on 06-10- 07.

NSSO (1997), *Economic Activities and School Attendance by Students*, NSS 50th Round, No. 412, Department of Statistics, GoI, May.

NSSO (1998), *Attending on Educational Institution in India: Its Level, Nature and Cost*, NSS 52nd Round, Report No. 439, July 1995-June, 1996, Department of Statistics, GoI, Oct.

NSSO (2001), *Literacy and Levels of Education in India*, NSS 55th Round, Report No. 473, July 1999-June, 2000, Ministry of Statistics and Programme Implementation, GoI, Sept.

NSSO (2006), *Status of Education and Vocational Training in India*, NSS 61st Round, Report No. 517, July 2004-June 2005, Ministry of Statistics and Programme Implementation, GoI, Dec.

Ramachandran, Vimala (2003), *Gender Equity in Education (India) Progress in the Last Decade*, EFA Monitoring Report, UNESCO, India Case Study, 16 May, Educational Research Unit, New Delhi.

Tilak, J.B.G (2006), "Education — A Saga of Spectacular Achievements and Conspicuous Failures, *India: Social Development Report*, Council for Social Development, Oxford University Press, New Delhi.

UNESCO (2003), Education – Educating Rural People: a low priority, UNESCO Publication accessed from *www.ev.php-URL-ID=30347 & URL-DO=DO-PRINTPAGE & URL- =201.html* accessed 02-10-07.

www.childinfo.org/MICS2/newreports/india/india.pdf accessed on 30-09-07 for Multiple Indicator Survey-2000 (MICS-2000), India Summary Report, Department of Women and Child Development and United Nations Children's Fund, November, 2001.

www.ncear.org/downloads/reports/ruralinfrareportdraft.pdf accessed on 22-09-07 for India Rural Infrastructure Report, National Council of Applied Economic Research, New Delhi.

www.mospi.nic.in accessed on 19-09-07.

www.indiatogether.org accessed on 09-11-07.

www.tribuneindia.com/2000/2000519/edit.htm accessed on 14-11-07.

http://prayatna.typepad.com/education/datastatistics/ accessed on 04-08-08 for MIMAP survey, 1994-95).

www.censusindia.net accessed on 22-09-07.

www.education.nic.in/cd50years/r/6H/HI/6HHI0701.htm accessed on 16-09-07.

www.manipur.nic.in/planning/DraftMSDR/Draft_SDR_pdf/ Chapter%2014_edu.pdf accessed on 07-10-07.

www.ssa.nic.in accessed on 13-10-07.

www.keralaplanningboard.org/ accessed on 31-07-08.

www.dise.in//downloads/ruralurban.html accessed on 16-09-07.

www.dise.in/Downloads/EDI.pdf accessed on 05-08-08.

3i Network (2007), *India Infrastructure Report, 2007, Rural Infrastructure*, Oxford University Press.

www.dpepmis.org accessed on 29-10-07.

20 Psychological Basis of Value Education

Reena Agarwal

Mahatma Gandhi, the Father of Nation, at the age of 7, timid and shy by nature, would not speak with other boys. He had, however, one friend – Uka – an untouchable, the son of a sweeper. Mohandas (Gandhiji's childhood name) was once given some sweet dish at home and he ran to share it with Uka. 'Please do not come near me' pleaded horrified Uka. Mohandas paid no heed to it; he pulled his friend's hand and heckled it with sweet dish. Putlibai, Gandhiji's mother had been watching all this from her window. She called him and objected to his son's behaviour but Mohandas would not agree. He asked his mother, "Isn't he also another boy like me? What difference do you see between us?"

Mother Teresa, a noble prize winner, one day saw a poor old woman sitting huddled on the pavement with her face covered. Sister Teresa bent down to talk to her and she was shocked to find that the woman was a leper and she had been thrown away by her own kinsmen. Sister Teresa was filled with compassion; she decided to set up a dispensary to treat leprosy and tuberculosis.

A. P. J. Abdul Kalam, twelfth President of India, in 1958, as an aeronautical engineer, had applied to Air Force Selection Board for the post of commissioned officer. After facing the interview, he was in for a shock. He had no Air Force personality. Kalam stood still with dreams shattered. But slowly recovering and refurbishing himself with the aid of positive thinking and faith in Allah, he reached Rishikesh to have a *darshan* of Swami Shivanand – a great man and *yogi*. Kalam narrated his sad tale to him and was told 'What you are destined to become is not revealed now but is predetermined, surrender yourself to the Will of God, rely upon the eternally unbroken promise of sunrise and of the spring. Abdul Kalam was reassured.

The above incidents of great men are focussing on certain values such as persistently proceeding towards the goal in spite of the failure, to work for a mission not out of selfish motive, faith in oneself and in Almighty.

Values are highly internalized structures. Internalization implies that values influence not only thoughts, feelings, expressions and actions but they form the core of one's personality. Morality, the sense of right and wrong, forms the base of the value system.

Value means worth attached to anything – object, person or act. Value makes men's life meaningful and gives them a sense of direction. The term value stands for intrinsic worth, whatever is actually liked, prized, esteemed, desired, approved or enjoyed by anyone, is valuable. Values are essentially effective, in the sense that strong feeling is central to value. But it has cognitive and conative dimensions as well. It means that while a strong feeling is central to any value, its base lies in one's system of knowledge and beliefs, and tends to induce certain forms of behaviour.

Present Scenario

Today we are passing through a critical stage of battle between the best possibilities and the worst possibilities, which give experience of value crisis in our lives. Rapid social changes, globalization, materialistic society, population explosion, goal oriented society, environmental pollution, difference between thinking and action, self centeredness are some of the causes leading to distortion of personality. Disregard shown to basic values like honesty, tolerance in personal and public life have become a matter of grave national concern. Crime, violence, cruelty, greed, meanness, selfishness and indifference and apathy to human sufferings have spread to all aspects of our living—political, social and economic. The values of idealism, altruism, selflessness, and service to fellowmen are becoming increasingly rare in the younger generation who are not able to find any meaning in life and adopt escapist means as drug addiction and alcoholism. Campus violence and indiscipline have become integral part of each and every working day. Pursuit of material wealth and selfish ends at any cost has become the lifestyle of modern man. Sensitivity to beauty, arts, literature, craft, nature and life has declined and the object of life is now considered to make oneself as comfortable materially as one can.

The goals of our Constitution *i.e.* Secularism, Socialism and Democracy to which the Nation has declared its ideological commitment have come under severe stream. Deculturisation, dehumanization and alienation are increasing day by day in our society. Forces of social and national integration have become inactive. Rationality has been taken away by the forces of unreason. At present, 'man-making' and 'nation-building' are relegated to the back-ground and 'money-making' and 'material-building' are high on agenda. Honesty, freedom of expression, respecting others' views, treating others equally, enjoying the beauty of environment, selfless love for others, and to have a sense of right and wrong are something to which some individuals give importance or value while some do not. At birth, no child has a sense of value and no child can be expected to develop a moral code alone. Instead, every child must be taught the group standard of right and wrong. Even more important, they must develop a desire to do what is right, to act for the common good and to avoid wrong. This must be done through education. The aim of education is to develop human personality in all its dimensions – physical, intel-lectual, emotional, social, spiritual, and moral. In recent times for various reasons, the affective domain of educational objectives has suffered serious neglect. Education is just providing information with primary objective of producing examination result.

Although various education commissions and committees of Government of India gave emphasis on value education, but with each passing year, report of the indicated number of juvenile delinquents, teen pregnancy, suicide and adult criminals have been rising steadily. This indicates that there is something wrong with the development of children.

Mere knowledge providing in the school and home does not guarantee good or right behaviour because behaviour is motivated by factors other than knowledge. Social pressure, how children feel about themselves how they are treated by family members and peers, desires at the moment and many other factors influence how child will behave in a situation. The behaviour of 'true morality' not only confirms to social standards but also is carried out voluntarily. It comes from the transition from external to internal authority and consists of conduct regulated from within. It is accompanied by a feeling of personal responsibility one's act. Learning to behave in a socially approved manner is a long and slow process. There are mainly three approaches to learning—Behaviouristic, Socio-cognitive and Constructivistic. All these approaches can guide teachers and parents about the learning process of their children, especially the learning of various values.

Behaviouristic approach believes that reinforcement is a necessary condition for the acquisition, maintenance and modification of behaviour. If a child's action or behaviour is followed by positive reinforcement, this indicates that his behaviour is right, correct or good and if behaviour is followed by negative reinforcement or punishment then the behaviour is wrong or bad. The behaviour of the child is externally controlled, so are the values.

According to Socio-cognitive approach, behaviourists neglect that behaviour arising from cognitive processes. Human beings have some superior capabilities which provide him/herself direction. The individual can also learn the new behaviour in the absence of external reinforcement.

Albert Bandura, one of the main architects of socio-cognitive theory gave importance to Learning by Observation in place of Learning by Direct Reinforcement. Observation factor is key in learning. Children learn to enjoy studying, to do household chores, and learn to play games. They may learn to be aggressive, altruistic, cooperative or even abnoxious. Learning by observation is actively judgemental and constructive process rather than a mechanical copying process. Observational learning is governed by four inter-related processes—attention process, retention process, motor-reproductive process and motivational process. In attentional process, learner has to accurately perceive the salient cues and distinctive features of model. This process is affected by many factors such as associational patterns, interpersonal attractiveness, model who appear high in competence, etc. All these factors directly contribute to the learning of values by a child. *e.g.* a child learns the behaviour of the person with whom he is associated or has regular interaction. He can learn altruistic behaviour, cooperation, honesty, sympathy, dignity to labour if he is in contact with such a person or persons. Retention process refers that learners must have memory of model's behaviour and he must have the capacity to recall. The motor-reproduction refers to the process of translating memories into behaviour. Bandura believes that when a child observes behaviour but makes no observable response, the child may still have acquired the modelled response in cognitive form.

Although Bandura opposes the behaviouristic approach of direct reinforcement, he was of the opinion that reinforcement can aid modelling but it is not vital to it. People are not only influenced by the experiences produced by their actions; they also regulate their behaviour on the basis of observed consequences (vicarious reinforcement) as well as those they create for themselves (anticipated consequences—self regulation). In his classical experiment of Bobo Doll (on students of K. G. class) one of the significant result Bandura (1965) found is that children who watched the film in which the aggressor's behaviour either was reinforced or went unpunished imitated the aggressor's behaviour more than did the children who saw the aggressor be punished. Joseph Joubert, a French essayist of nineteenth century reported that the children need models more than critics.

Self regulatory learning consists of the self generation and self monitoring of thoughts, feelings and behaviour in order to reach a goal. The goal might be controlling one's anger or getting along better with peers. Thus, students are responsible for their own behaviour for becoming educated and for becoming contributing citizens of society.

Constructivist approach believes that children construct and reconstruct their knowledge as a result of interactions with the environment. All development emerges from action. Under this approach, there are two prominent psychologists—Jean Piaget and Lawrence Kohlberg who provide the basis of value education. They consider morality as a development process.

According to Piaget (1932) moral development occurs in two stages. The first stage is Heteronomous Morality and the second one is Autonomous Morality. Before deriving a stage theory of moral development, Piaget extensively observed and interviewed 4 to 12 years old children. He watched them play marbles, seeking to learn how they used and thought about the game's rules. He also asked children about ethical rules, quizzing them about theft, lies, punishment and justice.

The stage of heteronomous morality lasts from approximately 4 to 7 years of age. Justice and rules are conceived of as unchangeable properties of the world removed from the control of people. The heteronomous thinker also believes in immanent justice, the concept that if a rule is broken, punishment will be meted out immediately. Young children believe that a violation is in someway automatically connected to punishment. They often looked around in a worried fashion after committing a transgression, expecting inevitable punishment.

Autonomous morality is Piaget's second stage of moral development, reached at about 10 years of age or older. At this point, the child becomes aware that rules and laws are created by people and that, in judging an action, the actor's intentions as well as the consequences should be considered, *e.g.* for a five years old child lying is always bad, but an older child recognized that lying is justified in some situation and is not necessarily bad. Older children being moral autonomists, recognize that punishment is socially mediated and occurs only if a relevant person witnesses the wrong-doing, and that even then punishment is not inevitable.

Children 7 to 10 years of age are in a transition between the two stages, showing some features of both.

Piaget said that moral development is mainly advanced through the mutual give-and-take of peer relations. In the peer group, where all members have similar power and status, results are negotiated and disagreements reasoned about and eventually settled. In Piaget's view, parents play a less important role in children's moral development because they have so much more power than children and hand down rules in an authoritarian way.

Lawrence Kohlberg (1976) like Piaget, believed that moral development primarily involves moral reasoning and unfolds in stages, Kohlberg arrived at his theory after interviewing children, adolescents and adults about their views on a series of moral dilemmas. According to him moral reasoning has six identifiable developmental stages and these are grouped into three levels. The three levels are :

Sr. No.	*Levels*	*Stages*
I	Preconventional (no internalization)	1. Punishment and obedience orientation 2. Individualism and purpose
II	Conventional (Intermediate internalization)	3. Interpersonal norms 4. Social system morality
III	Post conventional (Full internalization)	5. Community rights *v/s* individual rights 6. Universal ethical principles

Preconventional reasoning is the lowest level of moral development. At this level the child shows no internalization of moral values. Moral reasoning is controlled by external rewards and punishment. At the first stage of this level *i.e.* punishment and obedience orientation children obey because adults tell them to obey. They base their moral decisions in fear of punishment. At the second stage *i.e.* individualism and purpose, moral thinking is based on rewards and self interest. Children obey when it is their best interest to obey. What is right is what feels good and what is rewarding.

Conventional learning is the second or intermediate level. The child abides internally by certain standards, but they are essentially the standards imposed by other people such as parents, or by society's laws. At the third stage *i.e.* interpersonal norms, the person values, trust, caring and loyalty to others as the basis of moral judgments. Children often adopt their parents' moral standards at this stage, seeking to be thought of as a "good girl" or "good boy". At the fourth stage of social system morality, moral judgments are based on understanding and the social order, law, justice, and duty.

Conventional learning is the highest level in Kohlberg's theory. At this level morality is completely internalized and not based on external standards. The students recognize alternative moral courses, explain options, and then decide on the moral code that is best for him or her. At the fifth stage, the person understands that values and laws are relative and that standards can vary from one person to another. The person recognizes that laws are important for society but knows that laws can be changed. The person believes that some values like freedom are more important than the law. At the stage of Universal Ethical Principles *i.e.* sixth stage the person has developed moral judgments that are based on universal human rights. When faced with the dilemma between law and conscience, a personal individualized conscience is followed.

Kohlberg said that children construct their moral thoughts as they pass through the stages—that they do not just passively accept cultural norms for morality. He argued that a child's moral thinking can be advanced through discussions with others who reason at the next higher stage. Piaget and Kohlberg both believe that the mutual give-and-take of peer relations promotes more advanced moral thinking because of the role taking opportunities they provide children.

Kohlberg's theory has been the basis for a number of cognitive moral education programmes. In a programme high school students meet in a semester long course to discuss a number of moral issues. The instructor acts as a facilitator rather than as a director of the class. The hope is that students will develop more advanced notions of such concepts as cooperation, trust, responsibility and community. Kohlberg (1976) recognized that the moral atmosphere of the school is more important than the initially envisioned.

More than 70 years ago, educator John Dewey recognized that even when schools do not have specific programmes in moral education, they provide moral education through a "hidden curriculum". The "hidden curriculum" is conveyed by the moral atmosphere that is a part of every school. The moral atmosphere is created by school and classroom rules, the moral orientation of teachers and school administrators, and the text materials. Teachers serve as moral of ethical or unethical behaviour. Classroom rules and peer relations at school transmit attitudes about cheating, lying, stealing and consideration for others. And through its rules and regulations, the school administration infuses the school with a value system.

Strategies for Value Education

1. Students imitate what parents and teachers, do. *e.g.* if a teacher who comforts a student in times of stress is likely to observe students imitating her comforting behaviour.
2. Don't simply say "That's good" or "That's nice" to

students rather say specifically, "You are being helpful" or "You gave him a pen. That was very nice of you because he needed to write". Regarding antisocial behaviour, to a young child you might say something like "That's not being nice. How would you face if he messed up your papers like that?"

3. Attribute positive behaviours to each student. Attribute positive intentions to a positive act, such as "You shared because you like to help others."
4. Commenting on positive behaviours and attributing positive characteristics to students rather than using external rewards helps students to internalize pro-social attitudes.
5. Punishment tells students what not to do rather than what to do. If teacher makes a punishing statement such as "No, that's not right", always accompany it with positive feedback, such as "but why don't you try this".
6. Demonstrate and teach new behaviour like how to solve maths problems, read, write, think, control anger and perform physical skills.
7. Think about ways to use peers as effective models. Remember that students are often motivated to imitate high–status models. Older peers usually have higher status than same–age peers. Thus, a good strategy is to have older peers from a higher grade model to engage in the behaviours you want your students to perform.
8. For a change the pace of classroom life for teachers and students, guests can be invited who have something meaningful to talk about and demonstrate. Gardner in his theory of multiple intelligence talked about eight domains some of them are physical, musical, artistic etc. So out of such skills, in which the teachers do not have skills to serve as a competent model, invite competent model from

community to demonstrate and discuss their skills. If this can't be arranged, set up field trips in which students should be taken away where they are working or performing.

9. Children observe models on television, videos and computers. It is important to monitor children's T.V. watching to ensure that they are not being exposed to too many negative models, especially violent ones.
10. Models are important sources for conveying self regulatory skills. For example, students might observe a teacher engage in an effective time management strategy and verbalize appropriate principles. By observing such models, students can come to believe that they also can plan and manage time effectively, which create a sense of self-efficacy for academic self-regulation and motivates students to engage in those activities.
11. Value and emphasize consideration of others' needs encourages students to engage in more helping activities. Helping students notice and respond to others' feelings can increase their consideration of others.
12. Reason with students when they do something wrong. If a student is too aggressive and harms another student, point out the consequences of the student's behaviour for the victim. Avoid harsh, punitive behaviour with students.
13. Set up discussion sessions and let children evaluate how goods and benefits are distributed justly among people with varying needs, temperaments, talents and troubles.
14. Develop class and school projects that foster altruism. Let children come up with examples of projects they can engage in that will help others. These projects might include cleaning up the school yard, collecting toys or food for individuals in need, and making

friends with older people during visits to a nursing home.

15. Make a videotape of children behaving pro-socially and show it to the class to increase sharing.
16. Think about what type of model you will present to students. Everyday, students watch and listen to what their teachers say and do. They pick up teachers good or bad habits, their expectations for high and low achievements, teachers' enthusiastic and bored attitude, their controlled and uncontrolled manner of dealing with stress their learning style, their gender attributes and many other aspects of their behaviours.

Thus, it is necessary that value system must be integrated into the personality of an individual so that it may be characterized. Therefore, to acquire a value, a person should go through the following five stages which are levels of affective domain. These stages are –

(i) Receiving – getting aware of value,
(ii) Responding – responding value in appropriate situations,
(iii) Valuing – making judgment on preference,
(iv) Organizing – organize it to make stable in value system of mind,
(v) Characterization – making value as a part of character. All the elements whether teachers, administrators, parents, students should constitute the institutional climate where the students spend 7 to 8 hours per day.

REFERENCES

Bandura, A. (1965). Influence of models' reinforcement contingencies on the acquisition of imitative responses. *Journal of Personality and Social Psychology*, 1, 589-595.

Hilgard, E. R. and Bower, G. H. (1977). *Theories of Learning*. New Delhi: Prentice Hall of India.

Hjelle, L. A. and Zeigler, D. J. (1981). *Personality Theories: Basic Assumptions, Research and Applications.* Singapore: McGraw Hill Book Co.

Kohlberg, L. (1976). Moral Stages and Moralization: The Cognitive Developmental Approach. In T. Lickona (Ed.) *Moral Development and Behaviour: Theory, Research and Social Issues.* New York : Holt, Rinehart and Winston, pp. 31-53.

Piaget, J. (1932). *The Moral Judgement of the Child.* London : Kegan Paul.

Santrock, J. W. (2001). *Educational Psychology.* New York: McGraw Hill.

Saraf, S. (1999). *Education in Human Values,* New Delhi: Vikas Publishing House.

Seshadri, C. ; Khader, M. A. and Adhya, G. L. (1992). *Education in Values: A Source Book,* New Delhi : NCERT.

SECTION - IV

DEVELOPMENT OF THE MARGINALISED

21 Political Participation of Tribal Leaders

A.N. Panda

The theory of democracy is based on the premise that people know their interests best and they are capable of protecting those interests. The theory believes that people can select their own representatives and can represent their electorates and they are competent of taking decisions. Democracy has faith in the sovereignty of people and makes arrangements to ensure running of the government with the consent of the governed; it provides opportunity to all sections of people to take part in the decision-making process. Hence, the manner and amount of political participation is an essential ingredient of all democracies. "The success of democracy depends upon the extent of participation. The citizen, unlike the subject, is an active participant in the political input process—process by which political decisions are made"[1].

"Political participation refers to those activities by private citizens that are more or less directly aimed at influencing the selection of governmental personnel and/or the actions they take"[2]. Political participation comprises a vast range of activities those have political bearing. "The study of political activity can range from the consideration of a few overt acts such as voting, donating money to political causes, participating in activist groups, or simply talking about politics, to the analysis of all conscious or unconscious political thought and perception: the scope of the phenomenon is limited only by one's choice of definition"[3].

Through their political involvement people attempt to realise their objectives by affecting the policies of Government either by persuading or by pressurising the decision-makers and if needed, by replacing the decision-makers themselves. While people take part in political activities they become engaged in different electoral activities like voting, campaigning, etc. and other unconventional political activities like protest, demonstration, etc. Through political participation people can exhibit their consent and oppose the policies of government. Political participation is a means to provide legitimacy to the political system. "Citizen participation refers to purposeful activities in which citizens take part in relation to government"[4].

While people politically participate they interact with a number of organisations, authorities and individuals in multifarious ways and, therefore, the dimension of one kind of political participation may be different from another kind of participation. There are 'six dimensions of political participation such as cognitive, expressive, electoral, organisational, partisan and government participation dimensions'[5]. Similarly, the modes of political participation people vary from situation to situation. "There are four broad modes of political participation that are used, in ordinary circumstances, by citizens: voting, campaign activity, citizen initiated contacts, and cooperative participation. And each of these modes of activity can be engaged in through a variety of specific acts. This does not exhaust the totality of available political acts, but it covers a wide and significant set"[6]. Hence, political participation is multidimensional and it can be manifested in diverse ways as the forms of participation fluctuate from time to time.

Though participation of common people is very important and it is worthwhile to study political participation of leaders as political participation reaches its maximum range only in case of the leaders. "Some people are more likely to select risky alternatives than are others and clearly the benefit of leadership frequently involves risky prospects. Leaders, therefore, may have a higher propensity to seek those risky prospects than do followers, who prefer the costless alternative of doing nothing"[7]. "A second distinction between leaders and followers (or between participators and non-participators) is that leaders may be more future oriented than others. Typically, the rewards of collective actions are realised in the future, whereas cost must be borne immediately"[8]. "Finally, our third factor—relative freedom from constraints on resource—embodies the observation that leaders generally hold some advantage of resources. They often have more information; they are more likely than the others to hold public office; they are likely to have more financial resources and more access to the public media. For people with such resources, the initial cost of organisation and provision of the collective good is less of a constraint on choice than it is for others. Hence, the greater the resources the greater the likelihood that a person is willing to bear the cost of collective action"[9]. "These three features of leadership—risk taking, future orientation and abundance of resources—are, of course, interdependent"[10].

In this chapter, political participation of rural leaders of Kuchinda Scheduled Area has been analysed by making a case study of the positional leaders of different Panchayati Raj Institutions such as Gram Panchayats, Panchayat Samitis and the Zilla Parishad.

Universe of Study

Kuchinda Scheduled Area forms a part of Kuchinda sub-division of Sambalpur district in Orissa. It is constituted by the whole of Kuchinda sub-division except the N.A.C. area of Kuchinda town. It covers over 500 villages and an area of 924 sq. miles[11]. The whole Kuchinda sub-division in Sambalpur district has been declared as a Scheduled Area by the President of India in 1977[12]. The entire Scheduled Area constitutes only one Tahsil.

The headquarters of Kuchinda sub-division is located at Kuchinda town which is situated on Deogarh-Bamra Road and 85 kilometres away from the district headquarters, Sambalpur.

Kuchinda Scheduled Area is surrounded by Rairakhol sub-division of Sambalpur district in the south, Panposh and Sundargarh sub-division of Sundargarh district in the north, Jharsuguda sub-division of Jharsuguda district in the east and Deogarh district and Bonai sub-division of Sundargarh district in the west.

Out of the more than 630 tribes in India, 62 tribes are found in Orissa. The tribal people in the State account for 22.21 per cent of the State's population.[13] In Sambalpur district out of the total population of 9,35,613, 3,22,770 are tribal people[14], in terms of percentage the tribal people constitute 34.50 per cent of the population of the district. In Kuchinda sub-division of Sambalpur district, which has a population[15] of 2,41,024, 60 per cent of the people are tribal people. In the sub-division, though the Kissans form the majority tribe other tribes like Gond, Oram and Bhuyan are also found.

Methodology and Tool of Data Collection

In this research project, out of the total 561 positional leaders of the Panchayati Raj Institutions in Kuchinda Scheduled Area 376 leaders have been interviewed during field study with the help of a questionnaire. After the responses of leaders have been collected and analysed those are presented in a tabular form and conclusions have been drawn. Relevant information has also been gathered from other sources such as official documents, published books and articles in journals and newspapers.

As the main focus of this research work is on political participation of positional leaders, the political activities of the leaders during and after election have been examined. Also, their participation in the decision-making process has been probed into.

Participation during Election

Due to largeness in size all modern democracies are representative democracies. In a representative democracy, election plays the most crucial role because through election representatives are selected and the system gains legitimacy. For effective management of a democracy the prerequisites are the ability and willingness of people to select their agents and the willingness of others to be selected and act as agents.

Different political activities such as voting, campaigning, fighting for a political office, etc. are performed during election. It is also the conventional and more visible form of political participation. To know the participation of the respondents a number of questions have been included in the questionnaire on their political involvement during election.

Voting during Elections

Election enables majority of people to participate directly in the political process of the country by voting and select their representatives to take decisions on their behalf. Therefore, the first question to the leaders has been on their participation as regular voters during election. The responses of the positional leaders are presented in the following Table 21.1

Table 21.1: Distribution of Positional Leaders by Voting during Elections

Sl. No.	*Voting Participation*	*No. of Total Respondents*	*Percentage*
1.	Regularly voting	205	54.52
2.	Not regularly voting	171	45.48
	Total	376	100

As the above Table 21.1 shows out of the total leaders 54.52 per cent respondents are regular voters in elections whereas 45.48 per cent are not regular voters.

Encouraging others to Vote

By encouraging others to vote in elections one shows one's activeness in the political process. Hence, a question has been asked to know whether the leaders encourage others to vote during elections.

Table 21.2 : Distribution of Positional Leaders by their act of Encouraging others to Vote during Elections

Sl. No	*Encouraging others to Vote*	*No. of Total Respondents*	*Percentage*
1.	Yes	253	67.29
2.	No	123	32.71
	Total	376	100

From the above Table 21.2 it can be seen that 67.29 per cent of leaders encourage others to vote whereas 32.71 per cent of them do not. It means more than the majority inspire others to be engaged in political activities.

Acting as Polling Agents

Acting as polling agents is an important form of political participation as a polling agent helps the voters in the polling station to cast their votes, assists the polling officers to identify the voters and checks malpractices inside the booth. Persons with experience and well acquainted with the local area are generally appointed as polling agents. As the leaders have these qualities, they been asked a question on their association in the electoral process as polling agents.

Table 21. 3 : Distribution of Positional Leaders by their Acting as Polling Agents

Sl. No	*Respo nses*	*No. of Total Respondents*	*Percentage*
1.	Yes	116	30.85
2.	No	260	69.15
	Total	376	100

It can be found from the above Table 21.3 that 30.85 per cent of the respondents have acted as polling agents while 69.15 per cent have never acted as polling agents.

To a related question on how many times they have acted as polling agents; they have given the following responses.

Table 21.4 : Distribution of Positional Leaders by the number of times their Acting as Polling Agents

Sl. No.	*Encouraging others to Vote*	*No. of Total Respondents*	*Percentage*
1.	Once	68	58.62
2.	Twice	29	25.00
3.	thrice	16	13.79
4.	More than 3 times	3	2.59
	Total	116	100

As can be seen from the above Table 21.4 that majority of the respondents have acted as polling agents only once. They account for 58.62 per cent of the respondents who have replied the previous question in the affirmative. Only 2.59 per cent of them have acted as polling agents more than three times.

Participation in Campaign Activities

During election, though voting is a more visible political activity, campaigning is also another important activity. A campaigner propagates for a political agenda, convinces people of the worthiness of a candidate or a party and canvasses for votes in favour of a candidate and a party. As grass roots level leaders, the respondents are likely to be approached by political parties and candidates to campaign for them. To know their participation in campaigning, responses have been collected from the respondents and presented in the following Table 21.5

Table 21.5 : Distribution of Positional Leaders by their Participation in Campaign Activities

Sl. No.	*Responses*	*No. of Total Respondents*	*Percentage*
1.	Yes	102	27.13
2.	No	274	72.87
	Total	376	100

Out of the total respondents 27.13 per cent of them have participated in campaigning while 72.87 per cent of them have not done so.

Nature of Participation in Campaigning

A campaigner may be engaged in a variety of ways such as preparation and distribution of election materials, organisation of election rallies and door-to-door canvassing. The following Table 21.6 gives the leaders' involvement in campaigning.

Table 21.6 : Distribution of Positional Leaders by the Nature of their Participation in Campaigning

Sl. No.	*Activity*	*No. of Total Respondents*	*Percentage*
1.	Preparation of election materials	4	3.92
2.	Distribution of election materials	23	22.55
3.	Organising election rallies	8	7.84
4.	Door-to-door canvassing	65	63.72
5.	All activities	2	1.96
6.	Organising rallies and canvassing	-	-
7.	Material distribution and canvassing	-	-
	Total	102	99.99

It can be seen from the Table 21.6 that out of the total leaders involved in campaigning most of them are engaged in door-to-door canvassing. In terms of percentage it is 63.72. The rest, 3.92 per cent of leaders have participated in preparation of election materials, 22.55 per cent in distribution of materials, 7.84 per cent in organisation of election rallies and only 1.96 per cent of them have participated in all activities.

In India, direct elections are held to Lok Sabha, State Assembly and the local bodies and people get opportunity to be directly involved in these elections; however, the nature of their participation varies from one election to another as the size of constituency, proximity to the candidates, issues involved and other such factors differ from one election to another. It is necessary to know how the respondents play a part in these elections. Therefore, the leaders have been asked separate questions on their participation in elections to Lok Sabha, State Assembly and the local bodies.

Participation in Parliamentary Elections

Participation in the Parliamentary elections, which are held at regular intervals, is an integral part of political participation in India. These elections enable people to elect their representatives. A question has been asked to know whether the respondents have participated in the Parliamentary elections.

Table 21.7 : Distribution of Positional Leaders by their Participation in Parliamentary Elections

Sl. No.	*Responses*	*No. of Total Respondents*	*Percentage*
1.	Yes	211	56.12
2.	No	165	43.88
	Total	376	100

Out of the total respondents 56.12 per cent of leaders have participated in the Parliamentary elections and 43.48 per cent have not.

A related question has been asked to the respondents know the manner of their involvement in elections to Lok Sabha.

Table 21.8 : Distribution of Positional Leaders by their Participation in Parliamen tary Elections

Sl. No.	*Activity*	*No. of Total Respondents*	*Percentage*
1.	Voting	193	91.47
2.	Campaigning	-	-
3.	Candidacy	-	-
4.	Voting, campaigning	18	8.53
5.	All activities	-	-
	Total	211	100

From Table 21.8, it can be seen that out of the total respondents 91.47 per cent of them have participated in the election as voters and only 8.53 per cent of them have participated as voters as well as campaigners. There is no leader who has participated in the election in any other way. The participation of leaders in Parliamentary elections has been limited mostly to voting.

Participation in Assembly Elections

State Assembly elections allow the citizens of the State to directly engage themselves in the political process of the country. Hence, to know the involvement of leaders in these elections another question has been asked to them.

Table 21.9 : Distribution of Positional Leaders by their Participation in Assembly Elections

Sl. No.	*Respo nses*	*No. of Total Respondents*	*Percentage*
1.	Yes	239	63.56
2.	No	137	36.44
	Total	376	100

As Table 21.9 shows 63.56 per cent leaders have participated in Assembly elections and 36.44 per cent have not.

Another question has been asked to the leaders to know what kind of activities they have performed in Assembly elections.

Table 21.10 : Distribution of Positional Leaders by their Participation in Assembly Elections

Sl No.	*Activity*	*No. of Total Respondents*	*Percentage*
1.	Voting	168	70.29
2.	Campaigning	-	-
3.	Candidacy	-	-
4.	Voting, campaigning	71	29.71
5.	All activities	-	-
	Total	239	100

It can be seen from Table 21.10 that most of the leaders have participated in the Assembly elections only as voters. Out of the total respondents, 70.29 per cent of them have taken part in this regard as voters whereas 29.71 per cent leaders have taken part not only as voters but also as campaigners. None of them has ever participated in the elections as a candidate.

Participation in earlier Panchayat Elections

In all developing nations efforts have been made for achieving democracy and development in the rural areas because societies of these nations are predominantly rural in character. India is also no exception in this regard.

The Panchayati Raj system has been adopted in India to spread democracy at the grass roots level in the rural areas. It is believed that democracy becomes meaningful only when people are given scope to take the local decisions locally and allowed to tackle their own problems with their own initiatives. In India, people in rural areas get the opportunity to manage their own affairs through their involvement in the formation and functioning of the Panchayati Raj institutions, *i.e.* through their participation in grass roots politics.

As the respondents are grass roots level leaders their association in earlier Panchayat elections has been enquired into. The following Tables 21.11 and 21.12 present the earlier involvement of the respondents in the democratic process at the lowest level.

Table 21.11 : Distribution of Positional Leaders by their Participation in earlier Panchayat Elections

Sl. No.	*Responses*	*No. of Total Respondents*	*Percentage*
1.	Yes	263	69.95
2.	No	113	30.05
	Total	376	100

Table 21.12 : Distribution of Positional Leaders by the manner of their Participation in earlier Panchayat Elections

Sl. No.	*Activity*	*No. of Total Respondents*	*Percentage*
1.	Voting	117	44.49
2.	Campaigning	-	-
3.	Candidacy	-	-
4.	Voting, campaigning	87	33.08
5.	All activities	59	22.43
	Total	263	100

As two Tables 21.11 and 21.12 show, out of the total respondents 69.95 per cent of them have participated in the earlier Panchayat elections and 30.05 per cent of them have not. It is clear that they are more active in these elections than either the Parliamentary elections or Assembly elections. Out of the total respondents 44.49 per cent of leaders have taken part in the earlier Panchayat elections only as voters whereas 33.08 per cent of them have also participated both in voting and campaigning. At the same time, 59 respondents or 22.43 per cent of the total leaders have also contested earlier as candidates, besides taking part in voting and campaigning.

This proves that the respondents are more involved in the elections to the grass roots institutions in the rural areas. Parliament and State Assemblies being the two top levels of the Indian political system only persons with higher political reach contest in these elections and others are left with only voting participation, though a limited number of leaders also participate in these elections as campaigners.

Participation when there is no Election

Political participation is very prominent during election, but it does not end with it. One can be politically active even when there is no election and be associated in the political process of the country. It is more interesting to study political participation of the leaders as they have more scope to remain politically active even after election in a number of ways, such as propagating for a political cause, discussing political issues with others, keeping contacts with their followers and organising public meetings to protest or support some political issues.

Propagating for a Political Cause

As the elites of their localities the leaders play an important role in deciding many political issues in their own areas. They take sides in a political debate and lead their followers. They may also propagate for or against a political cause. A question has been asked to the respondents whether they take part in propagating for or against a political cause.

Table 21.13 : *Distribution of Positional Leaders by Propagating for a Political Cause*

Sl. No	*Responses*	*No. of Total Respondents*	*Percentage*
1.	Yes	64	17.02
2.	No	312	82.98
	Total	376	100

It is clear from the above Table 21.13 that only a limited number of leaders are active in this regard. Among all leaders only 17.02 per cent of them have propagated for or against a political cause whereas 82.98 per cent of them have not.

Discussing Political Issues with Others

Discussion can be regarded as a mode of interaction among different actors and is a way of political communication. The various participants in the discussion exchange their own ideas and thoughts among themselves and influence one another. Discussion of a political issue helps in political socialisation. Because of their relatively more exposure to different political aspects than other people the leaders can help in politically educating others.

Therefore, the leaders of the Panchayati Raj system have been asked a question in this regard.

Table 21.14 : Distribution of Positional Leaders by their act of Discussing Political Issues with Others

Sl.. No.	*Responses*	*No. of Total Respondents*	*Percentage*
1.	Yes	49	13.03
2.	No	327	86.97
	Total	376	100

As per Table 12.14, 13.03 per cent of leaders discuss political issues with others and 86.97 per cent of them do not do so.

Meeting with Electorates

As the representatives of the people, the leaders have to be aware of the problems of their electorates and to do so they have to keep regular contacts with their followers. Meeting serves the purpose of having a two-way communication among the participants. So meeting is important for both the leaders and their followers and a question has been asked in this regard.

Table 21.15 : Distribution of Positional Leaders by their Meeting with their Electorates Regularly

Sl. No.	*Respo nses*	*No. of Total Respondents*	*Percentage*
1.	Yes	324	86.17
2.	No	52	13.83
	Total	376	100

As Table 21.15 reflects a large majority of the respondents are in regular touch with their followers. In terms of percentage, 86.17 per cent of the leaders meet their electorates regularly while 13.83 per cent of them do not do so.

Mode of Meeting with Electorates

While such meetings take place the leaders may go to their followers or expect the latter to come to them or both can exchange visits. A related question has been asked to the leaders on the mode of such meetings.

Table 21.16 : Distribution of Positional Leaders by the Mode of Meeting their Electorates

Sl. No	Responses	No. of Total Respondents	Percentage
1.	Going to the electorates	55	16.97
2.	Coming of the electorates to the leader	17	5.25
3.	Both	252	77.78
	Total	324	100

In case of 16.97 per cent leaders, they go to the electorates, for 5.25 per cent of leaders, electorates come to them and for 77.78 per cent of leaders it is a two-way affair, *i.e.* the electorates come to them and they also go to the electorates.

Organizing Public Meetings

Public meeting gives the opportunity to the people to get politically involved. They get the chance to mix with other people, exchange their opinions, try to influence others and also get influenced by others. Therefore, attending and organising public meetings can also be regarded as a kind of political participation. A leader organises public meetings for different purposes. Through public meeting discussions are held and issues are decided and messages are spread among the people. It is also a way of keeping in touch with the electorate. To know this kind of activity, the leaders have been asked a question.

Table 21.17: Distribution of Positional Leaders by their Organizing Public Meetings

Sl. No.	Responses	No. of Total Respondents	Percentage
1.	Yes	66	17.55
2.	No	310	82.45
	Total	376	100

As the data reveals 17.55 per cent of the leaders organise public meetings whereas 82.45 per cent do not. It shows that a large number of leaders are not active in organising public meetings.

Taking Part in Procession

One can take part in a procession to support or oppose an issue. Therefore, a question has been asked to the leaders if they participate in any procession for or against any cause and specify whether it is inside or outside their own area.

Table 21.18: Distribution of Positional Leaders by their taking part in Procession

Sl. No	*Responses*	*No. of Total Respondents*	*Percentage*
1.	Yes	71	18.88
2.	No	305	81.12
	Total	376	100

Table 21.19 : Distribution of Positional Leaders by their taking part in Procession (inside and outside)

Sl. No	*Responses*	*No. of Total Respondents*	*Percentage*
1.	Only inside	49	69.01
2.	Only outside	2	2.82
3.	Both	20	28.17
	Total	71	100

It is evident from Table 21.19 that a limited number of leaders take part in procession. Out of the total 18.88 per cent of leaders take part in procession and 81.12 per cent of them do not take part.

Further, out of all the leaders who take part in procession 69.01 per cent of them do so only inside the universe of study, 2.82 per cent of them do so only outside it and 28.17 per cent of them do so in both outside and inside it.

Participation in Decision-Making

Participation in the decision-making process is considered as the highest form of political participation because certain scopes are available only to the decision-makers and not to ordinary citizens. The participation of ordinary citizens is limited but the leaders do something more apart from performing all the political activities which are performed by ordinary citizens. The leaders are continuously and actively involved in the political process even when there is no election and they take different decisions as the representatives of the people. Therefore, it is all the more important to know the participation of leaders as decision-makers.

As the study is concerned with the participation of the decision-makers, it is quite pertinent to enquire into the nature of their association in the decision-making system. So they have been asked a number of questions in this respect.

Attendance in the Meetings of Local Institutions

As the representatives of people the respondents have the responsibility to take decisions on local issues and the local bodies are the important forums to decide local issues. Therefore, queries have been put to the leaders on whether they attend local body meetings and if so, how many meetings?

Table 21.20: Distribution of Positional Leaders by their Attendance in the Meetings of Local Institutions

Sl. No.	*Responses*	*No. of Total Respondents*	*Percentage*
1.	Yes	376	100
2.	No	-	-
	Total	376	100

All leaders attend the meetings of the local bodies.

Table 21.21: Distribution of Positional Leaders by their Attendance in number of Meetings of the Local Bodies

Sl. No.	*Responses*	*No. of Total Respondents*	*Percentage*
1.	All	163	43.35
2.	Some	213	56.65
	Total	376	100

As Table 21.21 shows 43.35 per cent of leaders have attended all meetings and 56.65 per cent leaders have attended some meetings.

Raising the Local Problems in Local Body Meetings

A true representative has to raise the problems of the area, he or she represents and try to solve those problems. As the local bodies are the best forums at the grass root level for such a purpose the leaders have to raise the issues of their localities in the local bodies. A question has been asked in this regard.

Table 21.22 : Distribution of Positional Leaders by their Raising the Local Problems in the Local Body Meetings

Sl. No.	Responses	No. of Total Respondents	Percentage
1.	Yes	376	100
2.	No	-	-
	Total	376	100

As Table 21.22 shows all leaders have raised the local problems in the meetings of the local bodies.

Raising Local Issues the number of times in the Local Body Meetings

A related question has been asked to the leaders to know how many times they have raised the problems of the people in the local body meetings.

Table 21.23 :Distribution of Positional Leaders by their Act of Raising Local Issues the number of times in the Local Body Meetings

Sl. No.	No. of Times	No. of Total Respondents	Percentage
1.	1-5	276	73.40
2.	6-10	52	13.83
3.	11-15	30	7.98
4.	More than 15	18	4.79
	Total	376	100

Majority of the leaders have raised the problems of the

people 1 to 5 times and they account for 73.40 per cent of the total. 13.83 per cent of leaders have raised issues for 6 to 10 times, 7.98 per cent for 11 to 15 times and 4.79 per cent for more than 15 times.

Protesting when Opinion is Ignored

Sometimes the proposals given by a leader are not given due importance by others. In such a case it is interesting to know the reactions of the leaders.

Therefore, another interesting question asked to the leaders is whether they protest if their opinions are not given due importance.

Table 21.24: Distribution of Positional Leaders by their Protest when their Opinions are Ignored

Sl. No.	Respo nses	No. of Total Respondents	Percentage
1.	Yes	263	69.95
2.	No	113	30.05
	Total	376	100

It is clear from Table 21.24 that when their opinions are ignored, 69.95 per cent of leaders protest and 30.05 per cent of them do not.

Meeting with Government Officers

To solve the problems of people of their areas the leaders have to keep contact with government officers and communicate the grievances of people. They have to meet the officers concerned. Hence, the respondents have been asked a question in this regard.

Table 12.25 : Distribution of Positional Leaders by their Meeting with Government Officers to Solve the Problems of People

Sl. No	Respo nses	No. of Total Respondents	Percentage
1.	Yes	252	67.02
2.	No	124	32.98
	Total	376	100

As Table 21.25 shows 67.02 per cent of the positional leaders meet government officers to solve the problems of people while 32.98 per cent of leaders do not meet the officers.

Complaining when Local Officers do not Act

Sometimes the officers ignore the suggestions of the public representatives. To know whether the leaders protest against such actions of the officers at the higher levels a related question has been asked.

Table 21.26 : Distribution of Positional Leaders by their Complain when Local Officers do not Act

Sl. No.	*Responses*	*No. of Total Respondents*	*Percentage*
1.	Yes	136	53.97
2.	No	116	46.03
	Total	252	100

As Table 21.26 shows 53.97 per cent leaders protest when the officers do not act. 46.03 per cent of them do not protest.

Communicating the Problems of the Areas to Higher Leaders

To know the positional leaders' links with higher political leaders of the area and whether they communicate the problems of people to the higher political leaders, queries have been put to the respondents. Their responses can be found from the following Tables 21.27 to 21.29.

Table 21.27: Distribution of Positional Leaders by their Link with Higher Political Leaders of the Area

Sl. No.	*Response*	*No of Leaders*	*Percentage*
1.	Yes	179	47.61
2.	No	197	52.39
	Total	376	100

Table 21.28: Distribution of Positional Leaders by their Communicating Problems of the Areas to the Higher Leaders

Sl. No.	*Response*	*No of Leaders*	*Percentage*
1.	Yes	107	59.78
2.	No	72	40.22
	Total	179	100

As Table 21.27 shows 47.61 per cent leaders have links with political leaders of their areas while 52.39 per cent do not have such links.

Out of all the leaders who have contacts with higher political leaders of their areas 59.78 per cent of them communicate the problems of their areas to the higher political leaders and 40.22 per cent do not do so. It proves that majority leaders with political links use their connections for the benefits of people.

Complaining to Higher Leaders when Opinion is Ignored

Leaders give many suggestions at the local bodies to improve the condition of their electorate; but those are not always given importance by others. When the opinions of the leaders are not given importance generally they complain against such disregard. The leaders have been asked whether they complain to the higher leaders when their opinions are ignored.

Table 21.29: Distribution of Positional Leaders by their Complain to Higher Political Leaders when their Opinion is Ignored

Sl. No.	*Response*	*No of Leaders*	*Percentage*
1.	Yes	107	59.78
2.	No	72	40.22
	Total	179	100

As Table 21.29 shows out of all the leaders with political links 59.78 per cent of them complain when their opinions are ignored. 40.22 per cent of them do not complain.

Leading the People to Meet Higher Leaders

The leaders have been asked a question whether they lead the people to meet the higher political leaders to pressurise the latter for some favourable decisions. Their responses are given in Table 21.30 below.

Table 21.30 : Distribution of Positional Leaders by their act of Leading the People to Meet the Higher Leaders

Sl. No.	*Response*	*No of Leaders*	*Percentage*
1.	Yes	32	17.88
2.	No	147	82.12
	Total	179	100

As the Table 21.30 shows out of those leaders who have links with higher political leaders 17.88 per cent of them lead the people to meet higher political leaders while 82.12 per cent of them do not do so.

Talking to Media

One of the ways of redressing the problems of the people is talking to the media and making others aware of the problems of a locality. It is a way of communicating the grievances of people. A question has been asked to the leaders in this regard. Their responses have been presented in the following Table 21.31.

Table 21.31: Distribution of Positional Leaders by their Talking to Media

Sl. No.	*Responses*	*No. of Total Respondents*	*Percentage*
1.	Yes	45	11.97
2.	No	331	88.03
	Total	376	100

As Table 21.31 shows 11.97 per cent of leaders talk to the media whereas 88.03 per cent of them do not do so.

It is often complained that the level of political participation of people in India is not up to the expected extent even after so many years of Independence and adoption of the principle of universal adult franchise. There is always a debate on how to increase the level of political participation in India. An open ended question has been asked to the leaders in this regard. But none of them has been able to give a satisfactory reply; though some claim that due to publicity, some kind of punishment or inducement may have a positive result in bringing about more participation by people.

Conclusion

It can be concluded that the positional leaders of the grass roots level in Kuchinda Scheduled Area are active in the political process of the country. They are performing their responsibilities as the common citizens of the country besides doing their duties as the representatives of people, though there may have been deviations in some cases. They are not only active in doing their jobs at the grass roots institutions but also try to solve the problems of the people by taking recourse to meeting officers, higher political leaders and utilising their contacts. Some of them also engage themselves in propagating for some causes and politically socialising others.

Thus, the tribal leaders of the Kuchinda Scheduled Area are politically active not only at election time but also play dynamic roles at the time when there is no election. They are politically active in all respects though in some cases they are more active.

NOTES

1. Almond, Gabriel A. and Verba, Sidney, *Civic Culture: Political Attitudes and Democracy in Five Nations*, Princeton University Press, Princeton, 1963, p. 161.
2. Verba, Sydney and Nie, Norman H., *Participation in America*, The University of Chicago Press, Chicago, 1987, p. 2.

3. Manheim, Jarol B., *The Politics within*, Prentice-Hall, Inc., New Jersey, 1975, p. 111.
4. Langton, Stuart, "Citizen Participation in America: Current Reflections on the State of the Art" in Langton, Stuart edited *Citizen Participation in America*, Lexington Books, Toronto, 1978, p. 17.
5. Oslen, Marvin E., *Participatory Pluralism*, Nelson-Hall, Chicago, 1982, p. 48.
6. Verba, Sidney and Nie, Norman H., *Participation in America*, University of Chicago Press, Chicago, 1987, p. 47.
7. Riker, William H. and Ordehook, Peter C., *An Introduction to Positive Political Theory*, Prentice-Hall, Inc., Englewood Cliff, New Jersey, 1973, p. 75.
8. *Ibid.*, p. 76.
9. *Ibid.*
10. *Ibid.*, pp. 76-77.
11. *Brochure for 1987-89*, Integrated Tribal Development Project, Kuchinda (Introduction), p. 1.
12. *Gazette of India, Extraordinary*, Part II Section– 3 sub-Section (i), dated the 31st December 1977 as constitution Order No. 109.
13. Tiwari, A.N., *Reference Orissa*, Enterprising Publishers, Bhubaneswar, 1999, p. xxi.
14. *Sambad* (Oriya Daily), Sambalpur Edition, 16.7.2004, p. 2.
15. *District Statistical Hand Book*, Sambalpur, 2001, p. 8.

22 Political Communication and the Mass-media

A Conceptual Analysis

Tripurari Narayan Pati

Man, says Aristotle, is a social animal destined by Nature for political life. The social instinct of Man is the outcome of the Nature's gift of faculty of speech that initiates the process of communication and interaction, and that facilitate the formation of Human Society. Hence communication is the web of human society, it is the cement that makes the society and it also tends to account for the stability, growth and development of the society.[1] "With the advent of modern technological advances and the inception of industrialization leading to large scale modernization, man has necessarily become a communicating animal. This is in this backdrop Almond and Powell observed all forms of human interactions involve communication"[2]. Communication has different perspectives out of which Political Communication is distinct and special, because political communication is the functional prerequisite of the dynamics of the political system. In a nutshell political communication is the lifeline of a political system.

What is Communication

Communication is the process that transfers information[3]. It is, therefore, the process 'by which one mind may affect another[4] by way of transmission of information including messages, symbols, signs and signals between persons[5].

These transmissions initiate pave for, and facilitate human interactions and relations.

The Concept of Political Communication

In the communication process when explicitly political information and also politically relevant non-political information get transmitted, there ensues the process of political communication. Political communication refers to the process of communication that takes place in political context, that is, in the context of the Political System. It, therefore, involves communication of explicitly political information as well as politically relevant non-political information that tends to impinge upon the Political System, and influence its dynamics. Of course, definitions and notions on the concept of "Political Communication" are many and varied. Hence some of the important notions may be noted and analyzed.

Gabriel A. Almond considers 'Political Communication' as the process of "flow of information from the society to the polity, and in the polity, form political structure to political structure".[6] He links the political communication function to the function of circulation of blood in the body polity wherein demands are transmitted through the veins to the heart, and from the heart through the arteries flow the outputs of rules, regulations and adjudications[7]. As it involves the transmission of information "both within the political system, and between the political system and its environment"[8], the Political System, as a consequence, is enlivened and set into motion, and hence, the political communication function constitutes "a necessary pre-requisite"[9] for the performance of other systemic functions.

Karl. W. Deutsch views 'Political Communication' as the process of "collection of external and internal information" as well as "its transmission to the point of decision-making" in a Political System[10]. This process of information, according to him, influences and controls the performances of the political system in the context of attainment of societal goals, because political information as transmitted through the process of political communication may help form desired habits in the people for rendering habitual obedience to authoritative decisions. Therefore, the survival, growth and development of the Political System Deutsch believes, tend to depend, to a great extent, on its working as a network of "communication channel"[11] for formation of desired habits, *i.e.* supportive attitude and behaviour in the people towards it.

Political Communication as viewed by David Easton[12], involves transmission of influences and information within the Political System as well as between the Political System and its environment. It facilitates the formation and flow of the inputs into the Political System, conversion of inputs into outputs, and also flow of the outputs from the political system into the environment. The political system is, thus, enabled to work as a self-steering and self regulating system, and to persist in a situation either of stability or change. According to Easton, the political system may be said to persist as long as it is able to allocate values for the society, and to get these allocations accepted as authoritative by most of its people. The retention of these two life conditions or essential variables may become possible provided demand and support stresses are kept under bearable limit. This function of stress reduction may be done effectively, on one hand, by informing and educating people not to make irrelevant and recalcitrant demands detrimental to the life of the Political System, and on the other, by generating and fostering in them supportive attitude and behaviour toward the Political System through performance of the function of political communication by the communication mechanisms.

Lucian W. Pay[13] considers 'political communication' as the process of communication within the domain of politics. The flow of information in the political communication process, according to him, determines not only the individual's political behaviour but also the performance of the political system as well as the direction and pace of socio-political development. Political communication, for the individual, facilitates his comprehension of the substance of politics at any particular time, and simultaneously it is through "the organization of communication process that the host of random actions which represents the pursuit of power by the people throughout a society are placed in some form of relationship with each other, that order is established in the sphere of power considerations and a society finds that it has a polity"[14]. Therefore, the individual's political behaviour as well as the pattern of political life of a people, the structure and performance of their Political System, and the level of their political modernization and development tend to be crucially influenced by the content and flow of political information in the communication process.

R.R. Fagen defines political communication as "communicatory activity considered political by virtue of its consequences, actual and political, that it has for the functioning of the political system"[15].

Ithiel de Sola Pool[16] opines that 'Political Communication' involves transmission and dissemination of political information including signal, symbols and messages that influence the individual's political behaviour, and also the performance of the Political System.

Dan D. Nimmo views 'Political Communication' as "Communication (activity) considered political by virtue of its consequences (actual and potential) which regulate human conduct under conditions of conflict"[17] Nimmo identifies conflict as the essence of politics, and hence, all those communication activities related, more or less, to conflictual situations in society, according to him, compose the process of political communication. He puts it more succinctly when, along with Kieth R. Sanders,[18] he presents Political Communication, as a process encompassing all politically relevant communication activities. R.B. Meadow defines 'Political Communication' as "any exchange of symbols or messages that, to a significant extent, have been shaped by or have consequences for the functioning of the political systems"[19].

Jean Blondel portrays 'Political Communication' as "the dynamic movement of demands and decisions from one part of the political system to another"[20]. He emphasizes on the overriding importance of communication in the life of the political system as he finds that 'neither inputs nor outputs can take form, exist, or be related and affect the polity, at large, without the thread of communication. According to him, "communication links together the parts of the system, and also the present with the past and future so that demands are followed by policies", and hence, "no operation of the political system can take place unless the parts of the system communicate with each other".

Michael Rush and Philip Althuff consider "political communication' as 'transmission of politically relevant information from one part of the political system to another"[21] and between the social and political systems. They point out that political communication imparts dynamism to the political system as it initiates and influences not only the formation of the individual's political orientations and dispositions but also the performance of the systemic functions by their corresponding structures.

Features of Political Communication

A scanning of these notions and definitions preferred by some distinguished scholars and thinkers reveals some of the important features of political communication.

1. Political communication is a special type of communication that takes place in political context, that is in the context of working of the political system.
2. Political communication involves the transmission of

information within the political system and its environment both intra -social and extra-social.

3. As it is all pervasive it acts as a bridge between the political system and the social system.
4. All the functions of the political system are performed by means of political communication. Thus, it is termed as the lifeline of a political system.
5. The political system survives, grows, develops and maintained its salability in the environment due to political communication.

Types of Political Communication

Political communication may be classified into two broad categories such as Manifest Political Communication and Latent Political Communication.

Manifest Political Communication refers to the transmission of explicitly political information, news views whereas Latent Political Communication involves transmission of non-political information, which may be subsequently relevant. For instance, stories and articles published in the books and magazines, cinema plays, songs and music and other non-political programmes transmitted through the Television and Radio, event and information concerning social cultural events and games and sports transmitted through different agencies of communication.

Political Communication Structures

The function of Pol-communication in a political system are performed by means of different common structures. The Communication Structures which may perform the function of political communication, according to Almond are of five major types such as :

(i) Informal Face to Face contact,
(ii) Traditional Social Structures,

(iii) Political output structures,
(iv) Political Input Structures, and
(v) Mass-media.[22]

Informal face to face contact are informal channels of communication which emerge and operate when individual interact with one another informally. In such informal interactions, a vital role is played by the opinion-leader who, because of his higher social status or position, is listened to by others with great attention and admiration. The opinion-leader, as the term suggests, becomes instrumental in forming opinion in the members of the informal group because he interprets information concerning political and public affairs received through the mass-media or other sources interprets and transmits such information to his friends, co-workers, or neighbours with whom he interacts regularly and informally.

Traditional social structures are organised traditional social groups, characterized by formal structure, membership and leadership. Instances of such structures are tribal caste groups, religious and ethnic groups, as are found working in an organized way mostly in traditional societies. The primary function of these groups is discussion and deliberation on group related issues, and transmission of group related values and information. In these traditional social groups, key role is played by the group leader such as the tribal head in the tribal group, the caste head in the caste group, or the priest in the religious group. The leader of these traditional groups, apart from deliberating on group related issues, also discuss on public and political affairs, and thereby, they help transmit political and politically relevant information to the members of their respective groups.

Political output structures are formal governmental structures of the political system concerned with the making and implementation of authoritative decisions or outputs. Example of such structures are the Legislature, the Executive and the Judiciary, and their primary functions are Rule making function, Rule application function, and Rule adjudication function respectively. However, these output structures also perform the communication function because people are to be informed of the laws, rules, policies and regulations as enacted by the Legislature, Executive order as issued and implemented by the Executive, and Judicial decisions and adjudications as made by the Judiciary. The performance of the communication function by the output structures, thus, provides for governmental unity and integration, and also makes possible co-ordinated implementation of laws, the mobilization of societal resources and acquisition of legitimacy by the government by way of formation of supportive attitude and behaviour in the people.

Political Input structures such as Pressure Groups and Political Parties constitute other significant information channels though their primary functions are Interest Articulation and Interest Aggregation respectively. Pressure Groups articulate the demands and interest of their members, and Political Parties aggregate such articulated interest into policy alternatives, which constitute the basis for making of authoritative decisions by the Authority of the Political System. Thus, the input structures are concerned with transmission of demands of the people to the political system, and as such they come to play vital roles in the process of political communication.

Mass-media such as Newspaper, Radio, Television, Books and Magazines etc. constitute specialized structures for political communication because their primary function is transmission of information. It is through Mass-media that the people and also all components of the political system specifically get informed of political as well as politically relevant information. Therefore, the emergence of Mass-media as specialized structures for political communication seems to be a vital indicator of modernity of the Political Society.

These communication structures such as informal face-to-face contacts, Traditional social structures, Political Output structures, Political Input structures, and Mass-media are, thus, involved more or less, with transmission of political information. However, performance of the function of political communication with efficiency requires that they must have autonomy[23]. An autonomous structure is one which is free of domination and control either by the government or by particular vested interests in the society. Enjoyment of autonomy, therefore, enables a communication structure to transmit information with fidelity, and without distortion. However, among these various communication structures, only the Mass-media may be expected to function with autonomy whereas other communication structures naturally come under the control and domination either by the vested interest or by the government. Even, in case of mass-media, enjoyment of autonomy may be denied in a society where either the vested interest or the government or both dominate and control them. In such a society where there is domination or control, over the Mass-media, these specialized communication structures cannot perform the function of political communication with efficiency and effectiveness. Consequently, because of lack of transmission of true and relevant information, an increasing gap may be created between the people and Government and the political system may experience instability. Therefore, a Political Society, if it intends to remain stable for long through acquisition of legitimacy from the people, must provide autonomy to the communication structures, especially the specialized mass-media, so as to enable them to transmit and disseminate true and adequate information, and thereby, to create the right kind of environment that would be conducive for political stability and viability. This may be possible, according to Almond, only in a democratic society as he emphatically points out "Effective Political action must be based on rational calculation, which in turn requires information. A democratic system provides for a relatively free-multi-directional flow of information, thus making it possible for all structures to calculate and to act effectively."[24]

Role of Mass-media

In popular usage the term Mass-media refers to the media for mass communication such as Radio, Television, Newspaper, Cinema, Books, Magazines etc., which transmit and disseminate varieties of information to the people at large, and that too, easily, quickly and with minimum expense. These media are thus, mainly concerned with mass communication as they publicly address the collected information to a relatively large heterogeneous audiences that are anony-mous. The concern for reaching out to the audience quickly necessitates construction of a complex formal organization equipped with modern technology so that the information collected thus far may reach the people, within a time frame, through the print as well as electronic media. Thus, there seems to be two principal components of mass communi-cation viz. (i) Mass-media characterized by a complex formal organization, equipped with modern technology, and the concern for transmission of information publicly, and (ii) Audience who are relatively large in size, heterogeneous and anonymous in nature[25].

In real terms the audience thus, constitutes the target of mass communication for the information transmitted by the Mass-media through the application of modern technology. For this purpose the Mass-media are required to collect varieties of information through the performance of four major types of activities such as (i) Surveillance of the social environment (both intra-societal and extra-societal environ-ment), (ii) Correlating the parts of the society in responding to the environmental information, (iii) Intra-generational and inter-generational transmission of social values and heritage, and (iv) Entertainment[26]. Surveillance refers to the collection and distribution of information relating to varieties of information corresponding to varieties of events occurring in the environment, both within the society and outside it. Such information, thus, collected from the society and outside would, then, be interpreted and prescription for solution would be provided for maintaining the unity and integrity of the society, and to ensure its viability, stability and development. This may be termed popularly as editorial or propagandistic activity. Mass communication through the media also includes transmission of social values and norms from generation to generation for the survival and viability of the society. Another significant activity of the Mass-media is also to transmit varieties of information intended for the entertainment of the audiences. These activities may have tremendous consequences and implications for both the individual and the society as a whole. For the individual, the communication transmitted through the Mass-media may help form his orientation, which, in turn, tend to determine the dispositions, behaviour and role of the individual as a member of the society and also for the political system. Since the functioning of the society and polity depends largely on the basis of the role and functioning of their members, media communication tend to influence significantly their performance by way of influencing the role and behaviour of the individual. Thus, in the socio-political process, Mass-media may play roles as political socializer political communicators, and performance of these roles by the Mass-media may entail significance for the salability, viability and overall dynamics of the political society.

Mass-media and the Process of Political Communication

Mass-media, while transmitting and disseminating varieties of information, may play their roles as very important agents in the process of political communication. The information communicated by them may be explicitly political, or non-political with subsequent political implications. Accordingly, the roles of Mass-media in the process of political communication may be classified into two broad categories such as roles in the context of Manifest political communication, and roles in the context of Latent political communication[27]. Manifest political communication involves transmission of explicitly political information by the Mass-media, whereas Latent political communication involves transmission of non-political information which may be subsequently politically relevant to the audience. Both the Manifest political communications and Latent political communications as transmitted by the Mass-media may help form cognition, affect and evaluation in the individual toward politics and his political system, and thereby, the individual's political culture is formed and his political-self is shaped and moulded. The pattern of political culture as formed in the individual consequent upon his exposure to, and acquisition of Manifest political communications and Latent Political Communications seems to be a vital determinant of his political roles and activities, and such patterns of political roles and activities of the people as a whole tend to influence significantly the performance of the political system. Thus, Manifest political communications as well as Latent political communications transmitted by the Mass-media to the audience appear to have tremendous implications for the formation of the individual's political behaviour and roles, and also for the dynamics of the political society.

Latent Political Communication

Non-political information and communication transmitted by the mass-media may contain implicit political lessons for the audiences. For instance, stories and articles published in books and magazines, cinema, plays, songs and music and other non-political programmes transmitted through the Television and Radio, news and information concerning social and cultural events and games and sports transmitted through the audio-visual media and published in the newspapers, or even the advertisement of companies transmitted through the audio-visual and the print media for the sale of products may indirectly and inadvertently instill in the audience varieties of socio-cultural values such as cultural and social identities, peace, communal harmony, co-operation, fraternity, equality, social justice, conflict or even violence. Non-political communications may also serve to form and develop in the audience a self potency, efficacy and competence. Such non-political values learned and acquired by the individual as a consequence of media-exposure may be generalized and transferred by him to political arena. For instance, an individual who learns the value of violence from the Mass-media as a consequence of his regular media exposure may transfer it to the sphere of politics, and may, as a consequence, develop an aptitude for political violence and may even commit it actually. Similarly, an individual who learns the sense of self potency as a consequence of his regular exposure to such media communications may develop a high sense of political competence and play his role in the sphere of politics as an active and participant citizen. Therefore, media communications which are designed mainly to inform or entertain the audience, or even to sell a product and make money for the producer may well serve the function of Latent political communication[28].

Moreover, non-political communication transmitted by the Mass-media may indirectly contribute toward the political learning of the individual in another important way. Such transmission may serve as the buffer[29] between the audience and the political world. If the individual would be continuously exposed to political information and news as transmitted by the Mass-media, he may get bored and consequently, his receptivity to political information may diminish. Also continuous exposure to political information may heighten his anxiety level by making him aware of grimmer political realities and consequently, the individual may avoid such exposure[30]. In this context, the non-political communications transmitted by the Mass-media may serve as the buffer between the audience and his political world, and may insulate him from undesirable effects of an over-dose of political information, and may thus "produce a responsive audience for political news"[31].

Manifest Political Communication

Communications transmitted by the Mass-media may also include explicitly political information, news and views. The audio-visual media such as the Television and the Radio regularly transmit news bulletins, and discussions on political and public affairs. Similarly, the print media such as newspapers and magazines also transmit political news, views, commentaries. These explicitly political information, news and opinions transmitted by the Mass-media may not only help increase the level of political awareness and knowledge of the audiences, but also help form their political preferences, attitudes and opinions. Therefore, Manifest political communications transmitted by the Mass-media may directly contribute towards formation of the individual's political culture which is composed of his cognitive, affective and evaluational orientations about politics, political objects and the political system.

Thus, Mass-media may play, their roles in the process of political communication by transmitting and disseminating explicitly political information as well as politically relevant non-political information, and consequently, they may contribute toward the patterns of political culture in the audience.

Mass-media and Political Socialization

One of the most vital functions of the Mass-media is political socialization. Being an agent of political socialization mass-media may play a crucial and significant role in the process of political socialization which may be defined, in the words of Gabriel A. Almond as "the process of induction into the political culture" [32]. It is the process of political learning by which individual learns and acquires orientation and disposition to political objects. Thus, through this process the people of a political society learn and acquire that pattern of political culture, which is congruent to the structure or form of the political system, and accordingly, they are socialized, in it, in the sense that they internalize it, and manifest it in their political roles, behaviour and activities. Political culture may be said to be congruent and allegiant to the form and structure of the existing political system, according to Almond, "when political cognition in the population would tend to be accurate, and where affect and evaluation would tend to be favourable"[33] on the other hand it may be said to be incongruent and alienated if most of the people acquire negative affect and evaluation toward the political system[34]. It is the type of the relationship between the political culture of the people and the structural pattern of the political system, whether congruent and allegiant or incongruent and alienated, that seems to be an important determinant of stability or charge of the political system. It is most likely that, a political system would remain stable and viable as long as its structural arrangement is supported and sustained by people's supportive behaviour which evolves out of their allegiant orientations towards it. For instance, the democratic structural arrangement of a political system may remain stable and viable if most of its people are democratic in their political activities and roles which, in turn, emerge from their democratic political culture. Therefore, for a democratic political system, the congruent and allegiant political culture is democratic political culture, and such cultural structural congruence would, most likely, pave for stability and viability of the political system. As every political system, for its survival, stability and viability, needs legitimacy and supportive behaviour of its people, it tends to induct its people and accordingly socialize them in that pattern of political culture which is congruent and allegiant to its existing structural arrangement or form through the process of socialization. Therefore, the process of political socialization plays a very vital role for the survival, maintenance and stability of the political system. In this process of political socialization the mass-media like TV, Radio, Press may play significant roles in the context of formation of congruent and allegiant political culture in the citizenry by way of transmission of Latent and Manifest political communications supporting the political system. Thus, the media while playing their roles as political communicators, also tend to play their all important roles as political socializers, and thereby, may contribute significantly towards the formation and development of congruent and allegiant political culture in the people through the process of political socialization, which may lead to the stability and viability of the political system.

Extent of Media Impact

Mass-media, no doubt, have great potentiality to influence significantly the process of formation of political culture of the audience through transmission and dissemination of both latent and Manifest political communications. However, their roles as effective political communicators and political socializers tend to be determined by three major preconditions such as exposure, communication and receptivity[35]. For exerting influence upon the audience, the first precondition is the pattern of exposure regular or occasional, of the audience to the Mass-media. Non-exposure to the media would certainly not entail any influence upon the individual, whereas the extent of impact upon the audience may vary depending upon his pattern of exposure to the media. The audience who is regularly exposed to the media is likely to come under greater media influence than he who is exposed to the media occasionally. Apart from exposure, it is the pattern of media-communication to which the audience gets exposed seems to be a vital precondition for the extent of media-influence. The pattern of media communication may be manifested in case of transmission of explicitly political information, and it may be latent in case of transmission of politically relevant non-political information. In this context, Manifest political communications transmitted by the Mass-media directly and deliberately may exert greater influence upon the audience than non-deliberate transmission of non-political information that may be subsequently politically relevant for the audience. The third major precondition for the extent of media impact is receptivity of the audience to the media communications. The audience would, most likely, receive the media communication well and internalize it provided he understands it, and the level of his understanding seems to be crucially determined by his cognitive maturity which in turn, develop usually with his biological maturity, as well as his literacy and education. Thus, exposure, communication and receptivity appear to be three major preconditions which conjointly tend to determine the extent of impact of the Mass-media upon the audience.

Apart from these three major preconditions, there are also some other important factors which tend to determine the extent of media influence upon the audience. In this context, as Joseph T. Klapper[36] points out, media may extend influence upon the audience if his attitude, values and beliefs are not deeply rooted. In case of deeply rooted attitudes, for instance, basic attitudes toward one's identity and attitudes and beliefs held by the individual for prolong period of time, may be resistant to media induced change. Therefore, in case of deeply-rooted attitudes, values and beliefs, media-communications may have little impact for bringing any change in the individual, but they may have some impact on the individual's socio-political values, beliefs and attitudes already acquired by him through earlier socialization experiences. Another important determining factor for the extent of media impact relates to the social environment of the audience as it may affect his pre-dispositions, beliefs and values which, in turn, may determine his selection of the media as well as the content of the transmitted information.

Moreover, the role of the Mass-media as a set political communicators and political socializers may be affected by the nature of their ownership and control[37]. In case of privately owned and managed Mass-media communications are likely to be transmitted within the broad consensus of popular acceptability. Such media tend to avoid transmissions of controversial views and values because offending information may result in their non-acceptability by the audience at large and therefore ultimately in their financial bankruptcy. Hence, privately owned and managed Mass-media tend to transmit acceptable views and values and thus, tend to reinforce political values and beliefs of the audience. But, for the mass-media which are owned, managed and controlled by the State, and for whom profit is irrelevant, such constraint do not exist. Therefore, State owned and controlled Mass-media may transmit political communications, if necessary for socializing the audiences in political values and ideals held and championed by the State.

Thus, the role of the Mass-media as political communicators and political socializers and the extent of their influence upon the audience tend to be determined by a number of factors among which variables such as exposure, communications, receptivity, social environment and the nature of media ownership and control seems to be of crucial importance.

Mass-media, Political Communication and Political Development

Political communications as transmitted by the Mass-media may facilitate or hinder the pace of political development in a society. Political Development, in general, refers to the overall development of the Political System. Of course there is no unanimity among scholars as to a common definition on "Political Development" and a common set of criteria for measuring and assessing the level of development of a political system. Amidst such semantic confusions and diversity of definitions on the concept of political development, the Comparative Politics Committee of the Social Science Research Council of U.S.A. has undertaken a pioneering endeavour in identifying a set of political development criteria what is known as "The Development Syndrome"[38], that seems to provide a rational conceptual construct for the study and analysis of the level of development of a political system. The Development Syndrome is composed of three principal criteria such as (i) Equality, (ii) Capacity, and (iii) Differentiation and Specialization[39]. The criterion of equality encompasses three sub-criteria such as the nature and extent of political participation, the nature of the legal system, and the nature of the recruitment system. In respect of this criterion of equality, the development indicators are mass participation and popular involvement in political activities, prevalence of universal, secular and rational laws and prevalence of achievement oriented system of recruitment for public and political offices. The criterion of capacity is related to the outputs of the political system, and it encompasses four sub-criteria such as extractive, regulative, distributive and responsive capabilities of the political system. In respect of this criterion of capability, the development indicator is high level of systemic capabilities. The criterion of differentiation-cum-specialization encompasses two sub-criteria such as structural differentiation and functional specialization. In respect of this criterion of differentiation-cum-specialization, the development indicators are high degree of autonomy and differentiation among the structures of the political system, and also high degree of functional specialization undertaken by these structures.

These criteria and indicators that compose the 'Development Syndrome' may facilitate scholarly assessment of the level of Political Development of a society. However, these criteria of development may be exhibited by the political system provided the political culture of its people become developed[40]. The development political culture, therefore, seems to be a vital determinant of political development of a society, and it may be brought about, as Almond points out, through the process of secularization whereby people become increasingly 'rational, analytical and empirical' in their political orientations and disposition[41], and they become characterized by secular political culture that may be termed as "the Civic Culture"[42].

In the process of cultural secularization, what may also be termed as the formation of civic culture, Mass-media may play significant role by transmitting and disseminating political information and communication in such a way that people would become increasingly rational, analytical and empirical in their political orientations, disposition and actions. Thus, media communication pattern may be so designed and transmitted as to facilitate the formation of civic culture in the people that may in turn, pave the way for development of political system, and also the society as a whole. Hence, as Lucian W. Pye rightly points out, "the process of political communication and the process of political development and a fuller understanding of the essential of political development can be uniquely gained by studying the political process in terms of the communication process"[43].

Conclusion

The aforesaid discussions and analysis reveals the nexus between political communication and the Mass-media. Undoubtedly, political communication may play a vital role in the survival, stability, growth and development of the political system. In the process of political communication, Mass-media such as the Newspaper, the Radio and the Television and Cinema tend to play significant roles. While playing roles as political communicators, they may contribute significantly towards the formation of patterns of political culture in the individual as well as the collectivity by way of transmission of explicitly political information, news and views and also politically relevant non-political information and values. Such transmissions and communications may help shape the individual's political self of political culture which, in turn, may influence the performance of his political roles and behaviour. Simultaneously, the political behaviour and roles of the people tend to determine political dynamics and working of the political system. If the pattern of political culture of the people is congruent and allegiant to the structure or form of the political system, the latter is likely to remain stable and viable. On the contrary, if the pattern of political culture is incongruent and alienated to the structure of the political system, the latter is likely to experience instability and to undergo change. Therefore, culture-structure relationship, either allegiant or alienated tend to determine the prospect of stability or change of the political system. In the formation of the pattern of culture-structure relationship, the most important component is political culture which is shaped in the people as a consequence of their exposure to political communications transmitted by the varieties of political communicators. Among them, Mass-media seem to occupy a place of prominence because of their specific and specialized function is political communication, and their transmissions may reach the people easily, quickly and that too, at a low cost. Moreover, explicitly political communication as transmitted by the Mass-media are usually addressed to adult individuals who have already developed cognitive maturity to receive, understood and analyse such communications including explicitly political information, news and views, as well as politically relevant non-political information and values may contribute a lot toward formation and development of pattern of political culture in the people. The pattern of political culture thus formed in them tend to influence significantly their political behaviour and roles which in turn, tend to influence the dynamics and the performance of the political system.

Political culture is shaped at the individual level of and the community level through the process of socialization. In the process of socialization the Mass-media may play a significant role in the formation of congruent and allegiant political culture in the people by way of transmission of political information and politically relevant non-political information in support of the political system. Thus, the Mass-media may also perform the role of political socializers and thereby may contribute towards the stability and viability of the political system by developing congruent and allegiant political culture in the people through the process of socialization.

The role of the Mass-media as political communicator and socializer can be best realized provided the Mass-media become wedded to the national interest, and through their communications, they endeavour to create an allegiant, and integrated citizenry. People, through Mass-media communication, ought to be informed of and educated that the national interest is paramount, and that, therefore, their demands for social political change must not jeopardize the national interest, and must not undermine the capability of the Political System. The values of national unity and integration, patriotism, co-operation, harmony, peaceful coexistence and social justice ought to be inculcated in the people through media communications. However, for performing appropriate roles for realization of these goals, the Mass-media ought to enjoy autonomy, and freedom from control in the true sense of the term. They ought to be free from governmental control and undue censorship, and also from the vested interests so that transmission and dissemination of true and relevant information may become feasible. Of course, enjoyment of autonomy does not mean isolation and transmission of information even at the cost of national interest. Autonomy and freedom must be correlated with responsibility. Therefore, while enjoying autonomy necessary for the performance of their roles the Mass-media ought to develop work ethics characterized by commitment to national interests so that they play meaningful role in the context of both social change and stability of the political system. Hence, their roles as Political Communicator ought to be balanced by their roles as Political Socializers and these two types of roles ought to be harmoniously synthesized so that the Mass-media may substantially contribute toward the survival and stability of the polity and also toward the development of the society as a whole.

NOTES

1. Lucian W. Pye, "Introduction'. in Lucian W. Pye (ed.), *Communication and Political Development,* Indian Report (New Delhi : Radha Krishna Prakashan, 1972), p. 4.
2. Dr. Saneev Kumar Sharma, "Political Behaviour and Communication media in Rural Setting - A Case of Kumaun", *South Asian Journal of Socio-Political Studies,* Vol.6 No. 2 Jan.-June, 2006, p. 9.
3. Karl W. Deutsch, *The Nerves of Government. Models of Political Communication and Control,* New York, The Free Press, 1963, p. 82.
4. Claude E. Shannon and Warren Weaver, *The Mathematical Theory of Communication.* (Urbana, University of Illinois Press, 1959), p. 95.
5. Ithiel de Sola Pool, 'Political Communication' : Introduction in David L. Sills, (ed), *International Encyclopedia of the Social Science,* Vol. 3 (New York : The Mcmillan and the Free Press, 1968), p. 90.
6. "A Functional Approach to Comparative Politics", in Gabriel A. Almond and James S. Coleman (ed.), *The Politics of Developing Areas. Princeton,* N.J. Princeton University Press, Paperback Edn., 1970), p. 47. originally published by the Princeton University Press.
7. *Ibid.,* p. 47.
8. Gabriel A. Almond and G.B. Powell, Jr. *Comparative Politics: A Developmental Approach* (New Delhi : Amerind Publishing Company, 2nd Indian Reprint, 1975), p. 29.

9. *Ibid.*, p. 166.
10. Karl W. Deutsch, *The Nerves of Government, Models of Political Communication and Control*. New York : The Free Press, 1963), p. 16.
11. *Ibid.*, p. 150.
12. Easton David, *A. Framework for Political Analysis*, Englewood Cliffs, N.J.: Prentice Hall 1965, P-III also Easton David, "A System Analysis of Political Life" : New York : John Willey & Sons, 1965), pp. 29-33, pp. 117-127 and pp. 411-429.
13. L.W. Pye, 'Introduction', in Lucian W. Pay (ed), *Communication and Political Development* (New Delhi Radha Krishan Prakashan, India Reprint, 1972), p.6 and p. 4-6.
14. *Ibid.*, p. 6.
15. R.R. Fagen, *Politics and Communication*. (Boston : Little Brown & Co. 1966) p. 20.
16. Ithiel de Sola Pool, 'Political Communication. Introduction in David L. Sills (ed). *International Encyclopedia of Social Sciences*, New York. Macmillan Company and the Free Press, (1968) Vol. 3, pp. 90-95.
17. Dan,. D. Nimmo, *Political Communication and Public Opinion* in America (Santa Monica, C.A. Good year, 1978) p. 7.
18. Dan, D. Nimmo and Keith R. Sanders, Introduction : The Emergence of Political Communication as a Field, on Dan D. Nimmo and Keith R. Sanders (eds), *Hand Book of Political Communication* (Beverley Hills, California, Sage Publications, 1981), p. 27.
19. R.B. Meadow, *Politics as Communication*, (Norwood, N.H. : Ablex Publishing Company, 1980), p. 4.
20. Jean Blondel, *'An Introduction to Comparative Government'*, (London : Weideofeld and Nicolson, 1969) p. 223.
21. Michel Rush and Philip Atlhoff, *An Introduction to Political Sociology*, (London : Thomas Nelson & Sons, 1971), p. 160.
22. Gabriel A. Almond and G.B. Powell, *Comparative Politics : A Developmental Approach*, *op. cit.*, pp. 165-166.
23. *Ibid.*, p. 167.
24. *Ibid.*, p. 170
25. *Ibid.*, p. 29.
26. Charles R. Wright, *Mass Communication : A Sociological Perspective*, (New York) Random House (1989).

27. Ted Robert Gurr, *Why Men Rebel.* (Principles, N.J. Princeton University Press, Paperback Edn, 1972.
28. Richard E. Dawson and Kenneth Prewitt, *Political Socialization* (Boston : Little, Brown & Co., 1969) p. 63-64. Also Herbert H. Hyman, "Mass-media and Political Socialization : Role of Patterns of Communication in Lucian W. Pye (ed) *Communication and Political Development, op. cit.,* p. 128.
29. Herbert H. Hyman, "Mass-media and political socialization : The Role of Patterns of Communication", in Lucian W. Pye (ed) *Communication and Political Development, op. cit.,* p. 129.
30. *Ibid.,* p. 132.
31. *Ibid.*
32. *Ibid.*
33. Gabriel A. Almond, "A Functional Approach to Comparative Politics, in Gabriel A. Almond and James S. Coleman (eds), *The Politics of Developing Areas op. cit.,* p. 27.
34. Gabriel A. Almond and Sydney Verba, *The Civic Culture : Political Attitudes and Democracy in Five Nations,* Princeton N.J.: Princeton University Press, 4th Printing 1972, p. 21.
35. A Paul Allen Back, "Role of Agents in Political Socialization", In Stanley Allen Renston, (ed), *Hand Book of Political Socialization, Theory and Research,* New York : The Free Press, 1977, p. 117.
36. Joseph T. Klapper, *The Effects of Mass Communication,* New York : The Free Press, 1960, pp. 15-16 also pp. 45-49.
37. *Ibid.,* pp. 39-43.
38. Lucian W. Pye, *Aspects of Political Development,* New Delhi : Amerind Publishing Company, India Edition, 1972, p. 45.
39. *Ibid.,* pp. 45-47.
40 *Ibid.,* p. 48.
41. Also Gabriel A. Almond and G.B. Powell Jr., *Comparative Politics : A Development Approach, op. cit.,* p. 59.
42. *Ibid.,* p. 24.
43. Lucian W. Pye, Introduction in Lucian W. Pye (ed.), *Communication and Political Development, op. cit.,* p. 18.

23 Role of Panchayats in Alleviating Rural Poverty

A Case Study of West Bengal

Niranjan Mandal and Asit Kumar Banerjee

The notion of poverty in a country can be analysed on the basis of certain socio-economic conditions. It is a time specific and space specific notion. That is why we come across different conceptualization of poverty from different countries. Usually, poverty occurs when people fail to receive sufficient resources to support a minimum of maintaining physical health and efficiency, often expressed in terms of calories for nutritional levels. It is called as absolute poverty. Relative poverty, on the other hand, is defined by and relative to the general standards of living in different societies and what is culturally defined as being poor rather than some absolute level of deprivation. When poverty is defined relatively by reference to the living standards enjoyed by the bulk of the population, poverty levels vary between societies and within societies over time. It was popularly believed that poverty had been eradicated in Britain in the quarter century following the Second World War. Absolute poverty was abolished by high and sustained level of economic growth, which provided full employment and high wages and a state welfare system that cared well for those who were not part of the labour market or received low incomes from their employment. Relative poverty was much lessened by more equal distribution of income and wealth.

Sociologists and economists have challenged this belief, who suggest that poverty still exists and is rising. The Indian context in this regard is different from that of its western counterpart.

According to Prof. A.K. Sen, "The first requirement of the concept of poverty is of a criterion as to who should be the focus of our concern. The specification of certain consumption norms, or of a 'poverty line', may do part of the job: the poor are those people whose consumption standards fall short of the norms, or whose incomes lie below that line. But this leads to a further question: is the concept of poverty to be related to the interests of: (1) only the poor, (2) only the non-poor, or (3) both the poor and the non-poor?"[1]

To Sen, poverty and effects of poverty will be important issues to study in their own rights, and the conceptualization of poverty in terms of the condition only of the poor does not affect the worthwhileness of studying these questions. He puts forward some approaches to study poverty. The 'biological approach' defines families as being in primary poverty if their total earnings are insufficient to obtain the minimum necessities for maintenance of mere physical efficiency. He argues that the translation of minimum nutritional requirements into minimum food requirements depends on the choice of commodities. The actual incomes at which specified nutritional requirements are made will depend greatly on the consumption habits of the people in question. The second approach is the 'inequality approach'. Here the existing idea is that the concept of poverty is essentially one of inequality which has some immediate plausibility because after all transfers from the rich to the poor can make a substantial dent on poverty in most societies. Sen discards this approach too. According to him, analyzing poverty as an issue of inequality would do little justice to either. Inequality and poverty are not of course, unrelated. But neither concept subsumes the other. Third approach is concerned with 'relative deprivation'. It means that being poor has clearly to do with being deprived, and it is natural that for a social animal, the concept of deprivation will be a relative one. The choice of conditions of deprivation cannot be independent of the feelings of deprivation. Material object cannot be evaluated in this context without reference to how people view them. This approach, according to Sen, supplements rather than supplants the analysis of poverty in terms of absolute dispossession. It is certainly true that with economic development there are changes in the notion of what counts as deprivation and poverty, and there are changes also in the ideas as to what should be done. For Sen, while the exercise of identification of the poor can be based on a standard of minimum needs, that of aggregation requires some method of combining deprivations of different people into some overall indicators. In the later exercise some relative scaling of deprivation is necessary. "The much maligned biological approach, which deserves substantial reformulation but not rejection, relates to this irreducible core of absolute deprivation, keeping issues of starvation and hunger at the centre of the concept of poverty".[2]

Professor Sen wants to follow two alternative methods in identifying the poor—one is simply to check the set of people whose actual consumption baskets happen to leave some basic needs unsatisfied. This we may call direct method. It does not involve the use of any income notion, in particular, not that of a poverty line income. In contrast in what may be called the income method, the first step is to calculate the minimum income at which all these specified minimum needs are satisfied. The next step is to identify those whose actual incomes fall below that poverty line.

India is facing the problem of poverty even after sixty years of independence. India now comprises of 22 per cent of the world's poor. Nearly 260 million people in India are deprived of the bare minimum needs of life. Though the incidence of poverty has come down from 45 per cent to 26 per cent between 1950 and 1990-2000, poverty is still a challenge for the Indian economy and has become a controversial issue because the process of growth is often accompanied with increase in intensity of poverty. The Planning Commission of India has been estimating the incidence of poverty at the national and state levels using the methodology contained in the report of the expert group on estimation of proportion and number of poor and applying it to consumption expenditure data from the large sample survey on consumer expenditure conducted by the National Sample Survey Organization (NSSO) at an interval of approximately five years. In the earlier surveys the NSSO estimated monthly consumption expenditure on the basis of responses using a thirty-day recall period for all food and non-food items. In the 55th Round a 365-day recall period was used.

There have been various attempts to measure the extent of absolute poverty in India on the basis of the concept of poverty line *e.g.* Dandekar & Rath, Bardhan, Minhas, Ahluwalia, Planning Commission, etc. All these studies have defined poverty line on the basis of cost of minimum diet to maintain nutritional level of subsistence and used NSSO data to measure per capita consumption expenditure of the poor families.

The Planning Commission of India has defined the poverty line on the basis of nutritional requirements of 2,400 calories per person per day for rural area and 2,100 calories per person per day for urban areas. On the basis of these requirements the poverty line turns out to be a monthly estimated expenditure of Rs. 228 and Rs. 264.00 for rural areas and urban areas respectively at 1993-94 prices. At 2002-03 prices, the expenditure is estimated at Rs. 383.18 per month in rural areas and Rs. 442.10 per month in urban areas (Planning Commission).

Measuring the incidence of poverty or poverty line using income or food has two kinds of weaknesses. The first type stems from the many detailed methodological assumptions or choices that have to be made in the estimation procedure *i.e.* about the composition of the food basket; adult equivalent scales; inter-sectoral and inter-regional diets and prices; income distribution data to be used in the estimation process; etc. M. Guruswamy and Ronald Joseph Abraham in their study (June, 2006) rightly observed that there is a need to upgrade the concept of food security to that of nutritious food security. In addition, it should also be the right of every Indian citizen to have access to safe shelter, water, sanitation, healthcare, education and clothing.[3]

"The robustness of any poverty estimation using the poverty line approach, therefore, needs to be checked for its sensitivity to variations in these choices and assumptions"[4]. The second set of problems raises doubts about the meaningfulness of the poverty line. These criticisms go beyond practical objection and suggest that the approach totally distorts the very meaning of poverty.

The poverty eradication strategies must now focus not only on creation of additional employment opportunities but have to explore self sustained nature of such efforts through a single dose of assistance in order to increase the availability of resources for greater intervention. The grass root democratic institution that is Panchayati Raj Institution (PRI) can play an important role to improve the livelihood of impoverished and marginalized households in the countryside. The plan for public investments including self-employment and wage employment creation should be to supplement private employment opportunities so that the entire labour force in the economy is fully employed.

Objective of the Study

In our study we have not tried to measure poverty following income calculation method, consumption method or calorie intake method. Here we have tried to examine how Gram Panchayats play a positive role in reducing rural poverty by adopting and implementing different developmental schemes from time to time in villages under our study. Our main objective of this study is to show the trends in the incidence of rural poverty by studying some sample villages by taking family-wise data and by studying the perceptions of the beneficiaries of different developmental schemes. As we shall eventually find out, this trend is a steadily declining one.

Methodology

Relevant data regarding the role of Panchayats in reducing poverty by adopting and implementing different centrally sponsored PAPs have been collected from both primary and secondary sources of information. Primary data are collected directly from the field of enquiry by means of structured interview method. Panchayat records are also used as secondary data for identifying the rate of poverty in the study area since 1981 to 2006 and for analyzing the impact of PAPs on rural poverty alleviation. Our study area covers the geographical boundary of two blocks – Garbeta I & II of Paschim Midnapore district of the State of West Bengal. A total of 80 beneficiaries taking 40 from each of the two blocks are interviewed. Their responses are noted and analyzed to assess the PAPs in respect of their success or failure.

Case Study (Villages under 8 No. Saraboth Gram Panchayat) : Analysis and Findings

Before analyzing different Poverty Alleviation Programme (PAPs) undertaken by Gram Panchayats under survey, we need to go through some records regarding the rate of poverty in the villages since 1981 to 2006. Table 23.1 shows the percentage of poverty-stricken people over the years. To collect relevant data we have studied all the villages under 8 No. Saraboth Gram Panchayat in Paschim Midnapore District of the State of West Bengal.

Table 23.1 : Percentage of Poverty-Stricken People Over the Years (Villages Under 8 No. Saraboth Gram Panchayat)

Year	*Total Population*	*Percentage Increase in Population*	*No. of BPL Families*	*Population below the Poverty Line*	*Percentage of Poverty-Stricken People*
1981	6304	—	782	3878	61.52%
1991	8223	30.44%	941	3768	45.82%
2001	12024	46.22%	1032	3612	30.04%
2006	14805	23.00%	1237	3463	23.49%

Sources: Own Survey, 8 No. Saraboth Gram Panchayat Office, 2007: BPL — Below Poverty Line Decadal variation of population in Paschim Midnapore District : 1981—1991 - 23.57%, 1991-2001 — 15.35% (Statistical Abstract, 2002-03, Government of West Bengal).

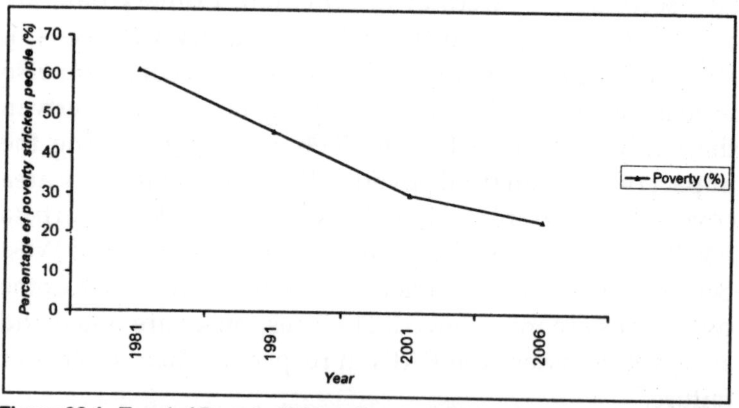

Figure 23.1 : Trend of Poverty-Stricken People of All Villages Under 8 No. Saraboth Gram Panchayat.

From Table 23.1 and also from Figure 23.1 it is seen that declining trends in poverty in those study villages. In the year 1981 there were 6,304 people in those villages under the Gram Panchayat out of which 3,878 people were below the poverty line as enumerated by the Government at that time. In that year (1981) 61.52 per cent of the total population of villages under study was poverty-stricken. In 1991 population reaches to 8,223 out of which 3,768 *i.e.* 45.82 per cent fall under the category of BPL though population increases by 30.49 per cent (decadal), percentage of poverty decreases by 15.70 per cent. In the year 2001 total population become 12,024 out of which 3,612 were under the poverty line *i.e.* 30.04 per cent of total population in the study villages. Here it is found that decadal variation of population is 46.22 per cent from 1991-2001 whereas in those years the rate of decrease in poverty is 15.78 per cent. From 2001-2006 i.e. in half decadal the rate of poverty comes down to 23.49 per cent. In the district as a whole decadal variation of population in 1981-91 was 23.57 per cent and in 1991-2001 it was 15.35 per cent (Statistical Abstract 2002-03 Government of West Bengal). Therefore, the data collected from the study villages is roughly matching with the governmental data. The table also shows fast reduction of the rate of poverty in those study villages. However, 23.49 per cent of the total population has been under the curse of poverty still today. It does not probe the success story of the entire developmental programme undertaken by the 8 No. Saraboth Gram Panchayat in Paschim Midnapore.

Earlier we have argued that a decrease in poverty may be an effect of various schemes/programmes undertaken by the Gram Panchayat to create mandays, which is shown in Table 23.2 below :

Table 23.2 shows that there was only one developmental programme under the head of NREP for which Rs. 59,286 spent and from that programme about 3,952 mandays were created. In the year 1991-92 under JRY Scheme Rs. 1,32,168 was spent which created 4,067 mandays. Under the same scheme Rs. 1,04,658 was spent in the year 2001-2002 from which 748 mandays were created. In that year also other programmes were taken up under the heads of IAY, EAS, JGSY from which 7,859 mandays were created. Since 1981-2006 it is found that a total of 37,116 mandays have created by those developmental schemes/programmes, which have immensely assisted in reducing the rate of rural poverty in our study villages. 8 No. Saraboth Gram Panchayat has achieved a success in this regard. However, if this Gram Panchayat wants to wipe out poverty from the villages under

Table 23.2 : Creation of Mandays through Different Centrally Sponsored Poverty Alleviation Schemes and Programmes (in 8 No. Saraboth Gram Panchayat)

PAPs	*1981-82*	*1991-92*	*2001-02*	*2005-06*	*2006-07*	*Mandays creation*				
						'81-82	*'91-'92*	*'01-02*	*'05-06*	*2006-07*
IAY	--	--	2,20,000	5,37,500	8,26,078	--	--	770	1,881	2,892
EAS	--	--	49,247	--	--	--	--	703	--	--
JGSY	--	--	4,95,400	--	--	--	--	6,386	--	--
JRY	--	1,32,168	1,04,658	--	--	--	4,067	748	--	--
SGRY	--	--	--	2,09,741	3,83,503	--	--	--	3,598	3,384
NREP	59,286	--	--	--	--	3,952	--	--	--	--
NFFWP	--	--	--	2,26,256	6,06,067	--	--	--	3,879	4,856
Total	59,286	1,32,168	8,69,305	9,73,497	18,15,648	3,952	4,067	8,607	9,358	11,132

Source : Records (Cash Book, etc.) of 8 No. Saraboth Gram Panchayat Office, 2007, (own survey).
IAY - Indira Awas Yojana
EAS - Employment Assurance Scheme
JGSY - Jawahar Gram Samridhi Yojana
JRY - Jawahar Rozgar Yojana
SGRY - Sampoorn Gramin Rozgar Yojana
NREP - National Rural Employment Programmes
NFFWP - National Food For Works Programme

its jurisdiction it must have other programmes to generate more rural employment which can support strongly in removing poverty from those villages. What Gram Panchayat needs is to implement Centrally-Sponsored Employment Generation Schemes, it should not distribute fund money to the poor villagers for their survival, which destroys the objectives of the schemes. Every scheme likes to sustain the life support system of the rural mass, which could not be provided only by offering cash benefit to them. Providing cash to the villagers cannot be a panacea to ills of poverty. The increasing trend of mandays creation from1981 to 2006 is clarified more vividly in Figure 23.2 below :

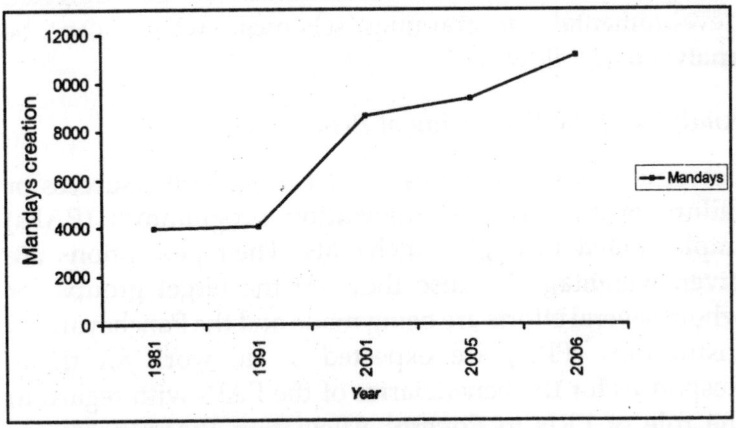

Figure 23.2 : Trend of Mandays Creation through Different Centrally Sponsored PAPs in 8 No. Saraboth Gram Panchayat

Panchayats have taken other measures to make the farmland multi-cropping, apart from schematic programmes undertaken from time to time by the 8 No. Saraboth Gram Panchayat, which creates enormous opportunities for rural jobs throughout the year. This multi-cropping culture was introduced in 1990's when minor irrigation projects like river pumps, electric shallow, and deep tubewells were installed in the fields. All these have produced a green revolution like situation, which enhances production as well as creates mandays. This process has resulted in reducing poverty in a faster scale. Farmers are now found to shift over from traditional cropping to unconventional cropping like producing different species of vegetables, oilseeds etc. for which a new market has been fast developing in the villages and small trading business has also been slowly taking place. These new opportunities of sustaining life of the villagers have reduced the rate of poverty in these study areas. Production of oilseeds and vegetables supply nutritious foods to the poor villagers, which is also an indicator of the reduction of poverty.

This declining trend in poverty has also been reflected in the perceptions of the beneficiaries of the different developmental programmes/schemes, which can be analyzed as follows :

Analysis of the Perception of Beneficiaries

Perception of beneficiaries is vital to know the success or failure of the Poverty Alleviation Programmes (PAPs) implemented through Panchayats. Their perceptions are given weightage because they are the target groups for whom several efforts are being made and the Panchayati Raj Institutions (PRIs) are expected to do work for them. Responses for the beneficiaries of the PAPs with regard to the role of PRIs in Poverty Alleviation Programmes are presented here.

Impact of PAPs on the level of income of the beneficiaries has been estimated and the data relating to this are presented in Table 23.3. Here we note the improvement in the income level by way of the difference between the income level 'before receiving assistance (B)' and the income level 'after receiving assistance (A)'. The data presented in Table 23.3 reveals that 56.25 per cent beneficiaries are in the income group of Rs. 4,501-6,500 before receiving assistance. It is the highest percentage among the four income groups. The percentage of beneficiaries having annual income upto Rs. 8,500 was about 29. The annual income of the beneficiaries after receiving assistance is also presented in Table 23,3. Now there are only 12.5 per cent beneficiaries in the income group of Rs. 4,501-6,500 after they got assistance as compared to 56.25 per cent, which was much higher. It is also observed from Table 23,3 that the beneficiaries (before assistance) in the income group of Rs. 8,501 and above was only 15 per cent whereas after assistance from the Panchayat the percentage of beneficiaries with higher income group has risen significantly that is from 15% (= 6.25 per cent +8.75 per cent) to 43.75 per cent (= 26.25 per cent +17.50 per cent). This tremendous increase in the number of beneficiaries in the higher income groups is a positive sign on

Table 23.3 : Income Status

Annual Income (in Rs.)	*Beneficiaries of PAPs*				*Total*	
	Garbeta Block-I		*Garbeta Block-II*			
	B	*A*	*B*	*A*	*B*	*A*
4501-6500	17 (42.5%)	5 (12.5%)	28 (70.0%)	5 (12.5%)	45 (56.25%)	10 (12.50%)
6501-8500	16 (40%)	17 (42.5%)	7 (17.5%)	18 (45.0%)	23 (28.75%)	35 (43.75%)
8501-10500	3 (7.5%)	13 (32.5%)	2 (5.0%)	8 (20.0%)	5 (6.25%)	21 (26.25%)
10501 & above	4 (10%)	5 (12.5%)	3 (7.5%)	9 (22.5%)	7 (8.75%)	14 (17.50%)
Total	40 (100%)	40 (100%)	40 (100%)	40 (100%)	80 (100%)	80 (100%)

Note : 'B' indicates before receiving assistance.
'A' indicates after receiving assistance.

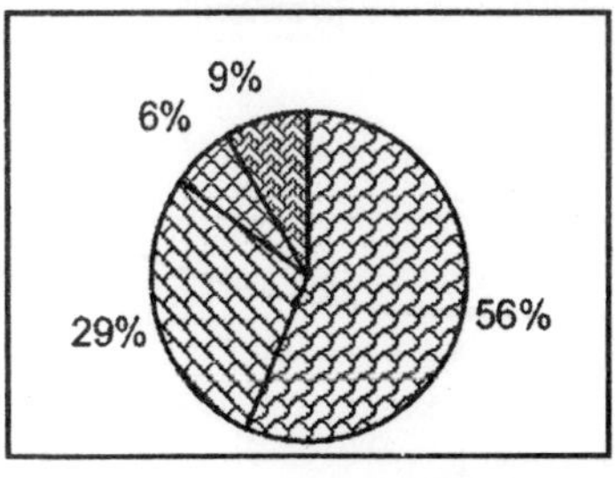

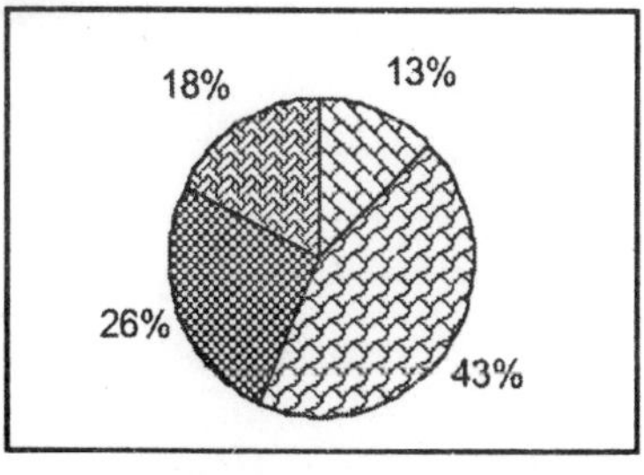

% of Beneficiaries before receiving assistance.
% of Beneficiaries after receiving assistance.

Beneficiaries were asked to mention the name of the programme under which they received assistance or wages. The answers given by the beneficiaries are presented in Table 23.4 :

Table 23.4 : Programme under which Assisted

Name of the Programme under which Assisted	*Beneficiaries of PAPs*		
	Garbeta Block-I	*Garbeta Block-II*	*Total*
JRY	11 (27.5%)	8 (20.0%)	19 (23.75%)
SGRY	3 (7.5%)	7 (17.5%)	10 (12.50%)
NFFWP	9 (22.5%)	13 (32.5%)	22 (27.50%)
IRDP	12 (30.0%)	5 (12.5%)	17 (21.25%)
DWACRA	–	–	–
IAY	2 (5.0%)	3 (7.5%)	5 (6.25%)
TRYSEM	3 (7.5%)	4 (10.0%)	7 (8.75%)
Total	40 (100%)	40 (100%)	80 (100%)

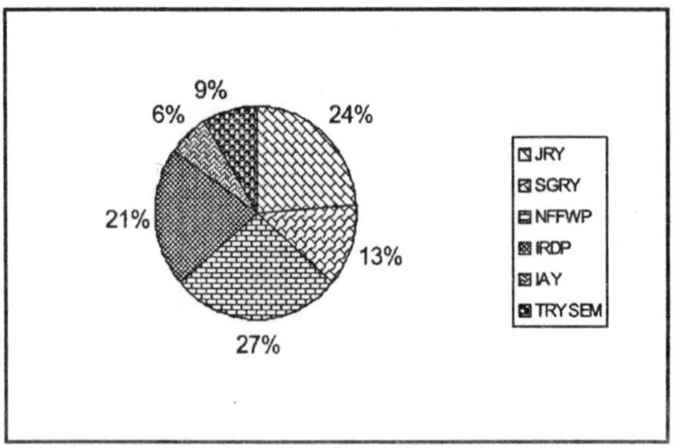

Beneficiaries — Programme under which assisted

Table 23.4 shows that about 21 per cent beneficiaries stated that they received assistance under IRDP. About 24 per cent beneficiaries get the wage employment under JRY whereas 12.50 per cent beneficiaries mentioned the SGRY as the programmes under which they were benefited. 27.5 per cent and 8.75 per cent beneficiaries were assisted by NFFWP and TRYSEM respectively. We find no beneficiaries who were assisted by DWACRA in our study area.

Inclusion of name in the BPL list is a prerequisite for receiving assistance under any PAP. Data relating to this aspect has been presented in Table 23.5.

Table 23.5 : Name in the BPL List

Name in BPL list	Beneficiaries of PAPs		
	Garbeta Block-I	*Garbeta Block-II*	*Total*
Yes	34 (85.00%)	36 (90%)	70 (87.5%)
No	6 (15.00%)	4 (10%)	10 (12.5%)
Total	40 (100%)	40 (100%)	80 (100%)

From Table 23.5, it is observed that there are 87.5 per cent beneficiaries who said that their names were included in the BPL list whereas only 12.5 per cent beneficiaries replied that they did not have the names in the BPL list. They are relatively poor, illiterate and less concerned about the importance of inclusion of their names in the BPL list.

Beneficiaries were interviewed about the source of information on PAPs. Their answers are presented in Table 23.6.

Table 23.6 : Sources of Information

Sources of information	*Beneficiaries of PAPs*		
	Garbeta Block-I	*Garbeta Block-II*	*Total*
1. PRRs	26 (65.00%)	23 (57.50%)	49 (61.25%)
2. Govt. officials	4 (10.00%)	9 (22.50%)	13 (16.25%)
3. Other villagers	6 (15.00%)	5 (12.50%)	11 (13.75%)
4. Media	4 (10.00%)	3 (7.50%)	7 (8.75%)
Total	40 (100%)	40 (100%)	80 (100%)

From Table 23.6 we see that Panchayati Raj Representatives (PRRs) are playing a significant role to carry several information relating to PAPs to the rural poor (61.25%). Media plays a relatively less significant role, as its coverage is only 8.75 per cent. Government officials and other conscious villagers have also the considerable role regarding the catering of information about PAPs to the rural masses, as their coverages are 16.25 per cent and 13.75 per cent respectively.

To know whether there has been any monetary corruption in the process of selection of beneficiaries interviews were made and the answers of the beneficiaries on this issue are presented in Table 23.7.

Table 23.7 : Expenses Incurred on Selection of Beneficiaries

Expenses incurred on selection	Beneficiaries of PAPs		
	Garbeta Block-I	*Garbeta Block-II*	*Total*
Yes	6 (15.00%)	7 (17.5%)	13 (16.25%)
No	34 (85.00%)	33 (82.5%)	67 (83.75%)
Total	40 (100%)	40 (100%)	80 (100%)

From Table 23.7 we find that most of the respondents (83.75%) said that there was no expenditure for their names to be selected among the beneficiaries and only 16.25 per cent beneficiaries put their allegation about monetary corruption in selecting the beneficiaries.

The central idea behind the introduction of new Panchayati Raj system was to utilize the PRIs to act as an agency of welfare state at the local level. PRIs are expected to initiate, plan and execute, developmental programmes keeping in view the local needs and thereby pave the way for social justice. Under the changed scenario it was important to know the views of the beneficiaries of PAPs whether they noticed any change as far as the implementation of PAPs was concerned. The views of the beneficiaries on this point are presented in Table 23.8.

Table 23.8 : Change

Changes Noticed	*Beneficiaries of PAPs*		
	Garbeta Block-I	*Garbeta Block-II*	*Total*
Yes	23 (57.50%)	27 (67.50%)	50 (62.50%)
No	17 (42.50%)	13 (32.50%)	30 (37.50%)
Total	40 (100%)	40 (100%)	80 (100%)

It is seen from Table-23.8 that 62.50 per cent beneficiaries noticed positive change in this respect.

Responses of these beneficiaries, who are of the view that there are positive changes, have been presented in Table 23.9, which are also shown in Table 23.9.

Table 23.9 : Changes Noticed (positive)

Changes Noticed	*Beneficiaries of PAPs*		
	Garbeta Block-I	*Garbeta Block-II*	*Total*
1.	2 (8.70%)	3 (11.11%)	5 (10%)
2.	8 (34.78%)	5 (18.52%)	13 (26%)
3.	4 (17.39%)	8 (29.63%)	12 (24%)
4.	0 (0%)	4 (14.81%)	4 (8%)
5.	3 (13.03%)	2 (7.41%)	5 (10%)
1 & 2.	1 (4.35%)	2 (7.41%)	3 (6%)
2 & 3.	1 (4.35%)	0 (0%)	1 (2%)
2 & 4.	2 (8.70%)	1 (3.70%)	3 (6%)
3 & 4.	2 (8.70%)	2 (7.41%)	4 (8%)
Total	23 (100%)	27 (100%)	50 (100%)

Note : 1. Indicates got labour works/wage paid jobs.
2.. Indicates overall welfare of village/cannot explain.
3. Indicates construction of building has been done.
4. Indicates more persons are getting benefits.
5. Indicates approach to Zilla Parisad and Panchayat Samity become easier.

From Table 23.9 it is found that 26 per cent beneficiaries mentioned that now the overall welfare of the villages has been possible. However, when they were asked to explain what they include in the overall welfare, they did not have a clear idea of it. 24 per cent respondents stated that construction of government building like school building, Anganwadi building, Panchayat building, etc has been undertaken on priority basis. Other changes mentioned by them are : (i) got labour works/wage-paid jobs (10%), (ii) more persons are getting benefits (8%); approach to Zilla Parishad and Panchayat Samity become easier (10%). Some of them have mentioned more than one change respectively. Hence, our observation is that the PRRs have their accessibility and acceptability among the rural people to a large extent.

We also have the responses of the beneficiaries to the question relating to the impact of PAPs in the rural areas. It is observed that 90 per cent of the total respondents have opined positively about this issue, which is quite encouraging. It clearly indicates Panchayat's role in the desired manner in rural areas (Table 23.10).

Table 23.10 : PAPs Helped

PAPs helped in eradicating poverty	*Beneficiaries of PAPs*		
	Garbeta Block-I	*Garbeta Block-II*	*Total*
Yes	34 (85.00%)	38 (95.00%)	72 (90.00%)
No	6 (15.00%)	2 (5%)	8 (10.00%)
Total	40 (100%)	40 (100%)	80 (100%)

As regards attitude towards rural masses the beneficiaries were asked whether Panchayati Raj Representatives (PRRs) were helpful or not. Their responses are presented in Table 23.11.

Table 23.11 : Attitude of PRRs

Attitude of PRRs	*Beneficiaries of PAPs*		
	Garbeta Block-I	*Garbeta Block-II*	*Total*
Helpful	23 (57.50%)	27 (67.50%)	50 (62.50%)
Unhelpful	9 (22.50%)	7 (17.50%)	16 (20.00%)
Indifferent	8 (20.00%)	6 (15.00%)	14 (17.50%)
Total	40 (100%)	40 (100%)	80 (100%)

From Table 23.11 it is seen that 62.50 per cent beneficiaries are satisfied with the attitude of PRRs. 20.00 per cent and 7.50 per cent respondents explain their attitude towards rural masses as unhelpful and indifferent.

At the same time beneficiaries were asked about the attitude of the Government officials whether they are helpful or not. The responses of these beneficiaries are shown in Table 23.12.

Table 23.12 : Attitude of Officials

Attitude of Officials	*Beneficiaries of PAPs*		
	Garbeta Block-I	*Garbeta Block-II*	*Total*
Helpful	22 (55.00%)	26 (65.00%)	48 (60.00%)
Unhelpful	5 (12.50%)	3 (7.50%)	8 (10.00%)
Indifferent	13 (32.50%)	11 (27.50%)	24 (30.00%)
Total	40 (100%)	40 (100%)	80 (100%)

From Table 23.12 we also see that 60 per cent beneficiaries have the feeling that the attitude of government officials is helpful and 30 per cent of them react nothing about the attitude of government officials. Thus, it is found that the majority of the officials in the two blocks under consideration have become conscious about their role under the changed situation of democratic decentralization and started discharging their functions with sincerity.

Success or failure of any PAPs depends on the assistance provided to the intended beneficiaries under the programme. The data relating to the adequacy of assistance is presented in Table 23.13.

Table 23.13 : Adequacy of Assistance

Adequacy of Assistance	*Beneficiaries of PAPs*		
	Garbeta Block-I	*Garbeta Block-II*	*Total*
More than adequate	2 (5.00%)	1 (2.50%)	3 (3.75%)
Adequate	15 (37.50%)	10 (25.00%)	25 (31.25%)
Less than adequate	23 (57.50%)	29 (72.50%)	52 (65.00%)
Total	40 (100%)	40 (100%)	80 (100%)

It is seen from Table 23.13 that majority of the beneficiaries (65%) are not satisfied with the assistance given to them. However, 31.25 per cent beneficiaries feel that the assistance given to them is adequate. Percentage of beneficiaries with the reply of 'more than adequate' is only 3.75 per cent. The analysis of the data underlies the fact that there is need to enhance the quantum of aid under various PAPs. They will, therefore, be above the poverty line which ultimately our target to achieve through successful implementation of PAPs.

Conclusion

From the discussion and analysis so far it may be concluded that in implementing centrally sponsored Poverty Alleviation Programmes (PAPs), the Panchayats have played a formidable role for alleviating rural poverty in our study area. Experience shows that Gram Panchayats could play an effective role in PAPs through the process of planning, execution, monitoring and evaluation. At the same time the Panchayati Raj (PR) leaders could provide help to the PRIs in identifying the beneficiaries, in selection of priority areas and also in monitoring the works of the Panchayats. Sometimes it is reported that PRRs and government officials behave negatively with the general masses. Their attitude towards the rural people is not favourable for smooth functioning of the Panchayat. Inadequacy of fund is reported to be another constraint in the implementation of plans and programmes. To combat the situation there is a need to enhance the quantum of aid under various programmes, thereby enabling the beneficiaries to generate enough income to raise Above the Poverty Line (APL). In our analysis it is also observed that in some of the cases, proper care has not been taken at the time of preparing BPL list. It appears that some non-poor are included wrongly in the BPL list instead of including real poor and, therefore, non-poor are relatively getting higher benefits than the poor. In West Bengal, PRIs have become synonymous with rural development. They have become perfect agencies of welfare state system. From the study it is noticed that only thing PRI's need is to reduce political interference, which sometimes becomes unhealthy for democracy.

NOTES

1. Sen, A.K. (1981), Poverty and Famines, Oxford University Press.
2. Dreze, Jean and Sen, A.K. (1995): India: Economic Development and Social opportunity; Oxford University Press.
3. Puthenkalam J.J. (2004): Empowerment: Sustainable Human Development Strategy for Poverty Alleviation, Rawat Publication, New Delhi.
4. Datt, Ruddar and Sundaram K.P.M. (2004): Indian Economy S. Chand & Company Ltd., New Delhi.
5. Guruswami and Abraham R.J. (2006): Redefining Poverty: A New Poverty Line for a New India, *Economic and Political Weekly*, June 24.

24 Milk Co-operatives and Rural Development in West Bengal

Ranjit Karmakar and Bhola Nath Ghosh

A cooperative is defined by the International Co-operative Alliance's Statement on the Co-operative Identity as an autonomous association of persons united voluntarily to meet their common economic, social, and cultural needs and aspirations through a jointly owned and democratically controlled enterprise·A co-operative may also be defined as a business owned and controlled equally by the people who use its services or who work at it. Co-operative enterprises are the focus of study in the field of co-operative economics. Cooperatives have a sponsored top-level internet domain , cooperative,which identifies legally registered or recognized co-operatives.

Co-operative has been viewed as an agency of rural development particularly of upliftment of poor or weaker sections. Milk Co-operative has been one of them and since 1970 this programme has been in progress in India. Though first milk co-operative was formed in Kaira district of Gujarat as far back as 1945. co-operative has been considered as effective means to reduce inequality but studies have shown in some cases it has exacerbated the inequality and various authors have pointed out that co-operative has some difficulties as well as it does not promote individual freedom. Still it is thought that poor people uniting together may stage a come back in the economic frontier with the help of it. But whether small farmer and big farmer can come together and co-operate has been questioned by researchers (Gupta:1987). Co-operative's role in rural development has to be measured by their services to members so as to protect their interest against exploitation by others (Baviskar :1980). Kole (2007) has emphasized the need for review the working of dairy co-operatives in India, as co-operative movement has completed its century, the role played by private as well as co-operative organizations in dairy sector has been discussed at length so as to comprehend the nature of services it is rendering. Poor people has no other alternative than to form co-operative on the basis of membership to serve themselves (Bhowmick : 2000).

Milk is an essential substance, which is required by both child and elderly. Milk is not a polluting substance like water in Hindu religious ideology. So any development concentrating on the milk marketing and production can bypass the constraints of caste and religion. Even lowest caste, tribals and persons from other religion can take part in this venture and benefit. So the cooperative milk production has been considered as the only viable alternative than the earlier rural development strategy, which frustrated in many ways due to non-participation of the poor and weaker sections. It has also been argued that even the landless can participate if he/she has only one or two milch cows at their disposal. In the earlier land based agro-developmental programme only the landholder could participate. But this is of very different nature from the earlier programme. From this point of view, strategy for milk production and dairy development can become a viable developmental programme in throughout the country. Before the advent of milk co-operatives in the rural area, the private dairy used to function as both vendors and collecting agency. The private dairy used to make profit by cheating producing households in many ways. To bypass the exploitation, the notion of co-operative dairy development has come into the picture. Co-operative not only brings about group business but it gives individual partners some honour of being a member of joint or collaborative effort. This gives strength to not only individual but also to group to which they belong.

Milk-business has an age-old tradition in India. During the epical period we find mention of milk trading caste like Jadavas to which Lord Sri Krishna was brought up and grown. However, that is mythological and any one can deny the existence of Lord Sri Krishna from scientific ground. We are not interested to argue in this line and do not want to extend the controversy.

Milk co-operative had been started first in Gujarat State of India. The famous AMUL was the first milk co-operative in India, which had long tradition of milk production in the surrounding villages of Gujarat.

The Navali co-operative is one of the 175 milk co-operative across India and affiliated with a dairy conglomerate—Anand Milk Union Ltd., better known as AMUL. The Anand pattern is an integrated cooperative structure that procures, process and markets produce. The village is the start of a supply chain that goes to the district and then to the State Milk Union. AMUL is a household name in India that produces milk and milk products like cheese, powered milk, butter, clarified fat, ghee and so on.

Pre-Co-operative Situation in Gujarat

The milk co-operative was not in existence during the British period. During the colonial period there was Polson Dairy, which used to collect milk from the surrounding producers and used to sell to Bombay city. The milk producers used to sell to the dairy and there were not many private enterprises, which used to do business on milk and milk products. As a result they had to face little competition and they had full control over the market. The situation of the farmer producers was not changing because they had to depend on the private dairies for selling. The private dairies were exploiting the producers to a great extent. As a result they had more grievances but could not do much about the state of business. The private dairies did not extend loan and any input services as we see today. That is why the situation was all the same and there was no sign of change in the life of the people. To organize the milk producers along the co-operative line was not an easy task. But the leaders like Late Prime Minister Morarjee Desai and Sardar Ballav Bhai Patel had tremendous influence over the organization of milk co-operatives and milk producers that also had taken part in national struggle as well. By this time the Polson Dairy had ceased to function and Kaira District Milk Producers Co-operative Union emerged as first milk based co-operative business organization in the country. The after story is very much known to many. But the expansion of the business of AMUL is enormous and it has gained domestic and international fame.

The Urge for Replication

In 1964, the Late Prime Minister Sri Lal Bahadur Sastri visited the Kaira District Milk Producers Co-operative Union Ltd. at Anand, Gujarat and he was astonished to see the potentiality of the AMUL. Having been impressed by the excellent performance of three levels of functioning of the milk cooperatives Mr. Sashtri expressed its replication in other States. Since then, the construction of milk co-operatives is being in progress. A large number of farmer producers are being brought under the fold of milk production and its co-operative structure. The figures of co-operative outlay are now exceeding lakhs of rupees in some areas it has exceeded crores of rupees.

Organisational Structure of the Milk Co-operative

The milk co-operative organization is composed of three tiers. At the apex it is State level Milk Producers Co-operative Federation Ltd. and followed by it, there is district level Milk

Producers Co-operative Union Ltd. and at the village level there are primary societies, which are the original foundation of the milk co-operatives of which farmer producers are the members. The village level milk co-operative sends milk to the district level Union Ltd., which then tries to market the milk in the nearby towns and cantonments. There are many stages of milk processing. The main process involved Homogenization and Pasteurization. The former indicate a process which milk evenly distributes molecules through the liquid medium and the latter means a process by which germs and bacteria are killed through a certain temperature and sudden chilling process. The next important stage of milk processing is packaging which is made by machine. After filling milk of certain amount in sachet it is closed by pressure and heat. The mechanization of milk marketing is very interesting. Entire process is very well maintained.

Allied Organizations involved in the Milk-Cooperative Organization

The milk co-operative organizations in different areas has also some allied organizations, which help, promote business of milk and milk products. The organizations are National Dairy Development Board (NDDB), Indian Dairy Corporation (IDC), European Economic Union and Mother Dairy. With the help of these organizations Government tried to alter the traditional milk sector and intended to provide farmer producers better pricing of milk and some input facilities. The dairy development programme was launched as Operation Flood and White Revolution. Operation Flood programme was divided into Phase I and Phase II. The first Operation Flood Programme was launched in 1970 and the Second Operation Flood programme was launched in 1985. In 17 States of India the Operation Flood programme was initiated either in the first phase or as an extension of second phase of Operation Flood. But how far the farmers have been benefited from the programme of Operation Flood is the basic research question. Of course the programme has merits and demerits. But whether the farmers and milk bureaucracy has any contradictory interests or they can act together to go ahead may be another dimension of the research being pursued. Indian Dairy Corporation was set up by Government of India to change radically the milk sector and its production. By this time India had come to know that there would be donation from EEC in terms of skimmed milk powder and butter oil produced in the European countries which had tremendous surplus of milk and milk products. To capture this donation various countries tried to vie with other countries. AMUL was the first which had the infrastructure and fame to receive this donation. As a result with this donations AMUL has been able to capture the market of milk and milk products all over the country and it has become the pioneer in co-operative milk trade.

The Modern Dairy Practices

The modern dairy practices itself is a different concept which varies greatly from the traditional dairy practices limited to household level but it has an objective of milk marketing from the same umbrella. Instead of household level production, the dairy production was given a fillip. The modern practices not only included dairy production but it has taken care of the marketing as well. The production was based on some input services including cultivation of Napier grass which enhances milk yield as well as machine made cattle feed which is scientifically produced to suit both for adult milch animal and calf for which calf starter is specially produced by the cattle feed unit of Co-operative Milk Union. Free veterinary services also are provided to the cattle of the milk producers at nominal costs. This has far-reaching consequences to milk production in India. All these measures has obviously made co-operative milk production an ever popular programme in India at the same time milk production in India has exceeded several times as is claimed.

But the present researcher doubts the truthfulness of the claim because if the production had increased then there would have been less dependence on EEC for skimmed milk powder and other donations. But in fact it is not so. Rather the Operation Flood programme's duration is being enhanced and dependence is increasing if not more. In Karnataka milk co-operatives run by women are drawing attention and being encouraged from the concerned ministry by giving grants (*The Hindu*: 2002).

Debate on the Issue

'Development planners and academics have wondered why co-operative organizations set up to serve the rural poor fail to elicit their co-operation. In view of the role co-operatives can play in providing patient and peaceful alternatives to more violent revolutionary alternatives in developing countries, the answer to this question seems central to the developmental debate' (Gupta : 1987). The transformation of dairy sector has also raised debate among the politicians, planners and researchers in the country. The line of argument runs like that benefits from the transformation of traditional milk production system. Is it urban consumer? Or the rural producers? Because milk is needed for children of both rural and urban community. When rural producers sells all the quantity of milk to the co-operative how the children or infirm of the rural area will survive? Because it is not only energy giver but also it gives strength also to them. Food and Agricultural Organisation of UNO has argued that there will not be any dearth of calorie in the rural households who can depend on carbohydrate and other protein sources instead of milk. Same argument can also be given for urban consumers who may depend on carbohydrate and vegetable sources instead of milk and under that situation rural producers can only keep this rare commodity for their household members. But rural development paradigm only state that how to increase the household income but not to upkeep the health status of the rural people. This is a great lacuna of the rural development policy being pursued in India. Why rural people will suffer for development? This question will continue to come again and again as long as present policy will not be altered. How long the policy of tapping of rural resources would go on and benefit the few? This milk producer co-operative has been a curse to the marginal and small farmers who sell all the milk to the co-operative but don't keep milk for their child and old people. So these milk co-operatives are also biased to the large producers who can keep sufficient amount of milk for household level and sell the surplus to the co-operative. So how far the farmers of all categories have benefited from this programme may be a matter of empirical study, which will be helpful to verify the claim that it has benefited all sections of the people involved in the programme irrespective of caste and size-class category. In addition to this issue of general economic benefits there are other issues like farmers' control and equality of voice and participation by all sections. Is it so? If so then there is no necessity of taking further rural development programme because development has occurred in its entirety. But no development is end in itself it leaves some impression good or bad and in the light of that further programme is chalked out to go ahead. In fact development is a continuous process and all development is not beneficial to people rather some has anti-people characters. People at the grass root are the prime force and they have to be given utmost importance so that they do not become victim to the onslaught of development. Development without care of the people does not make any sense and they are not to be object of development instead they should be subject of development and participants in the process. Bennet (1978) has observed that the poor lack of money, and since institutional co-operatives require participants with resources sufficient to carry on viable agriculture, it has been difficult to devise an approach which genuinely benefits poverty population.

This is different kind of observation, which does not fit with the very objectives of any kind of co-operative.

How far Milk Co-operative acts as Equalizer

Milk-cooperative has advantage that it is farmers' own organization and unlike joint stock companies there is one man one vote. So concentration of power by virtue of share holding is not possible. But traditional caste hierarchy has definite role in the affairs of the co-operatives it has been observed that high caste try to get the important portfolios of the co-operatives at the primary societies level in Khunia Busty M.P.C.S. in Jalpaiguri district in West Bengal. And on this issue there are grudging grievances among the general members of that co-operatives at the village level. I had an opportunity to visit the above mentioned Nepali caste milk co-operative in a forest village. I had asked one general member about his participation and about keeping his opinion in the affairs of the co-operative. He does not like to tell in the meeting as his views are not given due recognition by the portfolio holders though he was a close associate of Co-operator of RSP party leader like Late Nani Bhattacharya from whom he learnt about the utility of the co-operative for the weaker sections. He expressed his views in Nepali as "Thula Thula Manshi Chha Bhannu Lai" (meaning there are big big persons to tell who are we). So this indicates though co-operative is supposed to extend equal opportunity and voice to all members but actually it does not happen. This is obviously in contradiction of co-operative ideal.

Another aspect is veterinary treatment offered to the producers for their diseased cattle at nominal prices. But it is not possible to offer the minimum prices for veterinary cover for the animal of the landless and marginal farmers because in most cases they fail to offer the fixed visit. But the big and large producers who supply considerable amount of milk to the co-operative are mostly in a position to draw more benefit due to their closeness with the veterinary official and affordability. Here is also co-operative has not been able to bring equal justice to all the beneficiaries and it has revealed its bias towards the large producers.

Another aspect is Artificial Insemination Programme. Through the Artificial Insemination Programme the local breed of cow is turned into improved variety of cow due to placement of preserved bull semen into the ovary of the cow. Attempt is made to fertilize the ovum of the local variety with bull semen of higher variety. This is a good programme to change the dairy scenario. Some calves have also born out of this artificial insemination and in the first generation the change become 50 : 50 and in the second generation it becomes 25 : 75 and in the third generation the breed change is complete *i.e.* 100 per cent improved variety. But it has been noticed that calf born and brought up out of such insemination has been sold to Bangladesh in lieu of high price. Sometimes it has been observed that insemination programme has become a profession as it brings money to the inseminator for each case done privately. In these way member-beneficiaries of the village co-operative has been denied of this benefits due to monetary offer of the non-beneficiaries. That is why the selection of person for training programme of Artificial Insemination has been a lucrative offer as it is a technical knowledge which edge over the general knowledge of dairying. This observation was made in Jalpaiguri district and Darjeeling district respectively.

Competition among the Milk Co-operatives

There were 15 milk co-operatives in the Dooars region of the Jalpaiguri district during 1990-95 and at the same period there were 12 milk co-operatives in the Terai region of the Darjeeling district. But it was very interesting that each co-operative used to try to send milk to District Union in excess amount than the other. I had surveyed one such co-operative named Khunia Busty Milk Co-operative Society Ltd. which used to sell 200 litres of milk in every shift (in the morning and in the evening) but Shaongaon Milk-Co-operative Society which was a tribal co-operative in the Dooars region also had send 100 litres initially to 200 litres to the District Union. This kind of rivalry between milk co-operatives was healthy in terms of procurement situation. In the former milk co-operative there were 65 members including 15 tribal members along with different Nepali caste members. While the latter had all tribal members about 56 persons of Munda, Oraon and Mahali tribes. In the former case all the members were forest labourer and in the latter case all the tribals were tea plantation workers in the tea garden. Among the tribals there was no tradition of milking the cow as milk was meant for the calf and it is an offence to deprive the calf from their mother's milk. It was their belief. But after the introduction of co-operative and arrival of the vendors in the village they had started to milk the cow. So tribal did not know milk as a commercial substance earlier. So the co-operative has become a blessing to them bringing in new knowledge.

Some Socio-Ecological Consequences of Milk Co-operative

Khunia Busty Milk Producers' Co-operative Society Ltd. (Jalpaiguri District)

As the Khunia Busty Milk Co-operative Society was located in a forest village. The villagers informed that they had to cultivate the Napier grass given by District Level Union Himalayan Milk Co-operative Union Limited (HIMUL) near the household land. But this has brought the menace of wild elephants that had eaten up the Napier grass planted near the house and also have destroyed the nearby houses for salt. So one can understand how one kind of development programme has caused difficulties to the villagers. As the village Khunia Busty is located in the forest the wild animal damage greatly the cattle. The wild animal try to catch the cattle on the shoulder and suck the blood and flesh and thereby causing death to the costly cattle and sometimes the wild animal hurts the cattle by nails and paws for which villagers had to bear extra expenditure in treating the animal with veterinary doctor who comes in the village once in a week or at a call on payment of greater fees. But another thing is to be noted here due to being a forest village that the animal of the producers can graze in the forests where fodder is plenty. This has been possible due to closeness of the forest, which has a direct impact on the Khunia Busty Milk Co-operative Society for its success. So here surrounding nature has a positive impact on a milk co-operative's success. But forest officials were against the grazing in the forest, as it would cause forest depletion. Another incident which was very important from which it was evident that milk co-operative's role was highly commendable. In Khunia Busty there was a forest workers' union under the banner of a union of a left party. They had started cessation of work and went on strike in order to raise the forest worker's wages. The strike continued for a long duration and ultimately the Forest Authority had to increase the wages for the forest workers who were at the same time members of the milk co-operative in the village. When the local forest Bit Officer was asked about the strength of the strike and continuation of it for such a longer duration, he replied that the forest workers could continue strike as they had economic support from the milk co-operative, which was not stopped during the strike. So it is interesting to note that even a small milk co-operative can play a positive role in increasing the bargaining power of the workers. Another success of co-operative is elimination of private vendor if not entirely. The private vendors used many tricks to deceive the rural milk producers and usually tried to keep them bound to sell milk by providing the advance money in times of need. This aspect of milk co-operative has been criticized as in absence of credit facilities rural producers find it easy to sell to the private vendors. It was noticed that many milk producers used to sell milk partly to private vendors and partly to milk co-operative. This was in order to get loan from the private vendors and to get input services like free veterinary services, cattlefeed at nominal prices and Napier grass from the Himalayan Milk Producers' Co-operative Union Limited (HIMUL) under which the Khunia Busty Milk Producers Co-operative Society was registered. Though it seems that the villagers' commitment to the co-operative was partial but villagers favoured the presence of milk co-operative as they thought in absence of it the private vendors would increase their control.

Saongaon Milk Producers' Co-operative Society Limited

The Saongaon is a tea estate in the Bagrakot area of Dooars in Jalpaiguri district and most of the members of the Saongaon Milk Co-operative were tribal who had come to work in the tea garden from Chhotonagpur area. Actually, their forefathers had come to this place during the British period. After the lockout and closure of the tea garden by the then owner, the workers were put to serious plight. To rescue them from this situation the Trade Union of a Left Party had given leadership to form a Co-operative in the tea garden. It had got registration from Co-operative Societies Registrar, Government of West Bengal. The trade union leaders trained the workers in the management of the co-operative. The tea co-operative at Saongaon had a large savings more than Rs. 6 lakh and the workers had built up assets like Tractor. But the success story did not last long as the rejuvenation of the garden brought back the earlier owner who left the garden and misused the workers' provident fund and put them in plight. After seeing the success the owner challenged the registration of the Co-operative at the Jalpaiguri Court and the Court had deputed a receiver and thus the co-operative had to put off the activities by the order of the Court and started to function under the receiver. But meanwhile the tribal workers had learnt the technique of managing the co-operative affair on their own. The same experience and loyalty to the trade union leaders of the tribal workers had led to the formation of Saongaon Milk Producers' Co-operative Societies Ltd. in the village. It was registered under the Himalayan Milk Producers' Co-operatives' Union Limited (HIMUL). The same services were extended to the Saongaon MPCS by the HIMUL and at the initial stage of its formation the milk co-operative had daily collection of milk at 200 litres per day. Artificial insemination and other input services were also extended to the local cattle of the members. The DRDA loan was arranged to some members who were interested to rear Jersey breed. But after some days the tribal members realized that it is not easy to rear Jersy cow by them as it needs more care and shed but they are habituated to rear local variety which are driven out from the cowshed in the morning and graze themselves and return in the evening. By two years duration they had deposited some amount of money in the bank. But the act of Secretary of the Co-operative was doubtful in the eyes of the tribal and they started to reduce the quantity of milk they used to supply. Ultimately the quantity of milk collected at the cooperative had come to 20-30 litres a day and the authority of HIMUL stopped to collect milk from the Saongaon Milk Co-operative society. But they did not enquire about the reason behind this reducing quantity of milk form the member producers or they did not hold any meeting with the members. This arbitrary decision of HIMUL has become responsible for closure of a viable co-operative. When HIMUL feels that the transport cost would be higher than the collected milk then it decides to stop procuring from remote area. But there was a possibility of co-operation between the tribal and non-tribal in respect of milk-business and co-operative would have flourished if the local staffs of HIMUL properly nurtured it. These are the problems of the co-operatives in short and here also the role secretary was more important than the elected board of members and secretary had drawn salary and after misusing the co-operative funds, as suspected, tried to close the co-operative by creating frustration among the members.

Conclusion

So from the above discussion it is clear that there are many aspects of milk co-operatives, which need to be probed critically, and how it is affecting or benefiting the rural producers who always have been the victim of market mechanism, are they farm producers or milk producers. As in the age of market economy market plays a very important role and whoever has more control over the market will gain in the long run. But the farmers in many times do not get fair prices due to lack of control and infrastructure for their produces. The milk co-operative is free from these handicaps as the Milk Marketing Federation at the State level wholly controls the marketing affairs. But it is a matter of serious concern that Co-operative Milk business is being dependent on the donation of the EEC and technology imported from foreign countries. This has a serious implication on the indigenous milk production and health of the people. As milk procured long back in Guntur in Andhra Pradesh is coming to the market of West Bengal and the local market milk of West Bengal is being captured by other States. So it may have impact upon the local producers who are not in the co-operative fold. Theoretically co-operative has many advantages over the individual entrepreneurship but who controls the co-operative is to be looked into. Is it really a farmers' organisation? Instead bureaucracy is controlling the milk co-operatives? As general members are the vital force of the milk co-operatives operating in the villages but over bureaucracy of milk business will not encourage the general members who may suffer from lack of participation under such situation. Sometimes it was observed that the Secretary who is a paid staff of the village milkco-operative guides the Chairman who is elected person in the co-operative. As in the case of Khunia Busty Milk-Producers' Co-operative Society Ltd., the elected board of members of the co-operative are all from higher castes like Chettri, Bahun etc. So they try to keep control of co-operative within themselves and Secretary who was from Chettri caste was convening the meeting and taking all important decisions ignoring the elected board of directors. This indicate the fact that if the micro level milk co-operative is dominated by paid staffs or local bureaucracy then we can assume what may happen in the apex bodies of the milk co-operatives. This raises a pertinent question—are the farmers really owns the milk-co-operative or they are just maintaining the bureaucracy at the cost of their own energy and labour? Milk-producers are also eligible to vote and elect the District Union Level Organisation. According to bye-laws, there would be Chairman elected by the producers themselves and the Chairman would be their own person preferably from the producers themselves as the problems of co-operative would be best understood by their own men. But in only one occasion, a legal practitioner of Darjeeling was elected as Chairman but it was heard that he had misused the co-operative's fund and then he was removed and since then the District Magistrate has been becoming the Chairman by virtue of his official capacity. And no dispute has been raised in this regard so far in the management of the Himalayan Co-operative Milk Producers' Union Limtied. But obviously it does raise the question whether the farmer producers would be able to really control and manage their own affair regarding co-operative or they will fall prey to the victim of external forces and its internal allies. It should be remembered there are many factors responsible in the success or failure of the co-operative. In some States co-operatives function smoothly and can flourish in some congenial situation but in some States the socio-political environment does not allow co-operative to flourish or they face lack of encouragement and even bad impression

(Baviskar *et al.*, 1996). But in every enterprise there are corruption or mismanagement or misuse of power and finance to some extent and there are merits and demerits of every enterprise. In spite of some success of cooperatives, it is mostly blamed for inefficiency and corruption but it is co-operatives, which have social objectives and best quality control capacity. Process of co-operation also exists alongside the competition in the society. But unhealthy competition not only ruins oneself alone but it accelerates another process, which is known as isolation. So let us give co-operation a chance to succeed.

REFERENCES

Baviskar, B.S. & D.W. Attwood, 1996. *Who Shares? Co-operatives and Rural Development.* Oxford University Press

Bhowmick, Sharit K., 2000. *Social Security for Street Vendors,* Seminar, Internet Edition.

Gupta, Anil. K., 1987. 'Why Poor People Don't Co-operate: Learning from Traditional System', in *The Research Relationship: Practice and Politics in Social Policy Research* (ed. G. Clare Wenger), London, Allen & Unwin.

Koli, P.A., 2007, *Dairy Development in India : Challenges Before Co-operatives,* D.K. Publishers.

The Hindu, Friday, May 24, 2002.

25 National Rural Employment Guarantee Act
A SWOT Analysis

Vishnu Bhagwan

Right to work is in fact right to live. For a long period of time India had been recognized as Golden Sparrow at international level but with the passage of time this Golden Sparrow had been reduced to a mere skeleton which is in dire need of food and cloth. Poverty is prevailing in this prosperous country and its sharp claws make it bleeding pathetically. All other rights are meaningless in the absence of right to work which is in fact right to live because when we have nothing to earn then how can we have any thing to eat and survive. Therefore, in this light the National Rural Employment Guarantee Scheme which is in lump-sum the right to work has become the most important right in the present scenario. We can boast of our progress in the field of technology and science, sports, agricultural production and international trade but we cannot turn our face from the other *i.e.* ugly side of the coin where thousands of farmers are committing suicide in various parts of the country due to excessive poverty, where millions of people are striving and millions of children and women are malnourished, where childhood and old age is being spent in the excessive physical work leading to nothing, where 26 per cent of the population is living below the poverty line and is not able to earn even two square meals. There is a wide gap in the national progress and poverty alleviation programmes. In such circumstances a ray of hope lies in the National Rural Employment Guarantee Scheme. Poverty is one of the dangerous problems because when the devil of hunger arouse all other things become dwarf. To satisfy this devil a person is ready to sacrifice anything *i.e.* his ethics, morality and humanity. He can easily mortgage his patriotism. Criminals are emerging day by day in a great pace and root of all this lies somewhere in the poverty.

Rural Economic Scenario : Present Status

India is no doubt a developing and poor country. Out of 260 million poor people in the country, approximately 200 million poor people are in rural areas. Around 100 districts are under the constant threat of drought and semi-famine like situation every year and other 90 districts are facing floods and torrential rains. While about 25 per cent rural house-holds of landless labourers and bonded labour, have either no income generating assets, 80 per cent farmers being small and marginal have inadequate and/or poor quality of assets with meagre or no irrigation facilities. Rural artisans have no access to modern tools/equipment and marketing. Problem of perpetual and pernicious poverty more particularly in rural areas has been deeply rooted into the large-scale unemployment among rural households during half of the year. Chronic unemployment for a large part of the year is prevalent in hilly, tribal, desert and drought prone areas. The situation becomes very pathetic when monsoon fails. According to National Social Watch, there are 45 per cent villages in India where people do not work for six months in a year and 20 per cent villages do not have work opportuni-ties for people in any form. Even revamped Public Distribu-tion System does not reach to 68 per cent villages. 48 per cent people in 13 States of India do not get two meals a day. Thus, need for enshrining the provision of right to work or employment has very aptly gained tremendous importance in the recent years.[1]

National Rural Employment Guarantee Act : Introduction

A number of programmes, namely National Rural Employment Programme (NREP), Rural Landless Employment Guarantee Programme (RLEGP), Food For Work (FFW), Jawahar Rojgar Yojana (JRY), Ensured Employment Scheme (EEC) were launched with a view to provide direct supplementary wage employment in rural areas. Later on, during the year 2000 and 2004 three more programmes, namely Sampoorna Gramin Rojgar Yojana (SGRY), Rashtriya Sam Vikas Yojana (RSVY) and National Food For Work (NFFW) were launched all over the country with a view to provide supplementary wage employment in rural areas, create durable public assets and to ensure food security. These labour intensive programmes could provide some relief to the rural poor through short duration casual wage earning employment and provide some food security during the period of acute drought conditions.[2] But these could neither provide any guarantee to regular employment, nor durable public assets could be created leading towards sustainable development. The situation of unemployment has been compounded by the absence of any social security mechanism. There was, therefore an urgent need to ensure a certain minimum days of employment that too guaranteed in the shape of manual labour to every household in the rural areas and it came in the form of National Rural Employment Guarantee Act (NREGA).

The National Rural Employment Guarantee Act is a revolutionary step for India's poor. Since Independence, it was being demanded that right to work should be included in the list of Fundamental Rights. It was a matter of concern for all governments that in spite of their best effort, the problem of unemployment and poverty never came under control. It is noteworthy that a large number of rural youth have been migrating to the cities since Independence. Therefore, it always remained the priority of the government to stop this exodus of population to the cities[3].

Therefore, the National Rural Employment Guarantee Act is being implemented to enhance the livelihood security of people in rural areas by generating wage employment through works that develop the infrastructure base of that area. The objective behind this is to rejuvenate natural resources to stimulate the local economy and to stop local population from migration to the cities. Even today, 72 per cent of households belonging to rural India account for nearly 75 per cent of total population. In rural areas, about 66 per cent of employed males and 84 per cent of employed females are engaged in the agriculture sector. This way, we are still depending on agriculture which in turn depends on monsoon. It was, therefore, imperative to assure the rural lot that are part and parcel of our developing economy[4].

Dr. Manmohan Singh and the UPA Chairperson Mrs. Sonia Gandhi launched on February 2, 2006 the first-ever ambitious bid to tackle rural poverty by seeking to guarantee a hundred days of employment each year to rural families. It was launched in a remote village Bandlapalli in Anantpur district in Andhra Pradesh where thousands of farmers have committed suicide in the past two years due to mounting debts. In the first phase, the programme was implemented in 200 districts across the country. In the second phase it is being implemented in 130 more districts. The entire country will be covered within five years from its implementation.

It is the first time in the history of post-Independence India, Panchayati Raj Institutions are expected to be directly involved in this scheme in such a way that they would implement the scheme as an integral part of rural development plan. Gram Panchayats and Gram Sabhas would decide types of work to be undertaken in the villages and use of funds earmarked under the scheme. Gram Sabha would discuss and approve this plan. Gram Sabhas would also supervise and monitor the implementation of the NREGA.

A to Z of National Rural Employment Guarantee Act

The National Rural Employment Guarantee Act, 2005

guarantees 100 days of employment in a financial year to any rural household whose adult members are willing to do unskilled manual work. The A, B, C, of National Rural Employment Guarantee Scheme[5] in the form of its features are as follows :

(a) Application for Work

To get employment the registered adult must submit an application on a plain paper in writing to Gram Panchayat or the Programme Officer (at Block level) and get a dated receipt of the application.

(b) Basic Eligibility

The scheme will be open to all rural households in the areas notified by the Central Government. The entitlement of 100 days of guaranteed employment in a financial year is in terms of a household. This entitlement of 100 days per year can be shared within the household; more than one person in a household can be employed (simultaneously or at different times). 'Household' will mean a nuclear family comprising mother, father and their children, and may include any person wholly or substantially dependent on the head of the family. Household will also mean a single-member family.

(C) Citizens' Charters

A model citizens' charter covering all aspects of the duties of Panchayats and officials under the act is required. The citizens' charter should describe the specific steps involved in implementing the provisions of the act and lay down the minimum service levels mandated by these provisions on the Panchayats and the officers concerned.

(D) Day for Employment Guarantee

A particular day of the week in each Gram Panchayat is earmarked as "Employment Guarantee Day" for processing work application and related activities such as disclaimer of information, allocation of work, payments of wages and payment of unemployment allowances etc.

(e) Employment Guarantee Fund

There is a provision of National Employment Guarantee Fund. The grant to State Governments and District for implementing of NREGA shall be released from this fund. Similarly State Government may also, by notification, establish a fund to be called the State Government Employment Guarantee Fund.

(f) Financing Pattern

The Central Government will bear the entire cost of wages for unskilled manual workers, 75 per cent of the cost of material and wages for skilled and semi-skilled workers and administrative expenses of the Central Employment Guarantee Council. The State Government will bear 25 per cent of the cost of material and wages for skilled and semi-skilled workers, unemployment allowance and administrative expenses of the State Employment Guarantee Council.

(g) Grievance Redressal

The Programme Officer will be the grievance redressal officer at the Block level and the District Programme Coordinator at the district level. A system of appeal will be designed to deal with grievances at each level.

(h) High Wage-Low Material Ratio

The ratio of wage costs to material cost should be not less than the minimum norm of 60 : 40 stipulated in the Act. Wages of skilled labours and mates should be included in the material costs.

(i) Incentives and Provision for Workers

At work site safe drinking water, shades for children, periods of rest and first-aid box shall be provided at every work site by the implementing agency. A person may be entrusted with childcare responsibilities, if there are more than five children brought along on the site. If a worker gets injured working on the site, free medical treatment will be given by the State Government. In case of hospitalization of the injured labourers, he will be entitled for daily allowance which shall not be less than 50 per cent of wage rate applicable.

(j) Job Card

Upon registrations, a Job Card will be issued by the Gram Panchayat with photographs of adult members of the registered household. It will be valid for five years and will have the registration number of the household. A Job Card is a document that gives an applicant an entitlement for employment.

(k) Key Implementing Agencies

Gram Sabha and Gram Panchayat at village level; Intermediate Panchayat and Programme Officer at Block level; District Panchayats and District Programme Coordinator at district level; Employment Guarantee Commissioner and State Employment Guarantee Council at State level and Ministry of Rural Development and Central Employment Guarantee Council at Central level are the key implementing agencies.

(l) Laymen's Act

The National Rural Employment Guarantee Act is a "Laymen's Act" or "People's Act" in several senses. It empowers ordinary people to play an active role in the implementation of Employment Guarantee Schemes through Gram Sabhas, social audits, participatory planning and other means. More than any other law, NREGA is an Act of the people, by the people and for the people.

(m) Minimum Wages

The statutory minimum wage applicable to agricultural workers in the State to be paid but should not be less than Rs. 60 per day. Wages are to be paid not later than a fortnight after the date on which work was done.

(n) Notification

From time to time Central Government and State governments may by notification specify the areas in which the scheme shall be implemented, nature of works to be undertaken in the scheme and for the establishment of Employment Guarantee Fund etc.

(o) Objectives

The objectives of this scheme is to enhance livelihood security in rural areas by way of guaranteed wage employment, generating productive assets, protecting the environment, empowering rural women, fostering social equity and reducing rural-urban migration.

(p) Permissible Works

As per Schedule I of the Act, the focus of the scheme shall be on water conservation and water harvesting; drought proofing including afforestation and tree plantation; irrigation canals including micro and minor irrigation works; provision of irrigation facility to land owned by households belonging to the SC/ST or to land of the beneficiaries of land reforms or to land of the beneficiaries under the Indira Awas Yojana; renovation of traditional water bodies including desilting of tanks; land development; flood control and protection works including drainage in waterlogged areas; rural connectivity to provide all-weather access and any other work that may be notified by the Central Government in consultation with the State Government. No contractor or machinery will be allowed to work under the scheme.

(q) Quick Service

Whether it is giving of employment, wages, unemployment allowance, any daily allowance or *ex gratia* payment of Rs. 25,000 in case of death or permanent disability to registered labourer there is a quick service provision of time bound aspect.

(r) Right to Information

For ensuring commitment to transparency and account ability NREGA ensures Right to Information in its letter and spirit and proactive disclosure as per the provisions of Section 4 of the Act.

(s) Social Audit

All agencies implementing NREGA will be accountable to the public for their work. Social audit will apply to each aspect of implementation. Social audit may be seen as a means of promoting transparency, participation, consultation, consent, accountability and redressal of public grievances.

(t) Time Bound Employment

Within 15 days from submitting the application or from the date when employment is sought, employment should be provided by the Gram Panchayat. Gram Panchayat will inform applicants where and when to report for work within 15 days, by means of a letter. Public notice of this will be displayed on the Gram Panchayat's office.

(u) Unemployment Allowance

If the eligible applicant does not get employment within 15 days of demand of work or the date from which he sought work, he shall be provided unemployment allowance.

(v) Vigilance and Monitoring Committees

For every work sanctioned under the scheme, there should be a local vigilance and monitoring committee, composed of members of the locality or village where the work is undertaken, to monitor the progress and quality of work while it is in progress. The Gram Sabha will elect the members of this committee and ensure that SC/STs and women are represented on it.

(w) Woman Empowerment

Women will get priority to the extent that one-third of persons who are given employment are women who have asked for work.

(x) X'tra Wages Provision

Work will be provided within 5 km of applicants' residence. If employment is provided beyond 5 km radius of the applicant's residence then he is entitled to 10 per cent x'tra wages towards transport and living expenses.

(y) Yearly Reports

The Central Employment Guarantee Council and every State Employment Guarantee Council is required to prepare a Yearly or Annual Report. The Annual Reports should be placed before Parliament and the State Legislatures by 31st December of the succeeding year.

(z) Zeal for Record Maintenance

Under this programme the Gram Panchayat has to maintain records like Application Registration Register, Job Card Register, Employment Register, Asset Register, Muster Roll Receipt Register and Complaint Register.

National Rural Employment Guarantee Act : Progress Profile

The NREGA, which was launched with much fanfare on 2-2-06

to free India from poverty, has completed two years of its implementation. It has among its beneficiaries 36.44 per cent SCs and 25.35 per cent STs in 2006-07 and 31.06 per cent SCs and 27.23 per cent STs in 2007-08 (Upto Dec. 2007) and 41 per cent of women in 2006-07 and 44 per cent in 2007-08 (Upto Dec. 2007). Millions of mandays of employment has been provided under the programme through execution of about 12,31,000 works upto Dec. 2007 of which almost half have been completed. About 50 per cent of the work is implemented by Gram Panchayat. Contractors and Machinery are out of bounds from NREGA works which have to labour intensive. In total 2.10 crore families in 2006-07 and 2.57 crore families in 2007-08 (Upto Dec. 2007) have been provided employment. 90.50 crore mandays of employment during 2006-07 and 85.51 crore mandays of employment during 2007-08 (Upto Dec. 2007) has been created. During 2006-07 in total Rs. 8823.35 crore and in 2007-08 (Upto Dec. 2007) Rs. 9105.74 crore has been spent. Care has been taken to dispense with apprehensions expressed from time to time about slippage of NREGA funds or robbing the poor workers of their hard earned wages

National Rural Employment Guarantee Act : A SWOT Analysis

With an enlightened vision on literature related to NREGA and personal research and experience it is pertinent to highlight success and failure of the scheme as well as future prospects in all its pros and cons through SWOT Analysis. *i.e.* Strength, Weakness, Opportunity and Threat.

Strengths

So far as the strengths of NREGA is concerned the above mentioned feature of NREGA in the form of ABC of NREGA are its full proof strength. In addition to that, there are some more strength which need attention *e.g.* :

- It is empowering the people by granting them a right

to livelihood which is able to transform their dreams into reality.

- It entitles our rural poor to guarantee employment, to a means of sustenance, a means to avert distress, a means to secure two square meals and a means to lift them out of the lap of poverty.
- According to the Act[6], the summary of the scheme shall be published by the State Government in vernacular language which indicates the importance given to communication, the very life-blood of success.
- As per the Act[7], the preparation of labour budget in the month of December for the next financial year indicates the importance given to planning, an other off-shoot of success.
- As per item number 5 of Schedule 1 proper maintenance of the created public assets is leading way to sustainable development[8].
- The system of advance, multiple and group applications under the provisions of the Act substantiates its multi-dimensional approach.
- NREGA is a Guarantee not merely a scheme and that too demand-driven substantially differentiating it from earlier programmes and schemes of employment generation and poverty alleviation.
- According to the analysis made by the government agencies, the key to this Act lies in the word "Guarantee." There are so many schemes for the poor. But in those schemes there are many loopholes for interference from politicians. A guarantee seeks to take this power away from the hands of politicians. It makes it a right, something that people will expect and demand, something they can complain about or in extreme cases, sue the government.
- It has the potential to profoundly alter the ways bureaucrats treat the people they are supposed to serve.

- One of the most positive development emerging from the social audit is the creation of new partnership between the government and civil society organizations benefiting all parties. Social audit—a transparent, participatory and active evaluator process has the potentiality to attack the corruption that plagues anti-poverty programmes.
- NREGA also gives impetus to micro-planning coupled with decentralized planning as most of the plans are prepared at Gram Sabha level.
- As we know that any future edifice of success will be based on three W's *i.e.* Work, Women and Water and NREGA incidentally covers all the three ingredients of future progress in the form of unskilled manual work (Work), women empowerment (Women) and priority to water conservation and water-harvesting projects (Water).

Weaknesses

On the basis of keen and minute study of theoretical and practical aspects related to NREGA following observations highlighting the weaknesses may be taken into consideration to awaken and aware *hoi polloi* in general and the paraphernalia responsible for its execution and implementation in particular.

- The objectives achieved and benefits accrued under NREGA were not as expected as well as in proportion to the funds invested. Most significant reasons can be attributed to utter lack of involvement and participation of local people, for whom these schemes were evolved, in the matter of planning, implementation, monitoring-cum-concurrent evaluation, ex-post impact evaluation and modifying the projects to suit to local conditions and people's needs.

- Like other schemes and Acts, this Act is also suffering from the lack of awareness and social mobilization among the poor sons of Mother India due to illiteracy and passive attitude of these victims of poverty and unemployment.

  Job Card which is known as the spinal-cord of NREGA is suffering from the genetic disease *i.e.* corruption as from the very starting of the Act most of the Job Cards are without photographs openly laughing at the provision of accountability and transparency.
- It came to notice that during the harvesting time unskilled workers prefer to work in the field leaving NREGA a scheme only existing in the papers.
- The contact farming has been reduced leading to aggravating the problem of peasantry.
- On the horizontal and vertical pretext of the Panchayati Raj Institutions a new tension area in the form of *Sarpanch-Majdoor* relationship has been emerged in line with *Politics-Administration* relationship and *Generalist-Specialist* relationship.
- Under this scheme exhaustive paper work is required but there is lack of adequate staff and lack of training of available staff make it more complicated.
- Workers in the villages near to city prefer to work in cities due to better working condition as compared to NREGA.
- Some of the village Panchayats do not have *Panchayat Bhoomi* so the permissible works cannot be executed.
- Due to implementation of this scheme other routine works of administrative staff hamper resulting into the less dedication of the staff.
- Under this Act, the Government has offered a modest gainful employment which will fetch Rs. 500 per month for a family. There are people who believe that Rs. 500 per month is not sufficient to run a family nowadays[9].

- As there is a wage-material ratio of 60 : 40, some times it becomes difficult to maintain this ratio particularly in the States where infrastructure is already created. There exists administrative *versus* technical disputes also due to the petty interests of the fishes swimming in the river of corruption leading to delay and red tapism in the technical and administrative approval of the project.
- Appointment of *Panelled JEs* and *Rojgaar Sahayaks* through outsourcing leads to embezzlement in estimation of the project, quality measurement of the project, fake muster role preparation etc.
- Record maintenance which is the very base of success of any scheme is kept by *Rojgaar Sahayak* a person appointed purely on temporary basis through outsourcing agencies. Moreover provision of *Mate* is useless when *Rojgaar Sahayak* is there to supervise the work.
- There exists no norms regarding *pucca* work as most of the *pucca* work is done at the fag end of February. Moreover *pucca* work is permitted only after the completion of *kutcha* work of Rs. 5 lakh and it also came to light that the nature of work undertaken is not good as many of the work needed at local level requires use of machinery and contractors which is prohibited under NREGA.
- Practically only 10 per cent of the works are inspected on the other hand there should be 100 per cent inspection.
- Medical facilities as per the provision of the Act are provided in the beginning but later on there is no follow up. Similarly crèche centres provision is there but biscuits, milk etc. are not provided.
- Attendance of water carrier etc. are not taken into consideration as there exists no provision under the Act.
- As there exists piece rate wages so an old person has

to work from 7AM to 7PM for completion of one unit of work *e.g.* 100 cft in case of Haryana for Rs. 99.21.

- The concept of family is creating disturbance as some cases came to light of disputes in the family set-up as most of the husbands demanding money for work done by wives.
- It came to light that as per Act[10] under the heading unskilled manual work there does not exist any provision for physically handicap.
- Disbursement of daily wages shall be made on weekly basis or in any case not later than a fortnight[11] clearly negates the social justice where a worker should get his wages before his sweat wipes off.
- Minimum unemployment allowance[12] for 100 days will be Rs. 2,550 as against the minimum wages of 100 days of Rs. 6,000 which clearly shows the double character of NREGA.
- In the Central and State Councils there is a provision for non-official members from organisation of workers but irony is that the unskilled labour force at village level is highly unorganized.
- Functions of the Panchayats at district level and intermediate level are defined but not of Panchayats at village level [13].
- Penalty of upto Rs. 1,000 for non-compliance[14] is negligible from the deterrent point of view.
- Protection of action taken in good faith[15] has wider and ambiguous connotations.
- Power to remove difficulties[16] by order published in the official Gazette only upto the period of three years is against proper nurturing of this child *i.e.* NREGA.
- As per item 14 of Schedule I the word '*quality*' is used for completion of the work and that too from an unskilled labour force.
- As per item number 31 of Schedule II wages may be

paid in cash as well as in kind which seems to mock at its objective to provide self-dependency as wages paid compulsorily in kind may not be useful to the person concerned.

Opportunities

So far as the opportunities are concerned, some of the opportunities may be discussed as under :

- The Act offers an opportunity to empower weaker section of our society. Scheduled Castes and Scheduled Tribes and beneficiaries of land reforms can benefit through irrigation works on their fields.
- Women have been given priority in the allotment of employment opportunities.
- The economic security offered by the Act can be leveraged for social equity as well.
- It has the capabilities for making effective use of so far unutilized physical resources of the villages.
- A careful selection and execution of works has the potential to transform the rural economy of the State and to change the very geography of poverty.
- Income of the Panchayats can be increased up to 20 per cent to 40 per cent which may lead to internal resources mobilization and coupled with project-shelf and work-force at its disposal, the main stumbling block to the growth of Panchayati Raj Institutions of there F's *i.e.* Funds, Functions and Functionaries may be solved to a considerable extent.

Threats

Considering the threats aspect of SWOT analysis we can say that :

- How a family will decide who should get the job

under this scheme. This may disintegrate the families and brotherhood will be at stake.

- It is feared that under this scheme, the physically weaker could be left out.
- Keeping in view the precedents of politician — bureaucracy dismal relationship it is feared that tension may exist in their relationship in the implementation of this scheme.
- The question is also being asked as to how poor States will afford to shell out 10 per cent for this purpose. Moreover, unemployment allowance is also given by the State exchequer.
- The scheme has also to be implemented very cautiously, otherwise it will be eclipsed by corruption particularly in the form of demanding bribe for giving job and in the form of preparing fake muster rolls.
- Registration of bogus families/individuals and asking for money for registering names may be there leading to corruption. Further issuance of false Job Cards, issuance of Job Cards to ineligible persons *e.g.* to non-resident and to minors and delay in receiving Job Cards may aggravate the problem.
- Selection of work may serve a vested interest due to selection of low priority or inappropriate work as the Gram Sabhas are not actively participating.
- Neglection of urban unemployed at the horizontal level and skilled worker at the vertical level may cause a great threat to this noble cause oriented scheme.
- Increasing trend of Special Economic Zones (SEZ) and LPG *i.e.* Liberalization, Privatization and Globalization if not treated properly may cause a great hurdle in attaining its goal.
- Inflation and instability in the economy of the nation are also causing threat to this Act. There are people

who believe that the huge cost of the project might not be affordable for country like India. They feel that this might lead to a sharp increase in interest rates and will have divastating effect for the country's fiscal deficit.

Some Suggestions Leading to Highway of Success

If we want to fulfil the desire of our Prime Minister who has described NREGS as 'a landmark in our history in removing poverty from the face of the nation', then some suggestive aspects should be kept in mind :

- For the emergence of Gram Sabha as a body to whom the Gram Panchayat is accountable there is need to define the powers and functions of Gram Sabha in great detail, specifying its role as planner, decision-maker and auditor for the success of the scheme.
- Print and electronic media may consider necessary to release full report on a quarterly basis giving scope for constructive criticism for the smooth functioning of NREGs.
- Last year's implementation in 200 districts would provide feedback and experiences which may be written as case studies by subject experts to improve future policy and strategy.
- All the 29 items of XI Schedule in respect of 3F's *i.e.* Funds, Functions and Functionaries should be devolved to PRIs for coordinated development of rural areas as a whole in tune with NREGS.
- It is worthwhile to understand the present status of their functioning and initiating the most desired and essential components *viz,* participation, empowerment and capacity building of Gram Sabhas and Gram Panchayats through need-based training and evolving human resources development policy.
- For this purpose it would be necessary to assign the

role to National Institute of Rural Development and State Institutes of Rural Development to design training syllabus focussing sharply on all aspects of planning, implementing, managing financial resources, accounting, audit, monitoring-cum-concurrent evaluation, capacity building etc. for all the key implmenting agencies.

- Under the NREGA the capacity building should result into effective participation of all rural households, more importantly women and other marginalized groups in GS meetings and discussion leading to decision-making process.
- Elimination of caste, class and gender divide in the constitution of GP.
- Evolution of result oriented plan of activities, strategic execution and monitoring system in line with the objectives of the NREGs.
- Efficient mobilization of local resources for the development of village economy and better understanding of local self-governance and democratic values while taking decision.
- Effective coordination and communication between GP and GS to resolve problems and avoid misunderstanding/communication gap.
- Better networking and coordination between voluntary organizations and the GS/GP to share experiences for mutual benefits.
- Effective delivery of development programme leading to achieving the expected objectives/results.
- Adequate transparency in respect of scheme implementation including selection of targeted beneficiary, use of funds/resources and accountability of planners and implementers to GS.
- Information technology in the form of e-governance intervention is necessary to create data base as well as ensuring transparency.
- Monitoring-cum-concurrent evaluation of the

scheme on a regular and continuing basis should be entrusted to independent professional institutions and deficiencies noticed must be corrected on time by adopting appropriate policies.

- Review and monitoring of the implementation progress may need to be done on a monthly basis at PRI level. It should also be done quarterly at the State level and half yearly at the national level by a High Power Committee chaired by the Cabinet Minister for Rural Development concerned.
- Carefully planning the process of the implementation of the scheme may go a long way towards earning a bread for the empty bellies.
- Political will is required for the successful planning and implementation of NREGA. It should be honoured by every political party, irrespective of its status-ruling or opposition.
- Last but not the least, in spite of traditional methods of performance appraisal there should be 360° feedback for making this scheme in real sense a scheme of the people, by the people and for the people.

NOTES

1. Patil, Amrit, "Role of PRIs in implementing Rural Employment Guarantee Scheme", *Kurukshetra*: A Journal of Rural Development, New Delhi, August 2006, Vol. 54, No. 10, pp. 24-25.
2. Singh, J. N. and Mishra, Anurag, "Backward Linkages of Rural Employment Guarantee Scheme", *Kurukshetra*: A Journal of Rural Development, New Delhi, August 2006, Vol. 54, No. 10, p . 30.
3. Puri, Manohar, "The NREGA: Rural People to Grow With the Nation", *Kurukshetra*: A Journal of Rural Development, New Delhi, April 2006, Vol. 54, No. 6, pp.17-18.
4. *Ibid*, p. 18.
5. Bhagwan, Vishnu, "National Rural Employment Guarantee

Scheme: Transforming the Geography of Poverty", *Partiyogita Darpan*, Agra, May 2007 issue, pp. 1911-1913.
6. Section 4(2), National Rural Employment Guarantee Act, 2005.
7. Section 14(6), National Rural Employment Guarantee Act, 2005.
8. Section 4(3), National Rural Employment Guarantee Act, 2005.
9. Puri, Manohar, "The NREGA: Rural People to Grow With the Nation", *Kurukshetra*: A Journal of Rural Development, New Delhi, April 2006, Vol. 54, No. 6, p. 19.
10. Section 2(12), National Rural Employment Guarantee Act, 2005.
11. Section 3(3), National Rural Employment Guarantee Act, 2005.
12. Section 7(2), National Rural Employment Guarantee Act, 2005.
13. Section 13, National Rural Employment Guarantee Act, 2005.
14. Section 25, National Rural Employment Guarantee Act, 2005.
15. Section 30, National Rural Employment Guarantee Act, 2005.
16. Section 34(1), National Rural Employment Guarantee Act, 2005.

SECTION - V

POLITICS, DEVELOPMENT AND REGIONALISM

[illegible]

[illegible]

Politics

[illegible]

28. Role of the [illegible] Panchayat in Assam [illegible] Politics and the Future of [illegible]

[illegible]

29. [illegible] Water Dispute : A Historical Background

[illegible]

26 Manufacturing of Spaces
The 'Others' in Zo/Mizo Politics

Anup Shekhar Chakraborty

The 'North-East' of India in general and Mizoram[1] in particular provides a unique experience in understanding the trends in everyday politics 'as a living space' (Lefebvre, 1991) in contemporary India. The very term 'Mizo'[2], evokes in the minds of the mainland Indians an 'alien culture', backward tribals, 'Open sex societies', underdeveloped area inhabited by *'junglees'*, tribes with weird food habits infamously known as the 'dog-eaters' and so on (Hluna, 1985a). Beyond these stereotypical images mainland India is hardly aware of the reverberations of the underlying 'Politics of Silencings'[3] in the *Zo tlang ram*[4]. This chapter attempts to historically locate the 'Vai'[5], the 'Poi'[6] and the 'Gorkhas'[7] who constitute the *nebulous* category of the 'Others'; and also reflect on the experiences of the 'Politics of Silencings' on the *'Triad of the Marginals'* as propelled by the hegemony of the *'Nexus of Patriarchy'* in Zo/Mizo society. The *'Triad of the Marginals'* is a term I use for convenience to denote the similar experiences of women and the *'Others'* of victimhood, subjugation and the domination of the hegemony of the majority community (ies) which is very male *i.e.* Patriarchal in nature and experience, which I term as the *'Nexus of Patriarchy'*. The Zo tribes and their sub-clans form the majority and dominate all the socio-politico-eco-cultural arenas of the society. The Church and the State are the instruments through which the majority dictates their terms to the minorities including the women and 'Vais'. I call the coalition of the majority, the Church and the State 'the *Nexus of Patriarchy*' because it represents the functioning of the patriarchy which tries to dominate the others. The *Nexus of Patriarchy* dominates and marginalizes women and by the same token marginalizes the "others" — men and women inclusive.

The state-building process in the Mizoram requires the systematic mapping of the discourses and narratives of inclusion and exclusion at all levels. Interestingly the whole process as such is thoroughly dictated[8] by those in power in short the *Nexus of Patriarchy*. North-East India with its complex pre-colonial, colonial and post-colonial history(ies) reminds one, of the layered challenges and contestations (Udayon, 1988; Monirul Hussain in Samaddar, 2004, 292; Bhaumik in Banerjee, *et al.*, 2005, 144-174) involved in attempting to fit the region's 'Histories' of statecraft and policies into the distinct narrative of mainland India (Barooah and Scott, 1970; Guha, 1977, 1991; Dubey, 1978; Sanjib Baruah, 2005). To the mainland Indians, the name Mizoram 'rings the faint bell' of 'the protracted insurgency in the Christian dominated area led by the legendary Laldenga of the Mizo National Front'; and the success of India's democratic mechanisms as reflected through the dual processes of (1) the signing of the Peace Accord (1986) (Jyotirindra in Basu and Kohli, 1998, 183-214) and (2) the implementation of 'Cosmetic Federalism' (Sanjib Baruah, 2005). To the other less informed majority it remains a geo-political puzzle, mapping its geographic location and its habitants becomes a quest in itself [9].

I
LOCATING THE 'OTHERS' HISTORICALLY IN THE ZO/MIZO SOCIETY

The notion of *'Others'* just like that of *foreigners* as perceived by the Zos is apparently confusing and very broad. The category of the 'Others' can be broadly sub-divided into '*permanent pariah*' and '*temporal pariah*' and thus in general includes the '*Vais*', the '*Pois*' (Burmese, '*Burma Mi*') and at times incorporates the '*Gorkhas*' who have attained the status of 'Denizens'. The category also includes at times the internal tribes or ethnic communities/minorities who maintain cultural, linguistic distinctiveness or exclusiveness whether or not they believe in 'the mythical origin of the Zo tribes' *i.e.* Chhinlung Theory. Thus the Mara (Lakher), the Lai (Pawi), the Hmar, the Chakma, the Reang etc. also form the *nebulous* category of the 'Others' in Mizoram.

The 'Others' in the Zo Oral History

The Zo oral traditions or the *Kuki-Chin-Mizo Folklores* reflects to an extent the stereotypes and prejudices acting against the triad of the Marginals. Several *Kuki-Chin-Mizo Folktales* speak of the initial contacts with the 'Vais' (the Plainsmen) for instance the story of *Lalruanga and Keichalal* (Thanga, 1978) mentions that on the way to *Zangkaki's* village on a hot summer day, *Lalruanga* swam across the Tuiruang (Barak) river and accidentally dropped his box containing the secrets of magic which he had got from *Keichalal*. *Lalruanga* sent a rat known for its speed on a leaf to fetch the box but unfortunately both the box and the rat rifted downstream to the plains to be captured by the 'Vais'. The plainsmen learnt the art of magic from the box and that of building boats and rowing from the rat. The Zos believe that it is because of this incident that the 'Vais' are better at magic and building boats and rowing. Similarly the story of *Tualvungi and Zawlpala* and also that of *Remenhawii* (The beautiful lady who lived upstream with her husband and the lustful King from the Plains) (Thanga, 1978) speaks of the contacts of the *Zos* with that of the 'Vais'.

The *Kuki-Chin-Mizo Folklores* reflect the diverse range of marginalisation of the 'triad of the Marginals' in the Zo oral traditions. The stereotyped depiction of women as greedy, materialistic, vain and immoral (sexual) and the projection of

Vai's as cunning, shrewd, lustful, always looking for sexual favours from Zo women and the Poi's (Burmese) as greedy, rich and foolish in most of the folktales and sayings reflect the underlying patriarchal biases acting against the triad.

Locating the 'Others' through the lenses of Written History

The 'Others' in the Pre-Colonial Zo/Mizo World

The early contacts of the Kuki-Chin-Lushai tribes with the neighbouring tribes of the region have been traced to the *Rajamala or the Chronicles of Tripura* (Sangkima, 2004, 11). Suniti Kumar Chatterji in his '*Kirata-Jana-Krti*' refers to them as the *Kiratas* who were employed by the Hindu kings of Tripura and Cachar to suppress their enemies time and again. The history of the initial contacts of the 'Kuki-Chin-Lushai tribes' with the rest of the tribes in the North-East is still a contestable terrain and multilayered. It is safest to have a panoramic vision of the whole historical process as a multilayered process of migrations of tribes and non-tribes; and inter-tribal warfare for having a command over the same 'game-territory'.

The history of the early contacts between Cachar and the Zo/Mizo tribes by focussing on five prime issues: First, on the issue of head-hunting expedition[10] of the tribes into the plains, on the occasion of their Chief's death. Second, the 'Kheda' (elephant chasing) organized by the Military Department of Cachar which sometimes encroached upon the territories of the Zo Chiefs and created misunderstanding on the boundary issue. Third, the ever expanding frontiers of the British Tea Plantations which was an encroachment: on the game territory of the Zo/Mizo tribes of the region. Fourth, the large scale migration of the tribes into the plains after the death of Suakpuilala in 1818 and the atrocities inflicted on his people by his son Lalkhama. Fifth, the great famine of 1881 that forced the Zo Chiefs to seek help from the authorities in Silchar, Cachar (Sangkima, 2004, 175-83).

The pre-colonial 'Vai'-'Mizo/Zo' contacts can also be analysed through the accounts of the trade relations of the Zo/Mizos with that of the 'Vais'. Modern system of economics was not known to the Zo/Mizo tribes and they relied on barter trade at the 'Bepari Bazaar' in Sylhet border and Kasalang in the Chittagong border [Lewin, (1912)1977; Mac Kenzie, (1979) 2005; Lalrimawia, 1995)]. They welcomed the traders as friends as they used to get their supplies of sulphur, gun and flint glass from them. Enterprising tradesmen, familiar with the topography of the Hills and language, rendered valuable services in bringing the British into closer ties with the Lushais[11] . However, the pre-British contacts of the 'Vai' and the Zo/Mizo tribes were *temporary* and of short durations as evident from the seasonal visit to the tribes to the trade marts in the plains and the movement of the tradesmen to the interiors of the Hills.

The 'Others' in the Colonial 'Zo' World

The annexation of the Zo territory by *the British* along with the introduction of Christianity[12] and a *written history:* more powerful than the Oral Tradition led to the birth of a new Psychology. The two *external symbols of power,* namely the British Superintendent and Christian Missionaries ruled like independent sovereigns and were considered to be *superior*[13] by the primitive tribes because of numerous reasons (Goswami, 1979, 104-109). The superiority of the British was felt most evidently because the British were able to defeat and subdue the most powerful and revered Zo Chiefs at the physical level; and partly also because the Whiteman's way of life and religion *delivered them from fear of evil, death and uncertainty* of a war prone migratory life at the psychological level. As evident from the names given by the Zo tribes to these colonial symbols for instance *'Lal man tu'* (one who catches the chiefs) implying to the Superintendent; and *'Thlarau man tu'* (one who catches the spirit) implying to the Missionaries. Christianity thus began to play an overwhelming role in Mizoram because of these *internal* and *external factors* (Downs, 1983, 47-48). The colonial era also witnessed the *twin process* of the systematic replacement of the 'Traditional Elites'[14] by the 'New Elites'[15] *i.e.* the 'Black Coats' at *the religious arena* and the retention of the Traditional Elites at the *political-administrative arena* (Lalrimawia, 1982; Thomas, 1993; Ray, 1993; Nag, 1998, 25-29). The British skilfully manipulated both these elites to maintain its *indirect* hold over the Zo territory (Acharyya, 1984; Lalchungnunga, 1994, 35-36; Nag, 1998, 67-72).

The coming of the British marked an interesting phenomenon in the form of the *permanent entry* of the 'Vais' and the 'Arakanese', 'Hakka' tribes of Burma conveniently clubbed as 'Poi' or 'Burma Mi' (Burmese); and also of the Gorkhas into the Zo territory. Lalrimawia in his *'Mizoram History and Cultural Identity'* cites W.W Hunter's *'Statistical Account of Assam 1879'*, mentioning Captain Lewin's efforts of encouraging the 'Vai' traders to set up permanent marts in different places in Chittagong Hill Tracts. These traders would pay rent in kind, which would be a permanent source of income for the Chiefs; and as a token of goodwill gesture, the Chiefs, on their turn would guarantee the traders security of life and property. The coming of the 'Vais' *via* the British rule marked another hallmark in the Zo/Mizo society: the change in the nature and mode of Zo economy from a barter system to a permanent economy. However, the entry of the 'Vais' was limited by the restrictions imposed on the entry of the outsiders inside the Lushai Hills by the Chin Hills Regulations of 1896 and the Inner Line Permit (Acharyya, 1984; Sangkima, 2004, 180).

The direct result of the entry of permanent economy in the form of 'Vai' settlement was that the Lushais became totally dependent on external resources for the daily commodities and this phenomenon continues even to this day. The 'self-sufficient primitive economy' gave way to 'modern economy', and introduced along with it the phenomenon of Commodity and Cultural Fetishism. The 'Vais' as a result were stereotyped as *'Sum dawng'* (traders/ businessmen), economic animals; guided by profit mentality and *'Ui Kawm'* (misers). The permanent entry of the 'Vai' was very soon equated by the mushrooming of local business (shops) run by Zo/Mizo women. Trade centered around the flow of goods like cotton, woollen yarns, brass, enamel, aluminium utensils, iron, *pan* (Betel leaves), tobacco, matches, soaps, chillies, ginger, oranges, forest products and other fancy goods etc. (Lalrimawia, 1995; Rosanga, 1996; Sangkima, 2004, 178-79). The gradual yet sure, entry of the 'Vais' into the Zo/Mizo economy: provided for a greater degree of interaction between the 'Vais' and Zo/Mizo women. The change in the mode of economy in the Zo society can also be interpreted as an easy means to emulating the 'life-styles' of the white masters. The Neo-elites, who were salaried category and the emerging middle class found it convenient for a leap towards modern life. The arena of economics in the public sphere, in the case of Zo/Mizo society thus became the realm for the activities of Women and 'Others', *i.e.* for all those who were excluded from the realms of *spirituality* and *politics*.

The third arena namely, *Economics* was automatically ascribed a secondary existence and women being excluded from the realms of spirituality and politics (Mahajan, 2000, 1899) became *fit* along side the marginal groups like the 'Vai' and the Poi' (Burmese) to occupy the realms of economics[16] and form the 'Triad of the Marginals'. The Zo/Mizo patriarchy under the impact of Christian traditions began to view economics and the notions of business and profit to be both sensuous and materialistic and linked them with the notions of *original sin* and *sexuality*. The *'Nexus of Patriarchy'* associated the *'Triad of the Marginals'* with moral degradation, sin, immorality and everything signified by the word *'Khawvel'* (worldly). Controlling the sexuality and mapping the spatial domain[17] of the *'Triad of the Marginals'* thus became the holy goal of the Zo Christian society. In other words notions of spirituality, divinity and *God* are used as weapons to oppress (Daly, 1973, 19-20) the members of the '*Triad of the Marginals*'. Religion and Politics thus began to be considered superior, powerful and, therefore, more alluring; this led to the 'male-fying[18]' of religion and politics and the creation of the *'Nexus of Patriarchy'*.

The history of the Gorkhas in Mizoram followed a distinct and unique narrative than that of the other migrants namely the 'Vais' and the 'Pois'. The Gorkhas migrated to Mizoram with the sequel British Expeditions into the Zo/ Mizo territory in the late Nineteenth Century (Sen, 1977; Sunar, *et al.*, 2000.; Bareh, 2001) for administrative functions and expanding the British frontiers with the sole motive of *proselytization* so as to tame the wild tribes of the frontier regions to serve the commercial interests of the *British Tea Plantations in the North- East of India* (Zairema, 1978, 1; Allen, 1979, 2001; Chatterjee, 1990, 144). The history of the permanent settlement of the Gorkhas in Mizoram began in the year 1891 though they had been active in the region throughout the initial encounters between the British and the 'Kuki-Chin-Lushai tribes'. The boundary tussle between the frontiers of the Raj and the Tribal game land led to a series of punitive expeditions of the British. The first of such expeditions was headed by Lister in 1849 followed by Nuthall's in 1869; the two Column Expeditions of 1871-1872 to the Chin-Lushai Expedition of 1889-1890 and the Expedition against Kairuma in 1895-96[19].

'The British Government had at last come to the final decision that here as elsewhere the only effective method of protecting the frontier was the establishment of fortified posts in the hills' (Prasad, 1987). Col. Skinner selected Aizawl for the construction of a permanent post in the North Lushai Hills. Once the construction of the post was completed the column retreated back to Silchar leaving behind a garrison of 200 riflemen mostly Gorkhas of the Surma Valley Military

Police Battalion (SVMP). This garrison was later renamed the First Assam Rifles and set its base in the North Lushai Hills. Likewise in the South Lushai Hills the 400 Gorkha soldiers of the 2/2 G.R attached to the 9th Bengal Infantry led by Brig. F.V.G. Treagears set their base in Lungleh *via* Demagiri (Tlabung). With these expeditions began the official migration of the Gorkhas into the Zo Hills (Sunar, *et al.*, 2000).

The British employed the 'Gallawalahs' (middlemen) to convince the Gorkhas to migrate to the Zo Hills and assured them 'security and prosperity'. For instance the attractive pay, *'Doodh le mooh dhunu'*(mouthwash with milk), *'Patha ko sikar rah pakwah'*(lots of mutton), and ample opportunity for *'Ladai khelnu'* (to play battle for in the Gorkha tradition a battle is to be played and not fought) etc. T. H. Lewin summed up the reasons for the migrations of the Gorkhas into the Zo Hills as follows: 'I had formed a high opinion of the little Gorkha, who under Col. Macpherson, had done the fighting of the expedition, and I obtained permission to send to Nepal and get immigrants from there to colonize my frontier wastes' [(1912)1977)].

Lewin also mentions that 'the country where the villages were located had previously been uninhabited, through fear of maraunding Lushais, and my idea had been to establish there good stockaded villages of courageous, stiff-necked people like the Gorkhas, who should serve as the buffer between the Mong Raja's territory and the independent Lushais to the east' [Lewin, (1912)1977)]. 'To establish a number of villages along the frontier between the plains and the hills so that a well defined boundary between them and the British territory could be established' (Prasad, 1987). After the construction of stockades at Lunglei and Aizawl, peace was restored in most of the parts of the hills especially near and around the stockades by the spring of 1891. The expansion work at Aizawl and Lunglei as well as the administrative machinery required the increase in the inflow of immigrants *i.e.* the trusted 'Gorkhas' (Chambers). The migrant population thus were encouraged to settle in the buffer zones [Lewin, (1912)1977; Ray, 1982, 10, 12)] to serve two prime functions first, that of providing security to the Sahebs ('Saps') and second, to demarcate the worlds of the 'Colonised Masters' and 'the Natives'.

II
IDEAL ZO CHRISTIAN STATE-BUILDING, CITIZEN-BUILDING PROGRAMME AND ITS REVERBERATIONS ON THE 'OTHERS'

The post-colonial state-building process in Mizoram like the rest of the North-East India in general has tilted heavily on the notions of self-governance and autonomy. In keeping with this spirit the whole process of 'Zo state-building' has been aimed at freeing or liberating *physically as well as mentally*, the Mizo/Zo Christian people and their territory from the *dual* prejudice and hegemony functioning synchronously at two levels – the Administrative and Religious level. At the Administrative level the dual prejudice and hege-mony referred to the attempts at 'Indianisation' by India (meaning the Centre, New Delhi) and 'Ahomisation'[20] by Assam[21] and at the Religious level it referred to the predominant Hindu religion and the wave of Sanskritisation. Thus the desire to create an *Ideal Zo Christian State*[22] has been strongly portrayed and at times has led to the voyeuristic intervention of the church and its agencies in both the *private* and *public arena*.

The Post-Colonial 'Zo world' has witnessed the dual operation of *Proselytization* and *Colonialism* and the introduction of marked *structural* and *functional changes* in the Zo/Mizo society (Downs, 1983, 14-15; Thomas, 1993). The loss of indigenous Zo way of life and the fear of being usurped by *alien cultures* compelled the Mizos/Zos to live under the spectre of the *Pan Optics*[23] through the watchful eyes of the State, the Church and its agencies. The youth and students' organizations like the Young Mizo Association (YMA), the Khristian Thalai Pawl (KTP) and also the Mizo Zirlai Pawl (MZP) have been functioning as instruments of '*systemic* or *structural control*'. These agencies in the attempt to build the ideal Zo Christian state project a spectrum of varying attitudes ranging from prohibiting liquor and drugs, controlling sexual behaviour and checking prostitution, controlling HIV/AIDS to checking *foreigners*[24] and calling 'Vai Bandhs'[25] etc. The 'Vai Bandhs' refers to the frequent *bandhs* called either by the MZP, or any other agencies acting on behalf of the Church and the State *i.e. the nexus of patriarchy*. These bandhs or curfews are unique for they are meant for or targeted at specific groups within the *triad* namely the Vais. During these Bandhs the 'Vais' are supposed to stay in-doors and restraint from venturing out-doors which can stretch from 12 hours to 48 hours or more. Sometimes these 'Vai Bandhs' are preceded by 'quit Mizoram notices' to the non-tribals, for instance in 2004 the YMA served notices to the non-Mizos to quit Mizoram within a month. (Thangliana, *The Telegraph*, 2004, http://www.northeastvigil.in/archives/? p=6919; also see J.B Lama, *The Statesman*, 30 July, 2007, 'The inside and out of Mizoram's ethnic skirmishes').The enforcement of these attitudes contributes to the further marginalisation of the already marginalized sections of the Mizo society and snip their chance to play an *active role in politics*. Thus the spectre of Pan Optics haunts the Mizo society forcing the people to live in constant delirium.

A minute analysis of the attitudes projected for state-building reflects not just the loopholes in the policies of the '*Nexus of Patriarchy*' but also the continued victimization of the '*Triad of Marginals*'. For instance, a meticulous survey of several enactments ever since the imposition of 'Total Liquor Prohibition' under the strategy of prohibiting liquor and drugs (Vanlalhluna, 1996); and the State Excise Department Records (1997-2005) shows a constant rise in illegal liquor trade and drug trafficking in the region (Statistical Handbook(s), 1994, 1998, 2002; 2006, <India News Webindia 123com.htm>; Press Trust of India/*The Assam Tribune* 2000, http://www.northeastvigil.in/archives/? p=7475: 7643: 7948). An interesting observation in almost all these cases of illegal liquor and drug trafficking is that, women and the counterparts of the *triad* are picketed and victimized as *'Zu Zuars'* (liquor sellers, vendors), drug peddlers; even though State records and surveys reveal the active participation of Zo/Mizo men in such dealings.

The organizations like the Young Mizo Association (YMA), the Khristian Thalai Pawl (KTP) and also the Mizo Zirlai Pawl (MZP) have been functioning as the self proclaimed 'moral guardians' of the Zo society. The superficial imposition of archaic rules based on Christian ethics and against the 'will' on the people *for fighting social evils* results in the blatant violation of Human Rights. The enforcement agencies selectively target women, the Burmese and the Vai's and project them as *'the nexus of evil'*, conspiring to destabilize the *Ideal Zo Christian State*. These strategies of selective targeting, 'scapegoat mechanisms' that are employed to camouflage the loopholes and failures of the various attitudes projected for building the *Ideal Zo Christian State* serve as evidences of the *'reduction of human freedom'* (Popper, 1966) in the Zo/Mizo society. The hurdles posed to the building of the *Ideal Zo Christian State* often echoes frustrations and directly manifests itself in *the quest of finding the enemy* and perverse need of creating *'the Other'* as an object of condemnation so that those who condemn can judge themselves to be 'Good' (Szasz, 1970). The *varying attitudes* projected at state-building harps thoroughly on *morality, moral codes* (Foucault, 1987, 28) and *spirituality* (Singhal and Rogers, 2003, 223-224, 228). In all these readings of persecution, marginalisation and victimization of women and the *'Others'*, the hegemonic tendencies of the nexus of the church-the state-patriarchy cannot be ignored. The line between the public and the private domain becomes fused, and the nexus of the patriarchy becomes overwhelmingly hegemonic. The Mizo situation reflects the *dynamic strategies employed* in different societies for the construction, justification and continuance of the patriarchal hegemony, and the strategies adopted by the marginals to create their *own spaces*. The Mizo society today is in a dilemma whether to opt *for the glitters of the contemporary globalized liberal societies* or to tread the path of the Holy Gospel and strive for the *life beyond*[26] or strike a balance between the two. The question of ethical projection and construction of the *'Self"* to *'Other' vis-à-vis* these moral codes has led to *ethical subjectivation* (Foucault, 1987) and the continuation of the *Politics of Silencings* and the hauntings of the spectre of the *Politics of Panoptics* on the Marginals in Mizoram.

III
THE MANUFACTURING OF SPACES OF THE 'OTHERS' IN THE ZO/MIZO SOCIETY

The 'Vais', the 'Pois' (Burmese) and the 'Gorkhas' constitute the nebulous category of the 'Others', in Mizoram and have channelised their own strategies to overcome the hegemony of the *'Nexus of Patriarchy'*. The Vais and Pois through the *politics of camouflaging* ; which include a wide spectrum of strategies ranging from adopting Zo names, to converting to Christianity, to marrying local tribal women etc. bargain their existence in the Zo world. The politics of camouflaging is adopted for a plethora of reasons from that of personal security to that of private business or for being accepted as a *'Denizen'*. The ability to assume the position of Denizens thereby sets *oneself free* from being constantly ostracised as the *'Permanent Pariah'* as is the case of the Vais, the Chakmas, the Reangs or the *'Temporal Pariah'* as is the case of the 'Poi' (Burmese) and the other Zo tribes from beyond the borders of present day Mizoram. The 'Poi' also referred to as 'Burma

Mi' have at times successfully crossed the threshold of the ostracisation through the *politics of camouflaging*; and attained the status of *'Temporal Pariah'* best signified by cynical term 'Zo/Mizo Two (2)' used to refer to their partial acceptance into the Zo/Mizo society.

The 'Denizens', in Mizoram are: the 'Gorkhas' or the Nepalese community who migrated during the Colonial Raj (Sen, 1977) to present day Mizoram [(Lewin, (1912) 1977; Ray, 1982, 10, 12)]. The Gorkhas have to an extent assimilated themselves to the local customs, practices and food habits (Singh, *et al.*, 1995; Bareh, 2001) and naturally have succeeded at crossing the threshold of the stigmas of the boundaries faced by the 'Vai' or the 'Poi' (Burmese). The Gorkhas have more or less successfully assumed the status of Denizens in Mizoram as reflected through the everyday use of language by the Zos to refer to them (Gorkhas) such as *'Mizo ang chiah'* (Just like the Mizos), *'Zo rilru an pu'* (They think and feel like the Mizos). The Gorkhas have attained the status of 'Denizens' in Mizoram in the sense that even though they are a migrant population they have successfully camouflaged their identity with the majority Zo/Mizo identity. The Gorkha organisations for instance the 'Mizoram Gorkha Youth Association' (MGYA) formed on the lines of the YMA aim at cultural assimilation with the majority Zo/Mizo culture while maintaining its distinct Gorkha flavour. The acceptance of the Gorkhas as being Denizens of the 'Zo World' has to be understood in the context of Colonial legacy as well as the race factor (white skin, good features etc.) coupled with their conversion to Christianity and acumen of the local Duhlian dialect. The Gorkhas for the Zo/Mizo tribes in Mizoram symbolize the memories of the Colonial past and the rule of the 'Sap' (Whiteman) (Goswami in Dubey, 1978, 104).

Conclusion

The State of Mizoram has witnessed vast *constitutional,*

political and *administrative changes during the years*[27]. The State has grown form a hills district to a Union Territory to full Statehood, from a three-districts State to an eight-districts State. The Peace Accord apparently seems to have ended in success but the fact remains that ethnic identities are further mushrooming and minorities including women in Mizoram *today,* are raising their voices against the domination of *the majority* i.e. the Zos/Mizos and the Church and the State. These dissenting voices reflect themselves through the *various strategies* ranging from that of *whisperings* at the private spaces; to camouflagings and that of violent anti-Mizo/Zo movements spearheaded at the public spaces as a response to the State-led *Politics of Silencings* operating against the *marginals.* Mizoram serves as the contesting terrain of multi-ethnic communities/identities like the Hmar, Pawi, Mara, Reang, Chakma, Gorkhas, the 'Vai' etc. who form the nebulous category of 'Others' depending upon the dictates of the *'Nexus of Patriarchy'*. The rise of the Hmars through the Hmar People's Convention (HPC) movement[28]; the cultural consciousness of the Mara (Lakher) and Lai (Pawi); the armed mobilization of the Reang; silent but uncompromising attitude of the Chakma and the claim of a certain section of the population as belonging to the *'Lost Tribes of Israel'* and propagating the cause of migration to Israel under Israel's Law of Return (Zaithanchhungi, 1990) etc. all seems to reflect in varying degrees the disillusionment with the dream of an 'Ideal Zo Christian State' and the functioning of the 'Politics of Panoptics' and *'Nexus of Patriarchy'*. The strategies adopted by the Vais, Pois, and Gorkhas reflect the survival strategies to counter the *Politics of Silencings* at various levels and the 'Manufacturing of Spaces' for the 'Others' in the post-Colonial Politics in Mizoram.

NOTES

1. Mizoram, one of the federal States of India located at the extreme northeastern fringe has experienced diverse socio-

political upheavals ranging from secession to acceptance of the constitutional mechanism of India to being 'an Island of Peace', within a span of three decades. The whole territory officially came under British rule in 1895. The area was bifurcated into *South Lushai Hills* under the Superintendent or Assistant Political Officer of Chittagong Division of Bengal Province, and the *North Lushai Hills* under the control of the Political Officer who worked for the Chief Commissioner of the Assam Government. The North Lushai Hills and the South Lushai Hills were amalgamated as one district — *'The Lushai Hills District'* in 1898, and kept under the charge of one Superintendent who in turn worked under the Chief Commissioner of Assam (Ray, 1982, 12-17, 20-24; Lalrimawia, 1983; S.N Singh, 1994, 113-114).

2. The term 'Mizo' is a generic term and it stands for several major and minor tribes in Mizoram. Etymologically Mizo means Hillman ('mi'meaning man and 'zo' meaning hill), liberal interpretation of the term is inclusive of all ethnic hill tribes living in Mizoram including the Chakmas, Gorkhas, Reangs and the 17 'Zo' tribes and their sub-clans. The 'Zo'/ Mizos were migratory tribes living in the area between the Chittagong Hill Tracts in the West, Chin Hills in the East and Cachar Hills in the North and Arakan Hills in the South. Since the Lushai Hills District (change of name) Act of 1954, a number of communities have preferred to identify themselves as Mizos. However, recently the 17 Zo tribes who form the majority have been advocating for an inclusive Zo identity exclusively meant for the 17 Zo tribes and their sub-clans. There is a general tendency among those who call themselves Mizos to impose the 'Mizo/Zo identity' on other minor tribes like the Mara, the Pawi, the Chakma and the Reangs. One of the binding factors for this Zo identity or 'Zomi' identity is the nostalgia of having originated from the mythical cave of 'Sinlung' ('Chhinlung', or 'covered stone cave') somewhere in the north. 'The term Mizo/Zo is difficult to explain and has been interpreted in many ways according to one interpretation, 'Mi' means person and 'Zo' means highland *i.e.* highlander or people living in the high hills. Another interpretation says 'Zo' may also mean cold region and, therefore, Mizo signifies people of the cold region. Lehman,

however, argues that the interpretation of Mizo as 'Cold', stems from an error of understanding on the part of the missionaries and administrators. Another view is of the opinion that the people were named after the area of their habitation called 'Zopui', West of Tiau valley. However, it is difficult to accept this argument as because various Chin groups and Lushais use the word 'Zo' for themselves and all these Chin people do not come from that village. According to another interpretation the word 'Zo' is traced back to the Burmese word "Yaukkya" meaning man, and is supposed to have been derived from the Tai Chinese word "Yoe". The word is pronounced as "Dzo". B.S Carey, then the political officer of the Chin Hills, said in his accounts of the British invasion of the Chin Hills that the Chins used to call their race by the general name "Yo" (pronounced as "Zo") meaning 'man'. However, the above interpretation does not appear to be philologically 'sound'. Lehman opines that the word 'Zo' has a basic meaning relevant to the symbolic context of the plains cultivation of the 'Vai'. 'The Chins are described as Zomi because they lack the civilization of the Burman whose culture they envy, however, still will not emulate' (Lehman). So by this account Zo means, 'uncultivated, relatively crude and unsophisticated' (Lalchungnunga, 1994; Sangkima, 2004, 15-17, 30-32). The term Mizo ignores important divides between ethnic groups such as the Chakma, Reang, Pang, Mara, Lai and Gorkha etc. These minority tribes loom large into the politics of Mizoram. I use the term Zo/Mizo to refer to all tribes living in Mizoram excluding the Chakma, Reang, Magh, Pnar, Gorkha, and the 'Vais'.

3. I use this term *'the Politics of Silencings'* to refer to wide ranges from *exclusionist* and *inclusionist* policies of politics of identity, religious persecutions; State-led victimization of women and the marginals etc. that are justified in the name of 'State-Building' in Mizoram. The *'Politics of Silencings'* is a systematic process of deleting and silencing of historical processes and social-religious-politico-economic realities. The whole idea of *'Politics of Silencings'* can be understood in the context of a deliberate silencing mechanism acting for the benefit of patriarchal hegemony, which I call *'Deliberate Amnesia'*. For details see Chakraborty, Anup Shekhar, (2007). Politics of

Silencings: Echoes of the Margins from Mizoram. *Indian Journal of Political Science*, Vol. LXII, No. 4, Oct.-Dec.

4. The 'Zo hills' or 'Zo tlang ram' has special significance in the sense that the 'imagery of the Zo region and Zo unification' goes as far as the echoes travel in the hilly terrains of the region between Chittagong Hill Tracts and the Chin Hills. The sense of a boundary and international borders hardly makes a reality to the tribes of the region for affinities of primordial identities are far stronger and deeper. The sense of a boundary makes sense only when contextualized in terms of the 'others' which is again a large and fluid category and at times overlaps with the image of foreigners. In other words the boundary makes sense only when placed in the light of insider and outsider debate. Even though the Zo territory within India has been named Mizoram, the term Zoram or 'Zo tlang ram' continues to be in use to refer to 'the land of the Zos', in other words the term 'Zo tlang ram' or Zoram has a kind of emotional nostalgic appeal and attraction.
5. The term 'Vai' is a Mizo word used to describe the people of India who have Aryan features. The term is derogatory and signals anger, scorn, and racist overtones. B.B Goswami looks at the construction of the Vai from the perspective of 'out-group' – 'in-group' psychology. For the Mizos the term Vai as an out-group has three broad meanings. In one sense all non-Mizos including the British people are Vai. In another sense, all the people living in the plains of India are Vai. In the third sense the plains people of Burma are also considered to be Vai but in contrast to the Indian, the notion is more positive and traditional. For detailed reading on the Vai and 'in-group - out-group' problem in Mizoram, see B.B Goswami, "out-group from the point of view of in-group: A Study of Mizos", in Dubey, S.M. (Ed.). *North East India: A Sociological Study*.1978. 99-110.
6. The 'Poi' or 'Pawi' are a sub-section of the tribes called 'Chins' living in Indo-Myanmar border. They live in the Southern fringes of Mizoram and refer to themselves of late as 'Lai'. The coming of the British introduced settled life especially symbolized by the boundary. These migratory tribes were forcibly compelled to live in fixed territories and as is the case of almost all tribes in the North-East, the Poi or Pawi have their

kinsmen or sub-clans speaking the same dialect on the other sides of the International border (Myanmar). For further clarifications see Sangkima. *Essays on the History of the Mizos, chapter-26 'The Coming and Settlement of Myanmarese in Mizoram Since the beginning of the Twentieth Century A.D to the Present'.* 2004. 283-294. I use the term 'Poi' to specifically refer to the section of this particular tribe living in present day Myanmar (Burma) and 'Pawi' or 'Lai' interchangeably to refer to the section living in present day Mizoram.

7. The term 'Gorkha' or 'Gorkhali' in the Zo/Mizo case is used to denote all ethnic tribes who migrated from Nepal to present day Mizoram during the British times and who speak the 'Khas Kura' the *lingua franca* of Nepal. 'Gorkha' thus is a blanket term to refer to all migrant 'Nepali' population in Mizoram.
8. I agree with Michel Foucault's notion of a spatialized history which reflects the arena for power contestation, 'A whole history remains to be written of spaces', which would at the same time be the history of powers' (Rabinow, 1987; Soja,1989, 21) *which in the case of the North-East determines the criteria for inclusion and exclusion*. Emphasis added: A.S.C
9. Lalhmingthanga former Finance Minister of Union Territory of Mizoram has mentioned similar experiences in his Foreword to Dr. A.C Ray's *Mizoram Dynamics of Change*. Calcutta: Pearl Publishers, 1982.
10. The first recorded raid on Cachar took place in 1849 and was committed by Lallianvunga, Vanpuilala and Lalngura; they attacked a Thado-Kuki village named Palsang 10 miles south of Silchar. They killed 29 people and took 42 men as captives [McKenzie, (1979) 2005, 291; Sangkima, 2004, 176)].
11. Suhas Chottopadhyay's unpublished Ph.D. Thesis titled 'The Lushais and the English (1844-1904)', Gauhati University cited in Lalrimawia. *Mizoram History and Cultural Identity (1890-1947)*, 1995.
12. The sole motive of the Christian Missionaries and the British Raj was *proselytization* so as to tame the wild tribes of the frontier regions and annex their land so as to serve the commercial interests of the *British Tea Plantations in the North-East of India* [Zairema, 1978, 1; Allen, (1979), 2001; Chatterjee, 1990, 144)].

13. The Zo tribes used the word 'Sap' a corrupted form of the Hindustani word 'Sahib' to refer to the Europeans *i.e.* white men. B.B Goswami observed during his field work and interaction with the local people in Mizoram that 'There is not a single Mizo either in urban or in rural areas who told that the Mizos in general can become better or superior than *saps*'; and also that 'the *saps* are better than the Mizos for they have golden hair, beautiful eyes, tall and white complexion' etc. For detailed reading on the construction and imagery of the superiority of the white races in the minds and psychology of the Zo tribes Mizoram, see B.B Goswami, "out-group from the point of view of in-group: A Study of Mizos", in Dubey, S.M. (Ed.). *North East India: A Sociological Study*. 1978, 99-110.
14. Prior to the British annexation of the Zo territory, the 'Traditional Elites' — the *Lal* (Chiefs), the *Lalupas* (Elders) and *Village Officials* were the medium through which, religion, culture, administration, jurisdiction, economy and politics were determined. For instance the Village Officials like the *Puithiam*, the *Sadawt* and the *Tlakpawi*, who were different categories of priests, helped the Chief to perform the religious functions. While the *Khawchhiar*, the *Tlangau*, the *Zalen*, the *Ramhual* etc. helped the Chief to perform administrative-judicial and socio-economic functions (Lalrimawia, 1982; Thomas, 1993, 1994; Ray, 1993, 72-74; Nag, 1998, 15-21).
15. The New Elites were the *direct product of British colonialism* and their existence totally depended on their allegiance to the foreign rulers [McCall, (1949) 2003, 216; Elwin, 1964, 210].
16. Gurpreet Mahajan, "A Gendered Diary: Subject Dharma Kumar", in *Economic and Political Weekly*, June 3, 2000, 1899, gives a similar explanation for the exclusion of women from the realms of spirituality. My argument carries forward Mahajan's lines and locates the ultimate option left for the women in the Mizo society *i.e.* the realms of economics, which according to the Mizo patriarchy is both sensuous, and materialistic. Women in subsistence economies are allowed to participate in the whole process of 'economic pooling' as long as it is profitable to patriarchy to get the economic sphere enlarged. So long as the resources are enlarged the patriarchy does not feel threatened by the activities of the women and marginals. I owe this insight to my discussion with Sohini

Sengupta, (then working as Lecturer in the Department of Sociology, St.Joseph's College, North Point, Darjeeling) in an *'Adda' Session'* (informal tea table discussion).

17. I owe this insight to Professor Rudo B. Gaidzanwa. 'Silence becomes useful to both— those who inflict it as well as those on whom it is inflicted. That is to say 'silence' becomes a weapon for male hegemony (maintained through 'Fear Psychosis') and at the same time it also becomes a weapon for women in her *own domain* – the household, the private arena. *(At the CODESRIA/SEPHIS Extended Workshop, Dakar, 2006).* Emphasis added: A.S.C

18. This is a term I use to denote the whole process of making an already patriarchal system more chauvinistic, manlier. For instance the British consciously or unconsciously helped in the construction of the image or the myth of the "*Head-Hunters – the Looshais*". Thereby in the process, creating the fear among outsiders about the Zo tribes and their barbaric nature. The direct result of this external construction was that the Zo tribes especially the *Lushai clans* began to think of themselves as brutally heroic and thoroughly manly in their own construction about themselves. The direct result of such misconceived perception about the 'self' was that the projection of the self and also the clan and the tribes in total was always in terms of manliness as evident of the casual use of the phrase *'A Pa'*, in everyday language in Mizoram. The ritualized everyday practice of coercing young teenage boys to talk in a manly (*'Pa'*) manner/ tone and public exhibition of the *'Til Pawr Aw'* (the deep, broken tone of the voice that boys attain at puberty), is another instance of such display of manhood in the Zo society. The importance attached to the stage of *'Til Pawr Aw'* (*i.e. 'A Pa'*) can be understood from the fact that a boy with a *'Til Pawr Aw'* is considered *'hmeithai rai tham' i.e.* fit to impregnate a widow. The construction of the image of the *'Pa'* (male, masculine) in the Zo society systematically degrades the image of the *'Nu'* (female, feminine).

19. B.B Goswami's 'The Mizos in the context of state formation' in Surajit Sinha (Ed.) 'Tribal Politics and Systems in Pre-Colonial Eastern and North-Eastern India' cited in Sunar *et al.*, 2000, 9.

20. On October 24, 1960, Laldenga made a public speech at Aizawl urging the people not to accept Assamese language as the State

language as proposed by the Assam Official Language Act and led demonstrations against the high handed attitude of Assam Government. The MNF movement relied heavily on the twin issues of 'Anti-India' and 'Anti-Assam' feelings.

21. Assam it is argued suffers from elder sister syndrome among the Seven Sisters of the North-East States. Few scholars argue that as an elder sister *i.e.* Assam has been always hegemonic and argue that it was this hegemonic tendency that lighted the secessionist tendencies amongst the other minor tribes in the North-East. The elder sister tag has been given keeping in mind that almost all States in the North-East have been born out of the reorganisation of the territorial boundary of the State of colonial Assam. This argument has naturally been challenged from different quarters and those who counter-pose this trend argue that being the eldest sister Assam has suffered the most for all the sake of protecting the rest of the younger, weaker, feeble siblings. Assam as an elder sister has been misunderstood both at the Central and at the North-East level and has faced the brunt of a dual ill-feeling. I owe this insight to Professor Dyutish Chakraborty, Department of Political Science, North Bengal University.
22. This has been the dream of every Mizo and ever-political party in Mizoram. Even though India boasts of being a secular democracy and so also Mizoram, the speeches and the pre-electoral promises made by every political party in Mizoram tends to be overlaid with religious overtones.
23. The Mizo society serves as the good example for Bentham's Panoptic Society, where all persons are fearful of being watched by the Church and the moral agencies. The only difference being that in the case of the Mizo society the observer can be seen and sometimes partially invisible.
24. The notion of *foreigners* as perceived by the Mizos is apparently confusing and very broad it includes all *'others'*. It is very difficult as to exactly pinpoint who would be labelled as a foreigner by the Church and its agencies. The general accepted notion is that it includes the 'Vais', the Chakmas and the Burmese and at times it also includes the 'Zo' tribes from the other side of the borders. Here it must be noted that they make no distinction between Bangladeshis, Pakistanis, and Indians etc. Emphasis added: A.S.C.

The Inner Line Permit (ILP) that has been in existence in Mizoram since the colonial days has been used and misused by different groups to victimize the minorities time and again. The ILP has in fact become a weapon in the hands of the hegemonic tribes to extort money and exploit the minorities, especially the 'Vais' and the Burmese. For detailed reading on the issue of checking Foreigners in Mizoram, see http://www.Mizzima.com/MizzimaNews, 'Burmese Migrants in Mizoram worry threat of deportation'; http://www.angelfire.com, 'Chakma Refugees pushed back from Mizoram'.

25. The latest of these 'Vai Bandhs' were called by the MZP, the Mizo Students' Union and the YMA following the killing of a Mizo youth on 18th July, 2007 by suspected *Bangladeshi goons* at Dholai in Cachar District, Assam. Quit Mizoram notices were issued to the 'Vais' and a blanket curfew was imposed on the 'Vais' which was lifted only on the 25th of July 2007. The MZP, however, claimed that it had not imposed any curfew, but merely requested non-Mizos to stay indoors for their own safety. It also called a 24 hour *Bandh* at Vairengte the nearest town to Silchar, Cachar or the plains had demanded Rs. 15 lakh as compensation for the slain youth. (See J.B Lama, *The Statesman*, 30 July, 2007, 'The inside and out of Mizoram's ethnic skirmishes' for details).

26 This dilemma is specially found among the young educated youths who have completed their education in other States of India and have returned back to Mizoram to work in their home State. It becomes very difficult for the Mizo youths to digest the dictates of the Church and the moral police especially when it comes to dress code and watching television programmes etc. There are instances where the Church has imposed restrictions on inter-community relationships, for instance a Mizo girl should not marry a man from other community ('Vai'). The voyeuristic attitude of the Church and its agencies can be considered to be a contributory factor to the rapidly increasing rate of corruption, drug abuse and sexual liaisons in the Mizo society. People want a way out of the oppressive restrictive social system and want to flow away into the realms of fantasy taking refuge to drugs and other means to enjoy the life they have been denied by the moral police.

27. The changing nature of the Administrative experiences of Mizoram can be traced from the British times itself from the introduction of Inner Line to Excluded Area and Partially Excluded Areas to that of 'Circle Administration' during the Colonial times (Acharyya, 1984; Ray, 1982, 42-50) to 'Village Regrouping' during the insurgency (S.N. Singh, 1994, 88-133; Singh *et al.*, 1995, 9).
28. The Hmars tribes in the northern Mizoram consist of two groups (1) Completely Mizoised group and (2) Partially assimilated/Mizoised group. The Hmars collaborated with the MNF secessionist movement on the issue of 'Greater Mizoram'. However, as the Mizo Peace Accord of 1986 failed to integrate the Hmar inhabited areas into the new State of Mizoram, the partially assimilated Hmars, launched the Hmar People's Convention (HPC) movement which took a violent form.

REFERENCES

Acharyya, N.N. (1984). Modernisation of Mizoram. *Proceedings, NEIHA*, 5th Session.

Aleaz, Bonita (2005). *Emergent Women Mizo Women's Perspectives.* New Delhi: Mittal Publications.

Allen, B.C., Gait, E.A., Howard, H.F., & Allen, C.G.H. (Ed.) (1979). (2001). *Gazetteer of Bengal and North-East India.* New Delhi: Mittal Publications.

Banerjee, Paula. Sabyasachi Basu Ray Chaudhury & Samir Kumar Das (Ed.). (2005). *Internal Displacement in South Asia – The Relevance of the U.N's Guiding Principles.* New Delhi: Sage Publications.

Bareh, H.M. (2001). *Encyclopaedia of North-East India, Vol. V, Mizoram.* New Delhi: Mittal Publications.

Barooah, N.K & David Scott (1970). *North-East India 1802-1813: A Study in British Paternalism.* Delhi: (NA).

Barpujari, S.K. (1996) Bamboo-Flowering in Mizoram – A Historical Review. *Proceedings, NEIHA,* 17th Session.

Baruah, Apurba. K. (2002). *Student Power in North-East India.* New Delhi, Regency Publications.

Baruah, Sanjib (2005). *Durable Disorder – Understanding the Politics of Northeast India.* New Delhi: Oxford University Press.

Basu, Amrita., & Kohli, Atul. (Ed.). (1998). *Community Conflicts and the State in India.* Calcutta: Oxford University Press.

Baveja. J.D. (1970). *The Land Where the Bamboo Flowers.* Gauhati: Assam Publication Board.

Cesaire, Aime (First published in French 1955). *Discourse on Colonialism.* (Translated by Joan Pinkham) New York: New York University Press.

Chakraborty, Anup Shekhar (2007). Politics of Silencings: Echoes of the Margins from Mizoram. *Indian Journal of Political Science.* Vol. LXII, No. 4, Oct.-Dec.

Chakraborty, Anup Shekhar (2008). Emergence of Women from 'Private' to 'Public': A Narrative of Power Politics from Mizoram. *Journal of International Women's Studies*, Bridgewater, Vol. No. 3, May.

Chambers, Captain. O.A. (1899), (Reprinted 2005). *Hand Book of The Lushai Country* (Compiled under the order of the Quarter Master General in India in The Intelligence Branch). Calcutta: The Superintendent of Government Printing, India. Kolkata: Firma KLM Pvt. Ltd. on behalf of TRI, Department of Art and Culture, GoM, Aizawl, Mizoram.

Chapman, E. and Clark, M. (1968) .*Mizo Miracle.* Madras: The Christian Literature Society.

Chatterjee, Suhas (1990). *Mizoram Encyclopaedia,* Vol.-I. Bombay: Jaico Publishing House.

Chatterji, N. (First Indian reprint 1978). *The Lushais 1878-1889.* Aizawl: Tribal Research Institute.

Chatterji, S.K. (1974). *Kirata-Jana-Krti.* Calcutta: The Asiatic Society.

Chhangte, L.H. (1987). *The Life and Witness of the Churches in Mizoram.* Bombay: GLS Press, Serkawn, Lunglei: Baptist Church of Mizoram.

CYMA (1994 Revision). *Young Mizo Association Dan Bu. CYMA No.* 22. Aizawl, Mizoram: Y.M.A Press.

Daly, Mary (1973). *Beyond God The Father – Towards a Philosophy of Women's Liberation.* Boston, U.S.A: Beacon Press.

Datta Ray, B. (1983). *The Emergence and Role of Middle Class in North-East India.* Delhi: Uppal Publishing House.

Directorate of Economics and Statistics (1994), (1998), (2002). *Statistical Handbook(s) of Mizoram.* Government of Mizoram.

Downs, Frederick S. (1983). *Christianity in North East India.* Delhi: ISPCK.

Downs, Frederick S. (1971). *The Mighty Works of God – A Brief History of The Council of Baptist Churches in North East India: The Mission Period (1836-1950)*. Assam.

Dubey, S.M (Ed.), (1978). *North East India: A Sociological Study*. New Delhi: Concept Publishing Company.

Elliott, Carolyn. M. (Ed.). (2003). *Themes in Politics: Civil Society and Democracy– A Reader*. New Delhi: Oxford University Publication.

Elwin, Verrier (1955). *Religion of an Indian Tribe*. Bombay: Oxford University Press.

Elwin, Verrier (1964). *The Tribal World of Verrier Elwin – An Autobiography*. New Delhi: Oxford University Press.

Foreman, Martin. (Ed.), (1998). *AIDS and Men: Taking Risks or Taking Responsibility?*. London: Panos Institute and Zed Books.

Foucault, Michel (1987). *The History of Sexuality, Vol. II*. Harmondsworth: Penguin.

Goswami, B.B. (1979). *The Mizo Unrest : A Study of Politicisation of Culture*. Jaipur: Aalekh Publishers.

Guha, Amalendu (1991). *Medieval and Early Colonial Assam – Society, Polity, Economy*. Calcutta: K.P Bagchi & Company, Center for the Social Science Studies.

Guha, Amalendu (1977). *Planter Raj to Swaraj: Freedom Struggle and Electoral Politics in Assam 1826-1947*. New Delhi: Indian Council of Historical Research.

Hasan, Mushirul (Ed.). (2000). *Inventing Boundaries: Gender, Politics and The Partition of India*. New Delhi: Oxford University Publication.

Hill, Bennett D. (1970). *Church and State in the Middle Ages*. New York, U.S.A: John Wiley & Sons, Inc.

Hluna, John Vanlal (1985a). *Church and Political Upheaval in Mizoram (A Study of The Impact of Christianity on The Political Development in Mizoram)*. Aizawl, MHA – (Mizo History Association): Synod Press.

Hluna, John Vanlal (1985b). Mizo Problems Leading to Insurgency. *Proceedings, NEIHA*, 6th session.

Hluna, John Vanlal (1986). Role of Missionaries in Mizoram Education. *Proceedings, NEIHA*, 7th Session.

Houseknecht, Sharon K., & Pankhurst, Jerry G. (Ed.), (2000). *Family, Religion and Social Change in Diverse Societies*. New York: Oxford University Press.

Khiang, Mi Mi (1984). *The World of Burmese Women*. London: Zed Books Ltd.

Kim, Sebastian. C.H. (2003). *In Search of Identity: Debates on Religious Conversion in India*. New Delhi: Oxford University Publication.

Lalchungnunga (1994). *Mizoram: Politics of Regionalism and National Integration*. New Delhi, India: Reliance Publishing House.

Laldinpuii, K. (1996). The Mizo Non-Cooperation Movement, 1948-49. *Proceedings, NEIHA,* 17th session.

Lalrimawia (1983). A Brief Survey of the Administrative Development in the Lushai Hills (1890-1947). *Proceedings, NEIHA,* 4th session.

Lalrimawia (1984). Missionaries and Education in Mizoram. *Proceedings, NEIHA,* 5th session.

Lalrimawia. (1995). *Mizoram History and Cultural Identity*. Guwahati: Spectrum Publications.

Lalrimawia. (1981). Pre-Historic and Historic Migration of the Mizos. *Proceedings, NEIHA,* 2nd Session.

Lalrimawia (1982). The Lushai Chiefs under the British Rule. *Proceedings, NEIHA,* 3rd Session.

Leach, E.R. (1954). *Political System of Highland Burma – A Study of Kachin Social Structure*. Boston, U.S.A.: Beacon Press.

Lefebvre, Henri (1991). *Critique of Everyday Life, Vol.1*. London: Verso.

Lewin, Captain. T.H. (1912).(Reprinted 1977). *A Fly on the Wheel*. Calcutta: Firma KLM on behalf of Aizawl: Tribal Research Institute.

Lewin, Captain. T.H. (1870). (Reprinted 1978). *The Wild Races of South-Eastern India*. Calcutta: Firma KLM on behalf of Aizawl: Tribal Research Institute.

Lorrain, Reginald (1912). (Reprinted 1988). *Five Years in Unknown Jungles: For God and Empire*. London, Guwahati: Spectrum Publications.

McKenzie, A. (Reprinted 1979). (2005). *The North-East Frontier of India*. Delhi: Mittal Publications.

Mahajan, Gurpreet. (2000). A Gendered Diary: Subject Dharma Kumar. *Economic and Political Weekly,* June 3.

McCall, A.G. (1949),(2003). *Lushai Chrysalis*. Aizawl: Tribal Research Institute.

McCall, A.G. (1980). *The Lushai Hills: District Cover*. Aizawl: Tribal Research Institute.

Misra, Udayon (1988). *North-East India Quest for Identity*. Guwahati: Omsons Publications.

Mizoram Presbyterian Kohhran (1999). *Hmeichhe Inkhawmpui Lian-Vawi 39 – Na, Reports*, Thingsulthliah, Mizoram: Synod Press.

Nag, Chitta Ranjan (1998). *Mizo Polity and Political Modernisation*. Delhi: Vikas Publishing House.

Nag, Chitta Ranjan (1993). *The Mizo Society in Transition*. Delhi: Vikas Publishing House.

Nibedon, Nirmal (1981). *North-East India: The Ethnic Explosion*. New Delhi, Lancers Publishers.

Popper, Karl (1966). *The Open Society and its Enemies*. London: Routledge.

Prasad, R.N. (1987). *Government and Politics in Mizoram 1947-1986*. New Delhi: Northern Book Centre.

Rabinow, Paul. (Ed.). (1987). *The Foucault Reader*. London: Peregrine.

Ralte, Lalrinawmi. (1993). *Crab Theology: A Critique of Patriarchy – Cultural Degradation and Empowerment of Mizo Women*. Episcopal Divinity School, UMI Dissertation Services, Michigan, U.S.A: A. Bell & Howell Company.

Ray, A.C. (1982). *Mizoram Dynamics of Change*. Calcutta: Pearl Publishers/ICSSR.

Ray, Animesh (1993). *Mizoram*. New Delhi: National Book Trust.

Rosanga, O. (1996). 'British Trade Relations with Mizoram Till 1930, and its Impact'. *Proceedings, NEIHA*, 17th session.

Ruether, Rosemary Radford (1993). *Sexism and God Talk: Towards a Feminist Theology*. Boston: Boston Press.

Samaddar, Ranabir (2004). *Peace Studies – An Introduction to the Concept, Scope and Themes, South Asian Peace Studies. Vol. I*, New Delhi: Sage Publications/MCRG, Kolkata.

Samuelson, Rami Sena. (1991). *The Mizo People: Cultural Analysis of Life in a Mizo Village in the 1890s*. Ann Abhor, U.S.A.: University of San Francisco, UMI.

Sangkima (1992). *Mizos: Society and Social Change – 1890-1947*. Guwahati: Spectrum Publications.

Sangkima (2002). Oral Sources of Mizo History. *Seminar on Sources of the History of North-East India*. Guwahati: ICHR-NERC, March 12-14.

Sangkima (2004). *Essays on the History of the Mizos*. Guwahati: Spectrum Publications.

Schall, Rev. James. V., s.j. (1981). *Christianity and Politics*. Boston, U.S.A: St. Paul Editions.

Sen, Jahar (1977). *Indo- Nepal Trade in the Nineteenth Century*. Calcutta: Firma KLM Pvt. Ltd.

Singh, K. S.; Goswami, B. B.; Nunthara, C.; Sengupta, N .N. (Eds). (1995). *People of India – Mizoram, Volume – XXXIII. People of India – Anthropological Survey of India*, Calcutta, West Bengal: Seagull Books.

Singh, S.N. (1994). *Mizoram – Historical, Geographical, Social, Economic, Political and Administrative*. New Delhi: Mittal Publications.

Singhal, Arvind, and Rogers, Everett. M. (2003). *Combating AIDS*. New Delhi: Sage Publications.

Soja, Edward. W. (1989). *Postmodern Geographies: The Reassertion of Space in Critical Social Theory*. London: Verso.

Stedman, Murray. S., Jr. (1964). *Religion and Politics in America*. New York, Burlingame, U.S.A.: Harcourt, Brace and World, Inc.

Stevenson, H.N.C., F.R.A.I. (1943, Falam). (First Indian Reprint 1986). *The Economics of the Central Chin Tribes*. Aizawl, Mizoram: Tribal Research Institute: Everly Press.

Sturzo, Luigi. (1962). *Church and State, Volume I & II*. Notre Dame, Indiana: University of Notre Dame Press. (Translated by Barbara Barclay Carter, Printed in the U.S.A.).

Sunar, Pradip., Jeevan Kawar and I.K. Subba. (2000). *The Gorkhas of Mizoram. Vol.I*. Aizawl: Mizoram Gorkha Students' Union (MGSU).

Szasz, Thomas S. (1970). *The Manufacture of Madness*. New York: Harper & Row.

Thanga, L.B. (1978). *The Mizos: A Study in Racial Personality*. Guwahati: United Publishers.

The Synod Executive Committee. (1950) *Mizoram Presbyterian Kohhran – Nupa Chungchang Dan*. Aizawl, Mizoram: Synod Press.

Thomas, E.J. (1993). *Mizo Bamboo Hills Murmur Change (Mizo Society Before and after Independence)*. New Delhi, Daryaganj, India: Intellectual Publishing House.

Vanlalhluna, D.H. (1996). Mizoram Assembly as an Instrument of Social Change. *Proceedings, NEIHA*, 17th session.

Verghese, Brig. C.G., and Thanzawna, R.L. (1997). *A History of the Mizos. Vol. I & II*. Delhi: Vikas Publishing House.

Woodthorpe, R.G. (1873, UK). (First Indian Reprint 1980). *The Lushai Expedition 1871-1872*.Guwahati: Spectrum Publications.

Xaxa, Virginius. (2005). Politics of Language, Religion and Identity: Tribes in India. *Economic and Political Weekly*. March 26– April 1, pp.1363-1370.

Zairema, Rev. (1978). *God's Miracle in Mizoram (Glimpse of Christian Work among Head-Hunters)*. Aizawl, Mizoram: Synod Press.

Zaithanchhungi. (1990). *Israel– Mizo Identity*. Aizawl: J.R Bros., Offset Printer.

Internet Sources

'1122 deaths related to drugs and liquor poisoning in Mizoram', Aizawl, January 10, 2006, IST<India News-Webindia 123_com.htm>

'89 drug deaths in Mizoram', Guwahati, January 6, 2000, PTI/TAT, http://www.northeastvigil.in/archives/?p=7475

'AIDS victims buried in bags', Aizawl, December 4, 2005, IANS, <http://www.navhindtimesonthewebIndia.htm. >

'Aizawl back to normal after flare–up over girl's murder', Guwahati, May 18, 2004, PTI/TAT, <http://www. northeastvigil.in/archives/?p=3163>

'Bandh affects normal life in Mizoram', Guwahati, May 1, 2004, Press Trust India/The Assam Tribune, <http://www. northeastvigil.in/archives/?p=3222>

'Burmese Migrants in Mizoram worry threat of deportation', July 22, 2003, <http://www.Mizzima.com/MizzimaNews>.

'Chakma Refugees pushed back from Mizoram', Jana Samhati Samati <http://www.angelfire.com>.

'Mizoram drug deaths', Guwahati, March 30 2000, Anon, The Assam tribune, http://www.northeastvigil.in/archives/?p=7948

'North East- worst drug- affected area', Guwahati, February 2, 2000, Special correspondent, TAT, < http://northeastvigil.in/archives/?p=7643>

'Teenagers new HIV-AIDS threat group in Mizoram', - News - Webindia123_com.htm Mizoram Aizawl December19, 2005 <http://www.webindia123_com.htm>http://www.Avert. org HIV and AIDS in India.htm

Bhattacharya, Sukhendu. 'Women at a Disadvantage in Mizoram',

Aizawl, PTI, November 15, 2003 <http://www.rediff.com/election/2003/nov/15mizo.htm>

Chhakchhuak, Linda., 'Women of God Want a Place in Church', June 2002.htm. 'Patriarchy in Religion – Gender bias in the church makes women theologians unhappy' <http://www.indiatogether.org>

David. M. Thangliana, 'Non-Mizos asked to vacate State', Kolkata, The Telegraph, March 9, 2004: http://www.northeastvigil.in/archives/? p=6919

J.B Lama, 'The inside and out of Mizoram's ethnic skirmishes', *The Statesman*, 30, July, 2007,

Rajeev Bhattacharya, 'Hope flickers for Reangs', Kolkata, *The Telegraph*, May 6, 2004 <http://northeastvigil.in/archives//p=3307>.

Thangliana, David. M., 'Non-Mizos asked to vacate State', Kolkata, March 9, 2004, The Telegraph, <http://www.northeastvigil.in/archives/?p=6919>

27 Coalition Politics in India

A Study of Punjab Politics

Bhupinder Singh

The multi-ethnic and culturally plural character of our society and multi-party system of our polity seems to rule out the possibility of a single party government, strong enough to govern the country effectively. Rather, it requires the coalition politics for adjusting various social formations in the power-structure. Although, the Congress Party dominated India's national and State politics for a long period. However, this was not a permanent phenomenon. The hegemony of the Congress Party came to be challenged in the fourth General Assembly elections held in 1967 in which approximately half of the States of the Union, it lost its majority character. The coalition governments were formed by the non-Congress political parties in these States. So far as the case of Punjab politics is concerned, it has a history of pre-election coalition, electoral adjustments and post-election coalitions since 1967. The coalition governments were formed in Punjab during the 1967, 1969 and 1977 Assembly elections but no coalition government could complete its full tenure. The coalition politics once again revived in Punjab, when the Shiromani Akali Dal (Badal) (SAD-B) and Bhartiya Janata Party (BJP) decided to contest the 1997 Assembly elections by making an alliance. The SAD(B)-BJP coalition had won thumping majority during the 1997 Assembly elections. As a result, the SAD(B)-BJP coalition government led by Parkash Singh Badal was formed in Punjab. This was the first successful coalition experiment noticed in the Punjab (1997-2002). The SAD(B)-BJP coalition remained during the 2002 and 2007 Assembly elections in Punjab. However, the SAD(B)-BJP coalition could not succeed in winning the 2002 Assembly elections. But, the SAD(B)-BJP coalition had succeeded to win clear majority during the 2007 Assembly elections. As a result, the SAD(B)-BJP coalition government led by Parkash Singh Badal was formed in the State.

An attempt has been made in this chapter to analyse the SAD(B)-BJP coalition in Punjab. Both primary and secondary sources have been used in this chapter. The objectives of this study are as follows:

1. To know the factors which helped to combine the SAD(B) and the BJP.
2. To know the impact of the SAD(B)-BJP coalition on the electoral performance of the political parties in Punjab.
3. To highlight the certain issues which created the differences between the SAD(B) and the BJP during the 1997-2002
4. To evaluate the performance of the SAD(B)-BJP coalition government (1997-2002) in Punjab.
5. To know the impact of the coalition politics on Centre-State relations.

Historical Perspective

The chapter of coalition politics was started in Punjab as a result of the 1967 Assembly elections. The Shiromani Akali Dal (SAD) had been split up into two parties before these elections. One of these was led by Master Tara Singh and the other by Sant Fateh Singh. Congress Party and both SADs were the major contenders in these elections.

Table 27.1 : Performance of Political Parties in 1967, 1969 and 1977 Assembly Elections

Name of Party	*1967 Seats Won/% of Votes Polled*	*1969 Seats Won/% of Votes Polled*	*1977 Seats Won/% of Votes Polled*
Congress	48/37.7	38/39.2	17/34.7
SAD •	26/24.7	43/29.4	58/31.41
BJS/BJP	9/9.8	8/9	—
CPI	5/5.3	4/4.8	7/6.6
CPI(M)	3/3.2	2/3.1	8/3.5
PSP	0/0.5	1/0.5	0/0
Janata Party	—	—	25/15

• The figures of 1967 have been calculated by clubbing the seats won/% of votes by the SAD (Sant) and the SAD (Master).

Source: Office of the Chief Electoral Office, Punjab, Chandigarh, 1967, 1969 and 1977 Assembly Elections.

As Table 27.1 shows that though the Congress emerged as a single largest party in the State during the 1967 Assembly elections, it could not succeed in getting the majority. All the non-Congress political parties decided to form a United Front under the leadership of the Akali leader, Gurnam Singh. As a result, Gurnam Singh was sworn in as Chief Minister on March 8, 1967. But, this coalition government did not last long. About 7 months after its formation an Akali Dal leader, Lachman Singh Gill defected from the party along with 19 MLA's and formed the Punjab Janata Party. This brought Gurnam Singh government in minority. He tendered his resignation to the Governor. Lachman Singh Gill, who had the support of the Congress Party, was invited to form the Ministry and was sworn in as the Chief Minister on November 25, 1967. However, he had to resign on August 21, 1968 when the Congress Party withdrew its support. The Punjab Legislative Assembly was dissolved and President's rule was imposed in the State on August 23, 1968. As a result, mid-term elections to Punjab Assembly were held in February 1969. Both SADs (Master and Sant) were merged on October 7, 1968 before these elections. The United SAD declared that its main objective was the demand of the Sikh Homeland. The SAD not only entered in an electoral alliance with the Jan Sangh but also decided to have electoral adjustment with the CPI, CPI (M) and Swatantra Party. Like the 1967 Assembly elections, no political party could get majority in mid-term elections. As Table 27.1 shows that though the Akali Dal had failed to get majority of seats, it was able to emerge as the largest single party in Punjab Legislative Assembly. Since the United Front led by Akali leader Gurnam Singh was able to get clear majority in Legislative Assembly, Gurnam Singh was sworn in as the Chief Minister on February 17, 1969. However, this coalition government could not stay in power for long. The dissensions surfaced in the SAD after some time at the time of the elections to the Rajya Sabha for three seats. Gurnam Singh extended secret support to Bhupinder Singh, a nominated candidate by Master group, who won the election due to this factor and one of the two SAD candidates were defeated. As a reaction Sant Fateh Singh expelled Gurnam Singh from the SAD. As a result Gurnam Singh had to resign from his office. Parkash Singh Badal was invited to form the new Akali-Jan Sangh coalition government by the Governor. The Akali-Jan Sangh coalition government functioned smoothly till the emergence of differences between the SAD and Jan Sangh, in June 1970 on the question of affiliation of the Colleges of Jalandhar district with G.N.D.U., Amritsar. This led to the withdrawal of the support of Jan Sangh from the Government. As a result, Badal government was converted into an Akali government. But this government had to resign on June 13, 1971. The President's Rule was imposed and the Punjab Assembly was dissolved on June 15, 1971.[1] Coalition politics in Punjab once again revived during the 1977 Assembly elections. The SAD, Janata Party and CPI (M) made an alliance to contest these elections. As Table 27.1 shows that Akali-Janata coalition had got absolute majority in the 1977 Assembly elections. As a result, an Akali Dal-Janata coalition government was formed in the State after these elections. The CPI (M) decided to give support to it without joining the government. But this coalition government came under a strain when Janata Party withdrew support from it after split in it at the national level in July 1979. The decision was made by it because the SAD had decided to support Charan Singh government instead of the Janata Party. Since Charan Singh government could not prove its majority in Lok Sabha after the Congress (I) withdrew support from it, the Lok Sabha was dissolved and mid-term elections to Lok Sabha were held in 1980. The leader of the Congress (I), Indira Gandhi came to power in the Centre after these elections. The Indira Gandhi government dismissed the Akali government on this ground that it had lost the legitimacy after the defeat of the Akali candidates in 12 out of 13 Lok Sabha seats of the State. As a result Punjab Legislative Assembly was dissolved and the President's Rule was imposed in the State.[2] To be short, as discussed above, no coalition government could complete its full tenure. It was due to the following reasons:[3]

1. Personal political ambitions of the Akali leaders.
2. Struggle for power within the SAD.
3. Differences among the coalitions partners including the ideological differences.
4. Role of the then Central Congress Leadership to destabilizing the coalition governments.

Although as above discussed coalition governments (1967, 1969, 1977) could not complete their full tenure but it did not mean that they had not done any commendable work during their different phases of functioning. The best achievement had been that the Akali-Jan Sangh cooperation had eased out pains of adjustment between the Sikhs and the Hindus on the language policy which was long overdue. Besides, communal peace was maintained for most of the time.[4]

The 1997 Assembly Elections

The 1997 Assembly elections once again revived the coalition politics in Punjab. Approximately all the political parties decided to contest the elections under the alliances. The Shiromani Akali Dal led by Parkash Singh Badal [SAD(B)] and the Bhartiya Janata Party (BJP) decided to contest the 1997 Assembly elections by having a coalition. The coalition was considered beneficial for the SAD(B) from the following angles[5] :

1. It would ensure share to the SAD(B) in the political power at the national level because the BJP had emerged as the main national party in the 1996 Lok Sabha elections and had formed a short lived coalition government in which the SAD(B) had been given a share.
2. The role of the BJP on the eve of anti-Sikh riots and the resolve of the BJP government of national capital territory of Delhi to bring to book the guilty of anti-Sikh riots had brought BJP closer to the SAD(B).
3. The SAD(B) was confident that the BJP would be reliable in transfer much needed Hindu votes in the semi-rural and rural constituencies.
4. The coalition with the BJP based no problems regarding sharing of seats.

The BJP was too in favour of a coalition with the SAD(B) for various reasons[6] :

1. The national leadership of the BJP had realized the need of wooing the support of regional party like SAD(B) for attaining power at the national level.
2. The BJP leadership also considered coalition with the SAD(B) necessary for getting rid of its anti-minority image.
3. The alliance with the SAD(B) was regarded by the BJP as essential for protecting and promoting the interest of its constituency *i.e.* the Punjabi Hindus.
4. The national leadership of the BJP gratefully

acknowledged that the SAD(B) had supported it at a time (after 1996 elections) when no other regional party was prepared to do so.

This is what appears to have influenced the SAD(B) and the BJP in joining hands. Despite strong differences between the two on the issue of Anandpur Sahib Resolution, they formed an alliance on the basis of Common Minimum Programme (CMP)[7]. The SAD (B) contested 92 seats and the BJP 22. Four major issues (peace and development, communal harmony, corruption free administration and economic and other concessions to the people) were made the key issues in their campaign by the SAD(B)-BJP coalition and the Congress in these elections[8]. In fact, both vied with each other in resorting to populist policies by promising free electricity and free water to the farmers[9]. The SAD(B)-BJP coalition and Congress were the major contenders in 1997 Assembly elections.

Table 27.2 : Performance of Political Parties in the 1997 Punjab Assembly Elections

Name of Party	1992		1997	
	Seats Won	% of Votes Polled	Seats Won	% of Votes Polled
Congress	87	43.80	14	26.59
SAD (B)*	-	-	75	37.64
BJP	6	16.50	18	8.33
CPI	4	4.10	2	2.98
CPI (M)	1	1.90	0	1.79
BSP	9	16.40	1	7.48
SAD (K)**	3	–	–	–
SAD(M)***	–	–	1	3.10
Janata Dal	1	2.10	0	0.56
Independents	6	9.90	6	10.87

* The SAD (B) had boycotted the 1992 elections to Punjab Assembly.
** The SAD (Kabul) did not exist in 1997 Punjab Assembly elections.
*** The SAD (Maan) had boycotted the 1992 Punjab Assembly elections.

Source: Office of the Chief Electoral Officer, Punjab, Chandigarh, 1992 & 1997 Assembly Elections.

As Table 27.2 shows that the SAD(B)-BJP coalition scored a landslide victory; it secured ¾ majority in 1997 Assembly elections. Despite the fact that the SAD(B) had secured 75 out of a total of 117 seats in Assembly, it decided to form a coalition government with its alliance partner, the BJP which had won 18 seats. It could be regarded as a restoration of Accommodation Model of Politics. The accommodation of the BJP proved beneficial for Badal to check the struggle for power within the party. The landslide victory for the SAD(B)-BJP alliance was possible because it received support from all sections of society[10]. A sample survey confirms that among the people who preferred to vote for the SAD(B), 38 per cent were Sikhs, 27 per cent Hindus, 12 per cent Hindu S.Cs and 23 per cent Sikh S.Cs. Similarly, among those who preferred to vote for the BJP, 45 per cent were Hindus, 34 per cent Sikhs, 11per cent Sikh S.Cs. and 10 per cent Hindu S.Cs[11]. In fact, this coalition proved beneficial to both. The defeat of the Congress and victory of the SAD(B)-BJP in these elections may be ascribed by the following reason[12] :

1. The peace card played by the Congress did not work.
2. Negative aspects of the role of Beant Singh's government in overcoming militancy in Punjab cannot be overlooked.
3. The intensification of factionalism proved very costly to the Congress in the battle for the ballot.
4. The populist promises like free electricity and water for agriculture could help the SAD(B).

The 1998 Lok Sabha Elections

The SAD(B)-BJP coalition government led by Chief Minister Parkash Singh Badal began its functioning with a promise to provide clean, efficient and corruption free administration. The populist promises made in the CMP, such as free electricity and free power for the agriculture sector and the Shagun of Rs. 5100 on the marriage of scheduled caste girls, were implemented. The government decided to provide free education for the boys' upto matriculation and for the girls upto graduation level. The decision was also taken to give the old age pension to men and women above 65 and 60 years respectively. The State Human Rights Commission was established for enquiring the atrocities by the security forces and police during the militancy. The government managed to get from the Union Government, a waiver of Rs. 8,500 crore loan incurred by the State in fighting militancy[13].

The SAD(B) and BJP decided to contest the 1998 Lok Sabha elections in alliance with each other. The pro-rural and pro-peasantry populist policies adopted by the SAD(B)–BJP coalition government proved beneficial for it during the 1998 Lok Sabha elections in Punjab. It strengthened the rural support-base of the SAD(B). Besides, the BJP has its support-base mainly in the urban areas.

Table 27.3 : Performance of Political Parties in 1998 Lok Sabha Elections

	1996		*1998*	
Name of Party	*Seats Won*	*% of Votes Polled*	*Seats Won*	*% of Votes Polled*
Congress	2	35.10	0	25.85
SAD (B)	8	28.72	8	32.93
BJP	0	6.48	4	11.67
Janata Dal	0	2.66	1	4.18
SAD (M)	0	—	0	2.73
CPI	0	1.60	0	3.40
BSP	3	—	0	—

Source : Office of the Chief Electoral Officer, Punjab, Chandigarh, 1996 and 1998 Lok Sabha Elections.

As Table 27.3 shows that the SAD(B)–BJP coalition was succeeded in winning 12 out of a total of 13 seats in Punjab during the 1998 Lok Sabha elections. The victory of the

SAD(B)-BJP coalition and the defeat of the Congress in these elections may be ascribed by the following reasons[14] :

1. The pro-rural and pro-peasantry populist policies adopted by the Badal government strengthened its rural support-base.
2. The success of the BJP to retain support of its traditional upper caste Hindu urban voters also led to the defeat of the Congress.
3. The decision of the Congress to withdraw its support from the Central Government led by I. K. Gujral adversely affected its electoral performance during the 1998 Lok Sabha elections.
4. The coalition between SAD(B) and the BJP benefited for both. The coalition helped to join the rural-urban votes.

The SAD(B) joined the Central Ministry of NDA government led by A.B. Vajpayee which came to existence as a result of 1998 Lok Sabha elections. It was turning point in the Akali politics. It may be noted that the Shiromani Akali Dal's stance had been anti-Centre for a long period.

However Badal's popularity began to wave soon after the 1998 Lok Sabha elections due to the nepotism, favouritism and corruption in administration. Intra-party conflict was also started within the SAD(B). The faction led by Gurcharan Singh Tohra revolted against the leadership of Chief Minister Parkash Singh Badal soon after the 1998 Lok Sabha elections because he was unhappy over the induction of Badal's son Sukhbir Singh Badal in the N.D.A. Government. Tohra wanted the inclusion of his close associate, Prem Singh Chandumajra instead of Badal's son. He alleged that there was unprecedented corruption in the State. He even held the members of the Badal's family guilty for it. The fight between Badal and Tohra intensified over the celebrations of the birth centenary of the *Khalsa*[15]. Another factor that affected their relationship was the controversy over the intervention of *Akal Takht*. The S.G.P.C. Executive Committee which was dominated by the Badal group, suspended the then *Jathedar Akal Takht*, Bhai Ranjit Singh and appointed Giani Puran Singh as the acting *Jathedar* of *Akal Takht*. Later on, Gurcharan Singh Tohra, the then S.G.P.C. President, was also removed by the members of the S.G.P.C. in a meeting of the General House. Bibi Jagir Kaur was elected as a new President of the S.G.P.C. The fight between the Badal and Tohra factions was undoubtedly a struggle for power. This culminated the split in the SAD(B). Gurcharan Singh Tohra formed his own Akali Dal, the Sarb Hind Shiromani Akali Dal (SHSAD)[16]. This split adversely affected the electoral performance of the SAD(B) in the 1999 Lok Sabha and 2002 Assembly elections in Punjab. But this vertical split in the SAD(B) did not cause any instability to the SAD(B)-BJP coalition government in Punjab. This was first time in the history of Akali Dal that despite suffering vertical split within its ranks the SAD(B) government could maintain its stability and thereafter could complete its full term. The factors which helped Akali government to survive were its huge majority in Legislative Assembly and support of alliance partner (which had no sympathy with Tohra faction)[17].

The 1999 Lok Sabha Elections

The mid-term Lok Sabha elections were held in 1999. The split within the SAD(B) adversely affected the performance of SAD(B)-BJP coalition in these elections. After breaking away from SAD(B) and establishing its own identity as political party, the SHSAD tried to establish its moderate outlook. The SHSAD asserted its faith in unity and integrity of India, opposed all separatist demands and fissiparous forces and wanted to see strong India where all religious, linguistic and cultural denominations particularly minorities could prosperous. This approach was adopted by the SHSAD because it wanted the maximum damage to the SAD(B) by cutting into its moderate vote bank. The SHSAD also used the coalition politics as electoral strategy to defeat the SAD(B) in any future electoral fray. During the 1999 Lok Sabha elections the SHSAD was able to form United Front consisting BSP, SAD (Democratic), SAD (Panthic), SAD (M) and Bharatiya Kisan Union (Maan).

Table 27.4 : Performance of Political Parties in 1999 Punjab Lok Sabha Elections

	1998		*1999*	
Name of Party	*Seats Won*	*% of Votes Polled*	*Seats Won*	*% of Votes Polled*
Congress	0	25.85	8	38.44
SAD(B)	8	32.93	2	28.59
BJP	4	11.67	1	9.16
Janata Dal	1	4.18	0	0.10
SAD(M)	0	2.73	1	3.41
CPI	0	3.40	1	3.74

Source : Office of the Chief Electoral Officer, Punjab, Chandigarh, 1998 and 1999. Lok Sabha Elections.

As Table 27.4 shows that SAD(B)–BJP coalition could win just 3 out of a total of 13 Lok Sabha seats in Punjab. It may be noted that the coalition had won 12 seats during the 1998 Lok Sabha elections. Besides, the Congress which had won no seat in the 1998 Lok Sabha elections gained 8 seats in the 1999 Lok Sabha elections. The United Front was able to secure 12.35 per cent of the votes polled in the State. The Front was able to snatch one Lok Sabha seat (Simranjit Singh Mann defeated Surjit Singh Barnala) from ruling SAD(B) and was responsible for ruling coalition defeat in Patiala and Ropar Lok Sabha seats. According to an assessment, the SAD(B) lost 23 constituencies in 1999 Lok Sabha elections due to this split[18].

The defeat of the SAD(B)-BJP coalition and victory of the

Congress in 1999 Lok Sabha elections may be explained by the following reasons[19] :

1. The split adversely affected the performance of the SAD(B).
2. The alienation of the large section of the urban Hindu voters from the BJP.
3. The apathy of the rural based landless scheduled caste population to the SAD(B).
4. A significant shift of the Dalit voters from the BSP to the Congress also led to the defeat of the SAD(B)-BJP coalition.

The SAD(B) and the BJP had differences of opinion on certain issues. In April 1997, a controversy arose between the two coalition partner on the issue of granting 'Saropas' to the family members and relatives of Sant Jarnail Singh Bhindrawale on the 'Baisakhi' day in the presence of Captain Kanwaljit Singh, the then Finance Minister of Punjab. The BJP took this development very seriously and raised the matter with Akali leadership on various forums. As a result, the Akali leadership felt sorry for this development. The mid-term Lok Sabha elections were held in 1999. The Jalandhar Lok Sabha seat had become a bone of contention between the SAD(B) and the BJP. While the SAD(B) offered this seat to I. K. Gujral the then Prime Minister, the BJP opposed to this proposal. But political affair committee of SAD(B) ultimately decided to allot this seat to I. K. Gujral for the 'generosity' shown by him towards Punjab. Both the parties had also different perception on the role of Punjab police in the changed Punjab situation. While the SAD(B) was in favour of curtailing the powers of police and wanted that the police officers facing inquiries in terrorist cases should not be defended on the government expenditure. The BJP did not agree with this perception of SAD(B) and wanted a more effective role for Punjab police even in the situation so that militancy is not revived again. An unfortunate and unsavoury controversy had been sparked off over the acceptance and implementation of the *Nanakshahi* Calendar which was prepared by a Canada based Sikh Pal Singh Purewal. The calendar was based on universally accepted solar system. The S.G.P.C. decided to implement this calendar. But the R.S.S. opposed of its implementation and the BJP supported R.S.S. on this issue. This development deteriorated the relationship of the coalition partners[20]. Another important irritant in the relationship of the two coalition partners was BJP led N.D.A. Central Government decision to include U.P.'s Sikh populated Udham Singh Nagar district into the proposed Uttaranchal State. After the inclusion of Udham Singh Nagar district in Uttaranchal, the question arose as to whether SAD(B) should continue its support to BJP led government at the Centre? But P.S. Badal on this development argued that "continuing alliance with the BJP is much important as it is not based just on political considerations but stood for unity and amity of Punjab people." He also stated that "it was the alliance which ended the alienation of the Sikhs at the national level after years of militancy in Punjab". The differences cropped up between the ruling coalition partners over the contents of the memorandum proposed to be submitted to the Constitutional Review Commission on behalf of the Punjab Government. The Punjab Cabinet Minister and senior BJP leader Balramji Das Tondon issued statement that the Punjab cabinet had not been able to reach a consensus on the issue as the BJP Ministers felt very strongly against the demand of the SAD(B) regarding the scrapping of Article 356 and the demand for greater autonomy for the State. On the other hand, the Akali Dal decided to submit the memorandum to the Constitutional Review Commission on behalf of the party on 28th August, 2000. It was based on Anandpur Sahib Resolution which was passed by the Akali Dal on 1976[21]. On the whole, SAD(B)-BJP coalition government worked smoothly (1997-2002) despite the differences on the various issues among them.

The 2002 Assembly Elections

The coalition government led by Parkash Singh Badal did not take any lesson from the outcome of the 1999 Lok Sabha elections. No efforts were made to check the rampant corruption in the administration. No steps were taken in reforming the miserable condition of the State economy. Rather, the Chief Minister started his *Sangat Darshan* Programme. The parliamentary system in Punjab acquired the form of Chief Ministerial system. The power was concentrated in the hands of Chief Minister, his wife, his son and other close relatives of the Chief Minister. All key posts of the State at various levels were given to the officers personally loyal to the Chief Minister. This type of centralized, personalized and family rule had not existed during the earlier regimes. Although, Punjab was already facing a resource crunch when this government came to power, the populist policies further adversely affected the financial position of the State. The decision to provide free power and free water to the farmers proved very costly. Besides, the policies of populism introduced a new competition among various strata of the population. It was alleged that Badal's populism is pro-peasantry and it discriminates against the other sections of the society. The decision to abolish the octroi left the urban-local bodies resourceless. Consequently, no development plans could be undertaken. No care was given to revamp infrastructure needed for putting the State on the path of development. The programmes like *Sangat Darshan* were exercised in the wastage of funds. Consequently, neither care was given for resolving the crisis in agriculture nor was attention paid to restore the health of industries. Problems such as unemployment received little attention. The political and administrative corruption assumed new heights. The recruitment to jobs, transferring and posting etc. had become purchasable commodities[22]. Thus, the hope that Badal led SAD(B)-BJP government would bring prosperity to the State was belied. As a result, the SAD(B)-BJP coalition defeated during the 2002 Assembly elections.

Table 27.5 shows, the SAD(B)-BJP coalition could win only 44 seats out of a total of 117 seats contested by it. Besides, the Congress won 62 out of 105 seats contested by it. As a result, Congress government headed by Captain Amrinder Singh was formed in the State.

Table 27.5 : Performance of Political Parties in 2002 Punjab Assembly Elections

	1997		*2000*	
Name of Party	*Seats Won*	*% of Votes Polled*	*Seats Won*	*% of Votes Polled*
Congress	14	25.59	62	36.5
SAD(B)	75	37.64	41	30.5
BJP	18	8.33	3	5.7
CPI	2	2.98	1	1.7
SAD(M)	1	3.10	0	—
BSP	1	7.48	0	5.4
Panthic Morcha*	—	—	0	4.4
Independents	6	10.87	9	11.35

* The United Front was converted into Panthic Morcha in 2002 Assembly elections.

Source: Office of the Chief Electoral Officer, Punjab, Chandigarh, 1997 and 2002 Assembly elections.

The defeat of the SAD(B)–BJP coalition and victory of the Congress during the 2002 Assembly elections in Punjab may be attributed to the following reasons[23] :

1. The widespread corruption during the SAD(B)-BJP regime (1997-2002) immensely harmed their electoral prospect alienating them from the common masses.
2. The nepotism in the form of 'Badal Parivar' rule – comprising of his son, his wife, his son-in-law and his

nephew since 1997 caused widespread resentment among the voters.

3. The split within the SAD(B) also contributed to their fall as it eroded their base.
4. The anti-incumbency factor had also been put forward by the SAD(B) leadership to explain their setback.
5. The failure of the BJP to retain the support of its traditional upper caste Hindu urban voters also led to the defeat of the SAD(B)-BJP coalition.

The 2004 Lok Sabha Elections

The erosion of the electoral base complled P.S. Badal to make compromise with Jathedar Tohra's SHSAD to save further decline of SAD(B)'s political fortunes. The unity was an electoral compulsion for both Akali Dal parties (SHSAD and SAD(B) keeping in mind that the elections for the Lok Sabha was slated to be held in 2004. As a result both parties were merged on 27 July, 2003. It has been well established fact that Akalis fall apart whenever they come to power and come together in the name of *Panthic* unity whenever out of power[24].

Table 27.6 : Performance of Political Parties in 2004 Punjab Lok Sabha Elections

	1999		*2004*	
Name of Party	*Seats Won*	*% of Votes Polled*	*Seats Won*	*% of Votes Polled*
Congress	8	38.84	2	34.17
SAD(B)	2	28.59	8	34.28
BJP	1	9.8	3	10.48
Janata Dal	0	4.18	0	0.10
CPI	1	3.74	0	2.55
United Front	1	12.35	0	–
Panthic Morcha	0	–	0	–

Source : Office of the Chief Electoral Officer, Punjab, Chandigarh, 1999 and 2004 Lok Sabha Elections.

The elections for Lok Sabha were held on 14 May, 2004. The reunited Akali Dal was able to bounce back in the State politics by routing the Congress Party and Panthic Morcha in Punjab during the 2004 Lok Sabha elections. As the above Table 27.6 shows that the SAD(B)–BJP coalition won 11 out of a total of 13 seats during the 2004 Lok Sabha elections in Punjab. The SAD(B) won 8 seats and its alliance partner BJP won 3 seats. The Congress could win only 2 seats, whereas Panthic Morcha drew blank. It was clear that besides other factors; the merger of Tohra's SHSAD into SAD(B) was paying political dividends. It may not be out of place to mention here that though Panthic Morcha could win only 4.4 per cent votes during the 2002 Assembly elections but these votes were mostly at the cost of SAD(B). The Congress–CPI alliance was able to win 63 seats with 38.2 per cent votes and SAD(B)–BJP alliance could win 44 seats with 36.6 per cent votes. One can understand the importance of 4.4 per cent votes where less than 2 per cent swing in votes would have reversed the electoral outcome[25]. The defeat of the Congress and victory of the SAD(B)-BJP coalition during the 2004 Lok Sabha elections in Punjab may be attributed to the following reasons[26] :

1. The anti-incumbency factor had also been put forward by the Congress leadership to explain their setback.
2. The success of the BJP to retain the support of its traditional upper caste Hindu urban voters also led to the defeat of the Congress.
3. The merger of the SHSAD into the SAD (B) played crucial role in defeating the Congress. This united the Akali votes.
4. The factionalism within the Congress adversely affected its electoral performance.

The 2007 Assembly Elections

The coalition which was made between the SAD(B) and the

BJP in 1997 remained during the 2007 Assembly elections. The SAD(B) fielded candidates in 87 constituencies and its alliance partner the BJP in 30. It is important to note here that SAD(B) fielded seven Hindus and the BJP four Jat Sikhs in these elections[27]. It shows the importance of the coalition politics. Besides, the Congress decided to contest the elections on its own. Both, the SAD(B)-BJP coalition and the Congress released the populist manifestoes to win the Assembly elections. The most visible issue in the Assembly elections in Punjab was *Atta Daal* (flour and pulse). The SAD(B)–BJP coalition had promised with the poor to provide the flour at Rs. 4 per kg. and pulse at Rs. 20 per kg. The coalition used inflation, especially the rising prices of basic food items, as a heavy stick to beat the Congress government. During the election campaign they showed the comparative charts of prices of food items now and in 2002 when the SAD(B)-BJP was in power. The newspaper advertisements and pamphlets were used to show the comparative charts of prices of food items[28].

Table 27.7 : Performance of Political Parties in 2007 Punjab Assembly Elections

Name of Party	*2002*		*2007*	
	Seats Won	*% of Votes Polled*	*Seats Won*	*% of Votes Polled*
Congress	62	36.5	44	40.90
SAD(B)	41	30.5	48	37.09
BJP	3	5.7	19	8.28
CPI	1	1.7	0	0.76
CPI(M)	0	—	0	0.28
SAD(M)	0	—	0	0.52
BSP	0	5.4	0	4.13
United Front	0	4.4	0	—
Independents	9	11.35	5	6.82

Source : Office of the Chief Electoral officer, Punjab, Chandigarh, Punjab Assembly Elections 2002 and 2007.

As Table 27.7 shows that though the SAD(B) has

emerged as a single largest party in the 2007 Assembly elections by winning 48 seats; it could not succeed to get the clear majority on its own. However the SAD(B)–BJP coalition was able to get the majority by winning the 67 out of a total of 117 seats during the 2007 Assembly elections. The SAD(B) won 48 and its alliance partner the BJP got 19 seats in these elections. However the SAD(B) and the BJP both the parties had succeeded to increase their seats during the 2007 Assembly elections. It is pertinent to mention here that the SAD(B) could get 41 seats in 2002 Assembly elections. Its alliance partner the BJP had obtained just 3 seats during the 2002 Assembly elections. The Congress which had won the 2002 Assembly elections by winning the 62 seats, defeated in the 2007 Assembly elections. It could win only 44 seats in these elections. The victory of the SAD(B)-BJP coalition and defeat of the Congress in 2007 Assembly elections may be attributed to the following reasons[29] :

1. The unification of the two Akali Dals of P.S. Badal and G.S. Tohra before the elections united their votes.
2. The populist promises by the SAD(B)-BJP coalition during the election campaign strengthened their base.
3. The coalition between the SAD(B) and the BJP united the rural-urban votes.
4. The BJP succeeded in managing to woo back the urban Hindu voters which it lost to the Congress 5 years ago.
5. Captain Amrinder Singh was not successful in his attempts to woo the Sikh votes through his involvement in the celebrations of religious events. Rather, it may have done more harm than good by alienating Hindu voters.

Although the SAD(B) and BJP has succeeded to form the coalition government in Punjab but there are serious challenges before this government. The agriculture sector has long been heading to a deep financial and ecological crisis. The State has witnessed a steady decline on important fronts such as health, employment and education. Government schools have never been as shabby as now and only the poor people send their children in these schools. Public health institutions suffer from a lack of vision, not to mention resources. Unemployment levels have been described as 'explosive,' with thousands of young people angling to go abroad for jobs and many of them getting cheated in the process. This was, in fact, a major election issue in the central Doaba belt. Narcotics are another huge issue and little has been done to tackle the drug trade and the underlying factors that may have led to the widespread problem of addiction[30]. The necessary steps should be taken by the SAD(B)-BJP coalition government to solve the above said problems of the Punjab people.

Conclusion

From the above analysis it could be discerned that the era of coalition politics emerged as an offshoot of decline of Congress party in the fourth General Assembly elections held in 1967. Punjab was not exception to this phenomenon. But the first successful coalition experiment was noticed in this State only from 1997-2002. The SAD(B)-BJP coalition was remained during the 2004 Lok Sabha and 2007 Assembly elections. It was because the coalition was not based on the ideological underpinnings between them. Rather it was based on the sole compulsion of electoral victor. This coalition was mutually advantageous for them. On the one hand, it provided a good combination of rural-urban voting arithmetic, whereas on the other hand it provided the SAD(B) to be projected at the national level and BJP an opportunity for strengthening the rural base. This coalition is likely to continue till a serious challenge is posed to them with the emergence of such new combinations in Punjab politics or any one of the partner take a strong ideological shift in its electoral game plan. But at present both of these kinds of scenarios are unlikely to develop. Hence possibility of continuation of this coalition is not ruled out at present. The SAD(B)-BJP coalition government has been working in Punjab during the 2007 Assembly elections. On the whole, The SAD(B)-BJP coalition made a healthy impact on society of Punjab. The divide that had been created between the Sikhs and the Hindus during the militancy and had continued for more than a decade was bridged by this coalition. The coalition also strengthened the roots of the democracy in the State. Besides, it has opened a new chapter in Centre-State relations, ushering in the age of co-operated federalism in the country. The era of confrontations has been effectively ended and replaced with a forward-looking thrust on working together for the overall good of the State and the nation.

REFERENCES

1. J. C. Anand, "Politics of Retreating Communalism" in Iqbal Narain (ed.), *State Politics in India*, Meenakshi Prakashan, Meerut, 1976, pp. 275-298. Also see S. Bhatnagar and P. S. Verma, "Coalition Governments (1967-80)", *Punjab Journal of Politics*, Vol. V, No. 1, January-June 1981, pp. 125-140 ; Harbir Singh, "Mid-Term Elections in Punjab: Emerging Trends" in Verinder Grover and Ranjana Arora (eds.), *Encyclopaedia of India and Her States*, Deep & Deep Publications, New Delhi, 1996, pp. 388-410, and Subhash C. Kashyap, *The Politics of Power : Defections and State Politics in India*, National Publishing House, Delhi, 1974, pp. 381-443.
2. Bhatnagar and Verma, *op. cit.*, pp. 125-140; Surjeet Singh Narang, "Elections and the Shiromani Akali Dal— A Socio-Psychological Approach", *Punjab Journal of Politics*, Vol. V, No. 2, July-December 1981, pp. 19-31, and Arun Mehra, "Akali-Janata Coalition: An Analysis" in Verinder Grover (ed.), *The Story of Punjab: Yesterday and Today*, Vol. II, Deep & Deep Publications, New Delhi, 1995, pp. 479-490.
3. For further details see Dalip Singh, *Dynamics of Punjab Politics*,

Macmillan India Ltd., New Delhi, 1981, pp. 242-252. Also see Gopal Singh, "Factional Politics in Akali Dal and the Homelanders", *Punjab Journal of Politics*, Vol. XIV, Nos. 1-2, 1990, pp. 47-62; Bhupinder Singh, "Politics of Factionalism in Punjab: A Critical Study of Shiromani Akali Dal", *Indian Journal of Political Science*, Vol. LXVII, No. 4, Oct.-Dec. 2006, pp. 839-848, and Bhupinder Singh, "Punjab Me Sattarood Akali Dal Me Fut: Karn Avm Parbhav", *Politics India*, Vol. 1, No. 11-12, August-September, 1999, pp.13-15.

4. Sutapa Lahiry, "Ethnicity, Party System and Coalition Politics in Punjab in 1990s", *Punjab Journal of Politics*, Vol. XXVI, No. 1, 2002, p.34. For details on negative impact of coalition governments on State politics also see Anand, *op. cit.*, pp. 297-298.
5. This observation is based on discussions with the experts on Punjab politics.
6. *Ibid.*
7. For details on CMP see, "SAD-BJP Announces CMP", *The Tribune* (Chandigarh), January 23, 1997.
8. Ranbir Singh, "Politics in Punjab: Restoration of Accommodation Model", *Politics India*, Vol. 1, No. 10, April 1997, pp. 37-38.
9. For details see *Times of India* (New Delhi), February 18, 1997; *The Tribune* (Chandigarh), January 28, 1997, and *Hindustan Times* (New Delhi), January 29 and 31, 1997.
10. Parmod Kumar, "Punjab: Changing Political Agenda" in Ramashray Roy and Paul Wallace (eds.), *Indian Politics and the 1998 Election*, Sage Publications, New Delhi, 1999, pp. 293-294, and Sanjay Kumar, "Punjab: A Vote for Change", *Politics India*, Vol. 1, No. 10, April 1997, pp. 39-40.
11. *Ibid.*
12. For further details see Bhupinder Singh, "Electoral Politics in Punjab: A Study of Vidhan Sabha Elections 1997", Ph. D. Thesis (unpublished), Department of Political Science, Kurukshetra University, Kurukshetra, 2002.
13. Lahiry, *op. cit.* No. 4, pp. 34-35.
14. This observation is based on the reports published in the newspapers during and after the 1998 Lok Sabha elections.
15. Bhupinder Singh, "Impact of the 1997 Assembly Elections on

the Political Development in Punjab", *Punjab Journal of Politics*, Vol. 25, No. 2, 2001, pp. 166-167.

16. *Ibid.* pp. 167-170.
17. Janmeet Singh, "Akali Politics since Amritsar Declaration: A Synoptic View", *Indian Journal of Political Science*, Vol. LXVII, No. 1, January-March, 2006, pp. 157-159.
18. Jamshid Ali Khan, "The Akali-BJP Coalition: Bases and Working in the Punjab during 1997-2002", *The Punjab Past and Present*, Vol. XXXVI, No. 72, October 2005, p. 107.
19. See Parmod Kumar, "Electoral Politics in Punjab: From Autonomy to Secession", in Paul Wallace and Ramashray Roy (eds.), *India's 1999 Elections and 20th Century Politics*, Sage Publications, New Delhi, 2003, pp. 385, and Anne Vaugier-Chatterjee, "Strains on Punjab Governance: An Assessment of the Badal Government (1997-1999)", *International Journal of Punjab Studies*, Vol. 7, No. 1, January-June 2000, pp. 106-108.
20. Khan, *op. cit.*, pp. 107-108.
21. *Ibid.*, pp. 108-110.
22. For further details see Chatterjee, *op. cit*, p. 102; Nilanjan Mukhopadhyay, "The Price of Popularity", *The Statesman* (Delhi), February 25, 1997; "Free for All", *Times of India* (New Delhi) ,February 18, 1997; Hari Jai Singh, "Punjab's Battle of the Ballot", *The Tribune* (Chandigarh), January 25, 2002; Hari Jai Singh, "Populism is not Dynamism", *The Tribune* (Chandigarh), April 14, 2000; PPS Gill, "Populist Steps May Laid Punjab in Debt Trap Again", *The Tribune* (Chandigarh), August 5, 2001, and Hari Jai Singh, "Punjab Me Bhrashtachaar Hi Hai Mukhya Mudda", *Dainik Tribune* (Chandigarh), February 10, 2002.
23. *Ibid.* Also see Ashutosh Kumar and Sanjay Kumar, "The Recent Assembly Elections in Punjab: Some Reflections on Results and Changing Voter Preferences", *Indian Journal of Political Science*, Vol. 9, No. 1, 2002, pp. 113-127; P.S. Verma, "Punjab Assembly Elections: Sharply Polarised Electorate", *Economic and Political Weekly*, Vol. XXXVII, No. 15, June 15-21, 2002, pp. 2281-2284, and Ashutosh Kumar and Sanjay Kumar, "Assembly Elections: Decline of Identity Politics", *Economic and Political Weekly*, Vol. XXXVII, No. 15, April 13-19, 2002, pp.1384-1388.
24. Singh, *op. cit*, No.3. For further details on the issues raised by the political parties during the 2004 Lok Sabha elections also

see Surinder S. Jodhka, "Return of the Region: Identities and Electoral Politics in Punjab", *Economic and Political Weekly*, Vol. LX, No. 3, January 15-21, 2005, pp. 224-230.

25. Singh, *op. cit*, No. 17, p. 159.
26. This observation is based on the reports published in the newspapers during and after 2004 Lok Sabha elections.
27. Shekher Gupta, "Something Happened in Punjab", *Indian Express* (Chandigarh), March 10, 2007.
28. Annie Zaidi, "Paying the Price", *Frontline*, March 23, 2007, pp. 18-20.
29. Purnima S. Tripathi, "Lessons in Defeats", *Frontline*, March, 23, 2007, p. 19.
30. Zaidi, *op. cit*.

28 Role of the Asom Gana Parishad in Assam Politics and the Future of Regionalism

Jogendra Kumar Das and Haren Ch. Kalita

Assam is one of the most backward, underdeveloped and destabilized States of the Indian Union in general and Northeast India in particular. The State society is severely plagued by insurgency, economic underdevelopment, ethnic strife, resurgent sub-nationality movements, natural calamities like devastating flood and erosion of the mighty Brahmaputra and its tributaries and unabated foreign infiltration. As the capitalistic path of development and modernization is consolidated in India after Independence, the peripheral societies like Assam have to face acute regional disparities, Assam, in fact, becomes the most deprived region and has remained the most economically dispersed and politically subjugated State within the federal democratic polity of India. Assam polity today suffers from destabilization, non-consensus, mutual distrust, violence and normlessness. Democracy is severally injured here due to continuous negligence of the Centre and inefficiency of the state leaderships and consequent governments operated by mostly the national (all India) political parties as a result of which regional feelings gradually consolidating in the minds of the people.

The State is situated in the North East region of India – bordering States such as Arunachal Pradesh, Manipur, Meghalaya, Mizoram, Nagaland, Tripura, West Bangal and two countries like Bangladesh and Bhutan. Most of the State population lives in the lush and verdant valleys of its two major river systems in the 22 districts of the Brahmaputra Valley, and the three districts of Barak Valley. For administrative and revenue purposes, the State has 27 districts including the newly created Kamrup (Metro) and 4 districts under the newly created BTC areas such as Kokrajhar, Baska, Chirang and Udalguri.

Assam is a plural society composing of various religious, linguistic, ethnic and racial groups. The demographic diversity has been a crucial factor in the process of socio-economic and political development in the state[1]. The major social groups in Assam are the high caste Hindu Assamese composed of the Brahmins non-caste ethnic groups such as the Bodos, the Sonowals the Mishings, the Karbis, the Rabhas, the Lalungs, the Dimacha Kachais and the Dewris. The non-caste Assamese is called the OBC's. There are oppressed and socio-economically disadvantaged groups in the state, who are included in the Fifth Schedule to the Constitution of India known as the SCs. The non-Assamese groups are the Hindu Bengalis and the Muslim Bengalis. There are some significant migrant groups living in the State such as the Marwaris, the Gujratis, Orias, and Punjabis etc. The linguistic groups are the Assamese speaking, Bengali speaking, Nepali speaking and Hindi speaking. Thus migration from different places into Assam has made the population structure of the State most diverse and complex[2]. This resulted in the heterogeneous composition of the society. Frequent demographic changes especially since the colonial rule that have been taking place make it difficult to remove the impediments of developments of all the ethnic groups.

With the modest density of population prior to 1901, Assam grows spectacularly to be one of the most densely populous States of the nation in succeeding periods. It is a most diverse region and its heterogeneity results primarily in the population pattern. According to the 2001 Census, population of Assam stands at 2,66,55,528 of which 1,37,77,037 are males and 1,28,78,491 are females. The decadal growth of the population works out to 18.92 per cent during 1991-2001 as against 21.54 per cent for the country[3]. But the decadal population growth rate of the State during the earlier decades remained higher than that of the national level. It is a matter of great concern that the continuous Muslim migration from neighbouring Bangladesh poses a great threat to socio-economic development. The two decades growth rate of Muslim population in Assam is 30.4 per cent, which is abnormal and quite higher than the growth rate of Hindu population being 14.9 per cent[4]. With the census figure showing a decline of Hindu population in the State from 67.1 per cent in 1991, to 64 per cent in 2001 and a corresponding increase in Muslim population from 28.47 per cent in 1991 to 30.9 per cent in 2001, the emerging demographic picture in the State in the light of ongoing influx from Bangladesh is a matter of great concern.

The Indian National Congress largely dominated the government and politics of Assam during 1946-78.Further, except for a short break of 19 months between 1978-79 and nearly 5 years break 1985-91 and 1996-2001, the Congress has been the ruling party in the State. During this long history of rule, the succeeding Congress governments have largely failed to fulfil the rising expectations of the people. It is important to note that large scale migration from neighbouring Bangladesh has been taking place predominantly during the Congress rule in the State which resulted in the outbreak of the 6 years long Assam movement. Then the Assam movement ostensibly gave a solid foundation to regionalism in Assam with the emergence and of the AGP, which was reflective of the gross failure of the national political parties to resolve the burning socio-economic problems that the people are facing here since Independence.

Under the circumstances, it is necessary to undertake a

study on the role of the AGP, the apex nativist Political Party, which comes into existence in 1985 at a very crucial stage of Assam Political history as an alternative to the all India (national) political parties, with sky-high electoral promises. The present study seeks to review the genesis the role of the party in State politics, its present status and the future of regionalism in Assam as such. We have taken up a historical–documentary approach in dealing with the issues relating to the role of the AGP.

Genesis of the AGP

The genesis of the AGP was developed among the leaders and the course of the historic Assam Movement. The party in fact, was the by-product of the Assam Movement itself. During the period of the Assam Movement, the leaders and the participants acquired political experience and realized the necessity of forming a regional platform through which the aspirations of the *Asamiyas* could be carried out in the post-movement era. One of the chief objectives behind the formation of this first ever pioneering regional platform, was to fulfilling the regional aspirations of the people through the proper implementation of the Assam Accord. One perceptive scholar observes that although it may seem that the AGP is the result of the anti-foreigners' movement (1979-1985), its origin may be traced back even earlier to the movement[5]. There has been a long history of struggle of the Assamese people for their distinct socio-cultural and political identity which virtually started since the twenties of this century[6]. In fact, the anti-foreigner movement is the latest phase of this struggle[7]. Thus, the genesis of the AGP, being the apex regional platform of *Asom,* lies in the deep rooted and long standing regional feelings and native sentiments of the Assamese people of the mainstream Brahmaputra Valley of the State.

Hence, the regional aspiration, of the *Asamiyas* was culminated in the formation of AGP in 1985 following the

Assam movement and its resultant Assam Accord. The emergence of the party was really a significant development after the long Congress rule in the State. Though the AGP is the result of the anti-foreigner movement, yet it provides an occasion to work closely at the phenomenon of regional parties and the allied phenomenon of Assam's cultural pluralism and sub-nationalism.

We have already stated that the AGP was emerged in Assam politics as a result of the six years' long Assam movement during 1979-1985 on foreigner's issue. The Assam movement was gearing up outside the political party framework and leadership. The movement was organized and launched by the student communities of Assam of almost all the ethnic groups. It was, initially a mass movement and was led by the umbrella students organization, the All Assam Students Union (AASU) and its political wing, the All Assam Gana Sangram Parishad (AAGSP), which in a combine effort, gathered mass political mobilization and social support on a very large scale. It is important to note that Assam has both land and river border with Bangladesh on the frontier district of Karimganj and Dhubri. The border is more or less open there, being no physical barrier between the two countries conducive for border crossing. The Assam movement ostensibly aimed at stopping this unabated inflow to Assam. The question of foreign nationals arose out of this illegal infiltration of largely the Bengali Muslims from the erstwhile East Pakistan now Bangladesh that actually began during the partition of India in 1947 and thereafter continued unabated. Apart from the whooping number of Bangladeshis, a large number of internal migrants come to Assam in search of jobs. In course of time both the internal and external migrants settled permanently in the State and legitimized their position by entering their names into the voter list. By 1979, these migrants were in absolute majority in seven districts, which created existential problem to the indigenous people. As a result, the Assamese people developed in themselves a fear psychosis of being totally swamped in their own historic homeland both by the internal Indian migrants as well as the external (foreign) migrants. Consequently, prior to the Assam movement, *Bahiragata Bitaran Andolan* (Movement for deportation of Indian outsiders) was launched by the Purbanchalia Lok Parishad and Assam Jatiatabadi Dal during 1978-79 and later this movement was transformed into the movement for deportation of foreign nationals by the AASU and the AAGSP, which is called the Assam movement[8].

After a lot of bargaining, the movement leadership came to an understanding with the Central Government that resulted in the signing of the Assam Accord on 15 August 1985, between the movement leadership and Central Government. When the movement leadership compromised on the cut-off year, came to an end to the Assam movement. Two regional political parties were formed; one is in support of the Accord, called the AGP, while the other was against the Accord called the United Minorities Front (UMF)[9]. Though, the AGP was democratic and secular in orientation it came into existence with a strong native ideology. There were two significant aspects in this regard. The leadership of the movement accepted that detection of foreigners from 1.1.1966 should be the base date and year to deport the illegal migrants. The leadership of the movement also accepted the decision to allow the entrants between 1966-70 to be stayed in Assam, and to defranchise them for 10 years first and then again to recognize their voting rights after the stipulated 10 years were over. Secondly, the leadership of the movement accepted the Illegal Migrants Determination Tribunal (IMDT) Act 1983, to detect the names of the foreigners from the voter list, delete the names from the voter list and accordingly expel the foreigners who came to *Asom* on or after 25 March, 1971 onwards[10]. This particular aspect of the Assam Accord have become the major political issue that rocked the State society and politics during the last 20 years. It may not be irrelevant to mention here that since the IMDT Act is highly defective, no single foreigner could be detected and deported from *Asom* during the last 20 years rather millions of foreigners infiltrated illegally in the State and causes existential problem to the native people. Though the controversial IMDT Act was struck down by the Supreme Court of India on July 2006, yet the government is yet to create new Tribunals on the basis of Foreigners' Act 1946 and Foreigners' Tribunal Order 1966 to expel the foreigners from the State.

Thus we find that the AGP was formed by the four political formations such as the AASU, AAGSP, PLP, and the AJD with the sole objective of implementing the Assam Accord in general and to deport the foreigners from the State in the greater interests of the people.

Impact and Role of the AGP in Assam Politics

Since the formation, the AGP has been playing a very significant role in the State by participating actively in electoral politics. It captured political power twice and sits in the opposition thrice in the Assam Legislative Assembly and even plays an equally important role in national politics from Assam. In 1989 it took part in the formation of the National Front government led by V.P. Singh.

The party contested in both the State Legislative Assembly elections and Lok Sabha elections held in 16 December 1985. The people of Assam gave their verdict in favour of the AGP in the party's first electoral experiment and won 63 seats, as Tables 28.1 and 28.2 reveal. The Table demonstrates the end of Congress rule in Assam, which won only a meagre 25 seats. The Congress (S) could win only a microscopic four seats[11].

The AGP having a strong support base among the caste Hindu-Asamiyas, in the Brahmaputra Valley polled 34.54 per cent of votes as Table 28.1 has revealed. While the IND

Table 28.1 : Performance of the Political Parties in the 1985 State Assembly Elections

Name of the Parties	*No. of Seats Contested*	*No of Seats Won*	*Total Valid Votes Polled*	*Percentage of Poll*
INC	125	25	17,28,043	23.47
AGP	105	63	25,43,102	34.54
JNP	83	—	1,07,077	1.45
ICS	73	4	2,35,572	3.20
BJP	34	—	79,068	1.07
CPM	38	2	3,19,832	4.34
UMF	56	17	7,98,558	10.85
PTCA	27	3	2,67,640	3.68
CPI	20	—	72,877	0.99
LKD	19	—	16,806	0.23
UTNLF	15	1	—	—
IND	533	10	11,94,222	16.22
Total	1128	125	73,62,797	100.00

Source : Government of Assam State Election Office, Dispur, 1988.

Table 28. 2 : Performance of the Political Parties in the 1985 Lok Sabha Elections

Name of the Parties	*No. of Seats Contested*	*No. of Seats Won*	*Total Valid Votes Polled*	*Percentage of Poll*
INC	13	4	17,49,688	23.43
AGP	10	7	25,05,377	33.55
ICS	8	1	4,57,705	6.13
UMF	4	1	9,71,663	13.01
PTCA	3	1	3,10,150	4.15
JNP	9	—	2,64,876	3.55
BJP	2	—	27,916	3.37
CPM	2	—	2,56,254	3.43
CPI	2	—	1,03,323	1.38
LKD	3	—	55,685	0.75
IND	50	—	7,65,598	10.25
Total	106	14	74,68,235	100.00

Source : Government of Assam, State Election Office, Dispur, Guwahati, 1988.

got 16.22 per cent of votes; the UMF got 10.85 per cent of votes; and the position of other parties are negligible. The AGP formed the first ever-regional party government in the State bringing an end to the long standing Congress rule.

Most of the AGP Ministers and MLA's were either post-graduates or graduates and rush to political field from the University hostels. Most of them were unmarried and just 25-30 years old[12].

The performance of political parties in the 1985 State assembly elections can be observed in Table 28.1 and Table 28.2 respectively. The Table 28.1 demonstrates the political depression and consequent end of the Congress rule in Assam, which won only a meagre 25 seats. The Congress (S) another national party could win only a microscopic 4 seats.

A significant aspect of the Eighth ALA elections was that of the unprecedented and overnight victory of a minority dominated political party, the UMF, which was formed against the Assam Accord and in support of the doubtful citizens or the Bangladesh oriented minority domiciled to hurriedly capture 17 seats in the 126-member Legislative Assembly[13]. It should also be noted that almost all the elected members of the UMF were defectors largely from the Congress (I). This particular aspect was reflective of the Congress (I) tacit political bargaining with the Bangladeshi Assam-based lobby, which became the vote bank of the party. As and when the Congress government signed the Assam Accord, the minority vote bank as well as the Bangladeshi-lobby inside the Congress Party considered it detrimental to their existential interest and posing a great threat to the Congress (I) social bases, they hurriedly formed the UMF.

Table 28.1 also highlights a large number of IND candidates contesting the 1985 State Assembly Elections. However, as the single largest party in the legislature, the AGP succeeded in attaining support from 7 IND elected members later joining the AGP. Thus, the AGP got absolute majority with 70 seats and comfortably formed the government[14]. The AGP, having a strong support base among the caste Hindu *Asamiyas* in the Brahmaputra Valley polled 34.54 per cent of votes as Table 28.1 reveals. While the

IND got 16.22 per cent of votes, the UMF got 10.85 per cent of votes. The position of other parties are negligible.

The 1985 State Assembly Elections was in fact, an unprecedented political event in Assam. The number of regional political parties was considerably increased. In 1972, Plain Tribal Council of Assam (PTCA) was the only regional political party to contest elections. Similar situations occurred in 1978 and 1983 elections respectively. Thus, the victory of the regional parties like AGP, UMF, and PTCA and the formation of government in the State for the first time, since Independence by the AGP consolidated regionalism in a solid base from the earlier nascent position.

Though the people of Assam expected much from the newly formed AGP government the government in return totally failed to meet the popular expectations because of the inherent limitations of the party government and the structural constraints of the Assamese society and politics. The AGP failed to provide *weltangscuung* to the Assamese people, as they had to work in the old institutional arrangements with their zero political experience, which they could not change. The major problems remained unresolved rather some newly emerged burning problems rocked the State society. Law and order situations was extremely deteriorated which was beyond the control of the government especially with the indiscriminate violence perpetrated by the United Liberation Front of Assam (ULFA). It is very crucial to note that the government drastically failed to implement the Assam Accord, which was their sole commitment during the formation of the party and their main electoral plunk, mainly because of their lack of experience and efficiency. Here, we can draw up an inference that though a popular social movement and issues generated by it largely determined the outcome of elections to legislature, yet the consequent government may not be able to translate the very agenda of such social movement into reality.

It should be stated that the prominent members of the

Cabinet allegedly involved in various scandals and rampant corruptions and government strategy was largely directed towards personal interests of the AGP Ministers and the MLA's. As a result the party lost popularity as the party organizational network at the grass roots level had collapsed and party activity remained exclusively around Dispur, the capital of Assam. As we have already indicated, during the AGP rule, the ULFA, an extremist organization became very much active which almost destabilized the government The AGP government was blurred in tackling this pertinent issue and the Chief Minister Mr. P.K. Mahanta had to play a double role and all the time he was double spoken in dealing with this issue. Even, the next AGP led coalition government between (1996-2001), also failed to resolve the insurgency problem of the State. While the AASU-AGP combine, organized many agitations against the Central Government during 1985-2001, the response of this dyad was weak and even compromising[15].

Later, President's rule was imposed on 27th November, 1990 and the AGP government was dismissed on the ground of its failure to maintain law and order situation in the State in the wake of violence perpetrated by the ULFA. Most of the AGP supporters began to feel insecure about the party but even many top ranking leaders began questioning the future of the party. Such uncertainties coupled with the lack of deep ideological commitment made the AGP weak to work as a political party. Meanwhile, the AGP was divided into two hostile camps, the AGP and the Natun Asom Gana Parishad (NAGP), just before the 1991 State Assembly Elections mainly because of intra-party rivalries and leadership crisis. As a result, the Congress (I) won 65 seats in the 1991 State Assembly Elections and formed the government under leadership of Hiteswar Saikia. The Congress Party polled 24,01,349 votes, the percentage being 29 per cent that can be observed in Table 28.3. The Table 28.3 demonstrates that this time the AGP won only 19 seats, the percentage being 18.07 per cent, while its twin brother the NAGP won only a meagre seats, 5.5 per cent per cent[16]. Table 28.3 demonstrates the depressive picture of the divided parent AGP along with the depressive picture of other regional parties. The unexpected party split, non-performance of the party as a government acute law and order situation, non-implementation of the Assam Accord, failure to translate the other egalitarian election promises into reality, rampant corruption and gross failure to remove regional imbalances among the ethnic groups were the main causes behind the fall of the AGP government.

Table 28.3 : Performance of the Political Parties in the 1991 State Assembly Elections

Name of the Parties	*No. of Seats Contested*	*No of Seats Won*	*Total Valid Votes Polled*	*Percentage of Poll*
INC	124	65	24,01,349	28.98
AGP	120	19	14,97,615	18.07
BJP	47	10	5,31,926	6.42
NAGP	85	5	4,56,192	5.50
JD	95	1	3,98,628	4.81
CPI	37	4	3,20,655	2.46
CPM	28	2	2,03,997	3.87
ASDC	8	4	1,33,280	1.61
ICS	45	—	1,20,927	1.46
URMCA	54	—	1,09,443	1.32
UMF	29	—	1,08,620	1.31
PTCA	15	—	88,496	1.07
Others	108	—	1,26,184	1.52
IND	855	15	17,90,176	21.60
Total	1650	125	82,87,489	100.00

Source : Government of Assam State Election Office Dispur. 1992.

However, in the 1996 State Assembly elections, the AGP marginally managed to retain its prestige by securing 59 seats, and that too, because of non-campaigning of the Congress (I) in the elections due to the sudden death of Sri Hiteswar Saikia just one month before the elections. Had the Congress (I) launched full-fledged election campaign with its political heavyweight Hiteswar Saikia, the AGP would have been pushed back into the trap of political marginality.

However, good luck came to the AGP and they won the majority seats, while the Congress (I) won only 34 seats. The AGP formed the government for the second time under leadership of Mr. P.K. Mahanta as Chief Minister with the support of the CPI, CPM and some other Left and democratic parties. It is worth mentioning here that during the Assam movement the former AASU leaders and present AGPs considered the Congress and the CPM leaders as the main enemy of the movement, interestingly this time they all met together to enjoy power and pelf draining out all their historic enmities. This virtually reveals that their hostilities and friendship were not ideological rather essentially opportunistic. We find that in the 1996 elections the UMF won only 2 seats, while the Autonomous State District Council (ASDC) based in Karbi Anglong won all its bigoted 5 seats. The details of 1996 State Assembly Elections can be observed in Table 28.4. The AGP remained as a ruling party till the 2001 assembly elections.

Table 28.4 : Performance of the Political Parties in the 1996 State Assembly Elections

Name of the Parties	*No. of Seats Contested*	*No of Seats Won*	*Total Valid Votes Polled*	*Percentage of Poll*
INC	122	34	27,78,627	30.56
AGP	96	59	27,00,934	29.70
BJP	117	4	9,46,235	10.41
CPI	11	3	1,77,750	1.96
ADC(T)	106	2	241	3.70
CPM	10	2	1,76,721	1.94
JD	32	—	51,721	0.56
JP	2	—	829	0.01
Samata	1	—	285	0.00
Party	5	5	1,79,877	1.98
ASDC	12	—	3,709	0.04
Samajbadi Party	5	—	2,605	0.03
CPI (ML)	5	—	4,656	0.16
AB	5	—	746	0.01
URMCA	9	—	15,131	0.07
UMF	19	2	1,01,817	1.12
RCPI(RB)	6	—	5,513	0.06
IND	657	11	15,88,153	17.47
Total	= 1228	122	90,92,800	100.00

Source : Government of Assam State Election Office, Dispur, 1996.

The 2001 State Assembly elections scenario in Assam took a significant turn with the decision of the AGP and the BJP leadership to forge a pre-electoral alliance despite the strong opposition from the State BJP unit. As a result of the electoral alliance with the BJP, the AGP had to face political erosion and lost three of its former important allies, the CPI, CPI (M) and the United People's Party. The AGP, beyond its expectations, had lost popular mandate and the Congress (I) was voted to power in the State. The Congress (I) contested for 125 constituencies and had won 70 seats. The Congress (I) polled 41,90,001 votes, the percentage being 39.60 per cent. The 2001 elections brought to an end, to the regionalist AGP rule and invited the nationalist Congress (I) rule in the State. The AGP contested 77 seats and won only a scanty 20 seats. Table 28.5 indicates a remarkable depression of the performance of the AGP and other regional parties. Needless to state that the performance of the AGP-led coalition during 1996-2001 was not up to the expectation of the people, which virtually reflected in the outcome of the election results.

After the 2001 elections were over, intra-party rivalries were croppedup which destabilized the party solidarity. Party president P.K. Mahanta alleged to have been involved in several anti-party activities and the party followers, including top-brass leaders were extremely dissatisfied with his doubtful role. In fact, Mahanta was failed to lead the party honestly in the right direction because of his narrow personal interests and dictatorial outlook. This crisis ultimately compelled him to resign from the post of the party president and he had to face severe criticism within and outside the party. Every member of the AGP expected that Mahanta would realize his mistakes and takes up a path of self-introspection and repentance. The people also felt that Mahanta as an experienced politician could lead the party in the right direction, render valuable contribution in the stability of the party and the society as such. But to the contrary Mahanta started more confrontation with the

Table 28.5 : Performance of Political Parties In 2001 State Assembly Elections

Name of the Parties	*No. of seats Contested*	*No of Seats won*	*Total valid votes Polled*	*Percentage of Poll*
INC	125	70	41,90,001	39.60
AGP	77	20	21,30,118	20.13
BJP	45	8	9,80,290	9.26
CPI	19	0	1,16,889	1.10
CPM	22	0	1,89,349	1.79
NCP	62	3	2,65,941	2.51
AITA	23	1	58,361	0.55
ASDC (P)	5	0	98,032	0.93
ASDC (U)	5	2	1,18,610	1.12
CPIML	8	0	19,862	0.19
JD (S)	5	0	1,690	0.02
JD (U)	6	0	7,645	0.07
MUL	5	0	1,230	0.01
RJD	5	0	2,121	0.02
RSP	3	0	2,905	0.03
SAP	19	1	83,815	0.79
SP	22	1	1,09,391	1.03
AMB	1	0	422	0.00
LJNSP	11	0	9,051	0.09
LS	3	0	1,764	0.02
PDF	7	0	35,147	0.33
RCPI(R)	2	0	576	0.01
SJP(R)	8	0	2,345	0.02
UBNLF	13	0	16,687	0.16
UMF	9	0	43,712	0.41
URMCA	7	0	16,901	0.16
UTNLF	1	0	4,185	0.04
IND	389	19	20,74,746	19.61
Total	907	125	1,05,81,786	100.00

Source : Government of Assam State Election Office, Dispur, 2001.

democratically elected party president Brindaban Goswami who succeeded Mahanta in an extraordinary political exigency though on an *ad hoc* basis. Mr. Mahanta continued his act of confrontation with Brindaban Goswami to become party president once again by ousting the latter. With the single aim to become the party president without an intra-party support base, Mr. Mahanta contested for the post of party president against Brindaban Goswami, at the annual conference held at Tezpur in the year 2002. But, as was expected he was defeated and got the first ever official humiliation since he took over the charge of the post of party president at the dawn of the AGP in 1985. It is surprising to note here that even after his defeat in a big margin, he was reluctant to accept the party mandate continued his zeal to dominate the party against popular will and continued his anti-party mission, violating party discipline flouting out all the democratic norms in order to destabilize the party leadership.

It is worth stating here that due to his conspiracy, the AGP had to face heavy loss in the last Rajya Sabha elections. Sri Mahanta without respite continued his anti-party activities by adopting different strategies in different constituencies in the last Lok Sabha elections with the sole aim to defeat the party candidates. Even Mr. Mahanta with the tacit help of two of his follower MLA's, who were violating the party whip in the last Rajya Sabha elections, arranged his wife Jayashree Goswami Mahanta to contest from Dhubri Lok Sabha constituency as an independent candidate which was straight forward detrimental to party interest and a gross violation of party norms as such.

Despite such a foul play he was invited to the steering committee of the party in 25 January, 2005 and for the last time he was cordially requested to maintain party discipline. In the later stages the party had given him mild punishment. But Mr. Mahanta instead of responding to marginal disciplinary action against him, he published a press note on 9 June, 2005,where he severely criticized the party leadership and made very harmful comments against the steering committee. The steering committee then issued a show cause notice as per norms to Mahanta for the second time. While replying to the notice, he denied the allegations rose against him and avoided the matter. On 27 June, 2005 Mr. Mahanta started his unauthorized political mission with the Nationalist Congress Party to constitute an alternative political forum in the State. Subsequently, Mahanta, in exhibiting a parallel leadership within the party, kept busy to hold dialogue with various like-minded political parties for a future self-styled political alternative in Assam. Mahanta and his followers were also busy in convincing to all concerning people by giving an impression that regional party under leadership of Brindaban Goswami would not be able to form government in the State in the coming days. On the other hand, against the good relation that existed during his leadership with the regional forces and organizations, Mr. Mahanta is now maintaining the attitude quite detrimental to the interest of the party. It is also astonishing to note here that he, instead of clarifying the stand of the AGP in respect of the IMDT Act, he was maintaining abnormal silence[17]. This act of humiliation virtually distort the party image in the minds of the people. As a result, this vehement anti-party role, the line to expel him from the party was clear. Finally, the curtain rung on 3 July, 2005 on the long 20 years of party leadership of majestic manner, when, the chief architect of the six years long Assam Movement, the founder president of the AGP, former Chief Minister of Assam for two alternative terms, and the leader of the opposition of the Assam Legislative Assembly for the second time Mr. P.K. Mahanta was expelled from the party for ever.

The expulsion of Mahanta from the party has brought about a new turn into the political history of the AGP, which results into a great crisis of regionalism in Assam. It should be stated that during his first term (1985-90), he was alleged to have been involved in the notorious LOC scam followed by a series of other allegations including secret killings. A few top level AGP leaders were also the victims of his narrow political interests.

Whatever may be his motive, his expulsion makes the party weak and in a fix in determining the future course of the party role, since he had after all, a deep rooted influence in the State and even at the national level. He was also influential among the minority communities. Considering all these counts, his termination is a great loss to the party. Needless to state, this untoward event was also indicative of the future split in the AGP.

Consequently, just after the expulsion drama was over, Mahanta and his followers formed a new political party, the Assam Gana Parishad (Progressive), on 14th September, 2005 few months before the 2006 State Assembly elections. Thus, the party split formally being carried out posing a threat to the parent AGP. The newly emerged party was to be headed by Mahanta himself, while the executive committee includes 4 existing legislators and several former MLA's. An executive committee comprising of 79 members was formed to lead the party ahead to achieve victory for regionalism in the forthcoming electoral politics. It should be mentioned here, that, as is mentioned earlier, a similar situation occurred just before the 1991 State Assembly elections when the party had to face the first split only on leadership conflict between P.K. Mahanta and the former Home Minister of Assam, late Bhrigu Kumar Phukan.

Thus, at the formal emergence of the AGP (P), the parent AGP has to face the dastardliest split, which paid heavy price to both the twin brothers. Most of the educationists, intellectuals, eminent journalists and conscious sections of the Assam society raised questions as to which of the either factions could achieve the goals of regionalism in the crisis-ridden State. But the most prominent question was raised as to whether it would be feasible for either of the two regional platforms, the AGP and the AGP (P), to make a clear sweep of the 2006 State Assembly Elections single handedly distancing one faction from the other when it was most pertinent to form a strong and stable government to work towards achieving the goal of regionalism. But interestingly, and most ironically, as against popular belief at that moment, the Congress (I) became the single largest party in the poll capturing 53 (28.35 per cent of votes) seats in the 126-member ALA, while the parent AGP secured only a meagre 24

(18.83 per cent of votes) seats. The AGP (P) could win only a microscopic one seat, which really a great political setback for the political stalwart at the regional level like Mahanta. Thus the AGP got the actual price for their haphazard split before the elections and virtually the AGP political culture was neglected and collapsed as such, which is indicative of unexpected decline of regionalism in Assam at the political level.

The performance of the political parties in the 2006 State Assembly Elections can be gleaned in Figure 28.1. The figure shows that none of the parties gets clear majority and the House goes a hung Parliament. However, the Congress (I) being the largest political party securing a respectable 28.35 per cent of votes somehow managed to form the government with the support of 11 elected members of the Hagrama Mahilary faction of the Bodo People's Party. The AGP got a sort of humiliation and suffering from frustration sits in the opposition like the earlier term. Thus the AGP has failed to capture political power in the State for the two consecutive elections.

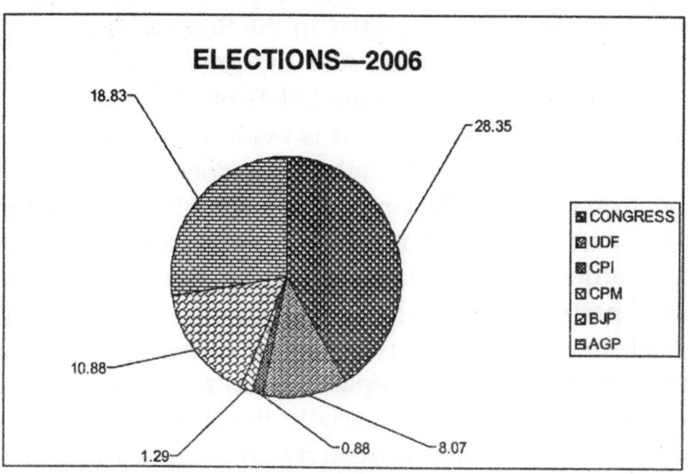

Figure 28.1 : Performance of Political Parties in 2006 Assembly Elections.

Source : *The Assam Tribune*, Guwahati, 14th May, 2006.

The post-2006 ALA elections reveal a serious disorderly position of the AGP. Now, the party becomes unstable and the party high command displays a very poor performance in strengthening the party organization at all levels. Internal party wrangling dissidents, mutual hatred, rivalries among the top-brass leaders, disbelief, are now rampant. Recently, the leadership of Mr. Brindaban Goswami, the present party president has also been questioned, from a large section of the party workers. Mr. Goswami's weak and most feeble leadership has been vehemently criticized not only by the party members but also by conscious sections of the Assam society. Even the think-tank of the party dare to held Goswami's inefficient leadership responsible for the unprecedented downfall of the AGP in the just concluded 2006 Assembly Elections. It is very interesting to note that of late a section of the parent AGP top level leaders, frankly convey their desire that the ousting stalwart P.K. Mahanta should be brought back to the party in order to save it from its present dilapidated condition. However, the matter is yet to be discussed seriously, at the party level. Very recently, an attempt has been made to forge a pre-electoral alliance between all the regional parties in the State including the AGP, AGP (P), and Trinamul AGP to fight unitedly against the Congress in the forthcoming Lok Sabha Elections.

Under the circumstances, it is evident that the AGP's political future is quite uncertain, so does the future of regionalism in Assam. Past experiences reveal that unless the regional parties are united, and both intra-party and inter-party rivalries are avoided it may not be possible for a single regional party like the AGP to carry out the very agenda of regionalism. In fact, as the recent trend reveals, the present party leadership, is not acceptable even to the committed voters of the AGP itself, especially the *Asamiya* speaking caste Hindus, who, once, wanted it to remain as a well-knit and well-organized regional political platform. Though a section of the Assamese society still calling upon both the two splitting factions to be reunited for the greater interest of progressive regionalism in the State, in reality, it appears that it is impossible as the leaders of the two camps are ideologically and psychologically pole apart from one another[18]. Thus, the AGP has lost a comprehensive past record of corporate fight against over centralism and extreme Unitarian motive of the Indian Central Government to retain regional entity. Once, the Congress was considered as the enemy of Assam, but now this enemy has ruled the roost for the fault of regionalists themselves. Now it is evident that only a clear egalitarian scheme with a definite and faithful programme of action can work to attract the voters, which the AGP has missed clearly indicating the non-relevance of regionalism parallel to the federal polity of the nation. It should be recollected that the vertical split in the AGP has served to cause a major break-up in its traditional vote bank in the 2006 Assembly Elections and this will definitely benefit both the ruling Congress and the BJP in future too. The Congress seems to gain far more from it in terms of securing a respectable total of seats. This was a major political blunder the AGP has committed in its pre-poll calculation. Hence, the election outcome reflects the destabilization of regionalism and its grim future at the decline of its apex platform the AGP, for its inherent limitations to work as a stable political party.

Conclusion

From the above discussion it appears that the present status of regionalism in Assam is quite unhealthy and the future is also not bright as is expected and as it was during 80's. The failure of the leaders of the AGP to fulfil the regional hopes and popular expectations along with its failure to work as a stable political party with a determinate programme of action are reflective of the futile effort of a regional movement. The decline of the AGP clearly shows that regionalism in isolation of a larger nation-wide democratic movement in the federal democracy like India is barren. It is also evident from the fact of the past, that regionalism parallel to national politics is sick, cripple and in fact, a fruitless attempt. Moreover, regionalism, as is evident from the specific historical exigencies of Assam society, is a difficult task where sub-national and innumerable ethnic movements are endemic. Now Assam-oriented regionalism in a comprehensive order is extremely difficult to achieve in the face of resurgent sub-nationality questions, where, Assamese comprehensive regionalism based on *Asamiya* Nationalism, has been challenged by the smaller ethnic groups with their vigorous autonomy movements on sub-nationality-questions[19]. Initially, though the AGP projected itself as the umbrella-comprehensive regional platform, now, it has lost its luster and the former glossy political surface and its social base is largely reduced. Besides, regionalism turning to chauvinism is more dangerous than parochial dictatorship. The fact that the AGP regional movement was no longer a collective and comprehensive political movement, covering all the autonomous movements organized by the sub-nationalities within this region. The large Assamese nationalism is in the trap of tremendous pressure from the resurgent sub-nationalities in recent times, and even the ethnic groups especially the first inhabitants, the tribal reluctant to identify themselves as Asamiyas[20]. Therefore, *Asamiya* identity, as it was during the Assam movement, is at the cross-roads, since, the Bodos, Rabhas, Mishings, Koches, Lalungs, Karbis, Deuris and other ethnic groups tend to believe that they are not belonging to the Assamese nationality. Thus, they have developed their separate sense of regionalism on the basis of their sub-nationality existence[21]. Therefore, the present AGP oriented regional movement, in order to make it more comprehensive, popular will have to cover up all the sub-nationalities recognizing the ethnic assertions by widening its social bases. Now, we find that factional or divided regionalism prevents comprehensive and enriched regionalism of Assam as a united entity to launch a vigorous regional movement. Lastly, the rapid development of science and technology and the ongoing trend of globalization makes the people extremely passive onlookers to the external stimuli brought by technology, especially, before the cable TVs and internet framework which bring people away from any collective resistance as it was during the yesteryears· Observing all these facts it can be said that regionalism has lost relevance and viability in the present age of globalization where people have started to think globally cutting across all local, regional and national boundaries, therefore, regionalists now, have to adapt themselves with the fast changing circumstances, that though they have right to organize themselves locally or regionally, they must think and act at the national level, as well as at the global level.

Coming back to the case of the AGP, it can be said that if the AGP further wants to upheld regionalism in a more solid basis, it has to widen its social bases, which become extremely narrowed down during the last 15 years because of its inherent class limitations and structural constraints of the Assamese society. Moreover, the AGP has to stop further erosion of its support bases meted out by the sub-nationality questions and resultant ethnic political formations, the minority lobbies backed by the foreign hands and the Congress (I). However, it should be noted that if the AGP compromises with the doubtful citizens and illegal inhabitants infiltrated from neighbouring Bangladesh, it may face more and more political erosion in the days to come at the hands of its major and original supporters among the caste Hindu *Asamiyas* since unabated infiltration from Bangladesh causes existential concern to both the indigenous majority and the minority domiciled of Assam, which the AGP and other regionalist forces cannot ignore for any kind of political gain , in the name of regional ideology.

NOTES

1. See for a discussion in this regard, Das, J.K. " Society of Assam: A Study of Groups, Their Structures and Status," *Indian Journal of Politics*, Vol. XXXV, Nos. 1-2, Jan-June 2001, pp. 85-103.
2. For an understanding of the history of internal and external migration into Assam, see *ibid.*
3. Government of Assam, Statistical Handbook, Assam, 2005, Directorate of Economics and Statistics, pp. 14-18.
4. *Ibid.* pp. 32-34. Also see for a systematic understanding about the migration and the problem of population growth in Assam Das, J.K. "Migration and the Problem of Population Growth in Assam", *South Asian Journal of Socio-Political Studies*, Adoor, Kerala, Vol. 8, No. 2, January-June, 2008, pp.19-25.
5. Phukan, Girin, "Genesis of the Asom Gana Parishad", in Bhatnagar, S. ed. *Regional Political Parties in India,* Ess and Ess Publications, New Delhi, 1988, pp. 51-52. Also see for a discussion in this regard, Dutta, Anuradha, "Growth and Development of a Regional Political Party, The AGP" in *ibid.* pp. 72-82.
6. Phukan, Girin, *ibid.* p. 51.
7. *Ibid.* p. 51.
8. It is here necessary to state that prior to the beginning of the Assam Movement, another vigorous youth movement was launched in Assam jointly by two youth organizations such as the Purbanchalia Loka Parishad and the Assam Jatiatabadi Dal from February 1978 against the non-Assamese Indians and this movement was called as the " *Bahiragata Bitaran Andolan*" (Movement for deportation of the Indians outsiders). In fact this movement was largely spearheaded for the expulsion of migrants Indian social groups such as Marwaris, Hindu Bengalis, Gujratis, Nepalis and other Hindi speaking people. Later, when the All Assam Students Union launched the Assam Movement, then this *Bahiragata Bitaran Andolan* was transformed into the movement against illegal foreign infiltrators, *i.e.* to deport *Bangladeshis* from India/Assam. However, we must mention that the Assam Movement had an anti-Bengali bias that was considered as a great setback to a mass movement like the Assam Movement. For a detailed and systematic understanding of this aspect see Hussain, Monirul., "*The Assam Movement : Class Ideology and Identity*", Manak Publications, New Delhi, 1993, pp. 101-105.

9. For the understanding of the genesis, role and impact of the United Minorities Front (UMF) in Assam politics and society, see Das, J.K. *Society and Legislature: A Study of Social Background of the Members of the Eighth Assam Legislative Assembly,* Forthcoming, Mittal Publications, New Delhi, pp.98-117.
10. Kalita, H.C. *Role of AGP in Assam Politics,* Unpublished Ph.D.Thesis , Gauhati University, 2005, p. 74.
11. See for a good electoral analysis, Goswami, R.R. *General Election to Assam Legislative Assembly* (1978-85): *A Study in Electoral Politics and Voting Behaviour,* Unpublished Ph.D.Thesis, Gauhati University, pp. 43-44.
12. See Das, J.K., "State Assembly Elections in Assam, 1985", *Punjab Journal of Politics,* Vol. XVIII, No. 2, December 1994, pp. 43-44.
13. *Ibid.* p. 44.
14. See for a detailed discussion of this aspect, Das, J.K.," Assam : The Post-Colonial Political Development", *The Indian Journal of Political Science,* Vol. LXVI, No. 4, Oct.-Dec. 2005, pp. 873-900.
15. Bhambhri, C.P., *Elections 1991: An Analysis.* B.R. Publishing Corporation, New Delhi, p. 122.
16. Das, J.K. *ibid.,* 2005, p. 890.
17. The authors have collected this information from the central office of the AGP in Guwahati.
18. Dwaipayan, "Split in the AGP and the Assembly Poll", *The Assam Tribune,* 22 September, 2005 and also see Dwaipayan, "Mahanta's Expulsion and Future of the AGP", *The Assam Tribune,* 19 July , 2005.
19. Here it would be pertinent to delineate the Assamese regionalism is the offspring of the century old Assamese Nationalism, which was emerged out of the British colonial exploitation, but Assamese nationalism was consolidated in Assam as a reaction to hegemonic Bengali nationalism. But, significantly, once nascent and now matured Assamese Nationalism is in tremendous crisis in the face of sub-nationality questions and their resultant sub-regional politics, see Das, J.K., "Assamese Nationalism in the Face of Resurgent Sub-Nationality Questions", *The Resurging India,* Centre for Nehru Studies, Aligarh, UP, Vol. 1, No. 1, January-June 2004, pp. 89-110.
20. *Ibid.* pp. 89-90.
21. *Ibid.* pp. 89-96.

ABBREVIATIONS

AAGSP	-	All Assam Gana Sangram Parishad.
AASU	-	All Assam Students Union
AGP	-	Asom Gana Parishad
ALA	-	Assam Legislative Assembly
ASDC	-	Autonomous State Demand Committee
AGP (P)	-	Asom Gana Parishad (Progressive)
BPP	-	Bodo Peoples Party
BJP	-	Bharatiya Janata Party
BTC	-	Bodoland Territorial Council
CPI (M)	-	Communist Party of India (Marxist)
CPI	-	Communist Party of India
IMDT	-	Illegal Migrants Determination Tribunal
IND	-	Independent
LOC	-	Letter of Credit
MLA	-	Member of Legislative Assembly
NAGP	-	Natun Asom Gana Parishad
OBC	-	Other Backward Classes
PLA	-	Purbanchalia Loka Parishad
PTCA	-	Plain Tribal Council of Assam
SC	-	Scheduled Caste
UMF	-	United Minorities Front
UDF	-	United Democratic Front
ULFA	-	United Liberation Front of Assam
UPP	-	United Peoples' Party.

29 Krishna Water Dispute
A Historical Background

Midatala Rani

Water is the most precious and critical element for satisfying basic human needs and maintenance of global economic systems. According to the United Nations by the year 2025 as many as 500 crore of people will be facing water shortage, as many as 270 crore will face severe water shortage, if the world continues consuming water at the present rate. With the misuse and overuse water is becoming scarce all over the world. Several prognostications made from knowledgeable quarters indicate that there could be a war over it in not too distant a future. To quote Kofi Annan "Fierce national competition over water resources has prompted fears that water issues contain the seeds of violent conflict".

Most of the world's major civilizations have flourished on the banks of rivers only. Historians believe that the emergence of human civilization was associated with organised efforts to control water supplies necessary for irrigation. Civilizations created and supported by rivers have enhanced the per capita use of water depending upon the economic strength of countries. But water is fast becoming inadequate due to rapid growth of population and multiplication of its use. With the march of civilization, the use of water is steadily increasing but the quantity of water remains more or less the same.

Environmental degradation, climate change, pollution of available water, inequitable distribution of water reserves often lead to discord or crisis between countries or between States within a country. Many observers have expressed concern about conflicts among basin countries in regions with water scarcity. As the former UN Secretary General Boutros Ghali observed, "in the next 50 years we will see a shift from oil to water as cause of great conflicts between nations and peoples".

In India agriculture is a major part of the economy. So water is one of the most critical component of India's integrity as a Nation. The National Water Policy of 1987 recognizes river basins as a unit for the purpose of harnessing the water potentials. Almost all the major river basins in the country are inter-State in character. This has contributed to inter-State water disputes in the country. Such disputes have often led to mass hysteria adversely affecting Inter-State and Centre-State relations.

The Constitution of India has various provisions relating to inter-State water disputes. Irrigation is a State subject. Under Article 246 (3) of the Constitution and entry 17 of List II of the Seventh Schedule every State Government has power to legislate in respect of water. When the source of the water of a river is not wholly within the State but encompasses more than one State such as river is an inter-State river (River Boards Act). The Constitution empowers the Parliament by law to adjudicate any dispute on complaint with respect to inter-State river water disputes. Article 263 provides for the establishment of Inter-State Council. Efforts to resolve the inter-State water dispute is contained in Article 262 of the Constitution. In pursuance of Article 262, the Parliament has enacted the Inter-State Water Disputes Act 1956, the River Boards Act 1956.

Invoking the Inter-State Water Disputes Act, the Parliament has so far constituted Five Tribunals to solve inter-State water disputes. They include Godavari Water Disputes Tribunal (in April 1969), Krishna Water Disputes Tribunal (in April, 1969), Narmada Water Disputes Tribunal (in October 1969), Ravi and Beas Waters Tribunals (in April 1986) and Cauvery Water Disputes Tribunal (in June 1990).

Social conflicts over water can be analyzed at different societal levels. Inter-State conflicts are generated when water projects of upstream States influence the quality and quantity of water flow in the basin and reduce the possibilities of water use by downstream States. Major inter-basin water transfers in rivers flowing through many States also generate conflicts by disturbing the riparian rights of States.

Water Management and Irrigation Works in British India

The tank system of South India is among the indigenous alternatives which has survived over centuries. This system consists of several hundred and in some cases over a thousand reservoirs linked together and forming such continuous chains of works that not a single drop of water falling in the catchment is lost in times of drought and very little is lost during normal periods. Major Sankey (one of the first engineers of Mysore State) stated that, "to such an extent has the principle of storage been followed that it would require some ingenuity to discover a site within this great area for a new tank". These tanks play a central role in irrigation even today. In the Rayalseema region, in the southern part of the Krishna basin tanks irrigate 620,000 acres while major and minor irrigation projects cover 427,000 acres.

The irrigation works in pre-British India were managed by Water Committees within the village community. The structure of these Committees included collective of all the beneficiaries of irrigation works and was headed by a leader. In Andhra Pradesh these Committees were known as 'Pinnapeddandarule' or 'Peddandarule' system. The difference between the two was in terms of the members who constituted them. In the 'Pinnapeddandarule' system youth were preferred as the desilting of canals involved hard physical labour. In Krishna district, less labour intensive work was involved, hence the membership rules were flexible. Each member or beneficiary was supposed to do his share of work in proportion to the land held. The Committee levied a fine on any one who failed to do his share of work, irrespective of the size of his landholding.

When the British arrived in India, they had no expertise in water management since agriculture in Europe has never been dependent on irrigation. Arthur Cotton, the founder of modern irrigation programmes wrote, "There are multitudes of old native works in various parts of India. These are noble works and show both boldness and engineering layout". Greenway, while writing on farming in India, commented on the lack of advanced engineering knowledge of the British. The British, however, had to control river water in India keeping in view their economic interest in increasing revenue. Water politics was thus as transient as the resource itself, to create obey areas and command areas, *i.e.* areas and people inhabiting them which are callously devastated to cater to the needs of areas and people which are industrialised, urbanized and politically and economically powerful.

Water Conflict in the Krishna Basin

The river Krishna is the second largest of the east flowing rivers of Peninsular India. It rises in the Mahader range of the Western Ghats, north of the hill station of Mahabaleshwar in Maharashtra and flows east through the States of Maharashtra, Karnataka and Andhra Pradesh. The waters of the river system after travelling nearly 1,400 km find their outlet in the Bay of Bengal. The Krishna basin extends over an area of 99,980 sq miles which is nearly 8 per cent of the total geographical area of India. As the boundaries of the river Krishna the Western Ghats 2,134 to 610 m (7,000 to 2,000 ft) high running parallel to the coast, form a continuous watershed on the west. On the north, the Balaghat and Mahadeo ranges stretching forth from the eastern flank of the Western Ghats and Anantagiri and other ranges of hills and ridges separate the Krishna basin from Godavari. On the eastern side, the broken ranges of the Eastern Ghats dissect the country and proceeding south-west have broad flat tracts of land between the hills and the sea. On the south, the Uravakonda and Mitta Konda ridges and the Erramalai hills separate the Krishna basin from the Pennar basin and the Nallamalai and the Veligondla hills separate the Krishna basin from other minor basins. Other ridges on the south separate the Krishna basin from the Cauvery basin.

The Krishna river is joined in its course by a large number of tributaries draining a total basin area of 256,000 sq km of which the share of the three riparian States of Maharashtra, Karnataka and Andhra Pradesh is 26.8 per cent, 43.8 per cent and 29.4 per cent respectively. The basin drains a length of approximately 700 km of the Western Ghats which is the predominant source of water of the river. As the river flows about 135 km from its origin near Mahabaleshwar Hills, the Koyna river flowing from the western side of the same hill joins it. Further along its course, it is joined by tributaries like Varna, Panchaganga and Dodhganga draining about 150 km of the Western Ghats. As the river emerges from the eastern slopes of the Western Ghats, it is joined by Ghataprabha and Malaprabha from the south at a distance of approximately 500 km from the origin. After traversing the Deccan proper the east flowing Krishna then enters the alluvial lands and at a distance of about 800 km from the source just from it enters Andhra Pradesh, a major tributary Bhima draining the Western Ghats, north of Mahabaleshwar joins it from the north. Near Kurnool the river is joined by another major tributary, Tungabhadra from the south, draining a major section of the Western Ghats in Karnataka. Within a short distance from this confluence the river enters the Naliamali Ranges characterised by peep gorges. At this place the Srisailam Dam and further downstream the Nagarjunasagar Dam have been constructed. At this point the major water sources of the Western Ghats have all been united. Tributaries like Dindi, Musi, Palleru and

Muneru draining the dry north-eastern parts of the basin join the river between Srisailam and Vijayawada but do not add much water. Below Vijayawada where the Krishna is blocked by the barrage constructed during the British period, the river spreads out into the delta and below the last major village Nagailanka it joins the Bay of Bengal.

In the Krishna basin comprising mostly of arid and semi-arid regions water management had reached a high level of sophistication, both for surface as well as groundwater utilisation. An aerial view of the basin reveals a network of a large number of tanks, some pre-historic, others constructed by the local people or the rulers at different times of history. The needs of the Vijayanagar Empire led to the first major intervention in the natural water flow. In the sixteenth century during the reign of King Krishnadevaraya there were many attempts to divert the water of Tungabhadra through seven canals in the Bellary district, these are known as the Vijayanagar Canals. The canals provided water for irrigation as well as satisfied the needs of the large army stationed in the capital city of Hampi. The interests of the Vijayanagar rulers were not limited to canals. Understanding the crucial role of tanks in food production as well as in providing drinking water supply, the kingdom undertook a systematic programme of tank construction. The Daroji tank and the Vyasayaraya Samudram in Cuddapah district are the result of this programme.

The first large scale intervention in the natural flow of water in the Krishna river basin was seen in the late nineteenth century. It was motivated both by the irrigation needs of export crops like cotton and groundnut, as well as for transporting these products easily to major ports like Madras. The Krishna delta canal system based on the Vijayawada barrage was constructed in 1855. The Nira Canal in Maharashtra was constructed in 1885 to irrigate about 1,50,000 acres and the Kurnool Cuddapah Canal was constructed in 1886 to irrigate 1,00,000 acres. With the passage of time an increasing number of Government aided large and medium projects came up and today the Krishna river has numerous dams including the Dhom Dam which is at a distance of 5 km from its source. Midstream we find the Alamatti and Narayanpur Dams of the Upper Krishna Project while further downstream Srisailam and Nagarjunsagar Dams generate electricity and divert water for irrigation. The tributaries have also been used extensively in this respect.

Apart from the above mentioned irrigation works, there have been a large number of tanks and wells used for purposes of irrigation in the Krishna river basin. There were about 27, 000 small tanks and diversions on the Krishna river system mostly in Andhra Pradesh and Karnataka. The position of diversion of waters from the river as existing in 1951 was 411.4 TMCF annually. The State-wise diversion was Andhra Pradesh (290.1 TMCF), Maharashtra (43.0 TMCF) and Mysore (78.3 TMCF).

With the attainment of Independence, the country embarked on a large scale, development of water resources for irrigation and power. The then States of Bombay, Hyderabad, Madras and Mysore commenced investigations and planning of some large projects on river Krishna and its tributaries. This required an Agreement between the concerned States for allocation of waters of the river Krishna. To facilitate the Agreement among the States, the Planning Commission convened an inter-State conference in July 1951, with an objective to discuss the utilisation of supplies in the Krishna river basin.

After the general discussion of the issues involved, the engineers of the participating States submitted the Memorandum of Agreement which allocated amongst the participating States the entire flow of the Krishna river. The dependable annual flow in the Krishna basin based on the recorded gaugings at Vijayawada was agreed at 1715 TMCF. The existing utilizations by the States were calculated at

744.5 TMCF. The balance of flow for new projects remained 970.5 TMCF which was rounded off to 1,000 TMCF and allocations were made between the different States including Bombay 240 TMCF, Hyderabad 280 TMCF, Mysore 10 TMCF and Madras 470 TMCF.

The balance flow in excess of 1,000 TMCF if any, the allocation for the above States was in the ratio of 30:30:1:39. The State of Bombay was allowed to divert the waters to the west across the Western Ghats for the hydroelectric project at Koyna upto a limit of 67.5 TMCF. The Agreement provided for a review of the allocations after 25 years. The Governments of Madras, Bombay, Hyderabad subsequently ratified the Agreement. However the Government of Mysore did not do so.

The new Constitution came into force in 1950. Consequently the entire Krishna basin fell within the States of Bombay, Mysore, Hyderabad and Madras. As a result of subsequent reorganisations through the States Reorganisation Act, 1956 the new States of Bombay (Maharashtra), Mysore (Karnataka) and Andhra Pradesh were formed and later the States of Maharashtra, Karnataka, Andhra Pradesh, Orissa and Madhya Pradesh emerged as parties to the dispute over Krishna waters up to 19 April, 1971.

In view of the territorial changes, demands were made to recast the allocations made in 1951. The Central Government appointed the Krishna Godavari Commission in 1961 and the three-man Commission headed by N.D. Gulhati submitted its report in August 1962. But the report could not provide a clear solution to the problems involved due to lack of sufficient data.

In spite of the interim reallocations of the Krishna river waters differences among the States continued and negotiations done by the Union Ministry of Irrigation and Power through Inter-State Conferences could not prove successful. The States of Maharashtra, Mysore and Andhra Pradesh requested the Central Government to set up a Tribunal under Section 3 of the Inter-State Water Disputes Act 1956.

Krishna Water Disputes Tribunal

The Krishna Water Disputes Tribunal (KWDT) headed by Justice Bachawat was constituted on 10 April, 1969 for adjudication of Inter-State Water Dispute regarding sharing of Krishna Waters. The Tribunal gave its award in 1976. As per this award 75 per cent dependable flow of Krishna Water upto Vijayawada was assessed as 2060 TMC which was allocated as below :

State	*Flow*
Maharashtra	560 TMC
Karnataka	700 TMC
Andhra Pradesh	800 TMC
TMC – Thousand Million Cubic Feet	

In addition, the above States were allowed to use return flows to the extent of 25, 34 and 11 TMC respectively. Further it gave liberty to Andhra Pradesh to use the unutilised waters of the upper States but with the provision that it shall not acquire any right whatsoever over and above its share of 800 TMC ft. The Tribunal has allowed the States to utilise their allocated share of water for any project as per their plans.

The Tribunal in its report has discussed about two schemes namely, Scheme "A" and Scheme "B". However in its Final Award the Tribunal has mentioned only about the Scheme "A". In the Tribunal report, it has been mentioned that Scheme "B" can be implemented if all the three States agree. (As per the KWDT Scheme "B", Karnataka, Andhra Pradesh and Maharashtra would be eligible after May 2000 for specified proportions of water, depending on the flow over and above the 75 per cent dependability yield.) There is also provision of setting up of Krishna Valley Authority under Scheme "B". Scheme "B" also specifies allocation of surplus water amongst three States.

Development in Post-1970s

As a post award development, a scheme to supply water to Chennai city was evolved and an agreement was signed among the three basin States on 14 April, 1976 to spare 5 TMC ft each out of the share of each to enable Tamil Nadu draw 15 TMC ft of water for this purpose through the Telugu Ganga Canal.

Since 1997, Karnataka has been pleading for the notification of Scheme "B" praying for restraining Andhra Pradesh from executing projects based on surplus waters. The Supreme Court dismissed its suit stating that Scheme "B" was not a decision taken by the KWDT and, therefore, could not be enforced. Later Andhra Pradesh prayed for restraining Karnataka from increasing the height of the Alamatti Dam.

The height of the Alamatti Dam (Stage II of the Upper Krishna Project) is a contentious issue in the sharing of the Krishna Waters between Karnataka, Andhra Pradesh and Maharashtra. The Alamatti Dam is designed to store 173 TMC ft of the total 734 TMC ft of Krishna Waters allocated to Karnataka by the Bachawat Tribunal under Scheme "A". Alamatti is the only dam where Karnataka can store the surplus waters of the Krishna. It was because of this that the Alamatti Project was designed for a height of 519 M to hold the storage with the option of an additional 5 M to provide for the storage of surplus water.

Andhra Pradesh raised objection to Karnataka's move to store the surplus water. It took the matter to the Supreme Court seeking directions to restrict the height of the Alamatti Dam at 509 M, the height to which the dam had been built (with 15 M high crest gates coming over it) saying that it is illegal in the absence of non-compliance with mandatory requirements of dam break analysis and disaster management plan. The height should have been restricted to a maximum of 515 M at which point the storage is sufficient to use Karnataka's allocated quantity of 160 TMC ft under the Upper Krishna Project. Although Karnataka has been allowed to raise the dam's height to 519.6 M, the Andhra Pradesh Government feels that storage capacity should be restricted to 509 M.

The Supreme Court in April 2000, passed Orders pegging the height at 519 M. The State has been impounding water up to the 519 M mark for the past two to three years. This has prevented the free flow of unutilised water to Andhra Pradesh. In the midst of its legal fight with Andhra Pradesh, Karnataka found Maharashtra also trying to create a controversy. Maharashtra started complaining of the backwater effect of the Alamatti Dam in its border districts.

Interestingly, although the Government of India requested that Scheme "B" also be made part of the Award and the KWDT itself felt that it provided for a fuller and better utilisation of the Krishna waters that was not done. This was because there had to be consent among the riparian States or an Act passed by Parliament. In the absence of either of these, the task has been left to a new Tribunal.

If the three States were slow in asking for a new Tribunal, the Centre was even slower in acting. It finally constituted one under the Chairmanship of Justice Brajesh Kumar on April 4th, 2004. The Tribunal has 3 years – with a two – year grace period to finish its task. One of the crucial points before the Tribunal will be the unutilised waters. All the three States have a delicate task in safeguarding their interests before the New Tribunal.

Perceptions of Water Rights

There are four theories which have been put forward with regard to the water rights of different riparian States. The theories include the Territorial Sovereignty theory also known as the Harmone doctrine. This theory holds that riparian States have exclusive or sovereign rights over the waters flowing through their territory. The Natural Water Flow Theory is also known as the Territorial Integrity

Theory. Under this theory every low riparian owner is entitled to the natural flow of the river unhampered by the upper riparian owners, otherwise it results in violation of territorial sovereignty. The Equitable Utilisation and Community of Interest Theories are closely interrelated. The idea is the sharing of an international river by various States on an equitable basis. Besides the Helsinki Rules and the UN Convention of 1997 deal only with one aspect of the water theme namely the sharing of international rivers ('drainage basins' or 'water courses') by the countries concerned. They do not setforth a view of water in all its complexity.

Conclusion

The dispute in the Krishna basin between Karnataka, Maharashtra and Andhra Pradesh has brought into sharp focus the issue of scarcity and struggles with regard to water resources and other important issues like water politics, displacement of people by raising the dams, large scale farmer suicides in the States. The riparian States in the river basin are making attempts to establish their water rights. The existing situation demands a clear cut National Water Policy with a Constitutional stand on waters and Scientific Water Management Control. It also calls for a review of Inter-State Water Disputes Act, 1956 consistent with the changing trends of disputes. Further the Inter-State Council needs to be given more impetus in resolving inter-State river water disputes. The proposed inter-linking of rivers is still in a speculative realm and its feasibility depends upon adventurous course of an unimaginable magnitude which may face more interruptions and insurmountable barriers when it comes to the stage of implementation involving a budget estimate in astronomical figures.

REFERENCES

Balekundry, S.G. (1992), Optimum Development of Krishna and Cauvery Basin, Karnataka, Vikasa Vedike, Bangalore.

Chauhan, B.R. (1992), Settlement of International and Inter- State Water Disputes in India, N.M. Tripathi Private Limited, Bombay.

Dodda Srinivasa Rao (1998), Inter-State Water Disputes in India - Constitutional and Statutory Provisions and Settlement Machinery, Deep & Deep Publications, New Delhi.

Government of India Notification, Ministry of Water Resources, 14 January 2002, New Delhi.

Gulhati, N.D. (1972), Development of Inter-State Rivers: Law and Practice in India, Allied Publishers, New Delhi.

Jain, S.C., Alice Jacob, Subhas C. Jain (1971), Inter-State Water Disputes in India, N.M. Tripathi Private Limited, Bombay.

Nanje Gowda, H.V., "Sharing Rivers Sans Policy", *The Hindu*, 11 August 1998.

Nanjundappa, D.M., "The Evolving of a National Water Policy — Something Long Overdue", *Deccan Herald*, 28 August, 1996.

Narasimhan, T.N., Water and India's Constitution, *The Hindu*, 15 December, 2005.

Ramanna, M.V.V., Inter-State River Water Disputes in India (1992), Orient Longman, Madras.

Ramaswamy Iyer, "Towards Universal Guidelines on Water Use", *The Hindu*, 27 December 2005.

Ravi Sharma, "Scarcity and Struggles", *Frontline*, 6 May, 2005, 31-46.

Sadasivan, S.N. (2003), River Water Disputes in India, Mittal Publications, New Delhi.

Sathiya Moorthy, N., "Water Wars in the South", *Industrial Economist*, 1994.

Steen Folke, "Conflicts Over Water and Land in South Indian Agriculture — A Political Economy Perspective", *Economic and Political Weekly*, 14 February 1998, 341-349.

"Water and Federalism: India's Institutions Governing Inter- State River Waters", IRIS, *India Working* chapter, 22 August 1996.

Index